WORLD RESOURCES

2002–2004

WORLD RESOURCES
2002–2004

UNITED NATIONS DEVELOPMENT PROGRAMME

UNITED NATIONS ENVIRONMENT PROGRAMME

THE WORLD BANK

WORLD RESOURCES INSTITUTE

WORLD RESOURCES INSTITUTE   Washington, D.C.

World Resources 2002–2004: Decisions for the Earth:
Balance, Voice, and Power

Paperback edition published by
World Resources Institute
10 G Street, NE
Washington, D.C. 20002
© 2003 World Resources Institute.
Printed on recycled paper.
First printing June 2003

The **World Resources Series** is a collaborative product of four organizations: the United Nations Development Programme, the United Nations Environment Programme, the World Bank, and the World Resources Institute. The views expressed in this volume are those of staff from each organization and do not necessarily reflect the judgments of the organizations' boards of directors or member governments.

The full report is available online at www.wri.org/wr2002.
Materials may be reproduced with the permission of World Resources Institute, 10 G St., NE, Washington, DC 20002.
ISBN: 1-56973-532-8
ISSN: 0887-0403

PHOTO CREDITS: (x-xi) AP/Wide World Photos. **Chapter 1:** (opposite p. 1) Frans Lanting/ Minden Pictures; (p. 2) AP/Wide World Photos; (p. 6) Franco Mattioli/IFAD; (p. 8) Anwar Hossain/IFAD; (p. 15) Frank Cezus/Getty Images; (p. 16) World Bank Photo Library; (p. 20) Franco Mattioli/IFAD. **Chapter 2:** (p. 27) UNHCR/A. Hollmann; (p. 35) Franco Mattioli/IFAD. **Chapter 3:** (p. 48) Giuseppe Bizzarri/IFAD; (p. 49) Robert Grossman/IFAD; (p. 50) Anwar Hossain/IFAD; (p. 55) Anwar Hossain/IFAD; (p.. 59) Franco Mattioli/IFAD; (p. 60) Louis Dematteis/IFAD; (p. 64) Franco Mattioli/IFAD. **Chapter 4:** (p. 66) Franco Mattioli/IFAD; (p. 73) Anwar Hossain/IFAD; (p. 81) Grameen Communications Village Computer and Internet Project; (p. 83) Franco Mattioli/IFAD; (p. 84 both) Franco Mattioli/IFAD; (p. 85 left) Sahar Nimeh/IFAD; (p. 85 right) Radhika Chalasani/IFAD; (p. 86) Katia Dini/IFAD; (p. 88) Anwar Hossain/IFAD. **Chapter 5:** (p. 105) IFAD. **Chapter 6:** (p. 133) Marcelo Soubhai. **Chapter 8 Case Studies:** (pp. 174, 176, 178, 180, 181) Courtesy of Jean Harris; (p. 182) ©2001, *Washington Post* photo by John Ward Anderson. Reprinted with permission; (pp. 188, 190, 192, 194, 196) Mineral Policy Center; (pp. 198, 200, 204) Greg Mock.

REPRINTED WITH PERMISSION: Chapter 5: (Figure in Box 5.5) from NWP as authored by USAID et al. 2002. **Chapter 6:** (Figures 6.1 and 6.2) KPMG 2002.

WORLD RESOURCES 2002-2004

CONTENTS

F O R E W O R D

MAKING WISE DECISIONS FOR THE EARTH

We recognize endangered species and degraded habitats as signs of environmental failure, but we rarely acknowledge them as the results of governance failures. Corruption and patronage. Backroom deals and land grabs. Development decisions made without local information, consultation, or support. These all-too-common governance failures don't just erode our civil and economic rights, they erode our natural heritage as well.

Degraded forests and dying coral reefs often reflect a flawed environmental decision-making process. Illegal logging thrives where forest managers have little accountability. Mining decisions taken in secret often attach too little value to protecting local water supplies or crucial habitat. Plans to exploit any natural resource prepared without input or review by local inhabitants and other affected groups all too often enrich a few but dispossess the larger community and disrupt the ecosystem. Poor environmental governance—decisions taken without transparency, participation of all stakeholders, and full accountability—is a failure we can no longer live with in an era when human decisions, not natural processes, dominate the global environment.

The importance of good governance is, of course, not restricted to environmental decisions. It goes to the heart of our social and economic progress. Good governance is now recognized as one of the most important factors in realizing a nation's development potential and reducing poverty–in part because public or private investors want the stability and transparency that good governance brings. That is essentially the conclusion endorsed by ministers when they gathered in Monterrey, Mexico, in March 2002. They concluded that money alone doesn't guarantee sound development with benefits shared by all. Rather, success also depends on sound institutions, prudent policies, transparent processes, open access to information, and equitable participation in decision-making–all salient features of good governance.

In this issue of *World Resources*, we focus on *environmental governance*–the processes and institutions we use to make decisions about the environment. Our four organizations endorse the Monterrey Consensus, which contains clear commitments to good governance, and challenge the international community to bring that mandate to bear on the crucial area of managing ecosystems and natural resources, both locally and globally. Our decades of experience dealing with environmental problems in rich and poor countries have shown time and again that good governance is crucial for the sustainable management of ecosystems, which are a key underpinning of sustainable economic growth and human development.

The building blocks of good environmental governance are the *access principles*, first spelled out in 1992 in the Rio Declaration–the official document of the United Nations Conference on Environment and Development. Principle 10 of the Rio Declaration calls for access to information concerning the environment, the opportunity to participate in the decision-making process, and effective access to judicial and administrative proceedings. But these principles are only as strong as our implementation of them.

How well have we done since Rio? Measuring governance performance and trends is difficult, but essential if we are to make progress toward achieving our environmental and social goals. The Access Initiative, described in this report, represents a first effort to make such an assessment of environmental governance, elaborating and defining just what we mean by access to information, decision-making, and justice. The results reveal in some detail our uneven progress. To accelerate implementation, the Partnership for Principle 10 (PP10) was launched in September 2002 at the World Summit on Sustainable Development in Johannesburg, bringing together a wide range of organizations that have committed to accept accountability for carrying out specific actions and to provide resources to enable improved access.

Our organizations are founding members of the Partnership for Principle 10, and as such we endorse this activity and commend it to others as a salient and practical response to the challenge of environmental governance. We also endorse the concept of independent assessments, such as those supported by the Access Initiative. We believe the Access methodology offers the global community a framework that should be applied widely to the vital work of identifying where our governance mechanisms and institutions are weak, as well as where we have made progress.

Of course, access alone is not enough to ensure good environmental outcomes. Indeed, one of the most apparent failures over the decade since Rio has been the inability to mainstream environmental thinking into economic and development decisions. This lack of integration translates into a failure to balance economic, social, and environmental concerns. More deeply, it reflects a reluctance to appropriately value the contribution of ecosystem goods and services to human welfare. Good environmental governance will succeed in achieving better environmental outcomes only if it is seen as an essential contributor to better and more equitable development.

In this spirit, we as organizations recommit ourselves to a focus on good environmental governance as a wedge to push forward better decisions–decisions for the Earth. In our own organizations, we will work to improve governance of the environment through our programs, policy advice, project work, and funding practices. Our experience proves that bringing communities and individuals into the decision-making loop, and insisting on accountability of those ultimately responsible for environmental decisions, can lead to fairer and more effective management of natural resources. Now, we must carry this message to our partners around the world.

We recognize the urgency imposed by the Millennium Development Goals adopted at the United Nations Millennium Assembly in September 2000, including eradicating extreme poverty and hunger, and ensuring environmental sustainability. We affirm our conviction that these human and environmental goals must be integrated, just as people and ecosystems are woven together in the web of life. We cannot alleviate poverty over the long term without managing ecosystems sustainably. Nor can we protect ecosystems from abuse without holding those with wealth and power accountable for their actions, and recognizing the legitimate needs of the poor and dispossessed. This is the balance we must strike in all of our decisions for the Earth.

Mark Malloch Brown
Administrator
United Nations Development Programme

Klaus Töpfer
Executive Director
United Nations Environment Programme

James D. Wolfensohn
President
World Bank

Jonathan Lash
President
World Resources Institute

DECISIONS FOR THE EARTH

How we decide
and *who* gets to decide
often determines *what* we decide.

ENVIRONMENTAL GOVERNANCE
WHOSE VOICE?
WHOSE CHOICE?

Who decides the fate of ecosystems? Who manages nature?

Earth has no CEO. No Board of Directors. No management team charged with extracting resources responsibly or maintaining the living factories–the forests, farms, oceans, grasslands, and rivers–that underlie our wealth. No business plan for a sustainable future.

Of course, the biosphere is no standard corporation. But every day we make what amount to management decisions that affect the planet's bottom line–the habitability and productive capacity of ecosystems.

Who Makes Environmental Decisions?

Who should decide whether to build a road or a dam, or how much timber or fish to harvest? What difference does it make if the public is consulted? Do democratic rights and civil liberties contribute to better environmental management? Should local citizens or advocacy groups have the right to appeal a decision they believe harms an ecosystem or is unfair? What is the best way to fight corruption among those who manage our forests, water, parks, and mineral resources? These are all questions about *how* we make environmental decisions and *who* makes them—the process we call *environmental governance*.

In fact, managing Planet Earth is a collective and largely uncoordinated affair. It is the sum of the myriad decisions we make that directly or indirectly bear on the environment. In essence, the state of Earth's environment is a living reflection of our daily decisions.

The Scope of Our Decisions

Our environmental decisions occur in many contexts. They begin with personal choices like whether we will walk or drive to work, how much firewood we will burn, or whether we will have another child. They encompass the business decisions that communities or corporations make about where to locate their facilities, how much to emphasize eco-friendly product design, and how much land to preserve. They include national laws we enact to regulate pollution, manage public land, or regulate trade. They take in the international commitments we make to abide by fishing limits, regulate trade in endangered species, or limit acid rain or CO_2 emissions.

Our decisions also involve a wide range of actors: individuals; local, state, and national governments; community and tribal authorities; civic organizations, interest groups, and labor unions; national and transnational corporations; scientists; and international bodies such as the United Nations, the European Union, and the World Trade Organization. Each of these actors has different interests, different levels of authority, and different information, making their interactions complex and frequently putting their decisions at odds with the ecological processes that sustain the natural systems we depend on (see Figure 1.1).

Maybe that is why our record of environmental care is so poor. Year by year, as our population and consumption levels increase, our impacts on the environment spin out on a wider arc. More forests are converted to farmlands and suburbs; a greater share of freshwater resources is siphoned off, dammed, or diverted; the genetic wealth of species is lost to uncontrolled harvests and habitat loss; the global atmosphere is steadily compromised by greenhouse gases. Each of these trends marks a failure of our *environmental governance*–the term we use to describe how we as humans exercise our authority over natural resources and natural systems.

Governance Is Crucial

World Resources 2002-2004 explores the importance of environmental governance–how we make decisions about the environment and who participates in these decisions. *How* we decide, and *who* gets to decide often determines *what* we decide, so questions of governance are crucial. They can mark the difference between environmental improvement or harm, between an effective environmental policy or one that is ignored, between success and failure in managing ecosystems and natural resources (see Box 1.1).

Environmental governance is the exercise of authority over natural resources and the environment.

In this report we put forth the thesis that improving the processes and institutions we use to make important environmental decisions–from whether to build a dam to how to manage a park or where to build a road–will bring better results, with less environmental impact and a fairer distribution of costs and benefits. Likewise, if we do not address our governance failures–from corrupt or inept agencies to decision-making that doesn't reflect the needs of people or the complex nature of ecosystems–our attempts to manage the environment will continue to be ineffective and unfair, with little chance of finding a path toward sustainability.

World Resources 2002-2004 also asserts that one of the most direct routes to better environmental decisions is to provide easy access to environmental information and encourage broad participation–direct or indirect–in environmental decisions. When those affected by a decision can participate in the process, we believe the result is likely to be fairer, more environmentally sound, and more broadly accepted. This "environmental empowerment" of the public can bring accountability to local, regional, and international decisions and can harness the energy and creativity of those with the greatest stake in successful environmental management: the people who live in or depend on the affected ecosystems.

In its examination of environmental governance, *World Resources 2002–2004* calls on a ground-breaking analysis of the openness and accessibility of environmental decision-making in nine nations. The results of the Access Initiative, a project undertaken by an international consortium of 25 public interest groups, give a detailed picture of how well the public in the surveyed nations can participate in local and national decisions about the natural environments they live in. They offer a road map to better governance by identifying the kinds of information and involvement people require to become active partners in ecosystem management.

Of course, poor natural resource management is but one factor in the world's diminished environmental state. The drivers of ecosystem degradation are rooted in an economic system that often rewards exploitation rather than stewardship of natural systems. They manifest in an inequitable distribution of property and power over natural resources and ecosystems, so that environmental benefits are not equally shared. They express themselves in rising per capita consumption in developed nations, and relentless population growth as well as a persistent legacy of poverty in the developing world—all factors that increase demand for what ecosystems can yield. But these drivers, too, are failures of governance—of inadequate

Box 1.1 Who Governs Nature?

How we make decisions determines how effectively these decisions are used to manage nature and how fair they are to the people affected. When people participate in nature-related decisions that affect them, they are more likely to support these decisions, and the decisions are more likely to be successfully implemented. When they are left out, it is often a recipe for conflict, inequity, and environmental harm.

When construction workers completed the Kedung Ombo Dam on the Indonesian island of Java in 1989, the rising waters displaced some 5,000 unhappy families in the villages of the Serang River Valley. The decision to build the dam was made far from the Serang Valley and without consulting the local population. A government-sponsored plan promised land and financial assistance to relocate to Sumatra, but many of the villagers chose to stay and fight rather than move thousands of kilometers away. Instead, the government was forced to establish villages in a nearby forest tract to accommodate those residents who insisted on remaining in the valley. Other families live in the greenbelt around the dam that was intended to prevent erosion. In this case, lack of attention to local concerns led directly to a higher human and environmental toll (Rumansara 2000:123–126).

* * *

In 1998, the residents of Rarotonga in the Cook Islands revived a traditional practice of protecting sections of the island's lagoons and coral reefs from fishing and the harvesting of shellfish, coral, and other marine life. Islanders had noticed a decline in the number and size of marine life, in addition to coral bleaching and an invasion of starfish—a sign of reef stress. Outside environmental groups suggested that action was needed to keep the island's marine resources from further depletion. However, it was local initiative by the island's traditional chiefs, supported by the community, that precipitated action.

The chiefs have no legal powers to control resources, but they do still command public respect, and exercise community leadership. After consultation with local communities around the island, five protected areas were established by common decree for an initial period of two years. Enforcement of the harvest bans is strictly by social means—through embarrassment—but local compliance is high. Community members are also responsible for monitoring the effects of the bans, which have brought quick recovery of sea cucumbers and other valuable species. Tourism has improved near the protected areas as well. The success of the bans has encouraged creation of two additional protected areas and extension of the harvest bans to five years. Fully 28 percent of the island's coastal area is now encompassed by protected areas, and community knowledge of and pride in the island's marine resources has risen measurably. Direct participation in the coastal management regime has brought wide public acceptance and effective local control of the marine resource (Evans 2002).

* * *

Autocratic decisions about who gets access to a country's natural wealth have the potential to prop up unpopular political regimes, spark armed conflict, and impoverish a nation.

In April 2002, President Charles Taylor of Liberia sold logging rights within the biologically rich Sabo National Park for several million dollars to Oriental Timber Company (OTC) of Hong Kong. The sale was made not as part of a deliberative process of park and forest planning, but as a unilateral measure to fund weapons purchases in contravention of a UN arms embargo against the country. UN reports show OTC logging ships transporting illegal munitions into Liberia and carrying timber out of the country for processing. The lucrative logging and weapons arrangement is part of a pattern of liquidating Liberia's forests and other natural resources such as rubber, diamonds, and iron ore to fund the government's war efforts. Liberia's impoverished citizens receive little payback in return, with the nation's education and healthcare systems destroyed and its economy in shambles (Farah 2002:A1; Global Witness 2001b:1–16; 2001a; 2001c; 2002).

Figure 1.1 A World of Influences on the Environment

Today's environmental conditions result from the interplay of a variety of physical, economic, and social forces and are affected by many different actors, from individuals to governments.

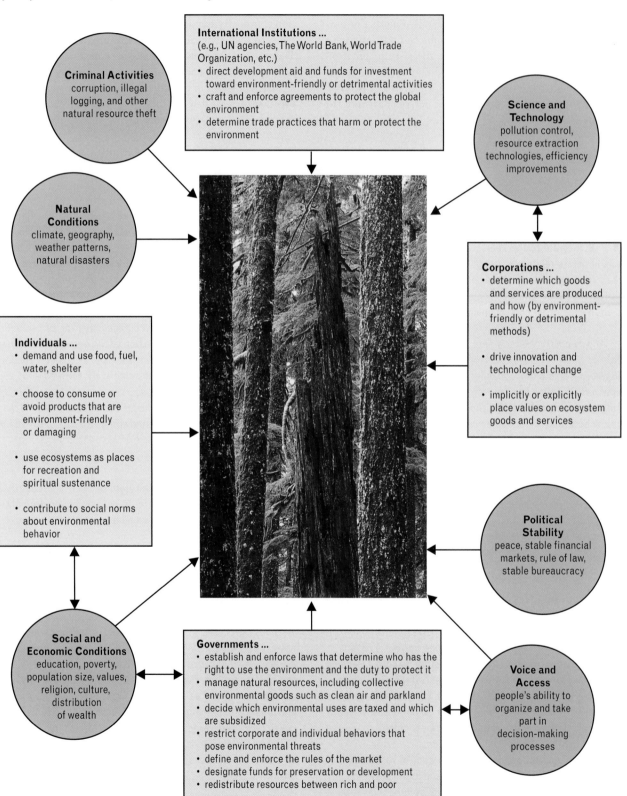

Criminal Activities
corruption, illegal logging, and other natural resource theft

International Institutions ...
(e.g., UN agencies, The World Bank, World Trade Organization, etc.)
- direct development aid and funds for investment toward environment-friendly or detrimental activities
- craft and enforce agreements to protect the global environment
- determine trade practices that harm or protect the environment

Science and Technology
pollution control, resource extraction technologies, efficiency improvements

Natural Conditions
climate, geography, weather patterns, natural disasters

Corporations ...
- determine which goods and services are produced and how (by environment-friendly or detrimental methods)
- drive innovation and technological change
- implicitly or explicitly place values on ecosystem goods and services

Individuals ...
- demand and use food, fuel, water, shelter
- choose to consume or avoid products that are environment-friendly or damaging
- use ecosystems as places for recreation and spiritual sustenance
- contribute to social norms about environmental behavior

Political Stability
peace, stable financial markets, rule of law, stable bureaucracy

Social and Economic Conditions
education, poverty, population size, values, religion, culture, distribution of wealth

Governments ...
- establish and enforce laws that determine who has the right to use the environment and the duty to protect it
- manage natural resources, including collective environmental goods such as clean air and parkland
- decide which environmental uses are taxed and which are subsidized
- restrict corporate and individual behaviors that pose environmental threats
- define and enforce the rules of the market
- designate funds for preservation or development
- redistribute resources between rich and poor

Voice and Access
people's ability to organize and take part in decision-making processes

4

regulation and outmoded subsidies, of undemocratic processes, of weak leadership and widespread apathy. Better environmental governance will mean dealing with these root causes, as well as with failed models of resource management.

Ecosystems: The Governance Frontier

Ecosystems are the life support of the planet and the ultimate basis of the global economy. These communities of interdependent organisms are the biological engines that sustain us and contribute to our sense of place. In our millennial report *World Resources 2000–2001: People and Ecosystems: The Fraying Web of Life*, we documented people's dependence on ecosystems and the goods and services they yield. These include the food we eat, as well as the water we drink and use for agriculture and industry. They also encompass the natural processes that purify water and air, decompose and recycle nutrients, prevent coastal erosion, and fulfill a hundred other essential functions that anchor our survival.

Because of their central and irreplaceable role in our well-being, ecosystems are the proper focus of environmental governance efforts. Without improving our environmental decision-making we can't hope to manage ecosystems both to provide for our current needs and remain viable for the future.

Such management is no easy task, given the current precarious state of global ecosystems (see Box 1.2). In *World Resources 2000–2001* we assessed the capacity of the world's ecosystems to sustain us. We reported the results of a systematic analysis of the condition of global ecosystems, concluding that ecosystems face a serious decline in their ability to provide the goods and services on which we depend. The current high production levels of ocean fisheries, temperate and tropical forests, and agricultural systems on every continent belie a progressive erosion in their biological capacity. Even as they support us, we are depleting them. At the same time, pressures on ecosystems relentlessly increase, with demand for land, water, wood, and grains projected to rise appreciably in the next two decades as population and consumption grow.

In this report–intended as a companion volume to *World Resources 2000–2001*–we assess the capacity of our social, economic, and political institutions to make decisions that will reverse these trends in ways that are both effective and fair. Governance is the essential human element of ecosystem management, with the task of interpreting the needs of all stakeholders within the biological realities of the ecosystem itself. Exploring how alternative methods of decision-making can bring about different–and better–outcomes is a starting point for improving ecosystem management.

What Is Environmental Governance?

"Who let this happen? Who's responsible for this mess?" These are typical questions people ask themselves when local environmental disasters happen or when the steady deterioration of the global environment makes the news. For most

Box 1.2 Governance and Ecosystems

An ecosystem is a community of interacting organisms and the physical environment they live in. They are the productive engines of the planet—the source of food, water, and other biological goods and services that sustain us. To be effective, environmental governance must lead to fair and sustainable management of ecosystems. However, ecosystems bring special governance challenges:

Ecosystem scales differ: Ecosystems exist at multiple scales, from a single stream, bog, or meadow, to a major river system or regional forest. How can management structures be tailored to match?

Uses and users vary: Ecosystems produce many different goods and services—fish, timber, crops, recreation—and must serve many different stakeholders, from local residents to commercial harvesters. Not all these uses and users are compatible, but what is the optimum mix? How are trade-offs made and disputes resolved?

Threats are cumulative: Many ecosystem threats, such as habitat loss or agricultural run-off into waterways, come from cumulative actions that occur at different scales and from different sources. How can environmental policies address these large-scale and integrated threats?

Recovery while in use: Most ecosystems are already impaired in some way, but they remain under heavy use. How can use be moderated to allow recovery without disenfranchising those who depend on ecosystems for subsistence and employment?

Dependence and Impact on Ecosystems

Annual value of global agricultural production (Wood et al. 2000:40)	$1.3 trillion
Percentage of global agricultural lands showing moderate to severe soil degradation (Wood et al. 2000:49)	52%
Population directly dependent on forests for survival (WCFSD 1999:58)	350 million
Decline in global forest cover since preagricultural times (Bryant et al. 1997:12)	46%
Population dependent primarily on fish for protein (Williams 1996:3)	1 billion
Percentage of global fisheries overfished or fished at their biological limit (FAO 2000:10)	75%
Percentage of world population living in water-stressed river basins (Revenga et al. 2000:26)	41%
Percentage of normal global river flow extracted for human use (Revenga et al. 2000:25)	20%
Percentage of major river basins strongly or moderately fragmented by dams (Revenga et al. 2000:17)	60%
Percentage of terrestrial ecosystem area (land area) converted to agriculture and urban uses (WRI 2000:24)	29%

people, it is not obvious who is "in charge" of the environment, and how decisions are made about developing, using, or managing ecosystems.

Governance is about decisions and how we make them. It is about the exercise of authority; about being "in charge." It relates to decision-makers at all levels–government managers and ministers, business people, property owners, farmers, and consumers. In short, it deals with who is responsible, how they wield their power, and how they are held accountable.

In this report, we look at governance specifically as it relates to the environment, and we try to evaluate it from the perspective of public empowerment and participation: Who has a voice? Who is empowered to make decisions that affect ecosystems and the communities that depend on them? Is it local communities? Private corporations? Government agencies? International organizations? (See Box 1.3.)

Property rights, including water, mineral, and other use rights granted by the state, are an important aspect of these questions. How are these rights awarded? To what extent should the public be involved when the exercise of these rights affects the surrounding environment and human communities? What about indigenous groups and the poor–who

are frequently deprived of these rights and robbed of a voice on local resource use? What if no one seems to "own" a resource, such as deep ocean fish stocks, and there is little effective control over its use? Absence of authority is a governance matter as well (see Box 1.4).

Environmental governance is also about the manner in which decisions are made: In secret or in public? Who has "a seat at the table" during deliberations? How are the interests of affected communities and ecosystems represented? How are decision-makers held responsible for the integrity of the process and for the results of their decisions?

Unfamiliar but Everyday

While the term "governance" may not be familiar, the themes of governance are all around us. U.S.-based Enron Corporation's misleading energy trading practices. Human displacement by China's Three Gorges Dam. "Salmon wars" between the United States and Canada over harvest limits for Pacific salmon. The struggle over whether genetically modified foods should be labeled or barred from trade. The political battle surrounding the Kyoto Protocol to address climate change. These cases deal with secret decisions, decisions that lack local backing, disputes over rules, over fairness, over protecting the public interest–all issues of authority and its consequences.

In fact, governance issues–and matters of environmental governance in particular–are extraordinarily dynamic today. The right of citizen participation; the transparency of organizations and processes; the need to address public corruption; the right to obtain information from governments and businesses about environmental conditions, pollutants, or land use decisions; the extent to which environmental protection should be included in global trade agreements: All of these are the subject not just of academic policy discussions, but of daily newspaper articles and heated public debate.

We see governance at work locally in decisions about whether we will log or graze a certain area, build a road through a park or a large undeveloped parcel, divert water from a river for farms or houses nearby. These decisions have obvious and immediate environmental impacts.

But governance reaches beyond these high-profile deliberations. It encompasses all the ways in which we exercise authority over the environment more generally, including the timing or overall strategy of management actions such as timber harvests or fishing limits; deciding financing and enforcement; and determining how the benefits from these actions will be allocated. Even the setting of economic policies–such as tariffs on imported logs, subsidies for fishing boats or renewable energy, or giving a green light to foreign investment in a natural gas pipeline–is an important aspect of environmental governance, since such policies determine the economic incentives that drive business decisions and influence their environmental and social impacts.

Sometimes we use the term governance very broadly to describe not just the process of decision-making, but the actual management actions–where and when to log, or how to limit fishing or distribute grazing permits–that come from that process. In other words, in our day-to-day experience we intertwine environmental governance and ecosystem management, which is where the real impact of decisions becomes visible. In truth, environmental governance goes beyond actual decisions on how to manage natural resources to include the decision-making framework—the laws, policies, regulations, bureaucracies, formal procedures, and codes of conduct—within which managers make their decisions. It sets the larger context that either enables or constrains management.

Does Governance Reach Beyond Governments?

A common mistake is to confuse governance with *government*—the set of institutions we normally associate with political authority. Clearly, governments are important players in how ecosystems are managed and how natural resources are exploited or conserved. National laws and regulatory frameworks set formal rules for managing natural resources by recognizing discrete property, mineral, or water rights. They also establish the legal mandates of government agencies with responsibility for environmental protection and resource management. These are the institutions that we frequently associate with major environmental decisions and the responsibility to govern nature.

Governments also act internationally (often through the United Nations) to set ground rules about pollution, water use, fishing, and other activities that affect resources across

Box 1.3 Seven Elements of Environmental Governance

1 Institutions and Laws: *Who makes and enforces the rules for using natural resources?* ■ *What are the rules and the penalties for breaking them?* ■ *Who resolves disputes?*
Government ministries; regional water or pollution control boards; local zoning departments and governing councils; international bodies such as the United Nations or World Trade Organization; industry trade organizations. ■ Environmental and economic laws, policies, rules, treaties, and enforcement regimes; corporate codes of conduct. ■ Courts and administrative review panels.

2 Participation Rights and Representation: *How can the public influence or contest the rules over natural resources?* ■ *Who represents those who use or depend on natural resources when decisions on these resources are made?*
Freedom of Information laws; public hearings, reviews, and comment periods on environmental plans and actions; ability to sue in court, lodge a complaint, or demand an administrative review of a rule or decision. ■ Elected legislators, appointed representatives, nongovernmental organizations (NGOs) representing local people or other environmental stakeholders.

3 Authority Level: *At what level or scale—local, regional, national, international—does the authority over resources reside?*
Visible in: Distribution of official rulemaking, budgeting, and investment power at different levels of government (e.g., district forest office; regional air pollution control board; national agriculture ministry; international river basin authority).

4 Accountability and Transparency: *How do those who control and manage natural resources answer for their decisions, and to whom?* ■ *How open to scrutiny is the decision-making process?*

Mechanisms: Elections; public oversight bodies; performance reviews; opinion polls; financial audits; corporate boards of directors; stockholder meetings. ■ Availability of public records of rules, decisions, and complaints; corporate financial statements; public inventories of pollutant releases from industrial facilities, power plants, and water treatment facilities.

5 Property Rights and Tenure: *Who owns a natural resource or has the legal right to control it?*
Visible in: Land titles; water, mineral, fishing, or other use rights; tribal or traditional community-based property rights; logging, mining, and park recreation concessions.

6 Markets and Financial Flows: *How do financial practices, economic policies, and market behavior influence authority over natural resources?*
Visible in: Private sector investment patterns and lending practices; government aid and lending by multilateral development banks; trade policies and tariffs; corporate business strategies; organized consumer activities such as product boycotts or preferences; stockholder initiatives related to company environmental behavior.

7 Science and Risk: *How are ecological and social science incorporated into decisions on natural resource use to reduce risks to people and ecosystems and identify new opportunities?*
Mechanisms: Science advisory panels (e.g., Intergovernmental Panel on Climate Change); natural resource inventories (e.g., Food and Agriculture Organization of the United Nations biennial State of World Fisheries and Aquaculture report); ground- and satellite-based ecosystem monitoring programs (e.g., Millennium Ecosystem Assessment); national censuses and economic tracking; company health, safety, and environment reports.

Poor communities are particularly vulnerable to failed governance, because they rely more heavily on natural resources for subsistence and income.

political boundaries. One of the most visible aspects of this global environmental governance is a large set of international environmental treaties, including the Convention on Biological Diversity, the Kyoto Protocol on greenhouse gases, the Convention on the Law of the Sea, and the Montreal Protocol to protect the stratospheric ozone layer. Multilateral bodies such as the World Bank and the World Trade Organization are also taking on greater environmental significance in an increasingly globalized and interdependent world economy. The European Union, which is able to enter directly into international negotiations on behalf of its soon-to-be 25 member states, will also play a growing role.

But environmental governance goes beyond the official actions of government diplomats, regulators, and resource managers. It also includes the considerable amount of decision-making and influence that occurs outside formal government structures and organizations. In some cases, it involves corporations or individuals acting in the state's place to harvest or manage resources. States may grant forest or mining concessions to companies for a fee, in some instances allowing them broad discretion to cut trees, build roads, or make other important land use decisions. Or the state may privatize once-public functions like the delivery of water, electricity, or wastewater treatment, again putting a host of environmental choices—from water pricing to power plant construction—into private hands.

On the other hand, environmental governance includes the activities of nongovernmental organizations (NGOs) such as environmental groups, civic groups, neighborhood groups, and labor unions that, in recent decades, have become potent advocates for better and fairer environmental decisions. It also incorporates the actions of industry groups, trade associations, shareholder groups, and professional associations that influence the way companies do business by promoting (or obstructing) cleaner processes, better environmental accounting practices, and standards and codes of conduct, or by pointing out the financial liabilities of business practices that harm the environment.

Governance includes our individual choices and actions when these influence larger public policies or affect corporate behavior. Voting, lobbying, participating in public hearings, or joining environmental watchdog or monitoring groups are typical ways that we as individuals can influence environmental decisions. Our actions as consumers

are also powerful governance forces. For example, the choice to purchase environmentally friendly products like certified lumber or a fuel-efficient car influences the environmental behavior of businesses through the marketplace. Consumer choices can sometimes be as powerful as government regulations in influencing business decisions that affect the environment.

What Is At Stake?

- The depletion of many marine fish stocks, such as cod, blue fin tuna, or patagonian toothfish, stems from the failure of government fishing ministries to effectively manage fishing rights. The fact that many fish stocks—such as

salmon and tuna—move between the waters of two or more nations magnifies the governance challenge and has led to conflict between countries.

- Disruption of the world's river systems with dams and canals that alter normal hydrological cycles is often the result of compartmentalized decision-making, in which plans to build dams, generate electricity, extend irrigated agriculture, and fill wetlands have been formulated without considering possible impacts on downstream water users or the aquatic environment itself.

- Forest degradation is often caused by timber companies that gain access to forest resources through corrupt

(continued on p. 12)

8

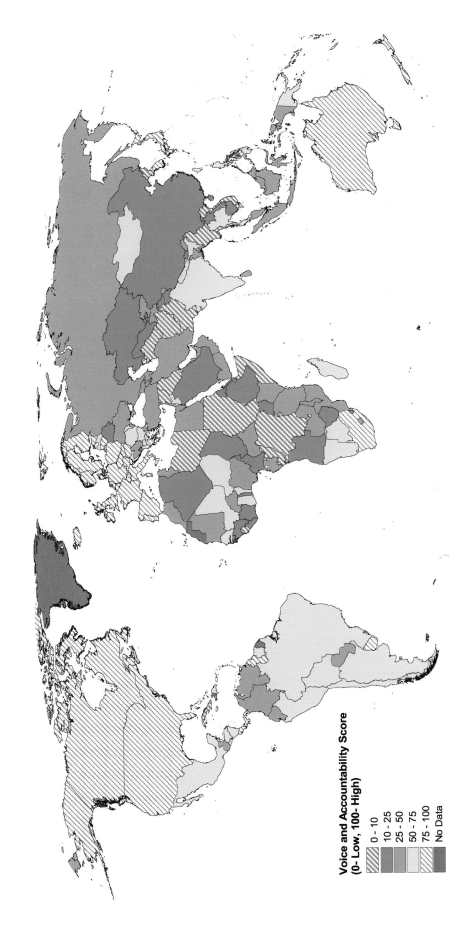

**Voice and Accountability Score
(0- Low, 100- High)**

0 - 10

10 - 25

25 - 50

50 - 75

75 - 100

No Data

Source: Kaufmann et al. 2002

The extent to which citizens are able to participate in the political and decision-making processes, give voice to their concerns, and hold their government representatives accountable is an important dimension of governance. The voice and accountability scores assigned here are based on indicators of political and civil liberties extended to a country's citizens, as well as the independence of media, which play an important role in monitoring governance performance. The scores were calculated by the World Bank.

Box 1.4 What About Ownership? Property Rights and Governance

Ownership is a common avenue to authority over resources. Ownership of land or the right to use a resource found on it—such as water, mineral, or harvest rights—means control. A land or resource owner often controls physical access to a site and has the principal say in all sorts of land use decisions: how often to harvest trees and whether to reforest, the number of livestock to graze, whether to clear land for crops and how much pesticide to use.

While it may seem simple, ownership actually has a complex relationship with environmental governance. How property rights or ownership are defined, who benefits from these rights, and how they are enforced are central issues. Insecurity of ownership, mismatches between state and indigenous forms of ownership, and unequal distribution of ownership are frequent sources of conflict and poor environmental decisions. Also, the problem of managing "common pool" resources like ocean fish stocks or groundwater supplies that do not seem to have owners is one of today's most vexing governance challenges.

Understanding Property Rights and Tenure

Property rights—the slate of rights that come with ownership—fall into a few basic categories. The most primary right is the *use right*—the right to harvest or exploit a land's resources, to occupy the land, and to make permanent improvements on it. The *transfer right* gives the owner the right to sell, give, lease, or bequeath the land and its resources, while the *exclusion right* gives the owner the right to keep others from using the resource. Finally, the *enforcement right* guarantees all other rights by providing for financial or social consequences when they are not honored (Rukuni 1999:3–4). Together, these property rights provide the basis of tenure—what we commonly think of as property ownership.

Tenure takes four basic forms (Rukuni 1999:4; McCay 2000:69; Burger et al. 2001:4–5). From an environmental governance standpoint, each has strengths and weaknesses:

- *Private*, or owned by an individual, corporation, or institution. Private ownership provides an incentive to maintain and continue to benefit from a property's resources, but also allows destructive land practices without giving a voice to others who may be affected by the owner's decisions.

- *Communal*, or owned in common by a defined group of individuals, such as a village, tribe, or commune. Communal ownership may more efficiently share resources among those dependent on them, but can be harder to define, govern, and enforce in the formal legal terms demanded by modern state authorities.

- *State*, or owned by the government. State ownership can allow diverse elements of the public to benefit from the land's resources, but states frequently lack the capacity to manage their land efficiently and sustainably in the face of public and commercial demand.

- *Open access*, or owned by no one. Most land that appears to be open access is actually state or communal land where the state or community lacks the ability to enforce rules about its use. Open access lands are often subject to heavy and unsustainable use, but constitute one of the few resources available for landless or low-income families.

In practice, these basic forms of ownership appear in a variety of combinations, often with competing rights and obligations (McCay 2000:69; Burger et al. 2001:4–5). For instance, private ownership is the most prevalent tenure arrangement in Western Europe and North America, with an emphasis on carefully drawn titles and formal leases. However, building codes, local zoning rules, and environmental regulations circumscribe the rights of the private property owner, giving the state—and often the public—a voice in private land use. In fact, how much the state should be able to modify private property rights to protect the environment is currently a controversial governance question in the United States.

In response, some new ownership arrangements try to accommodate public conservation and environmental objectives within the private property regime (McCay 2000:70). These include creation of conservation easements, where a private land owner sells or gives up the right to develop or harvest a site, while retaining other ownership rights. Land trusts—nongovernmental groups that negotiate conservation easements or acquire land outright to maintain as open space—help bridge the private property market and the preservation of public goods like open space, access to recreation, and intact natural habitat. In the United States, for example, some 1,200 nonprofit land trusts have protected more than 6.2 million acres from development (LTA 2003; TPL 2003).

In much of Africa, Asia, and South America, the situation is different. State-sanctioned, titled land ownership is a relatively unusual concept, especially for indigenous and rural populations. The historical norm was communal tenure, often mediated by local chiefs and elders. In Africa, for example, tenure systems allocated farming or grazing rights based on inheritance or the decisions of village elders, but the land itself was not owned in the sense of being a salable commodity (Bruce 1998b:3, 1998a:9; Agbosu 2000:13). In these areas, governance problems often revolve around the uneasy transition from traditional ownership practices to more formalized state arrangements.

The colonial era introduced the concepts of private and state ownership to many countries, and these practices were greatly expanded following independence (Bruce 1998a:4–5, 8). In many cases, the newly independent state claimed most of what had been communal land, but the land often continued to be controlled by local custom. This disjuncture between de facto local control and official state ownership often becomes a platform for conflict, leaves local residents unsure of their ownership rights, and opens an avenue for corrupt or unsustainable use of disputed land by opportunists (Rukuni 1999:2).

Individual vs. Communal Ownership

Security of ownership is important to anyone who relies on land or natural resources for livelihood, income, or shelter. *Secure tenure* is usually associated with having one's ownership or use rights formally recognized by traditional authorities in a community, or legally recognized by the state—often in the form of a title.

Security of tenure is often a deciding factor in how people use or abuse land and resources. Without confidence in their property rights, or lacking any guarantee of rights for a long duration—say, if involuntary removal from land seems likely—people have little incentive to invest in or improve the resource. For example, research shows that Sumatran rubber tappers with short-term leases tend to overexploit their rubber trees—compared to permanent owners—in order to increase short-term returns (Suyanto et al. 2001:1).

Promoting secure tenure can involve helping individuals to legally register or gain title to lands they are already using, though these may be state or communal lands. The private ownership that this titling confers can offer many incentives. The owner reaps the benefits of investments he makes in wells, terraces, soil amendments, and other good stewardship practices. Under the right market conditions, formal land ownership also allows farmers to borrow against their land, making capital available to fund improvements that would otherwise be beyond the reach of small landowners.

However, private ownership is only one way to bring secure tenure and encourage sustainable decision-making. Communal tenure, for example, can offer full security within a collective framework. In Africa, communal ownership is at the heart of the traditional or customary tenure systems that still dominate land use in rural areas. In these customary systems of ownership, some use rights, such as use of arable or residential lands, may be held by individuals and passed on within a family, while access rights to pastures, forests, mountain areas, waterways, and sacred areas may be shared (Bruce 1998a:8–10; Rukuni 1999:1–5; Toulmin and Quan 2000:35–36).

Communal tenure systems are under increasing pressure to reflect changes in national economies and political structures. In Mali, for example, local land markets have sprung up in areas where cash crops like cotton have supplanted subsistence crops, reflecting the newly realized commercial value of the land (Bruce 1998a:10). Most national governments have also actively discouraged customary tenure systems in an attempt to encourage economic growth (Bruce 1998a:6–11; Rukuni 1999:1–2; Toulmin and Quan 2000:34). The assumption—largely disproved by recent experience—was that private ownership would better foster the investment and productivity increases that modern states depend on for growth.

Such shifts toward private ownership systems have frequently become the basis for battles among local residents, commercial interests, and government agencies. In Indonesia, for example, the central government has often ignored traditional forest tenure arrangements (known as *adat*) when selling timber concessions to private logging companies, incurring the anger of local residents who have lost use of the forest without compensation (WRI 2000:36–37).

Government land titling and registration programs meant to shift communal tenure toward private ownership and private enterprise have also met with difficulties. These policies have, in some cases, contributed to poverty and landlessness by undermining customary land rights and providing a route to concentrate land ownership in the hands of private interests and political elites. In Kenya, a land registration program active since the 1950s has been accompanied by heightened inequalities in land ownership, increased land disputes between title holders and holders of customary rights, and increased insecurity among widows and poor farmers who find the cost of registration prohibitive (Toulmin and Quan 2000:34–37).

Avoiding a "Tragedy of the Commons"

As Africa and parts of Asia grapple with the transition to new ownership patterns, the experience of local groups with managing communal property is perhaps more relevant than ever. "Common pool" resources like public grazing areas, fisheries, water resources, and forest areas are particularly difficult to govern, precisely because no one individual has an exclusive right to use them, yet each person's use tends to diminish the remaining resource.

In 1968, author Garrett Hardin highlighted the vulnerability of common pool resources when he popularized the concept of the "tragedy of the commons." He argued that open access resources will inevitably be overexploited (Hardin 1968:1244). The state of global fish stocks is perhaps the purest modern

(continued on next page)

Box 1.4 (continued)

expression of Hardin's thesis. In many areas, fishermen have relatively open access to fishing grounds and little effective regulation of their activities. Competition for fish and lack of sanctions for overuse have left many fish stocks depleted.

But in the 35 years since Hardin's analysis, research has shown that degradation of common pool resources is not inevitable (Feeny et al. 1990:1–19; Ostrom et al. 1999:278–282). In fact, many instances of community management of communal property show that where traditional ownership systems remain intact, few resources are completely "open access." Most are governed through social and institutional arrangements that recognize the advantages of sharing resources among a limited number of community members with prescribed rules of behavior. In Kenya, for example, each Maasai community reserves dry season pastures that can only be used when no forage is available elsewhere. By accommodating neighboring groups in times of need, each group increases the expectation that they will have access to pasture in lean times, thereby improving their own security (Seno and Shaw 2002:79–80).

What are the conditions that lead to good community management of common resources? Research on thousands of cases of community-based management shows that key factors in success include a community-wide understanding of the value and scarcity of the resource; good communication among community members; an effort to monitor whether rules for use are followed; a credible system of sanctions when rules are broken; and a mechanism to resolve disputes. Government recognition of the community's right to manage the resource itself, ensuring that local authority is not undermined, is also a crucial precondition for success (Ostrom 1990:90–102; Ostrom et al. 1999:281; Jensen 2000:642).

practices. The problem is exacerbated by the failure of government agencies to enforce forest protection laws, or by management approaches that emphasize commodity production at the expense of forest health.

- At the global level, the refusal of the United States and a few other nations to embrace the Kyoto Protocol or negotiate other measures to systematically cut greenhouse gas emissions thwarts international efforts to deal with a global problem.

The inability of government institutions to manage ecosystems for their health rather than simply for maximum yield, to apportion the costs and benefits of natural resource use fairly, to manage resources across departmental and political boundaries, or to confront the disease of corruption are hallmarks of poor environmental governance. Many business decision-makers have compounded these problems by marginalizing environmental concerns in their business models.

As a result, ecosystems remain at great jeopardy, and with them the livelihoods and continued well-being of communities everywhere. Poor communities are particularly vulnerable to failed governance, since they rely more heavily on natural resources for subsistence and income, and are less likely to share in property rights that give them legal control over these resources.

On the other hand, improved environmental governance holds promise for reversing ecosystem degradation by more carefully balancing human needs and ecosystem processes.

- In the Indian states of West Bengal, Orissa, and several others, a change in the states' forest policies has led to a significant recovery of degraded forests and the biodiversity they harbor. Rather than treat local people as interlopers on state-owned forest lands, the state is allowing local communities to manage some of the forests themselves. Local people share the increased productivity of the recovering forests with the state, providing a strong incentive for long-term stewardship and self-policing (WRI et al. 2000:192).

- In the Philippines, cooperation among government officials, NGOs, indigenous and local communities, religious leaders, and the media has helped reduce illegal logging (Hofer 1997:236–238).

- In the United Kingdom, a law requiring industrial facilities to provide information to the public about toxic releases has directly contributed to a 40 percent reduction in releases of cancer-causing substances to the air over the past three years (FOE-UK 2002).

- South Africa's recent water reforms take an unusually far-sighted, ecologically grounded approach to resource management. Laws enacted in 1997 and 1998 mandate that the country maintain an environmental "reserve"–the amount of water that freshwater ecosystems require to remain robust–while also ensuring access to a basic provision of water as every citizen's "right," and vastly expanding the scope for local participation in water management (WRI et al. 2000:200).

- At the international level, the Montreal Protocol on Substances that Deplete the Ozone Layer–a treaty concluded in 1987–has been instrumental in nearly eliminating the manufacture and use of chemicals that harm the stratos-

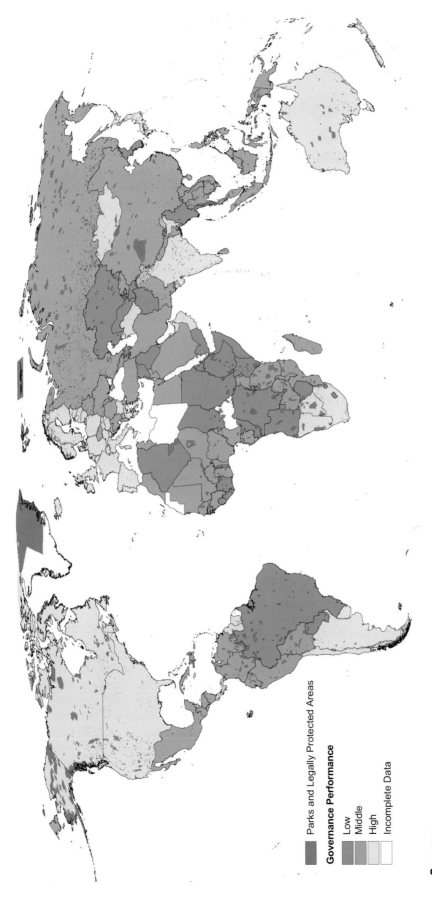

Parks and Legally Protected Areas

Governance Performance

Low
Middle
High
Incomplete Data

Sources:
UNEP-WCMC 2003
Kaufmann et al. 2002

Poor governance performance threatens the viability of protected areas over the long term. More than half of all protected areas occur in nations whose governance performance is poor or medium. Poor governance may translate to reduced capacity for park management, including planning, monitoring, and enforcement. It may also lead to greater risk of corrupt or illegal use of park resources, and a greater chance of conflict with local residents, who may not be given a voice in decisions about their tenure in and access to protected areas. Governance performance was calculated from the World Bank's Voice and Accountability index and the Government Effectiveness index.

pheric ozone layer in developed countries. And through the treaty's innovative financing mechanism, developing countries have cut their consumption of these chemicals by 25 percent since 1997, on the way to fully phasing them out by 2010 (Andersen and Sarma 2002:279).

Better Governance, Better Equity

One of the strongest arguments for encouraging better governance is that it requires us to focus on the social dimensions of natural resource use and ecosystem management, in addition to the technical details of how to manage. This includes how we value ecosystems, how we set management goals, how we negotiate trade-offs between conflicting uses or goals, and, finally, how we make sure the costs and benefits of our decisions—including impacts on the poor—are equitably shared (see Box 1.5). In fact, a focus on governance adds an explicit considera-

> A focus on governance adds an explicit consideration of fairness to the goals of ecosystem management.

tion of fairness to the goals of ecosystem management.

Science and technology can help us answer questions about what kinds of management actions are most effective in protecting or restoring ecological integrity. For example, conservation science can estimate how large an area of forest we should preserve to ensure the survival of various species of wildlife or plants. Atmospheric science can model how quickly greenhouse gas emissions must be reduced to stabi-

---

The Importance of Environmental Institutions

Environmental governance is inevitably associated with organizations such as government agencies, where official authority over the environment often resides, and where rules are codified, interpreted, and enforced. These commonly include local or provincial-level natural resource agencies and national ministries of environment, forestry, agriculture, mining, or finance, as well as environmental regulatory agencies.

At the international level are regional authorities such as the Mekong River Commission; multilateral development banks such as the World Bank or the Asian Development Bank; intergovernmental organizations such as the United Nations Environment Programme, the Food and Agriculture Organization of the United Nations, and the United Nations Development Programme; and international bodies that regulate trade and commerce, such as the World Trade Organization. Other organizations play important professional, legal, or scientific advisory roles, or set rules and standards that influence environmental decisions.

Because such organizations are critical to the official framework for environmental governance, their institutional failures are important contributors to today's environmental problems. Common failures include:

■ *Lack of coordination among organizations.* Many separate organizations may share overlapping environmental responsibilities, but fail to coordinate their activities. Aquatic, forest, grassland, and agricultural ecosystems may exist in close proximity and require integrated approaches for effective management, yet fall under the authority of different agencies. Often, these organizations compete for budget, jurisdiction, and influence within the government, increasing their insularity. Similarly, governing bodies at the local, national, and international levels frequently fail to integrate their management approaches and decision-making processes.

■ *Marginalization of environmental departments, programs, and ministries.* Environment ministries often become bureaucratic islands isolated from other ministries that affect the environment. Once a separate environmental unit is created—whether as a ministry in a national government, a department of a multilateral development bank, or a division of a private company—there is a tendency for all the other units to assume that concern for the environment is not their job. Yet, these separate environment units are seldom sufficiently powerful to influence most decisions that may have significant environmental impacts.

■ *Lack of transparency and accountability.* Some organizations have taken pains to create public communication channels and to establish processes, such as public hearings, that allow for participation in environmental decisions. However, many organizations still lack adequate mechanisms for transparency and accountability. Finance and trade, for example, are areas where public transparency and accountability have traditionally been limited. Thus, the World Trade Organization—whose decisions can profoundly affect national environmental standards and influence enforcement of treaties such as the Convention on International Trade in Endangered Species (CITES)—has typically kept its trade negotiations secret and without any meaningful avenue for public input.

lize their build-up in the atmosphere and avoid catastrophic changes in the global climate system.

However, conservation science cannot tell us how best to resolve conflicts between local communities and logging companies over the fate of a forest, and atmospheric science cannot tell us how responsibility for reducing emissions should be distributed. These are governance questions, involving the balance of ethical and moral concerns, social and economic goals, and the capacities of natural systems.

Similarly, economic analysis can answer questions about the most efficient methods for achieving various ecosystem management objectives. For example, economic analysis can inform the design of a system of taxes and subsidies to encourage electricity producers to build more efficient power plants, or to encourage polluting factories to reduce their emissions.

But economic analysis cannot tell us how best to respond to community concerns over the siting of those power plants and factories. Again, it is the challenge of governance to answer questions such as "What's fair?" "What's the right balance?" and sometimes "Who benefits and bears the consequences?"—in addition to giving insights into what is efficient and effective in the real world of competing interests.

Participation and Accountability

Participation and accountability are two key concepts underpinning the principles and practice of environmental governance.

Participation

Meaningful participation brings influence. Those who participate in decision-making that affects ecosystems stand the best chance of having their interests represented. Managing ecosystems frequently involves deciding among trade-offs. For example, damming a river may provide farmers more irrigation water but lower the river's fishing potential by interrupting annual spawning runs. Thus, participation by both farmers and fishermen is useful in negotiating how such trade-offs should be made and how the "losers" should be compensated.

Public participation also brings legitimacy, improving the credibility and effectiveness of decision-making processes. Stakeholders can identify conflicts and potential problems that resource managers may have overlooked at an early stage. When all stakeholders have a voice and time is taken to find acceptable solutions, public confidence in the fairness of the decision increases. Especially for large or controversial projects, public involvement in one form or another is required for any broad-based consensus behind the final decision (Bruch 2001:11390–11391).

Failure to provide for public input can bring just the opposite: conflict and resistance. For example, the resettlement of communities to make way for alternative land uses—ranging from hydroelectric dams to national parks—has been one of the most contentious public policy issues in both industrialized and developing countries. One reason is that the communities to be resettled often have not been consulted until *after* key decisions have been made.

In an attempt to address the root causes of such conflict, the World Commission on Dams proposed in its recent report a "rights and risks" approach to decision-making around development projects like dams. In this approach, anyone holding a right or facing a risk relevant to a proposed action must have the opportunity to participate in the decision-making process.

Mechanisms to ensure participation in environmental decision-making can take many forms. In democracies, the election or nomination of executives, legislators, or other representatives, and the selection of judges provide one way of giving citizens a voice in public policies related to the environment. However, the environment is often only one among many concerns of the electorate, and a candidate's environmental record is seldom the principal factor in determining the outcome of an election. Mechanisms for direct participation are often used to supplement or substitute for elections. For example, in many countries, national policies require that public hearings be held when the environmental impacts of proposed projects are being assessed (see Box 1.6).

A common challenge to ensuring participation in environmental decision-making is that not all affected stakeholders are equally well-positioned to express their views. For example, at the community level, cultural norms may discourage women from speaking in public, or even from attending a village meeting at which a proposed project is being discussed.

Box 1.5 Poverty and Environmental Governance

Better environmental governance holds special promise for the poor—the people most vulnerable to environmental degradation, and the people whose opinions and ideas are most often muted in environmental decisions. More than 1.2 billion people—including more than 40 percent of the population in sub-Saharan Africa and South Asia (World Bank 2001:23), and about one fifth of the population worldwide—live on less than $1 per day. Another 1.6 billion live on less than $2 (World Bank 2001:3).

But poverty means more than a lack of income. Poverty is also defined by increased vulnerability in a number of dimensions: vulnerability to environmental degradation or loss of access to natural resources, to employment scarcity, to property loss, to disease and ill health (IFAD 2001:2; World Bank 2001:15–21). Decisions about natural resources reach into all of these areas, and thus environmental governance failures often fall hardest on low-income families.

Marginal Lands, Marginal Voice

One of the greatest environmental vulnerabilities that poverty brings is a high dependence on natural resources for subsistence, particularly in rural areas. Low-income households typically rely much more on resources such as collectible forest products, fish, bushmeat, fodder, or surface water sources than better-off families. For example, a study of 80 villages in India showed that common property resources—such as community forest lands and grazing areas—provided 14–23 percent of total income for poorer families, while they provided only 1–3 percent of income for wealthier households (Jodha 1995). In Zimbabwe, studies in the 1990s showed that families obtained about one third of their income from environmental resources. The poorer the household, the greater the share of income from natural resources (Cavendish 1999:6–7; DFID et al. 2002:12). That means greater hardship when these resources degrade or disappear altogether.

The poor face even higher risks from environmental degradation because such a high percentage of poor families live on marginal lands. These lands may be arid, steeply sloped, or have low natural fertility—factors that limit their agricultural potential and make them subject to large swings in productivity as conditions change. Marginal lands are often prone to drought and are particularly vulnerable to land degradation, erosion, floods, and landslides. This makes them sensitive to changing land use patterns and increased population pressure, and increases the need for careful management (World Bank 2003:59-60).

The population on fragile lands has doubled in the last 50 years. Yet government decision-makers have paid only scant attention to these areas, and their governance records are unimpressive. Poor, rural families typically have very limited access to public services or decision-makers, and therefore have little effective voice. Decisions on mining concessions, water projects, and other resource issues that affect them often bypass their input. Further, since the rural poor living on marginal lands contribute little to the formal economy, these areas have garnered little economic investment, deepening the cycle of poverty (World Bank 2003:59–60).

Urban Exposure

Marginalization and heightened vulnerability to inferior governance are not confined to the rural poor. In urban areas too, poverty means fewer choices about environmental matters. Numerous studies show that low-income families are more likely to live in polluted areas, for example (Wheeler 2002:96–98). An inventory of pollution releases in England shows that 90 percent of polluting factories in London are in areas with below-average income (FOE-UK 1999).

The poor's lack of effective voice in environmental decision-making is also well-documented. Low-income families are less likely to register official complaints about contamination, and thus less likely to benefit from regulatory attention, such as enforcement actions against polluting industries by government inspectors. One World Bank study in China found that, for citizens with similar levels of pollution exposure and education, those living in high-income provinces were more than twice as likely to file complaints as those residing in low-income provinces (Wheeler 2002:95).

Lack of voice has real consequences in terms of environmental equity. Environment agencies are often very sensitive to public input in the form of complaints. For instance, the pollution control authority in the Brazilian state of Rio de Janeiro focuses almost 100 percent of its inspection efforts on investigating citizen complaints, and a similar situation prevails in Indonesia. Since wealthier and more educated residents tend to wield more influence and also to complain more, it is therefore no surprise that regulatory action to clean up pollution is often concentrated in wealthier municipalities or neighborhoods (Wheeler 2002:94–95).

Several factors contribute to the poor's lack of environmental voice. These include a lower capacity to organize for political action, a reluctance to take on government officials or business interests with political clout, and also a dearth of information about local pollution or other environmental problems and their effects. This information deficit and lack of political effectiveness mean that the interests of low-income families are frequently the last to be served in the decision-making process. Corruption only increases the marginalization of the poor.

Because of their lower social status, the poor are more likely to be subjected to exploitation, rudeness, intimidation, and even physical violence in their dealings with government institutions. The poor often complain of being demeaned and express the desire for greater respect from government service people and institutions (World Bank 2001:35–36). Given these circumstances, combined with their lack of voice, it is not surprising that the poor generally give government institutions low grades in terms of their fairness, accountability, and responsiveness.

Empowering the Poor

Since the late 1990s, strategies for tackling global poverty have begun to emphasize the importance of better governance, and the need to empower poor people to become their own advocates. The basic tools of poverty reduction are access to jobs, credit, education, and healthcare, as well as infrastructure like electricity, sanitation, roads, and irrigation. But delivery of these tools is inevitably affected by the efficiency and transparency of government institutions, and particularly by their accountability and accessibility to the poor (World Bank 2001:6–12).

The need for better access and participation is especially acute among the poor. When poor people are allowed to make their voices heard in political processes and local decision-making, and to insist on their rights in court, they are better able to protect their lands and claim a share of government resources. They are less likely to become victims of government decisions on parks, roads, dams, and forest concessions that often dispossess them of their lands without adequately compensating them (World Bank 2001:7, 9).

Making this kind of empowerment happen may at the beginning require specifically targeting the poor in participatory exercises, such as rural needs assessments, that build the capacity to participate. It will also require improving legal aid and disseminating information on legal procedures so that the poor know their rights. Promoting decentralization that devolves real control over local resources to rural residents can also be a powerful way to empower the poor, as well as bring government service agencies closer to poor communities. Attention to including women in decision-making circles will also be crucial for effective empowerment of poor communities, since women make up a high percentage of the poor (IFAD 2001:11; World Bank 2001:9–10).

Similarly, poorer households may not be able to afford to take time away from productive labor to attend such meetings. More broadly, barriers of distance, language, literacy, and connectivity can also prevent full participation.

Another difficulty is that, even if given the opportunity to participate, stakeholders may lack the capacity to become involved in as meaningful a way as they desire. They may not understand the costs and benefits of the management options or how those options could affect their own interests over time. Or they may not be able to call upon the same sophisticated planning tools or economic analyses that others may use to put forward a convincing case.

For example, when considering the benefits of a new road to an isolated community, some residents may have misgivings about environmental costs or changes to the community structure that road access could bring—but this may pale in comparison to official projections of economic benefits put forward by road advocates. Thus, capacity-building is often a necessary precursor to participation; the public may have to learn to be effective advocates for their interests. But even if many stakeholders lack the capacity to participate fully, the opportunity to participate at all can still increase public acceptance of the final decision.

A final challenge is how to represent the interests of nature itself in environmental decision-making. When negotiations over how to allocate limited natural resources take place, the need to protect ecosystem integrity or species survival does not always have a "seat at the table." For example, when rights to use surface water are being distributed, environmentalists have argued that downstream ecosystems should also have a guaranteed share. During a drought in 2001, a controversy of just this type erupted over whether the farmers—or an endangered species of salmon—should have priority use of the water in the Klamath River Basin in the United States (Schoch 2001:9; Bailey 2002:10).

Accountability

Accountability refers to the way in which public and private sector decision-makers are held responsible for their actions. In other words, what recourse is available when public officials or agencies fail to fulfill their mandate to protect ecosystems? Or when corporations deliberately mislead or fail to perform as promised?

There are many types of accountability, but all involve the ability to sanction the decision-maker or responsible party in some way—the ability to punish or bring pressure to bear (Keohane 2003). For example, elected officials can be voted out of office at the next election if constituents are dissatisfied with their environmental policies or performance. Companies can be fined for exceeding pollution limits. Within companies, supervisors can fire employees if they fail to comply with environmental policies, while boards of directors or similar oversight committees can insist that CEOs bring environmental considerations into their business models.

Withholding money is one of the most common means of holding officials or agencies accountable. Legislatures can cut or reconfigure the budgets of forest or environment ministries if they don't fulfill their mandates. Multilateral agencies such as the World Bank can also be held accountable by legislatures through their roles in appropriating funds. Many of the environmental policies and procedures that the World Bank adopted in the early 1990s were prompted by threats from the U.S. Congress to withhold a portion of Bank funding (Bowles and Kormos 1995:791–808).

On the other hand, courts can restrict or redefine the authority of government agencies, or impose remedial actions on those agencies if it finds them environmentally remiss. In India, for example, the Supreme Court has held the city government of Delhi accountable for enforcing limits on industrial pollution and has vigorously implemented a ban on certain types of vehicle fuels with the goal of cleaning up the city's polluted air (CSE 2002).

Environmental accountability comes into play at the broader societal level as well. Investors and consumers can use the marketplace to punish or reward corporations through their decisions about which companies to finance and which products to buy. For example, socially responsible investment funds offer investors a mechanism to invest only in companies that meet a certain standard of environmental performance.

Reputation is also a powerful leverage point for accountability. The desire to maintain a positive public image can be a major incentive for both government agencies and private corporations to improve their environmental practices. For example, unhappy with their growing international reputation for tolerating illegal logging in tropical rainforests, countries such as Indonesia and Cameroon have recently made public commitments to crack down on this practice (FWI and GFW 2002:x; WRI 2002).

All these levels of accountability depend on a flow of information about the decision-makers and the decision itself, so that it can be evaluated by the public, consumers, or individual stakeholders (Keohane 2003). Without knowing what decision was made, who was responsible, and what the intended outcome of the decision was, it is impossible to expect accountability. That is why environmental accountability is

Box 1.6 Avenues for Public Participation

Government staff may have the scientific expertise to decide whether to allow the construction of a new waste disposal site, or the marketing of a new pesticide, or to make any of a variety of other environmental decisions. So why is public involvement in such decisions so important? Won't public participation just be time-consuming, costly, and make it harder to reach an informed conclusion?

One key reason to involve the public is to ensure that government agencies are acting in the public interest, and that environmental policies reflect public values. Public participation can also help offset any undue industry influence over the regulatory system. Other ways that society benefits from public participation include (Beierle and Cayford 2002:4–6, 14–15):

■ improving the quality of decisions (the public may provide site-specific knowledge, or offer suggestions that satisfy a wider range of interests);

■ resolving conflict among competing interests (resulting in longer-lasting and more satisfying decisions, helping to overcome gridlock);

■ building trust in institutions; and

■ educating and informing the public.

Participation in environmental policy-making may be particularly beneficial because communities are often critical factors in the solutions to local environmental problems like transportation or watershed protection.

Public participation in environmental decision-making can take a variety of forms, depending on the kind of decision being made, the time and budget available to encourage public input, and the political and cultural circumstances of the decision. Some are relatively passive, with information flowing in only one direction. For example, a government agency may supply some specific information, such as a government report on air quality, in response to a citizen request. Other participation mechanisms are more interactive, involving discussions between decision-makers and citizens. Examples would be government consultation with citizens through town meetings, hearings, or advisory panels. Following are several typical avenues for public participation (ELI 1997:10–13):

Document review. The availability of project documents, policy analyses, or other background reports on the issue to be decided is an important element of informed and meaningful public input. Community members and other stakeholders increase their capacity to participate by reviewing background materials presented in a language and at a technical level they can understand. Available documents and reports also increase the accountability of decision-makers—as well as the perceived legitimacy of decisions—since there is a public record of project details and the decisions at issue.

inevitably tied to transparency—the openness of the decision-making process and its ability to be examined and judged.

Principles of Environmental Governance

The basic principles behind good environmental decision-making have been accepted for more than a decade. The 178 nations that attended the Rio Earth Summit in 1992 all endorsed these environmental governance principles when they signed the Rio Declaration on Environment and Development—a charter of 27 principles meant to guide the world community toward sustainable development. The international community re-emphasized the importance of these principles at the World Summit on Sustainable Development in 2002. The problem in applying these good governance practices is thus not their novelty, but the fact that they profoundly challenge our traditional government institutions and economic practices.

Make Decisions at the Appropriate Level

Often, decisions about ecosystems and natural resources are made far from those resources—perhaps in a capital city or an agency's regional headquarters—by people who lack local context or an understanding of how the decision will play out on the ground. In other words, decision-making tends to be centralized and isolated from the people and places affected. Sometimes a better approach is to let local communities or neighborhoods make decisions about the resources around them. In many instances, drawing on local knowledge can bring more informed decisions that serve local people and ecosystems better.

But local management may not always be appropriate or practical. Generally, the appropriate level for decision-making is determined by the scale of the natural system to be managed. Management of a small forested area could appropriately be undertaken by the communities that surround the forest, while management of a major river basin or an area of globally significant biodiversity might require cooperation across national borders.

Thus, finding the "appropriate level" for authority over ecosystem decisions sometimes requires devolving the authority to lower, more local levels of decision-making—what we have come to call decentralization. At other times it

Informational meetings. Natural resource managers can hold meetings at local, state, or national levels to provide basic information about proposed projects, such as where or how big a mine or road will be, or what kind of timber harvesting methods will be used. Such meetings can help build public support, identify local concerns, and develop collaborations with local groups.

Environmental Impact Assessments (EIAs). Environmental Impact Assessments are official analyses that detail the anticipated effects of planned projects or activities on local and regional areas, and explore options and alternatives for mitigating these effects. EIAs are critical planning documents in many nations, and often have important legal and political ramifications for whether the project goes forward or how it will be modified to reduce any negative impacts.

While the extent of public involvement in EIAs varies according to national laws, this tool can provide an opportunity for the public to comment on proposed projects and suggest alternatives. Some EIA laws include explicit procedures for government agencies to review and consider written comments, which are then factored into the agency's approval or licensing decisions.

The comment procedure not only allows participation of the general public and advocacy groups, but also provides a vehicle for other government agencies, or officials from neighboring jurisdictions, to contribute input and influence the debate.

Public hearings. Public hearings provide the opportunity for all interested parties to give public feedback on proposed projects, laws, or environmental policies. Such hearings, announced via radio, newspapers, or other media, are particularly important for stakeholders who may not be able to express their views clearly in writing. They can provide a forum where stakeholders can inform each other of their opinions and ascertain where they stand, as well as give decision-makers a sense of the diversity of community opinion. While some hearings may be simply informative, others may involve more substantive evaluation, where competing project ideas or proposals are vetted publicly, and details of project design are debated point by point.

Advisory committees. Advisory committees allow participation that is more in-depth and continuous, and thus potentially much more influential. These committees allow a diverse group of stakeholders to be involved in crafting policies and designing and modifying projects to reduce impacts and distribute costs and benefits equitably.

Public role in implementation and monitoring. Depending on the nature of the project or policy, there may be scope for NGOs or other local groups to participate in its implementation, including project maintenance, monitoring, or oversight. Monitoring may also involve ongoing public hearings or reviews to ensure that the project or policy is producing the benefits originally anticipated.

involves relinquishing authority to higher levels with greater geographic and political reach. This is especially true when tackling problems such as air pollution and acid rain that have transboundary effects and require regional solutions.

This principle of assigning authority to match the scale of the resource (sometimes called the *subsidiarity principle*) often requires unbundling decisions previously combined at one level. For example, it might be appropriate for a national wildlife management agency to retain the authority for setting annual hunting licenses quotas based on large-scale trends in wildlife populations. But decisions about whether, when, and how to award such licenses within the established quota might best be left to local

Drawing on local knowledge can bring about more informed decisions that serve local people and ecosystems better.

governments or community organizations that can respond to local hunting practices and conditions. In this case, a higher level authority specifies the *outcome* of decision-making (the maximum number of hunting licenses awarded), while a lower level authority specifies the *procedure* (how hunting licenses are awarded).

In other cases, it may be best to let a higher level authority specify the procedure for decision-making, while a lower level authority specifies the outcome. In a national rural development program in Vietnam, for example, village-level development committees are required to have at least one female representative (Dupar and Badenoch 2002:44). However, they are not required to allocate funds for projects specifically directed to women's needs. Thus, in this case, the national authorities influence how budget decisions are made, but the budget decisions themselves remain at the local level.

Provide Access to Information, Participation, and Redress
The heart of good environmental governance is accessible decision-making—that is, decision-making that is transparent and open to public input and oversight. The Rio Declaration established that access has three primary elements: access to information, access to decision-making and the opportunity to participate, and access to redress and legal remedy. These three *access principles* must all be present for an effective system of public participation.

The first foundation of access is *information*: about the environment, about the decisions at hand and their envi-

ronmental implications, and about the decision-making process itself. Without these, meaningful public participa-

> **The Rio Declaration:**
> **Key Governance Principles**
>
> **Principle 4**
> In order to achieve sustainable development, environmental protection shall constitute an integral part of the development process and cannot be considered in isolation from it.
>
> **Principle 10**
> Environmental issues are best handled with the participation of all concerned citizens, at the relevant level. At the national level, each individual shall have appropriate access to information concerning the environment that is held by public authorities, including information on hazardous materials and activities in their communities, and the opportunity to participate in decision-making processes. States shall facilitate and encourage public awareness and participation by making information widely available. Effective access to judicial and administrative proceedings, including redress and remedy, shall be provided.
>
> *Adopted by 178 nations, June 1992, Rio de Janeiro, United Nations Conference on Environment and Development*

tion is impossible. For example, communities have a right to know about contaminants in local drinking water supplies and their potential health impacts, so that they can make informed decisions about whether to drink the water or not. Communities also need to be informed about proposed actions that might threaten drinking water quality—such as the opening of a hazardous waste storage site—so they can ensure that their interests are represented when these actions are debated.

Access to information comes in many forms, including the right to examine public records, obtain the data from environmental monitoring, or read technical or policy analyses done by resource management agencies. Having these materials available in appropriate languages is also part of access, since such information is useless if it can't be understood and acted on in a timely fashion.

In highland areas of Viet Nam and Cambodia, for example, members of ethnic minority communities often do not speak the national languages, and frequently, officials of the government's natural resource-related agencies do not know the ethnic minority languages. Access to environmental information in an appropriate language—and in non-written form—is particularly important for ethnic minority women. A pilot program for decentralized planning in Cambodia's Ratanakiri province was relatively successful in increasing community participation in local environment and development planning because it included language and literacy training for non-Khmer speakers (Dupar and Badenoch 2002:44).

A second foundation of access is the *opportunity to participate* in the decision-making process itself—the chance to give input and influence the decision-makers. In addition to opportunities for input on specific projects, such as the siting of a dam or the size of a timber harvest, the public also needs a chance to weigh in on the design of more general laws, policies, or regulations. Thus, new framework legislation related to forests or mining, changes in policies on land use planning, and revisions to regulations governing automobile emission standards should all be subject to hearings, comment periods, or other mechanisms to solicit public input, beginning at the earliest stages.

The third foundation of access is the *ability to seek redress or challenge a decision* if stakeholders consider it flawed or unfair. Usually this translates into giving the public access to judicial or administrative remedies if public officials fail to perform their management or decision-making roles appropriately. For example, forest advocates may wish to challenge the accuracy of an analysis that managers have used to set the size and location of a logging concession. Or if a government agency refuses on the grounds of national security to provide information about a project or facility with significant environmental impacts, citizens may want to appeal that decision to an independent arbiter (see Box 1.7).

Box 1.7 The Aarhus Convention: State-of-the-Art Access

The Aarhus Convention is an environmental treaty that turns the 1992 Rio Declaration's vague commitments to the principles of access into specific legal obligations. Since its negotiation in 1998 as a regional agreement among the countries of the United Nations Economic Commission for Europe (UNECE), 24 nations in Europe and Central Asia have become Parties to the treaty, and 40 have signed it. It entered into force in October 2001, and is now open to signature by all nations of the world.

The Convention not only recognizes the basic right of every person of present and future generations to a healthy environment but also specifies how the authorities at all levels will provide fair and transparent decision-making processes, access to information, and access to redress. For example, the Convention requires broad access to information about the state of air and atmosphere, water, land, and biological diversity; information about influences on the environment such as energy, noise, development plans, and policies; and information about how these influences affect human health and safety. A person does not need to prove "legal standing" to request information or to comment on official decisions that affect the environment, and the Convention requires that governments respond to requests for information from any person of any nationality within one month.

The Aarhus Convention also gives citizens, organizations, and governments the right to investigate and seek to curtail pollution caused by public and private entities in other countries that are parties to the treaty. For example, a Hungarian public interest group could demand information on airborne emissions from a Czech factory. For most signatory countries, meeting the standards of the treaty will require authorities to change how they disseminate environmental information to the public, to create new systems of environmental reporting by businesses and government, to improve the practice of public notification and comment, and to change judicial processes.

Adopting and implementing the Aarhus Convention's principles beyond its European base could provide a straightforward route to better access at a global level. But while there is growing interest in endorsing the Aarhus principles in Latin America, southern Africa, and the Asia-Pacific region, many countries perceive the treaty's concepts of democratic decision-making about the environment as too liberal or threatening to commercial confidentiality. Some countries are also reluctant to adopt a treaty that they did not have a chance to shape initially. Nonetheless, the Aarhus Convention stands as an example of real progress toward a global understanding of what access is and how it can be manifested in national laws and practices.

Integrate the Environment into All Decisions

The *integration principle* asserts that consideration for the environment should be part of virtually every major business, resource, or economic development decision. This means making the environment a frontline factor in decisions rather than marginalizing it as something to be protected, if possible, after the fact. Because a wide range of decisions in every sector of the economy affect ecosystems, ecosystem management and environmental protection cannot be the concerns of environmental policy-makers alone. Ecosystems must be the responsibility of those charged with promoting agriculture and industrial development, as well as those focused on providing or regulating electricity, transport, and water services. They must be the concern of private businesses as much as public agencies, of financial investors as much as fisheries or forest managers.

Bringing the goals of environmental sustainability into the decision-making practices of organizations that do not see environmental concerns as part of their core mandates is thus a critical challenge. For example, how can government agencies responsible for navigation and flood control be encouraged to conserve biodiversity when they alter the natural contours of rivers? How can multilateral development banks like the World Bank be encouraged to combine environmental sustainability with their efforts to reduce poverty?

How can financial markets be altered to enable investors to include environmental performance as a factor in deciding which company's shares to buy? At least part of the answer lies in improving access practices and governing at the correct scale—the first two Rio principles. Participatory management and open, transparent decision-making regarding economic issues gives people with environmental concerns the chance to raise them—to integrate their larger goals and priorities for the ecosystem with business decisions.

Reconsidering Environmental Governance

The issues posed by environmental governance are complex. Many cannot be easily or simply resolved. But the alternative to improved environmental governance is continued mismanagement of Earth's natural resources—with consequences for both current and future generations.

WRR 2002–2004 analyses the state of environmental governance today. It considers public participation and access—including new efforts to measure meaningful access. It examines the roles of civil society and the private sector, and looks at what is required to strengthen both local voices and global governance processes. In-depth case studies explore environmental governance issues in more specific detail. A final chapter draws together recommendations from across the volume.

ENVIRONMENTAL GOVERNANCE TODAY

No one familiar with today's environmental trends could conclude that Planet Earth is well-managed. That truth alone hints at the troubled and often ineffective state of environmental governance at scales from local, to national, to global. Since the Rio Earth Summit in 1992, the capacity of Earth's ecosystems to sustain human well-being has deteriorated in nearly every category measured. This is in spite of painstakingly negotiated global environmental treaties and the considerable progress that has been made in understanding how ecosystems function. More often than not, human institutions still fail to make environmental decisions that work for both people and ecosystems.

What Influences Environmental Governance?

A significant part of the challenge of environmental governance is that it takes place in the context of a rapidly changing world. Those changes reach far beyond the accelerating decline of ecosystems to include economic, political, and technological trends that are redefining our relationships with ecosystems, often for the worse. Globalization, growing trade, and international investment magnify our actions beyond national borders. New fishing, farming, and extraction technologies enable rapid exploitation of natural resources and drive landscape-scale change. Yet, the spread of democracy and the emergence of a robust civil society in most nations have increased public expectations and the demand for "good governance." These trends give us new options for improving environmental governance as well.

Economic globalization—the growing integration and interdependence of national economies—has redefined our relation to ecosystems and extended the reach of our environmental decisions.

Governance in a Changing World

To understand the challenge of environmental governance today, we examine four broad trends. *Economic globalization* has placed new demands on environmental management across national borders and has raised new questions about the appropriate roles of the private sector and of international organizations in environmental governance. Increasing *democratization* of political systems around the world and the growing *acceptance of "good governance" norms* have opened the door to public participation in decision-making in a manner never possible before. At the same time, *the rapid growth of nongovernmental organizations* such as environmental groups and other public interest advocates has helped organize and enable the public to participate. Finally, the proliferation of *new information and communication technologies* is allowing social movements to coordinate at the global level and helping the public to hold governments and corporations accountable for their environmental performance. In addition, continuing armed conflict around the world poses an obstacle to stable and thoughtful governance (see Box 2.1).

Economic Globalization, Liberalization, and Privatization

Economic globalization—the growing integration and interdependence of national economies—has redefined our relation to ecosystems and extended the reach of our environmental decisions. The average consumer in London, for instance, can sit on furniture built from Asian forests, sip wine from South Africa, dine on Thai shrimp or New Zealand lamb, and set the table with cotton napkins from Egypt.

With some regional variations, the same is true in any number of cities large and small throughout the world, and, increasingly, in many rural areas. Globalization today is defined by growing access to goods and services from all over the world, large flows of capital between countries, and technological advances that can make vast distances a negligible factor in business decisions. Remote rain forests, mountains, and ocean ecosystems can be readily connected to commercial transactions and consumer choices thousands of miles away.

The world has experienced periods of globalization before, but never of the magnitude, complexity, and speed that have occurred since about 1980 (World Bank 2002b:23–24). Just as the development of the steamship aided the economic globalization of the late 1800s, communication and transportation breakthroughs are enabling today's consumers and businesses to tap far-flung goods, markets, and investment opportunities at reduced costs. Between 1920 and 1990 the average cost per ton for ocean cargo transport fell from $95 to $29, while the cost of a three minute telephone call from New York to London fell from $244.65 to $3.32 (Frankel 2000:46). The Internet has had a similar impact on the transmission of data and the management of global enterprises. Factor in developments like cell phones, containerized shipping, and overnight air freight, and the world seems to be shrinking and national boundaries fading.

New technologies are only one important factor in the increasing integration of world economies. Changes in trade and investment policy, as well as the changing role of the state in controlling the economy, are crucial as well. By the end of the 1990s, most countries, including those in the developing world, had implemented measures to liberalize domestic and international trade, lower tariff barriers, reduce the size and functions of the state, privatize state-owned enterprises, and introduce market economies.

One clear result has been the increasing importance of trade in the world economy. Trade now accounts for some 58 percent of the global economy—up from just 27 percent in 1970 (World Bank 2003). Notably, this bonanza has extended beyond high-income nations to include at least some of the developing world. Trade doubled as a percentage of the national economy (i.e., the trade/GDP ratio doubled) in 24 developing countries between 1980 and 2000 (World Bank 2002b:5). Brazil, China, Hungary, India, and Mexico are standouts among countries whose participation in global trade and investment increased (World Bank 2002b:5).

(continued on p. 28)

Box 2.1 Armed Conflict: Killing Governance

Along with the destruction of lives and livelihoods, war can also destroy croplands, forests, water systems, and other natural resources. Clean air and soils were casualties of the 1990–91 Gulf War after being polluted when Iraqis intentionally ignited hundreds of oil wells. Marine and coastal life was damaged too; spills of 6–8 million barrels of oil into the Persian Gulf and Arabian Sea killed 15,000–30,000 sea birds and contaminated mangroves and coral reefs (UNEP 2002:14, 204, 292; Omar et al. 2000:317). When Serbian forces systematically destroyed villages and towns in the 1999 Kosovo conflict, they also destroyed clean drinking water supplies and waste systems (UNEP and UNCHS 1999:5). And though decades have passed since U.S. forces cleared 325,000 hectares in the Viet Nam War by spraying the defoliant Agent Orange, biodiversity losses are still very much in evidence. Areas once covered by forests and mangroves now support just low-density grasslands and mudflats (McNeely 2000:362).

The toll on environmental governance is just as significant. War often destroys or weakens the institutions that make inclusive and informed decisions about the environment possible. The political and social turmoil that accompanies conflict can short-circuit systematic processes of environmental management. War creates refugees, leaves government and environmental agencies handicapped or destroyed, and substitutes short-term survival for longer-term environmental considerations. This means that ecosystems continue to suffer even after the fighting has stopped.

War or "armed conflict" is a governance problem for a distressingly large number of people, ecosystems, and institutions. Between 1990 and 2000, 118 armed conflicts worldwide claimed approximately 6 million lives (Smith 2001:1). People and the environment suffered the consequences for years after the wars ended. In 1999, more than two thirds of the ongoing conflicts had lasted for more than 5 years, and almost one third had lasted for more than 20 years (Smith 2001:3).

Most current wars are fought within national borders, not between nations, but the effects often spill over to neighboring countries (CAII 1997; SIPRI 2002). Resource wealth is usually a factor in the violence, with competition for valuable resources like gold, diamonds, and timber driving the conflict. By one estimate, one quarter of the roughly 50 wars and armed conflicts active in 2001 were triggered, exacerbated, or financed by legal or illegal resource exploitation (Renner 2002:6).

(continued on next page)

Armed Conflict and Refugees

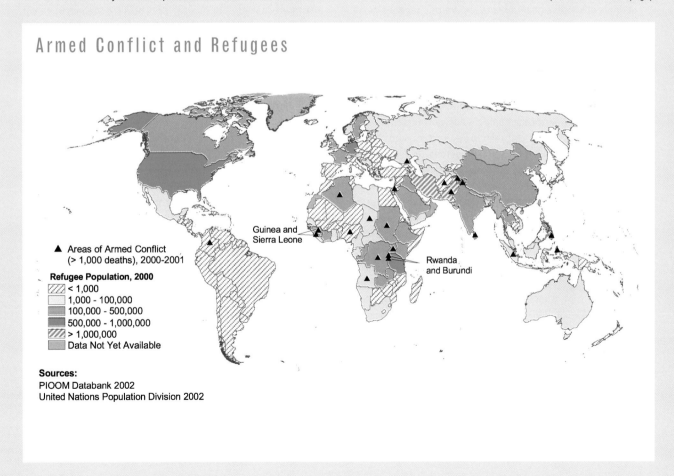

▲ Areas of Armed Conflict
(> 1,000 deaths), 2000-2001

Refugee Population, 2000
- < 1,000
- 1,000 - 100,000
- 100,000 - 500,000
- 500,000 - 1,000,000
- > 1,000,000
- Data Not Yet Available

Guinea and Sierra Leone

Rwanda and Burundi

Sources:
PIOOM Databank 2002
United Nations Population Division 2002

Box 2.1 (continued)

Disrupted Governments

During and after conflict, governments generally focus on meeting immediate human needs—food, shelter, and safety for citizens and displaced populations. Protection of the environment and sustainable resource management are inevitably relegated to lower priorities. Food shortages, disease, weakened health care systems, fragmented social networks, the destruction of people's livelihoods, and refugees who must be returned to their own homeland all take precedence over environmental concerns.

Even after conflict ends, well-informed environmental decisions are unlikely in the face of economic collapse, the need to rebuild infrastructure, and the disruption of commerce at the local, national, and international levels—common outcomes of armed conflict (CAII 1997; Kalpers 2001:21). War economies and destabilized governments perpetuate an ongoing cycle of violence and resource exploitation. Land and natural resources may be used as bargaining chips to gain allies during strife, in negotiations to end conflict, or as postwar paybacks to those who helped win the conflict. Little value may be accorded to intact ecosystems or ecosystem services in the process (Shambaugh et al. 2001:12–17).

In times of conflict, governments and warring factions need money to buy arms and supplies; high-value resources such as ivory and diamonds can readily satisfy that demand. This dynamic has worked to the detriment of elephant populations in strife-torn countries such as Sudan, Chad, and the Central African Republic. It has also driven forest liquidation in Liberia and Sierra Leone (Blom and Yamindou 2001:13; Shambaugh et al. 2001:7). After the conflict ends, governments need to kick-start the economy and rebuild key sectors, and one of the quickest ways is to mine natural resources.

Armed conflict can wreak havoc on government conservation efforts, especially in protected areas (Matthew et al. 2002:22). For example, during the Ethiopian-Eritrean war, parks and reserves lacked funds for staff, infrastructure, research, and management training (Jacobs and Schloeder 2001:19). In countries where nature tourism provides a major source of income for biodiversity protection, that source quickly evaporates when conflict begins. In Rwanda, income generated by tourists—many of whom come to see mountain gorillas—totaled about $4–6 million annually; this in turn funded conservation projects in parks and forest reserves. However, escalating conflict in the 1990s, and the 1994 genocide caused tourist numbers to plunge; they still have not fully recovered (Plumptre et al. 2001:19).

War often leads to the breakdown of law and order, leaving protected areas and species vulnerable to exploitation. During Sierra Leone's civil war in the 1990s, regional forestry officers, foresters, rangers, and guards went unpaid for long periods, while illegal mining and logging—and massive deforesta-tion—occurred in forest reserves (Squire 2001:21–22). And while the Ethiopian-Eritrean war raged, game hunting by the military in protected areas continued (Jacobs and Schloeder 2001:23). In the Central African Republic, hunting and poaching in war-torn provinces reduced the country's elephant numbers by 90 percent to just 5,000 and led to the disappearance of the rhinoceros (Blom and Yamindou 2001:14). And in Cambodia, the Khmer Rouge's trade in timber brought $10–20 million a month in funds for its civil war effort (Global Witness 2003).

Even after wars end, weakened political institutions may not have the authority, ability, or funds to effectively manage their country's natural resources (Orr 2002:139). Some reconstruction efforts may include environmental projects, but they are not likely to be a priority. Environmental ministries often lack the capacity to address environmental problems in any systematic way. The postwar turmoil can mean fragmented government ministries and new staff unaccustomed to working together or with other institutions. Years after the end of conflict in Bosnia and Herzegovina, environmental groups noted that new environmental legislation was forthcoming, but doubted the fledgling government's ability to implement and enforce it (REC 1997:35). Local governments may be equally shattered, making it difficult to decentralize the management of natural resources effectively. Two decades of conflict in Afghanistan left local community decision-making bodies without the information, infrastructure, money, or human capacity to cope with demands on the environment (UNEP 2003:95).

Refugees and the Environment

Refugees searching for safe haven can burden the ecosystems in their country of asylum and complicate environmental decision-making. In 2001, there were about 20 million uprooted people worldwide. Some 12 million were refugees and 5 million were "internally displaced persons"—people forced to flee their homes, but still living in their original country (UNHCR 2002:12, 19, 22).

Often, refugees are forced to settle in resource-scarce areas, putting further pressure on trees, land, water, and wildlife. The unstable in- and outflow of displaced people affects established patterns of rural cropping and food production, and upsets long-term agricultural investments (Messer et al. 2000). When rural communities are forced to flee, they may take with them knowledge of the harvest cycles of locally adapted seeds and the informal networks of seed swapping that help preserve the genetic diversity of agriculture (PRTADG 1999:12–14). Streams of refugees can overburden infrastructure for living quarters, clean water supplies, and waste systems.

When it is time to make decisions about natural resource use and conservation, refugees are unable to have a voice in those decisions because they are not citizens. Even if they return to their original homes, they may lose their say in land use and management decisions due to land ownership disputes or postwar changes in national land policy. For example, in postwar Mozambique, the government awarded commercial land concessions in many areas when local communities were still absent or were struggling to re-establish their livelihoods, and were thus unable to effectively join in the decision (Hatton et al. 2001:64). In addition, documentation regarding legal land rights and property ownership is often misplaced or confiscated during conflicts, as occurred in the southern Balkans when Kosovo Albanians fled to Albania and the former Yugoslav Republic of Macedonia in 1999 (UNEP and UNCHS 1999:5).

Civil Society Undermined

Civil society, so crucial to informed environmental management, is weakened during war. War thwarts the ability of nongovernmental organizations (NGOs) and the media to operate. It also makes it harder for people to assemble, to communicate within and outside borders, and to access information. Growth rates of NGOs have typically fallen during times of conflict and grown in the years after the fighting stops. In Bosnia and Herzegovina, for example, environmental NGOs thrived at local, municipal, regional, and national levels before military violence began. Local governments funded some of the work of various agricultural organizations, and NGOs had a voice in decisions that affected the environment and routinely worked with governments, religious groups, and scientific institutions. During the war, however, most NGOs were forced to cease their operations or were limited to local endeavors (REC 1997:35).

Conflict can mean the end of external funding and participation in environmental work. During wartime, foreign funders typically hesitate to support local NGOs. International organizations once active in environmental education, restoration, biodiversity monitoring, and natural resource management may pull out staff, abandon projects, or see their work destroyed by conflict, as experienced in Sierra Leone, Ethiopia, the Central African Republic, and other countries (Squire 2001:24). For example, the headquarters of a World Bank-sponsored project to manage natural resources in the Central African Republic was destroyed as a result of conflict, along with a large quantity of equipment, including the entire geographic information system (GIS) database of forest inventories covering the southwestern area of the country. The project was suspended and then discontinued (Blom and Yamindou 2001:18).

While government ministries and civil society groups are in disarray after conflict ends, the private sector is often able to mobilize quickly to take advantage of this void. After the Mozambique Peace Accord in 1992, for example, hunters and commercial loggers from urban areas followed construction teams as the road network was re-established, taking advantage of the new access to wildlife and forest areas. The quick profits they reaped left communities in the province a poorer resource base on which to rebuild their livelihoods (Hatton et al. 2001:11, 47–48).

The Defeat of Sustainability

Clearly, a country at peace is more likely to have the political, economic, and civil stability that fosters sustainable development. Simmering conflicts and eruptions of violence slow economic growth, and reduce the latitude for innovation and investment. Civil conflicts in Africa have deterred progress in introducing greater transparency and accountability into governments—critical to democratic and sustainable development. Political instability and conflict can result in a chronic lack of investment in environmental protection by governments, citizens, and businesses. In the Arabian Peninsula, political and military conflicts have hurt water sector development, contributing to water scarcity and the deterioration of water quality (UNEP 2002:175).

On the other hand, the aftermath of conflict can sometimes yield opportunities for improved policy-making and a fresh outlook that can actually benefit a nation's environmental prospects. This happened in Uganda and Mozambique when natural resource legislation enacted under new leadership enabled much greater opportunity for community participation in natural resource management (Oglethorpe 2002). In 2001, a new government in Afghanistan created a ministry for environmental management—the first time in the history of the country (UNEP 2003:92).

Under certain conditions, the disruptions of war can even work in the environment's favor (Matthew et al. 2002:42). Pressures for development and forest conversion may diminish as populations flee strife-torn areas, and resources may become inaccessible for exploitation in areas the military designates as off-limits. However, these benefits are entirely accidental and inadvertent, and rarely offset the direct environmental damage and destruction of the social and economic fabric that war brings (McNeely 2000:365).

Amid war's brutality, death, and deprivation, the environment may seem a minor casualty. Yet, the destruction of the environment, along with the demolition of democratic, informed decision-making, can prolong human suffering for decades, undermining the foundation for social progress and economic security.

Industrialized countries, too, are pursuing economic integration with greater fervor than ever. In January 1999, the European Union committed to a common currency—the euro. Research suggests that adopting a common currency can more than triple the volume of trade (Rose 2000:57).

But globalization has brought more than a trade boom. In fact, one of its most significant impacts has been, not from the movement of goods, but from the movement of money—in the surge of private investment capital from the boardrooms and investment banks of wealthy nations to developing nations. In 1991, private finance and official development aid (the total value of grants, loans, and other assistance) to developing countries were approximately equal at about $60 billion each. By 2000, private finance had multiplied by a factor of four, to $226 billion, while development aid had decreased by half to $35 billion (World Bank 2002a:32).

One factor driving this explosion in private North-South capital flows was a wave of policy changes promoting liberalization and privatization in the economies of developing and transition countries. Barriers to the free flow of trade and finance across national borders fell, while privatization of state-owned corporations and the creation of new stock markets in developing countries provided new opportunities for investors in industrialized countries. Then in 1997, with the advent of the financial crisis in Asia, and subsequent financial turbulence in Brazil, Turkey, and Argentina, both investors and recipient countries learned the downside risks of increased integration with the global economy.

Effects on Environmental Governance

Global integration has posed several challenges for environmental governance. These include the outpacing of environmental regulations by economic growth, the increasing power of the private sector to shape economic and environmental decisions, the environmental impacts of economic instability, and questions about the transparency and accountability of such international financial institutions as export-import banks, the World Bank, and the International Monetary Fund (IMF).

In several emerging market countries such as Indonesia and China, where international investment drove high rates of economic growth in the 1990s, the pace of economic development strained the institutions and regulatory frameworks designed to protect the environment. In China, for example, local officials were given a mandate to promote economic growth. They did not, however, face much countervailing pressure from environmental regulators to invest in pollution control equipment and clean manufacturing processes, or to enforce environmental regulations. As a result, uncontrolled industrialization has significantly worsened China's environmental conditions and increased related impacts on human health (Davis and Saldiva 1999:15; World Bank 1997:5–28; Lieberthal 1997:4–5).

Privatization of formerly state-owned assets and functions also created environmental governance problems in many countries. Since the mid-1980s, governments have increasingly transferred some of their powers to the private sector—to manage natural resources and provide services such as drinking water supply, wastewater treatment, and electric power. Water services are a good example of this trend. Private water companies have existed for nearly four centuries, but public authorities controlled water supplies and provided sewage treatment in the vast majority of jurisdictions until the 1980s (Brubaker 2001:1–2; Gleick et al. 2002:23–24).

However, by 2000, national, provincial, and local governments in 93 countries had begun to privatize drinking water or wastewater services (Brubaker 2001:1). In 1997, the Asian capitals of Jakarta and Manila awarded contracts to privatize their water services—just 2 of the 33 major water privatizations that year (Owen 2001:17). From 1995 to 1999, governments around the world privatized an average of 36 water supply or wastewater treatment systems annually (Owen 2001:17). Likewise, privatization has proceeded in the electric power sector, with some 40 percent of developing countries allowing the entry of private power producers into their electric utility systems by 1998 (Bacon 1999:8).

The potential benefits of privatization are both financial and practical. Privatization brings ready sources of private capital to invest in systems that are often cash-starved and in poor physical condition. Done right, this can bring better and wider service, greater efficiency, and increased financial viability. But the reality of privatization has been much more mixed and has prompted local backlash, even civil uprisings, in a number of locations. Decisions to privatize rarely involve public consultation and often have unpopular social repercussions, including job losses and price increases (Dubash 2002:x–xv).

Moreover, many governments are not prepared for the regulation of new private utilities—which are often monopolies—that is required to protect both social and environmental goals. Absent vigorous regulatory oversight, privatized utilities may not adequately consider environmental impacts when new infrastructure is built or when land use decisions are made. For instance, the decision to build a coal-fired power plant or to tap non-renewable water supplies may turn on short-term economic considerations such as ease of financing or the rapid recouping of investment, rather than long-term outcomes for the surrounding natural and human communities. For these and other reasons, the issue of how much state power should be put into the hands of private companies and what kinds of social and environmental obligations these companies should take on, is one of the most controversial governance topics today (Dubash 2002:x–xv; Gleick et al. 2002:29-39).

The economic and political instability resulting from the financial crises of the 1990s also challenged environmental governance structures. In Indonesia, for example, the breakdown of law and order and high unemployment following the fall of the Suharto regime in 1998—coupled with pent-up resentment of state control over natural resources—led to an explosion of illegal logging and wildlife poaching in the country's protected areas. At the same time, the economic collapse limited the government's ability to fund environmental protection and diverted the attention of normally vigilant public interest groups to the pressing issue of helping the newly impoverished (FWI and GFW 2002:60-64). Weak environmental governance institutions—including government agencies, community-level organizations, and public interest

groups—render ecosystems extremely vulnerable to economic and political disruption.

Finally, globalization has illustrated potential conflicts between the roles of institutions such as the IMF, the World Bank, and bilateral export credit agencies in promoting liberalization and privatization, and the part they play in global environmental governance. First, how can the activities that these organizations fund be made consistent with sustainable development? There are many instances where projects supported by these institutions promote unsustainable practices. For example, a World Resources Institute study found that export credit agencies in developed countries—which bankroll foreign projects intended to develop export markets abroad—were supporting energy projects with high greenhouse gas emissions in developing countries. This was in direct conflict with the professed desire of developed countries to encourage developing countries to lower the growth rates of their greenhouse emissions (Maurer and Bhandari 2000:1-6).

Second, there is concern that international financial institutions are not sufficiently open and accountable to the communities affected by their decision-making. While the World Bank and other multilateral development banks have introduced strong reforms related to information disclosure, public consultation, and appeals mechanisms, most export credit agencies and trade bodies remain closed to public participation and scrutiny (see Box 2.2).

Democratization

Over the last 30 years, the world has seen a significant trend toward democratization—the adoption of democratic principles of governance and public participation. Freedom House, which rates countries as "Free," "Partially Free," or "Not Free" based on a composite of political and civil liberties, estimates that while in 1973 only 81 countries were "Free" or "Partially Free," by 2003 that number had risen to 144. These numbers translate into a total population of 2 billion living under fully or partially democratic regimes in 1973, and 4 billion in 2003 (Freedom House 2003:2-3).

The relationship between democratization and environmental outcomes is complex (see Box 2.3). The more citizens are able to know about the environment, to express their opinions, and to hold their leaders accountable for their performance, the more likely it is that they will be able to prevent gross environmental mismanagement. For example, after 1989, the trend toward democratization in the countries of the former Soviet Union helped bring to light severe contamination of the landscape with radioactive and other toxic substances, and the exposure of unwitting citizens to extreme health risks. Despite some continued repression, environmental activists have forced governments in the region to begin to address environmental health concerns. In northwestern Russia, a community supported by advocacy

(continued on p. 34)

Box 2.2 Open Accounts? The Transparency of Multilateral Development Banks

Multilateral development banks (MDBs) such as the World Bank, the Inter-American Development Bank (IDB) and the Asian Development Bank (ADB) provide loans, loan guarantees, and grants to foster economic and social development in middle-income and poor countries. This lending typically supports projects that are intended to benefit rural development, infrastructure, and institution-building, such as the construction of power plants, dams, and pipelines; irrigation efforts to boost agricultural yields; and education and health initiatives such as AIDS awareness and anti-malaria programs.

But the MDBs don't just lend. Increasingly, they encourage countries to reform their markets and to make basic changes in their governance, health provision, and education policies (Tussie and Tuozzo 2001:106). One approach ties loan disbursements to requirements for government policy changes. Often, the banks provide loans, guidance, and conditions targeted at "restructuring" national economies to make them more open and increase their growth potential. Along with other changes, countries may be encouraged to privatize state industries, reform banking and monetary policies, and liberalize foreign investment measures. Some MDB loans support realignment of different sectors of a nation's economy—such as the forest or energy sector—by changing the government's policies, regulatory framework, or subsidies aimed at the sector.

Because of their macroeconomic effects on employment, trade, and government spending patterns, these "structural adjustment" or "sectoral adjustment" loans (also called "development policy support lending") can be among the most controversial in MDB loan portfolios. In the case of the World Bank, adjustment loans have grown in recent years to account for almost two thirds of fiscal 2002 disbursements (World Bank 2002b:27).

In 2001, MDBs provided net aid of $18.4 billion in grants and concessional loans (loans with an interest rate lower than from a commercial bank) (OECD 2002). This represents almost one third of the annual aid funneled to low- and middle-income countries, making MDBs highly influential in charting the direction and performance of national development policies.

The multilateral institutions also expanded their loan guarantee activities in the 1990s to help catalyze private sector activities in developing countries. World Bank programs alone guaranteed $18 billion in loans to developing countries from 1996–2000, twice the amount guaranteed in the prior five years (World Bank 2002a:107). In addition, MDBs leverage their lending through co-financing with the private sector and export-

Transparency in Multilateral and Regional Development Banks

How Open to Public Scrutiny and Involvement Are these Multilateral and Regional Development Banks?	World Bank	Asian Development Bank	African Development Bank	Inter-American Development Bank	European Investment Bank
Does an official bank policy or approved strategy address public participation in environmental decisions and policies?	Yes	Yes	No	Yes	Yes
Does a mechanism (such as an ombudsman) or procedure exist to receive complaints from civil society groups or affected populations?	Yes	Yes	No	Yes	No
Does the bank have an ombudsman or other mechanism that specifically acknowledges the importance of resolving *environmental* complaints or disputes?	No	No	No	No	No
Are the deliberations or meetings of the bank's Board of Executive Directors open to public scrutiny?	No	No	No	No	No
Do the bank's guidelines on Environmental Impact Assessments (EIAs) require disclosure of EIA findings *before* the bank makes a lending decision?	Yes	Yes	Yes	Yes	Yes
Are general project descriptions and project-related documents available to the public *before* the bank makes a lending decision?	Yes	Yes	Yes	Yes	Yes
Does the bank require that NGOs and other civil society groups be consulted while formulating its country assistance plan (the lending strategy for a country that embodies lending priorities)?	No	No	Yes	No	No

Source: Adapted from Maurer et al. 2003.

import banks (government-sponsored banks that fund foreign projects intended to open up export markets) (Gwin 2001:169).

In an interesting twist, multilateral development banks raise the majority of the money they disburse as loans by borrowing on the world's financial markets. The MDBs are able to borrow at low rates because they are backed by the financial guarantees of the banks' member countries, to whom they are ultimately accountable. Member countries also contribute some money directly to the MDBs to fund grants for the poorest countries.

Because of their central role in financing national development, multilateral development banks have a huge influence on natural resource use and the environment. For example, by funding carbon-intensive technologies, a bank's investment decisions can exacerbate climate change and put a country on a path to fossil fuel dependency. By contrast, MDBs can promote policies that include incentives for energy efficiency and renewable energy projects, such as wind energy installations or solar arrays in rural villages.

Bank decisions often involve trade-offs that have important social or environmental consequences. For instance, a bank can choose to support road construction that gives market access to remote villages or forests, but may displace indigenous people or damage biodiversity. By insisting on the use of standard accounting practices, reporting procedures, or consultation guidelines, banks can encourage greater local participation in project designs and discourage corruption and influence peddling among local officials.

The potential for MDBs' projects and policy prescriptions to affect a nation's environment, culture, and society has brought greater scrutiny to decisions that the banks, historically, have made quite secretly. Over the past decade, nongovernmental organizations (NGOs) have pressed the World Bank and other MDBs to become more transparent and accountable—to disclose information to people who are affected by proposed loans and projects, and to give them a

chance to participate in the project and policy design (Fox and Brown 1998:1–2; Gwin 2001:190).

WRI's evaluation of the official commitments or institutional policies of several large multilateral and regional development banks suggests that most have, indeed, made progress toward greater transparency (see Table). The majority of them now at least express general institutional support for access to information and public participation in their activities. The World Bank—the bank that lends the most money and has received perhaps the greatest criticism and scrutiny from environmental groups—has led the way in putting in place specific policies or commitments that promote public participation and transparency. Several other banks have followed suit. By contrast, the European Investment Bank, which has received limited attention from public interest groups, has few such specific policies in place (Maurer et al. 2003:5–9).

Some MDBs have also implemented mechanisms for redress, such as ombudsman offices or other formal procedures for responding to environmental complaints or resolving disputes. Yet, their generally cumbersome procedures and closed deliberation processes mean that NGO watchdogs or other groups have only limited ability to ensure that governments and banks honor their own policies or commitments. In addition, most banks do not offer the public or NGOs an opportunity to participate in the design of country assistance plans—the investment strategy that a bank uses to determine what kinds of in-country projects it will fund. Without such access, local public interest groups and private organizations find it harder to influence how their governments—who are guided by those strategies in their development planning—set priorities regarding resource use and the environment (Maurer et al. 2003:1–3, 8).

Disclosure: The World Bank, an editorial and financial partner in the publication of *World Resources 2002–2004*, did not participate in the design or conduct of the above analysis.

Box 2.3 More Democracy, Better Environment?

The political structure of nations—whether they have a democratic or autocratic style of government—is an important factor in their social and economic development. In the last half century, the world has moved steadily away from autocratic regimes that concentrate power in the hands of one or a few people, and toward democracies that grant broad civil liberties and freedoms of political participation. From 1950–2003, the number of electoral democracies—nations where governments were elected by popular vote—almost tripled from 43 to 121 (Freedom House 1999:1–2; 2003:5).

However, democracy is measured by more than simply the right to vote, and not all electoral democracies extend full democratic rights to their citizens. *Full democracies* are defined as granting a range of rights and institutions, such as elections, competitive political parties, the rule of law, independent media, limits on the power of government officials, and an independent judiciary. These mechanisms allow citizens to communicate and organize among themselves, choose their leaders freely, and participate in government decisions (Esty et al. 1998:9; Freedom House 2003:1).

Partial democracies have more limited respect for political rights and civil liberties. They share some of the characteristics of full democracies—such as elections—but also some of the characteristics of *autocracies*, such as an overly powerful chief executive, suppressed or restricted political parties, a state-controlled press, or a cowed judiciary (Esty et al. 1998:9; Freedom House 2003:1).

The nongovernmental organization Freedom House uses these definitions to rate countries as "Free" (full democracy), "Partially Free" (partial democracy), and "Not Free" (autocracy), based on the level of civil and political freedoms they grant their citizens. Freedom House's analysis shows impressive growth in the number of nations extending democratic freedoms over the last three decades, with those nations rated "Free" and "Partially Free" increasing from 81 in 1973 to 144 in 2003 (Freedom House 2003:2). (See Figure.) The accompanying map shows the current distribution of full democracies, partial democracies, and autocracies.

Democracy and Environment

Is there a causal connection between democracy and improved environmental quality? Between political freedoms and environmental sustainability? Assessing the influence of political liberties and civil rights on the environment is not straightforward. There is little empirical evidence of a direct link, and research is hampered by a lack of national-level data on environmental conditions outside industrialized countries.

Proponents of global democratization have asserted that such a connection exists (Gore 1992:179–180, 276–277), and a growing literature supports the idea that political freedoms may be as important as economic factors in improving envi-

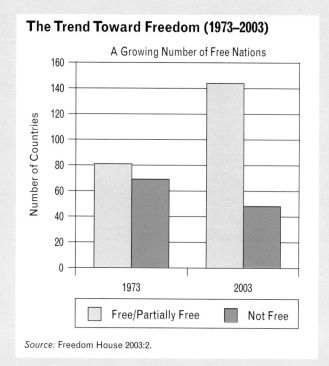

The Trend Toward Freedom (1973–2003)

A Growing Number of Free Nations

Source: Freedom House 2003:2.

ronmental quality, particularly in poorer nations (Barrett and Graddy 2000:455). For example, one recent analysis found that greater political and civil liberties were associated with improvements in air and water quality, such as reduced levels of sulfur dioxide and particulates in air, and lower coliform and dissolved oxygen levels in water (Torras and Boyce 1998:155).

The assertion that greater democratic rights can, in the right circumstances, result in better environmental policy and performance has been given powerful support in the aftermath of the terrible environmental abuses revealed in Central and Eastern Europe and the former Soviet Union after the fall of Communist regimes in 1989–1990. Environment was a rallying cry of reform movements in the region, and stricter environmental legislation has been rapidly enacted under new democratic governments.

The link between citizen rights and improving environmental trends has much to do with the power that democracies give to citizens to affect decision-making processes and hold government officials, corporate authorities, and other individuals accountable. Democratic freedoms encourage access to information—such as planning documents, budgets, reports on local environmental conditions, or pollution records—that can help citizens protect their environmental interests (Petkova and Veit 2000:3–5).

A strong correlation also exists between democracy and wealth. High-income countries are, with few exceptions, liberal democracies. Rising wealth, in turn, is associated with clear improvements in some environmental indicators. How-

Democratic Freedoms: Civil and Political Liberties, 2003

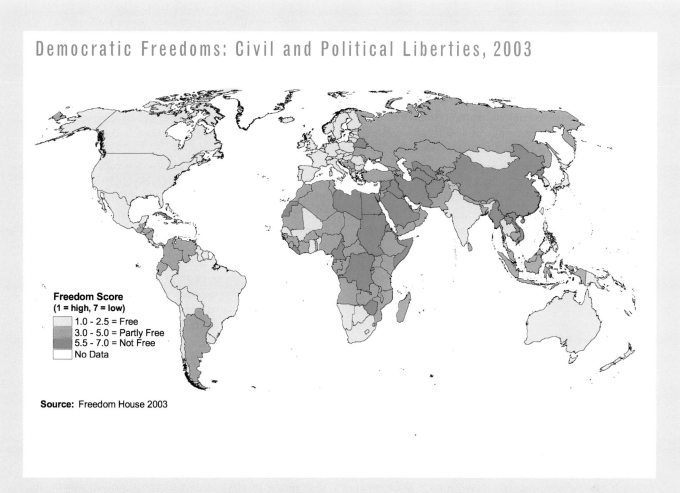

Freedom Score
(1 = high, 7 = low)
- 1.0 - 2.5 = Free
- 3.0 - 5.0 = Partly Free
- 5.5 - 7.0 = Not Free
- No Data

Source: Freedom House 2003

ever, experts caution against interpreting these results to mean that rising wealth *automatically* delivers improvements in environmental quality (Torras and Boyce 1998:147–160).

Rather, democratic institutions, levels of wealth, and citizen demands for environmental quality all appear to interact. The correlations among these three factors and better environmental policy appear strong (Grossman and Kruger 1995:353–377). However, it is important to distinguish among different environmental issues. The environmental benefits resulting from concerned citizens acting in a free society, and from investments made possible by rising wealth, tend to be local in nature. The first issues to be tackled are sanitation infrastructure, water and air quality, risks associated with toxic releases, and local habitat protection. Environmental problems that are more distant in space or time, such as biodiversity loss, overfishing, and climate change, have high awareness in democracies, but that awareness has not yet been translated into effective action (Max-Neef 1995:115–118).

Still more sobering is the fact that liberal democracies, as the richest nations on Earth, are themselves responsible for a disproportionate share of global resource use and waste generation. Democratic countries are built around the concepts of

individual liberty, freedom of choice, and the necessity of economic growth. The very success of liberal democratic and free market ideology has created a mighty engine of consumption. While there is no empirical evidence of a causal link between democracy and consumption, as opposed to the clear relationship between wealth and consumption levels, the three variables are strongly correlated. If developing countries replicate the Western model of liberal democratic governments and free market economies, environmental quality will likely improve in some respects but worsen in others.

A further consideration is that the transition from autocracy to democracy is often marked by political instability, rapid internal change, and even civil conflict. In many cases, political crises cause newly established democratic regimes to fail. In fact, during the second half of the twentieth century, about one quarter of all newly established democracies lasted for less than 5 years (Esty et al. 1998:viii). The environment is particularly vulnerable during times of transition and may suffer worse damage than occurred under autocratic rule. For example, eyewitness reports from Indonesia suggest that deforestation has dramatically increased since the fall of President Suharto in 1998 (FWI and GFW 2002:xi).

groups recently succeeded in blocking construction of a nuclear power plant by voting it down in a local referendum.

But there is also evidence that *partial* democratization–where some democratic practices (such as elections) are adopted without embracing a full array of civil and political liberties–may worsen environmental outcomes in the short term. Democratic elections in the absence of other mechanisms to hold politicians accountable for serving the public interest can drive destruction of natural resources through political patronage. For example, observers have noted an increase in the disposal of public forest land in Kenya in periods leading up to national elections, as the governing party rewards supporters with land that is supposed to be held in the public trust (Klopp 2000; Walsh 2002:A4).

Even in the most advanced democracies, effective regulation of extractive or highly polluting industries such as mining or power generation is often stymied by distortions of the democratic process. For instance, the campaign finance system in the United States is often blamed for allowing undue corporate influence in setting and enforcing environmental policies.

Emergence of Governance Norms

In addition to formal changes in political systems, the evolution and strengthening of global norms of "good governance" has also emerged as a significant form of democratization.

"Norms" are standards or practices that may not yet be codified in formal law, but that nevertheless influence the behavior of individuals, corporations, or governments. In this sense, norms become public expectations. They contribute to an individual's or organization's image as a responsible citizen, or a government agency's image of legitimacy or fairness. In the realm of environmental governance, emerging norms include decreased tolerance for corruption, and increasing expectations for transparency and public participation in decision-making.

Corruption is an important driver of natural resource degradation around the world. Corruption occurs when public officials abuse their regulatory authority, or appropriate public assets–land, timber, minerals, or other resources–for private gain. For a share of the profits, corrupt officials look the other way when corporations flout environmental protection laws, or may even directly participate in the illegal appropriation of natural resources managed by the state. For example, it is estimated that fully half of the logging taking place in Indonesia today is illegal (FWI and GFW 2000:xi).

Thus, it is significant that over the last ten years, the international community has lifted the taboo on discussions of corruption, and has recognized the role of industrialized countries and international institutions in attacking this problem. In 1993, a small group of former World Bank officials founded Transparency International, an organization that has effectively raised awareness of the corruption issue

and catalyzed citizen networks around the world to reduce it (Transparency International 2003).

In 1996, World Bank president James Wolfensohn highlighted the problem of corruption as a barrier to development and poverty reduction, and committed the Bank's resources and influence to address the problem in client countries (Wolfensohn 1996). Meanwhile, the industrialized countries represented in the Organisation for Economic Co-operation and Development (OECD) concluded an agreement in 1997 criminalizing bribery by corporations in their international operations (see Box 2.4).

The corporate community is also responding to changing norms of behavior related to its role in promoting sustainable development. An increasing number of domestic and multinational companies have committed to voluntary standards of corporate responsibility related to labor practices, dialogue with local communities, information disclosure, and environmental management. For example, 224 corporations are now participating in the Global Reporting Initiative (GRI)–an effort to standardize corporate disclosure of information about the social and environmental impacts of their operations (GRI 2003). Although many public interest advocates argue that voluntary guidelines are no substitute for mandatory regulations in governing corporate behavior, such consensus-building on appropriate norms may serve as the basis for more binding regulations in the future.

The Growth of Nongovernmental Organizations

Public interest groups that are independent of both government and private business can provide important checks on the failures of electoral democracy to protect ecosystems. *Civil society* can be defined as all organizations in public life above the household level that are neither government nor profit-oriented. Thus, religious organizations, professional associations, and universities are all part of civil society, in addition to nongovernmental organizations (NGOs)–a term often used to describe groups that focus on public interest advocacy or service delivery.

NGOs dedicated to promoting environmental protection have been at the forefront of democracy movements in many countries, including the countries of Central and Eastern Europe and the former Soviet Union as they have emerged from decades of socialist rule. In Indonesia and the Philippines, NGOs operating under authoritarian regimes have often used the limited political space available to advocate improved natural resource management as a politically acceptable entry point to address issues that were also about social justice and human rights.

Worldwide, the increasing number and influence of civil society organizations has been one of the hallmarks of environmental governance over the last decade, and is both a cause and effect of broader democratization trends. The number of NGOs recorded by the Union of International Associa-

Polls show that governments do not provide as much access to environmental information, or as much opportunity to participate in environmental decision-making, as their citizens would like.

tions has more than doubled since 1985 to over 47,000 (UIA 2000; 2001:1519). At the United Nations, 2,143 NGOs held consultative status in 2003 (DESA 2003), compared to 928 in 1992 and just 222 in 1952 (Willetts 1996:38; 2002).

In addition, civil society organizations have been increasingly effective in demanding a "seat at the table" in both the national and international policy arenas. The Rio Earth Summit in 1992 represented a quantum leap in NGO participation in setting the agenda and influencing the negotiations of a multilateral forum. Following the Earth Summit, civil society organizations have taken their place alongside government officials and business representatives in multistakeholder forums such as National Councils for Sustainable Development, and the World Commission on Dams.

Access to Information Technology and Connectivity

The recent revolution in information and communications technologies has profound implications for environmental governance. The Internet provides a powerful new vehicle governments can use to make information available to their citizens. Government websites have become convenient venues for posting official reports and analyses, Environmental Impact Assessments, and basic data on land use, air and water quality, industrial emissions, and census statistics.

A growing trend toward "e-government"–application of the Internet-based techniques of e-commerce to government services–also offers opportunities to increase the ease and transparency of government services such as land titling and registration. This can help empower low-income and rural residents in asserting their environmental rights. In the Indian state of Andhra Pradesh, for example, on-line property registration has reduced the time it takes to obtain a certified copy of a registered land title from days to a few minutes, and has shortened the entire process of official valuation and registration of land parcels to a few hours. Greater transparency in the process has helped discourage corruption and has increased state revenues from land registration by nearly 20 percent (Bhatnagar 2000).

New information tools also allow citizens to more easily share information in order to influence governments and private businesses. In the United States, Environmental Defense, an environmental advocacy group, has pioneered the use of interactive websites to post local pollution data. This allows citizens in any location to check on and take action against local pollution sources, such as hog farms that generate concentrated animal waste that may contaminate local waterways (Scorecard 2003).

New technology has also enhanced the power of maps in environmental decision-making. New mapping tools let researchers, advocacy groups, and government agencies combine specific land use or pollution data with geographic data to graphically portray environmental trends and impacts. These have often proved decisive in land use debates. In Norway, an NGO called Nature and Youth helped develop a map that illustrated the potential damage to a wilderness area from a proposed road. The map was so effective in swaying opinion that the road was not built (Denisov and Christoffersen 2001:5).

(continued on p. 39)

Box 2.4 Undue Influence: Corruption and Natural Resources

More than $1 billion of Angola's state oil revenue goes missing each year, at least a portion of which is apparently siphoned into private bank accounts off-shore (Global Witness 2002:3; Pearce 2002). In 2002, a powerful Kenyan cabinet minister seized 1,000 hectares of state forest land to build a memorial to his mother (Walsh 2002:A4). In Sumatra's Jambi province, corrupt civilian and military officials collude with private loggers to illegally harvest and export state timber. The collusion is so widespread and the impact so great that provincial legislators made a rare public appeal in 2000 to military, police, and justice officials to stop supporting the illegal timber operations (FWI and GFW 2002:31).

Whether it is high-profile embezzlement or a low-level bribe to a petty bureaucrat, corruption is a major force undermining environmental equity and destroying ecosystems. It is also the epitome of bad governance. Because corruption thrives away from public view and enriches only those involved, it naturally subverts the transparency, accountability, and inclusiveness that mark good decision-making. By offering special access to resources and decisions to a select few, it denies access to the wider public.

Broadly speaking, *corruption is the abuse of public office or public resources for private gain* (Gray and Kaufman 1998:22; Andvig et al. 2000:11). Bribe-taking, graft, sweetheart deals, political payoffs, influence peddling, cronyism, patronage, and nepotism are a few of its many faces. Corruption that makes the headlines frequently involves politicians, senior government officials, or military leaders—what is usually termed "grand" corruption. But "petty" corruption involving junior bureaucrats, local officials, or low-ranking military personnel is widespread and just as corrosive of sustainable resource management (Andvig et al. 2000:14–19).

In many countries, corruption is perceived to be rampant. Every year Transparency International polls businesspeople and analysts about the degree of corruption in a given country. Out of 102 countries rated in Transparency International's 2002 Corruption Perception Index (CPI), 70 scored less than 5 on a 10-point scale (with a score of 0 as highly corrupt). Eight countries—Azerbaijan, Indonesia, Kenya, Angola, Madagascar, Paraguay, Nigeria, and Bangladesh—received a score of 2 or less in the CPI poll (Transparency International 2002). The CPI findings and many other studies indicate that the problem of corruption affects all societies, rich and poor, but that the incidence is particularly high in many of the poorest nations (Transparency International 2001:7; 2002).

A Natural Target

Natural resources offer a rich opportunity for corruption. Indeed, environmental crime—illegal logging, theft of public lands, diversion of oil revenues, or other illegal appropriations of public assets—is a modern growth industry that is fre-

Corruption Perceptions Index 2002

10 Least Corrupt	10 Most Corrupt
Finland (9.7)	Bangladesh (1.2)
Denmark (9.5)	Nigeria (1.6)
New Zealand (9.5)	Paraguay (1.7)
Iceland (9.4)	Madagascar (1.7)
Singapore (9.3)	Angola (1.7)
Sweden (9.3)	Kenya (1.9)
Canada (9.0)	Indonesia (1.9)
Luxembourg (9.0)	Azerbaijan (2.0)
Netherlands (9.0)	Uganda (2.1)
United Kingdom (8.7)	Moldova (2.1)

Note: The CPI Score relates to perceptions of the degree of corruption as seen by businesspeople and risk analysts.
Source: Transparency International 2002.

quently facilitated by corruption. Natural resources often have high commercial value, making them a prime target for plunder. They are often governed by complicated regulations, require special permits for exploitation and export, and must be inventoried and accounted for to determine royalties and taxes—all entry points for manipulation and corruption (Ascher 2000:13–14; FAO 2001:90–91). For example, an official may accept a bribe to favor an applicant's request for a forest concession, speed the approval process, or grant more favorable concession terms or a higher harvest level. In other cases, officials may ignore breaches of the concession contract, allowing overharvesting or timber smuggling. Sometimes they may falsely certify illegally cut timber as legal, facilitating its sale or export (Callister 1999:12).

An added inducement to corrupt behavior is that there is often a low risk of being caught. Most natural resource exploitation takes place far from public view, in remote regions where monitoring and media scrutiny are low. The areas at issue may be physically vast and sparsely populated. Even if one is caught in the act, the penalties are commonly minimal relative to the potential returns. The people being victimized by the economic distortions and bad management that corruption brings are often the rural poor, who wield little political power and therefore pose little political danger (Ascher 2000:13–14; FAO 2001:90–91).

By their nature, corruption and environmental crime are hard to quantify, but available evidence makes it clear that the dimensions of natural resource corruption are large. The global timber trade, for example, is plagued by high rates of illegal logging in many important timber-producing nations, abetted by corrupt officials. Illegal timber comprised an esti-

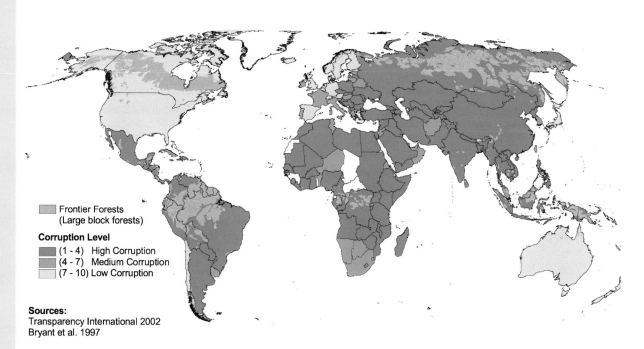

Frontier Forests
(Large block forests)

Corruption Level
(1 - 4) High Corruption
(4 - 7) Medium Corruption
(7 - 10) Low Corruption

Sources:
Transparency International 2002
Bryant et al. 1997

Corruption is a key factor in the misuse of forest resources. Two thirds of the world's remaining large blocks of intact forest—called *frontier forests*—occur in countries where corruption is perceived as high, putting these forests at high risk for mismanagement.

mated 80 percent of all harvested timber—some 25.5 million of a total 30 million cubic meters—in the Brazilian Amazon in 2000, according to IBAMA, the Brazilian Environment Agency (Smith 2003:Table 2).

In Indonesia, estimates of the percentage of illegal logging range from 50 to 70 percent; research shows that, in the mid-1990s, 84 percent of Indonesian timber concession holders were not in compliance with forest laws. Analysts believe that at least 20 percent of Russia's timber is harvested in violation of current laws, and that could increase to 50 percent in parts of Siberia and the Russian Far East. In Cambodia, where a robust illegal logging trade has flourished since the mid-1990s, payments to government officials in the form of bribes are estimated at $200 million for 1997 alone. That is more than 13 times the $15 million in revenue the Cambodian government took in from legal forest operations that year (Smith 2003:Table 2). Though corruption may not be implicated in every single incidence of illegal forest practice, the correlation between corruption and forest crime is believed to be remarkably high in many countries (Contreras-Hermosilla 2001:4).

The Roots of Corruption

A combination of economic, social, and administrative factors creates favorable conditions for corruption. In developing countries, for example, low salaries for civil servants—those responsible for the routine management of natural resources and enforcement of regulations—increase the motivation to earn additional income through corrupt activities (Andvig et al. 2000:112). In fact, bribes and other gifts and favors may form a significant percentage of a public employee's total income in societies where civil service pay is low (Mbaku 1996:100). Other aspects of public administration play a part as well. Hiring and job advancement, for instance, may be determined more by connections and payoffs than by merit, reducing the professionalism and competence of the bureaucracy and strengthening the cycle of corruption.

Corruption flourishes where the mechanisms of accountability and oversight are weak. These mechanisms can include independent audits, special investigative units or government inspectorates, NGO watchdog groups, a robust press, and vocal political opposition parties. When these institutions of detection and enforcement are lacking or are themselves corrupt, the chances of exposure are slim. The complexity of government regulations and the amount of discretionary power bureaucrats exercise factor into the corruption equation as well. Where rules are complex, vague, or frequently changing, administrators have more opportunities to use their influence to exact bribes (Kaufmann 1997:119; Gray and Kaufman 1998:26).

Expectations about the prerogatives of authority also vary. In many African countries, for example, corruption is common and quite visible, with most of those engaging in it believing they are entitled to the benefits they reap. Indeed, civil service

(continued on next page)

Box 2.4 (continued)

is frequently seen as a legitimate opportunity to enrich oneself and take care of one's family or other social obligations (Mbaku 1996:104; Andvig et al. 2000:63, 68–9).

Together, these factors can lead to an entrenched "culture of corruption," where the social stigma attached to such practices may be lower and tolerated by the public as part of everyday life and normal business practice, even if it does not wholly approve. An extreme example of this occurred when one African government eliminated the wages of its customs officials for six months, assuming they would earn sufficient income through bribes to support themselves (Tanzi 1995 as cited in Andvig et al. 2000:112).

A final and critical factor in the corruption cycle is the bribe-giver—the "supply side" of corruption. Bribe suppliers are frequently not simply victims of greedy officials, but active partners in the fraud (Vogl 1998:55). They may be local or international, since modern corruption is global in scope. In fact, complicity by multinational companies is often cited as a major factor in facilitating corruption in developing and transition nations (Transparency International 2002). On the World Bank's list of firms ineligible to receive Bank contracts due to fraud and corruption, more than half were based in the United States or the United Kingdom as of November 2002 (World Bank 2003).

Confronting Corruption

Since the early 1990s, public recognition and discussion of the problem of corruption has grown. From the World Bank, to watchdog groups like Transparency International, to the heads of state of the G-8 nations, calls for stronger action to confront this ingrained behavior have shattered the taboo on speaking out about a public scourge. In part, this new interest reflects the realization that corruption is bad for a nation's economic health. Research shows that corruption imposes significant costs and interferes with the pace and direction of development (Kaufmann 1997:118–120; Tanzi and Davoodi 1998:33–42; Andvig et al. 2000:91–102). For example, it discourages foreign investment by increasing the overall costs of doing business much like a new tax—a "corruption tax," so to speak (Kaufmann 1997:120; Andvig et al. 2000:94). As a result, international leaders now openly speak of directing aid and investment packages to nations with better records of transparency and financial accountability (Gray and Kaufman 1998:21–22).

The effort to combat corruption involves action on several fronts. Perhaps first and most difficult is the effort to change public expectations. Unless such practices are seen as unacceptable to practitioners and to the public at large, anti-corruption laws and procedural reforms are difficult to implement (Andvig et al. 2000:79).

The media, and public advocates such as Transparency International and Global Witness are key players in exposing corruption and raising societal norms with regard to bribe-taking and abuse of public resources. Investigative reporting and independent assessments of public performance heighten the visibility of questionable practices and introduce a measure of transparency to the actions of decision-makers. For this reason, press freedoms and reform of overzealous libel laws that can muzzle watchdog groups go hand in hand with corruption reform (Schloss 1998:15; Andvig et al. 2000:36–37).

Improvements in public administration and natural resource laws are certainly necessary parts of any attempt to reduce systematic corruption. These aim for greater financial transparency through such steps as simplifying procedures for issuing permits and granting concessions, reforming contracting practices for large infrastructure projects, or mandating independent audits (FAO 2001:96; Contreras-Hermosilla and Rios 2002:11–12, 33–36).

Other changes in public administration are important as well, such as higher pay and higher standards for civil service employees. Research shows that when hiring and advancement decisions are made on the basis of merit, corruption levels go down (Andvig et al. 2000:114).

Action against the supply side of corruption is also imperative. Some progress has already been made with the signing of the 1997 OECD Convention on Combating Bribery of Foreign Public Officials in International Business Transactions. This international treaty makes it a crime to bribe any foreign official and outlaws the practice of money laundering that often accompanies bribery. It also forbids the practice of deducting the cost of foreign bribes as business expenses on tax returns, a distressingly common practice in many developed nations until a few years ago. As of October 2002, 34 nations had ratified the treaty and all but two had adopted national legislation for its implementation (OECD 1998:1–18; 2003).

If it were strictly enforced, the treaty could be a significant tool against global corruption, since the signatory nations account for more than 90 percent of all foreign direct investment. Unfortunately, the Anti-Bribery Convention has yet to prove its usefulness, according to critics. Transparency International chairman Peter Eigen contends that since the treaty came into effect in 1999, it has not been responsible for a single fine or prison sentence, because of lack of enforcement (Eigen 2002:6).

Where the political will to act is strong, strict enforcement of anti-corruption laws brings results. In Singapore, for example, severe economic penalties against foreign bribes have contributed to the nation's successful cleanup campaign. In 1996, prosecutors convicted a middleman of paying nearly $10 million in bribes on behalf of five large international companies. The government banned those companies from bidding on government contracts for five years. It also banned any new firm the companies might set up to circumvent the penalty (Hawley 2000:18).

The NGO Global Forest Watch (GFW) has carried this power of imagery one step further by combining it with electronic networking of public interest groups concerned about forest loss. Through analysis of satellite imagery, government documentation, and on-the-ground investigation, GFW produces maps with overlays comparing actual changes in forest cover to the legal status of the forest, such as boundaries of protected areas and of legal logging concessions. Posting this information on the Internet provides a powerful tool for reform of forest policy and practice, when, as is often the case, significant discrepancies between government claims and actual practice are revealed (see Box 2.5).

Grading Environmental Governance

As the trends discussed above show, the context for environmental governance is far from static. The economic, social, and political conditions that shape environmental decision-making are evolving quickly, and the challenge of good environmental governance has become more complex. Adding to those challenges is new data that suggests a large gap between the public's interest in, and their access to environmental information.

In the face of these changes, how well has the world put into practice the key environmental governance principles endorsed at the Rio Earth Summit a decade ago? Analysis of governance trends like decentralization and the results of the Access Initiative—an effort to systematically measure people's access to information, participation, and justice in decisions that affect the environment—present a mixed picture: some progress, but much yet to be done.

Unmet Needs: The Public Demand for Access

A Gallup Poll commissioned by the Access Initiative interviewed more than 32,000 people in 46 countries around the world to gauge the strength of people's demand for information on environmental issues; their desire to participate in decisions that affect the environment; and their sense of how their governments are meeting those needs (see Box 2.6).

A clear finding from the poll is that, by a wide margin, citizens feel that governments do not provide them with as much access to environmental information, or opportunity to participate in environmental decision-making, as they would like. The gap is present in all regions, and is not confined to wealthy countries. As measured by this sampling of public opinion, then, access to environmental governance is clearly wanting.

Tentative Steps Toward Decentralization and Regional Cooperation

The task of shifting responsibility for natural resource decision-making to the appropriate level—that which is nearest to the resource and its users, but honors the scale of the ecosystem—is very much a work-in-progress around the world. Decentralization is a case in point. At least 60 developing

countries claim to be transferring political powers over local resources from a central authority to more local units of government (Ribot 2002:3). However, cases of true decentralization, where real authority is granted to a local institution that can be held accountable to local stakeholders—through elections or other means—are very rare.

National governments are seldom motivated to decentralize by an interest in protecting the environment. Instead, decentralization is often a response to pressures to downsize the civil service and reduce central government expenditures. As a result, decentralization often simply shifts the responsibility to manage natural resources to more local levels, but does not actually grant real authority to make decisions or allocate budgets. In other words, the local body does not provide local accountability, but acts simply as an agent to implement decisions made elsewhere.

Nevertheless, cases of more genuine decentralization in Bolivia, the Philippines, some states of India, and elsewhere give credibility to the belief that decentralization done well can bring decisions that are more acceptable to local people and more effective at meeting environmental management goals. In a pilot project in the Cambodian province of Ratanakiri, village committees who were given funds and

(continued on p. 41)

Box 2.5 Information Technology: A Map to Accountability

Around the world, individuals and civil society are gaining influence over resource decisions once made only by the elite. In part, this reflects a new ability to gather and wield environmental information as a lever for greater government accountability. Global Forest Watch (GFW), a nongovernmental organization dedicated to monitoring and publicizing what goes on in the world's forests, is an example of how new information technologies can change old governance patterns.

The Technology of Access

The satellite image that Susan Minnemeyer has created of Cameroon's forests is a treasure map: a detailed key to the region's timber resources and routes of access. Minnemeyer, head mapper for GFW, adds information layer by layer to enhance the image: she outlines areas leased by the government to private firms for harvest, park boundaries, and logging roads—both new and existing.

Using mapping capabilities (called *geographic information systems*, or GIS) developed over the last two decades and a network of on-the-ground observers, GFW has broken the usual government and industry monopoly on forest information. By providing independent oversight of how forests are used and who reaps the benefits, GFW encourages transparency in local forest decisions—such as who can harvest timber, build roads, establish plantations or farms—and helps to detect and restrain illegal logging and under-the-table deals by forest bureaucrats.

Information is Power

Oversight requires vigilance, technology, and teamwork. Many of the new forest roads on Minnemeyer's map are legitimate access roads into active timber concessions, but others impinge on parks and protected areas or zones not yet legally open to logging. When the mapping team finds those, they contact observers on the ground who can verify illegal activity. In each of eight critical forest nations, GFW teams up with local forest advocates who monitor the activities of loggers in their areas, access government and timber company records when possible, and press the case when irregularities are found.

This application of new technology, focused and interpreted with local expertise, has brought unaccustomed access to forest officials and government decision-makers. In the past, when local environmental advocates met with government regulators to discuss oversight of logging concessions, they were often dismissed, even though they had direct knowledge of abuses and infractions. Often, when they asked officials for maps of forest concessions to check their findings, they were told that they were not available to the public. Today, they can bring their own maps—credible, computer-generated, and easy to update. While forestry officials may not be authorized to release maps like GFW's, they may be willing to correct, update, or at least endorse the forest maps that GFW produces—in the process confirming data they would not have volunteered (Bryant 2001).

With accurate and timely data available at the click of a mouse, reporters are more willing to cover stories that would otherwise be vague. In Canada and the African nation of Gabon, Global Forest Watch maps, accessible via the Internet, have formed the basis for newspaper and magazine articles detailing trends in forest use. Using GFW's web-based maps and his own knowledge of Gabon's political scene, one journalist linked many errant logging companies to close associates of the country's top politicians (Vasset 2000; 2001).

In Cameroon during the late 1990s, GFW found that over half of all logging licenses in use were either expired or

located inside protected areas (GFW 2000:28). At the same time, one in five investigations into logging violations in Cameroon's eastern and central provinces was halted "by the intervention of an influential person" (GFW 2000:34). Published accounts of these irregularities, which were documented in GFW reports, brought considerable pressure to improve governance of Cameroon's forests. In mid-2002, in a breakthrough agreement aimed at increasing transparency, the Government of Cameroon and logging industry leaders formally requested GFW to monitor compliance with Cameroon's forest laws. Under the agreement—the first of its kind in Africa—the government will provide data on the country's forest concessions so that GFW's maps will become a more precise tool to identify illegal logging and monitor the state of Cameroon's forests (WRI 2002).

Brokering Change

By compiling information and making it freely available to all—governments, local citizen groups, industries, environmental NGOs, and international wood consumers—Global Forest Watch strives to be an honest broker of forest information. This comprehensive information can be a powerful force for better resource management. The Swedish furniture maker IKEA uses GFW data to avoid buying uncertified wood from the world's remaining intact forests. Reliable information is so important to their green marketing strategy and corporate image that they help fund GFW's data collection. Other large wood consumers such as Home Depot in the United States are also moving to support responsible forest management, and are eager for better information on the harvest practices of their timber sources. By giving these large customers the tools to pressure major wood exporting nations, GFW increases the incentives for good forest management.

The success of Global Forest Watch shows that technological innovation can be a catalyst for changing how decisions are made and who shares in the decision-making process. Unfortunately, new technologies can just as easily undermine sound decision-making and public participation. The same satellite data and mapping software that GFW relies on to track forest trends can also be used by industries to locate prime timber for quick extraction. And the same communication technologies that allow environmental networking and encourage media coverage can facilitate public graft and illegal logging, and make it easy to transfer ill-gotten gains offshore.

As new standards for disclosure make data more available, technology will play an increasing role in getting ecosystem information into the hands of the people who need it in a form they can use. At their best, neutral brokers such as Global Forest Watch allow the forest ecosystem to speak for itself, assuring regulators, stakeholders, and consumers that the data they are using are as complete and unbiased as possible.

For more information about Global Forest Watch, visit **www.globalforestwatch.org**.

autonomy by central authorities decided to map their local resources so they could manage them better—a direct response to the community's concern about protecting its resource base (Dupar and Badenoch 2002:30).

Besides decentralization, there has also been some progress in building regional institutions to manage ecosystems that cross national borders. River basin authorities such as the Mekong River Commission, the International Commission for the Protection of the Rhine, or the Nile Basin Initiative have evolved to coordinate development activities among the countries that share these watersheds.

Other mechanisms are also taking shape to address regional concerns. The European Union (EU) provides one of the best examples of what a regional body can accomplish in policy integration across borders, although it is only beginning to frame its environmental policies around ecosystems. Members of the EU have accepted a range of uniform environmental standards, monitoring criteria, and best practices to address transboundary pollution such as acid rain. The prospect of gaining membership has also pushed several European nations to bring their environmental standards and policies in line with those of the EU—often entailing significant improvement over their previous practices. Meanwhile, Europe's Espoo Convention provides a framework for conducting environmental assessments when proposed projects will result in impacts across borders.

Nonetheless, the development of regional mechanisms with real authority and mandates to sustain ecosystems is still in an early stage. By and large, these regional efforts are few in number, have limited experience and, with the exception of the EU, have powers that are often quite circumscribed in an effort to respect national sovereignty. Enforcement mechanisms may be weak or nonexistent, and thus compliance is largely voluntary. At this point, such agreements may function best as conduits for information-sharing among parties—itself an important achievement. However, these mechanisms have not yet become centers of management innovation or progressive transboundary thinking.

Access: A Gap Between Policy and Practice

Governments are making decisions that affect the environment with a degree of openness and transparency that would have been unthinkable just a decade ago. Forty-four developed and developing countries have adopted "access to information" laws, which impose obligations for disclosure on the government. New legislation is also starting to make more environmental information available to the public as a basis for informed participation.

Governments are also showing a greater understanding of the need to identify and incorporate public opinion when developing policies and plans. In the last 30 years, government agencies have expanded beyond just giving public notice or holding public hearings on high-impact projects, to using consensus-building exercises, policy dialogues, and stakeholder advisory committees. And some corporations, even major polluters, are beginning to publicly report in greater detail on their emissions, practices, and goals. The entry into force in October 2001 of the Aarhus Convention, which enshrines a detailed commitment to access principles in international law, reflects the progress made by some countries in embracing good governance norms since the Rio Earth Summit.

But the recent findings of the Access Initiative suggest that the evolution to systems of access that are truly open, participatory, and effective is a gradual one. Much more must be done to transform government promises and legal commitments into strong, integrated practices of access to information, public participation, and justice (see Chapter 3).

Many of the nine countries examined in the Access Initiative have enacted provisions guaranteeing access to environmental information and participation. Yet, the countries surveyed share common weaknesses in implementing those laws and commitments. The provision of access remains more passive than active. Countries collect data on facility compliance with pollution regulations, but then fail to integrate that data across agencies or make it publicly accessible. Governments track changes in environmental quality over time, but fail to give the public access to different levels of detail or various presentations of the information. Countries pass new access laws, but fail to train public officials and judges about the new rights, and tolerate a lingering culture of secrecy and indifference to the public interest.

Another problem is that the onus is on the public to identify opportunities to voice their opinions. They are generally responsible for initiating participation or exercising their legal rights. On the positive side, governments are increasingly trying to involve the public in decisions on new projects by soliciting input during the Environmental Impact Assessment process. However, all too often this input is limited in scope or occurs too late in the process to be useful. None of the countries surveyed by the Access Initiative has a mechanism in place to track whether or how public comments actually influence decisions.

In terms of access to justice, more and more courts are upholding people's rights to challenge environmental decisions, obtain information, and sue for damages. However, access to justice is limited in some countries by narrow interpretations of what is covered under freedom of information laws, or who has the legal standing to file a suit. High court costs and lengthy procedures are also formidable obstacles.

Lack of Progress in Mainstreaming the Environment

One of the most basic explanations for lack of progress in meeting the goals of the Rio Earth Summit is a continuing failure to integrate environmental thinking into mainstream economic and development decisions. At the national level, ministries of environment remain weak, and at best operate on the margins of significant policy decisions. Traditional economic models that fail to incorporate the costs of environmental decline continue to drive most decisions.

In addition, agencies charged with natural resource management, including ministries of agriculture, forestry, and mining, still prioritize short-term production of commodities over long-term delivery of ecosystem goods and services. In both the European Union and the United States, for instance, only a fraction of the enormous agricultural subsidies dispensed annually is targeted to ecosystem conservation.

This lack of integration at the national level is projected into international economic policies as well. International trade and investment agreements continue to be developed without attention to how they may unintentionally undermine national and international environmental objectives. For example, even though the North American Free Trade Agreement (NAFTA) has been hailed for including an innovative environmental side agreement, it also contains a provision that could stifle domestic environmental regulation by allowing corporations to sue for compensation if regulatory changes–such as new pollution rules–cause them to lose profits (ISSD and WWF 2001:15–21). The outcome of the 2002 World Summit on Sustainable Development (WSSD) also illustrates this lack of integration. While many governments and civil society organizations called for an examination of the relationship among trade, environment, and development, the WSSD failed to identify concrete measures to ensure that expanding international trade could contribute to sustainable development (La Viña et al. 2003:65).

On the other hand, one area of progress stands out. Many local communities worldwide have proven willing to adopt action plans that try to integrate social and economic goals with environmental goals. More than 6,400 local governments in 113 countries have adopted or are in the process of formulating "Local Agenda 21" plans; these identify ways that communities can move toward sustainable development by improving transportation efficiency, water and waste handling, and land use planning (CSD 2002:3). Largely self-motivated and self-financed, these initiatives show that the most creative energy for environmental integration is currently being generated at the local level.

An Ad Hoc and Ineffective System of International Environmental Governance

As environmental awareness has taken root over the last three decades, nations have struggled to assemble a coherent system of global environmental governance. The most visible elements of this are the 500 or so international environmental agreements now in effect. About 150 of these are global treaties and the others include a more limited set of parties.

Some of these agreements have amassed credible records of success, such as the Montreal Protocol, the Convention on International Trade in Endangered Species (CITES), and some of the regional treaties. Three decades of negotiations have also brought other benefits: Greater international awareness of environmental issues, agreements on common goals and definitions, elaboration of useful partnerships, and a body of applied experience that will make future progress easier. Perhaps one of the most significant advances has been the emergence, through cooperative monitoring and scientific consultation, of a global capability to assess environmental threats more quickly.

Unfortunately, our assessments usually stop short of action. In fact, our prodigious efforts at environmental diplomacy have largely failed to make serious headway against the world's most pressing environmental challenges–at least as measured by current trends. For example, the conference of the parties of the Convention on Biological Diversity–one of the prize outcomes of the Rio Earth Summit–recently admitted that in spite of the treaty, "biological diversity is being destroyed by human activities at unprecedented rates"(CBD 2002).

This poor overall record comes as little surprise. Few environmental treaties contain specific targets and timetables or adequate enforcement provisions, and financing is difficult. A more systemic problem, according to a recent United Nations University study, is that current environmental agreements have arisen in an ad hoc and largely uncoordinated fashion as each new concern–acid rain, ozone depletion, climate change–has entered the public consciousness. These agreements reflect a single-issue approach toward environmental stewardship rather than an integrated perspective that recognizes the common drivers of environmental decline, and the treaties are not generally framed with particular reference to ecosystems (Dodds et al. 2002:6).

International institutions created specifically to address environmental issues, such as the UN's Commission on Sustainable Development (CSD), the Global Environment Facility (GEF), and the United Nations Environment Programme (UNEP), also face daunting tasks in facilitating global consensus, efficiently discharging their broad mandates, and financing their activities. For example, while the CSD has provided an international forum for raising environmental issues, its effect on national policies and the implementation of Agenda 21–the Earth Summit's action plan for sustainable development–has been negligible (Upton 2002:20-29). Meanwhile, a recent evaluation of the GEF shows that it is maturing into a useful mechanism to help developing nations fund environmental priorities in a few key areas, and to make progress implementing the terms of the environmental treaties they sign–an accomplishment that should not be minimized (Streck 2001:93; GEF 2002:x-xvi). Yet, its success is necessarily bounded by its limited funds, and no one would contend that it can adequately address the great environmental financing needs of developing nations.

Efforts are now under way to harmonize the many international environmental agreements so that global resources and attention are focused more effectively. Other efforts are attempting to ensure that the global trading regime does not undermine national and international environmental laws. We can also take heart at the international community's determination to carry forward the final negotiations on the Kyoto Protocol to address climate change, in spite of the unilateral withdrawal of the United States from the treaty. This effort has been buoyed by global acceptance of the science-based approach and findings of the Intergovernmental Panel on Climate Change–an international group of scientists charged with assessing the evidence on this complex topic. But these positive events will do little to address nations' fundamental reluctance to shoulder the domestic political and financial costs of making environmental treaties enforceable and living instruments that can stimulate meaningful national action.

The Bottom Line

On a global basis, our capacity to consistently make environmental decisions that protect ecosystems, are informed by public input, and equitably meet human needs is severely limited. At the international level, there is rhetorical commitment to the goals of sustainable development and participatory decision-making. However, there is far less commitment to localizing these goals in national policies, decision-making practices, and the design of government agencies. As a result, public access to environmental information, to true participation, and to redress when the decision process fails is still scant.

Other findings reinforce the inadequacy of our current environmental governance. National decentralization efforts have yet to lead to significant devolution of power over natural resource decisions to the local level. The trade and investment policies that drive our decisions are largely opaque to the public and indifferent to environmental concerns. The international agreements and institutions meant to address global environmental problems have robust missions, but weak enforcement powers and insufficient funding. Successes at the local level show that good environmental governance is possible, but cannot be completely effective without strong national and international support.

Good Governance, Healthy Ecosystems

Beyond global treaties, trade policies, and transnational politics, ecosystems stand as the final test of our ability to govern nature with skill and fairness. Good governance principles thus have a special place in ecosystem management. For example, the participation of local, ecosystem-dependent people is one of the surest ways of giving ecosystems a voice. In a river basin that spans several countries, no nation may be in a good position to manage its section of the basin with the whole system in mind. On the other hand, river dwellers dependent on the fish or water that the river produces may be more attuned to the sensitivities of the ecosystem as a whole. The local public's role, then, may be to represent the

(continued on p. 46)

Box 2.6 The Unmet Demand for Access: Measuring the Information and Participation Gaps

Polling data from Gallup International show that, world-wide, there is a substantial gap between the amount of environmental information the public desires and the amount governments supply. Similarly, there is a large gap between people's desire to participate in environmental decision-making and the opportunities to participate that governments provide. Interest in environmental information and participation is strong in all regions and is not confined to wealthy countries.

■ More than 70 percent of people worldwide say they would like to invest time and effort to obtain and use relevant environmental information and to contribute their knowledge and experience to decision-making. Yet, only about 40 percent are satisfied with the efforts made by their governments to provide information or to engage them in decision-making.

Poll Particulars: In 2002, the World Resources Institute asked Gallup International to assess the strength of people's demand for information on environmental issues, and their desire to participate in decisions that affect the environment. The poll also asked about the extent to which citizens believe their governments are providing information and enabling

The Poll
Agree or disagree with these statements:
1. I would like to spend more of my free time learning about the impacts of environmental problems on me and my family.

2. Our government is providing enough information about environmental problems that could affect me and my family.

3. I would like to spend more of my free time participating in the decisions that affect the environmental quality of my community.

4. Our government is providing enough opportunities for people to participate in decisions that affect the environmental quality of my community.

public participation in decision-making. Designed in collaboration with Environics International and conducted from July to September 2002, the survey consisted of face-to-face or telephone interviews with over 32,000 citizens across 46 countries on 6 continents.

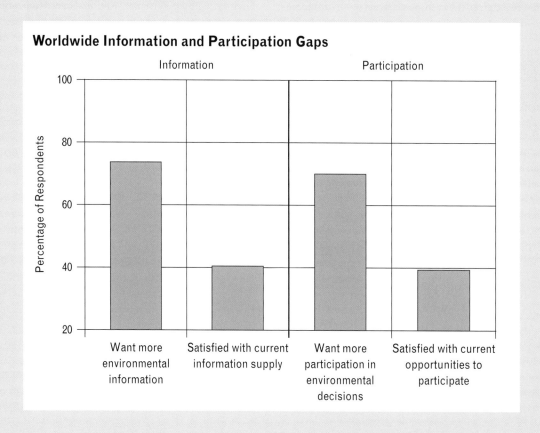

Worldwide Information and Participation Gaps

What Types of Information Do People Want Most? This figure provides a breakdown of public responses in different regions of the world. Participants were asked to pick the issue they would be most interested in learning more about from a short list of environmental issues. In other words, what types of environmental information do people really want?

■ Worldwide, there is a roughly even split among demand for four types of information: information about industrial accidents and pollution from industrial facilities (29%), information on ways to participate in economic decision-making that affects the local environment (22%),

information on general air and water quality (24%), and information on what national governments are doing to address problems (25%).

■ The emphasis changes among regions. In low-income countries, people appear more interested in information that would enable them to influence economic development choices. Concern about industrial accidents and pollution is highest in the European Union and Latin America. Interest in what governments are doing to address environmental problems is highest in North America, the Asia Pacific region, and Europe.

What Types of Information Do People Want Most?

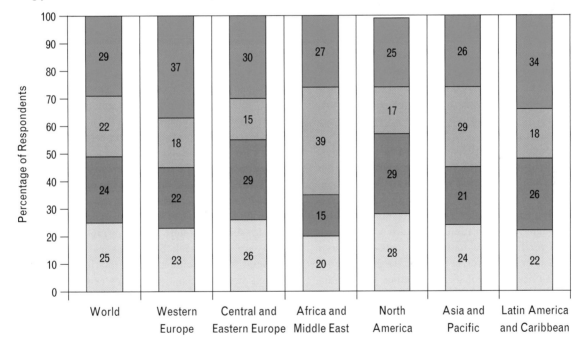

Information about:

■ Industrial accidents that could affect the environment, and pollution from facilities

■ Ways to participate in decisions on economic development that could affect the environmental quality of the community

■ General air and water quality

□ What government is doing to address environmental problems

Good governance principles are crucial tools
in dealing with the trade-offs that inevitably come
with ecosystem management.

ecosystem's interest–which they identify with their own well-being–over the national interest (Bruch 2001:11390). Thus, encouraging and giving weight to local input–a basic principle of good environmental governance–is also good ecosystem management.

Good governance principles are also crucial tools in dealing with the trade-offs that inevitably come with ecosystem management. Sometimes these trade-offs are between competing uses of a natural resource. For example, a forested area cannot simultaneously be used for intensive timber production and for wilderness recreation. Often such competition is between the production of natural products–"ecosystem goods," such as timber, grain, or fish, and the production of "ecosystem services"–hydrological regulation, soil fertility, or aesthetic value.

Most trade-offs have clear equity dimensions–there will be some winners who get more ecosystem benefits, and some losers who get fewer. When a river is dammed for irrigation, local farmers may see increased yields and profits, while fishermen go out of business. The goal of sound ecosystem management is to optimize the chosen bundle of goods and services and distribute it equitably, all while increasing the health and productive capacity of the ecosystem. But determining how to choose the goods or services to harvest and how to apportion the benefits and costs is as much a reflection of social values as it is a technical management question. The governance principles of access and participation are crucial in letting managers know which course to choose.

In the same way, following good governance principles promotes management at the correct scale–a scale that fits the properties of the ecosystem. Community-based forest management–where local village groups gain control over small forest areas–is a good example of granting decision-making authority consistent with the structure of the ecosystem. Experience shows that when people are given authority over a resource in which they have a long-term interest, both the community and the ecosystem tend to fare better.

Better governance can also bring science into its proper advisory role in management and can therefore lead us to a fuller understanding of ecosystem dynamics and the biological thresholds that determine how much ecosystem productivity we can expect. By increasing the visibility of and demand for environmental information, good governance norms create a constituency for ecosystem monitoring, which produces the kind of data that empower people to make informed choices about resource use, with some appreciation for the likely impact.

If we accept the tenet that reversing global environmental decline depends on more skillful ecosystem management, then we must begin to think in terms of adopting an "ecosystem approach" to environmental management. That means realigning our management practices so that we think in terms of ecosystem health–the basis of productivity–rather than commodity production. An ecosystem approach explicitly includes the needs and rights of people to share in and contribute to the productivity of this resource. Good governance principles ensuring access to and informed participation in management decisions, as well as a fair distribution of nature's bounty, are the only viable route to defining and applying such an approach.

PUBLIC PARTICIPATION AND ACCESS

In 2001–2002, a global coalition of 25 civil society groups called the Access Initiative measured the public's ability to participate in decisions about the environment. For this pilot assessment, the Access Initiative focused on laws and public experiences in nine countries: Chile, Hungary, India, Indonesia, Mexico, South Africa, Thailand, Uganda, and the United States. These countries vary in terms of income levels, development paths, literacy rates, natural resource dependency, and cultural and political traditions. The findings, summarized here, give a good indication of public access to environmental decision-making around the world.

Why Does "Access" Matter?

Access to environmental information is important because an informed public is more alert to problems, more apt to challenge assumptions of government or corporate decision-makers, more capable of discussing issues, and more likely to organize for social and political change. Access to decision-making matters because people want and need to shape the choices that affect their well-being—the quality of the air they breathe, the purity of the water they drink, the aesthetics of their neighborhood, the availability of forests that are a source of fuel or food, the wildness of their favorite place to hike. When people have access to justice—where independent courts supply remedy and redress free from politics—there is greater accountability for decisions that affect the environment.

The Access Initiative framed its assessment around the three elements of Principle 10 of the 1992 Rio Declaration, which asserts that access to information, to the decision-making process, and to a system of justice are all essential components of a comprehensive system of public participation. Assessment teams in each of the pilot test countries used a common methodology, including review of planning documents, legislation, and court cases; interviews with government officials and nongovernmental organizations (NGOs); questionnaires; requests for information; and media analysis (see Box 3.1). Using this material, the assessment teams examined how well public authorities provide:

1. ACCESS TO ENVIRONMENTAL INFORMATION. Public information is one of the cornerstones of sustainable development strategies. Access to environmental information enables the public to make informed personal choices, contributes to the protection of the environment, and encourages improved environmental performance by industry.

The Access Initiative focused on access to four critical types of environmental information:

■ *Information about day-to-day environmental quality, such as air and water quality*, which helps people decide whether children should play outside, whether to drink water from the tap, or whether to take other

actions to lessen environmental impacts on their health

■ *Information about environmental trends over time*, which creates a more enlightened public—one that is better able to connect its actions to environmental consequences, more likely to support policies that minimize environmental harm, and more able to hold decision-makers accountable

■ *Information about pollution from industrial facilities*, which empowers NGOs, investors, neighbors, and consumers to press for responsible corporate citizenship

■ *Information about emergency situations and risks*, which enables people to protect their health or environment during events such as a cholera outbreak or a fire at an industrial plant.

These categories represent a minimum standard for public authorities to use in providing environmental information.

Access Initiative researchers looked at specific cases of government practice and industrial reporting. They rated governments on how well they generate and manage environmental information and on how easily citizens can obtain comprehensive information in a timely manner,

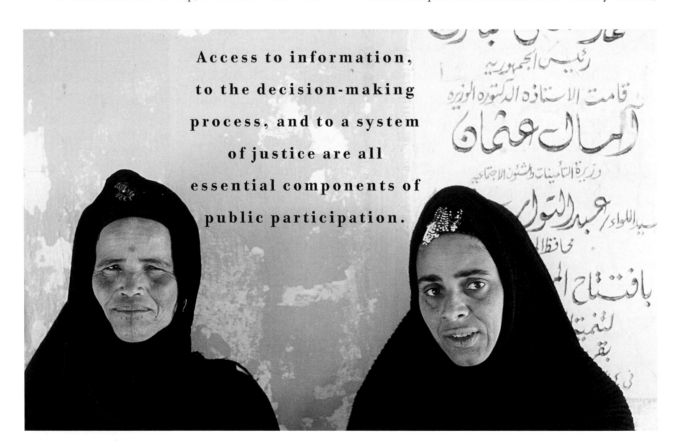

Access to information, to the decision-making process, and to a system of justice are all essential components of public participation.

usable format, and appropriate language. They did not specifically rate the accuracy of the information, but stressed the efforts made to collect and disseminate it. For example, in examining the response to a fire at a chemical factory in Viña del Mar, Chile in 2000, the Access Initiative found that public authorities provided neighboring communities information that was incomplete and too late to be useful. Accordingly, the Viña del Mar case rated "low" for access to information. The assessment teams also examined the framework of laws and regulations to determine each country's commitment to support people's access to environmental information through clearly defined and enforceable rights.

2. *ACCESS TO DECISION-MAKING AFFECTING THE ENVIRONMENT.* To get an indication of public participation in practice, the Access Initiative evaluated several specific kinds of decisions with environmental impacts and the degree to which a broad set of stakeholders or interested groups were able to participate early, easily, and substantively in each kind. Researchers examined how much opportunity the public has to influence:

■ *National policies and plans,* including broad environmental and economic policies, such as South Africa's water management policy, or Thailand's national provisions for siting power plants

■ *Provincial and local policies and plans,* such as regional development plans in Hungary, and other subnational decisions that affect natural resources

■ *The design of environmentally significant projects,* such as the licensing of a power plant in the United States, or approval of a discharge permit at a wastewater plant in Uganda.

Scores given for each of these categories were based on when and how easily people could participate, and the degree to which authorities took public feedback into account. For example, researchers looked at when, how, and who was notified about pending decisions and opportunities for input such as public hearings or comment periods. They also looked for the presence of laws and regulations ensuring people's rights to participate in environmental decisions.

3. *ACCESS TO JUSTICE AND REMEDY.* The Access Initiative evaluated whether individuals and organizations can seek legal remedy and redress when there is a failure to provide information or involve the public in decisions as required by law, or when citizens wish to dispute a decision or have it independently reviewed. Researchers scored countries on indicators of:

■ *Enforceable rights and legal standing,* particularly the legal guarantees and provisions for access to information and participation that enable individuals and organizations to build a legal case. Just as important is the matter of "legal standing," or the eligibility to defend one's rights in court, to file a suit, or post a grievance

■ *A process for review of disputed plans and policies,* including the presence of an independent, impartial, and ably administered judiciary, and the availability of review mechanisms in specific decisions such as the awarding of timber or mining concessions.

Access Initiative research teams also looked at practical considerations that can limit access to justice, such as the affordability of judicial and administrative services and legal help, or the time required for an appeal process.

The Access Initiative findings provide more than just a picture of the state of environmental democracy in individual countries. The results reveal common accomplishments and failures across countries, pointing to the challenges that face most nations as they try to create effective national systems of access for their citizens.

Box 3.1 Measuring Access

To assess how well a country is fighting poverty, you can turn to data on income, life expectancy, access to clean water, the percentage of people living below the poverty line, and undernourishment. Do you want to know how well a country is educating its citizens relative to other countries? It's fairly easy to find statistics on school enrollment and literacy rates. But what if you're interested in a country's performance on environmental governance? This is much harder to measure, with few objective, widely accepted indicators (UNDP 2002:36), since good environmental governance embodies not only environmental sustainability, but also human rights, political freedoms, transparency, and more.

Efforts are under way to fill this gap. For example:

- The Environmental Sustainability Index (ESI) is an assessment of 142 countries conducted by the World Economic Forum, Yale University, and Columbia University. It includes indicators of environmental governance such as people's "capacity for debate" estimated with data on democratic institutions, and civil and political liberties (World Economic Forum 2002:1).

- In the Human Development Report, the United Nations Development Programme offers a collection of objective indicators of governance (such as voter turnout or the existence of competitive elections) and subjective indicators (such as expert assessments of government effectiveness, corruption, and other aspects of a country's degree of democracy) for 173 countries (UNDP 2002:36–45).

- The World Bank calculates governance indicators for 175 countries that capture characteristics of the political process, civil liberties, and political rights, including citizen participation in the selection of government and the independence of the media (Kaufman et al. 2002:1).

- *The Wellbeing of Nations* is a survey of 180 countries conducted in collaboration with the International Development Research Centre, IUCN, and other research institutes. It combines measures of environmental conditions with measures of respect for human rights; the freedom to choose how decisions are made and who makes them; and the openness, accountability, and effectiveness of decision-making bodies (Prescott-Allen 2001).

These studies rely on existing data from surveys and from other organizations. There are also efforts to generate new data specifically on environmental governance, including country self-assessments organized by the United Nations Commission on Sustainable Development, environmental performance reviews organized by the Organisation for Economic Co-operation and Development and the United Nations Economic Commission for Europe, and an effort in Russia by a civil society coalition to assess governance practices related to freedom of information (UNCSD 2002; Russian Journalists' Union 2001).

The Access Initiative Methodology

The Access Initiative is also generating new country-level data on environmental governance. Specifically, the initiative has developed a framework of indicators that measure a country's progress toward implementation of the access principles articulated in Principle 10 of the 1992 Rio Declaration. The methodology was crafted by an international team convened by the World Resources Institute (U.S.), the Environmental Management and Law Association (Hungary), Corporación PARTICIPA (Chile), Thailand Environment Institute, and Advocates Coalition for Development and the Environment (Uganda).

Research questions are designed to assess both a country's policies on and practice of the access principles. Some of the resulting analysis is based on observable measures of access. For example, an observable measure of access to information is whether a government has published a State of the Environment Report in the prior three years, the degree to which that report contains comprehensive data, and the extent of proactive efforts to provide the report to the public and the media. Another measurable indicator is the number of groups a government consults before going ahead with a project. Other indicators are opinion-based. For example, to measure meaningful participation, Access Initiative teams surveyed experts on the degree to which public input influenced government decision-making related to a project or policy.

One aspect of access that the initiative did not measure is the role of legislatures and parliaments as a means of public participation in environmental governance. In many cases, citizens can lobby legislators on environmental issues of concern and influence legislative policies and oversight. However, the Access Initiative did not assess legislative performance or how well legislators represented their constituents' environmental interests. Instead, it focused on the efforts of non-elected government officials to extend access to citizens, and the access implications of government and judicial policies in practice.

The methodology for the nine pilot national assessments relied on more than 100 indicators; 79 were applied by all or most of the national teams and allow for some general conclusions about performance. These indicators form the basis of the Access Scorecard (see Figure 3.1).

The Access Initiative methodology has strengths and weaknesses. A strength is its relative ease of use and its global relevance: the nine national teams were able to apply most portions of the framework without making significant modifications. In most cases, assessments were completed in a matter of months and without excessive costs in spite of the great differences between countries. The assessment results have enabled several research teams to enter into constructive dialogue with national governments about ways to improve performance.

Although the Access Initiative offers a "standard" approach to measuring access, it also encouraged research teams to adapt the methodology to their own national circumstances. This sacrifices a degree of comparability across countries in the interest of country-specific relevance.

Another problem is that not all teams followed the suggested common criteria for case selection. Nor were all indicators applied by all teams. Sometimes teams proposed and pursued alternatives. South Africa, for example, assessed the investment of the government in environmental education using a survey. No other country used a survey method for this indicator, making it difficult to compare South Africa's findings with those from other countries.

The framework of indicators was revised based on the experiences of the nine pilot test countries. Ideally, additional countries will refine and use this set of standard indicators to conduct regular assessments of the performance of public authorities in implementing environmental governance. Wider application will provide more meaningful comparisons of compliance with the access principles across diverse cultural, socioeconomic, and political settings.

Access Initiative Findings: The State of Access

Every country examined by the Access Initiative has sought in significant ways to broaden citizen participation in environmental decision-making. However, people still have only limited opportunity to participate in the economic, political, and environmental decisions that affect their lives and their ecosystems. The Access Initiative findings show that governments in the nine countries surveyed scored highest at providing their citizens with access to information. They rated lower at providing opportunities to participate in decisions that affect the environment, and generally lagged on the provision of access to justice. A truly effective and empowering system of access requires the strong, integrated practice of all three principles.

Access to Information

Finding: Strong Laws, Weak Implementation

Strong laws guarantee access to information in all the countries examined—an important and encouraging finding. Since the Rio Earth Summit in 1992, the developing countries and transition economies included in the Access Initiative survey have introduced legal provisions and established the infrastructure for access to information. Three of the nine countries—Mexico, South Africa, and Thailand—have comprehensive legislation dealing with access to information, including constitutional guarantees to access, legislation addressing access to information generally, and legislation that specifically addresses access to environmental information. Three of the other countries examined have enshrined at least two of those three types of provisions in national law (see Table 3.1).

The constitutional right to information can offer advantages, such as a consistent basis for applying and enforcing this right, and protection from having the right arbitrarily revoked or abridged. Right-to-information laws are clearly valuable: they help meet strong demand for access to information. Following the enactment of the National Environmental Statute in Uganda in 1995, concerned citizens and environmental NGOs have increasingly requested and obtained environmental audits, the text of resource concession agreements, and other key documents not formerly available to the public from the National Environmental Management Authority (ACTS et al. 2000:5). In the United States, public use of the Freedom of Information Act (FOIA) continues to grow. In fiscal 1999, nearly 2 million FOIA requests were filed with federal agencies (National Security Archive 2002) and in Thailand, more than half a million citizens used the Official Information Act in its first three years of existence (Banisar 2002).

Figure 3.1 Access Scorecard

How Much Can the Public Participate in Environmental Decisions?

THE ACCESS INITIATIVE is a first effort to systematically take stock of people's access to information, participation, and justice in decisions that affect the environment. This scorecard presents a comparative analysis of national assessments conducted by research teams in nine pilot countries: Chile, Hungary, India, Indonesia, Mexico, South Africa, Thailand, Uganda, and the United States.

High

Most cases had scores in the highest range. A high score does not necessarily represent the best practice possible.

Medium

Cases had scores in the mid range or showed great variation among cases.

Low ●

Most cases had scores in the lowest range. A low score does not necessarily represent the worst practice possible.

Access and **Quality** scores are averaged to yield an **Overall** score. Not all indicators were measured in all nine countries.

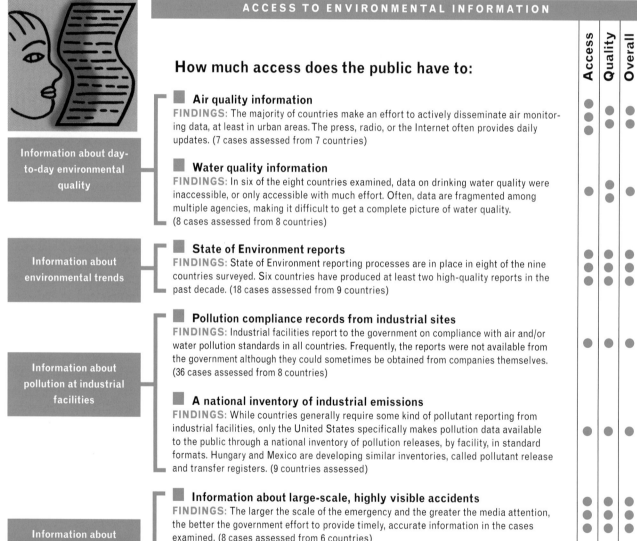

ACCESS TO ENVIRONMENTAL INFORMATION

How much access does the public have to:

Access | Quality | Overall

Information about day-to-day environmental quality

Air quality information
FINDINGS: The majority of countries make an effort to actively disseminate air monitoring data, at least in urban areas. The press, radio, or the Internet often provides daily updates. (7 cases assessed from 7 countries)

Water quality information
FINDINGS: In six of the eight countries examined, data on drinking water quality were inaccessible, or only accessible with much effort. Often, data are fragmented among multiple agencies, making it difficult to get a complete picture of water quality. (8 cases assessed from 8 countries)

Information about environmental trends

State of Environment reports
FINDINGS: State of Environment reporting processes are in place in eight of the nine countries surveyed. Six countries have produced at least two high-quality reports in the past decade. (18 cases assessed from 9 countries)

Information about pollution at industrial facilities

Pollution compliance records from industrial sites
FINDINGS: Industrial facilities report to the government on compliance with air and/or water pollution standards in all countries. Frequently, the reports were not available from the government although they could sometimes be obtained from companies themselves. (36 cases assessed from 8 countries)

A national inventory of industrial emissions
FINDINGS: While countries generally require some kind of pollutant reporting from industrial facilities, only the United States specifically makes pollution data available to the public through a national inventory of pollution releases, by facility, in standard formats. Hungary and Mexico are developing similar inventories, called pollutant release and transfer registers. (9 countries assessed)

Information about emergency situations and risks

Information about large-scale, highly visible accidents
FINDINGS: The larger the scale of the emergency and the greater the media attention, the better the government effort to provide timely, accurate information in the cases examined. (8 cases assessed from 6 countries)

Information about localized accidents at private industrial facilities
FINDINGS: Information about explosions and fires in private facilities is shrouded in secrecy. In four of five such emergencies examined, public authorities provided little or no information to local residents, or the information was supplied too late to be useful. (5 cases assessed from 4 countries)

Access is defined as:
• responsiveness by authorities to requests for information
• extent of active information dissemination
• provision of information in a range of formats and products
• timeliness and coverage during and after emergencies

Quality is defined as:
• clarity of content
• frequency of reporting
• breadth and coordination of coverage

ACCESS TO PARTICIPATION

	Access	Quality	Overall

How much opportunity does the public have to influence:

Participation in national policies and plans

■ **National environmental laws and plans**

FINDINGS: Governments generally made adequate efforts to solicit or allow the public to submit comments on national policies or proposals about environmental issues. Maps and policy documents were readily available for public comment. (3 cases assessed from 3 countries)

■ **National sectoral policies (e.g., mining, power)**

FINDINGS: Efforts to incorporate the public's environmental concerns into plans for power provision and other sectoral decisions are minimal in cases examined. In two of the four cases examined, plans and policies underwent no review or consultation with affected populations or public interest groups. (5 cases assessed from 5 countries)

Participation in provincial and local policies and plans

■ **Provincial and local policies and zoning plans**

FINDINGS: Participation and access vary widely at provincial and local levels; sectoral and issue-specific decisions are often made without broad input from stakeholders and without proactive efforts by relevant agencies to seek wider participation. (5 cases assessed from 4 countries)

Participation in the design of environmentally significant projects

■ **Projects requiring an Environmental Impact Assessment (EIA)**

FINDINGS: An EIA process does not necessarily ensure public accessibility to the decision process. In cases examined, more effort was made to solicit public input in high profile projects with significant environmental impacts, but typically too late in the process to influence the result. (11 cases assessed from 7 countries)

■ **Projects not requiring an Environmental Impact Assessment (EIA)**

FINDINGS: Without a formal EIA, the right of the public to participate in decisions can be easily forgotten or ignored; these cases demonstrated a range of accessibility and quality of participation. (5 cases assessed from 5 countries)

Access is defined as:
- existence of opportunities to participate and the ability of the public to learn about these opportunities
- opportunity to learn about the outcome of environmental deliberations

Quality is defined as:
- inclusiveness of consultation
- timeliness of notification of opportunities to participate

ACCESS TO JUSTICE

	Access	Quality	Overall

To what extent does the public have:

Justice for all affected people

■ **Enforceable rights and legal standing in courts**

FINDINGS: Most countries examined do not clearly define the scope of information in the public domain, agencies' responsibilities, or who has standing to pursue legal remedy. (9 countries assessed)

■ **A process of review for disputed plans and policies**

FINDINGS: In less than half the countries examined, the public can use administrative and judicial review to contest the way in which national or provincial policies were made. Justice is often expensive, complicated, and time-consuming. (9 countries assessed)

Access is defined as:
- legal standing
- affordability of legal help and fees
- the presence and diversity of mechanisms for dispute resolution and remedy

Quality is defined as:
- inclusiveness and clarity of legal mandates to disclose information
- inclusiveness of legal definitions of environmental information in the public domain

BOTTOM LINE: Governments scored high at providing their citizens with access to information, rated lower at providing opportunities to participate in decisions that affect the environment, and lagged on the provision of access to justice. A truly effective and empowering system of access requires the strong, integrated practice of all three principles.

Table 3.1 Grading Legal Guarantees to Environmental Information

The Access Initiative looked for:	Country Assessments		
	Weak	Medium	Strong
Constitutional guarantees of access to information	**Chile and the United States** do not constitutionally guarantee the public's right to information.	**India and Hungary** do not guarantee the public's right to information in their constitutions, but court decisions have interpreted the right to free speech and a free press to include the right to information.	**Indonesia, Mexico, South Africa, Thailand, and Uganda** constitutionally guarantee the public's right to information.
Legislation addressing access to information generally, such as Freedom of Information legislation	**Uganda** has no special legislation on access to information.	**India and Indonesia** have Freedom of Information legislation pending legislative approval.	**Chile, Hungary, Mexico, South Africa, Thailand, and the United States** have enacted Freedom of Information legislation.
Legislation addressing access to environmental information specifically	**Hungary, India, and Uganda** lack provisions specifically addressing access to environmental information. Or, access to different types of environmental information is treated in separate laws.	**No countries** in this category.	**Chile, Indonesia, Mexico, South Africa, Thailand, and the United States** have provisions that specifically support access to environmental information.

Despite the general strength of legal provisions for access to environmental information, the implementation of these laws is typically weak among the surveyed countries. Government bureaucrats and agencies have wide discretion to decide what information is secret, what to share, how to share it, and with whom. In their research and investigations, researchers discovered that many government agencies required parties to submit written justifications for requests for policy documents, and then determined whether or not to supply such information (Mexico and Thailand), or would supply only those excerpts they deemed relevant. In Hungary, Mexico, and Thailand, researchers found that gaining access to policy documents often required a fairly sophisticated knowledge of the agency in question, or a personal acquaintance with decision-makers or staff. Thai researchers who submitted identical requests through personal contacts as well as via formal letters from organizations not known to the agency, promptly obtained documents in the first case—but no replies, or late replies to the letters in the second case.

Many important concepts, such as what constitutes environmental information, are poorly defined. Few countries mandate that public agencies maintain a central environmental information service, and few have established requirements for public disclosure of industry reports on compliance and environmental performance. Ambiguous provisions can result in piecemeal access, as in Hungary and the United States, where laws governing different environmental media and types of pollutants each treat access to information differently.

Finding: Room for Improvement in Access to Information

In the countries surveyed, access to information about air and water quality—key elements of a citizen's day-to-day environment—is mixed. Citizens have good access to data on outdoor air quality, such as the level of airborne particulates and ozone. The majority of countries make an effort to actively disseminate air monitoring data, at least in urban areas. The press, radio, or the Internet often provides daily updates. By comparison, only in South Africa and the United States did researchers find that information on drinking water quality is actively disseminated to the public. Some countries, such as Hungary and Indonesia, disperse responsibility for collecting water data among multiple agencies and don't integrate the separate data collections into one comprehensive set of findings. For example, in Hungary, data on water quality are held

by both the environmental inspectorate and the health service. A citizen seeking a complete picture of Hungary's water situation must submit requests to both agencies.

State of Environment reports are an important way for governments to inform citizens about their nation's environmental status. The Aarhus Convention, for example, requires signatories to publish State of Environment reports every three to four years. Access Initiative findings show that State of Environment reporting processes in most countries are good, providing citizens with access to long-term environmental trend data. This does not necessarily mean that the data provided are always accurate or complete–often they aren't–but does imply an effort by authorities to communicate at least a modicum of environmental information. Most of the countries examined have produced two or more State of Environment reports in the past decade, in both print and electronic form. The United States, however, stopped produc-

What's in the Drinking Water?

In some countries, it's difficult to know. In Uganda, government authorities monitor the quality of drinking water, but don't share their findings with the public. In Thailand, it's impossible to find out from the Food and Drug Administration if bottled water contains contaminants—information particularly important to those who are pregnant, elderly, or caring for children.

Reversal of Information Access

A constitutional guarantee provides the most immutable means of ensuring public access to information. Nonetheless, even as a guaranteed right, access to information may have to be balanced against other state interests such as national security or privacy rights. In the absence of a constitutional guarantee, governments may be all the more likely to tip the balance away from access. In the United States, where there is no such constitutional guarantee, the executive branch of the government moved to take some information out of the public domain in the wake of the terrorist attacks of September 11, 2001. U.S. Attorney General John Ashcroft issued a memo to all federal agencies in October 2001 supporting their use of more restrictive standards of secrecy when considering requests submitted under the Freedom of Information Act. Also in October 2001, the United States Environmental Protection Agency removed from its website information related to Risk Management Plans for industrial facilities. These plans inform workers and communities about the potential consequences of a major chemical release and are aimed at preventing accidents.

ing meaningful federal-level reports in 1997, and Indonesia has produced only one in the past decade (in 1998).

Information about pollution at industrial facilities is the hardest information for the public to access, and is impossible to obtain in some of the surveyed countries. All the governments collect data on facility compliance with air and water laws, but of the nations surveyed only Hungary and the United States routinely make these data public. In Mexico, South Africa, and Uganda, researchers were unable to obtain any information about facility or sector performance from either companies or governments. Corporate rights of privacy are typically treated as paramount to individual citizens' rights to know about their environment, limiting access to information about what companies discharge from their smokestacks and pipes.

Businesses often make claims of confidentiality to shield proprietary research and protect trade secrets; these claims are frequently a barrier to the collection and sharing of facility data. Most countries examined do not have an explicit policy limiting a corporation's rights to claim that information is confidential and requiring justification of that claim.

Newer public disclosure tools are coming into play which, when more widely adopted, promise to improve accessibility of data on the environmental performance of private companies.

Emissions inventories–which provide a listing in a standard format of pollution emissions from each factory, power plant, or other private facility–are among the most progressive. Among the nine countries evaluated, only the United States operates a mandatory emissions inventory (which it calls the Toxics Release Inventory) specifically aimed at making information available to the public. Hungary has a legal mandate to establish a similar system. Under a new law, Mexico is drafting regulations for mandatory public reporting by industrial facilities starting in 2003 (see also Chapter 6). In recent years,

Indonesia has disclosed facility information through a public rating system that doesn't reveal specific data on company emissions, but does grade facilities on their environmental compliance (see Box 6.3).

Information on environmental emergencies such as large chemical spills into the water or air, explosions and fires at manufacturing plants, and even natural disasters like volcanic eruptions or earthquakes can have immediate bearing on citizens' health and safety, affecting their exposure to risk and their ability to evacuate disaster zones. Based on analyses of 13 emergency events, Access Initiative researchers found that access to information varies widely depending on the scale and nature of the emergency. In the majority of cases, the public received adequate and timely information. However, governments generally made a greater effort to provide timely information during large-scale and visible emergencies than during smaller or more confined industrial accidents at private facilities. One reason may be that the larger-scale disasters draw greater media attention and occasionally international attention, motivating authorities in the spotlight to provide more timely and often more accurate information to the public about the immediate threats to health and the natural environment. However, researchers also found that once the attention fades, the public has little or no access to information about the long-term impacts of most emergency events, regardless of their scale.

Access to Decision-Makers and Opportunities to Participate

Finding: Minimal Legal Rights to Public Participation

The right to public participation through hearings, Environmental Impact Assessments (EIAs), advisory groups, meetings with decision-makers, and other avenues is poorly articulated in the legal and constitutional frameworks of most of the surveyed countries. The majority of national legal frameworks:

- exclude certain groups or restrict them from participation

- don't require public participation in some sectors of the economy or for some development activities (such as the siting of forest or mining concessions)

- lack adequate provisions for participation at different stages of the decision-making cycle.

With the exception of Thailand, public participation rights are not explicitly guaranteed in any of the constitutions or legal frameworks of the countries surveyed (see Table 3.2).

Table 3.2 Grading Legal Rights to Participate

The Access Initiative looked for:	Country Assessments		
	Weak	Medium	Strong
Constitutional guarantees of public participation, freedom of speech, and freedom of assembly	**Chile, India, and Uganda** have constitutional guarantees, but the highest courts have limited their reach through decisions, or legal requirements limit how speech or freedom of assembly rights can be expressed.	**Hungary, South Africa, and Mexico** have strong constitutional guarantees for free speech and association, but they are not as well defined by the highest court's decisions.	**Thailand** includes the right to participation as well as broad freedoms of speech and assembly in its constitution. The **U.S.** Constitution includes strong protection of freedoms of speech and assembly.
Provisions for public notice and comment in sectoral policies and single development activities	**Thailand and Indonesia** have no such provisions.	**Chile, Hungary, India, and Uganda**: Notice and comment provisions are specified only for single development activities through EIA regulations.	**Mexico, South Africa, and the United States** have provisions requiring public notice and comment in specified types of both sectoral policies and single development activities.
Public notification and comment requirements for Environmental Impact Assessments (EIAs)	**Thailand** has no requirements for notification and comment for EIAs.	**Hungary, India, Mexico, and Uganda** require public notice and comment at the final stage of EIAs.	**Chile, Indonesia, South Africa and the United States** require public notice and comment at various stages of an EIA.
Broad legal definitions of the public and the public interest	**Chile, India, Indonesia, Thailand, and Uganda** do not define the public or the public interest in legal frameworks.	**Mexico** broadly defines the public interest in the constitution, but supporting legal regulations almost always restrict definition to persons affected or harmed by public or private action/decision.	**Hungary, South Africa, and the United States** broadly define the public and the public interest in legal frameworks.

Instead, public participation is usually articulated in government documents that are not legally binding, such as guidelines or manuals of "best practice."

Finding: The Burden Is on the Public

The Access Initiative finds that opportunities to participate vary significantly depending on the government agencies involved, the scale and scope of the project under debate, and the type of policy under review. What stands out across the majority of cases, however, is that the onus of initiating participation in a decision-making process is on the public.

In general, governments are not sufficiently proactive at seeking public input. This is true across the range of surveyed countries, regardless of economic development or income levels. For example, although Mexico provides broad constitutional guarantees for public participation, in practice, NGOs or affected communities must prove legal interest and submit formal requests to access documents about a decision or to ensure that a public consultation is carried out. Another common finding is that public participation is weak both at the early stages of decision-making and at the end of the process when a decision's impacts are monitored and its acceptability reviewed. In other words, notification of opportunities to participate, circulation of project documents like Environmental Impact Statements, and public consultations occur mainly in the middle stages of decision-making, when the parameters of the problem or possible solutions have already been defined, but before they are actually implemented or adopted (see Figure 3.2). This reduces "participa-

NGOs Lend Fresh Perspectives
When the government of Slovakia announced its intention to reform the energy sector, more than 20 Slovak NGOs jointly developed an alternative energy sector reform strategy. By the time the government strategy was ready, so were the NGOs. With help from the media, the two different approaches received much attention and discussion regarding their relative social and environmental merits. The final version combines elements of both the government and the NGO proposals.

tion" to refining already-defined policies, projects, and solutions. It can also lead to protracted conflicts with civil society, as occurred over the siting of the Hin Krud coal-fired power plant in Thailand. Despite the potential damage to nearby coral reefs from the release of water used in the cooling process, and negative impacts on the local economy from reduced tourism and fishing, the government selected the plant site without discussion with the public, external experts, or interest groups. Now that construction is under way, there has been tremendous public protest.

The use of Environmental Impact Assessments in most countries in the past 20 years has dramatically increased public access to decision-making that affects the environment (see Box 3.2). However, an EIA alone does not ensure adequate public participation. Access Initiative researchers

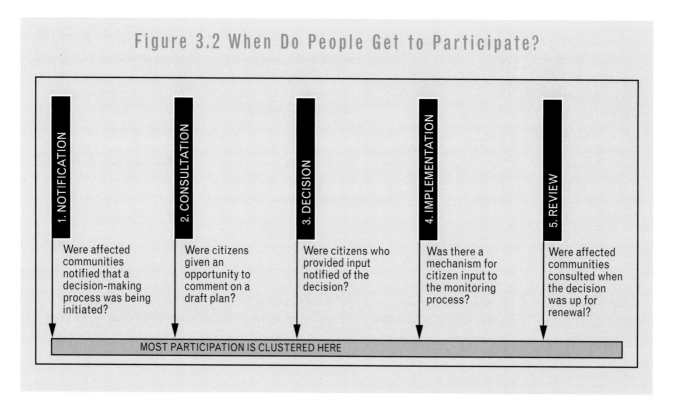

Figure 3.2 When Do People Get to Participate?

1. NOTIFICATION
Were affected communities notified that a decision-making process was being initiated?

2. CONSULTATION
Were citizens given an opportunity to comment on a draft plan?

3. DECISION
Were citizens who provided input notified of the decision?

4. IMPLEMENTATION
Was there a mechanism for citizen input to the monitoring process?

5. REVIEW
Were affected communities consulted when the decision was up for renewal?

MOST PARTICIPATION IS CLUSTERED HERE

Box 3.2 The Merits of Meaningful Participation

It is difficult to measure whether people have adequate, meaningful opportunities to participate. One proxy measure is the degree of public participation in Environmental Impact Assessments (EIAs). For example, in Hungary, there is widespread use of the EIA process, with early notification of and extensive participation by people and communities. Between 1995 and 1998, there were more than 600 EIAs carried out in Hungary, compared to just 16 in nearby Austria. Hungarian authorities rejected 4 to 6 percent of proposed projects where the EIA had detailed significant environmental impacts. This was mainly due to input the public provided. Across Europe, an average of just 1 percent of such projects are typically rejected (Fülöp 2002).

A recent analysis of more than two hundred cases of public participation in environmental decisions in the United States found that final government decisions incorporated public input about half the time. In these cases, better decisions resulted in less conflict among competing interests as a result (Beierle and Cayford 2002:17, 27–28).

The same study concluded that public participation is most successful when government agencies are flexible about the participation process itself and what they expect it to produce. Flexibility includes letting participants redefine the problem, focus on other issues, and change the nature of the questions being considered. In addition, when governments recognize the legitimacy of public values, the chances for successful participation improve. Finally, government agencies must understand that citizen input may lead to priorities and conclusions with which the agencies themselves do not agree (Beierle and Cayford 2002:64).

---

found that all surveyed countries had provisions for public participation in EIAs. However, in practice, the public isn't consulted early enough to really affect key decisions. Some authorities provide such a tight time frame for the public to provide comments that significant input is impossible. Officials often limit who is considered a "legitimate" participant, and projects are selectively exempted from the review process and assessments that would require public involvement. Even if citizens are allowed to participate in the assessment process, there are very few provisions for incorporating their input into the final EIA report.

The Access Initiative also analyzed EIA provisions in 15 Latin American and Caribbean countries. The findings confirmed that EIAs are not yet a consistent vehicle for meaningful public participation (see Box 3.3).

Access to Justice and Redress

When disputes arise over environmental decisions, or the public's rights to information and participation are ignored, a binding system of review and legal remedy is needed. Access Initiative researchers found that this kind of systematic dispute resolution by an impartial judiciary or administrative review was the weakest element of the three access principles.

Finding: Poor Procedures for Enforcement and Review

As mentioned earlier, countries have made much progress in the last decade in establishing a range of legal rights to environmental information and participation. Unfortunately, these rights are often not defined adequately enough to be legally enforceable, or the public is not given legal "standing" (the ability to appear in court or bring a legal suit). In other cases, there are no administrative procedures for reviewing decisions, registering complaints, and resolving disputes. The result is that the rights granted to the public in theory may not be effective in practice.

Access Initiative researchers found that in less than half the cases they assessed was the public able to use administrative or judicial review to contest how national or regional environmental policies were made. The situation is worse when logging, mining, grazing, or other resource concessions are awarded or Environmental Impact Assessments are conducted. In most of these cases, either no administrative or judicial review is available or legal standing is limited to "affected" people, giving courts and other administrative officials the discretion to limit who actually has access (see

Box 3.3 Comparing Environmental Impact Assessment Laws in Latin America and the Caribbean

An Access Initiative analysis of Environmental Impact Assessment (EIA) provisions in 15 Latin American and Caribbean nations concluded that the quality of public participation mandated in EIA laws and policies varies widely. Fourteen of 15 countries assessed have adopted EIA laws and policies at the national, sectoral, or even provincial levels to mitigate environmental damage from economic development. The majority include some requirements for public participation. However, only four Latin American countries mandate that the public be given the opportunity to comment early in the EIA process. The majority of countries only mandate provisions for public participation after the EIA findings are final or have been officially approved by the government. In general, Latin American EIAs provide governments with considerable discretion in deciding when to initiate or apply public participation provisions.

Public Participation Provisions in Latin American and Caribbean EIA Laws (X = In Place)

Indicator	Bolivia	Colombia	Ecuador	Perú	Argentina	Brazil	Chile	Paraguay	Uruguay	El Salvador	Guatemala	Jamaica	México	Nicaragua	Panamá
1. National law or policy exists that establishes the framework for the conduct of EIAs.	X	X	X	X		X	X	X	X	X	X	X	X	X	X
2. National (or at least two sectoral) EIA laws or policies clearly state that they apply to both public and private development activities.	X			X	X[1]	X	X	X	X					X	X
3. National (or at least two sectoral) EIA laws, policies, or guidelines provide for public participation after EIA is finalized.	X				X[2]	X		X				X		X	X
4. National (or at least two sectoral) EIA laws, policies, or guidelines provide for public participation before final approval of EIA.		X[3]		X			X		X	X			X	X	X
5. National (or at least two sectoral) EIA laws, policies, or guidelines provide for public participation at scoping or draft stages.	X			X										X	X
6. National (or at least two sectoral) EIA laws, policies, or guidelines provide for public participation in monitoring compliance or implementation of EIA mitigation measures.															

Source: Ibarra 2002.

[1] Argentina does not have a federal EIA framework. However, most of the provinces have their own frameworks. For those provinces that do not have their own, there are national sectoral frameworks, which they follow.

[2] Public participation provisions are included mainly within provinces' EIA frameworks.

[3] Colombia includes public participation provisions as mandatory, but only for ethnic minorities (Decree No. 1320/98).

Table 3.3 Grading Legal Rights to Review and Remedy

The Access Initiative asked:	Country Assessments		
	Weak	Medium	Strong
	Chile, Indonesia, Mexico, Thailand, and Uganda	**India and the United States**	**Hungary and South Africa**
Does a review process exist for decisions on projects with potential environmental impacts?	No review process is in place.	An administrative or judicial review process does exist.	Administrative review processes do exist.
	OR	**BUT**	**AND**
Who has legal standing to challenge these decisions?	Parties not participating in the decision-making process *have no standing* to challenge the decision.	Parties not participating in the decision-making process *have no standing* to challenge the decision.	Parties not participating in the decision-making process *do have standing* to invoke a challenge.

Access to Justice Is Vital

In 2001, WALHI, an environmental forum for NGOs and community organizations in Indonesia, went to court. WALHI argued that mining company Freeport-McMoran Copper and Gold, Inc. had provided false information regarding its responsibility for a landslide in Wanagoon Lake, West Papua. This was in violation of a national law requiring the provision of accurate information on environmental management. The court agreed with WALHI and held the company accountable.

Table 3.3). For example, in Mexico an individual or organization must show proof of harm in order to gain access to the courts for cases that pertain to the environment or access to information.

The efficiency, accountability, and independence of judicial systems also vary widely among the countries examined, undermining people's ability to enforce their access rights. In the United States, for instance, the judicial system has evolved as a strong, generally trusted, and widely used instrument for enforcing the law. In other countries, such as Indonesia, researchers found that the courts are seen as one of the country's most corrupt public institutions.

Finding: High Costs and Sluggish Processes

Legal costs are prohibitively high for the general public in all the surveyed countries. In Chile, fees to register environmental cases can cost more than 50 percent of the average monthly income, and in Hungary more than 20 percent. Pro

bono lawyers, who represent clients without charge for good cause, are usually concentrated in capital cities, not in rural areas. Only South Africa has a government-sponsored program with centers in the provinces that provide free legal help to the poor, and only the United States and Thailand have large national networks of pro bono lawyers.

Even where fees aren't a tremendous obstacle to justice, incidental legal expenses add up and the complexity and length of the legal process are a burden. This is a particular problem for the rural poor and community organizations that lack the time and resources to pursue long court cases or to travel to cities to press a case.

Improving Access: What's Needed?

Better access will require investments to increase the supply of information and opportunities to participate. Better access will also require greater demand for access rights from citizens, community organizations, and advocacy groups.

When residents of Szalánta, a village in Hungary, learned that their vineyards, wineries, and local economy were threatened by government approval of a hazardous waste incinerator in their area, they first tried protesting and lobbying against its construction. Then they turned to the judicial system. There they found an impartial ear for their argument that the permit needed reconsideration: their region's economy had special environmental needs that called for higher standards and requirements for the incinerator than the law required. The permit was refused.

Box 3.4 Access and the Internet

Where people have easy and affordable Internet access, governments have a ready means of supplying environmental data and alerts about opportunities to weigh in on projects, policies, and plans. For example, Bulgaria launched a website for "dialogues with the public" where comments and proposals related to environmental policies can be made on-line. To extend access to rural communities, Estonia is using a network of "telecottages"—rooms in a shop, school, library, home, or village center that offer free on-line access to the Internet and provide informa-

they help communities attain greater access and so help to protect the environment. In Tijuana, E-LAW members aided activists in drafting a municipal law that gives citizens the right to know the composition of factory emissions. They shared, on-line, examples of laws granting access to information from Australia, Canada, Kenya, Perú, and the United States (E-LAW 2002).

Unfortunately, the Internet is still limited in its reach. Internet usage for postings of information or agency rules, regulations, and data are helpful but not yet adequate to

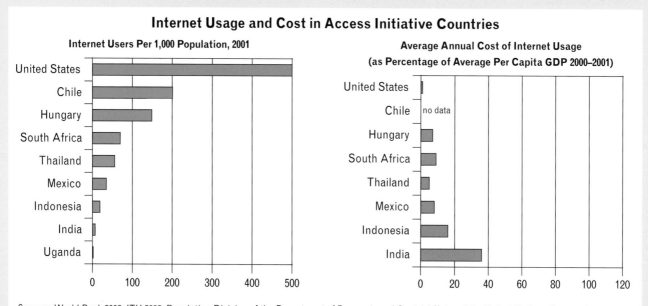

Internet Usage and Cost in Access Initiative Countries

Sources: World Bank 2002; ITU 2002; Population Division of the Department of Economic and Social Affairs of the United Nations Secretariat 2002.

tion on the state of the environment, plans, and policies. Countries that are signatories to the Aarhus Convention are considering creating a website for each country that would provide citizens with a single entry point for environmental information at the national level (United Nations Economic and Social Council 2000:7).

The Internet also provides a means for networking among the citizens, activists, and lawyers who seek to expand access rights. Public interest lawyers, for instance, stay connected through the on-line "Environmental Law Alliance Worldwide" (E-LAW) network. By sharing legal and scientific information

ensure access in all countries, and are particularly unlikely to serve citizens in poor countries or rural areas. Affordability and "usability" of the Internet varies greatly by country, and even within countries. In one-third of the countries examined by the Access Initiative, affordable or free Internet access is limited to major urban areas or capital cities. Low literacy rates also reduce the utility of the Internet in many of the poorest countries. Until the Internet is more widely accessible, governments must pursue alternative means of reaching the public, too.

Box 3.5 Public Interest Groups in Africa: Supported or Thwarted?

The Access Initiative assessed the ease with which public interest groups can form and operate in Botswana, Kenya, Mozambique, Tanzania, Uganda, and Zimbabwe. Each of these countries has constitutional provisions that guarantee freedom of association, but also has laws that restrict the activity of public interest groups. In all the countries, the national government assigned ministries exclusive oversight of registration or deregistration of NGOs. For example, Zimbabwe's Private Voluntary Organizations Act gives the Minister of Public Service, Labour, and Social Welfare the power to suspend the entire staff of an NGO without explanation (Viet 1999).

Some East African governments have created mechanisms that impede the process of NGO registration. For example, in Uganda, an NGO must obtain a letter of authorization from the appropriate ministry before official registration.

This oversight and regulatory power allows governments to act against interest groups that challenge them. In Tanzania, BAWATA (the National Women's Council) was registered in 1995 only after a battle to convince the Registrar of Societies to grant approval. Its early work—as articulated in its constitution—focused on issues such as inheritance rights, the right to own land, and political representation of women in parliament. Nevertheless, the government soon accused BAWATA of being a political party. In September 1996, the government, without affording BAWATA a chance to be heard, deregistered the NGO and demanded that the group amend its constitution and become a research institute. In March 1997, at a general meeting, BAWATA yielded and amended its constitution in accordance with the demands. Even so, the government deregistered BAWATA. While the case is still pending in court, the lengthy legal battle has taken a toll on the organization: its charismatic leader has left and donors have ended their support.

Improved Supply of "Access"

Strengthening legal provisions for access to information, participation, and legal remedy, and working with civil society organizations to implement those provisions are clearly critical steps toward more effective public participation in environmental decisions. But governments must also improve their capacity to generate and disclose information, and to solicit and respond to public feedback. This includes ensuring that the public always has access to adequate information in a usable format, including Environmental Impact Statements, prior to participating in public deliberations. (See Box 3.4.) The United Nations Environment Programme (UNEP) and the Aarhus Convention stress the need for countries to maintain a central environmental information service and to commit to a practice of early consultation with stakeholders on environmental decisions. UNEP established the INFOTERRA network of national environmental infor-

mation centers, currently numbering 177, to facilitate integrated access to information.

All countries must improve the capacity of government staff to make access to basic information easier. Agencies in some countries, such as Hungary and Indonesia, allow bureaucratic processes and attitudes of secrecy that can easily exhaust a citizen seeking information disclosure or attempting, for instance, to fight the siting of a new factory. Governments aren't adequately training staff so that civil servants are aware of new legislation and its implications for their work, or helping staff understand the value of public input in decision-making. South Africa and India were the only countries among those surveyed where three selected government agencies offered staff training on new rules about environmental information and public participation.

Donors can help with the task of building government infrastructure and capacity to make access a reality. Tracking and disseminating environmental information, for example, is expensive. Poorer countries that maintain centralized inventories of integrated environmental information typically rely on external funding. For example, Chile's environmental information system is supported by donor assistance, and Uganda maintains—with donor support—a highly effective and accessible public information system for health emergencies. Government commitment and the availability of resources also affect whether governments adequately train civil servants to provide information, involve citizens, or judge environmental cases.

Improved access is impossible without efforts by financial institutions—as the financiers of energy reform, electricity generation, water infrastructure, and other development projects with environmental impacts—to help nations apply the

In the Spotlight: Access and the Media

The media can drive demand for access to information and opportunities to participate (see Box 4.4). Unfortunately, in national assessments of media coverage of environmental issues, only three of the Access Initiative countries scored "strong" on the level of coverage, and four scored "strong" on the quality of coverage. Thailand alone scored "strong" in both categories, because during three randomly selected and non-consecutive weeks, a sampling of media outlets regularly provided features and analysis on the environment, with more than one point of view presented.

exercise their rights to information and participation. Proxy measures of how seriously governments take that responsibility include their investment in environmental education and their efforts to create a favorable climate for nongovernmental organizations. For the most part, governments are investing in environmental education. South Africa has trained staff to develop environmental education programs and incorporate them in regular curricula at all levels. Chile, Hungary, India, Mexico, and Thailand all support environmental education efforts.

principles of "good governance." Institutions that fund development must first adopt and apply the elements of public participation to their own operations, and then promote transparent and inclusive decision-making by their clients through their lending policies and requirements. In Uganda, for example, agencies that have access to World Bank financing are more open to engaging the public in decision-making than those that don't, because the World Bank has explicitly encouraged transparency through its lending policies there.

Increased Demand for "Access"

Most of the Access Initiative research teams commented on the limited levels of public awareness about environmental issues and access rights. Public authorities have a responsibility to build–directly and indirectly–the capacity of their citizens to

For More Information

Complete findings of the Access Initiative's pilot assessment can be found at **http://www.access initiative.org**. The website offers the full report, *Closing the Gap: Information, Participation, and Justice in Decision-making for the Environment,* and summaries of the national assessments. It also posts a *Guide* for groups interested in assessing the performance of their own governments.

However, the countries examined by the Access Initiative vary in their treatment and tolerance for environmental NGOs (see also Box 3.5). These groups often act as vital catalysts for public participation in environmental decision-making. They help citizens understand their access rights and obtain environmental information, and often represent individuals and communities in public deliberations and in judicial disputes. For example, the Advocates Coalition for Development and the Environment in Uganda educates communities about their rights, represents them in court, and is engaged in promoting access and participation in the East African Union.

South Africa offers an example of a supportive climate for NGOs. They do not have to register in court or with a government agency to be recognized as a legal organization and are permitted access to diverse domestic and international sources of funding. Not so in other countries. Onerous registration requirements in Chile, Hungary, Indonesia, and Uganda; the absence of local funding sources in Uganda; and restrictions on foreign funding for NGOs in India constrain the ability of public interest groups to form or operate. Consequently, most governments can promote greater access by enhancing the capacity of NGOs and working with them to draft new legislation, conduct education programs, and assess the strengths and weaknesses of access in government agencies.

C H A P T E R 4

AWAKENING
CIVIL SOCIETY

Governments and businesses no longer have
a monopoly on environmental decision-making. A third force–
civil society–is changing the power balance. Citizen groups of
all sorts now routinely participate in decisions about the environment and development. The growing influence of these
organizations is one of the most dynamic changes in environmental governance today, lending a stronger voice to the individuals, interest groups, and communities that must live with
the consequences of environmental decisions.

What Can Civil Society Offer?

Civil society brings pressure to make environmental decisions more inclusive and representative. And it brings new creativity to environmental problem-solving. Citizen groups
are capitalizing on expanding democratic liberties and press freedoms in many countries,
as well as new and cheaper communications technologies. They have used these tools to
shape public opinion, sway markets, mobilize political action, and provide services and
information—in short, to insert themselves into the decision-making process (Anheier et
al. 2001). This awakening of civil society is as important to the development of good governance as free markets are to boosting economic efficiency. Innovation and change are
often the result when individuals come together in the self-motivated activity that a robust
civil society fosters.

Examples of the growth of citizen power abound: A nationwide movement by traditional fishermen forced the Indian government to stop issuing licenses to environmentally destructive trawlers (Kothari 2000). Facing powerful financial interests, nongovernmental organizations and social movements blocked or reformed plans to construct huge dams in Asia (Khagram 2000:87–88, 99). Labor unions played a critical role in bringing about democratic leadership in Poland, which ultimately expanded the opportunities for environmental activism there. Churches have helped biodiversity-friendly coffee growers in developing countries connect to Western consumer markets and earn a living through the Fair Trade and Equal Exchange movements. Environmental groups have purchased tracts of rain forests to keep development and destruction at bay.

19th century. In fact, it was civil society groups that put environmental issues on the global agenda starting in the 1970s. Now, however, this sector is larger and more influential than ever before. This awakening of civil society is as important to the development of good governance as free markets are to boosting economic efficiency. Innovation and change are often the result when individuals come together in the self-motivated activity that a robust civil society fosters.

Of course, civil society is not always constructive and civic groups can engender contention as well as creativity and cooperation. More public participation can add inefficiencies and tensions to the decision-making process, and not all civic groups support a more "open" society or broader citizen participation. Many work for limited and parochial goals that can aggravate community divisions. But the achievements and potential of civil society outweigh its drawbacks. A

The growing influence of civil society is one of the most dynamic changes in environmental governance today.

All these groups are part of *civil society*—a term that encompasses voluntary, citizen-based groups that are autonomous from government and business (Fowler 1997:8; Edwards and Gaventa 2001:2). Civil society includes nongovernmental organizations, foundations, religious groups, consumer and shareholder groups, labor associations, sports or hobby clubs, and a variety of informal citizen groups established to address particular concerns. Independent press outlets (that is, media not controlled by the state), educational establishments, and independent political parties may also be included.

Civil society is marked by variety in its composition: Some groups are formally registered while many are informal. Some are membership-based, like unions, but many are smaller, self-contained organizations such as think-tanks, service groups, and science organizations. They operate at every scale: in the community, and at the national, regional, and international levels.

Civil society has a long history of involvement in environmental governance. Groups dedicated to nature conservation, such as the Royal Society for the Protection of Birds (UK), or the Sierra Club (U.S.), have been active since the late

vibrant civil society provides a vital democratic counterweight to the profit-driven impulses of businesses and the bureaucratic responses of states.

Civil Society: Power in Numbers

Of all the various types of civil society groups, *nongovernmental organizations* (NGOs) are perhaps the most prominent new force for improving environmental decisions. Environmental NGOs range from grassroots groups with just a few members to global organizations like the 5 million-member World Wide Fund for Nature (WWF) with offices in 48 countries (WWF 2003). Such groups serve as lobbyists, organizers, funders, researchers, networkers, and advocates, among other roles.

The number of environmental NGOs has grown significantly in the last few decades. This is part of a larger growth trend in NGOs in general, covering a wide range of sectors and issues. The precise numbers are difficult to ascertain because NGOs can be defined and counted in many ways. For example, some estimates include only officially registered groups. Others count the number of "nonprofit groups" or "private voluntary associations," which may not include all

(continued on p. 68)

Box 4.1 Democracy and Civic Renaissance in Central and Eastern Europe

The global trend toward democracy has been a key contributor to the growth of civil society and the flowering of environmental activism worldwide. Democratic movements, which have taken root in an unprecedented number of countries since the 1990s, typically increase the ability of citizens to voice their concerns. Freedom to organize, access to information, and press freedoms have contributed to the effectiveness of nongovernmental organizations (NGOs) and other civil society groups.

Several Central and Eastern European (CEE) countries illustrate the connection between democratization and environmental activism. During the 1980s, Communist regimes tolerated environmental organizations that were perceived as apolitical. The Czechoslovak Union of Nature Conservationists, for example, had hundreds of branch offices (Tolles and Beckmann 2000:8). But with the collapse of Communism in 1989, some 180 new environmental groups were founded each year to address the problems of dying forests, air pollution, undrinkable water, and threatened biodiversity as well as to seize the opportunity to have a larger voice in public policy

(REC 1997:16; Salamon et al. 1999:18; Tolles and Beckmann 2000). The total number of environmental groups in 15 CEE countries jumped from about 800 in 1992 to 3,000 in 2001; some 46,000 people now volunteer in environmental efforts in those countries (Atkinson and Messing 2002:11).

Just as democratization allows environmental organizations to thrive, sometimes environmental movements open the door to wider democratic and civil rights. In Central and Eastern Europe, environmentalism acted as a vehicle for nationwide rallies and an outlet for popular dissatisfaction with the Communist government. The Danube Circle in Hungary, Ecoglasnost in Bulgaria, the Lithuanian Green Movement, and the Polish Ecology Club protested Communist regimes in the late 1980s (OECD 1999:82) and helped shape the first democratic governments. In Slovakia in 1998, environmental NGOs campaigned to boost voter turnout and helped sweep democratic forces into power, including several green parties. Today, Slovakian environmental NGOs continue to battle corruption, and work to support open and transparent decision-making (OECD 1999:81–82; Tolles and Beckmann 2000:39).

Environmental NGOs in the CEE Region

Two thirds of environmental NGOs in the region are located in Hungary, Poland, and the Czech Republic. Most NGOs are based in small towns and operate mainly at the local level. About 60 percent have less than 25 members.

Country	Number of Environmental NGOs
Albania	45
Bosnia and Herzegovina	38
Bulgaria	100
Croatia	187
Czech Republic	520
Estonia	35
Hungary	726
Latvia	60
Lithuania	81
Macedonia	73
Poland	600
Romania	210
Slovakia	141
Slovenia	114
Fed. Rep. of Yugoslavia	90
TOTAL	**3,020**

Source: REC 1997:13.

1990s: A Period of Environmental Activism

About one fourth of the environmental groups operating in the CEE region today were already active in the 1980s, but far more were formed in the early 1990s. Now, with funding decreasing since the early years of the transition to a market economy, growth in environmental NGOs has slowed.

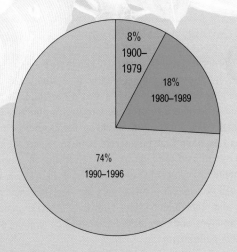

When were environmental NGOs in Central and Eastern Europe officially registered?

Source: REC 1997:16.

NGOs—often just those working for charitable objectives. Whatever definition is used, it is clear that the NGO sector is now significant worldwide. Once clustered mainly in Western democracies, NGOs have shown particularly dramatic growth in Central and Eastern Europe (see Boxes 4.1 and 4.2) and parts of Asia (REC 1997:13, 16).

The NGO sector's expenditures and employment rates are other indicators of its reach. A 1995 survey found that the combined expenditures of the nonprofit sectors in 22 coun-tries (excluding religious organizations) was $1.1 trillion—some 4.6 percent of these countries' combined GDP. The same survey found that more than 26 million people are employed by, or volunteer for, nonprofits in Western Europe, the United States, Japan, and Australia combined (Salamon et al. 1999:9, 479). As impressive as these numbers are, they don't really capture the most influential features of NGOs: their contributions of new ideas and the "social energy" and "social capital" they mobilize for environmental preserva-

Box 4.2 Partnering for the Environment in Central Europe

"To learn fundraising is not so difficult, but to learn from others—to really listen and think about what others are saying—that's a real problem. This inability to exchange experience is the biggest limit to the development of Czech conservation NGOs."

— Petr Dolejský, ČSOP, Bílé Karpaty, Czech Republic

Organizing citizens to take responsibility for the environment is difficult even when there's adequate funding, trained leaders, clearly understood environmental problems, and a public experienced in working together and with the government to propose alternative policies. Central European communities lacked these basic necessities and more in 1989 when Communist rule came to an end. A half-century of centralized decision-making had eroded the notion that one should or even could care for the land. People were unaccustomed to weighing other perspectives, forging compromises, and resolving conflicts. They didn't trust organizations or government, and they lacked a sense of community empowerment and initiative.

Three American foundations, however, recognized that helping to curb environmental deterioration was not only important in its own right, but could become a potent tool to foster democracy and build civil society. In 1991, the Charles Stewart Mott Foundation, the German Marshall Fund, and the Rockefeller Brothers Fund initiated the Environmental Part-nership for Central Europe (EPCE)—a consortium of five national foundations operating in the Czech Republic, Hungary, Poland, Slovakia, and, since 2000, Romania. Led and staffed locally, these independent foundations stimulate community-based environmental action and participation in the region (Tolles and Beckmann 2000:5).

Since its inception, EPCE has invested over $15.4 million to support more than 4,000 projects and to provide training, technical assistance, and study tours to 3,000 Central European organizations. Those organizations, in turn, have mobilized 30,000 volunteers, planted 175,000 trees, protected more than 150 endangered species of flora and fauna, and insulated approximately 1,000 homes, schools, and other buildings. The EPCE foundations are currently the most significant private source of funding for community-based environmental initiatives and advocacy projects in Central Europe (Růžička 2002). The EPCE is also the most important source of money in Central and Eastern Europe for advocacy projects.

The partnership has not only helped protect the environment, but has nurtured grassroots action:

■ In the 1980s, Kosenka, an NGO in an eastern Moravian town, tried to preserve rare species of orchids in the White Carpathians region by organizing volunteers to mow fields. Now, with support from EPCE, Kosenka takes a more holistic approach to biodiversity protection: the group partners with farmers to improve pasture health and helps commution, anticorruption efforts, democratic participation, or a myriad other endeavors (Putnam 1993:167; Brown 2002; Paxton 2002).

Environmental NGOs and Citizen Action

Although global data on environmental NGOs is scarce, one estimate suggests that by 1990 there were more than 100,000 groups working on environmental protection worldwide—most of them founded in the previous decade (Runyon 1999:13). The increasing number of domestic and international environmental NGOs and the growing membership base of many groups (see Figure 4.1 and Table 4.1) is a response to the worldwide attention given to environmental problems since the 1970s, along with rising incomes, and several major political and sociological factors. One such factor is the demand for opportunities to participate. For example, the number of Asian environmental NGOs grew rapidly in the 1990s as industrialization, pollution, and attendant environ-

nities and businesspeople develop and market traditional crafts and goods made from local produce, creating incentives to preserve the area's natural heritage (Tolles and Beckmann 2000:34).

- EPCE helped The Alliance of Greens in Hungary and MME (Birdlife Hungary) collaborate with other NGOs to establish a land trust—one of the first in Central and Eastern Europe—covering 500 ha of wooded steppe in the Bihar region. The first 28 nonprofit land trusts, totaling over 1,600 ha, have received official accreditation in the Czech Republic (Beckmann 2000:23).

- A group of environmental scientists from the Daphne Institute of Applied Ecology in Bratislava used EPCE support to engage local farmers and residents in restoring 130 ha of wetland habitats in the Morava-Danube floodplain in southwestern Slovakia (Tolles and Beckmann 2000:25).

- The Energy Conservation in Schools Program sponsored by EPCE involved over 9,700 schoolchildren and 1,800 teachers, parents, and other volunteers in local school energy conservation projects and educational activities. About 260 schools throughout Central Europe participated, with many receiving special grants to insulate windows, replace old lights and thermostats, and buy more efficient furnaces (Růžička 2002).

- The EPCE-funded Central European Greenways (CEG) project has involved hundreds of local communities, state and local representatives, businesses, and national government offices in creating a network of largely automobile-free recreational routes and trails. The 11 CEG routes total 3,000 km, and attract tourism and promote the region's natural and cultural heritage (Růžička 2002).

These and other initiatives supported by the partnership share a commitment to involve citizens in looking for and implementing sustainable land use practices and supporting public involvement in decision-making. In the context of post-Communist Central Europe, this is an approach that is nothing short of revolutionary.

The Roots of Success

Initially—and importantly—the Western foundations committed multi-year support to EPCE to give the partnership time to train local personnel, create a cadre of independent leaders, and broaden its funding. Staffing and start-up efforts consumed the consortium's first year as the founding leaders of the EPCE organizations struggled to find staff capable of managing local grant-making programs, and community members experienced enough to serve on the Boards of Directors of the new foundations. Beyond financial support, the three Western foundations cooperated closely with the EPCE groups to discuss strategy and create links between the EPCE consortium and established NGOs in Western Europe and North America.

In reviewing its progress over the last decade, the EPCE consortium stresses one lesson above all: let local communities themselves decide on their conservation priorities, rather than having them imposed from the outside. Finding effective local leaders to spearhead projects is also essential for successful action. The EPCE foundation staff see their task as facilitating discussion, advising on local decisions, and offering technical support to create projects that address these community-identified priorities.

As EPCE works through its second decade, it faces the challenge of a society still trying to develop a sense of civic engagement, initiative, and self-responsibility. Other challenges loom as well, including the need to increase its fundraising capacity. The coalition is now moving toward greater autonomy from its Western founders, whose financial support will phase out by 2005 (Scsaurszki 2002). Fortunately, the consortium has already secured funding from some European foundations such as the Dutch Foundation DOEN, and the Deutsche Bundesstiftung Umwelt Foundation in Germany. Businesses and governments have agreed to help, too, including a unique arrangement in the Czech Republic, where the government has set up a special endowment fund for Czech foundations (Růžička 2002). Meanwhile, EPCE has become a model for the former Soviet Union and the Baltic states in how to engage civil society to meet local needs through care for the environment.

mental risks increased and as a new middle class expanded. With an educated and better informed public and visible evidence of environmental degradation, more people are joining organized environmental efforts (Gan 2000:112–113).

Increasing access to a variety of resources has also created conditions ripe for the growth of environmental groups:

- Volunteerism is growing. One recent survey found that worldwide the number of volunteers devoting time to environmental NGOs increased by 50 percent in less than 10 years (Pinter 2001:200);

- The Internet and cell phones are helping individuals and groups get, share, and act on information quickly; collaborate across borders; hold institutions accountable; monitor environmental changes; and circumvent government controls on information (see Box 4.3);

- Total development funds channeled through NGOs by governments and international donors is growing (Anheier et al. 2001:26), though it's not clear what portion is directed to environmental NGOs. In the 1970s and 1980s many donors began to see NGOs in Africa and Asia as more effective at running health and development programs than government bureaucracies (Baron 2002). Now, more than $7 billion in private and government aid to developing countries flows through NGOs, compared to $1 billion in 1970 (UNDP 2002:102). Many European governments channel 10–30 percent of their aid through NGOs (Pinter 2001:201–202);

- During the 1990s, Western and international donors prioritized aid for civil society and for groups working in areas such as good governance, the environment, human rights, and the media. The U.S. Agency for International Development increased its support for "civil society" from $56 million to $230 million between 1991 and 1999 (Carothers 1999:210; Pinter 2001:201).

At the same time, democratization has contributed to the renaissance of civil society in general and environmental

activism in particular (see Box 4.1), and globalization has broadened awareness of environmental problems that cross borders (Wapner 1997:75; Brown et al. 2000:4, 6; Florini 2000:224, 227–228).

Beyond Environmental NGOs

Many strands of civil society other than formal, registered environmental NGOs influence environmental management and decisions. In fact, many civil society groups are not formally constituted or legally registered—yet they play a strong community role. One study in South Africa found that 53 percent of civic associations there were not legally registered (Swilling and Russell 2002:20). The proportion may be even higher in other countries of sub-Saharan Africa and parts of South and Southeast Asia. In these areas, informal NGOs such as rural savings associations and farming cooperatives are often key players in local decisions.

So-called "people's movements" are another influential element of informal civil activity. These movements may consist of hundreds of locally autonomous initiatives all focused on a common theme and using similar tactics. Examples include Kenya's Green Belt Movement in which citizens plant trees on public and private lands; the Sarvodaya Shramadana movement in Sri Lanka, which has organized more than 12,000 villages to produce small-scale improvement projects such as wells for drinking water and gardening; and the CHIPKO movement in India where villagers placed themselves between trees and the axes of timber harvesters (Salamon 1994:111).

Another important trend is the increasing diversity of civic activism on environmental issues. Though their objectives are not strictly "environmental," groups that focus on poverty alleviation, human rights, rural development projects, indigenous and women's rights, and world peace are increasingly collaborating with environmental groups to influence decision-making. The recent World Summit on Sustainable Development (WSSD) in Johannesburg drew a wide mix of issue-oriented NGOs. In contrast, the NGOs that attended the Rio Earth Summit in 1992 were predominantly environmental NGOs.

A variety of causes are bringing these diverse groups together. The effects of globalization on jobs, health, and the environment is one very visible issue uniting human rights groups, trade unions, and environmental groups (Boyle and Anderson 1996:2–3; Zarsky 2002:1–2). The environmental justice movement has also linked environmental and human rights communities with religious organizations.

Further alliances are forged as environmental organizations recognize that promoting civil rights can help to achieve their goals. For example, the right to freely associate and the right to a free press were both integral to the success of the environmental movement in the 1970s. In turn, many human rights organizations have come to see access to a

Figure 4.1 Growth of International Nongovernmental Organizations

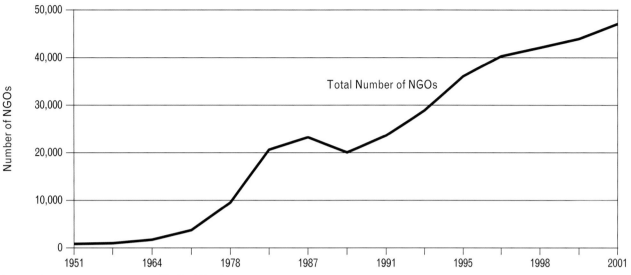

Source: UIA 1999, 2001:1519 as reported by EarthTrends.

decent environment—clean air, water, and a minimum standard of health—as a basic human right.

A Multitude of Roles

Civil society groups play a multitude of roles that affect the environment directly or bear on environmental decisions:

Snapshots of NGO Sector Growth

- The United States has 1–2 million NGOs, 70 percent of which are less than 30 years old.

- 60,000 NGOs were created in France in 1990 alone, compared to 10,000–15,000 in the entire decade of the 1960s. Associations in Germany have grown at a comparably high rate.

- New Zealand's civic sector includes at least 36,000 incorporated groups, with perhaps 20 new groups formed each week.

- Hungary boasted 13,000 associations two years after the end of Communism, at least half of them formed in the preceding two years.

- By the mid-1990s, about 1 million NGOs were operating in India, 210,000 in Brazil, 96,000 in the Philippines, 27,000 in Chile, 20,000 in Egypt, and 11,000 in Thailand.

Sources: Salamon 1994:111; Salamon and Anheier 1996:5; Robinson 1997:100; Runyon 1999:14; Silk 1999:16; Independent Sector 2001:3; UNDP 2002:5.

Implementing Programs and Providing Services

In many budget-strapped nations, NGOs are the institutions most capable of implementing environment and development programs. For example, some 1,500 neighborhood associations, called "Civic Exnoras," backstop the impoverished municipal government of the Indian city of Chennai by managing the primary waste collection for almost half a million people (Anand 2000:34–35). In Bangladesh the Rural Advancement Committee's 17,000-member staff works with more than three million people in rural communities. Its services reach nearly 60 percent of the country's 86,000 villages, and it has established some 35,000 schools (Weiss and Gordenker 1996:30; Gan 2000:126). Some NGOs help run ecotourism projects or help maintain parks and protected areas. The Belize Audubon Society manages 7 protected areas totaling approximately 150,000 acres for the Belize government (BAS 2003).

Educating and Informing

NGOs, informal grassroots groups, and academic institutions are all resources that help people, businesses, and governments make more informed environmental decisions. The information can be aimed at changing governance at the village level or the global level. For example, the Indian NGO Beej Bachao Andolan helped village farmers revert to using traditional seeds and agricultural practices that benefit biodiversity, while the U.S.-based Business for Social Responsibility provides tools, training, and advice to help companies incorporate responsible practices in their strategies and operations. Information dissemination can be geared toward crafting sound policy, rallying opposition to environmentally harmful projects or policies, increasing transparency in

Table 4.1 The Trend to Join: Variety and Growth of Selected NGO Membership Organizations

Organization	Mission	Date Founded	Current Membership	Recent Growth
Royal Society for the Protection of Birds (UK)	Creates and manages nature reserves and develops environmental policy alternatives.	1889	1 million individuals	25% (1990–2002)
Sierra Club (U.S.)	Pursues environmental activism and policy development, and promotes outdoor recreation.	1892	738,000 individuals	102% (1985–2003)
New Zealand Ecological Society	Promotes the study of ecology and the application of ecological knowledge in planning and management of the environment.	1952	600 individuals	33% (1985–2002)
Singapore Nature Society	Promotes the study, conservation, and enjoyment of the natural heritage in Singapore, Malaysia, and the surrounding region.	1954	2,200 individuals	182% (1983–2002)
World Wide Fund for Nature	Works to conserve nature and ecological processes worldwide through field projects, policy development, and research.	1961	4.5 million individuals	80% (1987–2002)
Hungarian Ornithological and Nature Conservation Society (MME-BirdLife Hungary)	Works to protect wild birds and their habitats through monitoring, nature conservation, and education.	1974	6,941 individuals	75% (1985–2002)
Grameen Bank	Provides credit to low-income individuals to promote economic and rural development.	1976	2.3 million individuals	1,279% (1985–2002)
Sanasa - Sri Lanka Thrift and Credit Cooperative Societies	Provides credit and promotes rural development.	1981	850,000 individuals	264% (1984–2001)
Environmental Law Foundation (UK)	Provides communities and individuals with information and advice on how the law can help resolve environmental problems.	1992	476 individuals	98% (1995–2002)
Korean Federation for Environmental Movement	Promotes environmental protection, peace keeping, and human rights.	1993	87,000 individuals	74% (1998–2002)
EarthAction	Mobilizes people around the world through a global action alert network to press for stronger measures to solve global problems.	1992	2,150 NGOs	329% (1992–2002)
Asia Pacific Forum of Environmental Journalists	Promotes honest and accurate reporting of environmental and development issues.	1988	46 organizations	318% (1988–2002)
Union de Grupos Ambientalistas (Union of Environmental Groups) (Mexico)	Promotes the conservation, rehabilitation, and improvement of the environment through awareness-raising and education.	1993	75 organizations	257% (1993–2003)
Forest Stewardship Council	Defines and promotes sound forest management and certification of forest products through a coordinated network of NGOs and community and trade groups.	1993	561 organizations and individuals	737% (1995–2002)

decision-making, or alerting citizens to threats to their health.

Governments often turn to NGOs for environmental data and analysis. In many cases, local NGOs have specialized knowledge of an area and the environmental threats it faces, but they can be important partners in larger-scale analyses as well. The UN Environment Programme's *Global Environment Outlook* (GEO), and the Millennium Ecosystem Assessment (MA) are examples of collaborative processes among NGOs, national governments, and international organizations to integrate local and regional data into a larger-scale assessment of environmental trends (Gemmill and Bamidele-Izu 2002:87).

Promoting Participation and Increasing Equity

NGOs can open doors to broader citizen participation in environmental decisions at all levels. Some NGOs focus on creating a climate conducive to participation. Many groups organize citizens for public hearings on environmental issues, or encourage their participation in Environmental Impact Assessments (EIAs). NGOs alert the public to opportunities for formal consultations with governments or international institutions on policies in agriculture, land use, or other sectors. They may help citizens prepare for these meetings, help

them articulate and advocate their views in writing, or even transport them to capital cities to lobby government representatives directly. In these ways, they bring grassroots voices directly to the ears of decision-makers.

Civil society groups also create channels for participation by people typically excluded from decision-making. For example, women's participation in microcredit cooperatives provides them with greater control over their livelihoods. Likewise, agricultural cooperatives in Latin America and Africa can give poor farmers a stronger voice in rural development plans that dictate farming techniques, agricultural policies, and pesticide use. In male-dominated societies, participation in civic groups can help women assume greater leadership roles (see Figure 4.2). For example, in Japan, where the business and government sectors are dominated by men, about 38 percent of nonprofit organizations are founded or headed by women (Kuroda 1998:9).

Watchdogs for Accountability

A vibrant civil society increases the demand for transparency and accountability of decision-makers in both government and business. Citizen groups and NGOs press for government reform and work to expose corruption. The NGO Transparency International taps a worldwide network to collect data on corruption and spotlight the most egregious examples. TRAFFIC–a partnership between the World Wide Fund for Nature and the World Conservation Union (IUCN)–aims to reduce illegal trade in endangered species by tracking and highlighting goods traded under the CITES treaty–the Convention on International Trade in Endangered Species of Wild Fauna and Flora. Other NGOs shame corporations into better behavior by documenting and publicizing their behavior. Global Witness, a London-based NGO, has played a central role in exposing corrupt practices in the oil industry in Angola and pressing transnational oil companies to adopt accounting practices to combat this corruption (Global Witness 2002:1–4). (See also Chapter 6.)

NGOs also enforce accountability at the local level. Between 1997 and 2000, a community-based monitoring project by an Indonesian NGO, Yayasan Duta Awan, uncovered problems with a multi-million dollar World Bank and Indonesian government project called "Integrated Swamps Development." The NGO exposed violations of the World Bank's policy on pest management, and documented farmers' increased dependence on chemical pesticides, the lack of information about the health effects of pesticides, and the exclusion of women from agricultural training. Their findings led to revisions in the project as well as efforts to implement recommendations from local farmers that the NGO had recorded as part of its monitoring work (PANNA 2001).

Working with the Private Sector

Rather than play an adversarial role, civil society can sometimes join with businesses in cooperative ventures. Together

Figure 4.2 Percentage of Full-time Positions Held by Women in South African Nonprofit Organizations

Women wield significant authority in South Africa's nonprofit organizations, dominating the ranks of professionals, managers, and support staff.

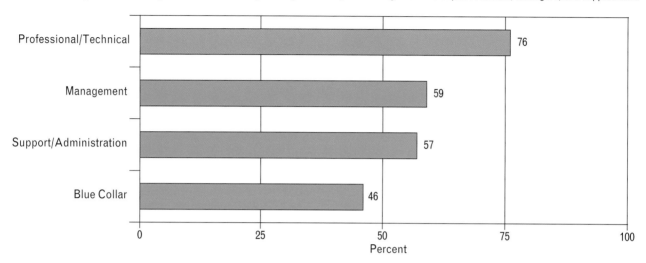

Source: Swilling and Russell 2002:25.

they can make decisions to protect the environment without significant government involvement. For example, the World Resources Institute is collaborating with leading businesses to build a market among corporations for "green power"—power generated from renewable sources. Since January 2001, member companies of WRI's Green Power Market Development Group have purchased over 50 megawatts of green power at over 200 U.S. facilities (Hanson 2003).

Conservation groups have also gained experience in brokering deals with financial lenders, paper mills, and other forest product companies to save land, and sometimes jobs. In 2002, the Nature Conservancy, a United States NGO, assumed $50 million in loans made to financially struggling Great Northern Paper. In return, the company turned over 200,000 acres of land in the state of Maine for conservation, recreation, and sustainable timber harvesting (Jiang 2002:B2).

Joining in Global Environmental Governance

In the 1990s, more than ever before, NGOs began to work on environmental issues beyond their own nation's borders. The number of international NGOs focusing on the environment grew almost 20 percent—from 979 in 1990 to 1,170 in 2000 (Anheier et al. 2001:300) and the number of all international NGOs more than doubled (see Figure 4.1) (UIA 2000; 2001:1519). Even countries typically considered withdrawn from international engagement, including Iran, Iraq, and Kuwait, have strong public participation in NGOs. Currently, individuals from high-income countries tend to dominate the membership and activities of international groups. However,

there has been dramatic growth in the number of international NGOs operating in sub-Saharan Africa and Asia, and the trend is toward greater parity in the participation of residents from all over the world (Boli and Thomas 1999:57, 77; Anheier et al. 2001:287–288).

One key to civil society's increased role in global governance is that these groups have forced international and regional governing bodies to officially acknowledge their presence and input. Some governments have actually made space for NGOs at the decision-making table by including NGO representatives in their official delegations. NGOs have successfully sought accreditation at international summits and other high-level meetings where they could lobby government delegates, organize briefings, officially address the governments, and submit official statements, commentaries, or research findings as guidance to delegates.

The 1992 Rio Earth Summit, in particular, provided a boost to NGO efforts to participate more broadly in international governance. Agenda 21—the blueprint for sustainable development that emerged from the Rio Summit—affirmed that the United Nations should expand the involvement of civil society groups in its decisions (Gemmill and Bamidele-Izu 2002:81–82). The response to this call has been impressive. While only 41 NGOs had "consultative" status with the UN system in 1948, almost 3,000 were accredited to participate in the 2002 Johannesburg Summit (see Figure 4.3) (Willetts 2002). (Consultative status affords at least some opportunity to propose agenda items, and to designate representatives to attend meetings of the UN Economic and Social Council and its subgroups.)

Civil society groups have also sought to have greater input into the work of multilateral banks such as the World Bank and the Inter-American Development Bank (IDB). These efforts have expanded opportunities for citizen participation in decisions about project financing for roads, dams, health-care, and agricultural development. Today, about half of all World Bank projects involve the input or direct involvement of NGOs, compared to only 6 percent 30 years ago (World Bank 1996; 1997:2). In December 2000, the World Bank's NGO-Bank Committee agreed to create a new Bank-Civil Society Global Forum to provide more opportunities for dialogue between the Bank and a cross-section of civil society organizations. In creating the Forum, the World Bank acknowledged that these groups have become "critical allies in designing innovative operations, implementing solutions, and monitoring results" of the Bank's work (World Bank 2001:105).

Civil Society Is Not Perfect

Civil society organizations don't always contribute to good environmental decisions. These groups are not immune from problems of legitimacy, transparency, and accountability—the same issues that NGOs often raise about governments and corporations. Nor are they universally effective, open to new ideas, or eager to collaborate with others. These weaknesses can leave civil society groups open to attack by government bureaucrats, politicians, and the media, and can damage their credibility in the eyes of many donors (Sinclair 2002).

Who Do NGOs Represent?

NGOs may claim to represent the "public interest" or "common good" and are often credited with some moral authority (Risse 2000:186). Yet, because of their diverse motivations and sources of funding, civil society groups aren't always legitimate or credible spokespersons for the broad public interest they claim to represent. Sometimes the public is appropriately skeptical of NGOs that are too closely identified with special economic or political interests. Indeed, NGOs don't always successfully maintain their independence and ability to speak freely when working with or accepting funding from corporate or government sponsors, or wealthy private benefactors. For example, an NGO called the Greening Earth Society—heavily sponsored by the United States coal industry—argues that global warming is good because it will enhance vegetation growth (World Watch 1999:2). The self-described grassroots organization People for the West! (now People for the USA) advocates broader access to land for mining, but it too is largely supported by mining companies.

(continued on p. 78)

NGO Coalitions: Networks of Influence

International coalitions of NGOs have widened their influence to the global stage. The number of international NGO networks has reached 20,000 according to the UN Development Programme (UNDP 2002:102). When they work best, transboundary NGO coalitions can help to transcend issues of national sovereignty, reconcile North-South differences, and bring the attention of a world audience to important regional or local issues. In some instances, these coalitions have achieved successes that many policy experts would have deemed impossible:

■ The International Campaign to Ban Landmines, a coalition of 1,400 NGOs from 90 countries, convinced 146 countries to sign a treaty to ban landmines at a time when private companies and government agencies in 52 countries were manufacturing antipersonnel mines and 2.5 million new landmines were being laid each year. Since the 1997 signing of the treaty, more than 30 million stockpiled mines have been destroyed (Mekata 2000:145; UNDP 2002:103; Wixley 2002).

■ A civil society coalition spanning more than 60 countries organized the "Jubilee 2000" campaign that alerted millions to the staggering debt of the poorest countries and caused G7 leaders to cancel more than $110 billion in foreign debt. The coalition included labor unions, physicians, religious organizations, environmental groups, food aid organizations, and peace and justice groups, and even enlisted the aid of rock star Bono as a spokesperson (Florini 2000:228; UNDP 2002:103–104; Jubilee 2000 2003).

■ Networks of NGOs from the West and from developing countries have successfully slowed or halted the building of large hydroelectric dams in India, Thailand, Malaysia, and other countries. These cross-border coalitions also influenced the World Bank's decision to give greater weight to the potential environmental and social impacts of a dam when making decisions on financing such projects (Khagram 2000).

Box 4.3 New Communication Tools for Environmental Empowerment

An international diffusion of affordable information technologies—Internet, mobile phones, pagers, faxes, e-mail, and mapping programs (Global Information Systems or "GIS")—is giving civil society organizations new ways to participate in environmental governance. In just the last decade, these new technologies have helped to alter the balance of power among governments, corporations, and civil society groups (Keohane and Nye 2001:22). The news media, for example, have actively embraced the on-line world, with about 40 percent of daily newspapers worldwide now offering their content on-line as well as in print (Norris 2001:180). Political parties have also used the Internet to spread their messages abroad, with "Green" parties especially quick to do so. As of 2000, 71 percent of Green parties had an on-line presence (Norris 2001:157–158).

Nongovernmental organizations (NGOs) have become particularly adept at using new technologies like the Internet and GIS. In fact, they have often proven to be quicker and better at exploiting these technologies than governments and businesses (Naughton 2001:147; Norris 2001:171). In a typical week, Greenpeace International's website gets 58,000 visitors (Norris 2001:187); the site provides information about issues ranging from whaling, to nuclear arms, to illegal logging. With a click of the mouse, the Sierra Club lets a visitor to its website e-mail letters to his or her political representatives expressing opinions on a variety of environmental topics. At NGO-sponsored "Village Information Shops," rural residents in India can use e-mail, Internet, phone, and CD-ROMs to learn about credit, seed prices and availability, transportation options, pest control and a number of other agricultural practices—information that benefits resource management decisions (Pigato 2001:31–32).

The advent of video cameras and growth in television ownership makes it easier to dramatize the scale and human impacts of environmental damage. In Honduras, an organization of small-scale fishermen sent a videotape to the Honduran Congress depicting the illegal destruction of mangroves by politically powerful commercial farmers, and protesting the loss of their livelihoods and habitat (UNDP 2001:32).

Activist groups have demonstrated that they can use Internet-based campaigns to quickly link people worldwide. In 1997–98, an Internet-based coalition of environmental NGOs, consumer groups, religious and human rights organizations, and trade unions from 67 countries came together to defeat the Multilateral Agreement on Investment (MAI)—an agreement that multinationals and the industrialized countries strongly supported. Many NGOs opposed the secrecy of the MAI negotiations process and the agreement's lack of environmental safeguards, among other shortcomings (Bray 1998). The NGOs used websites, e-mails, and "listservs" (electronic mailing lists) to quickly share strategies and detailed analy-

Access to Information by the Poor in Nepal

Sources of Information and Communication (based on surveys)	Percentage of Rural Poor	Percentage of Urban Poor
Radio	71	71
Newspapers	24	43
TV	2	57
Telephone	1	13
Computer	1	4
Fax	0	0
Friends	83	73
Family	81	83
Political Leaders	78	12
Local Leader	70	19
Schools	21	16

Source: Pigato 2001:29–30.

Mobile Phone and Internet Use, 2001

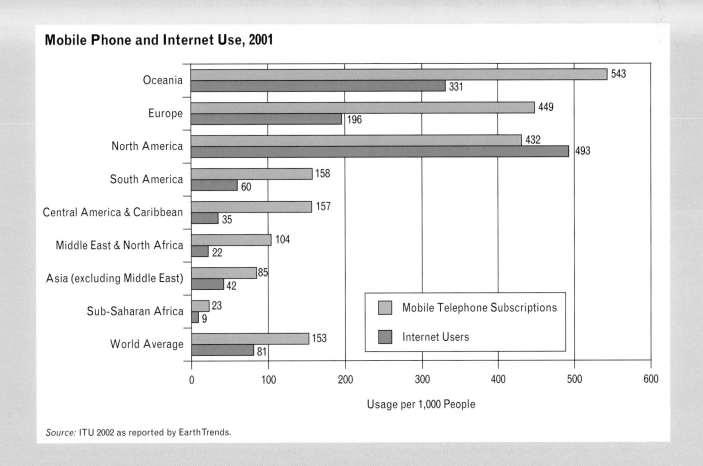

Source: ITU 2002 as reported by EarthTrends.

ses of draft MAI texts, mobilize citizens to contact decision-makers, and coordinate activists around the world. The Internet-based campaign enabled NGOs to shape the public debate, influence domestic media coverage in some countries, and made it harder for OECD officials to dismiss NGO positions as "fringe" (Smith and Smythe 2000).

Of course, the diffusion rate of new communication technologies varies by country and region (see Figure). The current "digital divide" means that only 6.7 percent of the world's population uses the World Wide Web, with the majority of users clustered in developed nations and urban areas (Freedom House 2001:1). But this number can be deceiving when judging the significance of Internet technology for environmental empowerment. In fact, there is evidence that NGOs may have a much higher level of Internet access than the general public, even in the developing world. A representative sample of 468 groups drawn from the Yearbook of International Organizations found that about one fourth can be reached through their own website (Norris 2001:189). Many

more undoubtedly have access to the Web and can spread the advantages of connectivity to their membership (Sinclair 2002).

Nonetheless, differences in access do have real implications for how the Internet is used by civil society. In North America and Europe, thousands of "connected" people with e-mail accounts can be quickly rallied to action or protest through e-mail alerts and discussion boards. Those same people can use the Web to share information on-line and access environmental data. By comparison, in poor countries, the power of the Internet may be more indirect. An NGO may indeed have access to environmental information and may be able to collaborate with other groups in far-flung places on-line. But the majority of citizens will be far more likely to rely on other technologies as their day-to-day information source. Surveys of communities in sub-Saharan Africa and South Asia have found that most people still rely on family, friends, and local leaders, or on the more basic technologies of radio, television, and newspapers (Pigato 2001:ii, 13). (See Table.)

It is sometimes difficult to determine exactly who a particular civil society group represents, and how effective they are as advocates for their constituents (Brown and Kalegaonkar 2002:25). Domestic and even international civil society groups may claim to represent local people–such as low-income families or indigenous groups–but may fail to consult them, or represent only one faction's interests.

This problem of representation extends to international NGO networks. In the past, large, wealthy Northern NGOs dominated such networks, calling into question how well they could reflect the priorities of the South. In the late 1980s and early 1990s, environmental and human rights groups joined in a battle against the oil company Conoco's plans to drill in the rain forests of Ecuador. United States and European NGOs were active and influential actors in this campaign, but typically had little contact with the local indigenous group–the Huaorani people–on whose territory the drilling was to occur. As a consequence, they often failed to take Huaorani interests adequately into account when they settled on action strategies or negotiating tactics (Jordan and van Tuijl 2000:2061).

The dominance of Northern NGOs has historically been projected into official circles as well. More than 85 percent of NGOs with consultative status in the ECOSOC are from the North (Edwards and Gaventa 2001:9). Similarly, of the 738 NGOs accredited to the World Trade Organization's (WTO) 1999 ministerial conference in Seattle, Washington, 87 percent hailed from industrialized countries (UNDP 2002:8). This problem seems to be diminishing as NGOs in the developing world grow in number and capacity (Florini 2000; Anheier et al. 2001:111). The majority of the NGOs who participated in negotiations on the Convention to Combat Desertification in the early 1990s were from the South (UNCCD 2003) and thousands of southern NGOs attended the WSSD conference in 2002.

Some NGOs lack both legitimacy and a real constituency. In some places, they have proliferated less out of community need than to take advantage of available donor funding, tax breaks, and employment opportunities. Such groups may not be serious about achieving a social mission or the public good. In fact, they may simply wish to compete with for-profit businesses (Brown et al. 2000:12; Anheier et al. 2001:198). The result can be duplication of programs and wasted effort.

Are They Reliable? Accountable?

Civil society groups are not always honest brokers. NGOs vying for media attention and donor funding may sometimes use tactics and information that is more alarmist than realistic. Greenpeace, for example, lost credibility in 1995 when it had to admit the inaccuracy of some of its claims about Royal Dutch Shell and its planned disposal of the Brent Spar offshore drilling rig in the North Atlantic (Keohane and Nye 2001:225). Greenpeace had greatly overestimated the amount of waste oil remaining on the rig. On the other hand, many NGOs realize that they risk discrediting themselves when they skew findings or supply inaccurate research, and therefore strive to make their information reliable and their biases clear (Diamond 1994:10).

Transparency and accountability may also be problems. Some civil society groups may not be vigorous in disclosing their sources of funding, or how they choose their projects and spend their budgets. They may not communicate regularly with their constituents or donors through newsletters, year-end reports, or other methods, and thus remain aloof from those they claim to serve. For example, a recent study of NGOs in Kenya found that it was impossible to trace the funding sources and expenditures of most NGOs, and often difficult to obtain information on their activities (Kunguru et al. 2002). Indeed, worldwide, many groups do not have any formal accountability mechanisms such as elections, auditors, or oversight committees. Often this is simply due to their small size, limited budget, and lack of capacity. But some do engage in corrupt practices, misallocating funds under the guise of community service.

Donors, members, and collaborating partners can help hold civil society groups accountable for their actions and the accuracy of their research by serving on boards of directors, demanding progress reports, and participating in internal strategy sessions. Funders hold a powerful tool for accountability through their capacity to remove financial support. Still, it can be difficult, if not impossible, for funders and constituents to know how decisions are made and moneys spent in the many remote venues where NGOs may work, or to determine whether the work accomplished was effective and appropriate.

Contention and Discord

NGOs don't always agree on how to tackle environmental problems. Southern environmental NGOs may have more pragmatic interests in environmental conservation than their Northern counterparts. Or, NGOs from both hemispheres may agree there's a problem, such as climate change, but not on the solution. Sometimes NGOs define their issues or goals very narrowly, or are blind to the possibilities of mutual gain from working with others. An NGO road-building program in the Dominican Republic, for example, helped some villagers get to the market, but also created erosion problems for neighboring villages not involved in the program (Brown and Kalegaonkar 2002:235–236).

Figure 4.3 More NGOs Can Participate in UN Meetings

Catalyzed by the impressive NGO presence at the 1992 Earth Summit in Rio, NGO mobilization gained speed in other conferences in the following decade, including the Vienna Human Rights Summit (1993), the Cairo Population Summit (1994), the Beijing Women's Summit (1995), the Istanbul Summit on Human Settlement (1996), and the Johannesburg Summit (2002).

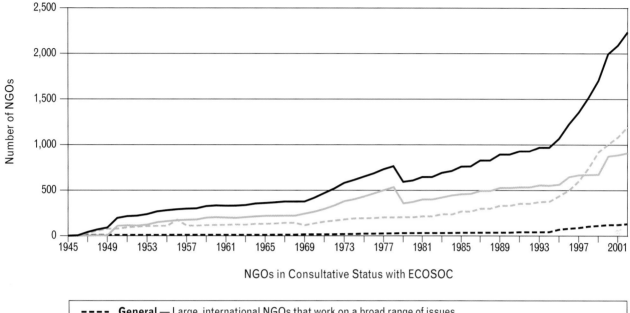

NGOs in Consultative Status with ECOSOC

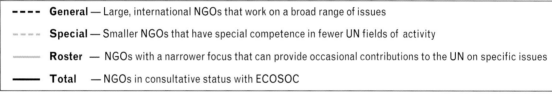

- - - - **General** — Large, international NGOs that work on a broad range of issues

- - - - **Special** — Smaller NGOs that have special competence in fewer UN fields of activity

—— **Roster** — NGOs with a narrower focus that can provide occasional contributions to the UN on specific issues

—— **Total** — NGOs in consultative status with ECOSOC

Source: United Nations Department of Economic and Social Affairs NGO Section, as reported by Willetts 2002.

Often NGOs simply have conflicting objectives and opinions. When the United States company Scott Paper proposed to develop a tree farm and pulp mill in southeastern Indonesia in 1988, a coalition of local NGOs eventually accepted the proposal, working with the company to reduce the project's environmental costs and increase its local employment benefits. However, some international-level NGOs campaigned to block the plantation altogether in the belief that large-scale forest development of any sort was unjustifiable (Jordan and van Tuijl 2000:2059–2060).

Some contention among civil society groups isn't bad. The contribution of civil society to good environmental governance is strengthened by a diversity of ideas, debate, and criticism. But discord and conflicting positions can mean lost opportunities to advance forward-looking policies and achieve environmental progress. A fragmented environmental NGO community is often an ineffective community, but united and coordinated, civic groups can articulate and pursue more influential strategies (Brown and Kalegaonkar 2002:236). In global and national politics, one of the major

constraints to NGOs exercising political influence is disunity at the bargaining table (Vanasselt 2002:157).

Empowered or Marginalized?

The capacity of civil society groups to organize and influence environmental outcomes varies widely by country and region. In some countries, NGOs are an accepted and empowered presence. They boast memberships and budgets in the millions and have ready access to the best and most up-to-date information technology. In other countries, government control remains very strong and civil organizations are weak.

Political and social contexts are important determinants of the power balance between governments and civic groups. For example, the United States has a long tradition of privately funded and managed public interest groups with a variety of mandates working on a wide range of issues. But in East and Southeast Asia, the centralized state typically has limited the scope for NGO participation in decisions about social issues and public policy. Nonprofit groups are met with suspicion about their motives and intentions, and government bureaucrats are reluctant to proactively work with NGOs (Baron 2002).

Governments may welcome NGOs that focus on social services, the delivery of aid programs, or those that don't threaten state authority, but they show hostility to advocacy groups that might challenge government policy (World Bank and ICNL 1997:3, 5, 9). For example, when the Tanzanian NGO known as Lawyers' Environmental Action Team exposed irregularities in connection with a cyanide-leach gold mine near Lake Victoria, the government issued warrants for the arrest of the NGO's leaders on sedition charges (Lissu 2002).

Some governments deny civic associations significant autonomy from the state. India restricts the amount of funds that domestic NGOs can receive from foreign donors. By keeping NGOs reliant on the state for financing, operation, and legal standing, civic groups are constrained as a force for independent information and oversight (Petkova et al. 2002:116). Egypt and Indonesia both have a history of authoritarian systems in which the government typically creates, organizes, licenses, and funds interest groups (Diamond 1994:13). China and other countries also have "government-sponsored" NGOs. While these "semi-public" or "semi-official" environ-mental groups may not be independent, they can still be effective, given their high-level connections. At the same time, such organizations are not likely to rally any large-scale activity against the state or business sector, and the scope of their work may be limited (Ho 2001:911, 915–916).

In general, governments generally have moved away from outright hostility toward environmental activism or civic organization. Still, they routinely use a variety of rules and regulations that hinder the sector's development and discourage the work of environmental advocates. In parts of Africa, the Middle East, China, and other countries, authoritarian governments severely curtail civil society's activities and influence (Mathews 1997:53). Some limit freedom of speech or the right to associate, effectively making it impossible to form a voluntary group (see Figure 4.4) (Anheier et al. 2001:263–266). NGOs in Ghana, Kenya, South Africa, Pakistan, and India have battled to stop governments from rolling back the legal space in which civil society operates (see Box 4.4).

Governments can also hinder the work of NGOs through the laws that regulate these organizations and determine their access to funds (World Bank and ICNL 1997:9). But tax laws can also help NGOs. The United States and Europe pro-

Box 4.4 In a Clear Voice: Press and Internet Freedoms

Press Freedom Is Growing

Freedom of the press and the Internet are important determinants of civil society's ability to influence environmental decisions and encourage broader public participation. For one, the news media are frequently the fundamental source of environmental information in a community. Greater media freedom often translates into more accurate and complete reporting and more reliable information.

In general, a free press is one of the most effective ways to expose environmental problems linked to government policy. It helps environmental groups and other nongovernmental organizations make their case to the public, and strengthens their oversight of government and corporate actions. For example, in 2000, NGOs from around the world focused media attention on a major cyanide spill from a Romanian mine into the Tisza River and the Danube. This media exposure brought public scrutiny to Romania's lax mine oversight and emergency planning, and led to government collaboration with NGOs in a new program to address environmental safety and risk issues (REC 2001:3–4, 13–15).

An active and free press can contribute to more fundamental social changes as well, and can help to limit government abuses, be they environmental or social. For example, in 2000, independent journalists publicized government corruption and human rights abuses in Peru and Yugoslavia, helping to bring down those government regimes. (Freedom House 2001:5).

The good news is that, in general, press freedoms are growing worldwide. According to Freedom House's annual survey of press freedom in 186 countries, the number of nations in 2001 with substantial freedom of the press rose to its highest level in a decade. The survey rated the press in 75 countries as "free;" 50 countries as "partly free;" and in 61 countries, national restrictions on journalists and publications meant the press was "not free" (Sussman and Karlekar 2002:5).

The overall upswing in the number of countries with a free press is impressive given the increased attention to state security after the terrorist attacks of September 11, 2001 in the United States. However, the new focus on security has not been entirely benign. In the United States, the Freedom House survey found that media access had declined somewhat in response to the "war on terrorism." In other countries, progress in granting press freedoms continued—for example, Chile repealed a controversial section of its State Security Law that criminalized anyone who "insulted" a state official. However, in many countries, strict libel laws and overzealous state security laws greatly impede media reporting on official corruption or malfeasance (Sussman and Karlekar 2002:7, 50).

In terms of the quality and extent of media coverage of environmental issues, trends are mixed. Environmental journalism in Asia now benefits from several umbrella organizations that provide services to journalists, including the Asia Pacific Forum of Environmental Journalists and the Environ-

vide favorable tax treatment, making financial contributions to NGOs tax-deductible and thereby encouraging donations. East Asian countries, on the other hand, typically limit tax deductibility on donations to NGOs or other nonprofit organizations (Baron 2002).

Registration laws vary, too. China's 1998 registration regulations for social organizations require an NGO to have a sponsoring institution, fewer than 50 members, and a minimum level of financial resources. They also disallow the existence of two organizations in the same field or sector, in the same jurisdiction. Those organizations that choose to avoid these restrictions and remain unregistered are unable to enter into contractual relations, such as obtaining telephone lines or leasing office space. Nor can they offer personnel benefits like pensions and medical insurance, or have their own bank account, making it harder to attract staff and funding (Ho 2001:903–905). In contrast, Japan eased financial requirements for the registration of NGOs in 1998 (Florini 2000:219).

Another controlling mechanism is government-imposed limits on a civic organization's existence. In Rwanda, an NGO can exist for no longer than three years and, in Kenya, an NGO must re-register and pay a fee every five years (World Bank and ICNL 1997:39). Sometimes, in the purported interest of accountability, governments exercise burdensome oversight on NGO activities. Viet Nam and Thailand require nonprofit organizations to file minutes of annual meetings. Japan and Korea require filed statements of proposed activities and budgets for the following year. Indonesia requires nonprofits to obtain government consent prior to receiving funds from abroad (Silk 1999:32, 37). Worldwide, many countries–particularly the countries of the South–lack an adequate framework of laws and regulations that would enable, rather than restrict, the operation of NGOs.

Building the Capacity of Civil Society

Nurturing New NGOs

Many NGOs working on environmental issues today were born of the democratic revolution and the economic changes of the past two decades. The challenge today is to support these new organizations as they develop the skills to become effective, well-managed, and self-sufficient (see Box 4.5). This includes learning how to partner with other institutions (including government), how to fund-raise, how to engage

mental Communication Asia network (ADB 2001:36). This is significant because environmental stories in the news media have been a key factor in the growth of the environmental movement in the Asia and Pacific region (ADB 2001:36). In the Central and Eastern European countries, some newspapers and television programs have established regular reporting on the environment. But, in most countries, newspapers and other media tend to cover the environment only occasionally, focusing mainly on accidents and controversy rather than on substantive environmental issues or the policies required to address them (SustainAbility et al. 2002:8–14).

Internet Freedom Is Mixed

Though relatively new, the Internet is already a significant element in expanding environmental democracy and empowering NGOs. But, like the media, Internet users can be subject to government constraints on who they can contact, what websites they can visit, and what information they can pass on.

Results from one of the first international assessments of Internet freedom show that while government restrictions on Internet access or content are uncommon, Internet freedoms are by no means universal. Of 131 countries examined, 58 provide liberal access to the web and generally do not control the content of material available on-line. Another 55 countries have moderate restrictions on web access and content. Eighteen countries, including China and Russia, significantly restrict Internet freedoms. In these countries, the state may provide the Internet service directly or intervene in commercial Internet service. Citizens may be fined, harassed, or imprisoned for messages deemed seditious or expressing dissent from government policies (Freedom House 2001:1).

Surprisingly, the results show that a high or moderate level of Internet freedom can often be found in nations where press freedom is low. In Oman, for example, there are many press restrictions, but Internet users are subjected to few. In 12 other nations with low press freedom, the government applies only moderate restrictions to the Internet. In these countries, the Internet may prove a critical tool for the effectiveness of civil society groups, and a major source of access to environmental information (Freedom House 2001:1–4).

the media, how to deliver services efficiently, and how to communicate results.

A recent analysis of civil society in 22 countries emphasized the need for capacity building in most of them (Salamon et al. 1999). But capacity building itself requires financial resources, and many civic groups struggle to secure even a shoestring budget. In fact, finding funding is the root problem plaguing new NGOs, and many older ones as well. The Regional Environmental Center for Central and Eastern Europe (REC) reported in 1997 that almost half the NGOs in that region were operating with budgets of under $1,000 a year, and three quarters reported their financial situation as either unstable or poor (REC 1997:8). With an increase in the size of the environmental sector and a decline in international funding to Central Europe since 1996, NGOs there now rely on even fewer resources.

Funding problems are compounded by the fact that most of the money from external donors goes to groups that focus on national and international issues, rather than to those working on local problems (OECD 1999:85). Meanwhile, few donors are willing to commit their support for longer than a few years despite the fact that NGOs–particularly new ones–require long-term funding to effectively address most social or environmental issues. Donor initiatives to establish longer-term relationships with NGOs are thus one way to deal with the problem of financial insecurity. Donor support can also include direct capacity building. For example, a donor agency might host an internship where NGO personnel can undertake research and training or produce a handbook or other field materials for use in their home country.

Government Action

Governments can facilitate civic action on environmental issues by improving the legal and regulatory frameworks that enable NGOs to grow and mature. Several nations in the Asia-Pacific region are making efforts in this area. For example, changes made to Thailand's constitution in 1997 guarantee freedom of association and specifically grant the freedom to assemble in the form of NGOs. In the Philippines, the government has enacted generous tax deductions for charitable contributions by individuals and corporations (Silk 1999:7, 12–16). However, progress needs to spread to other regions. This includes greater attention to press and Internet freedoms, which are vital to civic debate and the ability of civil society groups to communicate with and organize their constituents. Governments can also be proactive in seeking civic input in developing policies and pursuing projects with significant environmental impacts.

Developing Local Support

Support from external donors such as bilateral aid agencies or development banks often helps new civil society groups to

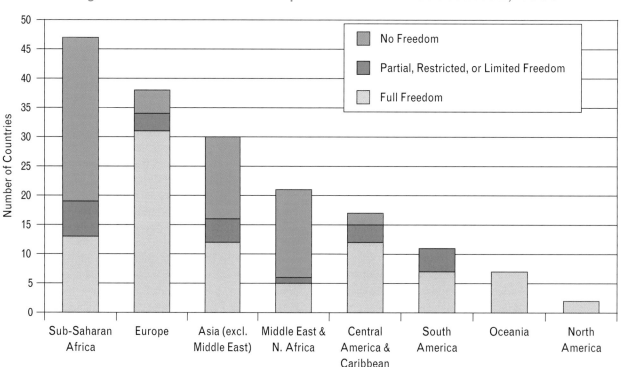

Figure 4.4 Freedom of Expression and Association, 1999

Source: U.S. State Department, as reported by Anheier et al. 2001: 263–266.

A vibrant civil society increases the demand for transparency and accountability of decision-makers in both government and business.

get off the ground and older groups to undertake special projects or build capacity for effective action. But in order to survive and thrive, civil society groups must eventually enlist local support and involvement. They must establish roots in their communities, engaging local interest and acceptance and securing financial support.

Establishing those local roots can be challenging. In many countries limited public understanding of the legitimacy of civil society organizations makes it difficult for new groups to stimulate indigenous support and participation (Brown and Kalegaonkar 2002:233). NGOs and other groups may be unaccustomed to reaching out to the public and other stakeholders, as an assessment of Russian NGOs found (see Box 4.6). Similarly, an examination of the sustainability of Latin

American NGOs concluded that NGOs can't expect to gain acceptance, legitimacy, and support by leading projects in isolation. They must learn to work effectively in a support role by coordinating community activities, forging alliances, and integrating themselves into the social fabric of the community (Valderrama 1999).

Building a broad base of indigenous financial support is a particular challenge in countries where there is no history of private philanthropy or nonprofit organizations, or where per capita income is very low. Yet, access to diversified sources of funding–local, international, and self-generated income from fees–is a key to NGO sustainability and autonomy. Analysis of environmental NGO financing in Central Europe shows an overwhelming dependence on foreign

donors. Unless local charitable support expands, these groups are left vulnerable to impoverishment as a growing number vie for a finite or shrinking pool of international support (Atkinson and Messing 2002:13). In five Latin American countries, researchers found a similar need to encourage the growth of local charitable foundations to enable further expansion of the nonprofit sector (Salamon et al. 1999:35).

Transparency and Accountability

One step toward overcoming doubts about civil society's legitimacy and effectiveness is for environmental NGOs and other civic groups to measure their own impact in clear and simple terms. More in-depth and transparent self-evaluation and peer evaluation can help defray questions of accountability or responsiveness to their primary constituencies. Similarly, transparency and openness in the areas of funding and work agendas can allay concerns that NGOs are merely agents of foreign interests.

There are fledgling efforts to make NGOs more transparent and to assess their effectiveness. These include scorecards that survey the performance and ethics of nonprofit organizations. *Worth Magazine*, for example, provides an annual list of the 100 best United States charities in several fields, including the environment, based on criteria such as return on investment and effectiveness.

Many efforts to improve accountability and transparency come from within the NGO community. Donors and some large conservation groups, such as the World Wide Fund for Nature, and the Nature Conservancy, are trying to develop accounting standards to audit the effectiveness of environmental projects (Christensen 2002:D2). InterAction, a membership association of United States NGOs engaged in international humanitarian efforts, requires its members to comply with set standards in such areas as governance, finance, communication with the U.S. public, and management practices. InterAction also promotes standard-setting

(continued on p. 86)

Box 4.5 African NGOs: A Kaleidoscope of Efforts

Africa's nongovernmental organizations (NGOs) mirror the wide variations in governance among the countries of the continent. Here, the best and the worst examples of NGOs can be found. Throughout much of Africa, strong NGOs have been on the frontline of the battle for civic freedom and better environmental governance, while in other parts of the region they are weak, insecure, and vulnerable to repression.

Yet, even in places where formal government structures are in disarray, such as in parts of the Great Lakes region, or Somalia, community organizations and NGOs have managed to address social and environmental concerns—against great odds. During the Rwanda genocide crisis in 1994, for example, local organizations worked in the communities that hosted refugee camps, helping people find alternative energy sources in order to reduce the destruction of local forests for fuelwood.

Similarly, in war-torn Somalia, local groups have been working with UN agencies such as the United Nations Educational, Scientific and Cultural Organization (UNESCO) and the United Nations Development Programme (UNDP) to help build a culture of reconciliation and peace, and a foundation for economic growth. In the oasis of Iskushuban in the Somalian desert, local groups using seed funding from UNDP have formed a water-users committee to rebuild irrigation channels, established a microcredit plan to finance new village enterprises, started a demonstration farm to spread organic farming techniques, and constructed retaining walls to pre-

vent erosion of the steep valley terrain. These locally led initiatives have become a model for civic action in other villages in the Iskushuban district.

Ghana, Kenya, Senegal, South Africa, and Zimbabwe are home to large numbers of NGOs, and many have played a critical role in advancing policy reform at the national level. In Zimbabwe, civil society found its voice during the years when the capital city Harare was the center of resistance to the apartheid regime in South Africa, and continues to address Zimbabwe's current civil troubles. Over the past decade, NGOs in Ghana and Kenya have defended the public's right of association in the face of government attempts to legislate a limit to this basic freedom. In Kenya in particular, NGOs such as the Mazingira Institute, Kenya Human Rights Commission, and the Green Belt Movement, in partnership with churches and other groups, have helped catalyze constitutional reform. Civil society also played a central role in the dramatic changes in South Africa's political system in the last two decades—a story that has somewhat overshadowed the important influence of NGOs as drivers of change elsewhere on the continent.

Much of the story of NGOs in Africa revolves around the relationship between civil society and government. Governments tend to look favorably on NGOs that provide services such as healthcare, education, or other activities that the state would ordinarily perform. On the other hand, politically active NGOs may provoke government ire. With the slow growth of democratic governance across the continent, civil society organizations are often seen as the only acceptable and effective vehicle to work for change in society. Consequently, many African governments have viewed NGOs with suspicion, if not outright contempt. But NGOs do not always work in opposition to the state. Since the 1992 Earth Summit in Rio, many African NGOs have worked to strengthen their governments' positions in international policy forums. And in

some countries, such as Senegal and Uganda, serious efforts have been made to bring civil society more meaningfully into the national policy-formulation arena.

Nonetheless, there remain many weaknesses in Africa's NGO sector. Despite the strength of ZERO in Zimbabwe, ENDA in Senegal, Friends of the Earth Ghana, Environmental Justice Networking Forum in South Africa, and Zambia Wildlife Society, to name a few, the vast majority of NGOs face critical financial constraints and capacity gaps. African NGOs argue that the high level of poverty makes it difficult to raise local funds, so they rely on international donors. Yet, charitable giving is not alien to most African cultures, and the difficulty of soliciting local funds is often simply due to a lack of fundraising skills, or the absence of strong support among local constituents.

What often *is* alien to Africans is the social concept of the nongovernmental association as it has developed in European cultures—a variety of citizens from different walks of life and often different communities, coming together to address a

specific set of social issues. Instead, many African NGOs reflect a narrower social base. Some have arisen from the activity of urban elites, along the lines of the European NGO model. Many others were created at the request of financial donors to carry out projects at the community level. Often, these NGOs have bypassed and alienated traditional social norms, which are community-focused and governed by traditional leadership structures, such as local chiefs. This cultural mismatch is one reason that NGOs in Africa are frequently accused by governments, as well as by some donor agencies, of lacking the capacity or mandate to succeed in their mission. Other shortcomings include corruption, tribalism, and the "Big Man syndrome"—where most decision-making power is vested in one individual or leader. These problems can become obstacles to fostering democratic norms, transparency, and accountability among the continent's civil society groups.

Although these concerns are real, they are often overblown by critics. This focus frequently leads to unfair or inappropriate treatment of NGOs by African governments, while a great deal of effective work by civil society organizations goes unrecognized. The many success stories among NGOs in Africa indicate that creative and culturally sensitive approaches to capacity development—such as fostering mechanisms for accountability, or nurturing democratic and effective leadership—have strong potential to broaden the response of civil society groups to Africa's environment and development needs.

Contributed by Robert Sinclair, capacity development consultant, Nairobi, Kenya.

Kenya's Healthy Civil Society

Number of voluntary nonprofit organizations in Kenya, 2002 (including informal organizations) (Hakkarainen et al. 2002)	150,000
Number of government-registered NGOs in Kenya, 2003 (Sinclair 2003)	2,511
Percentage of Kenyan hospitals run by NGOs, 1999 (Government of Kenya Ministry of Health 2001:63)	50.2%
Percentage of Kenyan health clinics and medical centers run by NGOs, 1999 (Government of Kenya Ministry of Health 2001:63)	87.1%
Percentage of Kenyan nursing and maternity homes run by NGOs, 1999 (Government of Kenya Ministry of Health 2001:63)	100%

Civil society groups create channels for participation by people typically excluded from decision-making.

processes for comparable groups in Canada, Japan, Asia, and Central and Eastern Europe (InterAction 2003).

At the same time, One World Trust, a London-based charity, is designing indicators to measure the accountability and transparency of a range of global institutions, including international NGOs. Using these indicators, an organization might measure how accessible its meetings and formal decision-making processes are to members, or the independence and transparency of its evaluation process. Or it might measure whether the group has adequate stakeholder representation from the North and the South (Kovach et al. 2003). Although many of these efforts focus on international NGOs or take place in developed countries, they provide approaches that might be adapted and used elsewhere.

Specialized Support Organizations

Some NGOs have taken it as their mission to help other civil society groups become more effective. These "support organizations" provide a variety of services. Some provide research and training to NGOs or increase the public's awareness of their contributions. Others build alliances or bridge the differences among government, business, and civil society groups. The work of these support organizations has catalyzed fundamental changes and maturation throughout the sector. Some notable successes include:

■ The Society for Participatory Research in Asia fostered the development of regional and international networks to promote capacity building and training for grassroots organizations. The Delhi-based organization responded to the demand for its services by developing a network of regional support organizations throughout India. It also forged alliances with organizations throughout South Asia that provide training, information, and other resources to strengthen NGOs and help women and disadvantaged populations participate in local and national governance (Brown and Kalegaonkar 2002:240).

■ The Philippine Business for Social Progress (PBSP), organized by business leaders, provides financial support to NGOs working on rural development and encourages learning from past initiatives to improve effectiveness. On a larger scale, PBSP has also generated awareness that improving relations between NGOs and businesses is critical to improving funding (Brown and Kalegaonkar 2002:241).

■ The Council of National Indigenous Associations of Ecuador (CONAIE) shares information among members and represents them in negotiations with govern-

Box 4.6 Russia's NGOs: Learning to Engage

To successfully advance their interests, nongovernmental organizations (NGOs) need to build relationships and be connected—to the public, to government officials, to the business community, and to each other. Yet, engaging the public and other stakeholders is easier said than done. Engagement is especially difficult in countries where civic groups are a relatively new force and there is general public distrust of such institutions and of government bodies.

Russia typifies this situation. Russian NGOs who work on environmental issues have traditionally been distant from the public and the communities in which they work. The leaders and members of these NGOs are often scientists, technical experts, and other professionals who tend to value their links to the scientific community, but who may not be inclined to consult "ordinary citizens." Indeed, a 1999 survey of Russian environmental NGOs found that 70 percent of these groups routinely consult with scientists to advance their work, while only 30 percent routinely seek involvement from the public (see Table) (Wernstedt 2002a:31).

The survey also found that most environmental NGOs don't work with other Russian or international NGOs on a regular basis. They consult even less frequently with anyone in local government. Weakest of all is their relationship with the private sector. Ninety-two percent of NGOs surveyed reported working with business or industry only "occasionally" or "never" (see Table). The absence of close working relations with these groups means that Russian environmental NGOs often lack an effective entry point to decision-making (Wernstedt 2002a:19, 31)

The problem of civic disengagement goes beyond the NGO community. Many Russian citizens do not actively seek to participate in environmental NGOs or in the political process. This is not due to any legal constraint on public participation. Russians have a constitutional and statutory right to participate in public decision-making and to give their input on environmental matters (Wernstedt 2002b:25). Yet, a recent poll indicates that only 5 percent of Russians currently participate in public organizations and nearly 75 percent say they have no interest in doing so (Wernstedt 2002b:24).

These results point to the difficulty of building coalitions for action around environmental problems in Russia today. But it may not always be so. Surveys show that the public is concerned about the role of the environment in health issues. Nearly 60 percent of 3,300 Russians surveyed in 2000 reported that they believed the environment caused or contributed to chronic illnesses in their family (Wernstedt 2002a:3-4). If it can be tapped, this concern may offer a viable path to public engagement. At the same time, Russian NGOs are clearly starting to understand the need to involve the public in their work. More than 40 percent of environmental NGOs now rank "increased public involvement" as a top priority for improving environmental policies (Wernstedt 2002a:29).

A Reluctance to Engage?

Percentage of Russian environmental NGOs surveyed who work with:

	Always	Usually	Occasionally or Never
Scientists	70	22	8
Other Russian NGOs	42	23	35
Educators	40	28	32
International NGOs	38	19	43
Local Public	30	30	41
Local Elected Officials	15	42	43
Local Government Institutions	15	41	45
Business/Industry	0	8	92

Source: Wernstedt 2002a:31

---

ments and international agencies when indigenous rights and resources are threatened. The CONAIE federation not only successfully revised a proposed law that jeopardized indigenous land-holdings, but also set the stage for a larger role for indigenous actors in future policy-making (Brown and Kalegaonkar 2002:243, 247-248).

These "support organizations" face their own survival challenges. They must create a constituency for their services—yet civil society actors are often unaware of their own shortcomings or reluctant to acknowledge their weaknesses (Brown and Kalegaonkar 2002:250, 254).

Coalitions and Alliances

Forming coalitions of environmental NGOs and other civil society groups can be a highly effective way to channel their energy and magnify their effectiveness. By adopting a common stance on key issues of national or international importance and by learning to work together, civil society groups can often achieve synergies that lead to more significant outcomes. They can convene diverse constituencies that sway

policy-makers far more easily than single groups. Influential coalitions include:

- The Danish 92 Group, which coordinated the work of Danish environment and development organizations in preparation for the 1992 Rio Summit and the 2002 Johannesburg Summit. Twenty domestic NGOs participate in the Group.

- The Norwegian Forum for Environment and Development, a network of 60 groups that develops common positions on issues such as global access to safe drinking water, and sustainable agriculture, and mobilizes participation and action on Agenda 21 efforts in Norway. For example, the Forum called for debt cancellation for developing countries, and for a larger portion of development assistance to be channeled to water projects (FwF 2002).

- The Caucus of Development NGO Networks (CODE-NGO) brings together some 2,500 NGOs and cooperatives from the Philippines to discuss issues facing the sector, promote professionalism, and build member consensus on development, NGO, and community issues.

One example of a particularly large and effective international coalition is ECO-FORUM—an alliance of more than 200 environmental organizations from all over Europe. The coalition enjoyed full negotiating powers in the drafting of the Aarhus Convention from 1996 to 1998. This was the first time that NGOs could sit with equal status alongside governments to draft an international treaty. Now that the Aarhus Convention has entered into force, ECO-FORUM remains involved in the implementation process and contributes to decisions on how to interpret and refine the treaty. For example, ECO-FORUM has been active in negotiations on a new treaty that will require signatories to compile annual inventories of pollutants from industrial sources (called Pollutant Release and Transfer Registries, or PRTRs). (See Chapter 6.)

Ultimately, effective participation of civil society groups in environmental governance won't come from simply having larger coalitions or more environmental groups. A greater voice in government and corporate environmental decisions will come as much from the *quality* of civil society efforts as from the *quantity* of people participating or projects undertaken.

The legitimacy of environmental groups—old and new— will depend on their ability to develop sophisticated strategies, to offer substantive knowledge and organization skills, to better measure their own performance, and to better forge connections with each other and with other stakeholders.

DECENTRALIZATION
A LOCAL VOICE

One key to smarter environmental management at the community level is to tap the ideas and energies of the community itself. In theory, the people who live closest to a natural resource stand to be most affected by its loss or alteration. They have a material interest in managing their environment sustainably. That's why *decentralization*–the steps that many central governments are taking to give regional, municipal, and local institutions responsibility for some public sector functions, from forest management to the provision of waste disposal services–is an important development in environmental governance.

How Can Decentralization Help Environmental Governance?

Decentralization—the transfer of powers or responsibilities from a central government to local institutions—goes directly to the question of who gets to make decisions about natural resources. Decentralization can make environmental decision-making more accessible to communities and their representatives, in turn increasing the relevance of those decisions and the likelihood they will be implemented. But decentralization can also occur in ways that leave the status quo—central government dominance of decision-making—largely unchanged, with little benefit to the environment or local empowerment.

For most of the world's citizens, having a significant voice in public decision-making would be a new experience (Ribot 2002c:5). Many African, Asian, and Latin American countries inherited centralized government systems from the nations that colonized them and maintained this emphasis on central government decision-making after they achieved independence. As a consequence, local governments–who have the means to bring decision-making closer to people–have often lacked the autonomy and resources to develop into competent, efficient, responsive institutions (Smoke 2000:3).

Recently, several waves of decentralization in developing and developed regions have provided opportunities for local governments to better respond to citizen concerns within frameworks of national environmental and natural resource policy (see Box 5.1). Central governments have often found it hard to enforce some policies–such as grazing allocations, fishing quotas, and restrictions on forest use–because of resistance at the community level to centrally imposed mandates. Under the right conditions, decentralization can bridge this gap by creating ways for local people to negotiate mutually acceptable environmental goals with state authorities.

But decentralization doesn't eliminate the central government's role in resource management decisions. Total control over natural resources at the local level is rarely a recipe for environmental success. Communities themselves can decimate resources out of desperation or ignorance, or through corruption or short-term profit-seeking.

Also, while natural resources such as forests and minerals are located in specific communities, their management has wider effects. These include downstream impacts on water supply, regional air pollution, global climate change, and biodiversity loss. Local communities may overlook these concerns or be incapable of addressing them adequately. For this reason, natural resources require the active oversight of many levels of government across many spatial scales (Larson 2003a:6).

Accordingly, the goal of decentralization should be to achieve an appropriate level of local input within a solid framework of national environmental policy. Effective local institutions are needed to negotiate community concerns with national authorities who represent the interests of society at large. Regional and national regulations and democratic processes should also help ensure that all those with a legitimate voice or concern about resource use get to participate in decision-making. The challenge lies in finding the right mix of local and national powers and responsibilities to achieve sustainability.

What is Decentralization?

Decentralization is the process where a central government relinquishes some of its management responsibilities or powers to a local government, local leader, or community institution.

About 60 developing countries are currently undertaking some form of decentralized natural resource management (Agrawal 2001:208; Ribot 2002b:1). At least in developing countries, the status quo prior to decentralization reforms is usually a central government with the power to make most major decisions about natural resources or land use. Commonly, central governments set the framework for environmental governance at the provincial, district, and local levels. For example, a conservation agenda for a park or reserve will frequently be made by a national parks service or a state wildlife conservation department–agencies operating at some distance from the actual resource and the people who rely on it for employment or subsistence. National forest ministries often assert legal authority over forest ownership and use policies. These determine who has access to forests, what timber resources are harvested, how revenues are used, and how well rules are enforced.

In most cases, all that is left to local governments or communities is the management of natural resources that are of little commercial value. For instance, a community may get to decide how to harvest non-timber forest products such as latex, mushrooms, rattan, or bamboo for household consumption, or how to allocate local fishing resources. In contrast, central government ministries tend to reserve the right to allocate timber, mining, or fishing concessions, provide hunting licenses, or manage tourist parks–all sources of significant revenue (Kaimowitz and Ribot 2002:5). Local authorities and citizens also may have little say when it comes to the siting of polluting industries and heavy infrastructure such as mines, airports, or roads, even though the pollution, noise, and traffic they create are felt locally.

Decentralization reforms can begin to break down such centralized–and sometimes highly exclusionary–decision-making systems in various ways. Reforms can range from grants of only small additional responsibilities to a subnational government, to significant empowerment of local leaders and previously underrepresented groups in major policy decisions or management. The powers that are typically decentralized to municipal or local institutions vary widely, ranging from regulatory and fiscal powers, to enforcement, and even some judiciary powers (see Box 5.2).

The local institutions that are granted these new decision-making powers also vary, and can include (Dupar and Badenoch 2002:3; Ribot 2002b:4-5):

■ elected local authorities, such as a mayor, a town or village council, or a planning commission

■ agents from government ministries of the environment, forest, wildlife, or other natural resources

■ elected or appointed user groups, such as agricultural cooperatives or wildlife management groups

Box 5.1 Tracing Decentralization in Developing Countries

The first in a recent wave of decentralizations swept developing countries in the late 1980s and early 1990s and was not specific to natural resources. Central governments were seeking to cut their budgets and find creative responses to economic crises. They hoped to transfer some planning and service delivery functions to local governments. Donors were eager to underwrite the experiment. Concerned about the grim fiscal problems of developing countries, lenders such as the World Bank pressured them to improve their administrative and fiscal performance and boost efficiency as a path to achieving economic growth. They advised governments to find new ways to administer costly programs ranging from healthcare, to education, to natural resources and parks management. Decentralization seemed a promising means for accomplishing these goals and went hand-in-hand with market liberalization.

Decentralization's potential to enhance political stability by satisfying citizen demands for greater participation is also attractive (World Bank 1999:107–108). Governments in South Africa, Uganda, Sri Lanka, Ethiopia, Bosnia-Herzegovina, and Colombia are among those adopting decentralization in an attempt to promote greater unity and gain grassroots support in the face of emerging geographic and ethnic divides (World Bank 1999:108). Sometimes decentralization enables governments to undercut political power in troublesome regions. For instance, the Indonesian government has deliberately empowered districts and municipalities rather than provinces because separatist tendencies run strongest at the province level (Resosudarmo 2002:3).

Some countries have specifically used decentralization as a tool to deepen grassroots democracy. Uganda sought to recreate its government in a way that was responsive to citizens and would revitalize local governments after years of repressive rule (Smoke 2000:8–9). In Thailand, which has embarked on some of the most ambitious decentralization reforms in mainland Southeast Asia, political parties sought to strengthen their support in rural areas by increasing the voice of rural constituencies (Dupar and Badenoch 2002:11). Bolivia's 1994 Popular Participation Law devolved a number of responsibilities to municipal governments, including some related to local land use and planning. The intention, at least in part, was to give communities, local farmers, and indigenous groups a greater role in government (Contreras-Hermosilla and Rios 2002:3).

From the mid-1990s onward, a second form of decentralization became popular thanks to the efforts of numerous donor agencies. Many of the policies and programs in this second wave were targeted at specific environmental and social sectors, rather than at local democratization more broadly (Manor 2002:1). They were intended to pinpoint particular environment and development challenges. For instance, donor agencies supported the establishment of river basin committees in Thailand (Pantana et al. 2001:34–37) and forest and wildlife management committees in Uganda (Namara and Nsabagasani 2003:17).

Today, decentralization is the centerpiece of policy reforms around the world. Some 95 percent of democracies now have elected regional and local governments, and countries everywhere are devolving administrative, fiscal, or political powers to tiers of governments below the national level (World Bank 1999:107). All but 12 of the 75 developing and transitional countries with populations over 5 million claim to be transferring political powers to local government units (Dillinger 1994:1; Agrawal 2001:208).

- local members of a political party apparatus

- local, national, or international nongovernmental organizations (NGOs), and

- traditional leaders, such as local chiefs, defined by local custom.

In short, decentralization can describe a variety of changes in who makes decisions about natural resources and how those decisions are made: A central government may grant some control over fisheries or tracts of state land to a local government, along with responsibility for infrastructure, such as water supply, sanitation, and irrigation. An agricultural agent, employed by the national government but based in a field office, may be allowed to issue rules on resource access for a tract of land, such as grazing permits. A central government may grant locally appointed bodies responsibility for surveying and leasing forest land to households. Or it may empower a nongovernmental organization (NGO) and a community

group to jointly set hunting quotas for elephants in a wildlife preserve.

Sometimes governments transfer responsibility over resource use to a private owner or enterprise—the process known as *privatization*. In Uganda, traditional forest users are being given outright ownership rights to many forests that were previously in the public domain—effectively privatizing them—in the name of decentralization (Ribot 2002c:7). However, privatization is not a form of decentralization (Dupar and Badenoch 2002:32; Ribot 2002a:v). Privatization removes decisions about nature from the public arena and transfers them to actors who may have less of a stake in environmental protection and equitable access to natural resources than public representatives do (see Box 5.3).

Effective Democratic Decentralization

Ideally, decentralization reforms help balance central government oversight and regulation with local input and empowerment. Done well, this effort should bring government closer to the people and increase opportunities for citizens to take an interest in public affairs because it devolves power to the local

Box 5.2 Defining Decentralization

What Are the Different Kinds of Decentralization?

There are a variety of ways in which a government can cede or share power over natural resources and the environment with other stakeholders, including local government agencies, nongovernmental organizations (NGOs), and even the private sector. These include:

Political or democratic decentralization: The central government transfers decision-making power and financial resources to elected representatives of people at regional or local levels. These local representatives gain significant discretion in making decisions and rules about resource use within prescribed limits.

Administrative decentralization (also called deconcentration): Central government ministries transfer some functions to regional or local outposts, perhaps by moving personnel to a particular location or assigning new responsibilities to staff in those branch offices. Deconcentration may bring services closer to citizens, but generally preserves the hierarchal relationship between central offices and field staff. It therefore does not necessarily increase the voice or involvement of citizens in resource management and government decisions.

In co-management arrangements, power over and responsibility for natural resources are shared between the government and local users. A local agency of a forest ministry working in partnership with village representatives or representatives from a resource users group would be one form of co-management. Government agencies and local groups may work together closely, but not necessarily as equals.

Community management programs include higher levels of discretionary authority and empowerment at the community level than do co-management programs. In cases of community management, a local group typically manages the resource under contract with a government agency. For example, an NGO might serve as guarantor of the community's ability to manage the resource. Systems of community management are often based on traditional institutional structures, such as local chiefs or councils, and may reflect traditional community tenure arrangements. Examples include community self-help groups working on agroforestry in Ghana and water management in Kenya.

What Powers Does Decentralization Involve?

Decentralization involves the transfer of several different types of administrative and political power from a central authority to a local institution:

The power to create rules or modify old ones—for example, to set land use and zoning rules, or to decide what kinds of trees can be harvested in a forest, or what days certain users can fish in a specified area.

The power to make fiscal and revenue decisions—for example, the power to levy fees at the entrance to a park, to set waste management or water treatment fees, or to decide how to spend revenues raised from hunting fees from a game preserve.

The power to implement rules and ensure compliance—for example, to penalize a factory for excess emissions, or to

and municipal level. Particularly in developing countries, opportunities to have meaningful input in resource use and decision-making are likely to decrease mutual suspicion and enable all major groups to participate in managing the shared environment on an equal footing (UNEP 2002:409). Decentralization should also benefit the environment and improve equity in natural resource management because it can tap local knowledge of the environment and bring a better appreciation of local people's needs. In addition, local groups are more likely to respect resource decisions made with local input (see Box 5.4).

But achieving decentralization's potential depends largely on how the reforms are designed and implemented (World Bank 1999:109). To best benefit the environment and improve equity in resource management, four minimum criteria must be met:

- Decentralization must result in a transfer of meaningful powers—including fiscal powers—to a local institution.

- The institution to which power is transferred must be representative of the local populace in its diversity—not just elite interests—and have a broad knowledge of local natural resources and people's dependence on them.

- The local public must be able to hold the institution accountable through elections, hearings, or other democratic means.

- Fiscal and regulatory incentives must be in place to promote sustainable management of natural resources over the long term.

Meeting all four criteria is not easy.

Perhaps the biggest hurdle is assuring the accountability of those to whom authority is transferred. Accountability implies taking responsibility for the decisions one makes. The key question is whether the local government body or organization to which a central government devolves power is accountable to the local community. In other words, will they have to answer to the people immediately affected by their decisions?

(continued on p. 96)

sanction townspeople who cut trees in a communal forest without permission, or hunt wildlife without a permit.

The power of adjudication—the right to resolve conflicts and oversee negotiations over resource use and rules.

Apparent decentralization can also occur with no real transfer of "powers"—just a transfer of responsibilities. For example, a local NGO or local government might inherit the responsibility to implement decisions and enforce rules made by the central government, but not the power to assign fines or make any rules of its own. This transfer of responsibilities without complementary powers does not result in true local control.

Who Is Involved in Decentralization?

The central state: Includes presidents, ministers, ministry personnel, and members of national assemblies. They define which powers are transferred from the central government, and to whom. Typically, one or more agencies with specific responsibilities for local government oversight may be particularly involved in decentralization, such as a Ministry of Local Government, Ministry of Home Affairs, or Ministry of the Interior.

Regional, district-level, or local institutions: Includes local branches of central government ministries, elected local governments, NGOs, traditional authorities, and community groups and cooperatives. These institutions or individuals receive power over the environment through decentralization reforms. For example, a country might create a new institution at the local level, such as a forest council made up of villagers. Or, a central government may grant new responsibilities to existing institutions, such as village, city, municipal, or district councils; town committees; county governments; watershed management boards; or village development committees.

Citizens: Citizens can be affected indirectly—say, through the implementation of new land use rules and access rights, changes in mining concessions, or the creation of new local governments. Or, decentralization may directly involve citizens—for example, through the election of representatives to a local institution designated to manage resource use or through a community-based watershed association. Citizen interests and abilities to participate in natural resource management may vary depending on their gender, age, class, race, religion, professional identity, or the culture of the community.

International donors and development banks: Many multilateral and bilateral donors provide funding for programs, projects, and policies that encourage decentralized governance and strengthen the capacity of local institutions to carry out decentralized responsibilities effectively and efficiently. For example, many programs of the U.S. Agency for International Development (USAID) promote local democracy and government efficiency and transparency, such as the project in El Salvador to modernize the accounting and administration of 28 municipalities and enhance citizen involvement through participatory planning processes and open city council and public budget meetings (USAID 2003).

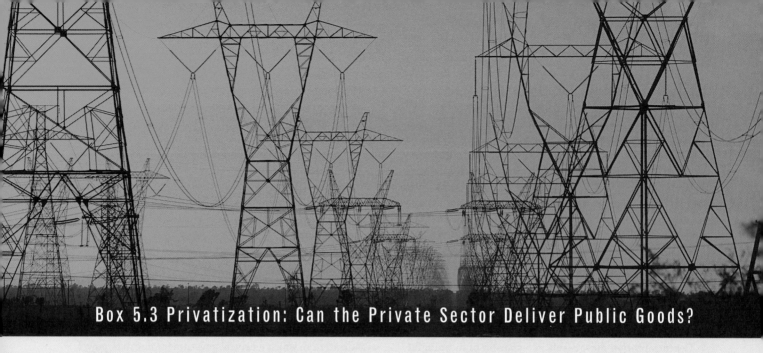

Box 5.3 Privatization: Can the Private Sector Deliver Public Goods?

Privatization—the sale of public assets such as a state-owned railroad or water utility to the private sector—is common worldwide. No services are exempt: banking, electric power provision, oil and gas production, healthcare delivery, water delivery, education, telecommunications, and transportation services are all frequently privatized by national, provincial, and local governments. Although the trend of privatization began in developed countries in the 1980s, today it is prominent in developing countries as well, where natural resources are often the assets targeted for sale. For example, 40 percent of the $44 billion in revenues that developing country governments raised through privatization in 1999 came from the sale of state-owned petroleum, mining, agriculture, and forest assets (World Bank 2001:183,188).

Governments privatize their assets for several reasons. One is to shed state enterprises that are operating at a loss and draining the government's coffers. Another is the hope that private owners will run the enterprises more efficiently, bringing better service than the state could provide by infusing the enterprise with new capital, improved management practices, and better technologies. However, the decision to privatize can be controversial, particularly when governments propose putting essential services like water delivery and electric power provision into private hands. The worry is that private companies may increase the efficiency of the enterprise, but ignore social objectives in the bargain, such as keeping the cost of water and power affordable, or providing bus service in poor areas.

The Theory of Privatization

Governments and international financial institutions typically promote privatization based on two arguments. First, theory suggests that public officials—politicians and bureaucrats—lack the incentive to run an enterprise efficiently. They can rely on public bailouts if bankruptcy is imminent. Also, there is no market competition or takeover threat as there would be in a typical business, and the public doesn't scrutinize perfor-

mance as shareholders in a public corporation would (Ram Mohan 2001:4865–4866).

Second, public managers often have to balance contradictory objectives. Efficiency may be sacrificed to increase social benefits such as employment, which may then translate into political support. For example, the poor state of the electricity sector in India has been attributed to public bailouts of bankrupt utilities, political pressure to allow nonpayment of bills, and below-cost electricity prices for politically influential farmer constituencies (Dubash and Rajan 2002:51–71).

Another impetus for privatization is the trend toward decentralization. Privatization proponents frequently conflate the two strategies. In fact, decentralization and privatization have very different effects. While decentralization, done well, can increase public input into local governance, privatization often leads to greater public exclusion from resource decisions, since it shifts ownership—and therefore control—to corporations and other actors that do not have to answer to the public. In the natural resources sector, privatization often incorrectly takes place in the name of decentralization. In Mali, for example, forests are being transferred to local elected authorities—an apparent sign of decentralization. However, these officials are being given the right to sell off the forests, taking them out of the public domain and reducing the public's future role in managing them (Ribot 1995:21).

Critics and Controversy

Critics of privatization question whether its promised efficiency gains are ever realized in practice (Ram Mohan 2001:4870–4871). They also charge that privatizing essential public services such as water and electricity, is fraught with near-insurmountable problems of governance (Hall 2001: 11–16). For example, when politically connected and powerful multinational corporations take over the provision of public services, governments may not be able to enforce competition or appropriately regulate these companies. The result may be higher prices for basic services, a lack of attention to environmental impacts, and a lack of commitment to public goals such as increasing access to water and sanitation services. These, in turn, may evoke a social backlash against privatization.

There are many examples of the controversy that can accompany privatization. Among the most publicized is that of Cochabamba, Bolivia. In 1999, when the city auctioned off its ill-functioning water system as part of this program, it received only a single bid—from a British-led consortium. But the government proceeded with the sale, handing over in the deal not only the water system but also the rights to all the water in the district—including underground water—and guaranteeing a 15 percent annual return on the company's investment (Finnegan 2002:45).

Taking advantage of these terms, the consortium quickly raised the price it charged for water, in some cases doubling water bills (Finnegan 2002:47). This sparked mass demonstrations in Cochabamba and escalated into confrontations with armed police. As unrest grew, the government eventually revoked the contract (on the grounds that the company had abandoned its concession) and rapidly implemented a new national water law that promised public consultation on rates, and provided protection to small-scale water systems (Finnegan 2002:51).

The Cochabamba example and other problem-ridden experiences in Buenos Aires, Manila, Johannesburg, and other cities have convinced some social advocates that privatizing such basic necessities as water is inherently problematic. These advocates suggest that essential services should not be privatized without greatly improved regulation by the state and participation by citizens to ensure that private firms are accountable to consumers and to the public at large (Kessler 2002:4–6, 8–12).

Economic Benefits?

On the other side, many economists believe that, judged on economic grounds, privatization's record looks good. They argue that statistical surveys largely show that it does, in fact, lead to greater efficiency (Megginson and Netter 2001: 345–360). For example, a study in the United Kingdom found that electricity privatization had resulted in a permanent reduction of 5 percent per year in the cost of providing electricity service (Newbery and Pollitt 1997:269).

However, these results are by no means definitive (Ram Mohan 2001:4865). For example, privatization often occurs at the same time as deregulation, and the effects of the two are not easily separated. Economic gains attributed to privatization may just as likely be the results of deregulation and could also reflect other macroeconomic trends, such as general economic expansion.

Most importantly, perhaps, while economists have focused on economic gains, they have not applied equal vigor to understanding whether the efficiency gains they measure are actually distributed equitably among the population (Birdsall and Nellis 2002:3–4). In the United Kingdom, for instance, electric-

ity producers and shareholders captured all the economic gains from privatization, while consumers and the government were net economic losers (Newbery and Pollitt 1997:269). The result of all these factors is a significant gap between the reported economic benefits of privatization and its apparent social costs.

Environmental Implications

From an environmental perspective, the outcomes of privatization rest heavily on initial negotiations between the government and the private company and particularly on the details of the contract drawn between the two. Inappropriate water privatization contracts, for example, might undermine conservation efforts and reduce attention to water quality. Or they might fail to insist on minimum water flows in rivers and streams that are needed to keep aquatic ecosystems healthy (Gleick et al. 2002:iv, 37–38). Conversely, when environmental considerations are factored in at an early stage, privatization has the potential to promote environmental goals. For instance, through a combination of environmental audits, detailed environmental provisions in contracts, and mandated compliance with existing environmental standards, the environmental performance of steel-making facilities in Mexico and Kazakhstan greatly improved after privatization (Lovei and Gentry 2002:63, 69–70).

While the available evidence is limited, experience from the electricity sector suggests that environmental concerns tend to get short shrift in privatization efforts (Dubash 2002:157). A review of recent sector reforms—which often feature privatization of power production and distribution—revealed that technocrats from energy and finance ministries have dominated the restructuring process in the countries studied. Representatives from environment ministries or civil society groups have had little or no voice in the design process, and opportunities to promote environmental outcomes have been missed. For example, Bulgaria's international commitment to reduce greenhouse gases was not factored into the country's electricity reforms, despite the considerable opportunity it had to reduce emissions by providing incentives to upgrade inefficient industrial plants and engage in other energy-saving measures (Doukov et al. 2002:97).

Experience in the electricity sector suggests a more general point about privatization. Economic reforms such as privatization have often arisen in closed processes. In these circumstances, privatization has sometimes been pursued to achieve narrow goals, rather than as a means to a range of public policy objectives including greater efficiency, wider access, better service, and reduced environmental impact. A more open and democratic process of economic governance that allowed for broad debate about the goals of reform would substantially increase the potential for incorporating social and environmental goals into privatization reforms (Dubash 2002:170).

In many cases of apparent decentralization, the answer is no. Ministry staff in a local branch office may answer only to their bosses in the capital city and have little local accountability. The same may be true of a local forestry cooperative, women's association, or NGO that needs answer only to its members, who are only a subset of the community (Agrawal and Ribot 1999:494; Ribot 1999:6).

In fact, a transfer of power to a local ministry, unelected committee, NGO, or similar institution may not bring real empowerment to the local level and thus may not necessarily be a beneficial form of decentralization. On the other hand, devolving power to a democratically elected body—an institu-

tion that citizens can hold responsible for its decisions through public hearings or by voting them out of office—can effectively broaden public participation and bring about more equitable natural resource management (Agrawal and Ribot 1999:478–479).

The role of the central government and its relationship to local governments and communities is another critical issue that can determine whether decentralization merely improves government efficiency or actually empowers citizens and engenders real participation. When the central government safeguards its right to make all major decisions or vests only branch offices of the government with authority,

Box 5.4 Why Does a Local Voice Matter?

One reason to think decentralization can lead to more just and satisfied communities is the fact that most people want to have a say in their own affairs. They resent the idea of a distant bureaucracy telling them what to do with their water, farms, or forests. The results of a 1996 study conducted in 14 municipalities in Nicaragua show a passionate support for grassroots environmental control: 65 percent of people surveyed opposed the concentration of resources and decision-making in the central government, and 68 percent believed that municipal governments could do things better. Ninety-seven percent believed the best way to solve problems was through citizen participation (Larson 2002:6).

But theoretically, decentralization reforms can do more than promote efficient government. Carried out in ways that genuinely increase citizen involvement in government and local environmental decisions, decentralization should also benefit the environment and social justice.

Real life experience also shows that decentralization can tap local environmental protection strategies. Communities that have the right to manage their own lands and are given a stake in the outcome of their conservation efforts can be very successful at managing ecosystems. Experience with community-based natural resource management—in which people work collectively to manage local forests, wildlife, or other resources—suggests that when communities are the primary implementers of a protection plan, they are more likely to make the plan work. They see tangible benefits in complying with harvesting rules, allocations of water rights, or other resource management plans. India provides many examples of communities that have adopted self-imposed restrictions on how local forests will be harvested to prevent the resource's destruction (Kothari 2000:3–4). In much of Southeast Asia, community forestry helps mitigate conflicts over use rights, reduce illegal cutting, and stabilize forest cover.

Local governments and community groups also may be more knowledgeable about the natural resources in their area and the demands on them than will the staff of a state or

national agency (Ribot 2001:5). For example, the people in the village of Bhaonta-Kolyala and other villages in the Arvari river basin in the Indian state of Rajasthan are regulating natural resource management as a "parliament" because they understand just how essential the forests are for water, fuel, and fodder. They try to manage the area using ecological, rather than administrative boundaries because they view development, land use, cultural, and other processes as interconnected (Kothari 2000:5,9).

In the same vein, several Indian villages involved in joint forestry management projects with the state have resisted government proposals to create commercial forest monocultures of single tree species. They believe a monoculture won't benefit nature or provide the diverse non-timber forest products they rely on throughout the year (Kothari 2000:11).

By contrast, when government bureaucrats in a central ministry office impose environmental rules or restrict local access to resources, the results are often disappointing. This is especially true when local communities disagree with the national government's strategy and feel excluded from participation in its design (Agrawal 2000:57). People may simply ignore the new rules—especially those that contradict their normal patterns of resource use—and find ways to surreptitiously break them. They may even accelerate their use of a regulated resource, fearing that they will eventually lose access altogether (McKean 2000:35).

When authorities declared a section of South Africa's coast a protected area and barred subsistence mussel harvesters from the resource they had stewarded sustainably for centuries, the harvesters began to gather the mussels secretly at night, damaging the mussel beds in the process (see Chapter 8). Similarly, throughout the 1990s, local fishermen in the Galapagos Islands fought harvest regulations on spiny lobster, sea cucumbers, and sharks that were meant to protect the ecosystem. Frustrated by the government's management process and angered by restrictions on access to the marine resources, the fishermen ransacked research stations, harassed tourists, and killed giant tortoises (Rohter 2000:A1).

the chances of increased local participation in natural resource management are reduced. Lack of secure rights to manage and benefit from natural resource management further diminishes the incentive for people to invest in natural resource conservation and sustainable use.

On the other hand, decentralization that is democratic and empowering does not necessarily come about when central governments simply hand management responsibilities over to local institutions and then step out of the picture. Effective decentralization usually occurs when central governments actively implement the necessary reforms, provide appropriate training for local actors so that they can use their new powers effectively, and defend the rights of marginalized citizens—women, the poor, ethnic minorities—to participate (Larson 2003a:19).

Decentralization Today: Partial Progress

Central governments around the world are beginning to relinquish some important responsibilities over natural resources to local institutions and communities:

- Since 1989, the CAMPFIRE program in Zimbabwe has given rural local authorities some rights to manage wildlife and collect revenues from such activities as game hunting and tourism (CAMPFIRE 2003).

- Viet Nam's 1998 Water Law calls for a more integrated approach to watershed management and has devolved irrigation management rights to local "Commune People's Committees" (Dupar and Badenoch 2002:14).

- In Mali, 1994 regulations give rural communes the right to protect all or part of their forest resources (Ribot 1995:1–2).

- Nepal's 1993 Forest Act legalized "forestry user groups," giving them the right to own the trees, although ownership of the land remains with the state. User groups develop management plans, set prices for forest products, and determine how surplus income is spent (Agrawal and Ribot 1999:483). By June 1997, there were 6,000 user groups managing 450,000 hectares of forests, with another 6,000 waiting for formal registration (DFID et al. 2002:39).

- Thailand's ambitious experiments in decentralized government include granting nominal responsibility for the sustainable management of land, water, and forest resources to new local government entities at the sub-district level called "tambons." Tambons are charged with formulating development plans and funding them based on proposals submitted by villages within their jurisdictions (Dupar and Badenoch 2002:12).

- Guatemala's regulatory framework for forest management grants municipal governments the right to 50 percent of the taxes levied on logging permits, plus subsidies for reforestation. Municipalities are also responsible for establishing environment commissions that work closely with the national agency in charge of the forestry sector to control illegal logging and supervise legal logging, and to develop municipal forestry plans with popular participation (Larson 2003a:12).

- In Honduras, the Law of Modernization and Development in the Agricultural Sector (1992) gave elected local governments the right to make decisions about logging and management plans (including controlled burning, land use plans, the creation of protected areas, and citizen watershed protection projects) for about 30 percent of the country's forests (Larson 2003a:9–10).

These and other decentralization reforms are beginning to change the process of making resource and conservation decisions and reshape the way natural resource management takes place. They promise to have profound effects on who manages, uses, and benefits from nature and on the subsequent impacts on the environment.

To date, however, the results of decentralization have been mixed. Decentralization clearly can be good for environmental stewardship, livelihoods, and local empowerment, but only if done properly—and that is rare. Some of the obstacles to successful decentralization are explored below.

The Difficulty of Meaningful Power Transfer

Decentralization reforms often enable only limited involvement of citizens in environmental governance. Typically, local governments or community groups are granted some rights, but with limited scope or subject to significant central government oversight (USAID 2002:29). Examples abound:

- In Senegal, 1998 forestry laws grant rural councils the right to manage forests within their jurisdictions. By law, the councils can refuse to permit timber production, or they can assign plots to individuals, cooperatives, or corporations to cut wood according to government-prescribed rules. However, despite these laws, the Forest Service still makes the most critical decision: whether or not a forest surrounding a community will be cut at all. In practice, local populations and village councils cannot forbid commercial use of forests within their jurisdictions (Agrawal and Ribot 1999:2,18–19; Ribot 2000:478).

- In mainland Southeast Asia, central governments let communities make day-to-day decisions about forest management, but the most influential decisions about land use are retained by the ministries. In Cambodia, for example, the central government sets annual logging quotas for each province (Dupar and Badenoch 2002:15).

■ In the Nghe An province in northern Viet Nam, central governments dictate so many guidelines that they leave little scope for local discretion by district officials who have inherited new responsibilities for forest land allocation and management. District officials can only distribute forest lands as smaller parcels to individual households, not in larger chunks to communities as shared lands. This is in spite of local preference for community-owned forests, which can provide whole communities with safety nets during times of poor crop production (Dupar and Badenoch 2002:36).

Sometimes local institutions are granted responsibilities for implementing decisions or administering services, but not the power to generate revenue, for instance by setting fees or levying fines (World Bank 1999:123–124). A local government might be charged with maintaining a water supply system, but lack the fiscal authority to adjust the price charged for water use. In the same vein, central governments sometimes retain the most lucrative fiscal powers—say, the right to assess wildlife hunting fees or the right to allocate revenue from a logging or mining operation—while granting rural community committees or governments less valuable rights to subsistence-scale harvesting, such as the collection of firewood or bamboo. Rarely do local

institutions receive substantial discretionary power over the disposition of a resource *and* its economic benefits.

Central government reluctance to devolve real decision-making power is based in part on the assumption that local populations lack the technical or scientific knowledge necessary to husband resources, and do not have the aptitude to learn (Agrawal and Ribot 1999:29; Ribot 2000:477). In addition, central governments often fear losing their own power, or believe local governments to be incompetent (Larson 2003a:19). Of course, problems of local government incapacity are real (see below). But too often, central governments use this as an excuse not to decentralize, rather than address the weakness of local institutions by providing more training for local governments, strengthening municipal associations, promoting fair elections, and trying to increase civic awareness and public participation (Larson 2003a:20).

More enlightened decentralization efforts recognize that many natural resource decisions require no special capacities beyond what local communities already possess (USAID 2002:30). For example, local watershed councils consisting of village residents in the arid northern reaches of the Indian state of Gujarat have shown themselves to be perfectly competent to manage local water resources, which they depend on for survival (see Chapter 8). Experts suggest that decentralization is most likely to succeed if the central government views the technical aspects of management as a partnership to which both the state and citizens contribute. In addition, the central government must be willing to actually seek and incor-

Table 5.1 Decentralization: Pro and Con

Decentralization must be carefully managed to yield good outcomes.

For	Against
• Promotes democracy because it provides better opportunities for local residents to participate in decision-making.	• Undermines democracy by empowering local elites, beyond the reach or concern of central power.
• Increases efficiency in delivery of public services—delegation of responsibility avoids bottlenecks and bureaucracy.	• Worsens delivery of service in the absence of effective controls and oversight.
• Leads to higher quality of public services, because of local accountability and sensitivity to local needs.	• Quality of services deteriorates due to lack of local capacity and insufficient resources.
• Enhances social and economic development, which rely on local knowledge.	• Gains arising from participation of local people offset by risks of increased corruption and inequalities among regions.
• Increases transparency, accountability, and the response capacity of government institutions.	• Promises too much and overloads capacity of local governments.
• Allows greater political representation for diverse political, ethnic, religious, and cultural groups in decision-making.	• Creates new or ignites dormant ethnic and religious rivalries.
• Increases political stability and national unity by allowing citizens to better control public programs at the local level.	• Weakens states because it can increase regional inequalities, lead to separatism, or undermine national financial governance.
• Acts as a spawning ground for new political ideas; leads to more creative and innovative programs.	• Gains in creativity offset by risk of empowering conservative local elites.

Source: Adapted from ICHRP 2002:8.

porate local input on how best to design resource management systems.

Accountability and Representation

Decentralization works best when the central government cedes responsibility for environmental management to an institution that must answer to the people, is subject to enforcement or sanctions for poor performance, and will be obliged to explain or justify its actions.

A good example can be found in Kumaon district of the Indian state of Uttaranchal in the Himalayas. Since 1931, the government has permitted villagers to form nearly 3,000 forest councils, which have the right to formally manage and control nearly one quarter of the forests in the district. The councils are elected directly by villagers. A forest council can be formed when one third of the village population petitions the District Collector, the head of revenue administration in the district. Councils have five to nine members, and all adult villagers are eligible to vote or run for election to the councils (Agrawal and Ribot 1999:481).

Elections are held at periodic intervals in the presence of a Forest Council Inspector, who is part of the Revenue Department. Villagers can attend meetings of the council and lodge complaints about its performance—a timely and specific constraint on the arbitrary exercise of power by council members. In addition, a council member's right to hold office can be challenged if evidence of wrongdoing is available. Councils are also accountable to the district administration for accurate recordkeeping and enforcement of Forest Council rules (Agrawal and Ribot 1999:481-483; Agrawal 2001:208-211).

But the Kumaon experience is far from widespread. As mentioned earlier, decentralization often simply transfers authority over marine areas, forests, or other resources to lower levels of the central government itself, such as a field officer of the forest ministry. In such cases, no local accountable institution that directly represents the citizenry is strengthened. The ministry agent is not accountable to local constituents, only to his or her superiors within the central government. Such reforms may bring decision-making or services closer to citizens, but they will not necessarily involve citizens more deeply in the design of the policies or resource management plans that guide local decisions.

A Dearth of Democratic Institutions

Sometimes decentralization's potential is frustrated by the lack of an appropriate institution to which powers can be successfully devolved. Democratically elected institutions are often considered the best candidates to receive decentralized powers from the central government. Elections give citizens the opportunity to judge the performance of an institution—whether it is a local government or village council. If elected officials cannot justify their decisions, they can be voted out of office (Dupar and Badenoch 2002:3).

However, elections alone do not necessarily ensure adequate representation of citizen interests. In Senegal, for example, rural councils have been granted some power over forest decisions and are elected bodies. Yet, candidates for these councils are selected by political parties, reducing their direct accountability to voters. Accordingly, many villagers feel that the elected councilors represent the interests of these parties rather than the local people (Agrawal and Ribot 1999:20). To make these rural councils democratic would require admitting independent candidates in local elections.

Elections are, therefore, a necessary but insufficient condition to establish the accountability of the local body, whether it is a rural council, NGO, government agency, or municipal government (Crook and Sverrisson 2001:7). Institutions can also offer other means of ensuring that their dealings will be transparent and responsive to the public interest, including (World Bank 1999:122; 2001:1-3):

■ Holding deliberations that are open to the public

■ Using internal practices that promote accountability, such as keeping open records of decisions and deliberations, using merit-based personnel policies, and requiring that financial records be fully auditable, and

Nicaragua: Decentralization Without the Power of the Purse

In 1990, Nicaragua created elected municipal governments. Reforms to the municipalities law in 1997 granted local officials important responsibilities for managing their territories in general, including natural resources. However, local governments were not given control over most income-generating aspects of natural resources, such as the right to enter into contracts for logging, mining, and fishing. These rights are reserved for the central government.

Municipal governments have the right to express their opinions prior to central government approval of resource exploitation requests, including both requests for concessions on national lands, and extraction permits on private lands. Up until recently, however, the central government did not always request local government opinion. In addition, a dissenting opinion by local government is not binding and can simply be ignored.

The central government has also failed to transfer sufficient funds to allow local governments to meet their obligations to constituents. In the case of forests, the law mandates that 25 percent of forest license revenues be returned to the municipal jurisdiction in which the logging takes place, but the central government only began to comply with this obligation in 2000, and some communities still claim that they do not receive their full share (Larson 2003b).

■ Publicly disclosing how they comply with central government laws, rules, budget constraints, and oversight.

Other mechanisms of keeping local institutions that manage natural resources responsive to the public include availability of legal recourse for citizens, open media coverage of local issues and government proceedings, and monitoring and evaluation of local government performance based on benchmarking and citizen feedback (World Bank 2003:127).

Capacity to Exercise New Responsibilities

Local governments often face serious challenges in handling their new responsibilities for natural resource management. They may need additional staff capacity or skills training to carry out the various aspects of public consultation and transparency required for a sound decision-making process. They may need more capacity to implement and enforce their decisions. For example, a recent analysis of Uganda found that the majority of local government officials have limited levels of education and resources and often do not understand what their new role entails when powers are decentralized to them (Watt et al. 2000:48).

In many cases, local governments also lack the budgets to carry out their new mandates. A recent analysis of decentral-

ized forest management in Latin America found this to be largely true (Larson 2003a:7, 10–11, 14). For example, when Costa Rica granted local municipalities authority over logging in some forests, the new responsibility came with no funding, supervision, information, or technical assistance (Larson 2003a:14).

Identifying sustainable practices at the community level can also present a challenge for local institutions. Central governments or other agencies that promote decentralization should not assume that local people and their representatives necessarily know how to manage natural resources sustainably (Enters and Anderson 1999). Decentralization's proponents sometimes make romantic assumptions about local people's ability to live in harmony with nature and utilize traditional practices to safeguard the environment. But in fact, local people often desire technical assistance from outside the community to improve their agricultural productivity and management of forests, water, and land. Indeed, decentralization's potential lies in empowering communities and their representatives to articulate their priorities, and to draw upon both appropriate local knowledge and suitable outside expertise to realize those objectives. That expertise could come from such diverse sources as government line agencies, international donors or NGOs, or the private sector.

Power Transfer to Elite Interests

Rather than amplifying the voice of the community, many decentralization reforms actually strengthen nonrepresentative local authorities, shifting decision-making power to local elites. This is common in some African countries, where power is often transferred to nondemocratic groups such as traditional chieftains, religious organizations, NGOs, or businesses. None of these is formally accountable to the wider community and may bring only a narrow section of the citizenry into the decision-making process (Ribot 2002c:12; 2003:55–56). An NGO might prioritize the interests of its members, donors, and leadership. A business might emphasize only its commercial interests. Traditional indigenous leaders might be inclined to maintain cultural norms of exclusion of the poor, minorities, or women from participation in local decisions or access to local resources.

Another danger is domination of the local electoral process or local institutions by the wealthiest citizens or business interests (Dupar and Badenoch 2002:46). From Burkina Faso to Cameroon, Mali, and Zimbabwe, there are cases of special interests dominating the governance process while local people's environmental interests are ignored. The same is true in Bolivia. There, municipal governments have gained a larger role in forest management. However, local merchants, professionals, ranchers, and sawmill operators often control the municipal government. Accordingly, they may focus on expanding access to timber royalties, rather than on restricting practices that degrade forests, or pursuing sustainable land use planning (Pacheco 2002:5).

Supporting Better Decentralization

As discussed earlier, whether decentralization successfully promotes fairer and greener governance depends primarily on transferring real discretionary power over resources to local institutions that are accountable to local resource users. This was the main conclusion from a 2002 conference that examined decentralized natural resource management in 15 developing countries in Africa, Asia, and Latin America (Ribot 2002b:1–3).

However, other factors are critical as well—factors that capitalize on the mutual strengths of central government and local institutions and give citizens appropriate incentives for conservation.

A Balance between Central Government Authority and Local Empowerment

As local institutions take on more day-to-day authority for decisions about natural resources, central and regional agencies must guide these efforts, supporting them financially and technically and insisting that sustainability is factored into local management plans. This may involve (Caldecott and Lutz 1998:176; Smoke 2000:20; DFID et al. 2002:31; Dupar and Badenoch 2002:3):

- Developing procedures and standards to help local governments improve operations and increase their transparency

- Facilitating more inclusive public participation processes within local institutions and promoting social equity to ensure that women, the poor, and minorities are not dissuaded from taking part in consultations or serving on councils or committees

- Building local governments' capacity to elicit and guide community participation, and to absorb and respond to the input they receive as a result

- Educating citizens about their responsibilities and their role in making government more responsive

- Dealing with market failures, such as agriculture or water subsidies, that are beyond the control of local governments yet factor heavily in environmental decisions, and

- Balancing local interests with larger-scale issues of biodiversity protection, and drafting national standards for sustainable resource use.

In practice, effectively balancing the power of citizens, local institutions, and regional and national governments is difficult. It may require changes in how these groups traditionally work, manage, or make decisions. Central government officials who are accustomed to making most major

Bolivia: Partial Decentralization's Partial Benefits

In 1996, sweeping policy and institutional changes in Bolivia gave municipal governments and citizens unprecedented authority over their local forests. Among the provisions of the new forestry law (Forestry Law 1700):

- Municipalities are charged with administration of up to 20 percent of public forest lands, which must be used for the benefit of Local Community Associations—groups of traditional forest users, peasant communities, and indigenous populations that depend on the forests within a municipality (Contreras-Hermosilla and Rios 2002:12).

- Municipal governments inherit some financial powers. They also receive 25 percent of royalties from forest concessions and fees from clear-cutting operations (Contreras-Hermosilla and Rios 2002:12).

- Municipal governments are charged with helping to ensure that timber concessions and sawmills comply with forestry regulations.

- The public can become directly involved in forest law enforcement. Private citizens can use a special authorization or warrant granted by the office of the Forest Superintendent (part of the Ministry of Sustainable Development and Environment) to inspect field operations (Contreras-Hermosilla and Rios 2002:11).

Although this move toward decentralized forest management in Bolivia is still in its nascent stages, it is clear that the partial empowerment of local community associations is giving a voice to many people who previously lacked the right to participate meaningfully. Municipal governments are also gaining a stronger role in environmental decisions. But, at least initially, these governments are constrained by legal ambiguities about their powers and a lack of funding to carry out their new duties. The central government's forest superintendents are reluctant to turn logging revenues over to the municipalities, some of which lack technical and managerial capacity to implement forest management plans. By mid-2000, the government had assigned just 560,000 hectares of forests (out of Bolivia's 53 million forested hectares) to 3 of the country's 104 municipalities (Contreras-Hermosilla and Rios 2002:22).

Who is Really Empowered to Manage Nepal's Terai?

Since the implementation of the 1993 Forest Act, villagers living in the buffer zones of protected areas in the Terai, a region in the lowlands of Nepal, have had the right to organize into community "users groups" of farmers, and timber and firewood gatherers. Through the elected leaders of these groups, villagers have the legal right to participate in forest management. Government officials had hoped that this initiative would reduce the level and intensity of conflicts between local populations and park rangers.

In practice, though, users groups mainly participate in activities sponsored by officials in the Department of National Parks and Wildlife Conservation, such as clearing underbrush, delimiting forest areas, and participating in protection committees. Those officials retain control of most decisions about resource management, while allowing local people the right to manage their users

groups and harvest some subsistence products from the protected area. Extensive regulations forbid the use of park resources except for a limited period during the year. Villagers and members of users groups can work in the park—maintaining trenches, planting vegetation, and related tasks—but as paid labor, not as participants in the design of any management plans. Illegal harvest of fodder and firewood from the protected areas continues apace, and benefits to locals have changed little since the program began.

So far, changes in natural resource management have not provided significant incentives to citizens to maintain the resources, or changed the balance of power between the central government and local institutions—some of the hallmarks of true decentralization (Agrawal and Ribot 1999:483–485).

decisions unilaterally and exerting control over local authorities must embrace more local participation–an approach that may meet with bureaucratic resistance (Brinkerhoff and Honadle 1996:26). At the same time, local governments must learn to cope with new demands from citizens for greater accountability and participation.

Many institutions, both at central government and local levels, are ill-prepared for the challenge of citizen participation. An analysis of the forestry sectors in India, Sri Lanka, and Zambia suggests that it is difficult for bureaucrats in the forestry sector to make the transition to more participatory engagement with citizens at the grassroots level. Typically, members of the forestry services in those countries serve as a police force for the forests, preventing illegal harvesting and arresting miscreants. Now, the same bureaucrats must work as part of joint forest management programs, sharing responsibilities with local groups. This is a major shift in their jobs, and requires very different skills (Manor 2002:2).

Citizens must also adapt to make decentralized natural resource management effective. They must be aware of and concerned about the new responsibilities that have been given to their local institutions. They must know what their leaders are doing and hold them accountable. Otherwise, decentralization can actually increase opportunities for corruption or waste, as public officials at lower levels gain new

powers without oversight, or are given the power to spend money without accordant responsibilities for revenue collection or budgets (World Bank 2002:108). Mechanisms for effective local oversight must gradually come into play as well, such as third-party auditing of financial records, the development of regional Inspectors General offices, and so on. The involvement of a robust investigative press is also helpful in making local accountability work (Ribot 2002a:29–31).

Decentralization that Respects Ecosystems

Central governments have the responsibility to make decentralized management work at an ecosystem scale. Ecosystems may span many local jurisdictions and serve many communities, each of which may take on some management responsibilities after decentralization. It may fall to the central government to coordinate these efforts, to introduce a large-scale perspective, and to establish mechanisms to resolve conflicts and establish communication networks. Otherwise, decentralization reforms will fail to capture a key potential benefit: the chance to take a larger, ecosystem-based view of environmental management.

China's series of reforms decentralizing management to villages in the Baoshan region of Yunnan Province, for example, have not improved the environment. Villages lack the capacity to address conflicts and competition for natural resources between upland and lowland communities. Nor have government agencies coordinated a plan within watersheds to protect clean water flows—for example, to monitor and limit the flooding caused by upland soil erosion and deforestation (Dupar and Badenoch 2002:33).

Similarly, in Bolivia, municipalities inherited a great deal more power under new forest laws. But many municipalities with abundant forest resources are relatively isolated, with few links to other levels of government. In some watersheds, several different municipalities control forest segments whose management should be coordinated if the resource is to remain healthy. Yet, these jurisdictions continue to operate in isolation (Contreras-Hermosilla and Rios 2002:22).

Transferring the Mandate for Sustainability

The rights and rules detailed in decentralization reforms themselves can provide tremendous incentive—or disincentive—for conservation by local people and institutions. Two incentives for sustainable management are the right of resource access, and the right to the revenue from the resource itself (see below). Local authorities and residents have little reason to help protect a resource that they cannot use or benefit from (see Box 5.5).

But along with rights of resource access, the central government must also transfer some specific responsibilities for resource protection to newly empowered local governments, councils, and users groups. Without some stipulation that they will be held accountable for sustainable development, local authorities may choose to use their new powers for quick resource exploitation and development, particularly in areas where the potential revenue from natural resources is high. Such is the case in Indonesia, where district governments' ability to allocate small-scale timber licenses and cash in on the revenues has effectively opened protected forests to illegal logging (Ribot 2002c:10). Similarly, in China, local authorities rapidly logged timber stands to generate quick cash. By 1998, the central government had to impose a logging ban to protect watersheds from further deterioration, since the highly decentralized policy had failed to do so (Dupar and Badenoch 2002:33,39).

Donors can help transfer the mandate for sustainability to governments—both national and local—as the World Bank did with a 1992 structural adjustment loan to the Philippines. To promote community-based law enforcement, the Bank included conditions for forest monitoring and enforcement and asked the government to create "Multisectoral Forest Committees." These committees were established at the village, province, region, and national levels and include representatives from local communities, the forest department, police, customs and other state agencies, NGOs, and civic groups. A village committee, for example, tracks activities in and around forest concessions, while a provincial committee tracks shipments of illegal logs between provinces. With support from a World Bank legal team, thousands of people

guilty of forest crimes have been apprehended and prosecuted, and almost all large-scale illegal logging has been halted (Brunner et al. 1999:7-8).

Secure Tenure Is Important

Grants of secure tenure over resources are an essential ingredient of community-level conservation. If the central government can easily revoke the rights of resource management or access that it has delegated, citizens have less reason to invest in soil fertility, watershed protection, forest regeneration, or other long-term conservation measures (USAID 2002:22). For example, as farmers make investments in irrigation systems or trees on a parcel of land, the importance of secure, long-term tenure over that specific parcel of land sharply increases.

Without having long-term tenure security embedded in decentralization laws, local authorities or residents may take advantage of a forest, marine fish stocks, or other resources while the opportunity lasts. In Indonesia, for example, local

Brazil's Participatory Budgeting

Some 140 of the 5,500 municipalities in Brazil have adopted the practice of participatory budgeting. The idea is to have community representatives—generally from low-income districts—get together to decide how to allocate a municipality's budget. This may involve determining how much to invest in education, health, water supply, or sewage, or where to locate a new park or what roads to pave. There are also distributive criteria to ensure that poorer areas receive more funding than well-off ones, no matter what the representatives want.

Porto Alegre has used participatory budgeting since 1989. As many as 40,000 citizens participated in public meetings to allocate about half the city's budget in 1999, taking part in several rounds of meetings and debates over 9 months, starting with district-based meetings in gyms and churches. The meetings begin with formal reports by the city government on the previous year's expenditures. Ultimately, through the democratically elected representatives, each district produces rankings of its priorities, such as paved roads, water lines, or beach clean-up. The process has prompted some interesting decisions. In one case, the city turned down the construction of a five-star hotel proposed for the site of a decommissioned power plant, opting instead for a public park and convention hall. Urban service provision has shown some positive signs, too, with sewer and water connections in Porto Alegre increasing from 75 to 98 percent of residences between 1988 and 1997, and the number of schools quadrupling since 1986 (Goldsmith 1999:1–4; Souza 2002:1).

Box 5.5 Namibia's Conservancies: Nature in the Hands of the People

In 1996, the Namibian government began encouraging its citizens to take the lead in managing lands that were owned communally. A landmark policy encourages Namibians to form "conservancies"—legally recognized associations governed by community members who live in designated areas. These conservancies are granted the right to benefit directly from wildlife resources in their particular areas, and are responsible for their sustainable use and management.

The process of establishing a conservancy is straightforward and transparent. Local communities mobilize and register community members, adopt a constitution and by-laws, identify boundaries of management areas, commit to a plan for sustained yield management of wildlife, organize resource monitoring, and agree on a plan for the distribution of benefits (Anderson 2003). The central government approves the establishment of the conservancies and their associated plans, a process that usually takes less than 6 months (Anderson 2003).

Since the late 1990s, this "decentralized" conservancy system has:

■ greatly increased wildlife populations, which were previously shrinking;

■ increased community income. The wages collected from wildlife tourism have grown from about 500,000 Namibian dollars in 1996 to more than 6 million in 2001 (USAID 2002:14). Benefits are evident in better provision of social services and greater ability of residents to pay school fees;

■ increased local participation in resource management. Fifteen conservancies are now registered, involving more than 30,000 people, and more than 35 others are being formed. The number of people participating in decisions, including the very poor, has more than tripled (USAID 2002:14), and

■ expanded institutional and technical support for community-based management. For example, the Ministry of the Envi-

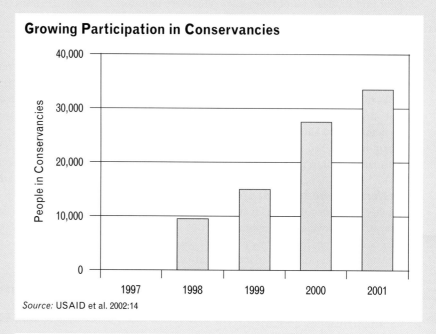

Growing Participation in Conservancies

Source: USAID et al. 2002:14

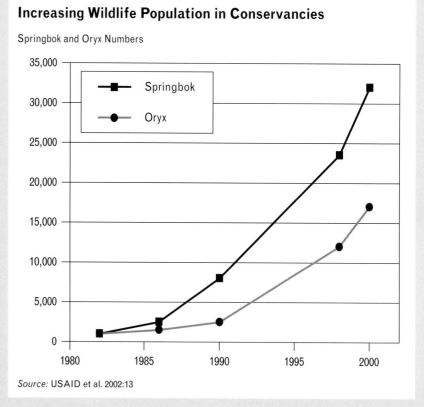

Increasing Wildlife Population in Conservancies

Springbok and Oryx Numbers

Source: USAID et al. 2002:13

ronment and Tourism has created and staffed a Community-Based Natural Resource Management Support Unit with 29 field officers (USAID 2002:14). This unit can help communities negotiate joint ventures with private sector investors for economic activities such as game hunting and ecotourism.

authorities who have been granted access rights to timber stocks are not confident these rights will last, resulting in a heightened level of forest exploitation (Resosudarmo 2002:5).

Encouraging Consultative Processes

Consultative processes–where government representatives and local people join in directed dialogue–can provide citizens with useful opportunities to take stock of local resources and deliberate about production systems and livelihood options together. For example, in the Dak Lak province of western Viet Nam's highlands, farmers have found that the creation of Water Users Associations has catalyzed new discussions about watershed degradation. The associations, which cooperate with local agencies of the central government, have encouraged farmers to view watershed problems more holistically. In working with government agency staff, villagers have increased their own awareness of integrated conservation and development priorities (Dupar and Badenoch 2002:42).

NGOs Can Help

Sometimes NGOs can provide critical incentives for effective natural resource management, the protection of biodiversity, and other local environmental governance challenges. Because of their specialized knowledge, NGOs can offer important information on resource issues to help local officials understand the environmental implications of their decisions. Their networking skills and contacts with international donors can also help link local governments to wider conservation interests, possible sources of funding for environmental projects, and contacts at higher levels of state government that can provide assistance in meeting local goals.

Furthermore, researchers and nongovernmental groups have an important role to play in documenting sustainable natural resource management systems at the community level and debunking policy myths that blame local people for resource destruction. They can also be a critical part of the pressure for real decentralization as they create alliances among donors and civil society to compel central governments to undertake meaningful change (Larson 2003a:20).

The watchful eyes of NGOs add an important level of local oversight to decentralization reforms. Where local institutions ignore conservation interests and public participation, NGOs can press for more inclusive governance and more accountability. In Nicaragua, NGOs have provided that pressure for good governance and attention to environmental interests where local governments have tended to accede to the interests of local elites. In the county of Cua-Bocay, a local NGO organized an alliance of community groups to oppose a mining concession; this convinced the municipal council to vote against the concession. Some NGOs and funders have pressured municipal governments to form Municipal Environment Commissions to advise on resource management decisions. Nicaraguan NGOs also add their influence in legislative affairs, drafting resolutions and ordinances regarding natural resource management and presenting them to the municipal councils for negotiation and consideration (Larson 2002:7).

Careful and Structured Implementation of Reforms

Decentralization is often implemented haphazardly and hastily in times of financial crisis or political stress, or using a model that has not been tailored to fit a particular region's unique circumstances (Smoke 2000:4). Poorly structured efforts actually threaten both environmental management and equity. In Zimbabwe, for example, the financially strapped central government abruptly stopped funding the maintenance of community-based rural water supplies, devolving this responsibility to the local level. But local communities and district councils were not prepared to take on these management and maintenance responsibilities, and the water supplies deteriorated (Conyers 2002:117). Transferring responsibility over resources carefully and gradually yields better results.

Overall, the case for the environmental benefits of carefully managed decentralization is still being assembled. But enough evidence already exists to reinforce its importance as a supporting condition for equitable and sustainable development. However, key to the success of decentralization is making sure that new local powers are conferred along with the mandate to manage resources sustainably and that this is supported with the resources needed to work out what this means in the local context.

DRIVING BUSINESS ACCOUNTABILITY

Business transparency and accountability are prerequisites for better environmental governance. They are the necessary complement to greater openness on the part of governments and more public participation in government policies. As is the case with government, one of the most potent tools to drive greater business accountability is public access to information. *Public disclosure*–from mandatory pollution reporting, to voluntary "sustainability reporting," to eco-labeling–is the face of a new and more participatory approach to regulating the environmental performance of businesses. Using the tool of disclosure, communities and consumers enter a new relationship with business that can speed the transition to a greener business model.

Getting Business on Board

The link between business and environmental governance is simple. Businesses are among the world's most influential institutions. As society's mechanism for production and consumption, their decisions have significant environmental effects. Those decisions have ever-greater reach as companies globalize and national resources are privatized. Better environmental governance simply isn't possible without business on board. That means sharing information with stakeholders, making decisions in an open and transparent process rather than behind closed boardroom doors, and actively seeking investments that can benefit both the environment and the bottom line.

Greater information disclosure by businesses can help address the weaknesses of traditional regulation.

Beyond Traditional Regulation

Government-imposed regulations, enforced with inspections and penalties for noncompliance, are the traditional means of ensuring that businesses are accountable for their environmental impacts. A typical approach is to limit the amount of pollutants that businesses can release or the rate at which they can extract natural resources. This "command and control" approach has greatly improved air and water quality in most industrial countries (Coglianese and Nash 2001:1, 7).

However, command and control regulation has many limitations. Its success rests on vigorous and timely enforcement. This is difficult in countries where state authority is weak, budgets are constrained, or technical capacity is low. The rigidity of these regulations is also a problem. Many companies and policy-makers contend that standard government regulation doesn't leave them the flexibility to fix environmental problems in the most efficient ways and doesn't encourage improvements beyond those specified by law.

In response, governments have begun to employ market-based approaches to regulation, such as pollution charges and tradable emissions permits. These can also pose serious challenges of design, implementation, monitoring, and enforcement, reducing their effectiveness in many countries (Tietenberg and Wheller 1998).

Nor do traditional regulations address the governance challenges posed by the increasing globalization of corporate activity. In the face of competition to attract business, some nations are less willing or able to regulate transnational corporations effectively. In this case, transnationals largely regulate themselves, with little accountability to communities or consumers for their impacts (see Box 6.1).

Greater information disclosure on the part of businesses can help address some of the weaknesses of traditional regulatory approaches, empowering civil society and local communities to join the regulatory process. There is a growing array of public and private efforts to increase the availability

Box 6.1 Growing Corporate Influence

More than ever before, the public is paying attention to corporate behavior. One reason is the dramatic growth and economic dominance of multinational—or "transnational"—corporations (TNCs). Today, more than 65,000 corporations are transnational, meaning that they do business and control assets in more than one country. Together, these companies control some 850,000 affiliates, or subsidiary companies (UNCTAD 2002:14). Between 1990 and 2000, the sales of the largest one hundred TNCs increased from $3.2 trillion to almost $4.8 trillion (UNCTAD 2002:90).

Foreign Direct Investment 1980–2001

Source: World Bank 2003

Transnationals were also significant local employers. Foreign employment by TNCs—people employed outside of a corporation's home country—grew from 24 million in 1990 to 54 million people in 2001 (UNCTAD 2002:xv).

Investment in foreign operations is a good measure of the increasing economic power of transnational corporations. The value of cross-border mergers and acquisitions—a transaction in which a foreign corporation acquires more than a 10 percent stake in an existing domestic enterprise—skyrocketed from $94 billion to $866 billion between 1996 and 2000 (UNCTAD 2002:12). In developing countries, the number of cross-border mergers and acquisitions increased by 50 percent from 1995 to 1999 (World Bank 2001:40–41).

Transnational corporations are considered to be both global and local citizens. In theory, they are accountable to numerous constituencies. They bring undeniable benefits to local communities, including investment, jobs, and sometimes healthcare, roads, and schools. Yet, they are often perceived as having little accountability to anyone except their shareholders. Some citizens and communities worry that global companies will use their power to evade national regulatory requirements, engage in unfair labor practices, or damage the local environment. Consumers also feel that it is difficult to make informed purchases—and hold companies accountable

of information about companies and their products—and to help consumers, shareholders, workers, and others use that information as a lever to encourage more environmentally friendly business decisions (WRI and USEPA 1999:11–13). These efforts include:

- *Government-mandated pollution disclosure programs,* such as the Toxics Release Inventory, which requires companies in the United States to detail the pollutants and wastes they discharge as a matter of public record.

- *Voluntary corporate disclosure initiatives,* such as industry-wide codes of conduct, or the Global Reporting Initiative, which provides companies with guidelines for generating a "sustainability report" that stakeholders can use to evaluate environmental and social performance.

- *Consumer- and investor-based efforts,* such as socially responsible investing, eco-labels, and product certifications that offer a market-based appeal to companies to make their operations more transparent and to embrace production methods that are less environmentally and socially damaging.

Business Tools for Environmental Accountability

Traditional Accountability Mechanism
- Government-mandated environmental regulations and permits

New Disclosure-Based Mechanisms
- Government-mandated disclosure of environmental performance
  - Pollution registers
  - Mandated corporate environmental reports
- Voluntary corporate initiatives
  - Corporate codes of conduct
  - Voluntary corporate environmental reports
  - Environmental management systems
  - Eco-labels
  - Voluntary industry-government agreements
- Public action and advocacy
  - Socially responsible investing
  - Eco-labels/green consumption

through the marketplace—when a corporation's operations are widely spread and information on their environmental performance in different countries is hard to obtain.

Another reason for the rising public concern about corporate citizenship is the trend toward privatization of natural resources in many countries. Increasingly, governments are allowing private companies to own or manage projects in the energy, telecommunications, transport, and water and sanitation sectors. Between 1990 and 2001, 132 low- and middle-income countries introduced private sector participation in these sectors (World Bank 2002:1). During this period, the private sector assumed the operation or construction of almost 2,500 infrastructure projects in developing countries, with investments totaling $750 billion (World Bank 2002:1). Such privatization shifts the decision-making processes for water and power provision, timber production, mining, and similar natural resource-based activities to organizations that the government and civil society may not have the capacity to hold accountable for compliance with environmental standards and acceptable customer service (Panayotou 1997:60–61). (See Box 5.3.)

Corporate influence on government politics is also a concern. Critics warn that corporations are using their economic muscle and close government connections to coax decision-makers to favor corporate interests over other stakeholders. In the United States, for instance, energy, mining, and waste management industries contributed $29.7 million to political campaigns in 1999–2000, and spent another $159 million on direct lobbying activities in 2000 (Center for Responsive Politics 2003).

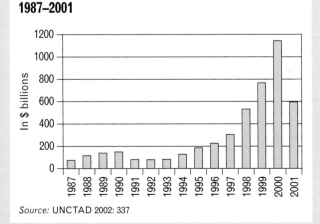

Cross-border Mergers and Acquisitions 1987–2001

Source: UNCTAD 2002: 337

Information Disclosure Is the Key

These information disclosure strategies are beginning to connect businesses to their stakeholders in a direct way. They help backstop and reinforce the minimum standards of environmental performance that governments set, and also help align business objectives with sustainable development goals. In other words, they do not replace standard regulation, but enhance its effectiveness, encouraging businesses to adopt greener behavior to guard their reputations and market power.

Disclosure tools work because they empower the public to hold businesses accountable for their environmental performance. For example, public information about an industrial facility's emissions gives NGOs and community groups the ammunition with which to pressure the worst polluters to improve, and helps government inspectors do their jobs more efficiently. Information about a company's practices in handling toxic chemicals or managing hazardous wastes helps investors avoid companies whose operations or products might expose them to major liabilities, government fines, and expensive lawsuits. In short, public disclosure prevents corporations from relying on invisibility to avoid accountability.

Just as importantly, disclosure offers businesses potential benefits. A company's efforts to track and disclose its wastes, for example, often leads to insights that can increase process efficiency and cut costs (Danish Environmental Protection Agency 2003). Some businesses see information disclosure as positive advertising, using environmental certifications or eco-labels to distinguish themselves from poor environmental performers and to reap rewards in the marketplace. When information disclosure benefits the bottom line in this way, it helps companies develop an internal rationale for making environmentally sound decisions.

The time is ripe for disclosure tools. The cost of information collection and dissemination is falling, while the demand for information about firms and products is on the rise (Ditz and Ranganathan 1997:1; WBCSD 2002:9). That

Box 6.2 A Community's Right to Know: The U.S. Toxics Release Inventory

On December 3, 1984, 45 tons of methyl isocyanate gas leaked from a Union Carbide plant in Bhopal, India. Four safety mechanisms failed to stop the escaping gas, due to inadequate maintenance. The accident killed 3,000 and at least 40,000 were seriously injured (Robins 1990:106; Shrivastava 1996:121, 125).

The tragedy at Bhopal made citizens and NGOs acutely aware of their ignorance about what local industries were producing. In the United States, workers and communities had called for the right to know about chemicals in their workplaces and neighborhoods since the 1970s. Political momentum peaked in 1986, when the U.S. Congress passed the Emergency Planning and Community Right to Know Act. The legislation required the U.S. Environmental Protection Agency to establish a publicly accessible electronic database that would allow users to track the quantities of pollutants released by major businesses to air, land, and water. The database also tracked pollutants and wastes that companies transferred for various "off-site" waste management treatments such as landfill disposal, incineration, chemical treatment, or recycling.

This Toxics Release Inventory (TRI) is specifically intended to make it easy for anyone—journalist, policymaker, investor, parent—to learn exactly what and how much companies are releasing from their smokestacks and discharge pipes. The data from each facility are reported in a standard format, with standardized names for each chemical listed. Thus, they can be compared over time to determine emission patterns and to rank facilities on their emission records.

The database has proven both popular and useful. A government website offers simple instructions for searching the database, making it easy to check the record of industrial facilities (see http://www.epa.gov/tri/index.htm). Other environmental groups also offer convenient access to the data as well as explanations of pollution regulations and human health risks to help interpret the information (see http://www.score card.org/).

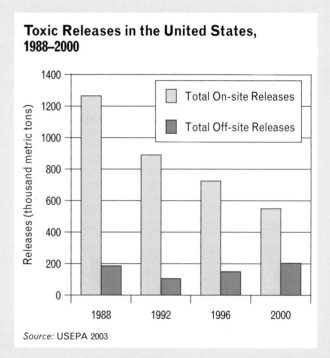

Toxic Releases in the United States, 1988–2000

Source: USEPA 2003

growing demand for corporate transparency and accountability is essential. Businesses don't change their behavior simply because more information about their environmental practices becomes publicly available. They change their practices when employees, consumers, NGOs, and government officials are motivated and able to use the information to force action. Or when companies themselves conclude that disclosing information will boost their competitiveness and protect their standing in the communities in which they operate.

Government-Mandated Disclosure

No business wants to be known as a big polluter. That reputation can hurt them in the marketplace, jeopardize the goodwill of neighboring communities, and invite scrutiny by regulators, investors, and environmentalists. Accordingly, governments increasingly employ the spotlight of public scrutiny to encourage businesses to behave responsibly. Rather than mandate reductions, they mandate that businesses publicly report the pollutants and wastes their facilities produce.

The TRI has inspired notable reductions in emissions from industrial facilities. Working in conjunction with other laws and regulations, the TRI has helped reduce total pollutant releases by 1.5 billion pounds (680 million kg) or 48 percent between 1988 and 2000 (USEPA 2002a:12). This comes despite the fact that the data were never intended to be used by government agents to check for regulatory compliance. Their purpose was simply to inform the public.

The power of public disclosure was clear from the start. When the first TRI data were reported, many firms showing large pollutant releases—making them polluters in the public mind—suffered declines in their stock prices (Hamilton 1995:109). The link between TRI data and public perception proved a powerful stimulus for some companies. In fact, those firms experiencing the largest stock price declines on the day that their TRI emissions were disclosed subsequently reduced their emissions more than their industry peers. Companies with the most significant drop in their stock price reduced 1.84 pounds of pollutants per thousand dollars revenue, compared to about 0.17 pounds by others in the industry (Konar and Cohen 1997:120).

Many companies found that in the long run, the TRI actually helped them. For example, TRI reporting requirements spurred the Haartz Corporation, a U.S. manufacturer of coated fabrics, to install a chemical recycling system to cut its releases of the toxic solvent MEK, saving $200,000 annually (Doa 2003:104). Other companies made reductions that saved them money in fines, and as they paid more attention to each step of the manufacturing process, the quality of their products often improved.

Of course, the TRI is not without flaws. One notable failure is that it does not require small businesses to report their emissions and wastes. Only facilities that manufacture or process over 25,000 pounds of at least one listed TRI chemical, or use more than 10,000 pounds of at least one TRI chemical need to file a report. That leaves many businesses like dry cleaners, gasoline service stations, and a variety of small manufacturers and service providers out of the public eye (Scorecard 2003). In addition, the lag time for making new emissions data available to the public averages 18 months—making it difficult for the public to track a company's current performance (USEPA 2002a; USEPA 2002b).

Another significant flaw is that the TRI offers a definite incentive to businesses to reduce certain kinds of toxic emissions, but not necessarily to reduce the total amount of waste they produce. For example, data show that the amount of "on-site" releases, such as pollutants emitted into the air in the vicinity of a factory, has decreased. But "off-site" releases—chemicals transferred for recycling, incineration, treatment, and landfill—have increased since 1988. This suggests that companies may be storing and treating more of their wastes rather than converting to processes that are inherently less polluting. While this may be an improvement over directly releasing pollutants into a sewer or from a stack, it does not reduce the overall waste stream, and may simply transfer problem substances to another community where final treatment—and potential exposure or contamination—takes place (Harrison and Antweiler 2001:17).

Table 6.1 Global Status of Pollution Registers, 2003

Countries Operating a Pollution Register

Data available to the public on emissions to all media (air, water, and land)

Australia	Ireland*	Korea	Norway*	United Kingdom*
Canada	Japan	Netherlands*	Slovak Republic	United States
Mexico (preparing regulations for new mandatory system)				

Countries that Have Taken Steps Toward a Pollution Register

Have taken concrete steps such as public reporting on pollutants in a single medium, a pilot project, or are members of EU and thus required to participate in the European Polluting Emissions Register

Austria*	Estonia*	Hungary*	Luxembourg*	Slovenia*
Belgium*	Finland*	Italy*	Malta	Spain*
Cyprus*	France*	Latvia*	Poland*	Sweden*
Czech Republic*	Germany*	Lithuania*	Portugal*	Switzerland*
Denmark*	Greece*			

Countries that Have Demonstrated Interest in a Pollution Register

Have worked with UNITAR, UNEP, or with bilateral assistance on designing a pollution register, or actively participated in preparation of the Aarhus Protocol on Pollutant Release and Transfer Registers

Albania	Brazil	Ecuador	Kazakhstan	South Africa
Argentina	Bulgaria*	Egypt	Romania*	Ukraine*
Armenia*	Chile	Georgia*	Russia	Uzbekistan
Azerbaijan	Costa Rica	Macedonia*	Serbia and Montenegro*	Taiwan
Belarus	Croatia*	Moldova*	Tajikistan*	Turkey
Bosnia and Herzegovina*	Cuba	Monaco		

Countries Using or Developing a Public Rating Program

Publicly rates compliance of industrial facilities with national pollution standards, without making public the compliance data

China	Indonesia	Philippines	Thailand

*Country signed the Protocol on Pollutant Release and Transfer Registers In Kiev in May 2003.

Note: A pollution register is also called a "pollutant release and transfer register," or PRTR.

Sources: OECD 2002; Fenerol 2003; Irwin 2003; UNECE 2003b; UNITAR 2003; vandermost 2003

Perhaps the best known example of this strategy in action is the Toxics Release Inventory (TRI) in the United States. The TRI is a plant-by-plant accounting of industrial pollution–a *pollution register*–that the government makes publicly accessible via the Internet and published reports. The TRI has been instrumental in cutting industrial pollutant releases of tracked chemicals by 48 percent from 1988 to 2000, pressuring some firms not only to comply with government regulations, but to reduce pollution beyond their legal obligation (USEPA 2002:12). (See Box 6.2.)

The United States, Canada, the Netherlands, Norway, and the United Kingdom all have at least a decade of experience operating comprehensive pollution registers like the TRI. In response to the success of these registers, other governments have instituted or are in the process of creating their own national pollution registers, which are generically termed "Pollutant Release and Transfer Registers" or "PRTRs."

Today, about 60 countries have developed or are in the process of developing such registers (Petkova et al. 2002:54; Irwin 2003). (See Table 6.1.)

Success of Pollution Registers

Pollution registers are clearly providing information that interests and empowers citizens, investors, and reporters. Since the first release of TRI data in 1989, these pollution listings have become the subject of media reports. Journalists were particularly likely to report on a company with pollution concentrated at a few facilities, or on large chemical releases from companies that were not traditionally considered big polluters, such as those in the paper industry (Hamilton 1995:107).

The TRI data has affected the decisions of stock market investors as well. On the day that TRI data first became available in 1989, the companies included in the inventory suf-

Within 2 days of its rollout, some 3 million Internet users visited the Canadian *Pollution Watch* website and sent 1,200 faxes to polluting companies listed there.

fered statistically significant declines in the market value of their stock. For companies whose emissions were the subject of a media story, the loss in stock value was greater—an average of $6.2 million, according to one analysis. The negative investor reaction reflected the change in expectations about a company's likely pollution-related costs (Hamilton 1995:109–110; Konar and Cohen 1997:112). In other words, investors were surprised by the quantity of pollution their companies produced, and worried about negative publicity and potential clean-up costs.

For communities with the capacity to organize themselves, TRI data can provide a useful bargaining chip to pressure companies to reduce emissions from local factories. Companies cite local activism as one significant factor in their management decisions (Hamilton 1999:106–7, 112, 118), and TRI data are clearly a tool that activists have begun to use. Between 1989 and 1994, for example, public

interest groups and local activists used TRI data in over 200 reports to give substance to their demands to lower pollutant emissions (Orum 1994:1). Today, citizens in any community in the United States can use the Internet to print a tailored emission report from the TRI database for their county, and can even send a message or question about their findings to the government.

The Canadian National Pollutant Release Inventory (NPRI) has followed a course similar to that of the TRI, providing communities and consumers with information that they have used to pressure Canadian companies to reduce their emissions. Within 2 days of its rollout, some 3 million Internet users visited the *Pollution Watch* website created by Canadian NGOs to give easy access to NPRI data, and sent roughly 1,200 faxes to polluting companies listed there (Antweiler and Harrison 2003:497).

Some Shortcomings

Although countries have adopted pollution registers with unusual speed, governments face numerous obstacles implementing them. For example, companies may not know how to estimate their pollutant releases. They are often unaccustomed to sharing information with the public and fear that the data will be misinterpreted, bring bad publicity, or reveal confidential information about their operations. Governments often find it difficult to align the data that companies report with the information governments collect separately for enforcement purposes. Enforcement-related data may be fragmented among different government departments focused on air emissions, water discharges, and waste, each with its own approach and monitoring criteria. The absence of common or legal definitions—for example, how to define waste—can be a problem as well.

In addition, while pollution registers are clearly a useful and accessible source of information on company behavior, they do not give a complete picture of all pollutant releases. In general, they track only a fraction of the more than 210,000 substances that are regulated or covered by chemical inventories worldwide (CEC 2002:75). For example, the U.S. TRI tracks about 650 chemicals (USEPA 2002:1). Most pollution registers do not apply to small companies or those that manufacture or process less than some threshold amount of listed chemicals, and most do not report toxic releases from use of consumer products such as automobiles.

Nor do the reporting requirements of pollution inventories apply to all economic sectors—a fact which can skew the public's understanding of pollution problems. For example, until 1998 the metals mining sector was not required to report to the U.S. TRI. Only when mining companies were added to the inventory did it become clear that that sector's emissions were higher than that of any other economic sector—accounting for 47 percent of total releases in 2000 (USEPA 2002:2).

Expanded Disclosure

There is momentum at the global and regional levels for wider adoption of pollution registers. In 2001, the environment ministers of the G-8 countries—large industrialized democracies who meet regularly to discuss major economic and political issues—committed to promoting compatible pollution registers. They agreed that these registers should include core chemicals like persistent organic pollutants, heavy metals, and ozone depleting chemicals.

Pollutant registers have garnered international interest since the Rio Earth Summit in 1992. As part of a broader call for public access to information, the Rio Principles—endorsed by all the nations attending the conference—specifically mention access to information on hazardous materials. Agenda 21, also adopted at Rio, urges countries to adopt chemical inventories based on a community's "right to know."

The Organisation for Economic Co-operation and Development (OECD) took up this call in the mid-1990s. Through a series of workshops involving NGOs, businesses, and national governments, OECD prepared guidelines to help governments construct pollution registers, and encouraged its 30 members to establish such registers and share their experiences in implementing them.

At the same time, regional organizations have begun to develop pollution registers as well. In the mid-1990s, the North American Commission for Environmental Cooperation started publishing an annual "Taking Stock" report, which tracks trends in pollutant releases in Canada and the United States (and Mexico, when its new pollutant register starts generating data). The European Union is also pursuing a multinational register, the European Polluting Emissions Register, which will begin reporting data in 2003. This new register will include greenhouse gases, but does not yet track toxic chemicals contained in waste.

A significant and ambitious advance in the adoption of pollution registers came in January 2003, when a broad coalition of countries completed negotiations on a binding "PRTR Protocol" under the Aarhus Convention (see Box 1.7). In May 2003, 36 nations and the European Union signed the PRTR Protocol—the most significant expansion of mandatory disclosure requirements to date (UNECE 2003c; 2003a). Nations ratifying the treaty, which was negotiated under the auspices of the United Nations Economic Com-

Box 6.3 The Polluters Exposed: The Power of Indonesia's Public Ratings Program

In 1995, Indonesian manufacturing was growing at 10 percent a year and the government had only limited ability to enforce its environmental regulations (Wheeler 2000:64). Then, the budget-strapped Environmental Impact Management Agency ("BAPEDAL") took a new approach to regulation. It designed the Program for Pollution Control, Evaluation and Rating, or "PROPER," to rate the water pollution produced by 187 medium and large industrial plants. Performance ratings were based on the government's existing data on compliance with water regulations, responses to a survey about effluent discharges, and rigorous on-site inspections (Afsah et al. 2000:7–8).

In June 1995, when BAPEDAL completed its initial analysis, it rated only 35 percent of the plants as "in compliance"(Afsah 1998:17). Rather than immediately publicize the names of the noncompliant plants, parent companies, and managers, BAPEDAL privately notified the offending facilities that they had six months to cut pollution and improve their rating before public disclosure (Afsah et al. 2000:9). By December 1995, half the bottom-ranked companies had reduced their pollution enough to improve their rating and avoid negative reactions from communities, and tarnished reputations (Wheeler 2000:65–66).

BAPEDAL then released the results to the media. By early 1997, more than 50 percent of the plants tracked were in compliance (Afsah 1998:18). (See Figure.) Eighteen months after the project's inception, total organic water pollution from the monitored plants had declined 40 percent—at a cost of only about $100,000 to the government and only $1 a day to the plants (Wheeler 2000:71). At the same time, BAPEDAL improved its pollutant tracking system and boosted its credibility with industry, NGOs, and the public (Afsah 1998:23; Wheeler 2000:68). Surprisingly, improvements at facilities were motivated as much by the information that senior management gained about their plant's environmental performance as by the external disclosure of ratings. In most cases, plant managers had simply not understood the level of wastes they were releasing and the associated business costs (Afsah et al. 2000:12–13, 17).

The PROPER program does not disclose raw data about factory emissions, just a rating of compliance with environmental standards. But because it provides government-certified performance information in a format that is easy for the media to report and the public to understand, it still helps communities negotiate pollution control agreements with neighboring factories, and points consumers and activists to companies with superior performance.

The PROPER approach is spreading rapidly in Asia as a low-cost and effective method of spurring better industrial performance. In 1997, a Philippines pilot program modeled on PROPER boosted compliance among the 52 factories it monitored from 8 to 58 percent in 18 months (Wheeler 2000:73). China, India, Thailand, and Vietnam are among the countries in the region that are interested in or currently testing systems of corporate ratings and public disclosure (Afsah 1998:22).

mission for Europe, commit to establish compatible registers that report pollution emissions and transfers of a core list of 86 pollutants. The protocol suffers from many of the weaknesses of other pollutant registers, including a relatively small list of pollutants and the public's limited ability to demand expansion of the list. In addition, it includes a provision whereby companies may claim some emissions as "confidential," barring information on these emissions from public release (ECOSOC 2000; European ECO-Forum 2003; UNECE 2003b).

However, the treaty also contains some progressive elements. Its pollutant list includes greenhouse gases, a number of pesticides and toxic metals, and even some chemicals shown to disrupt the human endocrine system. In addition, it demands emissions reporting from companies involved in a wider range of activities than do many current pollution registers. For example, it includes the energy sector (except the nuclear power industry), as well as intensive livestock and fish-farm operations (European ECO-Forum 2003; UNECE 2003b:1–2).

While the primary focus of the PRTR protocol is still large, concentrated point sources of pollution—such as individual factories and power plants—it also provides a framework for reporting on pollution from diffuse sources such as motor vehicles, agriculture, and small- and medium-sized businesses that usually escape reporting requirements (European ECO-Forum 2003; UNECE 2003b:1–2).

Beyond Pollution Registers

Pollution registers are not the only kind of corporate environmental disclosure that governments mandate. Since the mid-1990s, a number of countries have required some companies to report on aspects of their environmental performance. For example, a 1996 Danish law requires over 1,000 companies to submit "green accounts"–reports that detail raw materials used and waste produced. The reports must include specific types and volumes of a variety of pollutant discharges, including toxic chemicals contained in company products, and even noise and odors. In addition, companies are required to state any significant changes in releases from previous years and the underlying reasons for these changes, so that readers can better track trends over time (Danish Environmental Protection Agency 2003). A 2001 French law requires companies listed on the French stock exchange to issue reports detailing their environmental and social performance (KPMG

Scoring Indonesia's Industries: PROPER Ratings

☐ World class standards (no facilities received this rating)
▨ Exceeds compliance standards
▨ Meets minimum national regulatory standards
▨ Falls short of compliance
■ No pollution control effort, causes significant environmental damage

June 1995
Ratings of 187 Factories

6 Factories (3%)   5 Factories (3%)
115 Factories (61.5%)   61 Factories (32.5%)

March 1997
Ratings of 173 Factories

4 Factories (2%)   7 Factories (4%)
81 Factories (47%)   81 Factories (47%)

Source: Afsah 1998:17

Meanwhile, in spite of its success, the PROPER program went into "hibernation" in 1998 due to the financial crisis in Indonesia, and is only now re-emerging with a new round of ratings slated for 2003. The restarted program will benefit from several improvements meant to strengthen its value as a measure of corporate responsibility. In addition to its technical review of company compliance with pollution regulations, the new ratings will also use indicators meant to probe a company's relationship with local communities. These indicators may include the number of complaints the company receives, court cases filed against it, negative media reports, or the results of community surveys on company performance. Negative reviews from local communities will make companies ineligible for the highest ratings category even if their regulatory compliance is adequate (Afsah 2003; Wheeler 2003).

The return of the PROPER program after four years of hibernation is a testament to its inherent strength and continued relevance. However, the hiatus stands as an important lesson in the vulnerability of enforcement programs during times of economic contraction—particularly if they are not yet considered part of the core mandate of an agency or do not have a source of dedicated funding.

2002:14, 29; SustainAbility and UNEP 2002:12).

Some governments are experimenting with methods to encourage disclosure that are not as comprehensive or expensive as pollution registers. For example, Indonesia has created a pollution disclosure program that publicly rates the compliance of industrial facilities with national pollution regulations, but does not reveal specific data on company emissions as pollution registers do. Other nations in Asia have expressed interest in adopting this low-cost approach to disclosure (see Box 6.3).

Voluntary Corporate Disclosure

Since the 1980s, thousands of companies have voluntarily issued reports on their environmental performance. Some have commissioned environmental audits that disclose compliance with regulatory requirements and long-term environmental liabilities. Others have committed to environmental "codes of conduct"—sets of general principles and overarching goals meant to guide a company's day-to-day practices. Still others have sought to have their products or the way they run their businesses certified by independent third parties as "environmentally sound."

This growing array of voluntary initiatives provides routes to accountability that businesses themselves find more acceptable. To

"Setting standards is 5 percent of the work; ensuring compliance is 95 percent."

—Simon Billenness
Franklin Research and Development Corp.

some extent, adoption of these voluntary practices reflects the acceptance by many companies that they must address public expectations of their behavior forthrightly. On the positive side, evidence shows that some voluntary measures have helped reduce pollution, increase company eco-efficiency, or boost competitiveness. They may also have helped businesses avoid more costly regulation and saved governments some regulatory expense (Schmidheiny et al. 1997:148).

But in practice, voluntary initiatives have several weaknesses that limit their ability to drive better environmental performance on a significant scale. Despite huge growth in voluntary programs of disclosure and environmental certification, the number of corporate sectors and companies involved remains relatively small (Utting 2002:63). Codes of conduct and environmental certification schemes often lack clear targets, measurable outcomes, or deadlines for improvement. Corporate reports issued voluntarily may supply a wealth of data, but not necessarily the information that regulators, investors, consumers, and communities need to assess company performance, or to hold corporations accountable for their commitments to good environmental citizenship.

Corporate Codes of Conduct: Accountability or Public Relations?

In the last two decades, many corporations in the United States and Europe have adopted codes of conduct that publicly spell out general rules of corporate behavior on social and environmental issues (Jenkins 2002:1; SustainAbility and UNEP 2002:5). These codes vary widely, depending on whether the company itself designs the code, or whether it is crafted by an outside entity such as a trade association or a group of NGOs, investors, or other stakeholders.

Company-generated codes are developed primarily by corporate management. They are often broad statements of business ethics and commitments to responsible labor, environmental, and safety practices. An early and influential example is the "Global Sourcing and Operating Guideline" that Levi Strauss & Company adopted in 1991 to manage the labor practices of its global chain of apparel suppliers (Jenkins 2002:12). The code commits Levi Strauss to work only with suppliers who do not use child or prison labor, who maintain reasonable work hours and benefits, who permit union organizing, and who maintain adequate health and safety standards (Levi Strauss & Co. 2003). Levi Strauss consulted with NGOs and based its code on principles elaborated by the International Labour Organization and United States labor law (Butler 2003).

Another common approach is for a trade association to develop a code, which is then adopted by a group of firms. The idea here is to commit a whole business sector to a certain minimum standard of practice, with peer pressure helping to enforce compliance. For example, the Kenya Flower Council, representing a group of Kenyan growers and exporters of cut flowers, crafted a "Code of Practice" that commits members to minimize pesticide use, dispose of chemicals safely, and be audited on their commitments twice a year (Kenya Flower Council 2003).

Some codes are crafted through negotiations among diverse stakeholders, including non-governmental organizations, and these tend to be more exacting and insistent on accountability measures. One example is the Forest Stewardship Council's (FSC) code for forestry operations—a set of standards for sustainable management of timber-producing lands that harvesters must prove they meet in order to market their wood as "certified" and to use the FSC trademark logo (FSC 2003). Some NGOs also propose model codes of conduct that they'd like to see industries follow. Amnesty International, for instance, offers a set of human rights principles that companies can use in building their own code of conduct (Amnesty International 1998).

Finally, a few codes have been drafted by intergovernmental bodies, such as the Organisation for Economic Co-operation and Development (OECD). The OECD's "Guidelines for Multinational Enterprises" is a set of voluntary principles and standards for good business conduct in a range of areas such as product safety, environment, labor management, and public disclosure. Governments who accept the Guidelines agree to promote these principles to the multinational companies in their countries. However, the code and its principles remain advisory only, with no method for tracking or ensuring compliance (OECD 2000:6, 15, 17–24, 41).

Are Codes Effective?

To the extent that codes of conduct inspire corporations to examine their business practices, expand their disclosure to stakeholders, and offer substantive commitments for self-regulation, they can be valuable tools. For example, the "Responsible Care Program"—a detailed code of conduct followed by many of the world's major chemical manufacturers—has reportedly led to significant changes in how chemical companies conduct business and interact with local communities.

The Responsible Care Program was first adopted by Canadian chemical corporations in 1986 and subsequently by the International Council of Chemical Associations in the 1990s. It has since spread to chemical manufacturers in 47 countries. The code commits companies to responsibly manufac-

ture, store, and ship chemical products, and to actively communicate with the communities in which they work (ICCA 1999; ACC 2002; ACC 2003).

Although some experts question the effectiveness of Responsible Care, industry members cite significant results. The Canadian version of the Responsible Care program, which requires public reporting on emissions of certain pollutants, points to a 50 percent reduction in total discharges from 1992 to 1996 (Harrison 1999:37). The American Chemistry Council says that its members, which must all actively participate in the U.S. program, reduced their toxic chemical releases by 58 percent from 1988 to 1997, while increasing production by 18 percent (ACC 2002). It is not clear, however, how much these reductions stem from adherence to the Responsible Care code, as opposed to stricter government regulations or other factors (Harrison 1999:37).

If crafted properly, industry codes of conduct can provide civil society with a lever for pushing corporations to improve their performance, actively involve citizens and communities in key decisions, and provide more information on their operations and impacts. Comprehensive codes that are monitored and independently verified can give stakeholders a means of influencing corporate behavior in places where government policy or regulatory enforcement are weak. For example, in El Salvador, the Gap clothing company set up an independent monitoring group in cooperation with the Interfaith Centre on Corporate Responsibility, Business for Social Responsibility, and the National Labor Committee to verify the Gap's compliance with its corporate code (Jenkins 2002:44).

Codes of conduct that are the basis for product certification or eco-labeling programs can give consumers greater access to information about the environmental and social impacts of products. Many codes foster the "greening" of the supply chain by asking signatory companies to extend the concept of responsibility to the activities of their suppliers as well as their subsidiaries (Jenkins 2002:49).

A Limited Tool

To be meaningful, codes of conduct must contain clear provisions to implement the broad principles they espouse. To be credible to the outside world, they must also contain requirements for monitoring the performance of the companies that adopt them. Ideally, an independent party, rather than the company itself, should conduct the monitoring. Unfortunately, very few codes of conduct contain such provisions, leaving the public little means of assuring that companies really do what their codes promise (Jenkins 2002:43).

Codes of conduct are often vague, sometimes consisting of little more than broad declarations of business principles, and lacking specific targets or behaviors that can be measured. For example, fewer than 40 of 587 corporate action plans submitted to Canada's Voluntary Challenge and Registry for greenhouse gases contained targets for reduced emissions (Harrison 1999:44).

Codes also tend to be limited in their application. They cover only a limited number of industry sectors and, within those sectors, a limited number of companies. These companies tend to be clustered in industries with high profiles or controversial practices. In a 2000 survey, the OECD found that corporate codes of conduct focusing on the environment are concentrated in the chemical industry, the oil industry, the forestry sector, and the mining sector–industries with significant and visible environmental impacts and hazardous processes (Jenkins 2002:34–35).

Codes are also popular among large retail chains, especially those that do business in Northern markets where expectations about labor and environmental standards are high. These companies all tend to be name-conscious and thus easy targets for NGO and consumer pressure, making them more willing to go on record with their commitments. In those business sectors where public pressure is not as keen, codes of conduct are less popular (Jenkins 2002:34–35, 41–45).

One of the most significant shortcomings of codes as an accountability mechanism is the lack of independent performance monitoring. The OECD found that only 10 percent of the 246 codes it surveyed included provisions for external monitoring. Provisions for monitoring by outside groups are more common in sector-wide codes and codes initiated by NGOs than in those established by individual companies. Monitoring by companies themselves is somewhat more common. A survey by Kolk et al. found that in about 40 percent of cases, companies assigned themselves the task of monitoring code compliance, rather than require an independent monitor (Jenkins 2002:43–44).

Codes of conduct can become little more than public relations ploys when they lack monitoring and enforcement. In some cases, companies have adopted carefully worded codes, only to ignore their application. A *Wall Street Journal* investigation of clothing subcontractors in Guatemala–factories that supplied apparel for retail chains in the United States–found that compliance with code provisions was spotty, inspections rare, and inspectors usually more interested in assuring product quality than code compliance (Ortega 1995:A1; Broad and Cavanagh 1998:24).

Greater standardization and mechanisms for accountability would help codes fulfill their potential. As one researcher noted: "Setting standards is 5 percent of the work; ensuring compliance is 95 percent" (Ortega 1995:A1). Even the Global Compact, a United Nations-sponsored initiative of nine principles of corporate responsibility, leaves much open to debate about what the principles mean in practice. More than 700 companies have signed on so far. The compact may help multinational companies share experiences and set strategic goals, but does not insist that companies make specific commitments or achieve those goals. Monitoring arrangements are informal and the principles are general in nature (United Nations 2003).

Similarly, the OECD's Guidelines for Multinational Enterprises lack specific mandates for "good" company behavior,

legal sanctions for violations of the guidelines, or other formal modes of accountability. However, governments do promise to put in place a "National Contact Point" to investigate noncompliance. To date, 37 nations have signed the guidelines (OECD 2000:6, 11–22, 32; Aaronson 2001; OECD 2003).

Even the strictest code is no substitute for regulation. In fact, the effectiveness of codes of conduct relies in part on the regulatory structure already in place. Many corporate codes, for example, require compliance with local regulations. Even more important to effective codes is the credible threat of additional regulation in the future if corporations do not meet certain standards of expected behavior. A survey by the European Commission in 1997 found that roughly two thirds of the industries polled cited the potential to forego or postpone new regulations as the main reason they committed to voluntary environmental agreements such as corporate codes of conduct (Harrison 1999:45–46; Jenkins 2002:51).

Voluntary Environmental Reporting: Better Disclosure?

The environment has crept into corporate reporting in a big way in the last decade. A corporate report is no longer necessarily just a statement of profits and losses. In conventional annual reports and special "sustainability reports," businesses are also disclosing diverse elements of their environmental and social performance.

Reporting practices vary widely. Ricoh Japan publicly reports on the environmental impact of its key products, such as photocopiers, through their entire life cycle, rather than just after manufacture. Suncor Energy of Canada calculates the greenhouse gas emissions its products generate once in use. Chiquita, a tropical fruit grower, assesses the environmental aspects of its Latin American farms. Australian utility Sydney Water estimates the company's "ecological footprint"—a measure of its impact on the natural environment (SustainAbility and UNEP 2002:36–40).

To be sure, some of this new trend toward environmental reporting is driven by compulsory regulation, such as mandatory disclosures for state pollution registers, or France's new law mandating sustainability reports from publicly traded corporations. But thousands of companies are also *voluntarily* sharing information on their environmental impacts and policies. Many–but not all–of these reports demonstrate that companies are capable of meaningful voluntary disclosure.

In the early 1990s, perhaps only a few hundred companies produced environmental reports (Irwin et al. 1995:5). Globally, 7,000–10,000 corporations now publish environmental reports each year (Rikhardsson 1998). Forty-five percent of the 250 largest companies in the world produce such reports (defined as social, sustainability, or health, safety and environment reports) (KPMG 2002:6). In spite of this tremendous growth in reporting, the number of firms issuing environmental reports still represents only a small fraction of all companies.

The willingness to issue a voluntary environmental performance report varies across business sectors. Industrial sectors appear to report more than non-industrial sectors. Larger multinational companies with a high public profile are also more likely to report (Adams et al. 1999:315; KPMG 2002:13).

Figure 6.1 Voluntary Corporate Reporting by Sector; Level of Third-Party Verification, 2002

(Top 100 Companies in 19 Developed Countries)

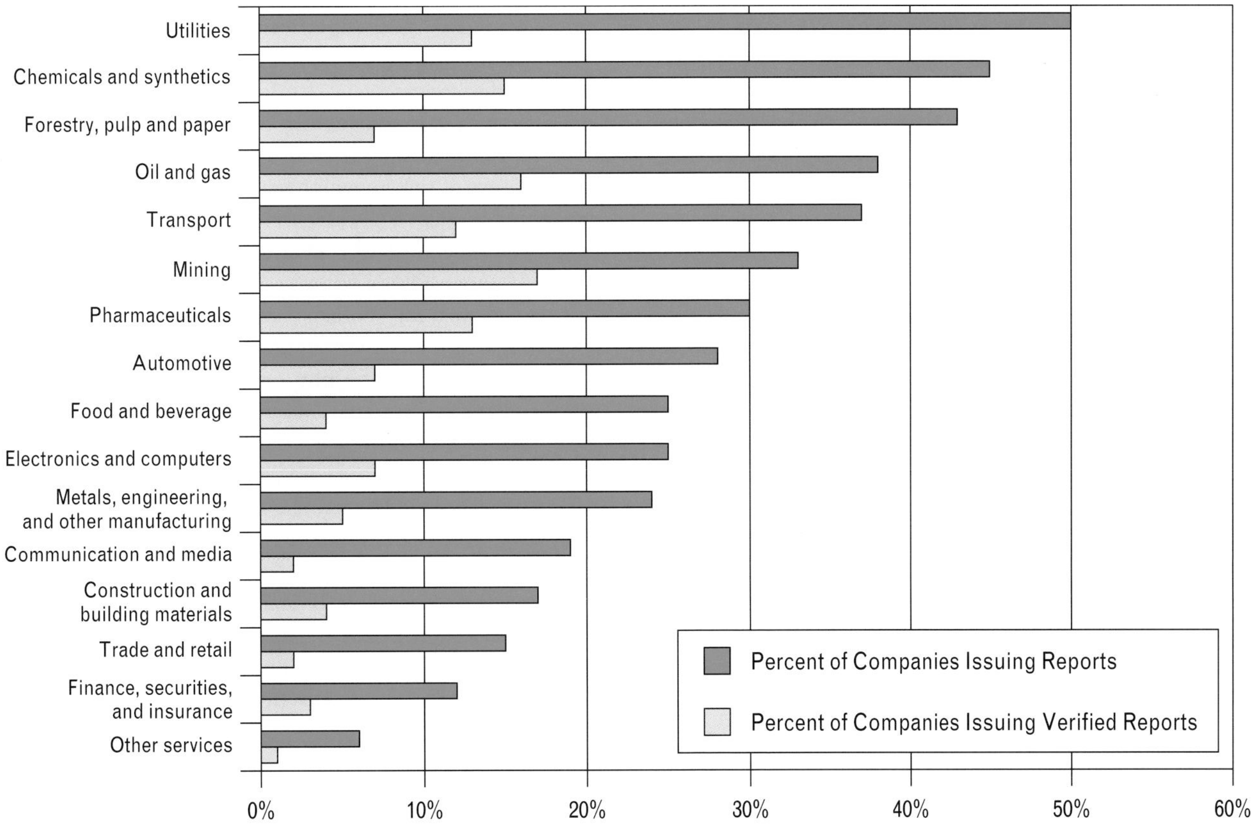

Source: KPMG 2002:19

(See Figure 6.1.) For small companies, the cost of reporting can be daunting. Preparing environmental or social reports can cost hundreds of thousands of dollars. Arranging for independent auditing of the results to increase a report's credibility adds even more to the cost. The Body Shop, for example, spends $750,000 annually on its sustainability report, and a large transnational corporation like Shell Oil could spend far more to gather, analyze, and disseminate its environmental performance data (Bennett and James 1999:62).

Increased voluntary reporting is a response to pressure from governments, NGOs, the financial community, and consumers. In the United Kingdom, the government uses the tactic of "naming and shaming" prominent companies that have not produced a corporate environmental report (Bennett and James 1999:53). The corporate accounting scandals that surfaced in 2002 in the United States, Europe, and Asia have also focused attention on the need for corporations to more fully account for their actions. In addition, some companies see their environmental reports as ways to distinguish themselves from less responsible or less savvy companies, or to identify cost-cutting opportunities.

Benefits and Problems

In theory, corporate environmental reports should be a key vehicle that companies can use to demonstrate transparency on their own terms, providing stakeholders with select but verifiable information they can use to assess company behavior. Some companies have gone far in achieving this end by measuring and reporting on key areas of performance, such as energy use or waste production, while also giving sufficient context to make the information useful.

Overall, however, environmental reporting by businesses has not come close to its potential as an accountability tool. To reach that potential, the quality of reporting must improve so that the information is more relevant and understandable.

At the same time, stakeholders must trust the reliability of this information and be able to use it to compare a company's performance over time and against other standard measures of performance (Bennett and James 1999:63; WRI and USEPA 2000:7).

Currently, the quality and content of corporate environmental reports varies widely. Some reports simply state the corporation's environmental commitment and goals for improvement, without significant data or interpretation. Others offer a wealth of data, but it is often focused on product safety, hazardous waste, or other compliance information taken from mandatory reports to the government, rather than environmental performance variables that would give a fuller picture of the company. Such variables might include energy and raw materials usage; the amount of waste packaging produced per unit of production; or how much material is recycled (Outen 1999:6; White and Zinkl 1999:118).

One notable trend is that company environmental reports are getting longer and more detailed. A 2002 survey of 100 corporate reports by SustainAbility and the United Nations Environment Programme found that the average length of reports grew 45 percent in two years. However, the surveyors concluded that the added girth did not, in general, improve the quality of reporting. In fact, the additional facts were more likely to confuse than illuminate readers (SustainAbility and UNEP 2002:2).

This is because much technical information does not lend itself to easy interpretation. For example, a report might include data on the total amount of materials a company uses in its factories. But unless the company offers statistics for multiple years or comparisons to the amount of materials used by other industry peers, the information may have little meaning to a local watchdog group or the general public.

The problem of comparability is also a concern. Because voluntary reports typically present dissimilar types of information in various formats, and use different measurement standards, it is virtually impossible to use these reports to compare firms, facilities, or products (Ranganathan 1998:3; Skillius and Wennberg 1998:39). For example, Monsanto Company does not report data on its energy use, so it cannot be compared in this aspect of environmental performance with Dow Chemical, which does (White and Zinkl 1999:119).

Financial analysts and shareholders—an audience companies identify as one of the targets of their environmental reports—also struggle to find information that is relevant to their interests. These users typically want to see information on the financial risks a company faces from its environmental liabilities, and the potential pay-off from its investments in environmental best practice (WRI and USEPA 2000:10; WBCSD 2002:19). This kind of information is hard to glean from many reports.

Box 6.4 The Global Reporting Initiative

The Global Reporting Initiative (GRI) is an internationally recognized standard for "sustainability reporting"—that is, reporting on the combined environmental, social, and financial performance of a company. The GRI's corporate reporting guidelines, which have been evolving since 1997, incorporate input from nongovernmental organizations (NGOs), corporations, accounting organizations, business associations, academics, and other stakeholders worldwide. The guidelines do not tell companies what they should and should not do, but lay out criteria for what kind of information to provide to investors and other stakeholders.

A set of eleven principles, including transparency, completeness, and comparability, as well as a list of key indicators—performance measures that companies can quantify and track over time—help firms structure their reports. The guidelines also contain special supplements for companies in different business sectors, as well as technical protocols on how to measure and report on the various performance indicators. Part of the GRI goal is to help an enterprise understand the relationship between its financial performance and its environmental and social performance. The GRI is also designed to provide reports that will invite further stakeholder dialogue and inquiry (GRI 2002:1–56).

More than 200 companies have released reports based on the GRI guidelines, with the highest numbers coming from

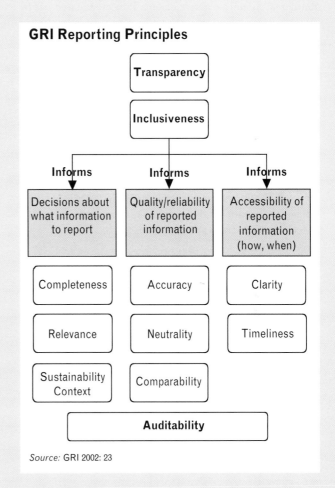

GRI Reporting Principles

Source: GRI 2002: 23

Regional Distribution of Companies Following GRI Guidelines, 2003

Latin America and the Caribbean (1%)
Oceania (9%)
Asia (20%)
North America (18%)
Sub-Saharan Africa (4%)
Europe (48%)

Source: GRI 2003

firms in the United States, Japan, the United Kingdom, and Australia (GRI 2003). The initiative clearly is motivating good reporting. A recent review of corporate sustainability reports found that 60 percent of the "best reporting companies" (based on completeness, innovation, and effort to integrate environment reporting into business decision-making) used the GRI guidelines (SustainAbility and UNEP 2002:14).

But the GRI has its shortcomings. Like most corporate reporting initiatives, the GRI does not require third-party verification that reports conform to the guidelines or are complete and honest (SustainAbility and UNEP 2002:17).

Audits and Reporting Guidelines

Can the information that companies voluntarily supply in their reports be trusted? The 2002 financial scandals–from Enron to WorldCom–increased public skepticism about the quality and honesty of corporate reporting (SustainAbility and UNEP 2002:2).

To increase confidence in their reporting, some companies, such as Chiquita Brands International, voluntarily have their reports audited or "verified" by a third party. In Chiquita's case this involves using two separate processes to certify performance against specific standards–one set by the Rainforest Alliance's Better Banana Project, and another by an international labor standard. Chiquita's report spells out its compliance, along with areas of concern expressed by the auditors, and the company's response to these concerns (Chiquita Brands International Inc. 2000). But auditing or verification is not common. Recent surveys estimated that just 27-28 percent of corporate environmental reports are independently verified (Elkington et al. 1999:337; KPMG 2002:18). (See Figure 6.1.)

The issue of credibility of company environmental reports is serious enough to discourage some companies from even attempting such a report. These businesses simply aren't convinced that reporting will benefit their reputation with customers or help the company to be more efficient–at least not enough to justify the cost (Bennett and James 1999:55). They believe that some stakeholders won't trust the information even if it is verified. In addition, many business leaders already feel besieged by requests to provide information to regulators, investors, and the public, and can't decide which data will be most useful to provide (Outen 1999:6).

To address these concerns, there is a concerted effort underway to provide companies with guidelines for structur-

Box 6.5 ISO 14001: A Standard for Environmental Management Systems

Almost 37,000 facilities have adopted the ISO 14001 standard for Environmental Management Systems since it was published in 1995 (ISO 2002:5). At a minimum, organizations that adopt the standard accept the responsibility to (Andrews et al. 2001:32):

■ Adopt a written environmental policy;

■ Identify all significant impacts of their activities, products, and services;

■ Set objectives and targets for continuous improvement in environmental performance;

■ Assign clear responsibilities for implementation, training, monitoring, and corrective actions;

■ Evaluate and refine the management system over time to achieve continuous improvement.

Just 17 percent of the companies adopting the ISO 14001 standard are in developing countries (ISO 2002:24–28). Nonetheless, this voluntary standard may ultimately prove most useful in rapidly developing countries such as China, India, Thailand, and Indonesia—places where compliance costs may make inflexible regulatory standards a poor choice, and where the capacity to enforce formal regulations is lacking (Panayotou 2001:113).

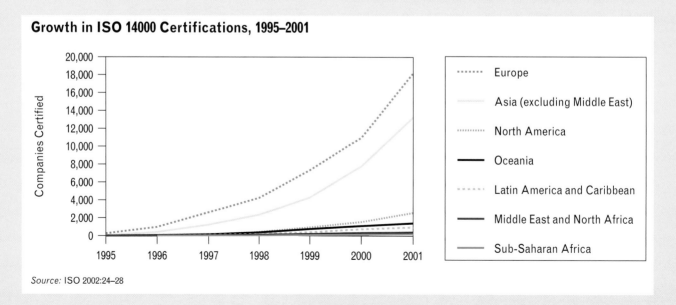

Growth in ISO 14000 Certifications, 1995–2001

Source: ISO 2002:24–28

ing their environmental reports. The intent is to encourage companies and customers to see environmental reporting as a standard business practice that is both predictable and trustworthy. More than 30 organizations worldwide have developed environmental reporting guidelines. Most offer loose guidelines for what should be reported, but some–perhaps less than one third–put forth specific standards and metrics (Ranganathan 1998:9-11).

One of the best-known and most specific set of guidelines comes from The Global Reporting Initiative (GRI), which offers both general reporting principles and specific guidance to different business sectors so that reports are more standardized, rigorous, and consistent. (See Box 6.4.) However, other guidelines exist as well, such as the World Business Council for Sustainable Development's set of indicators for tracking eco-efficiency, and Australia's Public Environmental Reporting Framework. This raises a concern that businesses may still find it difficult to converge on a reporting framework that is universally accepted (Ranganathan 1999:479, 489).

Environmental Management Systems

Since the mid-1980s, thousands of firms worldwide have developed Environmental Management Systems (EMS). An EMS is an internal set of policies and procedures that define how a company will manage the environmental impacts of its operations. For example, a company might rewrite its standard operating procedures to require employees to monitor not just plant cleanliness, but also compliance with its waste, air, and water permits. Or a firm could establish consistent rules for safer waste disposal at all its facilities. Or an EMS might commit company managers to regularly review the environmental impacts of their products as they are transported, resold, used, or thrown away, and to sever a business relationship with a customer that does not use the firms' products safely (Andrews et al. 2001:32; Coglianese and Nash 2001:12). (See Box 6.5.)

From the business perspective, an EMS can help managers exceed legal requirements for environmental compliance, but at a lower cost than formal regulation, since companies can design their own approaches. As with other voluntary measures, businesses may also adopt an EMS to help distinguish themselves from competitors, appease NGOs, and head off mandatory regulations.

But do Environmental Management Systems actually help promote corporate responsibility and increase their accountability to stakeholders? Some analysis suggests they might. A recent survey of almost 600 manufacturing plants found that factories using an EMS were more likely to have adopted improvements in the areas of recycling, air emissions, solid waste reductions, and electricity use. They were also two to four times as likely to share information about their environmental practices with neighbors and environmental groups, and much more likely to use Citizen Advisory Councils to help them address community concerns (Florida and Davi-

son 2001:91). But other evidence is less positive. A survey of chemical companies found that EMS adoption had generally helped firms improve their relationships with outside groups, but often without significantly changing the companies' internal behavior (Metzenbaum 2001:163).

An obvious factor in the effectiveness of an EMS is whether it meets certain recognized standards. Firms can design their own EMS, but thousands are opting to follow and gain accreditation by either of two international standards: the International Organization for Standardization's ISO 14001 standard, and Europe's Eco-Management and Audit Scheme (EMAS). The EMAS has more stringent requirements on disclosure. It requires companies to issue an independently verified site-specific report on its energy and materials use, waste generation, pollutant releases, and noise, among other impacts.

By comparison, the increasingly popular ISO 14001 standard is much less prescriptive. It simply calls for a company to have a system in place for examining its environmental impacts and to commit to continuously improving that system. It does not specify what environmental goals companies should set or what performance measures they should use, nor does it require facilities to publish a public environmental report. In fact, no reporting of facility inputs or outputs is required for certification under the ISO standard (Ditz and Ranganathan 1997:27; Nash and Ehrenfeld 2001:70-71).

Use of ISO 14001, EMAS, or other standards to set concrete goals and commitments to forthright communication with stakeholders could benefit corporate accountability and performance (Ditz and Ranganathan 1997:27-28). But as long as firms using an EMS don't have to report any environmental information in a standardized format, the impact of an EMS can't be measured from year to year or across companies or industries. In fact, it is quite possible that two companies certified to the same standard can be operating at entirely different levels of environmental performance. Nor does an EMS guarantee that a company is even meeting its legal obligations. Eight out of nine ISO-certified firms in Mexico failed to comply with Mexican environmental laws, according to a 1998 survey (Harrison 1999:40).

Regulation by Civil Society

One of the newest and most progressive approaches to greater corporate environmental accountability is direct intervention of consumers, investors, and civil society groups in business affairs. Two premier examples are socially responsible investing (SRI)–making investments on the basis of a company's environmental and social performance–and eco-labeling or product certification that guides consumers to greener products. Creative use of these tools can sometimes mimic the effect of government regulation, but with much less government intervention. Both tools are entirely dependent on information disclosure for their effectiveness, and are strengthened when businesses increase their transparency.

Box 6.6 Covenants: Voluntary Industry-Government Agreements in Europe

Covenants are voluntary contracts between the government and industrial sectors that address environmental impacts common to a large number of companies, such as the production of packaging waste (EPE 1996). The government typically negotiates with trade associations to meet industry-wide targets, and individual firms then sign on to sectoral covenants via letters of declaration.

The concept of voluntary business-government agreements began in the Netherlands and caught on across Europe in the early 1990s. As of 1996, there were 305 such agreements, with two thirds of them in the Netherlands and Germany (Harrison 1999:24–27). In the Netherlands, covenants have been negotiated with 18 industrial sectors responsible for most of the nation's industrial pollution, but there are dozens of other covenants that address energy efficiency and other environmental issues (Harrison 1999:24). In fact, these contracts have become a key mechanism in the government's environmental strategy.

Although voluntary industry-government agreements may be a valuable complement to traditional government policy and a means of engaging corporations directly in problem solving, they haven't traditionally emphasized transparency or accountability. In most cases, there are no sanctions for corporate failure to achieve commitments. A study of 154 covenants, including 85 in the environmental field, concluded that the majority lacked sufficient safeguards to ensure their success. In most, companies agreed only to "strive to achieve" their obligations rather than to actually achieve them. In half the cases, deadlines for achievement were unclear, and only one in seven required public reporting of results (Harrison 1999:25).

Even where clear provisions for sanctions are incorporated into agreements, the interconnectedness of European and world trade means that negotiating covenants is not simply a national matter. As part of the third Dutch packaging covenant, the Dutch government and the packaging industry agreed that by the end of 2003 businesses would reduce the number of beverage cans and bottles thrown away by two thirds. If the reductions were not met, a compulsory deposit of 0.25 euro (US$0.23) would be placed on cans and bottles on 1 January 2004. However, some European governments and

The Dutch Packaging Industry Covenant: Recycling Obligations and Results in 2001

Dutch covenants have met with mixed success as a tool to achieve environmental goals. According to the Dutch packaging industry, manufacturers exceeded the recycling target for wooden packaging, but failed to reach the targets for paper/cardboard, glass, metal, or plastic packaging.

Packaging material	Recycling percentages	
	2001 obligation	2001 actual
Paper/cardboard	85%	66%
Glass	90%	78%
Metals	80%	78%
Plastics	27%	24%
Wood	15%	27%

Source: EUROPEN 2002:4

industry groups have challenged the mandatory deposit fees, arguing that they are contrary to European Union law and a possible barrier to free trade (BAE 2003:11).

Another criticism of the covenant approach to regulation is the lack of third-party involvement in their crafting. Corporations and governments frequently agree upon pollution reduction goals with little opportunity for participation by citizens and nongovernmental organizations (Harrison 1999:45). And, unlike laws, informal agreements can be crafted by unelected government officials, with little involvement of democratically elected legislatures—again decreasing their openness to public input (Harrison 1999:17).

Analysis of covenants in Europe in 1997 found that environmental groups participated in the negotiation of only one in five agreements. Just two thirds contained any provision for monitoring, and just over half contained any provisions for verification of this monitoring by government officials (Harrison 1999:24–25). More recent agreements have placed greater emphasis on clarity of commitments, monitoring, and legal formality.

Socially Responsible Investing

Socially responsible investors–who base their investments on companies' social and environmental behavior–are no longer rare. Although socially responsible investing is still a niche market, it is growing rapidly. It is being adopted by mainstream investors–typically stock market investors–as evidence mounts that good social and environmental performance translates into better overall business performance (WBCSD 2002:9). (See Box 6.7.)

Socially responsible investing is a powerful lever for corporate accountability because it offers a direct route to the ear of corporate managers and boards of directors–those with the power to make company practices more responsible. Shareholders have access and economic leverage: they can meet with management, sponsor shareholder resolutions at annual company meetings, and divest their stock if they are not satisfied with management's response.

Disclosure by a company should be the beginning of a relationship with the surrounding community and other stakeholders—not an end to it.

Figure 6.2 Voluntary Corporate Reporting by Country, 2002

(Top 100 Companies in 19 Countries)

Percent of Companies Reporting

Source: KPMG 2002:14

A common approach to SRI is to positively or negatively "screen" companies. In negative screening, an individual investor or mutual fund manager avoids investing in companies whose practices are perceived to be harmful to people or the environment, such as tobacco or alcohol producers, munitions manufacturers, or businesses that don't provide healthcare for employees. Positive screening involves deliberately seeking out companies that offer solid financial returns and yet are leaders in social and environmental performance.

Another approach is to marshal shareholder power to actively press for change at the highest level of corporate decision-making. Shareholders can provide constructive criticism of corporate practices and suggest alternatives by filing what are known as "proxy resolutions." For example, they can file a resolution asking an oil company to promote renewable energy sources, or a mining company to analyze and report the impacts of its operations on biodiversity. Technically, shareholders "own" the company, so if enough shareholders vote in favor of the resolution, the company must act.

This tactic has become more popular and effective in recent years. In 2001, shareholders filed 261 resolutions on social issues (SIF 2001:16). Although these resolutions rarely receive a majority vote, the pressure they bring from shareholders—often in conjunction with work done by

Box 6.7 The Growth of Socially Responsible Investing

The United States is the world's biggest market for socially responsible investing (SRI), with perhaps $1 in every $8 invested in this manner (SIF 2001:2). Three strategies define socially responsible investing (SIO 2003):

- *Positive or negative screening* applies social or environmental guidelines to the investment process;

- *Community investment* entails support of community development or micro enterprise initiatives;

- *Shareholder advocacy* is the involvement of investors in bringing about positive social and environmental change within corporations.

In the United States, assets in funds utilizing one or more of these strategies have jumped from just $40 billion in 1984 to $2.34 trillion in 2001. The number of mutual funds that incorporate social screening grew from 168 in 1999 to 230 in 2001 (SIF 2001:4, 6). The growth in SRI in the United States is significant because U.S. investors invest globally and tend to make their voices heard in the boardroom. The U.S. mutual fund industry, where much of this investing takes place, is the largest in the world (Domini 2001:135).

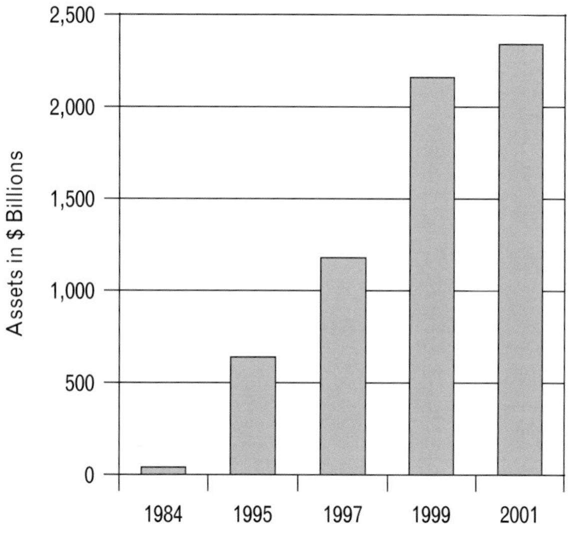

Socially responsible investing is also growing rapidly in Europe and Australia, and emerging in Asia (ABI 2001:8; ASrIA 2003). In Japan, four "green funds" launched in 1999 grew to an asset base of more than $1 billion in about a year (Domini 2001:134); Hong Kong has a nascent SRI fund market as well and Malaysia offers funds screened for Islamic principles. SRI fund options elsewhere are very limited. In Singapore, only one registered SRI fund exists, which invests in companies that show a commitment to empowering women. Taiwan offers one global "eco-fund." (ASrIA 2003).

SRI in the United States

Assets in $ Billions

Source: SIF 2001:4

Value of Screened Funds Under SRI Management, 2001

USA*	$1,350 billion
Europe	$38 billion
Canada	$33 billion
Japan	$1 billion
Asia (excluding Japan)	$1 billion
Australia*	$.5 billion

*When funds screened for shareholder advocacy and community investment are included, the total value for the United States exceeds $2 trillion; Australia's total SRI fund value increases to $5.4 billion.

Source: Kendall 2001. Based on data published in The Cerulli Edge— Global Edition.

NGOs, citizen activists, and consumers—has convinced some of the biggest companies to change their practices:

- In 2000, socially responsible shareholders convinced several Fortune 500 companies, including Ford Motor Company and Nike, to endorse the CERES Principles—a ten-point code of conduct that commits companies to improvements in environmental performance and reporting (SIF 2001:17).

- Shareholder pressure helped convince General Electric to make its new line of washing machines 20 percent more efficient in water and energy use by 2004, and 35 percent more efficient by 2007. GE's move led to major improvements in energy- and water efficiency across the appliance industry (Domini 2001:87).

- Fifteen institutional investors (investors owning large blocks of shares) joined an environmental coalition in 2000 that convinced Mitsubishi Corporation to abandon plans for a salt factory in the Gulf of California, Mexico that would have destroyed a calving site for grey whales (SIF 2001:15).

- Shareholder pressure in 2000–2001 helped convince the top five pharmacy chains in the United States, as well as other retailers, to phase out distribution or production of mercury-filled thermometers, which can release mercury when disposed of (SRI World Group Inc. 2001b:56).

Among the successes enjoyed by socially responsible investors in the 2002 proxy season were a record 19 resolutions filed with major companies on the topic of climate change. Shareholder resolutions to coax companies to address global warming are the fastest-growing category of socially motivated resolution (Innovest 2002:12).

SRI and the Bottom Line

SRI sends companies a message that their environmental behavior, reputation, and even their ethics and transparency policies can impact the price of their stock, and therefore the company's worth. Research shows that news about a firm's environmental performance—whether good or bad—can boost or diminish stock prices in the United States and Canadian markets by 1–2 percent (Wheeler 2000:61–62). Stock markets in developing countries react even more strongly. News about criminal or enforcement actions against corporations for environmental wrongdoings can depress stock prices 4–15 percent in these markets, according to one study. In response to good news—about awards for good environmental performance, for example—stock prices have been shown to increase as much

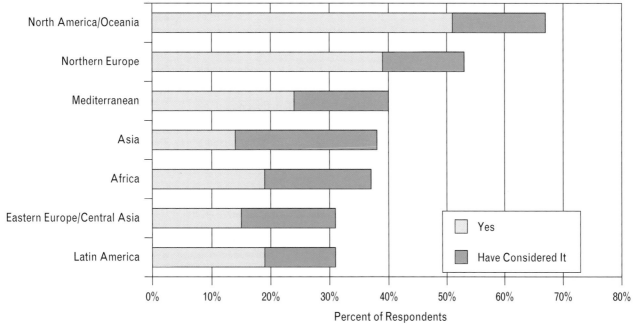

Figure 6.3 Public Perceptions Affect the Bottom Line

In the past year, have you avoided the products of, publicly criticized, or otherwise punished a corporation you don't consider socially and environmentally responsible?

Source: Environics 1999

as 20 percent in Argentina, Chile, Mexico, and the Philippines (Dasgupta et al. 1998:17).

Socially responsible investing was once seen only as a means of "doing good" with one's money. But today, proponents emphasize its potential as a smart investment, offering competitive financial returns (SRI World Group Inc. 2001b:xiii). In fact, environmental soundness may be a good indicator of a well managed firm, and hence useful as a broader measure of potential financial performance.

Although analysts still struggle to quantify the specific impact of a company's environmental risks on individual stocks, there is growing evidence that environmental factors can materially impact a company's financial performance. An analysis of 13 pulp and paper companies in 2000 revealed that half could face losses of at least 5–10 percent of shareholder value due to pending environmental issues like stricter logging restrictions and air pollution regulations (Repetto and Austin 2000:19).

Applying the same methodology to 16 oil and gas companies, economists in 2002 found that shareholders could lose 1–6 percent of the value of their investments in these companies because of the effects of new regulations and other

efforts to curb climate change (Austin and Sauer 2002:33). Another recent report warned that costs related to climate change could affect companies across a broad range of sectors—from transportation and forestry to manufacturing and agriculture—causing them to lose as much as 15 percent of their total market capitalization (Innovest 2002:10).

Such studies have begun to build a business case for SRI–a necessary step if SRI is to advance beyond its current niche market. Indeed, the strategy of emphasizing the "bottom line" benefits of socially responsible investing and the risks of ignoring exposure to environmental problems has made SRI appealing to a much more mainstream audience. This has even prompted a few large institutional investors to become active on environmental and social issues. The City of New York and the retirement system of the State of Connecticut both filed shareholder resolutions in 2002 aimed at getting companies to address climate change (Innovest 2002:13).

Nor is interest in SRI confined to North America. Major European investment houses such as Henderson Global Investors, and Friends Ivory and Sime PLC have developed sophisticated guidelines for assessing the management responses of companies to the climate change threat. These

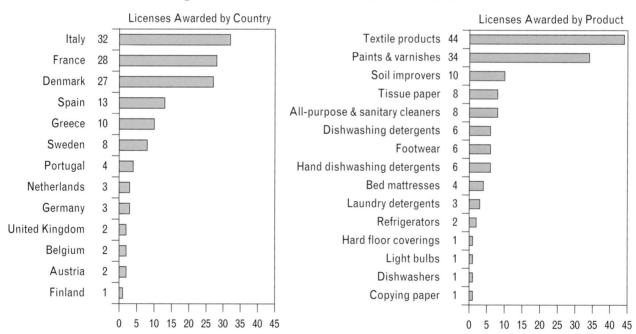

Figure 6.4 The EU Flower Eco-Label

What does the Flower Eco-label mean?

The label on footwear tells you...
Risk of allergic reactions from certain chemicals is minimized
Water and air pollution during manufacturing is limited
The product is sold in recycled packaging
The product is at least as hard wearing as conventional shoes

The label on paints and varnishes tells you...
The quantity of white pigment is reduced while still ensuring sufficient coverage
Pigments are produced according to strict ecological criteria
The product releases fewer solvents
The product does not contain heavy metals, carcinogens, or toxic substances

Note: A license is awarded to a company to produce one or more eco-labeled products.
Source: Bouvret 2003; EUEB 2003

Box 6.8 A Binding Convention on Corporate Accountability?

In some quarters, concern over the weakness of corporate codes of conduct and other voluntary measures to ensure good corporate behavior has sparked interest in a mandatory set of rules to which all transnational corporations would be subject—a binding convention on corporate accountability. Indeed, for many years, NGOs have been calling for a such a legally binding treaty to ensure that corporations comply with certain minimum human rights, environmental, and labor standards, and accept legal liability for the impacts of their business practices (Broad and Cavanagh 1998:19–26, 39; Phillips 2002:1–6).

Most recently, the idea for such a treaty gathered momentum at the 2002 World Summit on Sustainable Development in Johannesburg. The argument was backed by many developing nations and the European Union, but failed to result in an agreement. One proposal—put forward by the nongovernmental organization Friends of the Earth International (FOEI)—would have imposed environmental, human rights, and labor standards on transnational corporations and made it possible for anyone to sue or file criminal charges against them for alleged violations of the standards (FOEI 2002; Gardiner 2002:7).

FOEI's proposal contained the following elements (Bruno and Karliner 2002:6; FOEI 2002):

■ Corporate reporting requirements on environmental and social impacts. Prior consultation with affected communities, including environmental impact assessments and access to information;

■ Extension of liability to corporate directors for corporate breaches of national environmental and social laws; corporate liability for breaches of international laws or agreements;

■ Rights of redress for citizens, including the ability for affected people anywhere in the world to pursue litigation against parent corporations in the country where they are based;

■ Community rights to resources, including indigenous peoples' rights over common property, such as forests, fisheries, and minerals. Community veto rights over development projects, and compensation for expropriated resources;

■ Sanctions against companies in breach of the Convention. These might include fines, suspension of a corporation's stock exchange listing, withholding of state subsidies, and, in extreme cases, withdrawal of a corporation's limited liability status.

Although the FOEI proposal was rejected, participants at WSSD did eventually include language that some see as an endorsement of future discussions on a Corporate Accountability Convention (*Journal of Corporate Citizenship* 2002:4; La Viña et al. 2002:7). The WSSD Plan of Implementation—the set of agreements negotiated and signed by governments attending the Summit—included the following commitment:

"[We will]Actively promote corporate responsibility and accountability, based on the Rio principles, including through the full development and effective implementation of intergovernmental agreements and measures, international initiatives and public-private partnerships and appropriate national regulations, and support continuous improvement in corporate practices in all countries." (United Nations 2002:40)

investment houses have begun to communicate the importance of the issue and their concerns to clients (Cortese 2002:6; Innovest 2002:11). In the United Kingdom, the third largest pension fund, with US$30 billion in assets, is calling for other UK investors to take an active position on the financial risk associated with climate change. And in the Netherlands, ABP Investments–Europe's largest pension fund–recently began to address climate risk systematically in its stock selection process, beginning with a $100 million "experimental" portfolio. It is considering expanding its environmental risk "screen" to a larger proportion of its US$140 billion portfolio (Innovest 2002:33).

Whether SRI matures into a significant force affecting corporate governance depends, ultimately, on the scope and quality of information available to concerned investors (SRI World Group Inc. 2001b:81). Currently, SRI relies heavily on voluntary disclosure by companies and pension fund managers about the relevance of environmental issues for future financial performance (Austin and Sauer 2002:35).

This is beginning to change in some countries, where new government regulation is facilitating SRI. For example, starting in 2001, pension funds in the United Kingdom were required to declare whether and how they integrate social and environmental factors into their investment decisions. Many UK pension funds have since expressed a new resolve to engage corporations in dialogue on these issues. Canada, Norway, Sweden, and Denmark are among the countries considering similar regulations (ABI 2001:8; Domini 2001:144; SIF 2001:25). Beginning in 2003, an Australian law will require all investment firms to disclose the extent to which environmental and social considerations are taken into account (Baue 2003). A new regulation by the Securities and Exchange Commission in the United States requires mutual funds to disclose how they voted on shareholder-originated proxy resolutions–allowing investors to judge the environmental and social awareness of mutual fund managers (SRI World Group Inc. 2003). By bringing the question of social and environmental performance to the fore, these actions are likely to build awareness of and interest in socially responsible investment options.

Eco-labeling: The Power of Informed Consumers

Informed consumers can be a powerful force for better environmental governance. According to a 2001 survey, 79 percent of consumers take corporate citizenship into account when making their purchasing decisions, and 36 percent consider it an "important" factor (Hill and Knowlton 2001:3; SRI World Group Inc. 2001a). In 1999, another survey of 25,000 consumers worldwide found that 1 in 5 had either rewarded or punished companies in the past year based on their perceived social performance. That means they avoided a company's products or actually spoke against the company to others (Environics International Ltd. 1999). (See Figure 6.3.)

Even if consumers exaggerate their activism when polled, other analysis suggests that perhaps 10-15 percent of consumers truly integrate environmentalism into their lives and are regularly willing to pay higher prices for green products (Frankel 1998:140). At least for some companies, in some sectors and countries, an environmentally conscious public is driving change in company behavior.

The worldwide surge in organic food sales is a case in point. Consumers are sending a clear signal to food producers that they are willing to pay a premium for foods that are not contaminated with pesticides and are grown in ways that don't harm ecosystems. In 2000, global organic agriculture sales were worth about $20 billion, and growing 25 percent annually in major markets like the United States, Europe, and Japan (CSD 2000:6). This provides farmers with a real incentive to consider reducing their pesticide use and investing in soil and biodiversity conservation to increase their earnings.

But consumers are only able to use their market power–and, in turn, influence corporate environmental behavior–if they can make an informed choice when they shop. They need to be able to easily identify products that have been produced responsibly–such as organic food or sustainably grown lumber–and to distinguish between valid and spurious claims of producers. To meet this need, some independent organizations and governments have begun to certify and "eco-label" goods produced using sustainable practices (WRI and USEPA 2000:12).

Since West Germany launched the first environmental labeling program–the Blue Angel–in 1978, eco-labeling initiatives have emerged in more than two dozen countries, including Canada, the European Union, Scandinavia, Japan, and the United States (Harrison 1999:10). Eco-labels can cover a surprisingly broad range of items, from lawnmowers to vegetables. Germany's Blue Angel is found on over 3,500 products (The Blue Angel 2003). Europe's "flower label" is used by 135 manufacturers, retailers, and service providers and on several hundred products (Bouvret 2003; EUEB 2003). (See Figure 6.4.)

While governments are behind some eco-labeling programs, other well-known programs are privately sponsored. Typically, an independent organization–often a coalition of stakeholders including environmentalists and industry representatives–crafts an environmental standard that becomes the basis for product certification and labeling. One well-known example is the Rainforest Alliance's SmartWood Program. Using environmental, social, and economic standards established by the Forest Stewardship Council (an NGO), accredited certifiers assess the management of forest lands. This third-party certification helps ensure the SmartWood label's credibility. Forest products coming from areas managed in accordance with the standards can carry the SmartWood logo. That logo helps consumers, architects, manufacturers, woodworkers, builders, and municipal governments locate sustainably grown wood for everything from furniture

A clear, enforceable environmental regulatory regime provides the context for all disclosure, and the bar against which it is measured.

to flooring, and musical instruments to picture frames (SmartWood 2003).

Clearly, certification and labeling programs can benefit the environment. The West German government credited the Blue Angel program with reducing the amount of household paint solvents entering the waste stream by 40,000 tons. The program also spurred industrial changes to meet its environmental criteria and capture a larger market share (Salzhauer 1991:11–12). In several developing countries, eco-labeling schemes have reduced the intensity of fertilizer and pesticide use in the production of cut flowers (Grote 2002:289).

But, as a source of information to guide consumer decisions, eco-labels can still improve. Avoiding confusion and broadening consumer confidence in eco-labels are two continuing challenges. For example, there are more than 100 regional or national standards for organic products worldwide, meaning many products labeled as organic will not have met identical standards (CSD 2000:12). Which labels should consumers trust? In this instance, standardization is already beginning to occur among labels. Widely adopted guidelines issued by the International Federation of Organic Agriculture and the 1999 FAO/WHO "Codex Guidelines" for the production, processing, and labeling of organically produced foods have helped reduce the differences between these eco-labels (CSD 2000:14). But bringing clarity and consistency to other product areas will require continued effort.

Assuring equity among producers worldwide is also a significant challenge. Some producers in developing nations complain that labeling and certification programs can be costly, and sometimes require access to technical knowledge and organizational capacity that they lack. That can put them at a disadvantage, and reduce their ability to compete in the burgeoning market for green products. In the case of organic agricultural exports, for example, many developing-country producers lack information about regulatory requirements, prices, quality factors, and logistics (UNCTAD 2001:6, 8). Similarly, small-holder or community-based producers of forest goods find the costs of obtaining certification to be prohibitive, especially in remote areas. Addressing these concerns will help widen the acceptance of and participation in eco-labeling programs.

Supporting the Transition to Accountability

Public access to information on company performance has already become a major factor driving business accountability. The information comes through several channels, some compulsory, such as pollution registers, and some voluntary. Together they comprise a wave of disclosure that is slowly sweeping through company operations and altering business practice.

Some companies have acted aggressively, positioning themselves to take advantage of the disclosure wave. They have become "best reporters," seeing value in building their names as leaders in transparency and corporate citizenship. But many more companies have resisted the disclosure trend, unconvinced that it will benefit them now or in the long run. In fact, those companies who voluntarily and proactively make information on their performance available are still the exceptions.

It does not help that the range of disclosure efforts—from mandated pollution reporting to voluntary sustainability reports to consumer-targeted eco-labels—is fragmented, and does not form a coherent disclosure system. It is still very difficult, if not impossible, to compare the environmental performance of products, facilities, firms, sectors, and countries using the information currently available.

Amplifying the disclosure wave will require effort on at least three fronts. First, businesses themselves must begin to more fully embrace the business rationale for disclosure. Greater attention to quantifying the benefits of transparency to the bottom line is the only way to bring many businesses on board. More dynamic engagement of businesses with their neighbors and other stakeholders—through community advisory panels and other business-public partnerships—is a second area of need, allowing companies to turn the results of disclosure to their benefit. Finally, government regulators and policy-makers must play their part. Government regulation is the vital backdrop against which all disclosure—manda-

(continued on p. 134)

Box 6.9 Banking on Ecosystems: HSBC's Corporate Gamble

What inspires a corporation to become more environmentally responsible? The corporation's philanthropic programs can be one surprising answer. While corporate giving is sometimes criticized as "green washing"—primarily an effort to enhance environmental image or community relations—sometimes corporate philanthropy is a viable route to real internal change and better behavior. In the case of international banking giant HSBC, a philanthropic partnership with three environmental nongovernmental organizations actually led the corporation to examine its environmental practices, and to build the capacity of its employees to make better environmental decisions themselves.

Changing Perspective

With 8,000 offices in 80 countries and almost US$800 billion in assets, HSBC has local interests almost everywhere. Their advertising tagline, "the world's local bank," sums up one aspect of the business. However, the company, which has major subsidiaries in Hong Kong, Europe, the United States, and South America, is also heavily involved in commercial lending and investment banking (HSBC 2002).

Over the last several years, managers began fielding more and tougher questions from shareholders and stakeholders about the environmental impacts of the company's operations and lending policies (Beck 2002). Employees dutifully attended to issues like energy conservation and paper use, but HSBC had not done an environmental audit before 2002 and had made several questionable investments, including lending money for the Three Gorges Dam Project and supporting unsustainable oil palm plantations in Indonesia (Carrell 2002:6). At the same time, the bank began building an even more global institution. It acquired several new subsidiaries and aimed to associate its red hexagon logo with integrity, trust, and customer service (HSBC 2002:9). The group's chairman, Sir John Bond, began pushing to use HSBC's corporate philanthropy as a means to build that reputation (Beck 2002; Neville 2002).

While the company had supported local education and environmental projects for years, its London headquarters now began trolling for ideas with more global reach. The bank solicited proposals for partnerships from environmental organizations and developed a group of projects that could make a difference for the environment on an international scale. While the potential for real environmental improvement was a major criterion in choosing the projects, it wasn't the sole motivation. "We certainly don't mind if our actions make our customers think well of us, or if we're seen as a more attractive employer" says Chairman Bond (Bond 2002). And, while giving alone won't alter the effect of operations or lending policies, HSBC began to establish environmental partnerships that could promote a keener awareness of the company's impacts at many levels.

A Partnership with Global Reach

The new round of HSBC projects includes a company investment of $50 million in partnerships with three nonprofit conservation organizations. A grant of US$11 million to Botanic Gardens Conservation International (BGCI) funds biodiversity education and helps revitalize 16 botanic gardens in Asia and Latin America. A partnership with the World Wildlife Fund (WWF) worth US$18.4 million, focuses on freshwater management and restoration in the Brazilian Amazon, China's Yangtze River, United Kingdom farming communities, and the Rio Grande river basin. The third program, costing US$16 million, engages HSBC employees directly. It funds their participation in educational research expeditions sponsored by Earthwatch, a nonprofit environmental research and education organization. Like other Earthwatch participants, HSBC employees will donate much-needed labor to biological conservation and monitoring projects around the globe, gaining an intimate understanding of threatened ecosystems and a broader awareness of ecological issues in general (HSBC et al. 2003). Earthwatch has similar corporate programs with other companies, including Rio Tinto and Shell Oil (Hillyard 2002).

Adventures Near and Far: The Earthwatch Partnership

Over the next five years, as part of the Earthwatch partnership, HSBC will send 2,000 employees to study threatened frogs in Australia, track jaguars in Brazil's Pantanal, participate in reforestation projects, and help to monitor acid rain in the Czech Republic, among a range of choices. A portion of the bank's financial contribution will also support training for developing-country scientists in current conservation and monitoring techniques (Higgins 2002; HSBC et al. 2003).

As Earthwatch volunteers, participants often camp at remote sites and endure all the discomforts of doing field research while contributing to essential environmental work. After returning to HSBC, each employee plans a community conservation project and receives follow-up guidance from Earthwatch. To each employee's community project HSBC contributes $500 (Combes 2002). Typical projects have included a community composting scheme, a revitalization plan for a village pond, and a monitoring program for a local wildlife trust (Hillyard 2002). Timothy O'Brien, a technical manager for HSBC in Buffalo, NY, tracked mountain lions in Idaho with Earthwatch and is planning a project to improve ruffed grouse habitat in his home state (O'Brien 2002).

By encouraging employees to integrate their new skills and energy into their daily activities and to make a difference in their communities, HSBC hopes to leverage the substantial investment it has already made. Adding a financial contribution creates an extra incentive for employees to take responsibility for the outcome of their efforts.

Challenging Partners

Partnering with three such large and respected environmental organizations offers HSBC many advantages. Working together, the professional public relations departments of these large NGOs have spread the word of their HSBC partnerships far more broadly and effectively than had been possible under the bank's formerly patchwork approach to giving. The size of the projects and the NGOs' experience make it more likely that HSBC will be effective in its goals and that the difference will be noticeable on a global scale. In a typical results-driven approach, HSBC has retained an environmental auditing firm to monitor the projects, and continued contributions will be tied to demonstrable results (Beck 2002).

The grant-making negotiations, which lasted about 18 months, held a few surprises and challenges for the company (Beck 2002). Reputation is just as important to a global brand like WWF as it is to HSBC. And while US$18 million can make a huge difference in WWF's programs, one of the biggest opportunities in a partnership like this is the chance to engage a company in a candid, committed conversation about its practices (Neville 2002). All three environmental partners asked tough questions, not just about the bank's own operations, but also about the indirect impacts of their lending. They insisted on speaking with top management. But while they needed to assure themselves that the company was committed to the process and to change, they weren't looking for a company that had all the answers. "In some ways," says Earthwatch's Dave Hillyard, "working with companies who have a large environmental impact provides a greater opportunity for environmental gains" (Hillyard 2002).

Exposure to their new environmental partners may well inspire a few internal changes at HSBC. For example, until this latest initiative, managers at the bank had not put in place an Environmental Management System—a fairly common approach to monitoring, documenting, and ultimately reducing a company's environmental impacts (Beck 2002). (See Box 6.5.) Managers are generally hired and groomed from within and it is not uncommon for senior managers to have been with the company for 40 years (Beck 2002). The practice encourages a powerful loyalty and depth of experience, but it also means that company policies are rarely articulated or questioned as they would be elsewhere. "We're evolutionary, not revolutionary," says HSBC's head of external relations, Richard Beck (Beck 2002). When their new partners started asking about specific lending policies, managers could produce no documentation, though they maintained they had been more attentive to environmental issues in recent years (Beck 2002).

They may still be reticent about articulating their internal changes publicly, but HSBC embraced the challenges such a partnership presents when they initiated it, and they are apparently moving toward greater awareness and transparency. The UK division produced its first environmental management report in May 2002 and the bank is in the process of expanding systematic environmental reporting to its global operations (HSBC 2003:20).

If HSBC should be tempted to relax its efforts, there is some internal motivation built into the program. With 2,000 freshly educated and inspired employees returning from Earthwatch expeditions in the next five years, the bank is building a corps of knowledgeable, empowered employees eager to sustain that agenda. "That's approximately one percent of their work force," says Dave Hillyard, "I don't think they quite realize what impact that will have" (Hillyard 2002).

tory or voluntary–takes place. In addition, government action can help bring coherence to the diverse disclosure tools that exist.

A Stronger Business Case

In too many cases, businesses simply are not convinced of the strategic advantage of providing information on their environmental performance. This is not for lack of theory. For many years, business theorists, NGOs, and others have advanced the idea that openness adds to a company's reputation–its "branding" as responsible and deserving of the continued right to operate. They have also argued that companies should see performance reporting as an opportunity to improve internal processes and reduce potential liabilities, rather than as a threat.

Many outside of business find this convincing. A 2000 survey of 100 leading European investors, policy-makers, regulators, media, and NGOs found that two thirds of those surveyed believe that a company's reputation for social responsibility is crucial to business success. Nearly half also believe that it will have a direct impact on company share prices (Burson-Marsteller 2000).

But for many business managers, the argument remains theoretical. They may believe in the value of their company's brand name, but see little analytical evidence that the expenses related to disclosure will bring sufficient compensation in terms of better branding. They lack data on how much their efforts toward better environmental performance contribute to the overall value of the company's reputation. Nor is there much movement to rectify this analytical gap. A 2001 study found no corporate efforts or studies that quantify the link between corporate environmental actions and the company's brand value (Reed 2001:15).

Programs like the Global Reporting Initiative are guiding businesses to the indicators they need to understand how good environmental practice can connect to good financial performance. However, only a handful of companies have gathered and organized data that show the impact on earnings of various environmental programs, such as reducing or creating revenue streams from waste. Baxter International, a global medical products and services company, is among those estimating the net financial impacts of its environmental programs. Baxter reports that these programs contributed income, savings, and cost avoidance of about $75 million in 2000 (Baxter International Inc. 2001:45). IBM has released similar data showing that the operating margin from its environmental efforts is 1.1 percent (Reed 2001:10). Even so, neither of these companies attempted to quantify the added brand value that their actions created.

Some Japanese companies, such as Kirin, Matsushita, and Ricoh Japan are also linking sustainability investments to good business practice in their reports, perhaps because government guidelines encourage detailed reports on environmental costs and savings (SustainAbility and UNEP 2002:45–47).

There is also evidence that the effort to compile an environmental report can itself result in cost savings as businesses identify ways to refine processes and reduce waste. Some 25 percent of the businesses taking part in the Danish Green Accounts program, which requires corporate environmental reports from more than 1,000 Danish businesses, say their Green Account reports have helped them realize such savings (Danish Environmental Protection Agency 2003). To advance the internal rationale for disclosure, this kind of effort by businesses to quantify the benefits of their environmental investments to the bottom line and the brand name must expand markedly.

Greater Engagement with Communities and Partners

Disclosure by a company should be the beginning of a relationship with the surrounding community and other stakeholders–not an end to it. When companies offer information about their operations, they should also have the chance to put it in context and address the concerns it may raise. But the opportunity to provide that context often only arises in dialogue with stakeholders. That means reaching out to communities, NGOs, investors, and others who will be using the information provided.

Company outreach can take many forms, such as community advisory panels, company ombudsmen, participation in local disaster planning efforts, corporate philanthropy, and partnerships of various types with stakeholder groups.

Community advisory panels are one formalized structure that companies can use to maintain a working relationship with local communities and other stakeholders. Ideally, these independent bodies contain a cross-section of community members, with company management in attendance but not in control. They provide companies with a forum to listen to community concerns, explain company policies on contentious issues such as transportation of hazardous waste, get local reaction to facility expansion plans, and tackle the question of what information the community really needs in order to feel comfortable (ACC 2001:10-14, 29-31, 44-46, 61-72).

The chemical industry's Responsible Care program has met with some success in improving its community relations by stressing the importance of community advisory panels. As part of the U.S. Responsible Care program, more than 300 such local panels have been formed in the last three decades. In 1997, the community advisory panel in Channelview, Texas, successfully engaged two local chemical producers to negotiate a "source reduction project." The genesis of the project came from community concerns about the health effects of plant emissions. By 2000, the project had reduced toxic air emissions and cut back on the flaring of waste gases at the chemical plants (ACC 2001:71).

Partnerships with communities, NGOs, and other stakeholders can help to address the issues that environmental performance disclosure raises. Such collaborations, often

A survey of 100 leading European investors, policy-makers, regulators, media, and NGOs found that two thirds of those polled believe that a company's reputation for social responsibility is crucial to business success.

structured around a specific commitment or performance target by industry, can provide strong incentives for greater corporate responsibility and innovation. A partnership between the Environmental Defense Fund and McDonald's Corporation in 1989 led to a waste reduction program that eliminated 150,000 tons of packaging and recycled 1 million tons of corrugated cardboard between 1989 and 1999 (Environmental Defense Fund 1999).

Similarly, Starbucks Corporation partnered with the Alliance for Environmental Innovation in 1996 to increase use of reusable cups and redesign single-use cups to reduce the environmental impacts of coffee consumption (Frankel 1998:70). Multinational fish retailer Unilever teamed with the World Wide Fund for Nature in 1996 to form the Marine Stewardship Council (MSC), which has since established a certification and eco-labeling program for fish harvested in a sustainable manner. Consumers who select fish with the MSC logo know they have not contributed to over-fishing (Frankel 1998:70-71; OECD 2001:119). In all these cases, companies have acted to counter common perceptions–derived from informal disclosure and heightened awareness–that they were contributing to environmental problems.

Even corporate philanthropy–business donations that support charitable projects–can be an opportunity to engage in genuine dialogue with communities and civil society organizations. Projects that start as simple expressions of corporate good citizenship can evolve into learning tools for businesses. When the transnational bank HSBC entered into a recent partnership with three environmental organizations to fund biodiversity conservation, it also ended up improving its environmental reporting policies. (See Box 6.9.)

The Continuing Need for Government Regulation

Effective government regulation is behind all effective disclosure–mandatory or voluntary. Pollution registers and other mandatory disclosures by definition require a direct government role. But even companies that voluntarily publish environmental performance reports, commit to codes of conduct, or choose to partner with NGOs are motivated at some level by the potential to avoid regulation, or to gain the reputation of exceeding regulations. In other words, a clear, enforceable environmental regulatory regime provides the context for all disclosure, and the bar against which it is measured. This argues for the continued role of regulators in making information disclosure drive true business accountability (Harrison 1999:45-46; Jenkins 2002:51).

Beyond providing businesses with baseline environmental standards to be met–and the credible threat of additional regulation in the future–regulators also have a more direct role in effective disclosure. For one, governments are the only institutions with the power, through legal enforcement, to demand honesty from businesses in their disclosures. Without this oversight, the power of disclosure wanes dramatically. Third-party oversight from certification agencies and private auditors is an important adjunct to government efforts, but in the end, governments exercise final authority.

Unfortunately, effective oversight is often lacking. In the United States, for example, the Securities and Exchange Commission (SEC) only sporadically enforces its few environmental disclosure rules. A 1998 survey by the U.S. Environmental Protection Agency found that three of every four publicly traded U.S. corporations in the survey had openly violated the SEC's requirement to report their environmental liability exposure to shareholders (ENS 2002). Enron's high-profile reporting fraud further highlighted the importance of accurate public disclosure, and the role of governments in ensuring accuracy and transparency (SRI World Group Inc. 2001b:81).

Governments also have indirect roles to play in supporting disclosure. Government economic policies, for example, set the broad context in which business decisions are made. When they help companies to place economic value on resources like water and clean air, and environmental services like a stable climate and biodiversity conservation, they strengthen the business rationale for best practice. This in turn reduces resistance to environmental performance disclosure and eco-labeling. (See Box 6.10.)

A recent UNEP analysis of progress toward sustainability by 22 industry sectors found that many were reducing emissions and toxic releases and improving water efficiency–areas where tax and regulatory structures ensured a clear return on investment in clean-up and improved efficiency. However, where the value of environmental efforts were difficult to measure–such as protecting biodiversity or reducing the impacts of product use–progress was less obvious (UNEP 2002:5). Government has an essential role in helping industries quantify the economic value of biodiversity and other hard-to-value environmental services, and in crafting economic incentives–through regulation, tax policies, or market mechanisms–to protect such services. Disclosure then becomes a useful tool to encourage business to follow through on these incentives.

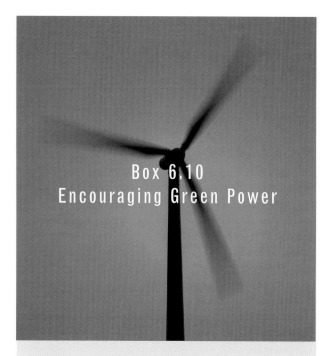

Box 6.10
Encouraging Green Power

Green power—generated from renewable sources such as hydroelectric dams and wind turbines—is now an option for many electricity customers. It is usually priced slightly higher than electricity from cheaper fossil fuel sources. The marketing of green power is an example of a voluntary information disclosure strategy: utilities can choose to advertise green power options to consumers, but it's not required by any law.

Consumers seem to be using the information to change their purchasing habits. Green power customers number 775,000 in the Netherlands, 280,000 in Germany, and 62,000 in Australia. Leeds Metropolitan University in the United Kingdom started buying 30 percent of its energy from green sources in October 1999. Edinburgh University signed an agreement in 2002 to purchase 40 percent of its power from green sources.

But the new availability of information about energy sources and the power to choose hasn't come about merely because of consumer demand and the clamor of NGOs. Governments have encouraged greater transparency and product information dissemination from power companies, and have greatly influenced public acceptance of green power through progressive legislation and regulations. The UK government made renewable energy sources exempt from a climate change levy enacted in April 2001, allowing customers to save money by buying green. The Netherlands' rapid growth in green power consumption is driven by a similar tax exemption. Germany, too, exempts green power from energy taxes and even pays private green power producers a premium rate for energy they feed into the electricity grid (Fischlowitz-Roberts 2002).

Governments also have an important educational function. Whether business disclosure in fact encourages good environmental performance depends, in large measure, on an informed public. Governments build the capacity of citizens to use information to hold companies accountable (see Chapter 3). Many governments have made information on company emissions and other performance measures easily available through the Internet and other public information sources. But they must also present objective analysis of what these results mean—including trends by pollutant and by industrial sector—and they must try to provide context for the information.

Needless to say, such information means nothing if the political space to act on it is absent. For disclosure to be an effective tool, basic civil liberties such as freedom of speech, the rights of civil society groups to organize freely, and an independent press need to be in place (Schmidheiny et al. 1997:151). Effective disclosure also requires an efficient and independent judiciary, so that the public can enforce its rights in court and press liability claims in a timely manner if the information warrants.

Finally, governments can play a useful role in streamlining the disclosure tools available today and integrating them into a more coherent system of information. For example, governments who adopt the new PRTR Protocol negotiated under the Aarhus Convention can establish a "Regional Pollutant Register" that integrates the pollutant data from all participating countries. Such a regional register has already proved useful in North America. The ultimate goal should be to provide the broadest set of comparable measures, both by facility and across industrial sectors, across the largest region. Disclosure at this scale would provide a variety of new uses for the data—to both the public and government regulators tracking industry trends.

Governments can also help bring order to the disclosure field by weighing in on the question of which sustainability indicators companies should use in their voluntary reporting, and by encouraging companies to adopt a standardized approach, as recommended by the Global Reporting Initiative. Governments might also play a useful advisory role in reconciling some of the different eco-labeling programs currently in the field.

CHAPTER 7

INTERNATIONAL ENVIRONMENTAL GOVERNANCE

The interconnectedness of the global environment is beyond dispute. Few would disagree that coordinated international action is essential to protecting Earth's climate, preserving its biodiversity, and managing its marine and other common resources. In short, the need for a coherent system of international environmental governance is clear. But constructing such a system, and maintaining its effectiveness in the face of the many competing interests of nations, has proven exceedingly difficult.

Governing at the Global Scale

It is not enough to confine our environmental governance to the local or national level only. The global biosphere behaves as a single system, where the environmental impacts of each nation ultimately affect the whole. That makes a coordinated response from the community of nations a necessity for reversing today's global environmental decline. But the challenges of international governance are substantial. Finding consensus among nations about what sustainable development means, how to finance it, and what international laws and institutions are required to facilitate it is an urgent, but unfinished task.

The difficulty of pursuing environmental governance at the global scale is made greater by the obvious fact that there is no global government–no central institution with authority sufficient to craft strong environmental protections at the international level and to insist on compliance. In its absence, a looser system of global environmental governance has emerged. The current system reflects the strengths and dysfunctions of global politics, and shows the difficulty of inspiring effective cooperation among the fractious community of nations–even on environmental matters that all agree require common action.

The current system of international environmental governance consists of three basic elements. One component is a collection of intergovernmental organizations, such as the United Nations Environment Programme (UNEP), the United Nations Development Programme (UNDP), and other specialized UN agencies and commissions that are responsible for coordinating policy on the environment at the international level. These organizations, controlled by UN member nations, are charged with formulating an international agenda that will protect the environment and promote sustainable development. A variety of other international organizations, such as the World Bank and the World Trade Organization (WTO), also play important roles in global environmental decision-making.

A second element of the international environmental governance system is the framework of international environmental law that has evolved over the last century or so. This takes the form of a web of environmental treaties, such as the Framework Convention on Climate Change or the recently negotiated Stockholm Convention on Persistent Organic Pollutants. These are legally binding agreements among countries to take joint action on different environmental problems, with each nation responsible for action within its own territory.

A third element is financing mechanisms–to build capacity to carry out treaty commitments, to supplement national efforts toward sustainable development in poorer countries, and to support the UN agencies and treaty secretariats that coordinate and carry out environmental efforts. Some of these mechanisms are more general, such as the system of dues and voluntary contributions that funds UN agencies, or the financing that the World Bank and other multilateral development banks provide for development activities with environmental components. Other financing mechanisms, such as the Global Environment Facility, are more specifically targeted to environmental activities.

Note: In drafting this chapter, World Resources Institute acknowledges the input and advice of its publication partners (UN Environment Programme, UN Development Programme, and World Bank), but takes final responsibility for the analysis presented here.

Together, the three components of international environmental governance are supposed to set priorities and facilitate steps to protect the environment and further sustainable development. Most of these steps must be implemented by individual nations themselves. From legislation to regulation to enforcement, it is the actions taken by nations at the domestic level that ultimately count most for success at the global level. But international organizations like UNDP, UNEP, and the World Bank also play major roles in implementation. Bilateral aid agencies and civil society groups also participate in important ways, as does the private sector.

Supplementing these elements is a continuing series of international environmental "summits," such as the 2002 World Summit on Sustainable Development in Johannesburg and the Earth Summit in Rio de Janeiro in 1992. These large gatherings are intended to provide highly visible forums that advance global resolve on the environment (see Box 7.1).

The record of governance this loose global regime has compiled is decidedly mixed. On the positive side, the international community has clearly accepted the environment as a key topic in global affairs, crafting hundreds of environmental agreements that promise cooperation on topics as specific as protecting certain species of sea turtles and as broad as preventing harm to the global climate. Supporting this growing will toward sustainability has been a gradual expansion of the capacity to assess global environmental threats through monitoring and analysis that the international community accepts as scientifically valid, and therefore a neutral basis for understanding and negotiation. Although far from perfect, this analysis has begun to bring the principle of access to environmental information to life at the international level–an essential enabling condition for action.

However, the international environmental governance regime has fallen short in many respects. Even internal UN assessments have concluded that the system is fragmented, with a host of policy-making organizations, treaties, financing mechanisms, and implementation projects whose efforts are often poorly coordinated and sometimes overlapping. There is a strong sense that "current approaches to global environmental management and sustainability are...ineffective" (UNEP 2001a:19). In many instances, international negotiations produce agreements with ambitious goals, but without realistic means of implementing or financing them. At a more fundamental level, international governance institutions are weakened by divisions among countries and regions, often manifesting themselves as North-South divides in terms of environmental priorities and perceived responsibilities. These weaknesses and divisions limit the capacity of the international community to respond to even the most pressing environmental problems–and may be an important reason why the combined efforts of dozens of organizations, hundreds of treaties, thousands of international meetings, and billions of dollars have failed, in most instances, to reduce environmental decline.

The international environmental governance regime has fallen short in many respects. Even internal UN assessments have concluded that the system is fragmented.

The relative ineffectiveness of international environmental governance is most apparent when compared to the evolving system for international governance of trade and investment. Not only does the World Trade Organization wield more concentrated authority over trade than any single environmental organization, but international trade agreements have strong enforcement and dispute resolution mechanisms. Moreover, international trade and finance policies have significant impact on the environment and real potential to trump international environmental policies when they come into conflict.

To be fair, the international environmental governance system is still a work in progress. Nearly all of it has come into being in the three decades since the environment began to be a common concern, and it continues to evolve, with new efforts to strengthen key elements agreed to at the Johannesburg summit. Civil society and the private sector have taken more active roles as the growth of "multi-stakeholder processes" has created a political space for the input of environmental, human rights, scientific, business, and other organizations in international decision-making processes. New partnerships that link civil society groups, businesses, and governments have also begun to make their influence felt at the international level, shifting some of the burden of implementing global solutions to groups that can tackle issues quickly and with special focus. These new coalitions have become a more dynamic force as the formal machinery of statecraft has shown its limitations.

Setting Environmental Policy: A Symphony of Organizations

The formal system of international environmental governance starts with the United Nations. The UN family of organizations includes the UN Environment Programme (UNEP), which has been given the principal environmental mandate but comparatively modest resources. It also includes the Commission on Sustainable Development (CSD), set up to monitor progress on Agenda 21—the blueprint for sustainable development adopted at the Rio Earth Summit. The United Nations Development Programme (UNDP) plays a major role in sustainable development and in implementing the Millennium Development Goals, one of which focuses on reducing environmental degradation. The formal system also includes a host of specialized agencies. Among others, it includes the World Meteorological Organization (WMO), which deals with atmosphere and climate; the Food and Agriculture Organization of the United Nations (FAO), whose purview includes agriculture, forests, and fisheries; the United Nations Educational, Scientific, and Cultural Organization (UNESCO), which has responsibilities in science and environmental education; and the International Atomic Energy Agency (IAEA), which monitors nuclear safety and radioactive wastes. (See Table 7.1.)

It is not just UN agencies that play roles in environmental policy-making at the international level. The World Bank has significant impact, both indirectly through the implications of its development activities for the environment and directly through its own environmental strategy. The Global Environment Facility (GEF), with its own governing council, sets priorities and processes for funding many environmental projects. In addition, a number of other intergovernmental and nongovernmental organizations (NGOs) routinely influence conservation and sustainable development policy. An important example is the World Conservation Union (IUCN), an international network of NGOs and governments that operates in 140 countries and has a mandate to help nations conserve nature and use it sustainably.

Regional organizations such as the European Union (EU) or the Organization of American States (OAS) contribute to international governance both through their own programs

(continued on p. 141)

Box 7.1 The World Summit on Sustainable Development: Pursuing a Global Agenda

Ten years after the Rio Earth Summit, the World Summit on Sustainable Development (WSSD) convened in Johannesburg, South Africa, in August 2002, with 191 countries in attendance. The Summit was designed to review progress in implementing the ambitious goals that emerged from the Rio Summit. Beyond heads of state and government ministers, a multitude of observers from civil society groups, academia, the scientific community, local communities, and the private sector also made their way to Johannesburg (IISD 2002). Many of them had taken part in the extensive local, national, and international preparatory meetings that were held to identify and build consensus on key issues in the year leading up to the Summit.

Both the cost and the scale of the Summit were unprecedented, with more than 20,000 participants registered (La Viña et al. 2003:54). Its role expanded beyond the traditional bounds of an environmental conference to address three interlinked agendas (Speth 2003:28)

- *Environment*, including social justice, ecological equity, and the limited scope and effectiveness of environmental treaties;

- *Development*, including financing, fundamental human rights, gender equity, poverty, and population; and

- *Trade*, including corporate exploitation, North/South economic divisions, the roles of international institutions, and privatization of public services and infrastructure.

Although it took place amid concerns about terrorism and a worldwide economic downturn, the Summit produced some tangible results. Intense negotiations resulted in commitments by governments in five priority areas: Water and sanitation, energy, health, agriculture, and biodiversity and ecosystem management. Governments approved two major negotiated documents: The Johannesburg Declaration on Sustainable Development and the Johannesburg Plan of Implementation. In the Johannesburg Declaration, heads of state committed broadly to take action to make sustainable development a reality. The required actions were spelled out in some detail in the Johannesburg Plan of Implementation. Although many of the commitments do not specify timetables and leave room for national interpretation, a few involve

specific targets and dates for achievement. These include (DESA 2002:2–4):

- **By 2010,** achieve a significant reduction in the current rate of biodiversity loss.

- **By 2010,** encourage the application of an ecosystem approach for sustainable development of the oceans.

- **By 2015,** cut by half the number of people with incomes less than US$1 per day and the proportion of people who suffer from hunger.

- **By 2015,** cut by half the proportion of people without access to safe water or sanitation.

- **By 2015,** reduce mortality rates for children under 5 by two thirds, and maternal mortality rates by three quarters.

- **By 2015,** maintain or restore depleted fish stocks to levels that can produce maximum sustainable yields.

- **By 2020,** use and produce chemicals in ways that do not lead to significant adverse effects on human health and the environment.

Notably, governments failed to reach agreement on a target for increasing the share of renewable energy in the world's energy mix, a topic of considerable negotiation due to its relevance to climate change (La Viña et al. 2003:63).

Both the Johannesburg Declaration and Plan of Implementation are political documents and, therefore, are not legally binding on governments. Like Agenda 21 before it, the Plan of Implementation is designed to guide development, financial, and investment decisions by governments, international organizations, and other stakeholders.

In addition to these official government commitments, a myriad of non-official parallel processes, drawing thousands of participants from around the world, were convened in and around Johannesburg at the same time as the official summit. The events included conferences of business leaders, civil society groups, local authorities, scientists, and chief justices. Two of the main parallel processes were the Global People's Forum (GPF) and the Kimberley Summit of Indigenous Peoples. The

GPF was attended by thousands of representatives from nongovernmental organizations, a majority of them from the South, and resulted in two documents:

■ *A Declaration* that calls on all governments to fulfill Rio commitments and civil society to participate in implementing these commitments, while reaffirming the rights of specific stakeholders (GPF 2002a).

■ *A Programme of Action* that makes recommendations based on principles of human rights, economic justice, and environmental protection (GPF 2002b).

Meanwhile, indigenous peoples came together for the Kimberley Summit, held during the four days leading up to the WSSD's official process. The Summit produced both a political declaration in which indigenous peoples reaffirm their relationship to Mother Earth and their responsibility to coming generations to uphold peace, equity, and justice (IIPSSD 2002), and an accompanying plan of action. These and the many other parallel events are a unique accomplishment of the Johannesburg Summit. They represent a diversity of voices and interests previously unseen, and highlight the success of the sustainable development concept in spreading beyond the purview of governments and gaining prominence on the international stage.

Overall, the form and outcomes of the Johannesburg Summit reflect a 30-year evolution of the idea of global environmental summits. When the UN Conference on the Human Environment convened in Stockholm in 1972, it represented the first serious international attempt to grapple with global environmental problems, and gave birth to new institutions such as the UN Environment Programme as well as inspiring new environmental treaties to save species and curb pollution. Twenty years later at Rio, the global agenda had matured, manifesting in the Rio Declaration of key governance principles and Agenda 21, which gave substance to the idea of sustainable development.

Ten years after that, in Johannesburg, the tenor of discussion had again changed, focusing more on the social and economic pillars of sustainable development, and less exclusively on the environment. At the same time, a far more diverse array of actors beyond governments had become involved in setting and negotiating the agenda. While many viewed the official outcomes of the WSSD as modest at best, their limitations probably reflect the difficulty of reconciling apparent conflicts between the environmental, social, and economic aspects of sustainable development as nations perceive them today (Speth 2003:28–29).

or legislation and through participation in global accords. At a national level, most countries now have ministries or other agencies responsible for environmental matters. A recent UN review provides a more detailed description of the many actors and mandates that comprise the international environmental governance system (See: UNEP 2001a:9–14).

In one sense, the complexity of this system reflects the complexity and diversity of environmental issues themselves. Environmental concerns span a huge range, touching almost every aspect of human existence: The clean drinking water that is essential to health; the soils, fisheries, and other natural resources critical to much economic activity; the continued viability of ecosystems and the stability of Earth's climate that affect all living things. Not surprisingly, a large number of entities, governmental and nongovernmental, have a stake in how international environmental issues are resolved. But the proliferation of international bodies that deal with one aspect or another of the environmental agenda also reflects the rapid evolution of that agenda over the past three decades and the proliferation of new entities and structures to deal with it. Regardless of the cause, the complexity poses a real challenge: setting coherent and achievable policies and coordinating actions. How well has the symphony played together?

Some Strengths and Achievements

Over the past 40 years, one clear achievement has been increased public concern and government attention to environmental issues at all levels. The diversity of agencies and agendas has meant programs and policy voices at an international level that respond to many concerns and touch many economic sectors. Diversity can be a strength and a source of resilience, in political and biological ecosystems alike.

Moreover, the international system has demonstrated that it can mobilize scientific and legal talent to expand understanding of environmental issues and build an impressive body of international environmental law. For example, many scientists around the world, coordinated by WMO and UNEP, contributed to the work of the Intergovernmental Panel on Climate Change, whose efforts in analyzing climate processes and projecting future trends under a variety of circumstances played a major role in building the consensus that brought nations to the negotiating table for the Kyoto Protocol.

UNEP has made major contributions to international environmental law, playing an important role in developing such legal regimes as the Montreal Protocol, the Convention on Biological Diversity, and the Convention to Combat Desertification. At the national level, it has helped more than 100 nations develop environmental legislation and institutions (Nagai 2003). IUCN also has an impressive track record in drafting and promoting national and international environmental legislation (Holdgate 1999:244). IUCN has helped over 75 countries prepare and implement national conservation strategies (UNEP 2002a:9–10) and participated in the drafting of the

Table 7.1: Selected Intergovernmental Organizations that Influence Environmental Governance

Organization	Estab.	Function	Website
UN Affiliated			
United Nations Environment Programme (UNEP)	1972	The voice for the environment within the United Nations system, UNEP acts as a catalyst, advocate, educator, and facilitator to promote the wise use and sustainable development of the global environment.	http://www.unep.org
United Nations Development Programme (UNDP)	1965	UNDP, the development arm of the United Nations, strives to connect countries to the knowledge, experience, and resources needed to meet the challenges of development.	http://www.undp.org/
Food and Agriculture Organization of the United Nations (FAO)	1945	FAO is the lead UN agency responsible for assessing the state of global agriculture, forests, and fisheries, and for promoting sustainable development and harvest of these resources.	http://www.fao.org/
Commission on Sustainable Development (CSD)	1992	The CSD is charged with follow-up to the Rio Earth Summit through monitoring and reporting on the implementation of the Earth Summit agreements.	http://www.un.org/esa/ sustdev/csd.htm
United Nations Educational, Scientific and Cultural Organization (UNESCO)	1945	UNESCO promotes collaboration among nations through education, science, culture, and communication in order to further universal respect for justice, for the rule of law, and for human rights.	http://www.unesco.org
United Nations Industrial Development Organization (UNIDO)	1966	UNIDO works to strengthen industrial capacities of developing and transition nations with an emphasis on promoting cleaner and sustainable industrial processes.	http://www.unido.org/
International Atomic Energy Agency (IAEA)	1957	The IAEA serves as an intergovernmental forum for scientific and technical cooperation in the peaceful use of nuclear technology, promoting nuclear safety and non-proliferation.	http://www.iaea.org
International Maritime Organization (IMO)	1948	The IMO is responsible for improving maritime safety and preventing pollution from ships.	http://www.imo.org/
World Health Organization (WHO)	1948	The WHO catalyzes international cooperation for improved health conditions, including a healthy environment.	http://www.who.int
United Nations Population Fund (UNFPA)	1969	The UNFPA assists countries in providing reproductive health and family planning services, formulates population strategies, and advocates for issues related to population, reproductive health, and the empowerment of women.	http://www.unfpa.org
Intergovernmental Panel on Climate Change (IPCC)	1988	The IPCC was established under the auspices of UNEP and the World Meteorological Organization to assess scientific, technical, and socio-economic information relevant for the understanding of climate change, its potential impacts, and options for adaptation and mitigation.	http://www.ipcc.ch/

Convention on International Trade in Endangered Species, the Convention on Biological Diversity, and other major treaties.

Another strength has been in monitoring and analyzing environmental trends and assembling the data and informa-

tion on which policy-making relies. UNEP has played a key role in these activities, publishing a long list of technical reports, atlases, and other specialized compendia, and its *Global Environment Outlook* report offers a broad overview of environmental conditions and trends. FAO has been a pri-

Table 7.1 (continued)

Organization	Estab.	Function	Website
Outside the UN System			
World Bank, International Monetary Fund (IMF), and regional development banks such as the Asian Development Bank or Inter-American Development Bank		Multilateral development finance institutions seek to reduce poverty in developing countries by formulating development assistance strategies and providing loans and technical assistance for a broad range of development activities.	http://www.worldbank.org http://www.imf.org
Global Environment Facility (GEF)	1991	As the designated financial mechanism for international agreements on biodiversity, climate change, and persistent organic pollutants, the GEF helps developing countries fund projects and programs that protect the global environment.	http://www.gefweb.org/
World Trade Organization (WTO)	1995	The WTO deals with the rules of trade between nations through the administration of trade agreements and by acting as a forum for trade negotiations and settling trade disputes.	http://www.wto.org
World Conservation Union (IUCN)	1948	The IUCN seeks to influence and assist societies to conserve the integrity and diversity of nature and to ensure that any use of natural resources is equitable and ecologically sustainable.	http://www.iucn.org/
International Council for the Exploration of the Sea (ICES)	1902	The ICES plans, coordinates, and promotes marine research, including the assessment of fish stocks, in the North Atlantic and adjacent seas.	http://www.ices.dk/

mary source of data and analysis on agriculture, fisheries, and forest trends. IUCN regularly publishes the Red Data Books–authoritative lists of threatened plant and animal species that inform much conservation policy at the national and international levels.

Catalyzing and publicizing new concepts is another strength. In 1983, by establishing the Brundtland Commission, the UN system helped catalyze new ways of thinking: The Commission's seminal report, *Our Common Future*, made "sustainable development" an important organizing concept and spurred the effort to integrate environment and development activities. IUCN was a leading voice in partnerships that produced the *World Conservation Strategy*, *Caring for the Earth*, and the *Global Biodiversity Strategy*, publications that helped popularize the terms "sustainable development," "ecosystem management," and "biodiversity," respectively. These are concepts that guide modern environmental policy-making. UNEP's *Environmental Perspectives to the Year 2000 and Beyond* was a driving force behind the convening of the UN Conference on Environment and Development, also known as the Rio Earth Summit.

Convening governments and setting guidelines or standards are special strengths of the international environmental governance system. This occurs on every scale–from small, technical workshops to international summits, and from procedural standards to "soft law" performance guidelines. In 1998, for example, World Bank President James Wolfensohn convened logging industry leaders to promote a shift to sustainable forestry. The World Bank also worked with IUCN and UNEP to convene the World Commission on Dams in an effort to develop international consensus on guidelines for decisions on building large dams (Dubash et al. 2001:1). The UN summits have not only focused international attention on environmental issues and brought government leaders and many other actors together, but also generated the political momentum needed to forge international treaties.

The World Bank Group has established requirements for Environmental Impact Assessments (EIAs) and other environmental "safeguard" policies and guidelines. These apply only to operations financed, cofinanced, or guaranteed by its constituent organizations, but often serve as de facto global standards, at least for developing and transition economies.

Many of the largest and riskiest development projects include World Bank participation, for example, and some private financiers adopt the Bank's procedures and guidelines to reduce risk even in privately financed projects. Voluntary or "soft law" guidelines are increasingly seen as means of generating consensus and action more rapidly than the time required to negotiate binding agreements.

Many developing countries have lacked the capacity to address environmental issues effectively. Here, development agencies such as UNDP and the World Bank have played major roles—by helping countries build the technical skills, legal instruments, and staff to manage pollution or natural resources more effectively. UNDP, for example, plays a direct role in environmental governance through its country offices, 90 percent of which have assisted governments with designing institutions and implementing policies to promote both poverty reduction and environmental goals (UNDP 2001:2). In Cambodia, for instance, UNDP worked with the government to develop a National Biodiversity Strategy and Action Plan, which was launched in July 2002 (UNDP 2003a).

UNDP also provides financial support, technical assistance, and training to intergovernmental organizations, research institutes, and nongovernmental organizations. For example, in the Nile River basin, UNDP has worked with 10 riparian countries, donors, and other international organizations to develop a legal and institutional framework for jointly managing the Nile's resources (NBI 2001).

In recent years, UNDP has become a pragmatic complement to UNEP's global environmental treaty-making efforts, and has helped countries take practical measures to implement global accords. For example, through its Montreal Protocol Unit, UNDP has provided 85 developing countries with technology, technical assistance, and training to help phase out ozone-depleting substances (UNDP 2003b). And in Europe's Danube River Basin, UNDP facilitated a partnership among 15 countries, regional commissions, the World Bank, NGOs, and other UN organizations to restore the badly degraded Black Sea ecosystem (ICPDR 2003).

These are tangible achievements. The symphony has clearly made meaningful music. But the present system of international environmental governance is not without serious difficulties.

Weaknesses and Challenges

One set of weaknesses stems from the virtual impossibility of coordinating such a complex set of actors to act in synchrony all the time. The results, according to a recent review of international environmental governance convened by UNEP, are gaps in international policy, fragmentation of effort, and sometimes competing or incoherent decision-making structures (UNEP 2001a:19). International policy has all too often focused on sectoral approaches: For example, separate approaches to land degradation, forest policies, and water management, often by different agencies, even though the

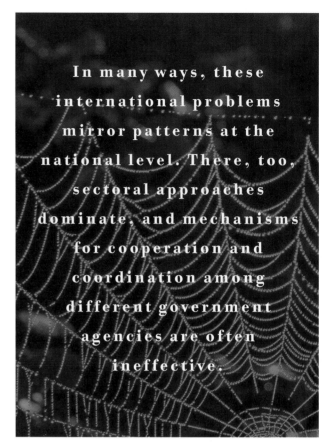

In many ways, these international problems mirror patterns at the national level. There, too, sectoral approaches dominate, and mechanisms for cooperation and coordination among different government agencies are often ineffective.

three areas are intimately related (clearing of forests is a major contributor to erosion, flooding, and water quality problems). Ecosystem approaches, like those reflected in the Convention on Biological Diversity, overlap with sectoral approaches and, in some areas, with those focused on species, such as the Convention on International Trade in Endangered Species (CITES).

UNEP, in theory the lead agency for policy coordination, in practice has a mandate that overlaps with those of a dozen other UN agencies. It has neither real authority to set the agenda nor resources to play a major role across the full range of environmental issues. Consultation and coordination efforts are on the increase, but in practice, each international organization tends to make its decisions independently, guided by the wishes of the national governments that are most influential on its council or governing board. The result, all too often, is fragmentation and inconsistency. As the UNEP-convened review concluded, the absence of coordination "seriously undermines the formulation of a strategic approach" (UNEP 2001a:20).

In many ways, these international problems mirror patterns at the national level. There, too, sectoral approaches dominate, and mechanisms for cooperation and coordination among different government agencies are often ineffective. Environmental ministries often have smaller budgets and weaker political voices than, for example, those that directly manage productive natural resources such as agriculture or determine economic policy–in developing and developed countries alike. And since it is predominately environment ministers who sit on UNEP's Governing Council, agriculture or forest ministers who have the greatest influence on FAO, and economic or finance ministers who talk to the World Bank, it is not surprising that policy gaps at the national level are repeated or reflected in the international system: In effect, it is fragmentation by design.

A second set of problems concerns weak support for existing institutions and oversight mechanisms. UNEP, for example, is financed mostly by voluntary contributions from UN member states. Participation fell substantially in the late 1990s–from 73 contributors in 1998 to 56 in 2000–but has since risen again (Cheatle 2003). At the same time, contributors have increasingly earmarked their money for special projects, reducing the agency's budgetary discretion. The result has been uncertainty and a reduced ability to plan and carry out core activities. Effective budgets for many UN agencies and the World Bank have also shrunk–even though budgets for environment-related activities at UNDP and the World Bank, for example, still dwarf that at UNEP. "Competing for scarce funds and political commitment, existing institutions are frequently torn between competing priorities... There continues to be a lack of financial resources for international environmental cooperation" (UNEP 2001a:20).

A third set of problems arises from the fact that decisions that govern production, trade, and investment often pay inadequate attention to protecting the environment and human needs. In effect, most development is not yet sustainable. This will be discussed in more detail later in this chapter, but one aspect of this problem also manifests itself within agencies committed to sustainable development, such as UNDP and the World Bank. Both organizations have attempted to integrate environmental concerns into all of their development efforts–an approach known as "mainstreaming." At the World Bank, for example, the portfolio of projects directly focused on the environment is substantial, valued at some $5 billion in 2000 (UNEP 2001a:21).

But beyond these explicitly environmental projects, the World Bank has met with more limited success mainstreaming environmental considerations into its loan portfolio. According to a recent analysis of the Bank's mainstreaming performance conducted by the Bank itself, there is still considerable ambivalence about incorporating environmental considerations into its lending (Liebenthal 2002:11). This reflects a lack of incentive and clear direction to make the environment a core consideration, as well as a lack of accountability for doing so. In the report's words, "The environment has too often been viewed as a luxury that can wait rather than a central part of the Bank's development strategy" (Liebenthal 2002:23). Again, these problems in the international system reflect a similar lack of integration of environment into broader economic decision-making at national levels.

Environmental Treaties: A Consensus for Stewardship

Environmental treaties–known as Multilateral Environmental Agreements (MEAs)–are the legal framework for international environmental governance. They are the official expression of the collective will of national governments to protect the environment and steward the Earth.

In theory, their rationale is relatively simple. Pollution across national borders and depletion of shared resources such as migratory wildlife, the stratospheric ozone layer, or the global climate threaten environmental quality and jeopardize economic prosperity and human welfare–both locally and, sometimes, regionally or globally. Controlling these harmful cross-border effects requires nations to limit their sovereignty somewhat for the common good. A nation agrees to sign a treaty because it believes the benefits of this mutual restraint–whether in the form of cutting pollution, sharing water resources, or the many other cooperative actions nations agree to in MEAs–will exceed the cost. Environmental treaties, then, depend on mutual understanding of what will be lost if nations do not cooperate, what will be gained if they do, and how much compliance will cost–in both economic and political terms (Haas and Sundgren 1993:402; Brack 2000:11; Barrett 2002:133–164).

Environmental treaties cover a vast array of international environmental issues. Some establish regimes for conserving wildlife, fish, or plant species. Others coordinate policies for preventing the spread of plant diseases like Dutch Elm disease, or of insect pests such as locusts or Mediterranean fruit flies. Many treaties, including several of the more familiar ones such as the Kyoto Protocol, require nations to curtail their emissions of air or water pollutants, or regulate their shipment and disposal of toxic wastes. Still others regulate trade in endangered species, set rules for transport on international waterways, or set formulas for sharing the water in international river basins (UNEP 2001c:3–4, 13–15; Barrett 2002:133–134). (See Table 7.2.)

International environmental agreements are not new. The first bilateral treaties on hunting and fishing were forged in the 18th century, and the first multi-country treaty focused on endangered species was signed in 1900–a treaty between the European colonial powers to conserve a number of African wildlife species (Sand 2001:3). Over 500 separate MEAs currently exist, even though many–over 300–concern regional issues such as regulation of local fisheries and have a limited set of signatories. Some 60 percent of these treaties have been signed since 1972, the year of the Stockholm Conference on the Human Environment, which is considered the beginning of serious consideration of the environment at the international level (UNEP 2001c:3). (See Figure 7.1.)

The rapid growth in adoption of MEAs reflects more than just an emerging realization of the scope of environmental decline and its consequences. It also stems from the significant

(continued on p. 148)

MEA	Purpose
Ramsar Convention - Convention on Wetlands of International Importance Especially as Waterfowl Habitat	To conserve and promote the wise use of wetlands.
World Heritage Convention - Convention Concerning the Protection of the World Cultural and Natural Heritage	To establish an effective system of identification, protection, and preservation of cultural and natural heritage, and to provide emergency and long-term protection of sites of value.
CITES - Convention on International Trade in Endangered Species of Wild Fauna and Flora	To ensure that international trade in wild plant and animal species does not threaten their survival in the wild, and specifically to protect endangered species from over-exploitation.
CMS - Convention on the Conservation of Migratory Species of Wild Animals	To conserve wild animal species that migrate across or outside national boundaries by developing species-specific agreements, providing protection for endangered species, conserving habitat, and undertaking cooperative research.
UNCLOS - United Nations Convention on the Law of the Seas	To establish a comprehensive legal order to promote peaceful uses of the oceans and seas, equitable and efficient utilization of their resources, and conservation of their living resources.
Vienna Convention - Convention for the Protection of the Ozone Layer	To protect human health and the environment from the effects of stratospheric ozone depletion by controlling human activities that harm the ozone layer and by cooperating in joint research.
Montreal Protocol - Protocol on Substances that Deplete the Ozone Layer (Protocol to Vienna Convention)	To reduce and eventually eliminate emissions of man-made ozone-depleting substances.
Basel Convention - Convention on the Control of Transboundary Movements of Hazardous Wastes and Their Disposal	To ensure environmentally sound management of hazardous wastes by minimizing their generation, reducing their transboundary movement, and disposing of these wastes as close as possible to their source of generation.
UNFCCC - United Nations Framework Convention on Climate Change	To stabilize greenhouse gas concentrations in the atmosphere at a level preventing dangerous human-caused interference with the climate system.
Kyoto Protocol - Kyoto Protocol to the United Nations Framework Convention on Climate Change	To supplement the Framework Convention on Climate Change by establishing legally binding constraints on greenhouse gas emissions and encouraging economic and other incentives to reduce emissions.
CBD - Convention on Biological Diversity	To conserve biological diversity and promote its sustainable use, and to encourage the equitable sharing of the benefits arising out of the utilization of genetic resources.
UNCCD - United Nations Convention to Combat Desertification	To combat desertification, particularly in Africa, in order to mitigate the effects of drought and ensure the long-term productivity of inhabited drylands.
Aarhus Convention - Convention on Access to Information, Public Participation in Decision-Making and Access to Justice in Environmental Matters	To guarantee the rights of access to information, public participation in decision-making, and legal redress in environmental matters.

Note: Status as of June 2003; European Union included in count of parties and calculation of world percentage.

Source: Stokke and Thommessen 2002 and Secretariat websites.

Date Adopted	Entry into Force	Parties to MEA	Percent of World Nations that are Party to MEA	Secretariat and Annual Budget
1971	1975	136	70%	IUCN, Ramsar Convention Bureau. Gland, Switzerland. Core budget: $2.4 million (2002).
1972	1975	176	91%	UNESCO, World Heritage Centre. Paris, France. Budget: $8.1 million (2002-2003).
1973	1975	162	84%	UNEP, CITES Secretariat. Geneva, Switzerland. Administrative budget: $6.7 million (2002).
1979	1983	84	44%	UNEP, CMS Secretariat. Bonn, Germany. Core budget: $1.8 million (2002).
1982	1994	142	74%	United Nations, Division for Ocean Affairs and the Law of the Sea. New York, United States. Division budget: $3.1 million (2003).
1985	1988	185	96%	UNEP, Ozone Secretariat. Nairobi, Kenya. Administrative budget: $1.2 million (2002).
1987	1989	184	95%	UNEP, Ozone Secretariat. Nairobi, Kenya. Administrative budget: $3.9 million (2002).
1989	1992	158	82%	UNEP, Secretariat of the Basel Convention (SBC), Châtelaine, Switzerland. Budget: $4.2 million (2002).
1992	1994	188	97%	United Nations, Climate Change Secretariat. Bonn, Germany. Total budget: $16.8 million (2003).
1997	Not yet in force	110	57%	United Nations, Climate Change Secretariat. Bonn, Germany. Total budget: $16.8 million (2003).
1992	1993	187	97%	UNEP, Secretariat for the Convention on Biological Diversity. Montreal, Quebec, Canada. Core budget: $10 million (2002).
1994	1996	187	97%	United Nations, Secretariat of the Convention to Combat Desertification. Bonn, Germany. Core budget: $15.3 million (2002–2003).
1998	2001	25	13%	Aarhus Convention Secretariat, Environment and Human Settlement Division (ENHS), United Nations Economic Commission for Europe (UNECE). Geneva, Switzerland. Core budget: $855,000 (2003).

Figure 7.1: Growth in Numbers of Parties to Selected MEAs

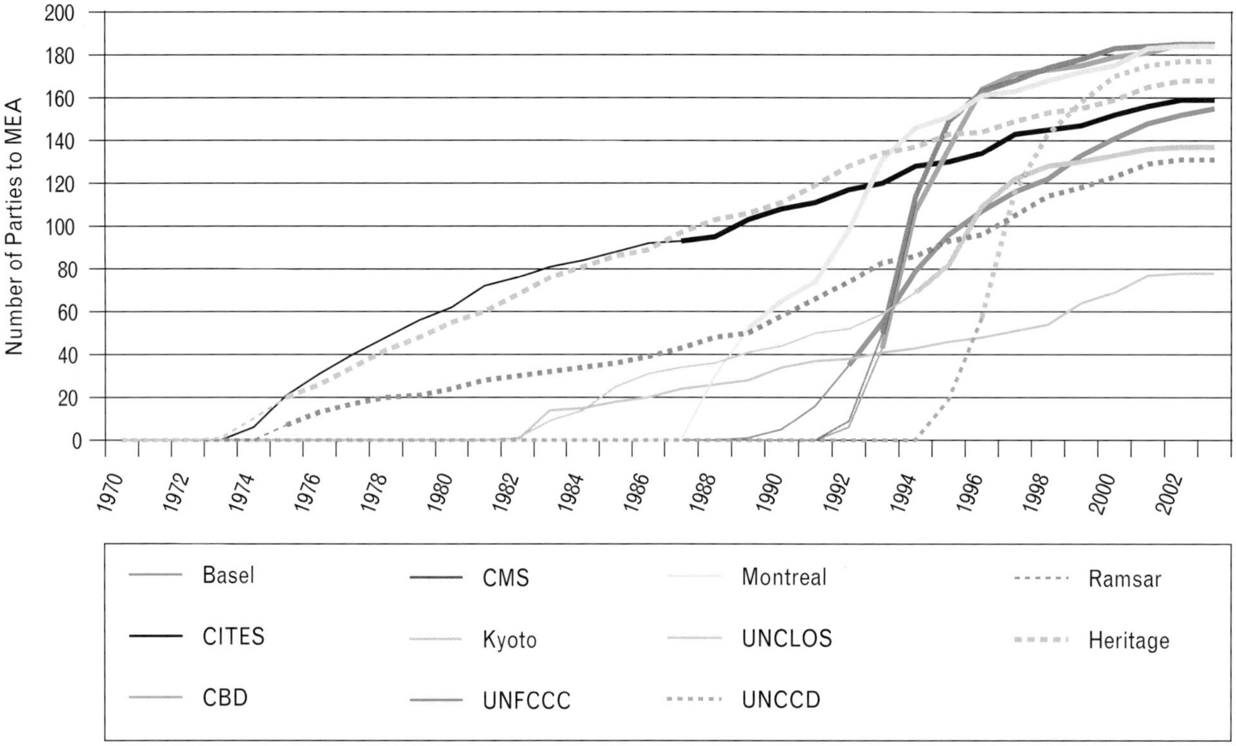

Legend:
- Basel
- CITES
- CBD
- CMS
- Kyoto
- UNFCCC
- Montreal
- UNCLOS
- UNCCD
- Ramsar
- Heritage

Note: Lines turn thick after a treaty enters into force.

Source: Adapted from UNEP 1999:201

increase in the total number of nations after the independence movement of the 1950s and 1960s. As the number of nations–and national boundaries–has grown, the occurrence of transboundary effects has been more pronounced and the need for treaties more apparent (Barrett 2002:136). The most important MEAs cluster into five areas: biodiversity, atmosphere, land, chemicals and hazardous wastes, and marine issues.[1]

The Changing Face of Environmental Agreements

Environmental treaties have changed in nature over the decades since 1972. Treaties negotiated in the 1970s and early 1980s were usually limited to single issues, such as pollution prevention or conservation of certain species (UNEP 1999:199–202). Important agreements from this era include the Convention on International Trade in Endangered Species (CITES), whose goal is to protect vulnerable species from depletion through illegal trade; the Ramsar Convention, which established a regime for protecting wetlands important to migrating waterbirds; and the Convention on Long-Range Transboundary Air Pollution, intended to address acid rain and other immediate air pollution effects.

By the mid-1980s and early 1990s, attention had shifted to broader treaties that provided "frameworks" for action on overarching topics such as climate change and biodiversity loss. The Rio Earth Summit in 1992 was the inspiration and launching event for MEAs of this type. These agreements treated the biosphere as an integrated system, rather than as disconnected forestry, marine, wildlife, and atmospheric sectors. The important role of ecosystems was acknowledged for the first time. Framework agreements launched at the Earth Summit were the UN Framework Convention on Climate Change–the mother of the Kyoto Protocol–and the Convention on Biological Diversity (UNEP 1999:202).

Both of these agreements were broad in their provisions and strove for nothing less than the sustainable use of the planet's climate and living resources. Both also stressed equity issues–the need to distribute equitably the benefits of conserving biodiversity and the costs of cutting greenhouse gas emissions. However, the detailed provisions for how to achieve these noble ends were, for the most part, left to be determined by later follow-on treaties or protocols–a task with which the international community is still wrestling.

Indeed, the current era in environmental treaties is shaping up as a time of refinement and increasing specificity in determining what actions treaty signatories must take to

---

[1] Detailed discussion of major treaties since 1972 can be found in UNEP's Global Environment Outlook 3 report (UNEP 2002a). On-line at: http://www.unep.org/geo/geo3/.

Environmental treaties have demonstrated some clear strengths. They represent in their sheer number a substantial body of international law—the very fabric of governance.

make these agreements effective, and what incentives are required to make nations participate and comply with their commitments. This could be called the "era of implementation and compliance," whereas the Earth Summit period aimed mainly to gain wide agreement on norms for environmental stewardship and the definition of sustainable development. Rather than negotiate a series of ambitious new MEAs, the belief among many observers is that it is time to make existing treaties work (Brack 2000:2; Speth 2002:20).

As the nature and goals of treaties evolved, the process for crafting these agreements changed as well. What had been a largely closed negotiating process where governments bargained in private began to open gradually to the influence of civil society groups. As environmental and human rights NGOs gained influence in society, they also started to play greater advisory and advocacy roles, particularly in the beginning stages of MEA formation, when the issues and possible solutions were still being defined. For example, the UN Convention to Combat Desertification requires nations to involve local communities in creating action plans to combat desertification, and to enlist them in reviewing the effectiveness of these plans (United Nations 1994).

Civil society groups have also become important contributors to the continuing life of treaties—the series of official meetings called "conferences of the parties" that address day-to-day problems of how to implement the provisions of a treaty and how to improve it through new provisions and refinements (Dodds 2001b:3).

Some Strengths of MEAs

Environmental treaties have demonstrated some clear strengths. To start with, they represent in their sheer number a very substantial body of international law—the very fabric of governance. MEAs also are not static documents, but living institutions—agreements that, while formally set down, are always subject to renegotiation as parties to the agreement change or new circumstances arise (Porter and Brown 1996:147). As a result, many environmental treaties have gradually strengthened their provisions and refined their procedures to improve performance. For example, the provisions of the Montreal Protocol on Substances that Deplete the Ozone Layer, which called for a gradual phase-out of ozone-destroying CFCs, were strengthened several times as new sci-

entific evidence surfaced showing the severity of global ozone depletion. The nations that signed the treaty agreed to speed up the phase-out and further restrict the most damaging ozone-destroying chemicals.

Negotiators have also successfully pioneered a variety of innovations to make environmental treaties more effective. One approach is to offer selective incentives to countries that might not otherwise sign a treaty. These typically involve payments of money, technology transfers, or access to trade. For example, the Montreal Protocol established a special fund, bankrolled by industrial nations, to help developing nations pay for the conversion to ozone-friendly chemicals. Additional funds were made available through the Global Environment Facility to assist transition countries. The Convention on Biological Diversity offers parties access to biological and genetic resources, and contains provisions for compensation and technology transfer in return for participation (Tolba and Rummel-Bulska 1998:17–18).

Use of such innovations, combined with the power of treaties to act as global convening forums, has resulted in some notable achievements. CITES, for example, put in place a global ban on trade in ivory to discourage illegal poaching of elephants, as well as a robust noncompliance procedure that has been successfully applied many times (Brack 2001: 14–15). Elephant recovery has shown the effectiveness of the ban, and limited return to ivory trade shows that the treaty is still actively evolving and responding in real time to changing conditions.

The Montreal Protocol is perhaps the most positive example to date of what the global community can achieve under the right conditions, through a treaty regime. Treaty negotiators crafted a plan to phase out ozone-depleting chemicals on an ambitious schedule, with a 10-year grace period for developing nations. Although CFCs and other ozone-depleting compounds were in widespread use in 1987 when the treaty was signed, less harmful substitutes were available and industry generally embraced the accord. The innovative financing efforts helped both developing and transition economies make the change (GEF 2002:14–16). As a result, compliance with the agreement has been high, the phase-out has gone as scheduled, and concentrations of CFCs in the atmosphere have started to drop—tangible progress toward the treaty's environmental goal (GEF 2002:14–16; WMO 2003:1).

Even where there has been relatively little progress, such as under the UN Framework Convention on Climate Change and its follow-on, the Kyoto Protocol (which is not yet in force as of mid-2003), preparatory activities and the mere existence of the treaty have had useful impacts. For example, efforts to prepare national inventories of greenhouse gas emissions have increased awareness and understanding of the threat to Earth's climate. The treaties have also spurred efforts to model climate change and its effects on ecosystems and created a credible scientific forum–the Intergovernmental Panel on Climate Change (IPCC)–to interpret this research and its implications for policy (IPCC 1995; 2001). Similarly, the Basel Convention on the Control of Transboundary Movement of Hazardous Wastes and Their Disposal provided a forum where the problems of toxic waste dumping from industrialized to developing nations attained a high profile, and the dimensions and economic drivers of the global waste trade were revealed (Agarwal et al. 2001:83–86).

An important addition to the formal legal framework of treaties are "soft law" approaches. "Soft law" refers to guidelines, norms, and even action plans that are non-binding and depend entirely on voluntary compliance. Not only are such approaches less difficult and time-consuming than formal legal treaties, they can also engage parties other than governments, such as civil society and private industry. An example is the UNEP-administered Global Programme of Action to address land-based sources of marine pollution. By holding meetings and engaging a wide range of participants, the action plan aims to build consensus and stimulate voluntary activity. Moreover, soft law approaches often help to create awareness, solution models, and other conditions that can, in time, lead to formal treaties. Just such an evolution led to enactment of the Basel Convention.

Limitations of MEAs

A two-year review of international environmental governance convened by UNEP (the IEG review) underscores some important problems related to environmental treaties. For example, although MEAs are legally binding instruments, international mechanisms to settle disputes arising from these agreements remain weak, and so does implementation. More than a decade after the high-profile signing of climate and biodiversity framework conventions at the Rio Earth Summit in 1992, nations are still struggling to bring definition to the broad provisions of these treaties, draft protocols that bring binding targets to their ambitious goals, hammer out action plans that can achieve political buy-in, find funds to pay for these activities, and design indicators to measure whether progress is being made (UNEP 2001a:19–21, 54).

Moreover, according to the IEG review, the existing array of environmental treaties lacks coherence, when viewed either in the context of today's important environmental policy issues or in the broader context of sustainable development. Largely because of the way in which MEAs have evolved

over the past few decades, they are not really a unified system of international law at all. There is no mechanism to bind the MEAs together in any formal sense or to develop common approaches. Nor have most environmental treaties arisen from holistic views of the environment, or coordinated attempts to address the relationships among environmental issues. This has resulted in a treaty system that is fragmented and focused sectorally, with separate agreements on pollution abatement, conservation, and other goals (UNEP 2001a:18). Both the IEG review and other assessments emphasize the need to move away from sectoral efforts toward a more integrated approach that reflects the "interconnectedness of the global environment" (UNU 1999:8–12; UNEP 2001a:18–19; Dodds et al. 2002:1–15).

Perhaps most important is that despite all the treaties, and the complex network of international organizations focusing on environmental matters, environmental conditions in much of the world continue to worsen. A forum of environment ministers (the Global Ministerial Environment Forum) meeting in Malmö, Sweden, in May 2000 adopted a declaration expressing deep concern about the increasing rate of deterioration of the environment and the natural resource base (UNEP 2000). From this perspective, the success of the Montreal Protocol in halting and beginning to reverse the environmental condition that gave rise to the treaty is rare, if not unique. Underlying these failures to achieve intended goals are a number of weaknesses in both the process of negotiating treaties and in their design and implementation:

- *Slow negotiation and ratification:* International negotiating processes must accommodate the differing views of as many as 190 governments. As a result, they are often excruciatingly slow, often with a decade passing between the time the international community begins to mobilize and the time a final treaty is signed. Even then, the treaty does not immediately enter into force, since it can take years to be ratified by some minimum number of countries. The negotiations for the UN Law of the Sea, one of the primary treaties dealing with management of coastal and deep sea waters, spanned a period of 9 years before its signing in 1982, and required another 12 to muster the ratifications it required to enter into force (United Nations 2003). This delay between identifying a problem and acting on it is particularly troublesome because environmental problems can amplify quickly, calling for rapid response. For example, governments who are party to the Biodiversity Convention recently acknowledged that "biological diversity is being destroyed by human activities at unprecedented rates" (CBD 2002).

- *Compromising toward the lowest common denominator:* Treaties are forged by consensus, so some compromises are to be expected. However, there is often a pronounced tendency toward lowest common denominator bargaining, where ambitious goals, mandated targets, and firm timelines are either removed or diluted. Consensus bargaining gives nations who want to preserve the status quo great leverage in treaty negotiations and later conferences of the parties, particularly if their cooperation is crucial to achieving the goals of the agreement. Such strategies weaken treaties to achieve greater participation, but risk forging an agreement that can't meet its environmental objectives.

- *Lack of monitoring for compliance or performance:* A high percentage of treaties do not insist that nations monitor their compliance in any systematic way or attempt to measure the impact of their actions. For example, the Basel Convention does not contain provisions for tracking either compliance or implementation (Agarwal et al. 2001:107–108). Even if nations wish to measure their performance, they often lack acceptable indicators to measure. In fact, UNEP reports that a lack of indicators to measure MEA effectiveness is a significant obstacle to better performance (UNEP 2001b:34).

- *Lack of provisions for enforcement:* With little mandatory monitoring of MEAs, it is perhaps not surprising that enforcement is weak as well. In large part, environmental treaties rely on an "honor system" with little, if any, accountability other than the public pressure that NGO watchdog groups can apply (Dodds 2001b:7). Indeed, even if governments are shown to be out of compliance, they are rarely called to account. Only a small number of environmental treaties actually include robust enforcement mechanisms, such as trade sanctions, fines, or withdrawal of technical or financial aid (Barrett 2002:164). Lack of compliance is often dealt with using "soft" approaches, including notices or warnings, or offering technical assistance to help the party comply (UNEP 1999:204). This may be helpful if parties are in fact striving to comply. But it may fail if the will to comply is weak.

- *Lack of technical and financial resources:* Many developing nations simply lack the technical capacity and financial means to fully carry out their responsibilities under the environmental treaties they have signed (Paoletto 1999:8–11). They may not, for example, be able to police their coasts to enforce fisheries conventions, subsidize the transition to cleaner energy technologies to cut carbon dioxide emissions, or carry out widespread campaigns to educate citizens about the need to conserve forest biodiversity. Systematic underfunding of treaty obligations—even such simple ones as filing

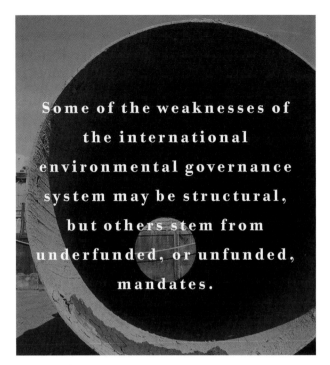

Some of the weaknesses of the international environmental governance system may be structural, but others stem from underfunded, or unfunded, mandates.

timely reports or attending conferences of the parties— is a common and significant obstacle to making treaties effective at national and international levels.

Problems of Scale and Unequal Influence

The sheer number of MEAs has become an increasing problem. In addition to the staff and money needed to design and carry out meaningful action plans, the day-to-day logistics of servicing so many agreements can be daunting. UNEP reports that European Community countries are currently parties to as many as 65 global and regional environmental agreements (UNEP 2001b:4). Each may involve its own reporting requirements, monitoring regime, trips to conferences of the parties, and annual dues for financing the treaty secretariat. For smaller nations, this can impose significant burdens on staff time and resources, and make it difficult to be substantively involved in the ongoing decision-making and negotiation that typify the life of an active treaty (Hyvarinen and Brack 2000:33).

In addition, major treaties usually establish substantial permanent offices, or secretariats, to manage their affairs and coordinate among the parties. As the focus of effort shifts to implementing the treaty, secretariats often begin to develop programs and agendas, becoming in effect little UN agencies with their own mandates, activities, and governance. This simply adds to the proliferation of agencies and fragmentation of governance. In addition, these secretariats are often physically and organizationally remote from one another, reducing exchange.

A potentially more difficult set of problems stems from the unequal influence of developing and developed countries in the system of negotiating environmental treaties—often to the perceived detriment of developing countries. First, industrialized countries are selective in their engagement in global environmental negotiations. For example, industrialized countries—and in particular the United States—exercised strong leadership to achieve international agreement on the Montreal Protocol in 1987 (Benedick 1991:6-7). Among other consequences, disappearance of the ozone layer would have increased the risk of skin cancer in the temperate latitudes where most industrialized nations occur. By contrast, industrialized countries have been relatively disinterested in the Convention to Combat Desertification, which is of most interest to African countries (Agarwal et al. 2001:1, 305).

Second, industrialized countries are also selective in the issues they address in global forums. For example, within the context of the UN Framework Convention on Climate Change, industrialized countries have neglected issues of equity, adaptation, and stabilization of atmospheric greenhouse gas concentrations—issues of interest to developing countries—while focusing on so-called "flexibility mechanisms" designed to reduce the cost of mitigation efforts, benefiting developed countries most (Sokona et al. 2002:2-3).

Third, developing countries are handicapped in their negotiating power by a variety of constraints (Gupta 1997: 132-149). For example, developing countries are often represented in international environmental negotiations by smaller delegations with less experience or knowledge than those from industrialized countries. And some environmental conventions, including both the Montreal Protocol and the Aarhus Convention, were negotiated solely by industrialized countries with developing countries encouraged to sign on later.

These multiple problems do not take away from the significant accomplishments of treaties. Without MEAs, the international community would be far less environmentally mobilized, and ecosystems would be at even greater risk. But it does indicate that the current collection of international environmental agreements is not likely to provide sufficient impetus for clear, coordinated action that can counter current environmental trends.

Financing for the Global Environment: Paying the Piper Poorly?

Support for addressing global environmental issues comes from several sources. They include bilateral aid agencies, multilateral organizations such as the World Bank and UN organizations, and the domestic budgets of individual countries. They also include international funding mechanisms set up specifically for environmental purposes, such as the Global Environment Facility (GEF) and other mechanisms associated with specific environmental treaties. NGOs, foundations, and other civil society organizations play increasingly important roles; so, indirectly, do private capital flows.

Among major agencies, the World Bank in 2000 had an active portfolio of more than $5 billion in environmental projects; UNDP had a portfolio of more than $1.2 billion, in addition to efforts in capacity-building and sustainable energy; UNEP managed about $285 million in GEF funds and another $85 million in its own projects (UNEP 2001a:21-22, 26).

The UN target for official foreign aid from nations is 0.7 percent of those nations' gross national products. This target was reaffirmed at the Rio Earth Summit. Yet, foreign aid levels fall far short of this goal, except in Nordic countries and the Netherlands, and have generally declined over the past decade (UNEP 2001a:21). Commitments made at a 2002 conference on financing for development held in Monterrey, Mexico, may begin to reverse this trend (Bush 2002). But with bilateral and multilateral budgets declining and increasingly directed toward new problems—from AIDS to rebuilding Iraq—the general climate has been one of increasingly scarce resources for official support of environmental concerns.

Innovation in Financing

In this context, the GEF has been an important innovation. Governments of the Organisation for Economic Co-operation and Development (OECD) established the GEF in 1991 as a "green fund" pilot program during the run-up to the Rio Earth Summit. The GEF was formally launched in 1994 with a mandate to help developing and transition nations implement the new climate and biodiversity treaties they signed at Rio, and to fund experimental or innovative approaches in those areas and also in ozone depletion and the sustainable management of international waters. Since then, additional mandates, such as addressing land degradation and persistent organic pesticides, have been added.

The GEF is designed to support projects with global environmental benefits, rather than projects that serve national development goals alone. It works by funding the "incremental costs" of these projects; that is, that portion of the cost over and above what the country would have spent on the project to achieve its own ends. In its first decade, GEF funded some 700 projects in 150 countries, spending $3 billion of its own money and attracting $8 billion in additional financing (UNEP 2001a:23).

The GEF works through a trio of implementing agencies—the World Bank, UNDP, and UNEP—and a small group of other international organizations, who originate and manage GEF-funded projects. Although technically the GEF operates as a trust fund within the World Bank, it has its own governing council comprised of representatives from 32 member countries. Because GEF funds are much in demand, particularly as other sources of multilateral funding have declined, this has given GEF leverage to strengthen the environmental component of many development projects.

Quite apart from its financing role, the GEF is significant from a governance perspective because it has become one of the most transparent international organizations. Independent reviews of its processes and progress are conducted every four years, and the GEF has noticeably shifted its internal balance of power by increasing developing country representation on its council and furthering its engagement with developed and developing country NGOs. The result has been described as a model of how "modern governance structures" might be designed (Streck 2001:93).

According to the most recent evaluation of its work in 2002, GEF-supported projects have produced "significant results aimed at improving global environmental problems" (GEF 2002:x). Notable successes cited by the independent review include a rapid phase-out of the use of ozone-depleting compounds in Eastern Europe and the independent republics of the former Soviet Union; considerable improvements in heating and lighting efficiency in a number of countries such as Hungary and Mexico; demonstration and eventual commercialization of coal bed methane retrieval in China; and formation of conservation trust funds to support operations in parks or other ecologically significant protected areas in many countries. More than 700 NGOs have participated in carrying out GEF projects. While noting its successes, the review also observed that it is not clear whether GEF projects have yet had a measurable impact on most of the global threats it seeks to address (GEF 2002:xi, 17, 19–20, 91).

But if the GEF has proven an important addition to funding mechanisms for the global environment, it has also added to the challenge of coordination described earlier. To support implementation of treaties, for example, the GEF has to coordinate with the treaty secretariats. Moreover, instead of using the GEF as a general purpose funding vehicle for new international environmental agreements, the international community has established a variety of additional trust funds and other mechanisms. For example, the conference of the parties for the Convention to Combat Desertification established its own separate funding entity called the Global Mechanism.

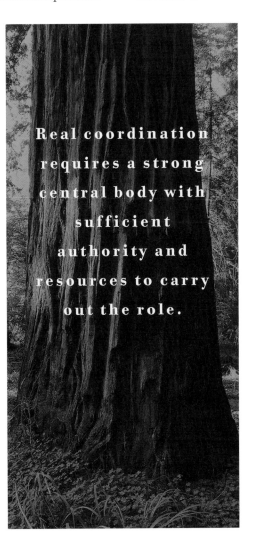

Real coordination requires a strong central body with sufficient authority and resources to carry out the role.

Matching Mandates with Resources

Some of the weaknesses of the international environmental governance system may be structural, but others stem from underfunded, or unfunded, mandates. International organizations can do little without the resources to hire expert staff,

collect and analyze data, hold meetings, or fund projects. But as the environmental agenda has expanded and the number of issues and treaties has grown, the resource base available to support it has not expanded comparably. The result is a mismatch of expectations and capacity.

UNEP is a case in point. Although designated as the principal environmental policy body for the UN system, its resources have fluctuated, limiting its capacity to lead or even to coordinate activities across the wide spectrum of its responsibilities. Compounding these difficulties has been the uncertainty of its budget from one biennial budgetary period to the next. The uncertainty arises because contributions to the core UNEP budget are voluntary and thus can change rapidly. Moreover, most of UNEP's other resources come from more than 68 separate trust funds established by donors who want to earmark the money for specific projects or purposes (UNEP 2003). As a consequence, this money may not meet the agency's needs or priorities. For the 2000–2001 biennium, core and earmarked sources together totaled just over $200 million (UNEP 2002b:60)—an amount that was higher than in recent years, but still dwarfed by the environmental resources of the Bank, of UNDP, of the GEF, and even of some environmental NGOs. In addition, UNEP is an implementing agency of the GEF, but here, too, manages a relatively small portfolio.

Other agencies report budgetary pressures in their environmental work, too. In some bilateral agencies, for example, emphasis has shifted away from environmental or natural resource concerns to other priorities, from addressing poverty to international security—a consequence of the preoccupation with terrorism. The bottom line for the global environment is that resources are tight, making reform of international environmental governance more difficult.

Strengthening International Governance: Priority Tasks

Strengthening the current system of international environmental governance will require a mix of incremental and more fundamental reforms. Common to nearly all these reforms is a recognition of the need for greater coordination and coherence among the multitude of existing international organizations that have environmental responsibilities. Even basic improvements in harmonization could bring benefits. For example, the Commission on Sustainable Development and the UN Commission on Social Development often meet at the same time in the same building, but the two bodies have no institutionalized means of interacting (Bernstein 2001:3).

Strengthen UNEP

However, the problem of coordination goes deeper than simply improving communication and joint planning among environmental institutions. Real coordination inevitably requires a strong central body with sufficient authority and resources to carry out the role. Thus, attention has focused on strengthening the capabilities of UNEP, which holds the UN mandate as the "leading global environmental authority" and is charged with coordinating international action on the environment in a manner that supports sustainable development (UNEP 2001a:4, 6, 29).

Strengthening UNEP's coordinating role could take several forms. One proposal is simply to bring all UN organizations with substantial environmental responsibilities under UNEP's aegis (UNEP 2001a:31). Other suggestions call for changes to UNEP's basic structure. For example, one idea is to upgrade UNEP from a United Nations "program" to a full-fledged "specialized agency" equipped with a new redefined mandate and its own budget funded from assessed contributions from UN members (UNEP 2001a:29). This would, presumably, both enhance its authority in the UN system and its financial stability. However, the political backing for such major restructuring is lacking at present. Indeed, nations at the recent World Summit on Sustainable Development in Johannesburg did not call for any major reform of UNEP's structure in their joint agreement at the summit's end.

A more incremental approach to improving UNEP's coordinating role may be to take better advantage of the annual Global Ministerial Environment Forum that UNEP convenes. In this forum, environment ministers from many countries convene with UNEP's Governing Council to review and revise the agency's environmental agenda and advise on areas for priority action. At its first session in 2000, more than 70 environment ministers attended, and subsequent sessions have also been well attended (Hyvarinen and Brack 2000:30, 55–56; UNEP 2001a:31; United Nations 2002:7, 9–10).

Since this forum holds the potential to command high-level government attention, broadening its role may be a ready way to increase UNEP's ability to set the international environmental agenda and to provide broad policy guidance. This could be done by expanding the range and depth of topics the ministers consider, supporting these deliberations with solid background research, and soliciting participation from civil society groups and the private sector. The effectiveness of the forum could be magnified with the inclusion of ministers from other government sectors that affect the environment, such as trade, finance, and agriculture. Otherwise, this forum risks the same kind of marginalization that already separates the environment from other economic sectors (Hyvarinen and Brack 2000:30, 55–56; UNEP 2001a:31; United Nations 2002:7, 9–10).

A necessary part of any attempt to strengthen UNEP is more substantial and reliable funding. As indicated above, UNEP's budget in 2000 and 2001 averaged just over $100 million per year—clearly incommensurate with its global responsibilities. Attention to this problem has increased in the last two years, and funding for the core budget has risen somewhat (UNEP 2002b:60). UNEP recently introduced a suggested scale for national contributions to its budget to help nations standardize their payments and add predictability to its budget (UNEP 2002b:60). Use of the scale is voluntary, but as many as 80 countries chose to comply and contributed accordingly (Drammeh 2003). While this represents progress, the mismatch between UNEP's mandate and budget remains a significant obstacle to its effectiveness.

Reorient the Commission on Sustainable Development

In the wake of the 1992 Rio Conference on Environment and Development, the UN General Assembly formed the Commission on Sustainable Development (CSD) and gave it the task of monitoring the implementation of Agenda 21–the Rio Conference's detailed plan for sustainable development. The CSD was also charged with guiding new sustainable development initiatives and developing the political impetus for nations to act on their Rio commitments. Unfortunately, in the years since its inception, the CSD has failed to become the catalyzing influence for sustainable development policy that many of its founders envisioned (Upton 2002:4).

Making good on the CSD's important mission will require refocusing its efforts so that it plays a more practical role in monitoring commitments that nations have made and reviewing progress in achieving agreed goals. This change has already begun. At its recent meeting in May 2003, CSD participants adopted a new work plan that focuses on helping countries share successful practices to implement Agenda 21 and examine the obstacles they meet and the policy options available to overcome them (CSD 2003a). This represents real progress in the longer-term transformation of CSD into an accountability mechanism.

Over the medium term, the CSD could also explore new ways to enhance the impact of future global sustainable development summits. Although summits are not strictly institutions, they occupy such a critical role in international environmental governance that reforming the way they are conducted is a priority. The Stockholm Conference in 1972 and the 1992 Earth Summit in Rio were landmark events in the history of global environmental governance. The WSSD, however, was perceived differently. Governments in Johan-

nesburg acknowledged that they need to do more to respond to the world's immense development and environmental problems. Nonetheless, they concluded weakly by ratifying existing efforts and approaches that have been found wanting (La Viña et al. 2003:62). High-level summits, especially those that involve heads of state, can be useful to galvanize action and resources. But they must be better organized, become more outcome-oriented and inclusive, and result in meaningful decisions. Otherwise, governments and the public will justifiably lose interest and the summits will become irrelevant.

Harmonize and Strengthen MEAs

Priority steps to improve the international framework of environmental treaties fall into three areas: Harmonizing international agreements and coordinating their implementation; putting into place practical mechanisms for treaty monitoring, compliance, and enforcement; and reforming the way treaty bodies, particularly conferences of the parties, do business.

Harmonizing and coordinating treaties is easier said than done. As long as there is no overarching institution responsible for overseeing all MEAs, complete integration of these treaties is unlikely. Nor is it even desirable. Experts note that the autonomous nature of most treaties has often led to greater innovation than a highly centralized approach would likely yield (Dodds et al. 2002:11). Nonetheless, some useful steps could easily be taken to increase coordination.

Clustering MEAs according to their content is one such step. MEAs naturally fall into a limited number of groupings, such as those focusing on biodiversity conservation, or those related to the atmosphere, or to the marine environment. Within these clusters, there should be opportunities to carry out a coordinated work plan that will help implement several treaties at once. This could come in the form of cooperative

research, shared capacity-building and education programs, mutual efforts to help nations draft legislation that supports the provisions of several treaties at once, or cooperative monitoring of compliance (UNEP 2001c:9). At the very least, clustering could allow better data exchange and overall information flow among related treaty secretariats.

Improved cooperation among treaties will not amount to much, however, without better mechanisms for monitoring and verifying the performance of countries in meeting their treaty obligations. One of the major features of modern MEAs is the requirement that countries report on how they have implemented their commitments. But these national reports are meaningful only if they are subsequently assessed based on a set of performance benchmarks agreed on earlier, such as the emission reduction targets and timetables specified in the Kyoto Protocol. Even meaningful benchmarks for progress and firm deadlines for attaining them are not enough. They must be matched with a credible monitoring program and robust enforcement mechanisms, including trade or other economic sanctions, in the event of substantial noncompliance. Mechanisms for settling disputes among parties are likewise essential.

Reforming some of the decision-making procedures that treaties employ is another more radical step that nations could take to improve the environmental treaty regime. Most treaties specify that the parties to the agreement hold a regular conference of the parties (COP) where interpretations of treaty provisions can be made, new rules and provisions adopted, and performance reviewed. Ordinarily, all the important decisions relevant to the treaty are made by the COP. The problem with this process is that agreement within a COP is typically difficult to achieve. Political interests often become paramount: North-South differences and conflicting political and economic interests among developed countries are frequently highlighted, and progress stymied.

Expanded trade is a key feature of economic globalization and an unmistakable trend linked to economic growth. More trade seems inevitable as the world economy grows. What this will mean for the environment is not quite as clear.

Two fundamental shifts in how decisions are made in MEAs that could potentially speed the negotiating at COPs and make treaties more responsive to quickly changing environmental trends have been suggested. One shift would be to abandon the need for full consensus among the parties, at least for some issues, by substituting rule by a super-majority, or even a simple majority. This would speed the negotiating process and make it less subject to preserving the status quo. A second shift that would facilitate on-the-ground implementation of treaty provisions would be to give more power to specialized expert groups appointed by the parties—such as science advisory groups—to make certain kinds of regulatory and scheduling decisions that would not need to be approved by all the parties at a COP (Speth 2002:23).

An additional way to increase the effectiveness of environmental treaties might be to make fuller use of regional mechanisms to implement the provisions of MEAs. There is already a consensus for increased regional cooperation on the environment, since transboundary issues such as water management and air pollution are often most effectively addressed at the regional level. Indeed, a majority of the environmental agreements negotiated over the last 30 years are regional in scope (UNEP 2001c:3). In addition, such regional bodies as the European Union, the Organization of American States, and the Association of South-East Asian Nations have developed their environment-related work through ministerial forums such as the Environment for Europe and the African Ministerial Conferences on the Environment (AMCEN). Beyond enhancing these existing mechanisms, there is also a real opportunity to foster new institutions, such as river basin organizations, that are constituted to manage at an ecosystem scale. By their nature, these organiza-

tions can address transboundary issues from ecosystem perspectives, and can directly incorporate the goals of MEAs into their institutional structures and work plans (see Box 7.2).

International Trade and Finance: Can Environment Be Integrated?

International environmental governance goes beyond the confines of global treaties and organizations that deal explicitly with the environment. In fact, the most crucial environmental decisions often come from outside the environmental sector, from the economic mainstream. The challenge of integrating environmental thinking into economic decisions—the *integration principle* outlined in Chapter 1—surfaces prominently in the areas of international trade and finance. These two drivers of the global economy have their own governance structures—institutions such as the World Trade Organization and the system of multilateral development banks and export credit agencies—that can either contribute to or come into conflict with the goals of sustainable development.

Trade and Environment in Conflict?

Expanded trade is a key feature of economic globalization and an unmistakable trend linked to economic growth. More trade seems inevitable as the world economy grows. What this will mean for the environment is not quite as clear.

There is no doubt that trade activities have direct impact on natural resources and the environment. However, the physical and economic links between trade and environment are complex. There is no conclusive evidence that trade in and of itself necessarily harms the environment. Rather, trade often magnifies the environmental effects of economic activities. If an activity like logging or fishing is unsustainable, trade can worsen its effects by increasing the scale of the activity. For example, global trade in fish products, which amounted to over $55 billion in 2000 (FAO 2003), contributes to overfishing of many valuable fish stocks such as blue fin tuna, cod, and red hake. Similarly, export-oriented cultivation of coffee, bananas, cotton, cut flowers, and many other crops can result in high pesticide and water use, drive conversion of natural forests to farm fields, and result in a loss of biodiversity (Thrupp et al. 1995:1–12).

Whether trade contributes to environmental degradation depends to a great extent on two factors: The strength of national environmental regulations, and the degree to which international trade regimes reinforce or undermine them. If a country's ability to regulate pollution and exploitation of natural resources is already weak, international trade can amplify existing problems. For example, a nation may ban the use of dangerous pesticides or logging of old growth forests. But if enforcement is rare, and world markets offer high prices for blemish-free fruit and hardwood timber, the economic incentive to violate the bans will be strong.

Whether trade rules strengthen or weaken environmental regulation depends on how trade and environmental policies mesh. The North American Free Trade Agreement (NAFTA) provides an example of each. On one hand, the environmental side agreement negotiated among Canada, Mexico, and the United States enables public interest groups to use the international forum to challenge governments that fail to enforce existing environmental laws. On the other hand, many fear that investment rules being negotiated under trade agreements will prevent governments from strengthening environmental regulations by limiting their ability to regulate in the public interest. NAFTA's Chapter 11 provisions, which allow foreign investors to recover losses incurred when regulations change, is a case in point (Brack 2001:10).

Meshing trade and environmental regulations is not straightforward. For one, the international structures that govern trade and the environment have developed in relative isolation and operate independently. In contrast to the loose global environmental regime, the global trade system is characterized by strong institutions—the World Trade Organization (WTO) and a number of regional trade regimes, such as NAFTA and the European Union (EU). These regimes have developed clear trade rules that garner nearly universal compliance, since the economic consequences of flouting the rules are severe.

The WTO, in fact, is the most powerful and effective institution for international governance that exists today. Some of its power comes from widespread participation in the world trade system, which nations cherish for its huge potential economic benefits. Yet, much of the WTO's strength comes from its ability to enforce its rules and resolve disputes among its members. If the WTO dispute settlement panel finds that a member country has violated its trade obligations, the economic sanctions it applies can be immediate and devastating.

In most cases, this makes WTO rules self-enforcing, as countries seek to avoid disputes and trade sanctions (Sampson 2002:6).

The strength of the global trading regime could benefit the environment, but only if trade rules and environmental policies can be made to support each other. Theoretically, this should not be difficult. The preamble to the agreement establishing the WTO expressly recognizes the need for trade to support sustainable development and "protect and preserve the environment" (Sampson 2002:5). Likewise, NAFTA's preamble states that member countries will undertake their trade obligations in a manner "consistent with environmental protection and conservation" (NAFTA Secretariat 1992).

But in reality, there are several points of conflict or potential conflict between the global trade regime and the global environmental governance system. Where these conflicts occur, trade commitments have the potential to trump environmental ones.

The Problem of "Discrimination"

One source of inherent conflict between modern trade practices and environmental laws is the concept of "discrimination." Free trade practices rely on the idea that countries should not discriminate against the products of other countries on the basis of where or how they were produced. Domestic products should not be favored over imports that look and perform the same (UNEP and IISD 2000:26; Sampson 2002:6–7).

But this nondiscrimination principle runs counter to the basic premise of many international environmental policies: That countries *should* discriminate against products and processes that harm the environment, and favor those that minimize harm. This idea was behind a U.S. law that banned the import of tuna caught in a way that endangers dolphins, which frequently swim near tuna schools and are easily killed if fishers do not take special precautions. The tuna ban was applied in a way that trade advocates deemed protectionist, and in 1991, a tribunal of the General Agreement on Tariffs and Trade (GATT)—a precursor to the WTO—ruled against the law on the basis that it was discriminatory (Brack 2001:7; 2004).

This and other similar rulings gave the early impression that the nondiscrimination principle was irreconcilable with environmental goals. However, more recent cases show that WTO rules may allow certain exceptions to the principle if the environment-related trade measures are applied carefully. A U.S. embargo on imports of shrimp caught by boats that fail to use sea turtle exclusion devices was upheld once the United States made it clear that the embargo was narrowly and even-handedly applied (Brack 2004). The measure was intended to protect sea turtles from entrapment and death in shrimp trawls.

It is also important to note that WTO rules do permit nations to restrict trade on environmental grounds if necessary

(continued on p. 160)

Box 7.2 Transboundary Environmental Governance: The Ebb and Flow of River Basin Organizations

What kind of governance arrangement best suits ecosystems that cross borders, such as large river systems? Local management alone is inadequate to sustainably manage natural systems that span many communities or even several nations. As a result, regional and multinational governance systems have begun to evolve to manage rivers and other natural resources that must be shared among many parties. River basin organizations (RBOs)—forums where governments that share rivers can come together to coordinate activities, share information, and develop integrated management approaches—are the most common expressions of such transboundary environmental governance.

Worldwide, there are 261 major river basins shared by two or more sovereign states, and even more river basins that cross local, state, or provincial boundaries within individual countries (Turton et al. 2000:1). Historically, shared rivers were governed through treaties at the international level, or interagency compacts at local or state levels. Today, river basin organizations constitute a fast-growing alternative. The International Network of Basin Organizations currently has 133 member organizations in 50 countries, and this does not include all RBOs at the local and state levels (INBO 2003).

A Growing Environmental Mandate

The traditional focus of international river governance has been fair water allocation, often aimed at preventing upstream states from taking more than their share. Maintenance of navigation rights and coordination of hydropower development among governments have also been important priorities. As the environment has become more of a concern, balancing interests has become even more challenging. Modern freshwater governance has begun to shift toward so-called "integrated river basin management"—a holistic approach that combines water and land management to develop and protect river basins as ecosystems. An important part of this approach is the goal of maintaining environmental flows, or water levels sufficient to sustain all the elements of aquatic ecosystems, such as wetlands and fish populations. This involves closer cooperation between upstream and downstream states to protect against basin-wide threats.

In principle, many RBOs acknowledge the need to adopt ecosystem-based approaches to basin management, recognizing that rivers and wetlands provide important ecological services like waste assimilation, floodwater storage, and erosion control. There is also increasing awareness that maintaining these services can provide social and economic benefits as well as environmental ones, including preservation of local livelihoods and alleviation of poverty within river basins (McNally and Tognetti 2002:9). In practice, however, RBOs have rarely succeeded in balancing social, economic, and environmental objectives.

Part of the problem is historical. Some well-established RBOs, such as the International Commission for the Protection of the Rhine, came into being before wide acceptance of the idea that a river's ecological services are as valuable as its water, hydropower, and navigation resources. The Rhine Commission was initiated in 1950 by the Netherlands, the Rhine's most downstream state, which was concerned about the quality of drinking water taken from the river. Since then, the Commission has gradually had to shift its agenda to accommodate wider concerns. Now, the organization's mandate encompasses "sustainable development of the entire Rhine ecosystem" (ICPR 2003).

The Murray-Darling Basin Commission (MDBC) in Australia has one of the most well-developed environmental mandates of all RBOs. The river basin falls entirely within Australia, but it spans five state boundaries, which makes integrated planning a considerable challenge. In 2001, the Commission adopted a series of objectives to make good on its vision for "a healthy River Murray system, sustaining communities and preserving unique values" (Scanlon 2002:11). These include the goals of reinstating some elements of the river's natural flow regime; maintaining sufficient flow to preserve fish runs and keep the estuary at the river mouth healthy; and managing salinity and nutrient levels to reduce algal blooms and relieve strain on the aquatic ecosystem. Notably, the Commission adopted social objectives as well, including consulting and ensuring participation from river communities. The goal is to take advantage of local knowledge of river processes, and acknowledge the historical and cultural importance of the river (Scanlon 2002:11–12).

The Mekong River Commission has also, at least in principle, recognized the importance of ecological concerns and the need to incorporate an environmental flow regime to maintain the river's enormous productivity. The Mekong basin is one of the most biologically diverse areas in the world and a major source of food and basic livelihood for 65 million people. Unfortunately, weak enforcement mechanisms and incomplete basin-wide membership keep the Commission from meeting its environmental goals (WRI 2000:206–209).

River basin organizations also have potential roles in conflict resolution, acting as catalysts for wider cooperation between countries (McNally and Tognetti 2002:16). The International Commission for the Protection of the Danube (ICPDR) has done just that. It has facilitated cooperation among Danube basin countries, lessened the division between Western and Eastern Europe in a post-Cold War political climate, and strengthened democratic institutions in the former communist bloc. The ICPDR sprang from the adoption by basin countries in 1994 of the Danube River Protection Convention, an acknowledgment of the river's importance to the region and its poor condition (McNally and Tognetti 2002:21).

Elements of RBO Success

Why are the mandates of some river basin organizations implemented more successfully than others? And what is it that keeps some RBOs from being champions of ecosystem-level governance? First, the levels of authority that governments grant to RBOs are obviously critical to their abilities to manage their respective river basins. The most successful RBOs have strong bases of support among basin governments, and high levels of authority through formal instruments like legislation. The success of the Murray-Darling Basin Commission, for example, can in large part be attributed to its ministerial authority, specific federal legislation supporting its operation, and united political backing. On the other hand, the absence of formal and binding provisions weakens the operational capacity of many international RBOs, such as the Mekong River Commission, which has no enforceable authority. Even the decisions taken by the International Commission for the Protection of the Rhine are not legally binding, though member nations generally act in good faith.

A second critical factor is the level of cooperation among members of the river basin organization. Great political and economic diversity among basin nations can cause mismatches in goals and make basin-wide decision-making difficult. An unequal balance of power between basin nations and disparate political and cultural heritages can also make it harder for an RBO to carry out its mission. For example, the Mekong River Commission (MRC) member states have diverse political agendas that have divided the basin (WRI 2000:208–209). Experience shows that when divisions among basin countries are likely to be a major obstacle, appointment of a neutral and independent chairperson to the commission can facilitate decision-making, as can the use of a technical advisory group to offer impartial expert advice (Pittock 2003).

Specific and achievable measures to implement basin-wide goals are a third important factor in the success of RBOs. Such specific measures exist in the case of the Murray-Darling Basin Commission, including a cap on water diversions and the establishment of a water market (Scanlon 2002:5). The result has been more efficient public water use as farmers are required to comply with set limits (McNally and Tognetti 2002:19).

Finally, it is becoming increasingly evident that river basin management requires strengthened mechanisms for transparency, public participation, and accountability to ensure that local concerns are incorporated into transboundary decision-making. The absence of such mechanisms may lead to inflexible or unenforceable basin-wide decisions that fail to engender local support or draw on local knowledge. The Murray-Darling Basin Commission has established channels for public participation, including an 18-month public consultation with river communities on three different plans for ensuring environmental flows in the river. A recent survey found that 95 percent of stakeholders surveyed supported the principle of returning more water to the river for environmental purposes, but that support dropped to less than 40 percent if the community was not actively brought into the decision-making process (Scanlon 2002:12).

Other RBOs have embraced the idea of public participation as well. In North Africa, the Nile Basin Initiative, which involves ten nations in the Nile basin, has incorporated openness and public participation into its discussions of the allocation of the Nile's water, a politically charged topic (Bruch 2001:11392–11393). Unfortunately, while requirements for openness and public participation are increasingly common in the mandates of RBOs, the steps to achieve these goals remain ill-defined, and public participation is still lacking in most cases (Milich and Varady 1998:37).

for protecting human, plant, or animal life, or to promote the conservation of natural resources. But in all cases, these exceptions to normal trade practices are narrowly interpreted, and subject to many conditions. In other words, environmental exceptions must pass high standards should disputes arise (Sampson 2002:6–7; Brack 2004). In effect, this gives the WTO considerable power to influence environmental policy, even if that is not the WTO's intent.

Environmental Treaties and Trade

Another source of potential conflict involves the ambiguous relationship between trade rules and environmental treaties. Over 30 environmental treaties place some type of restriction on international trade, mostly as enforcement mechanisms (Brack 2000:3). The Convention on International Trade in Endangered Species (CITES), for example, is intended to interrupt harmful trade in species. It requires export permits for all trade in endangered species, and can level trade sanctions on countries that don't comply. Indeed, as of 2000, CITES had applied trade bans in 17 cases with good results: All the offending countries returned to compliance (Brack 2000:8).

Although only a small proportion of treaties contain such trade measures, those that do may have significant effects on international trade flows (UNEP and IISD 2000:16). The point of these measures is precisely to discriminate between countries on the basis of their environmental performance. That, at least on its face, violates WTO principles (Brack 2000:13). However, environmental treaties are legally binding multilateral agreements in their own right, so it is not clear which regime should prevail in a dispute. In fact, no dispute over an environmental treaty has yet been brought before the WTO, but threats have been made, particularly against CITES (Brack 2000:3, 14).

Because of this uncertainty, many NGOs and governments suggested that nations at the World Summit on Sustainable Development should give a clear signal that WTO rules should not take precedence over environmental treaties if disputes arise. But governments were reluctant to send such a signal. In fact, a proposal was tabled that would have had the opposite effect—weakening environmental agreements by subordinating them to WTO commitments (Khor 2002). In the end, the conference adjourned with no resolution of the matter, although the wording of the Summit's final document specifically avoids subordinating environmental treaties to WTO rules.

Greening Trade: Opportunities in the Doha Trade Round

A potential start on greening global trade rules may come from the WTO's current negotiating round, called the Doha Round, which was launched in 2001 in Doha, Qatar. At the meeting, member nations provided some significant openings to address crucial trade and environment issues. In fact, the statement released by WTO member countries—the Doha Ministerial Declaration—is striking in its language on sustainable development and environmental protection:

"We strongly reaffirm our commitment to the objective of sustainable development... We are convinced that the aims of upholding and safeguarding an open and non-discriminatory multilateral trading system, and acting for the protection of the environment and the promotion of sustainable development can and must be mutually supportive" (WTO 2001a).

To make good on this commitment, the Doha Declaration established a new, though limited, mandate for negotiations on the trade-environment nexus. WTO members agreed to address the relationship between WTO rules and environmental treaties that contain trade measures. This includes

Examples of Trade Measures in Environmental Treaties

The Basel Convention: Parties are prohibited from exporting hazardous wastes to other parties unless the receiving party has not banned such import and gives its written consent. Parties are also obliged to prevent the import or export of such wastes if there is reason to believe that the wastes will not be treated in an environmentally sound manner at their destination.

CITES: The Convention bans commercial international trade of endangered species included in an agreed list. Trade in other species that might become endangered is also regulated and monitored. Trade sanctions can be applied to parties found in violation.

The Montreal Protocol: This agreement prohibits trade in identified ozone-depleting substances between parties and non-parties. The Protocol also has the ability to enforce trade sanctions against parties and non-parties who do not comply.

The Convention on the Prior Informed Consent Principle of Certain Hazardous Chemicals and Pesticides in International Trade (Rotterdam PIC Convention): Parties are allowed to decide, based on an agreed list of chemicals and pesticides, which substances they cannot manage safely and, therefore, will not import. When trade does occur, labeling and information requirements must be met.

The Cartagena Protocol on Biosafety: This recent agreement allows parties to restrict the import of some living genetically modified organisms unless Advanced Information Agreement (AIA) procedures laid down in the Protocol are fulfilled.

Source: UNEP and IISD 2000:16–17.

the issue of whether secretariats from environmental treaties such as the Convention on Biological Diversity, which is greatly affected by trade rules, can be granted "observer status" at WTO proceedings–a step that would give them non-voting voices in WTO deliberations (Régnier 2001:3–5).

Another important area for negotiation is the topic of reducing environmentally harmful subsidies, such as agriculture and fisheries subsidies. This is a possible point of convergence for trade and environmental regimes, since both consider such subsidies harmful (Régnier 2001:3–4). While agricultural subsidies have been a major concern in previous trade talks, the decision to include fisheries subsidies was seen by NGOs as a sign that negotiations might break important new ground. For years, environmental groups have advanced the case that fisheries subsidies are a root cause of overfishing and destructive fishing practices (WWF 2002:1, 3).

With these decisions, the WTO has clearly come to recognize the importance of dealing with trade and environment linkages and the special challenges they pose. However, it has also laid down very narrow parameters for what can be negotiated. The ministerial conference made it clear that the outcome of these negotiations on trade and environment had to remain "compatible with the open and non-discriminatory nature of the multilateral trading system," and that they must not "add to or diminish the rights and obligations of members under existing WTO agreements" (WTO 2001a). How much latitude this gives for real progress is not yet clear.

A Need for Greater Transparency

There is no certainty that the results of the WTO negotiations on the environment will be positive. Already, there is skepticism about whether they will truly benefit the poor and result in outcomes consistent with sustainable development (La Viña & Yu 2002:13; Malhotra 2002). While much depends on the political will and sincerity of governments, the role of civil society in ensuring good outcomes should not be underestimated. Many NGOs are active in WTO processes as activists, analysts, and protesters. In Doha, 365 NGOs attended the meeting–an impressive number, given that it took place shortly after the September 11th attacks, and security arrangements and travel were difficult (WTO 2001b).

In spite of the official NGO presence in Doha, WTO's record of transparency and openness to civil society input are not sterling. While the organization gets high marks for making its decisions and official documents publicly available online and in multiple languages, it does not score as well in receptiveness to civil society participation. In fact, much of its business continues to take place in informal sessions, announced only to those who are invited, and usually generating no written record of discussion (Maurer et al. 2003:13). With the Doha negotiations now accelerating, this mode of doing business is once again becoming a matter of active protest (Focus on the Global South 2003) (see Box 7.3).

Investing in the Environment?

The international system of investment and finance provides the capital that fuels global development. It includes the activities of both the private sector and multilateral funders such as the World Bank. It also includes the norms that govern international finance, the policies imposed on national governments by the International Monetary Fund, and the investment rules negotiated as part of trade agreements.

Because this system controls the global purse strings, its activity bears on the environment at many points, from funding specific projects–such as roads or manufacturing plants, which can have very negative environmental impacts–to shaping national economies and the way they are integrated into the global economy.

For this reason, mainstreaming environmental thinking into the institutions and rules that govern investment and finance is vital to the success of the international environmental regime. How well is the global finance regime doing in integrating environmental concerns?

International Rules Governing Investment

There is no single global treaty that governs international financial flows. But myriad bilateral, regional, and multilateral investment agreements serve to facilitate foreign investment, principally by reducing the risks faced by investors (Werksman et al. 2001:5). As with the global system of trade rules, international investment rules have developed without reference to their environmental consequences. This gives rise to several concerns about how investment rules could undermine environmental management regimes at both global and national levels.

One major concern is that international investment rules could conflict with important provisions of international environmental agreements. For example, under the Kyoto Protocol, a "Clean Development Mechanism" is envisioned to award emissions credits toward industrialized countries' emission reduction targets in exchange for climate-friendly investments in developing countries. However, such a mechanism could run afoul of investment rules by limiting the countries eligible to participate or the kinds of projects eligible for credits (Werksman et al. 2001:1–4).

Another major concern is that strengthening the rights of foreign investors can come at the expense of national-level environmental protection. NAFTA's Chapter 11 illustrates this problem. Chapter 11 is designed to protect the interests of foreign investors in the three NAFTA countries–Canada, the United States, and Mexico–from trade barriers that governments may erect in the form of laws or regulations.

Unfortunately, many of these "barriers" have been environmental laws meant to maintain clean drinking water, control the use of carcinogenic substances, and manage hazardous wastes such as PCBs (IISD and WWF 2001:15). Disputes under Chapter 11 are decided by an arbitration

(continued on p. 164)

Box 7.3: Trading Away Public Participation?

With both environmental problems and trade increasing in recent years, civil society has questioned whether the decisions made by institutions that influence international commerce are transparent—or whether they are secretive and undertaken in relative isolation from environmental and social concerns. Two trade regimes, the World Trade Organization (WTO) and the North American Free Trade Agreement (NAFTA), have been primary targets of civil society criticism. Although many of the rules they negotiate and the disputes they settle significantly affect the environment, public interest groups have found only limited opportunity to introduce environmental and other public interest concerns in their negotiations and dispute settlement processes.

To gauge the openness and accountability of trade and economic institutions to civil society input today, World Resources Institute (WRI) assessed a sample of five: The WTO, NAFTA, the Association of Southeast Asian Nations (ASEAN), the European Union (EU), and the East African Community (EAC). This selection includes international and regional bodies that deal with trade rules and negotiations. It also reflects diversity in age, with some well-established insti-

Transparency in Five Trade and Economic Institutions

How Open to Public Scrutiny and Involvement Are the Negotiations of these Trade and Economic Institutions?	World Trade Organization	North American Free Trade Agreement	Association of Southeast Asian Nations	European Union	East African Community
Does the institution post dates and locations of upcoming negotiations/meetings on its official website or publish them in another form more than three months in advance?	Yes	No	Yes	Yes	No
Does the institution post work programs or agendas for upcoming negotiations/meetings on its website, or publish them in another form?	Yes	No	No	Yes	No
Are the institution's articles of constitution available on the web or published in another form?	Yes	Yes	Yes	Yes	Yes
Are decisions or agreements taken by members posted on the web or published in another form?	Yes	Yes	Yes	Yes	No
Are negotiation processes presumed to be non-confidential unless agreed to by members, according to official documents?	No	No	No	Yes	No
Do institutional statements explicitly recognize the need for or relevance of public participation in their decision-making processes?	Yes	No	No	Yes	Yes
Do institutional documents and/or policies state that the institution seeks expert and technical advice from civil society groups/representatives?	No	No	Yes	Yes	No
Do institutional documents and/or policies include examples of institutional collaborations or partnerships with civil society to accomplish specific objectives?	No	Yes	Yes	Yes	No
Does an environmental unit/office specify how it incorporates public participation in its work?	No	Yes	No	Yes	No
Does the institution have a dispute resolution mechanism or court that settles cases of non-compliance with agreements or violation of rules?	Yes	Yes	Yes	Yes	Yes
Does the Secretariat publish or post on its official website a list of cases or petitions before the mechanism/court?	Yes	Yes	No	No	No
Does the Secretariat publish or post on its official website decisions or outcomes of individual disputes/cases?	Yes	Yes	No	Yes	No
Can citizens or individuals submit information to the institution's dispute resolution mechanism about member non-compliance with an agreement?	No	No	No	Yes	Yes

Source: Adapted from Maurer et al. 2003: 14-15

tutions like the EU, but also newer bodies like the East African Community, which was established in 2000 to create a common market among the countries of Tanzania, Kenya, and Uganda.

Specifically, WRI looked at the public's access to information about the negotiations undertaken by these institutions, access to opportunities to participate in negotiation processes, and access to redress (see Table).

Findings

Most of the economic and trade bodies surveyed are providing the public with general information about their negotiations. With the exception of the East African Community, all make available the decisions or agreements of their members on the Internet, and all post their articles of constitution on the web. However, timely disclosure of information on upcoming negotiations—such as dates, locations, and proposed agendas—is less consistent. For example, the WTO posts such information, but often too late for civil society to follow negotiations in real time.

Most of the institutions surveyed are codifying their information disclosure policies. Among the five, the EU makes the most extensive commitments to public information disclosure. The WTO has instituted disclosure policies similar to the EU, but with caveats, like restrictions on access to documents for six months or longer after production. NAFTA and ASEAN have less extensive rules for information disclosure, and the EAC has articulated few if any rules or policies on information disclosure.

Unfortunately, while disclosure of general information is improving, confidentiality of negotiations remains the norm. Only the EU presumes that most negotiations and deliberations are non-confidential unless otherwise established by members. The other institutions either keep deliberations confidential or have no clear confidentiality rules. A related problem is that a significant portion of the institutions' business takes place in informal sessions. These sessions are announced only to those who are invited, and they typically generate no written record of discussion. Nevertheless, real decisions take place in this informal context, leaving at a disadvantage not only civil society, but also countries that will be bound by decisions reached in forums to which they were not invited.

In the area of public participation, the strongest articulation of norms is found in the European Union. It recognizes the importance of public participation in its own decision-making processes, commits to consulting and exchanging information with civil society, and incorporates public participation procedures in its environmental departments and policies. Other institutions typically acknowledge the relevance of public participation, but do not formally integrate public participation into internal deliberations. For example, WTO documents and policies include general statements about the relevance of public participation, information exchange, and consultation, but limit participation to informal dialogues with NGOs. Some of those dialogues, like the WTO's public symposiums, have been discounted by civil society as public relations exercises with no impact on real decision-making.

None of the economic agreements or institutions reviewed requires its members to seek the input of domestic constituencies on agenda items or substantive issues on the docket for meetings or negotiations. In response, many civil society networks in industrialized countries routinely press their negotiators or representatives to listen to their views. The protests against the WTO ministerial meeting in Seattle in 1999 are a case in point. By contrast, civil society groups in developing countries, like their own governments, have less access to the human and financial resources that are needed to track and informally influence trade and economic policy negotiations. As a result, these groups are at least partially disenfranchised from international economic decision-making.

The five institutions surveyed present a similarly mixed-to-poor record of offering intergovernmental organizations and third parties the opportunity to intervene in or observe dispute settlements. All five institutions have created dispute resolution mechanisms such as official consultation and mediation processes. In addition, the European Court of Justice and the WTO's Dispute Settlement Body publicly disclose cases pending and rulings handed down. However, deliberations in the European Court of Justice remain confidential; similarly, NAFTA's dispute settlement and panel review procedures are confidential unless the parties involved agree to entertain third party submissions. ASEAN's dispute mechanism is the least transparent.

Few systems give much weight or opportunity to NGOs or non-parties that want to submit briefs or opinions to a court or out-of-court consultation. Only the European Court of Justice and EAC officially permit such submissions, and only the EAC posts them on its website. Also troubling is the trend at the WTO of accepting NGO or nonmember submissions while maintaining the Dispute Settlement Body's discretionary authority to ignore them—perhaps indicative that these submissions bring no real benefit or power to the submitting parties.

Source: Adapted from Maurer et al. 2003.

tribunal, and substantial monetary judgments have been awarded. For example, in October 2002, the NAFTA dispute panel awarded $6 million (Canadian dollars) to U.S. investor S.D. Myers, who had sued over a Canadian law banning exports of PCB waste (ICTSD 2002).

The most serious fallout from Chapter 11 far exceeds the actual disputes. It is the chilling effect that such judgments have on the enactment and enforcement of robust environmental laws with implications for foreign investors. Faced with potential suits, local and national policy-makers are reluctant to pass legislation that might be construed as "anti-investor." Critics complain that such effects make NAFTA's environmental language meaningless and undermine national, state, and local sovereignty (Public Citizen and FOE 2001:vii).

In 1998, similar concerns contributed to the collapse of negotiations on a proposed Multilateral Agreement on Investment (MAI). Initiated within the Organisation for Economic Co-operation and Development (OECD), the proposed MAI would have strengthened investor rights significantly compared to existing agreements. Negotiations foundered on substantive disagreements among countries, notably on provisions for environmental and social standards. They were also the target of a global campaign by NGOs opposed to unfettered economic globalization (UNCTAD 1999:5-25; Henderson 1999:38-53).

Nevertheless, there is concern that provisions similar to those in NAFTA's Chapter 11 will be incorporated into other trade agreements now in negotiation, such as the Free Trade of the Americas Agreement (FTAA), currently under discussion by 31 Latin American and Caribbean nations. This proposed trade pact includes an ambitious proposal to extend Chapter 11-type protections to the rest of the western hemisphere (Public Citizen and FOE 2001:i). Such investor protections would be unprecedented in an international trade agreement, and could greatly widen Chapter 11's chilling effect on environmental laws.

A similar debate is happening in the World Trade Organization. In its 2001 ministerial meeting in Doha, Qatar, the WTO agreed to consider new areas in which trade rules could be applied, including the relationship between trade and investment—a warning bell for many environmentalists (WTO 2001a).

Private Sector Investment

By far the greatest share of international finance flows through private channels. These include the foreign direct investment of multinational corporations, the stocks and bonds traded by international brokers, and the loans made by commercial banks. Other sources are contributions made through international charities and remittances sent home by foreign workers. Total outbound private investment flows from the United States—mostly to other industrialized countries—were estimated at more than $365 billion in 2001 (U.S.

Dept. of Commerce 2003). But data on the size and composition of these flows—which fluctuate significantly from year to year—is poor.

Nevertheless, it is clear that these financial flows have significant implications for environmental sustainability and social equity, in terms of both the ecological footprints of specific investments and the development trends they reinforce. Some impacts are clearly negative. For example, international finance of a coal-fired power plant will result in local air pollution and greenhouse gas emissions, as well as lock in a fossil fuel-based energy strategy for a generation. Other effects can be positive: For example, the environmental performance of a manufacturing facility acquired by a multinational corporation could be improved by installing cleaner technology (Seymour et al. 2002:175).

Ideally, the integration of environmental considerations into private international financial flows should be governed at the national level in countries where the investments are made. Sectoral policy frameworks—blueprints for how different economic sectors should be developed—can provide incentives for more environmentally friendly investments, while regulatory frameworks can ensure disclosure of information and public consultation prior to approval of specific projects. Unfortunately, however, the steep rise in international financial flows has outpaced the ability of many countries to put such policy and regulatory frameworks in place, and some would argue that governments' desire to attract investment has even retarded efforts to develop and enforce such frameworks (Zarsky 1997). In addition, many international investments affect transboundary or global ecosystems for which governance regimes are not yet in place.

As described in chapter six, several multinational corporations have voluntarily begun to track and report on the environmental implications of their businesses. Private international financial institutions have only recently begun to consider the environmental impacts of their investments or their accountability to stakeholders other than corporate shareholders. Most private financial transactions are not public, and information is available only through proprietary databases. Information on the environmental character of lending and investment practices is even harder to come by.

However, several international commercial banks have recently launched an initiative to promote better environmental practices in the industry. Ten banks—including ABN Amro Bank, Barclays, Citigroup, West LB, and Credit Suisse First Boston—have drafted environmental criteria to guide future investments. These so-called "Equator Principles" are based on the environmental safeguard standards of the World Bank's International Finance Corporation (The Equator Principles 2003). The banks involved in the initiative provided over $9 billion in loans for infrastructure projects in 2002. If the bulk of the international banking community follows suit and agrees to abide by such criteria, it could have a significant effect on both the environmental character of the banks' port-

Better governance means greater participation, coupled with accountability.
Therefore, the international public domain—including the United Nations—
must be opened up further to the participation of the many actors whose
contributions are essential to managing the path of globalization. Depending
on the issues at hand, this may include civil society organizations, the private
sector, parliamentarians, local authorities, scientific associations,
educational institutions and many others.

The UN Secretary General's Millennium Report

folios and on the ability of affected communities to have a say in the activities they finance (Phillips and Pacelle 2003:A1).

Regulations governing capital markets could go beyond such voluntary initiatives to render private international financial flows more transparent and accountable. For example, the Securities and Exchange Commission in the United States currently requires publicly traded corporations to disclose environmental legal proceedings pending against them. However, this regulation is seldom enforced domestically, much less against the international operations of U.S. firms or foreign firms listed in the United States (Seymour et al. 2002:194). A requirement that multinational corporations disclose their environmental liabilities worldwide would empower shareholder activists to promote the corporate responsibility of individual companies in the short run, and would harness markets to reward companies with superior environmental performance in the long run.

Public Sector Finance

The absolute volume of funds channeled through public international financial institutions, such as bilateral aid agencies and multilateral development banks, is dwarfed by private flows—by a factor of almost seven to one in 2000 (World Bank 2002b:32). Nonetheless, the potential of these public financiers to influence the character of private investment is significant. For example, the majority of loans for large infrastructure projects in developing countries are guaranteed by the export credit and investment promotion agencies of industrialized countries, such as the Overseas Private Investment Corporation in the United States (Seymour et al. 2002:177).

Multilateral development banks also leverage private resources by providing co-financing and loan guarantees to specific projects, and are able to impose their own environmental assessment, information disclosure, and public consultation practices on those projects. These environmental standards and procedures often serve as de facto international standards. For example, the Equator Principles mentioned above were based on the standards of the World Bank's International Finance Corporation.

In addition, multilateral development banks—often in collaboration with the International Monetary Fund (IMF)—exercise influence over the national policies of countries through structural and sectoral adjustment loans (see Box 2.2). Usually, conditions attached to such loans encourage governments to open their economies to foreign investment in the belief that this promotes economic growth and reduces poverty. Questions about the validity of this belief were amplified in the aftermath of the Asian financial crisis in 1997-98. In addition to opening the door to investors, Asian countries had relaxed their control over the flow of money in and out of their countries, making their currencies vulnerable to the whims of international markets. With the onset of the crisis, currencies crashed almost overnight, devastating economies and swelling the ranks of the poor.

Consequences for the environment included increased pressure on forests and other open access resources as people thrown out of work sought other sources of income. The World Bank and the IMF urged increased openness to foreign investment as a way out of the crisis, even in environmentally sensitive sectors. In Indonesia, for example, conditions attached to the IMF bail-out package included liberalization of investment in palm oil plantations, an important driver of deforestation (Seymour and Dubash 2000:90, 94).

Overall, recent progress in integrating environmental sustainability and public participation into the operations of public international financial institutions has been positive, but slow. Multilateral development banks are gradually putting into place policies that expand information disclosure, mandate environmental assessment and public consultation, and provide mechanisms for accountability at the level of specific project investments (Maurer et al. 2003:4-8).

Less progress has been made in ensuring consistent implementation of such policies, and in mainstreaming environmental considerations into all policy and lending decisions. For example, in a recent progress report on its efforts to implement an organization-wide environment strategy, the World Bank found that integrating the environment into poverty reduction strategies and structural adjustment loans were areas of continuing weakness (World Bank 2002:3).

Bilateral export credit and guarantee agencies (ECAs), which leverage hundreds of billions of trade and investment dollars annually, lag far behind multilateral development banks in integrating environmental concerns and public participation into their decision-making. A few such agencies—notably the U.S. Export-Import Bank and the Overseas Private Investment Corporation—require large projects to undergo environmental assessments, release the results of these assessments to the public, and disclose what projects and companies benefit from their financing. But most such agencies promote the commercial interests of domestic industry unfettered by public scrutiny or requirements to consider the environmental impacts of their investments. For example, Hermes, the German export credit agency, only requires environmental assessments if they are legally mandated by the country where the project is located. Hermes does not release the results of these assessments, and provides no information to the public on specific projects that it finances (Maurer 2002:9).

In 1999, the governments of industrialized countries agreed to negotiate common environmental guidelines for projects financed by ECAs. However, these negotiations have failed to achieve consensus on the standards to be used in environmental assessments or the information that should be disclosed to the public and affected communities (Maurer 2002:16–19).

New Players, More Inclusive Processes

As the challenges of international environmental governance have become clearer, and the inability of governments to fully meet these challenges more apparent, a variety of new actors and new approaches have come into play. The expanded role of civil society in international governance processes is probably the most visible aspect of this. Whether in high-profile summits or in conferences of the parties of environmental treaties, civil society attendance and participation has increased in volume and diversity. This expansion, in turn, has resulted in the emergence of officially sanctioned "multi-stakeholder processes." These forums are built around the idea of bringing all parties into the deliberation process in order to achieve real exchange between governments and civil society. Greater civil society involvement has also spawned many government-NGO and public-private partnerships. Such partnerships have become a significant new outlet for addressing environmental concerns and defining sustainable development.

But have these new developments really made a difference? Is civil society participation limited to mere attendance and observation of meetings, or is it truly substantive? Do multi-stakeholder processes address issues that governments care about, and do governments take heed of what they hear? Will partnerships supplant legal commitments by governments, and let them off the hook? Do partnerships open the door for vested economic interests to unduly influence governments and intergovernmental processes? Are the decisions that emerge really better—socially and environmentally—because of these innovations?

Expansion and Effectiveness of Civil Society Participation

Civil society's attendance records at the landmark environmental and sustainable development events of the last thirty years—the 1972 Stockholm Conference on the Human Environment, the 1992 Earth Summit in Rio, and the 2002 World Summit on Sustainable Development in Johannesburg—show how dramatically civil society participation has grown. Only 134 NGOs were accredited to participate in Stockholm, but by Johannesburg, the number had risen to nearly 3,000 organizations (see Figure 7.2), with some 8,000 individuals from these groups attending (Haas et al. 1992:32; DESA 2002; Willetts 2002).

The involvement of civil society groups has not been limited to these big UN summits. It is also a phenomenon in the major meetings convened under the various multilateral environmental agreements such as the Framework Convention on Climate Change (UNFCCC) and the Convention on Biological Diversity.

Diversity of civil society representation in governance processes has also been expanding steadily. In the 1980s and early 1990s, most nongovernmental actors participating in global environmental processes came from the North and usually represented large environmental groups, such as the World Wide Fund for Nature or Friends of the Earth. In Stockholm, only 10 percent of registered NGOs came from developing countries. By the Rio Earth Summit, that had risen to about one third (Haas et al. 1992:32). By 2002, at least 40 percent of NGOs that registered for the various preparatory conferences leading to the WSSD were from developing countries (CSD 2003b). This rise in the participation of developing country NGOs is also reflected in MEA processes.

The composition and range of NGOs participating in global environmental processes have also changed, with more development and poverty NGOs, as well as business and industry groups, in attendance. Human rights organizations, including those advocating for the interests of indigenous peoples and women, have also increased their participation in these processes.

Of course, greater volume and diversity of NGO representation only go so far. It is what these representatives do that matters. Civil society participation ranges from mere attendance to actual involvement in the negotiations governments are engaged in. This can come either directly, by membership in a national delegation, or indirectly, by active lobbying of delegations on specific issues.

It is difficult to assess the success of civil society in influencing the outcomes of global environmental processes. Certainly, civil society groups have played effective roles in developing and disseminating scientific information that has catalyzed many environmental treaties. For example, NGO scientists helped develop the scientific basis for our present

> "The United Nations once dealt only with governments. By now we know that peace and prosperity cannot be achieved without partnerships involving governments, international organizations, the business community and civil society. In today's world, we depend on each other."
>
> *UN Secretary-General Kofi Annan*

understanding of climate change and the global biodiversity crisis. Experts from civil society organizations routinely participate in the work of the Intergovernmental Panel on Climate Change, which keeps parties to the Kyoto Protocol updated on the latest climate change science. Likewise, the Convention on Biological Diversity is partially a result of many years of work by IUCN, which includes among its members a broad group of nongovernmental conservation organizations.

Civil society organizations have also been instrumental in putting forward new ideas and in lobbying for concrete actions by governments. The concept of addressing climate change by setting targets and timetables for reducing greenhouse gas emissions—an idea now incorporated in the Kyoto Protocol—can be traced to the so-called "Toronto Targets" pushed by key environmental organizations in the late 1980s and early 1990s (Grubb et al. 1999:53; Victor 2001:14). The input of NGOs in the negotiation of the Aarhus Convention was certainly a crucial element in its eventual adoption (Petkova and Veit 2000:5). As early as the first conference of the parties to the Convention on Biological Diversity in 1995, NGOs lobbied strongly for the adoption of a Biosafety Protocol to address issues around the safe use of genetically modified organisms; they participated extensively in the negotiations that resulted in its adoption in 2000 (Gale 2002:251, 258–261).

What is unclear, however, is the extent to which NGOs are able to influence specific policy decisions—what rule or target to adopt, for example—that governments make as they deal with the complexities of global environmental issues. In this area, the record is at best mixed. There have been successes, but there have also been significant failures. Many NGOs welcomed the adoption of the Kyoto Protocol, for example, even as they decried the failure of governments to adopt more stringent targets and timetables (La Viña 2003).

In assessing the effectiveness of civil society participation in global environmental processes, it is also important to consider whether alternative NGO summits, such as the Global Forum in Rio and the Global People's Forum in Johannesburg, are a viable tool. These events, held in parallel to official intergovernmental meetings, have become a focus of much civil society activity. To the extent that such gatherings facilitate networking and coalition-building among groups and act as vehicles for reflection and dialogue, they may be extremely useful. But as a strategy to influence governments, they may not be cost-effective and have not compiled a good record.

Are Multi-Stakeholder Processes Useful?

One response to the rise of civil society activism in environmental governance has been to organize and, as in the case of the Commission on Sustainable Development (CSD), to institutionalize multi-stakeholder processes (MSPs). In the context of international environmental governance, MSPs are designed explicitly to enable direct and meaningful interactions between governments and civil society stakeholders on specific topics. In the CSD and in meetings of multilateral environmental agreements like the Convention on Biological Diversity, MSPs are considered official parts of the intergovernmental process and are usually integrated into official meeting agendas. They provide opportunities for stakeholders to articulate their concerns, present proposals on the issues at hand, and discuss them in detail with governments. As a result, governments can become better informed and improve the quality of their decisions.

However, MSPs have not been popular with all stakeholders. Some governments and NGOs are skeptical about their usefulness. In the Commission on Sustainable Development, for example, some civil society groups continue to encounter official objections from governments to their meaningful inclusion in official forums. In addition, some NGOs are concerned that the prominent place given to businesses in MSPs could erode the role of governments in decision-making and enhance the influence of the private sector, which is not accountable to the public the way governments are (Dodds 2001a:37–38).

There are also concerns about how stakeholder representatives are selected. Who decides which groups will sit at the table, and how are their negotiating positions decided? But in the end, NGOs are most concerned about whether investing in MSPs is worth the effort. Do MSPs make a difference in decision-making?

The answer depends, of course, on how they are conducted. Some MSPs do seem to succeed. One example that is frequently put forward is the World Commission on Dams (see Box 7.4). But others are less fruitful. Suggestions put forward to improve the chances of success include formulating rules to govern the selection of participants. The use of an independent facilitator is also an option, so that MSPs can become more than mere venues for prepared speeches and instead engender genuine dialogue. Finally, accountability mechanisms to ensure that governments actually

Figure 7.2: Civil Society Participation in Environmental Summits

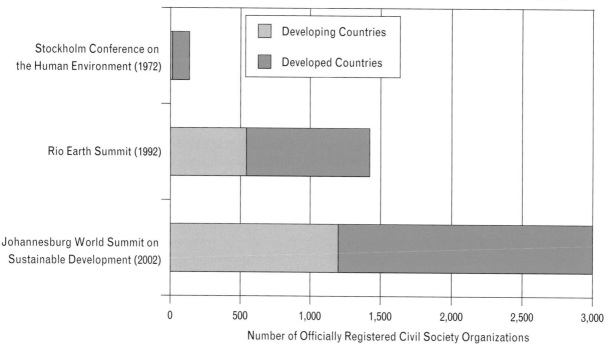

Source: Haas et al. 1992:32; United Nations 1992; 2002a; 2002b; ECOSOC 2002; Willetts 2002; WRI calculations

incorporate the outcomes of these dialogues in their decisions would improve the credibility of and justify participation in MSPs.

The Emergence of Partnerships

In recent years, partnerships–public-private initiatives, as well as coalitions of international organizations, governments, and NGOs–have become a favored UN strategy to motivate concrete action on many environmental problems. Partnerships are voluntary and self-organized. They are not formally negotiated and thus do not require universal consensus. Those directly involved willingly commit to take concrete steps and implement specific programs that define the partnership.

Partnerships range from simple agreements to exchange information to initiatives that plan and fund infrastructure projects, education programs, or scientific studies. Since 2002, partnerships have been elevated to a new, though still legally undefined, status. Much of this new attention was inspired by the prominent role partnerships played at the World Summit on Sustainable Development (WSSD). Governments considered the new partnerships announced in Johannesburg an important outcome of the Summit–essential to fulfilling the promises they made in the WSSD Plan of Implementation, the Summit's final list of agreed actions and intentions. On its website, the CSD Secretariat has posted a list of over 260 partnerships that relate to the commitments contained in the implementation plan (CSD

2003b). They include partnerships like the Water, Sanitation, and Hygiene for All Initiative, the Sustainable Agriculture and Development Partnership Initiative, and the Partnership for Principle 10, which aims to increase citizen access to environmental information, participation, and legal redress (see Box 9.1).

While many have welcomed the partnerships that emerged from WSSD, others have been more cautious in their endorsement. Some critics complain that these liaisons have been formed without any overall coordination, and that many reflect efforts already underway rather than new thinking or new resources. Participation is also uneven among nations, and some worry that the WSSD partnerships mirror the same disparities in power and priorities that have dominated international relations over the past decade (Andonova and Levy 2003).

Beyond the WSSD, the emergence of partnerships on the global scene has engendered a serious debate about their promise and implications for governments. Partnerships are controversial because of the apprehension that they could come to substitute for governmental commitments, allowing governments to abdicate responsibilities that are more properly functions of the state. Some fear that the acceptance of partnerships might herald a transition from traditional multilateral diplomacy to a voluntary approach to implementation, essentially letting governments off the hook. In this sense, they are seen as signs of the failure of diplomacy (CSD 2002).

Another major concern is that, without proper transparency and accountability, partnerships might become vehicles for the infusion of inappropriate corporate money and influence into the United Nations. Some see a danger that private interests might become able to exert influence over the public sector, for example by promoting privatization (Utting 2001:1–2). Partnerships could also serve as "greenwash," to be used by companies to establish credibility even if little is achieved.

While there is legitimacy to some of these concerns, partnerships–when properly designed and implemented, and accompanied by a legally binding framework for corporate responsibility and accountability–can be powerful vehicles for sustainable development. They must, however, be based on clear criteria, with well-elaborated lists of goals to be achieved, specific commitments by partners to attain them, and financial resources committed to fund them. A transparent and inclusive approach to developing partnerships, including obtaining buy-in by those communities intended to benefit, is essential. Finally, monitoring and accountability mechanisms must be put in place to document achievements and areas for improvement and to ensure that partners make good on their pledges.

Principles to Guide International Governance Reform

As this chapter has shown, many steps can–and must–be taken to improve the institutional framework for international environmental governance and mobilize new partners and practices for attaining global environmental goals. Two principles should guide the reform of international environmental governance in general. First, environmental objectives can only be met if they are compatible with the broader goals of sustainable development, and especially with the overriding aim of eradicating or reducing poverty worldwide. Second, any reform efforts should be guided by the principles of The Rio Declaration–in particular, the *common but differentiated responsibility principle* and the *precautionary approach.*

The Poverty-Environment-Governance Nexus

Progress in solving environmental problems can only be made if strategies to combat them are consistent with a priority objective of the international community and most countries: The eradication of poverty. Environmental policy must be integrated into and coordinated with development policy if it is to be effective. This is true at the local and national levels, and it is also appropriate for responding to global environmental challenges like climate change, biodiversity loss, and desertification.

The political motivation for this posture is that dealing with poverty is a top priority for many developing countries and one of the main goals of development cooperation between North and South. Environmental decisions and actions that are consistent with this priority are likely to gain wider acceptance from governments and stakeholders. Conversely, when such decisions and actions are perceived to be "anti-development" or contrary to poverty reduction goals, resistance to their adoption is predictable.

There is another reason for implementing approaches that integrate environment and development objectives at the global level. Global environmental threats harm the poor–and the poorest countries–disproportionately, because they undermine the natural resource base on which many poor people directly rely for their food security and livelihoods. Poverty reduction is therefore closely linked to sound management of the environment at local, national, regional, and global levels (OECD 2002:13).

At the global level, how can the principle of linking poverty and environment be implemented? Two ways immediately suggest themselves: First, by achieving the UN Millennium Development Goals within the agreed timeline; and second, by maximizing the synergies between development policy and the implementation of environmental treaties.

The UN Millennium Development Goals were adopted by the United Nations General Assembly in 2000 (United Nations 2000). Many of them, particularly those relevant to sustainable development, were subsequently reaffirmed during the recent Johannesburg Summit (WSSD) (UN/DESA 2002:2–5). Achieving these goals is important for the credibility of the international community and will represent a key milestone in realizing sustainable and equitable development.

Another practical step that could be taken to ensure that poverty and environment strategies reinforce each other is to link national development policies with the implementation of environmental treaties. OECD has identified various entry points and approaches to achieve such synergies. One of these is to integrate the national action plans drawn up to implement various MEAs with other national plans such as sustainable development strategies and poverty reduction strategies. Previously, these various government strategies have been conceived in isolation. Other approaches work at ecosystem levels to match development strategies with countries' physical and ecological conditions. These include better utilization of land use planning tools such as zoning; environmental assessment tools to evaluate infrastructure projects; and community-based natural resource management to assure local control over natural resources (OECD 2002:47–57).

In implementing environmental treaties, priority should be given to environmental activities that restore or mitigate the loss of natural resources on which the poor most depend, such as in rural areas, on marginal lands, or in informal peri-urban settlements. In particular, designing and implementing cost-effective responses to the impacts of climate change on the poorest or most affected nations, the least developed countries, and small island states, is an urgent task.

Implementing the Rio Principles

In reforming international environmental governance, it is important to return to the basic principles agreed upon by

(continued on p. 172)

Box 7.4 A Watershed in Global Governance?

The World Commission on Dams (1998–2000) brought together government officials, business people, scholars, and activists to assess the contributions of large dams to development and to formulate principles and guidelines for planning, building, managing, and decommissioning dams. This extraordinary assembly of diverse viewpoints to hash out a contentious problem makes the Commission a high-profile example of a multi-stakeholder process.

Multi-stakeholder processes have formed at the local, national, and international levels with a variety of objectives. Some aim to inform official decision-making processes, others to promote dialogue and understanding between diverse groups, others to monitor policy implementation (Dubash et al. 2001:21; Hemmati 2001:20–21).

The World Commission on Dams was formed to address increasingly frequent and intense international furor over the costs and benefits of large dams. Over the past three decades, civil society protests in Malaysia, India, Lesotho, and Nepal have slowed down or stalled work on dams, sometimes even leading to project cancellation. Proponents argued that dams were essential to meeting growing water, energy, and food security needs, especially in the South. Opponents argued that the negative environmental and social impacts of large dams and the availability of various alternatives (especially for power generation) rendered large dams anachronistic and unacceptable.

A Meeting of the Minds

As the Commission's chairman put it, all sides realized that a "hard headed analysis" of the evidence was required to get beyond constant conflict (Asmal 1999). In 1997, the World Conservation Union (IUCN) and the World Bank convened actors from different sides of the debate to discuss the main issues. At the request of these actors, the IUCN and World Bank helped create the World Commission on Dams shortly thereafter. The Commission's members were chosen to represent the viewpoints of industry, government, the IUCN and World Bank, and NGOs and social movements. Once the Commission and its secretariat were in place, the World Bank and IUCN withdrew to allow them to function independently.

The Commission brought together vastly different perspectives. Commissioners included a former chairman of the principal dams industry association, the CEO of a multinational corporation involved in dam construction, an indigenous peoples' advocate, and an anti-dam activist from an Indian grassroots movement. The inclusion of social justice activists at the negotiating table was a first for international commissions. The chairman and vice-chairman came from developing country governments.

The strength of opposing views within the Commission almost derailed the whole effort. But thanks in part to its com-

mitments to transparency, openness, and independence, the Commission was able to gather a large knowledge base on dams and produce a consensus report from its 12 members. One means of keeping the process open was the Commission's invitation to all stakeholders to share their views of how dams had proven effective or detrimental to their society's development. Commissioners solicited written submissions from all segments of society. From these submissions, they selected representatives from all sides of the issue to present their views in person to the Commission at four regional consultations: In Latin America and the Caribbean; the Middle East and Africa; South Asia; and East and Southeast Asia.

To demonstrate its independence, the Commission was not funded by any one source; it sought to raise funds from all sectors in the debate: Government, industry, and nongovernmental groups. To help keep the process transparent, the Commission posted on-line the terms of reference for the many commissioned papers in the knowledge base, as well as hundreds of other Commission documents. The website won awards for its comprehensiveness and navigability.

The Commission's Findings

In November 2000, the World Commission on Dams released its report, *Dams and Development.* The report makes human rights a central issue in dam development. The Commission argued that until now, governments have failed to apply established international norms to dam-building. Principles enshrined in the Universal Declaration of Human Rights (1948), the Declaration to the Right to Development (1986), and the Rio Declaration (1992) have been brushed aside in the rush to capture dams' perceived benefits.

The Commission proposed a framework for future water and energy decision-making that would explicitly recognize the rights and risks of different stakeholders to be affected by a proposed dam. The framework calls for policy-makers to clarify who has legitimate needs and entitlements, and to identify whose lives and livelihoods a project puts at risk.

Historically, stakeholders who take voluntary risks, such as governments and investors, have a say in decision-making and an opportunity for their concerns to be addressed. But people who bear involuntary risks, such as communities displaced by dam construction or fishers who lose their livelihoods, seldom have a say. The Commission argued that decision-making processes should respect the rights of all relevant stakeholders, take account of the risks they bear, and negotiate toward appropriate outcomes. This has become known as a "rights and risks approach" to making decisions about dams.

Within this broad framework, the Commission proposed seven strategic priorities to guide future decision-making (WCD 2000:214–256):

■ **Gain public acceptance:** Recognize rights, address risks, and safeguard the entitlements of all groups of affected people, particularly indigenous and tribal peoples, women, and other vulnerable groups.

■ **Comprehensive options assessment:** Identify appropriate development responses based on comprehensive and participatory assessments of water, food, and energy needs, giving equal significance to social and environmental, as well as economic and financial factors.

■ **Address existing dams:** Optimize benefits from existing dams, address outstanding social issues, and strengthen environmental mitigation and restoration measures.

■ **Sustain rivers and livelihoods:** Understand, protect, and restore ecosystems at the river basin level.

■ **Recognize entitlements and share benefits:** Use joint negotiations with adversely affected people to develop mutually agreeable and legally enforceable mitigation and development provisions that recognize entitlements and ensure that affected people are beneficiaries of the project.

■ **Ensure compliance:** Ensure that governments, developers, regulators, and operators meet all commitments made for the planning, implementation, and operation of dams.

■ **Share rivers for peace, development, and security:** Initiate a shift in focus from the narrow approach of allocating a finite resource to the sharing of rivers and their associated benefits.

The report offers 26 specific guidelines for putting these principles into practice when assessing water and energy options and planning and operating dams (WCD 2000:278).

Setting International Norms for Dams

The Commission's framework constituted a major advance in international thinking about who should participate in dam-related decision-making and why. It remains an open question as to whether the framework will become the basis for a set of international norms around dams. If so, these norms could apply not only to dams but to a host of other infrastructure developments and extractive industries.

The challenge for the Commission's supporters has been to promote the adoption of the *Dams and Development* framework internationally. In the two years since the report's release, some institutions, like the Indian and Chinese governments, have rejected the report outright, citing concerns that the proposed consultations and safeguards would indefinitely stall nascent dam projects.

Many other institutions have assessed their own principles, laws, and practices to ascertain where they converge with and diverge from the Commission's recommendations. Some have concluded that "business as usual" is the right course. For example, the World Bank's board of directors agreed to disagree with elements of the Commission's report. The Bank did commit to incorporating the report's seven strategic priorities into some of its sector strategies, into advisory information for operational staff, and into a new "Dams Planning and Management Action Plan," with outreach to client countries, World Bank professionals, donors and other interested parties. However, the World Bank will not adopt the 26 guidelines, as many nongovernmental organizations and people's movements would like. The Bank has opted instead to leave it up to individual governments or private sector developers to test the application of the Commission's guidelines in the context of specific projects (World Bank 2001). In other cases, lending agencies and corporations have decided to incorporate new guidelines into their practices.

The most comprehensive and action-oriented approaches have arisen from multi-stakeholder processes convened at the country level. In many respects, these processes are duplications of the World Commission on Dams' own model at a smaller geographic scale. In South Africa, a committee representing government, utilities, affected communities, NGOs, the private sector, finance, and research organizations is assessing how existing South African legislation meshes with the Commission's guidelines. The committee will issue recommendations for specific stakeholder groups on how they can remedy gaps in policy, implementation, and knowledge (South African Steering Committee 2002). In Pakistan, IUCN is convening a series of multi-stakeholder workshops at the government's request. Participants are reviewing the Commission's strategic priorities in order to assess their relevance and applicability to the Pakistani situation.

There have also been efforts to apply the World Commission on Dams guidelines at the project level. For instance, the consortium funding Laos' Nam Theun II dam and the American company behind Uganda's Bujagali dam contracted consultants to assess the degree of project compliance with WCD guidelines. The Swedish aid agency SIDA is assessing the environmental and social impacts of two SIDA-funded dams—the Pangani dam in Tanzania and the Song Hinh dam in Viet Nam—with a view to implementing additional mitigation measures. Consultants for these contracts will be required to abide by WCD guidelines. However, this agency, like many other multilateral and bilateral donors, considers that affected people's claims for compensation are generally a matter for national governments to address (Development Today 2001). The WCD report, however, suggests that bilateral aid agencies and multilateral development banks "review the portfolio of past projects to identify those that may have underperformed or present unresolved issues and share in addressing the financial burden of such projects for borrower countries" (WCD 2000:315).

An Approach to Global Problems?

In many ways, the World Commission on Dams was a product of our globalizing world. It was initiated by a multilateral development institution, the World Bank, and an international conservation alliance with more than 980 members, the IUCN (IUCN 2003). Its deliberative processes involved individuals and institutions that are active globally: Multinational corporations, international investors, and transnational social movements. But experience with putting the Commission's principles into practice shows that the influence of such global, multi-stakeholder processes relies upon ongoing efforts to democratize decision-making at the national and local levels.

Meanwhile, the World Commission on Dams process may serve as a model for advancing better, more equitable environmental governance in other sectors. The multi-stakeholder approach has been adopted by the Extractive Industries Review, a process housed within the World Bank to inform its future policy on the oil, gas, and mining industries. However, many NGOs monitoring the Extractive Industries Review process consider it a weak cousin to the World Commission on Dams. It is tied closely to—rather than independent of—the Bank and has far fewer resources in terms of funding and staff than did the WCD process (FOE 2002).

At the least, the Commission demonstrated that through a painstaking process of common learning and dialogue, individuals representing the extremes in a debate can overcome differences and craft a wholly new vision for an issue as volatile as dam construction.

countries during the Rio Earth Summit in 1992. These include Principle 10, as discussed at length throughout this book. Two other principles of particular relevance to international environmental governance are the *common but differentiated responsibility (CDR) principle* and the *precautionary approach*.

Reaffirming and implementing the CDR principle, which is a political priority for developing nations, is probably a prerequisite for joint action. This principle is based on the idea that countries differ in their historical responsibility for and, more importantly, in their current capacity to respond to global environmental threats. It requires industrialized economies with greater means and higher consumption levels to do more, at least initially, to meet global environmental challenges. It calls on rich countries to finance obligations under environmental treaties and to assist developing nations in implementing their commitments under such agreements.

While the CDR principle was accepted at the Rio Earth Summit (UNEP 1992) and has been incorporated into various agreements, it continues to be a key political issue debated by governments in many negotiating forums. The Montreal Protocol on ozone depletion is one legal regime where the CDR approach has worked. Through its Multilateral Fund, which is financed by developed countries, developing country parties are given financial assistance to phase out their manufacture of ozone-destroying compounds (UNMFS 2003).

In recent years, however, the debate over how to interpret the CDR principle has intensified. For example, in negotiations on the Kyoto Protocol, the question of how much developing nations should contribute to reducing greenhouse gas emissions was a contentious issue (Baumert and Kete 2001:1–9). Though contentious, the CDR principle continues to be a powerful tool to approach questions of equity at the global level.

Implementing the precautionary approach is also important. Under this principle, precaution must be applied in decisions where environmental risks are uncertain, but carry potentially large costs. The precautionary approach should be integrated into the legal and policy frameworks regulating human activities that affect the global environment—in particular, in drafting national development plans and negotiating environmental treaties.

While the precautionary approach was accepted by governments attending the Rio Earth Summit (UNEP 1992), incorporating it into specific decision-making practices has proven a challenge. Parties to the CBD successfully accomplished this when they negotiated and adopted the Cartagena Protocol on Biosafety. The Protocol allows governments to take a decision not to permit the importation of "living modified organisms" even "if there is lack of scientific certainty due to insufficient relevant scientific information" (CBD Secretariat 2000). Other convention bodies, including future negotiating forums, should be encouraged to take similar decisions.

CHAPTER 8

A WORLD OF
DECISIONS:
CASE STUDIES

How are people around the world rising to the
challenges of environmental governance? The case studies that follow
explore why it is so difficult to make inclusive and effective decisions
about ecosystem use. But they also demonstrate the infinite human creativity, adaptation, and experimentation that can bring success. Each
case contains a box that draws out the principal governance lessons
that can be learned from the story. Some of these lessons illuminate the
power of an informed community, some the difficulties and benefits of
integrating economic and environmental goals. Others reflect the tensions between traditional approaches and new ideas, between immediate human need and long-term environmental health, between lofty
goals and practical results.

   The stories told in these case studies range from the struggles of an
indigenous community in South Africa to the nascent efforts toward
environmental democracy in Iran. However, they represent only a fraction of the stories that could be told. The lessons they teach are valuable guides to improving environmental governance everywhere, but
they also serve to remind us that every situation is unique in its geographic, economic, environmental, social, and cultural make-up.
Achieving more equitable and sustainable use of ecosystem goods and
services demands patience and a deep understanding of local circumstances, as well as an appreciation of the broad principles explored
throughout this book.

MIND OVER MUSSELS:
RETHINKING MAPELANE RESERVE

The Sokhulu people know that when the *msintsi* tree is flowering, mussels are good and fat. They know the Zulu names for the rock ledges that mussels inhabit along approximately 30 kilometers of coast. Their ancestors have been harvesting mussels along this coast for years beyond counting and are buried in the nature reserve that is intended to protect it. Yet, for the past two decades, they have been called thieves and poachers and driven to harvest what they could get under cover of darkness (Harris et al. 2003:62–66).

Mussel shell middens on the coast of KwaZulu-Natal province where the Sokhulu people live date back 2,000 years (Horwitz et al. 1991:1), suggesting that residents have harvested and husbanded this resource for at least that long. They employed a system of rotational harvesting that allowed each mussel bed to recover for several years between uses. They occasionally closed the harvest season completely to preserve the mussel stock at vulnerable times, a tactic common in many scientifically managed fish and shellfish stocks. Before commercial forestry came to the region in the 1930s, women gathered mussels in the daytime, prying mature mussels from the rocks with a pointed stick, but foresters and loggers soon challenged their right to collect and drove them into hiding (Harris et al. 2003:64–66).

When Jean Harris, then a University of Cape Town researcher, arrived in the area in 1995, the situation for traditional mussel harvesters was dire. Harris had hoped, through her research, to determine a sustainable level of harvesting for the area's mussel beds. She soon realized, however, that the relationship of the Sokhulu community to the resource had been deeply distorted by the community's run-ins with outsiders. Her research into sound resource management would have to begin by grappling with the effects of this conflict. Clashes with vigi-

lante foresters, fishers, and the Natal Parks Board—the body that exercised legal authority over the province's park and coastal resources—had made mussel collection a high-risk activity. It took place only at night, by men willing to chance being beaten or arrested. In fact, few young Sokhulu women had ever gathered mussels, though women were the traditional harvesters, and mussels were regarded as a high-quality food, especially for children (Harris et al. 2003:73).

The conflict can be traced to 1933 when commercial forestry first came to the area, but tensions escalated sharply with the establishment in 1984 of the Mapelane Nature Reserve—an area that the Sokhulu community claims to own. Mapelane Reserve was intended to protect a region of rich habitat and biodiversity and is one of several smaller parks that were combined in 1997 to form the Greater St. Lucia Wetland Park. This World Heritage Site encompasses almost 240,000 hectares, including the foothills of the Lebombo mountains, lakes, coastal forests, massive dunes, and productive estuaries. Offshore, the park's coral reefs are home to 991 fish species, nearly 85 percent of reef fish species native to the western Indian Ocean region (WCMC 1999). Mapelane Reserve is on the extreme southern end of the Greater St. Lucia Wetland Park and is not itself inhabited, but has traditionally supplied fish and shellfish to adjacent communities.

The Natal Parks Board (recently reconstituted as Ezemvelo KwaZulu-Natal Wildlife, or EKZN Wildlife) has a powerful stake in protecting the resources under its authority, but its mandate does not—or did not—extend to accommodating the subsistence needs of local people. The region is biologically rich and visually spectacular. Leatherback and loggerhead turtles nest on the beaches. Whales, dolphins, and sharks ply the waters. Flamingos and pelicans put on dramatic displays in the wetlands. At just two and a half hours from the city of Durban, St. Lucia draws up to one million tourists annually (WCMC 1999) and ecotourism is expected to bring 500 million rand (more than US$60 million) and 1,200 new jobs to the region in the next several years, as a new road from Durban is completed and a concentrated malaria eradication campaign bears fruit (SAN-Parks 2002).

Governance Lessons from Mapelane Nature Reserve

Mapelane Nature Reserve on South Africa's northeast coast is a place of beauty, a refuge for wildlife, and a center of conservation. It is also a focus of conflict and contested rights. To tourists venturing north from Durban, the reserve is a haven of bird life, verdant forest, and unspoiled coast. But until recently, residents of the nearby Sokhulu Tribal Authority saw it only as a restricted zone where they were forbidden to harvest mussels along the rocky coast, in the custom of their ancestors. The conflict over resource access and tenure in Mapelane Reserve is not unique. It is mirrored in national parks and protected areas in many nations, and points to a conundrum in sustainable park management: How can parks work for—and be supported by—local residents, and yet still fulfill their conservation missions? Can park neighbors both use and help to preserve a park's biological assets? Or must they be kept out to safeguard the park's living legacy?

At Mapelane, the solution required a new relationship between park officials and the indigenous community. Sokhulu residents regained authority over mussel beds on a short stretch of coast. Their right to harvest mussels is now linked to their responsibility to demonstrate—in hard numbers—that the level of harvest is sustainable. The success of this agreement demonstrates that transmission of rights and responsibilities over park resources to local groups is one avenue to conflict resolution and greater equity, but that the transition must be negotiated with care.

■ Co-management by park personnel and local residents offers a viable route to empowering local subsistence use of coastal resources.

■ Successful co-management arrangements require the establishment of a local users group or management committee respected by the community and endowed with legal standing, allowing it to create and enforce management rules.

■ Democratic mechanisms such as elections of local representatives to the management committee are important to establish its legitimacy and accountability to the local community.

■ New harvesting regimes must be justified on the basis of joint fact-finding by both co-management partners to be credible. Harvest restrictions are more acceptable when validated by local experiments.

■ Local consensus-building processes need sustained financial and technical support for solutions to take hold.

■ An assessment of the current status of the resource is an essential precondition for co-management, followed by consistent monitoring over time, to determine if the resource is being used sustainably.

■ Subsistence harvesting rights, even when successfully negotiated, are fragile if they begin to compete with commercial harvesting.

Perhaps that influx of money will bring new opportunities and a different way of life to Sokhulu. But in the meantime, its residents continue to depend on the humble brown mussel as a subsistence food, and have made it clear that they will fight to retain access to the shores where they have always gathered them. It took an outsider, Jean Harris, to propose that the goals of the Parks Board and the harvesters really weren't so far apart, and that a collaborative approach might bring them closer to a solution than had decades of violence and resentment.

The Invisible Users

Class and cultural biases are often embedded in systems of fish and shellfish management (Bailey and Jentoft 1990:344). Rules on when, how much, and who can harvest these resources are usually drawn up by technical staff focused on commercial and recreational fishing, but divorced from subsistence use. Such biases were reflected in provincial legislation in the 1980s, which was clearly targeted to recreational harvesters. It required mussel collectors to purchase permits and limited their take to 50 mussels per day (Harris et al. 2003:64).

The cost of a permit was beyond the means of most villagers. Until very recently, there were few sources of employment in the region and many families needed to supplement their small salaries with free wild foods. In addition, the small daily limit meant that villagers had to walk the 2 hours to the coast and back for an amount that barely constituted a family meal. Unwilling to live with what they considered an unfair regulation, the villagers adopted a different approach (Harris et al. 2003:64, 77).

Groups of harvesters made the walk at night, stripped mussels from the rocks wholesale, and cooked them in drums over fires built in the nearby woods. They worked fast, using spades and bush knives, to avoid detection and arrest. The practice badly damaged mussel beds, reducing the stock of harvestable mussels and eliminating the protected spots among older mussels that serve as sanctuary for young mussels and attachment sites for mussel larvae. Conservation officers and vigilante fishermen, convinced that harvesters were damaging the beds, sought out and ambushed their camps, attacking and arresting them. As a consequence, a people who had long depended on mussels for subsistence was gradually divorced from its access to the resource and from its previous sustainable practices (Harris et al. 2003:66).

The conflict between the Sokhulu people and park authorities echoes similar clashes around the world where indige-

nous communities feel their resource rights have been violated by outsiders. In Central America, indigenous use of forest resources, including fruits, game, and medicinal plants, has often taken a back seat to the establishment of parks intended to preserve biodiversity and facilitate tourism. Commercial resource extraction has also played an important role. For example, treaty-based rights assigned to Mi'kmaq fishers in eastern Canada and Saami fishers in northern Norway were acceptable only until they began to interfere with state-imposed fisheries management systems (Davis and Jentoft 2001:225–231).

Elsewhere in Africa, the privatization of traditionally communal land rights has left many small-scale farmers with no means of support and resulted in bitter rivalries within families and clans and among townships and villages (Kamuaro 1998:302, 309–310, 313). These conflicts often have complex roots, involving rising demand on resources from population growth and economic development, conflicting objectives and poor communication among stakeholders and government authorities, lack of government recognition of customary and communal property rights, and inadequate or skewed enforcement of existing laws (Bennett et al. 2001:369–372). No matter what the mix of causes, however, indigenous communities tend to find themselves on the losing side of the conflict.

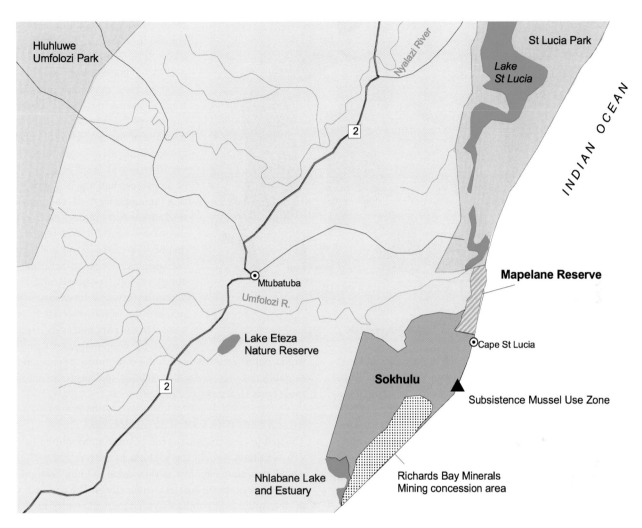

Source: Harris and Radebe-Mkhize 2003

Burying Old Enmities

The Sokhulu Tribal Authority comprises eight wards, mainly rural and poor, with bad roads, no electricity, and few telephones–a legacy of South Africa's long years of apartheid. A traditional *nkosi*, or chief, heads the Tribal Authority, while councilors provide leadership in the wards. Although the region is rich in timber and minerals, until recently it had little appeal to investors because of a high prevalence of malaria. In time, new and upgraded roads into the area may bring more economic opportunity. But, at present, most jobs are a 90-minute bus ride away at the mine near the town of Richards Bay.

The last time the Sokhulu people remember being able to harvest in peace was in 1933, before the arrival of loggers. After that, they were regularly harassed by white foresters, fishers, and recreational collectors who would camp along the rocky shore and hunt for mussels and rock lobsters. The establishment of the reserve complicated matters further, adding park personnel and the force of law to the existing conflict. Where formerly, recreational harvesters and subsistence gatherers might come to blows, harvesters now had to worry about being apprehended and incarcerated. Physical violence, rock-throwing, and arrests became common and subsistence gatherers looked for new ways to circumvent regulations they saw as unjust. They began harvesting even faster, with little regard for the old ways of preserving the stock. Ultimately, the efforts of park personnel to protect the shoreline were causing greater overall damage to coastal resources, and perpetuating tension and violence between park officials and the Sokhulu community (Harris et al. 2003:66).

In 1995, Harris and Mapelane's officer-in-charge, Terry Ferguson, convinced higher park authorities that there might be a better approach. Harris obtained outside funding for a five-and-a-half year project to examine what level of mussel harvesting might be sustainable and to find ways to put

tion process itself. Sokhulu members of the Joint Committee were elected within each ward by the harvesters themselves, and a Sokhulu harvester chaired the Committee, backed up by a vice chair from EKZN Wildlife, the provincial management agency. In order to keep any single individual from amassing too much power, it was agreed that the Committee chair would be re-elected each year, and the group would strive to act by consensus (Harris et al. 2003:74).

Both sides had much to gain from this arrangement. If the process worked, the community would regain use of resources it had long been denied, as well as training and logistical support, access to information about relevant political and legal developments, and the chance to participate in resource-related decisions. On the park authority's side, a successful co-management project would improve relations with the community, reduce unsustainable resource use and poaching, and decrease enforcement costs (Harris et al. 2003:68).

the responsibility for the resource back in the hands of those who depended on it. Through a park employee who was also a tribal member, they arranged a meeting with the *nkosi* of the Sokhulu Tribal Authority, who approved a gathering of harvesters and park staff. Officer Ferguson had recently arrested several of the harvesters and had been injured in a stoning incident. He stood before the harvesters and pleaded for their help in finding a different way forward. He proposed that if local harvesters would help park authorities ensure that the resource was being harvested sustainably, park administrators would secure them legal access to the mussel beds (Harris et al. 2003:67).

With some reservations, the Sokhulu community agreed to a scheme of "co-managing" the mussel harvest with park authorities. The agreement called for the formation of the Sokhulu Buhhlebemvelo ("Beautiful Nature") Joint Mussel Management Committee, known as the Joint Committee. The Joint Committee consisted of Sokhulu mussel harvesters, park representatives, researchers from University of Cape Town, and a few professional staff, including a community liaison officer to provide translations and keep the lines of communication open. The *nkosi* endorsed the agreement, on condition that he would be kept up-to-date on progress (Harris et al. 2003:67, 73).

Under the co-management scheme, the Joint Committee exercised control over most aspects of the mussel harvest. It identified subsistence collectors, issued harvest permits, specified collecting methods, determined the harvesting schedule, specified how many mussels could be collected per month, and hired monitors to record and oversee the collec-

An Experiment in Cooperation

The first few meetings of the Joint Committee required an outside facilitator to help the Sokhulu harvesters and park personnel communicate. But as they came to know each other, the group was able to lead its own meetings. The first task was to determine how community members currently used the resource and how dependent they were on it. This was accomplished through a survey of Sokhulu households.

Next, the Joint Committee tackled finding a suitable test location that could be opened to legal harvesting. The group decided on a series of rocky ledges that supported healthy mussel beds just south of the park border. The harvesting area—called the "subsistence mussel-use zone"—comprised only 2 of the 20–30 kilometers of coastline traditionally used. Still, the Sokhulu considered the ability to collect mussels legally without fear of harassment, a significant victory. On the first day of legal harvesting, an 80 year-old woman told a local reporter:

"Today is a big day. I eat mussels for the first time in many, many years. As a young girl, I used to collect mussels with my grandmother. Then came the restrictions. So after my mother-in-law was arrested and we had to sell the cow to get her from jail, we didn't get mussels anymore. I was worried that I would never eat a mussel again before I died (Harris et al. 2003:68)."

The Joint Committee then had to decide how to harvest in a way that would be both fair and sustainable. A strong disagreement surfaced over the kind of tool the harvesters should use to pry mussels off the rocks. A pointed stick had been the traditional tool and a screwdriver was the legal tool for recreational harvesters, both serving to dislodge only the mature mussels and leave younger stock attached to rocky outcrops. In the years when they gathered mussels in secret, however, Sokhulu harvesters had become used to using a *panga*, or bush knife, which they found to be more efficient. They saw suggestions that they should return to more "primitive" tools as efforts to hold them back (Harris et al. 2003:75).

To resolve the dispute, an experiment was proposed. Harvesting an equal number of edible-sized mussels first with a *panga* and then with a screwdriver, the Joint Committee recorded how long the harvest took and how many undersized mussels were dislodged and wasted. Although it did take almost twice as long using a screwdriver, as opposed to a *panga*, far fewer young mussels were lost. Furthermore, because the activity was now legal within the subsistence zone, the speed of harvesting was far less crucial. The experiment also inspired a re-seeding project, where members of the Joint Committee placed dislodged mussels under plastic mesh, allowing the mussels to reattach and continue growing to edible size.

Of course, the primary questions that confronted the Joint Committee revolved around determining a sustainable harvest level. How many mussels should harvesters be allowed to collect? Could they harvest year-round? Both sides had firm ideas, but neither side was basing its ideas on research. Jean Harris' original research project—sidelined by evidence of heavy poaching—had been to determine a sustainable level of use. So she helped Sokhulu women set up an experiment to answer that question. They established zones of different harvesting intensity along the shore, marking them with color-coded flags. They hired several youths from Sokhulu and, with help from park personnel, trained them as monitors to oversee the experiment and record harvest data in a scientifically rigorous manner.

The researchers and park personnel, used to communicating with literate professionals, soon learned that a different approach was needed here. Live demonstrations, models, and pictorial representations soon took the place of technical explanations. The harvesters, who were mainly women and accustomed to keeping their opinions to themselves, gradually began to speak up and ask probing questions as they gained trust that their input would be heard and respected. The local youths hired as harvest monitors also benefited in the new arrangement. Through instruction and hands-on experience, they developed concrete understanding of resource sustainability concepts. They also earned salaries and received training in English, conflict resolution, and computer skills.

The experiment with different harvest levels led to some unexpected changes in attitude. A wide range of collection intensities was chosen at the beginning of the experiment and some, of course, were not sustainable. As they saw the effects of the more intense harvests on mussel populations, and how slow the stocks were to recover, women who had wanted higher quotas at the start reconsidered their demand. In fact, they asked the Joint Committee to curtail further harvesting where collection levels had been highest and most damaging. Their participation in the experiment and their control over decision-making brought them to a very different perspective than that held only a year before. Harvesters also recommended a closed season of 3 months each winter, based on their memories of traditional practice (Harris et al. 2003:82–83, 85).

Establishing the Rules

Seeing the results of their own experiments, harvesters have readily accepted limits on the number of permits issued, size of the harvest allowed per permit, and the tools used to harvest. Monitors and Joint Committee members enforced the rules within the subsistence zone according to community norms until one recent incident, when they tried to apprehend a poacher and were physically threatened. Now they leave enforcement to park officials and law enforcement officers, but ask that offenders within the subsistence zone be brought to the Joint Committee and the *nkosi* before they are taken to a police station.

In one case the *nkosi* and the Joint Committee decided that a Sokhulu woman had breached the rules, but only because of great need: Her husband had abandoned her and she had young children to feed. She was not expelled from the group by the Joint Committee, although she was fined. The community, which bears the brunt of damages caused by resource overuse, is able to grant leniency where appropriate. The arrangement keeps responsibility for local resources and norms within the community, while reducing the potential for violent conflict and maintaining responsibility for overall resource protection at regional and national levels.

Until recently, the small size of the subsistence collecting zone remained a point of community discontent. The 2-kilometer zone was tiny relative to the area of traditional use, and inadequate to the community's needs, especially because sustainable harvest rates turned out to be lower than the community originally expected. However, in December 2002, the national government (which, under 1998 legislation, has overall responsibility for managing coastal resources) approved the Joint Committee's application to expand the collection zone to 10.5 kilometers—a credit to the community's successful co-management experiment (Harris 2003).

Beyond Subsistence

Attacking the problem from the other side, the Joint Committee is also working on developing new sources of income for the Sokhulu people in hopes of reducing their dependence on mussels. For example, the co-management project has spawned a "craft initiative" that has tapped government funds to train some harvesters in craft development and marketing. The group now sells its crafts to three tourist shops in Durban (Harris 2003).

The co-management project itself has also been an important spur to development in Sokhulu, bringing new skills and confidence to the women who participate in the Joint Committee. Many participants in the project have tried to build their own capacities to continue working in the field of resource management. Where possible, community members have taken on responsible positions in the Joint Committee, such as treasurer and secretary, even though they required additional training. One very successful strategy has been the training of local youths to be harvest monitors: One of them has gone on to college to study natural resource management (Harris 2003).

The co-management experience has also brought the mussel harvesters considerable empowerment. Gradually, harvesters have become more vocal, challenging and arguing with park personnel. Still, without institutionalizing the progress made, the power balance could easily shift back. Harvesters are uniformly poor and female, a factor undermining their influence in most decision-making circles. To address this risk, the Sokhulu community and KwaZulu-Natal park authorities have recently signed a contractual agreement that spells out the roles and responsibilities of the two co-management partners, and confirms their commitment to continue working together (Harris 2003).

A Model of Co-Management

A measure of the success of the Joint Committee and its subsistence harvesting regime is that it is being used as a model for similar management programs in 17 other coastal communities in KwaZulu-Natal where subsistence fishing and shellfish collection play important roles in local livelihoods. In addition, the experience gained by the people involved in the Sokhulu subsistence project has become a marketable asset that is already bringing the lessons of Sokhulu to a wider audience. Two of the mussel harvest monitors have been tapped to help run co-management projects elsewhere along the coast, and the community liaison officer of the Sokhulu project has been appointed the new provincial subsistence fisheries manager (Harris et al. 2003:92).

Indeed, the tide may be turning toward a more constructive approach to subsistence fishing and shellfish collection. In 1998, South Africa passed the Marine Living Resources Act, bringing authority over marine resources under the control of the central government rather than the provinces. One provision of the law requires a new plan—now being developed—for recognizing and managing subsistence use of marine resources. Implementation of the subsistence fisheries plan has been slow, but some progress is evident. Sokhulu's Joint Committee is the first local co-management group to be granted permits for legal subsistence collection under the law. Also, in crafting the new plan, park officials have introduced mandatory training for all field personnel in conflict resolution and the principles of co-management (Harris 2003; Harris et al. 2003:89).

Keeping the success of the Sokhulu project going will not be easy. It will require favorable interpretation of national marine legislation, local perseverance, and the continuation of an open and accepting attitude on the part of park personnel and Sokhulu community leaders. In addition, the Joint Committee's legal status will need to be further clarified, so that its rights to manage subsistence mussel collection become routine, rather than legal exceptions subject to revocation. This will require a modest amendment of national law. On the positive side, the national government has indicated that it will provide on-going funding for the Joint Committee's management expenses, including the mussel monitoring program. This indicates strong buy-in at the national level—an important precondition if the Sokhulu experience is to be viable over the long term.

Using the Sokhulu co-management model for resources other than mussels may be difficult as well. Mussels have fairly low commercial value, and thus subsistence mussel collection does not tend to compete with any commercial market. But other marine resources such as fish or lobsters may have higher value in the marketplace, creating more obstacles to equitable sharing, and requiring different modes of cooperation.

Still, the basic elements of successful co-management of coastal resources are becoming clearer from the Sokhulu

experience and similar cases. A critical prerequisite is the establishment of a forum where community stakeholders and resource authorities can meet and negotiate common goals. Also critical is an appraisal of the resource and its current uses that is credible to all parties. At the heart of the co-management arrangement must be a body like the Joint Committee that has respect in the community and legal standing with state authorities, allowing it to limit access to the resource, control the harvest, and enforce rules. Adequate enforcement support from authorities is vital. Consistent and objective monitoring of the resource and harvest activities is also important to assess whether the management plan is sound or needs to be adjusted. Finally, there must be adequate technical and scientific help available, as well as con-

sistent funding over more than just a few years to support the effort while it matures (Sowman et al. 2003:300–335).

For groups with violent or divisive histories, taking these steps requires courage and skillful mediation at first, as well as much outside support. But initial success can quickly lead to a freer process of management where local residents take leading roles in determining what and how much to harvest, and in policing their own resource use. Along the KwaZulu-Natal coast, this formula has brought greater security to subsistence users while reducing poaching levels. Instead of arrests and rock-throwing, the future of the Mapelane's mussel beds lies now with the Joint Committee, where the day-to-day meaning of sustainability can be hammered out in discussion, then double-checked at low tide.

THE NEW IRAN:
TOWARD ENVIRONMENTAL DEMOCRACY

The standard image of Iran abroad is of a centralized, Islamic state where women have little public standing and religious leaders exert far-reaching control over political and social life. Widely publicized incidents such as the jailing of political dissidents perpetuate this image in the outside world. Yet, the appearance is deceptive. Beneath the authoritarian surface, significant changes are under way in Iranian society. In recent years reformist politicians have begun a decentralization drive, handing more power and administrative functions to local government bodies. Since 1999, local elections have been held across the country, and several hundred women now sit on local councils.

These decentralization efforts have not been limited to the political arena. The Iranian government's desire to halt environmental degradation has also triggered a democratic experiment to involve rural communities in conserving scarce water resources and productive land.

Since the late 1990s, the Sustainable Management of Land and Water Resources Program, based in rural Tehran and Semnan provinces, has developed a model of participatory decision-making that is attracting interest around the world. The results have encouraged the government to replicate the project's community-led methods to counter natural resource problems such as soil erosion, land degradation, and drought, in other rural regions.

The initiative, jointly funded by the Iranian government and the UN Development Programme, targets communities in a 1.2 million hectare region along the Hable River. Facilitators have worked with villagers to identify local environmental problems and solutions in a region where overgrazing, desertification, and water scarcity are endemic. Results have been slow to materialize in some areas, highly impressive in others. The most marked success has been in the village of Lazoor, 75 miles east of the capital Tehran.

Community involvement in decisions governing the use of land and water in rural Iran marks a significant first step toward the decentralization of natural resource management in the Islamic state. In the village of Lazoor, 100 miles east of Tehran, and other communities this has produced real environmental and social benefits. These include women's inclusion in decision-making; community-led implementation of effective flood control and water conservation measures; and a growing belief in, and commitment to community stewardship of natural resources.

However, the experiences of these communities also reflect common barriers encountered during attempts to empower local people and achieve genuine decentralization of control over natural resources around the world (see also Chapter 5):

- Central government ministries can be reluctant to give up power and decentralize decision-making and control over natural resources.

- Government officials often focus on expert planning and technical solutions rather than utilize local knowledge in natural resource management.

- Wealthier households can dominate participatory decision-making processes.

- Government ministries that share responsibility for natural resource management may fail to cooperate or coordinate effectively.

- Expanding successful local, community-led projects to a regional scale often proves difficult.

Lazoor: Participatory Planning in Action

Four years ago, the mountain village of Lazoor was plagued by routine flooding, land erosion, and communal apathy. The 3,000-strong community had only 1,100 hectares of productive farmland, mainly producing wheat, barley, and potatoes, and the villagers also owned 12,000 sheep (Farzin 1999; 2002:10). Overgrazing by these livestock had degraded the rangelands (which are under national ownership) and triggered landslides. Government efforts to improve agricultural practices and output, imposed from Tehran, had not gained the support of local farmers. As elsewhere in rural Iran, poverty levels were high and young people were leaving for the cities in search of jobs, mainly as tailors and carpenters.

As a result, Lazoor was chosen for the land and water project—one of eight pilot villages within the Firouzkooh township of Tehran Province. The ambitious aim of program manager Seyed Heidarian was to equip villagers with the techniques needed to identify, analyze, and prioritize local problems pertaining to natural resources, economic development, and social welfare. They would then be asked to produce solutions, based on their knowledge of the local environment and social and cultural traditions.

This was no easy feat, as Firouzkooh township was a typical Iranian rural enclave, where all rural planning decisions were made by central government officials and women had little public role. The first step was to democratically elect 20 local residents as "animators," including two from Lazoor. In 1999, these volunteers attended a one-month training program on participatory rural appraisal techniques, organized by the Center for Sustainable Development and the Environment (CENESTA), an Iranian nongovernmental organization. They then returned to their villages to initiate community decision-making sessions with the help of expert facilitators funded by UNDP.

In Lazoor, public village meetings and workshops were organized to gauge community concerns and ensure an inclusive voice in decision-making. A 76-person coordinating committee, including 25 women, was established to filter discussion on the community's priorities. Every villager was encouraged to attend the public meetings, and female-only workshops were also held to encourage women and girls to take part. After months of debate, a list of 81 priorities was completed. It included demands for anti-erosion and anti-flooding measures, a micro-credit scheme, a high school, and a women's clinic. Meetings were then held between villagers and government experts to approve the top sustainable development priorities for action.

According to Mehdi Kamyab, former UNDP manager of the land and water program, the coordinating committee "fairly represented" about 500 families made up of 2,000 people, and the "whole process was consensus-based, nobody had the last say." When there was a disagreement between villagers and government project managers about a scheme's practicality, independent facilitators brokered a compromise solution. Although the village Islamic Council, the local elected body, did not play a direct role in implementing Lazoor's sustainable development priorities, it did provide additional legitimacy by officially approving the decisions made (Kamyab 2003).

Improving Land and Water Management

Supported by government engineers and agricultural experts, the villagers translated their decisions on priorities into a dozen practical projects. These were implemented beginning in September 1999, with oversight from an elected central committee of five men and two women. Government and UNDP funds bankrolled the projects, along with a small "sustainable development fund" contributed by residents.

Hable River Basin, Iran

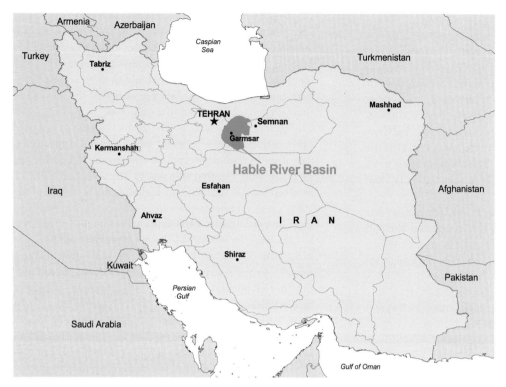

ing to develop the medicinal plants nursery, a scheme proposed by villagers and funded by the Global Environment Facility's Small Grants Program. "People describe the self-confidence generated by doing their own brainstorming and the ability to believe in self-organized problem solving as the best things that have happened to them" (Djazi 2002).

Shoukat Esfandiar was one of the Lazoor residents chosen to learn about public participation techniques and community-led problem-solving. Still working as an animator, she believes the villagers have not only gained confidence, but are also developing a sense of stewardship over their natural surroundings, suggesting an explicit link between empowerment and environmental responsibility. "The level of tolerance has increased in the village and the society's outlook is positive. Villagers have become aware of the issues related to the environment and resources, so much so that they are interested in maintaining, protecting, and sustainably using these natural resources" (Esfandiar 2003).

Lazoor's residents have since helped to build 42 small dams to control flooding, a water reservoir, five silt reservoirs to guard against soil erosion, and miles of anti-erosion embankments and irrigation canals. The community has also planted more than 7,000 fruit trees, including apple, cherry, pear, and plum, on a hillside overlooking the village. A second tree-planting program is also helping to improve soil quality and local biodiversity (Anderson 2001:A24; Farzin 2002:10; OCHA 2001).

By using rain and rivers more efficiently, Lazoor's residents are not only managing water resources more sustainably. They are also creating new opportunities for economic growth. Flood control, for example, has produced opportunities to cultivate new land. The community's entrepreneurship has so impressed state banking officials that they have opened a mobile bank branch in the village, approving several hundred small loans of $600–$1,200 and enabling around 300 families to open personal savings accounts (Anderson 2001:A24). Future programs include developing a medicinal plants nursery and exploring the feasibility of a mineral water bottling plant (Farzin 2002:11).

According to Hushang Djazi, one of the independent facilitators in Lazoor, the key to the village's success is active citizenship. "In the past the government was willing to do something for the villages, but since it made its own decisions without paying attention to the people who were affected, the projects failed. Our aim in Lazoor has been to improve rural people's skills and persuade them to participate in decisions and activities which directly affect them." Djazi is now help-

Empowering Women

Alongside these land management improvements, a social transformation has taken place. Only a few years ago, all village-related decisions were made by a group of elders with women playing no part. Since the project's facilitators ran female-only meetings, however, women have begun to demand more say in village affairs. Once a month, the village middle school plays host to the coordinating committee. Following opening prayers, members discuss progress and make suggestions for new activities. Several projects to improve women's independence and income, such as sewing classes, have been successfully established at their insistence. Mixed group meetings also now take place in the local mosque– where women were previously required to sit separately behind a screen (Anderson 2001:A24).

Twenty-five women actively take part in a public participation program run by Fatemeh Maafi, the second Lazoor facilitator. "Before our women didn't have access to facilities like men. They didn't access decision-making in village councils and other bodies. The Hable River project made this happen.

Women are not completely emancipated, but our situation is much better." The choice of projects, she says, has clearly been influenced by women's priorities. "Sometimes women's problems are different from those related to men. No one knows about these problems unless there is a voice, and the louder the voice, the more people will hear it" (Maafi 2003).

Malcolm Douglas, who led an international panel of experts commissioned by UNDP to evaluate the project in October 2001, also concluded that local women had been genuinely empowered. "It was impressive to see how women were involved in decision-making. Our impression was that the project facilitators' approach had given women more confidence and had helped them to get the message across to men in the community about women's concerns" (Douglas 2002). His panel report noted, however, that most women who actively participated in the project appeared to be from the community's wealthier families, suggesting that the views of poorer women were not receiving equal weight (Douglas 2002).

Success Beyond Lazoor

Lazoor's exercise in people-led resource management is not an isolated experiment. The village is one of several hundred actively involved in the Hable River land and water program, which covers a large swathe of land inhabited by 600,000 people across Tehran and Semnan provinces, south of the Caspian Sea. The watershed (and the project) is geographically segregated into three zones–the mountainous northern area, which reaches 4,000 meters above sea level; the southern desert plain, which falls to 700 meters; and a central area of hilly, inhospitable, and flood-prone terrain. The river runs northeast to southwest for 100 kilometers through this landscape, providing a magnet for agriculture and for the annual movement of migratory herdsmen and their livestock (Farzin 2002:4).

The project officially got underway in 1998-9 with public participation exercises in eight northern villages, including Lazoor, followed by similar exercises across the region. The emphasis throughout was on community involvement in identifying and addressing resource management problems such as flooding, erosion and water pollution. The results have not always been identical to the Lazoor experience, but many have yielded substantive accomplishments.

In the fertile plain in the south of the river basin, participatory planning projects have focused on efforts to increase agricultural productivity by improving drainage of waterlogged and saline land and the efficiency of irrigated areas. Farmers and water user groups have been enlisted in problem-solving exercises, although the emphasis from government managers has been very much on engineering solutions.

In the tiny villages of the rugged, mountainous central zone, small-scale road-building has helped reduce transport costs for fruit and vegetable exports, and villagers have come up with innovative schemes to improve their water supplies. For example, in the village of Ghalibaf, home to 40 families,

project funds and villagers' labor has been used to build 4,700 meters of rubber pipes channelling water from a nearby spring to the hamlet (Farzin 2002:12).

In three other mountain villages, cooperative women's groups have established bee-keeping enterprises with the encouragement of project managers and seed funding from UNDP. Each family contributes to buying the beehives. The original 200 hives have since grown to 600, with villagers recouping their investment several times over by selling honey (Farzin 2002:12).

Local Empowerment—Within Limits

The experiment under way in the Hable River watershed is best described as "partial decentralization." Although communities are setting priorities to improve natural resource use and devising local solutions to land management and water problems, the minimum conditions for full decentralization described in Chapter 5 have not been met. Villagers in Lazoor do not control most of the local program budget (the exception being the sustainable development fund made up of villagers' contributions) and there are concerns that wealthier families dominate the coordinating committee. Detailed land use planning and mapping is also done by outside experts.

Nevertheless, power and decision-making are now essentially split between communities and central government managers. As in other countries, such as Bolivia (see Chapter 5), it is clear that the partial empowerment of local communities is giving a voice to people in Iran who previously lacked the right to participate in a meaningful way.

Moreover, given that the concept of local empowerment is very new in the modern Islamic republic and that rural communities have been used to decades of centralized control over their daily lives, the limited nature of the decentralization process to date is hardly surprising. Further, some international experts argue that a mix of indigenous knowledge and central government expertise can sometimes prove more effective at protecting natural resources and promoting sustainable use than passing all power and control to local communities.

"It was the first time in Iran that people had tried using participatory planning for natural resource management," says Malcolm Douglas. "In my experience, under these kinds of circumstances, if you have a totally open process you end up with a simplistic wish list. People agree that they want a new road, a school, a clinic, a mosque and so on without any real consideration of local natural resource and social issues. Unless you have trained facilitators with some technical background, natural resource issues can often fade into the background" (Douglas 2002).

According to facilitator Hushang Djazi, the project managers in Lazoor have already learned valuable lessons that could be applied to rural communities across Iran. "The keys to the Lazoor method are: believe in local people; program with them, not for them; improve local institutions; and act as a real facilitator, not a program expert or manager"(Djazi 2002). Nevertheless, two expert panels commissioned by UNDP to evaluate the project in 1999 and 2001, while praising the extent of public participation, also raised concerns about the limits of local democracy. Both teams visited Lazoor and made similar observations, namely that (Koohafkan et al. 1999; Douglas et al. 2001):

- The village's 76-person project development committee appeared to be dominated by the wealthier residents. Poorer villagers, especially women and the illiterate, were not well represented, suggesting that their views were not being properly heard.

- There was too much emphasis on technical solutions, particularly engineering projects such as dams and detailed land mapping exercises, and not enough use made of villagers' indigenous knowledge about local biodiversity.

- The project managers relied too much on central government officials and experts from UN agencies and nongovernmental organizations (NGOs), rather than building up knowledge and expertise among community organizations and locally based central government administrators and technical staff.

- The project's purse strings were too tightly controlled from Tehran rather than by local administrators and the communities themselves.

All these factors have raised concerns among land husbandry and sustainability experts that local ownership of the project in Lazoor is not yet strong enough for it to survive without continued outside support from government, UN agencies, and NGOs. On a region-wide scale, concerns have also been raised that managers of the three project areas are failing to coordinate activities and pool experience and that there is no centralized database to help monitor progress and evaluate results.

Part of the problem—and a common failure of governance in countries attempting to decentralize power—has been the reluctance of some government officials to accept the validity of local empowerment and village-level decision-making. "The difficulty in implementing a new approach has not only been gaining the trust of communities, but also generating belief in such approaches in higher authorities," notes Mohammad Ali Farzin, an Iranian development economist (Farzin 2002:7).

To counter this endemic problem, the second panel of experts to visit Lazoor recommended that Iran's government conduct awareness-raising programs for senior officials on the benefits of participatory planning to promote its wider acceptance (Douglas et al. 2001:14).

Environmental Benefits—Within Limits

There is no question that the community empowerment experiment under way along the Hable River has produced environmental gains. In November 2001, for example, the UNDP-commissioned expert panel concluded that "the program is building up a wealth of valuable experience in tackling the problems of sustainable management of land and water resources...that is expected to be applicable to other parts of Iran." They also noted that small-scale activities were being initiated spontaneously by communities, women's groups, and even individual farmers and herders, demonstrating both a growing confidence in self-determination and a genuine commitment to sustainable resource management (Douglas et al. 2001:3-4).

Several factors, however, have been identified as holding back progress toward sustainable agriculture and water use. First, the resource management program only covers a small area of the watershed and its activities are dwarfed by the problems facing the region. The inhospitable terrain, regular occurrence of flooding, and sheer extent of land degradation and water scarcity after decades of poor management have all combined to offset the efforts of villagers and project staff. For example, the limited tree-planting and water conservation measures under way in the uplands are likely to have little impact on the amount of water and sediment discharging into the flood-prone southern plains (Douglas et al. 2001:8). Malcolm Douglas witnessed these limitations first-hand in November 2001. "The program so far was really just scratching the surface. All it would take was one major storm and you would get massive flooding downstream which would neutralize much of the work being done" (Douglas 2002).

Second, while steps have been taken to improve coordination among central government departments, gaps in the newly integrated system remain. The widespread degradation of rangelands through overgrazing has been acknowledged as a critical problem, for example. Yet, Iran's Department of Extension, Irrigation, and Livestock Affairs has not been involved in administering the Hable River project. Since this department is responsible for setting herders' animal quotas, it has not been possible for local communities and project managers to reduce livestock on over-burdened land.

Third, little effort has generally been made so far to tap into communities' own environmental knowledge and expertise. Villagers' knowledge of local soil conditions and ecology, built up over many generations, could play an important role in improving soils, combating land degradation, and successfully introducing new species. Yet, much of the land use planning continues to be done by outside experts, a trend noted by the expert panel (Douglas et al. 2001:9-10). To enable local farmers and herders to become more actively involved, the panel recommended developing simple indicators to measure land degradation and the impacts of different land use practices.

Demography and Democracy in Iran

Democratization in Iran is not taking place in a vacuum. It is occurring in the context of significant changes in birth rates, life expectancies, and educational opportunities, particularly among rural women. Advances in these social and demographic indicators provide a basis for social change.

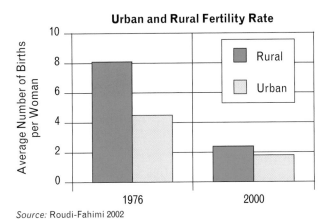

Urban and Rural Fertility Rate

Source: Roudi-Fahimi 2002

Life Expectancy at Birth, Female

Source: World Bank 2003

Rural Iran: Toward a Sustainable Future?

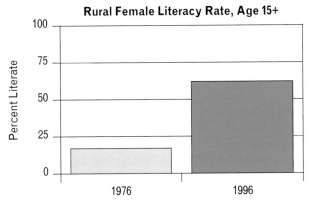

Rural Female Literacy Rate, Age 15+

Source: Roudi-Fahimi 2002

Rural Iran: Toward a Sustainable Future?

Despite the widely publicized success in Lazoor, there is a general consensus that the Hable River program still lacks an overarching "sustainability vision." This failure to develop a common purpose and agenda among community-led projects across the region has limited the program's impact. It is also jeopardizing the original objective: to produce a workable blueprint for sustainable land and water management applicable across rural Iran.

According to Hossein Jafari at UNDP in Tehran, "the elements of a national model for rural land and water management are in place, but we have been unable to fit [them] together" (Jafari 2003).

As a result, UNDP ended its involvement in the first phase of the project in 2002, with two thirds of the $1.2 million dollar budget still unspent. "There had been very good activities in the field producing very good results," says Mr. Jafari. "Trials in ten more villages would not have produced any added value. Our key objective now is to produce a national model based on the successes of Lazoor and other areas" (Jafari 2003).

To this end, senior UNDP and FAO officials met with key government officials in January 2003. Agreement was reached for the two UN agencies to prepare the program's second phase with government support. Work on producing a river basin-wide model for sustainable resource management, replicable across the country, is due to start during 2003. A participatory monitoring and evaluation system will also be established.

Whether such a regional blueprint will be able to generate a revolution in sustainable natural resource management across Iran will depend on many factors, not least the willingness of various government ministries to embrace decentralization initiatives and coordinate effectively (Jafari 2003).

Clearly, the early years of Iran's transition from bureaucratic, centralized control of natural resources to an environment where people play a leading role in preserving their own natural surroundings have not been entirely smooth or easy. There is a long way to go before partial decentralization of power over natural resources becomes full-fledged environmental democracy, with communities genuinely in charge of decision-making, program management, and budgets. Or before Lazoor and other Hable River communities become workable models for the whole of rural Iran.

Nevertheless, although the trend in Iran so far is toward granting limited powers and resources to local people, the results have been positive, delivering ecological benefits and improving dialogue between government and civil society.

"If the right lessons are learned from Lazoor and other successful areas," suggests Malcolm Douglas, "and they spread the effort across the whole region and go in with less of a technical fix, then there could be a major beneficial ecological impact" (Douglas 2002).

OK TEDI MINE:
UNEARTHING CONTROVERSY

The environmental and human tragedy that is still unfolding at the Ok Tedi mine in Papua New Guinea raises fundamental questions about the governance of natural resources. These questions concern the balance of power between inexperienced, cash-poor governments and powerful multinational industries; the provision of and access to information that is technical in nature; communication across language and cultural barriers; and the need for institutional structures that allow for effective complaint and redress when things go wrong. Such issues are directly relevant to the global mining industry's ongoing efforts to reduce its adverse social and environmental impact and to be more accountable for its actions.

The Story in Brief

Papua New Guinea, a country of only 5 million people, is a botanical treasure island. Its relatively pristine rain forests, mountains, rivers, and reefs harbor a host of rare plants, animals, and birds, including flying foxes, river turtles, the longest lizard, and the largest orchid, bat, and butterfly species in the world (NRI and World Bank 2002:8).

Yet, in the 1990s, the country became a byword for the ecological destruction that can result when a young, weak government and an international mining corporation ignore environmental concerns and the voices of local communities.

The main source of trouble has been the Ok Tedi mine, situated deep in the rain-forest-covered Star Mountains of Papua New Guinea's Western Province. Since the mid-1980s, the large copper and gold mine has released about 30 million tons of mine tailings (a fine sand of crushed rock and metals) into the Ok Tedi tributary of the Fly River every year (Kirsch 2001:1). The result has been ecological disaster. By the early 1990s, fish were dying, turtles disappearing, and canoes running aground midstream as sedimentation raised riverbeds. The overflow destroyed food gardens in down-

---

Ok Tedi Mine: Some Facts and Figures

Operating Life: 1984–2010.

Jobs: Ok Tedi Mining Limited (OTML) employs about 2,000 staff. About 1,800 are Papua New Guinea citizens and 800 live within a 40-kilometer radius of the mine.

Production: About 200,000 tons of copper and 500,000 ounces of gold a year. By December 2001, the mine had produced 7.5 million tons of copper concentrate.

Ecological Impact: About 40 million tons of waste rock and 30 million tons of tailings—a fine sand—are discharged annually into local rivers. Impacts on rivers and rain forest will last for decades.

Economic Impact: The mine is the single largest contributor to Papua New Guinea's economy, accounting for about 10 percent of GDP. In 2001, sales accounted for 18 percent of total national exports.

Profits: From 1984-2001 OTML's profits totaled US$338 million.

Source: OTDF 2001:6; Higgins 2002:1; Kirsch 2002:18; OTML 2003c:13; OTML 2003d

stream indigenous communities and killed thousands of trees.

The mine's main shareholders—Australia-based Broken Hill Proprietary or BHP (renamed BHP Billiton after merging with UK-based Billiton in 2001) and the Papua New Guinea government—failed for years to respond adequately to the ecological consequences of its operations. After the case became an international cause celebre, the indigenous peoples living along the Ok Tedi and Fly rivers sued the BHP and received $28.6m in an out-of-court compensation settlement (NRI and World Bank 2002).

Today, although a limited dredging operation has been introduced, mine waste continues to pour into local rivers. While the mine's operations—and along with them, its boost to the national economy—are scheduled to end in 2010, its ecological impact will linger for decades. Ok Tedi Mining Ltd. (OTML), the company that operates the mine, itself acknowledges that more than 2,000 square kilometers of rain forest could be stunted (OTML 2003b). BHP Billiton, however, has walked away from Ok Tedi. In February 2002, its 52 percent equity share in the mine was transferred to an offshore trust, set up on behalf of the Papua New Guinea people (Finlayson 2002:6). The government gave BHP Billiton legal indemnity from responsibility for future mine-related damage to the Ok Tedi ecosystem, although the legality of this deal may be challenged in the country's courts.

What went wrong? The answers—explored in the following pages—lie in the interplay of several factors, all related to governance. They include the linkage of the mine with nation-building and economic development in a newly independent country; the political marginalization of local communities and weakness of local government institutions; the government's over-reliance on BHP for information about environmental costs and benefits; and the government's conflicting role as both mine shareholder and regulator.

Ok Tedi Mine: The Political and Economic Context

Papua New Guinea's first central government was elected upon independence from Australia in 1975. The young nation experienced an abrupt transition to rule by a weak, centralized government whose authority was rivalled by traditional clan systems. The new government faced high expectations from its people; it also faced external pressure from multilateral lending organizations such as the World Bank and International Monetary Fund and from corporate partners in the mining industry.

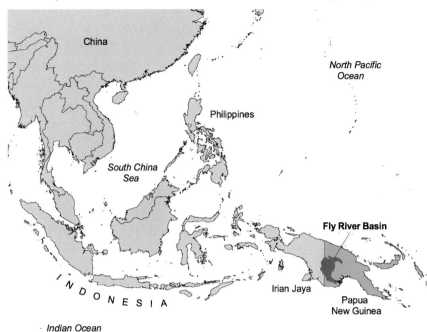

Papua New Guinea and Surrounding Region

Papua New Guinea is rich in mineral wealth. Large-scale mining began in the 1930s, under Australian colonial rule, in the Wau-Bulolo area. In 1972, a massive copper mine began operating at Panguna on the island of Bougainville, discharging its waste directly into the Jaba River. Over the next 15 years, the Bougainville mine became the world's biggest copper producer (Filer 1997:59; Finlayson 2002:1).

The copper and gold deposits at Ok Tedi on Mount Fubilan, almost 2,000 meters high in the rain forest-swathed Star Mountains, presented a daunting challenge. The terrain is inaccessible and prone to high rainfall, frequent earthquakes, and landslides (King 1997:96). But the ores presented a tantalizing prospect to Papua New Guinea's young government. By 1974, mining's contribution to the national income had already increased substantially, and a new mine at Ok Tedi promised to raise it even more.

The government wanted to use income from the mine to develop infrastructure and services and to boost Papua New Guinea's international standing as a major minerals exporter. It was encouraged in this by the World Bank and the Australian government, whose Export Finance and Insurance Corporation helped fund exploratory studies at Mount Fubilan (IWT 1994:60; MPI and AID/WATCH 1999:23).

In 1976, the state of Papua New Guinea authorized BHP, Australia's biggest mining corporation, to prepare a development plan for the mine. Four years later, the government committed to a partnership in Ok Tedi Mining Limited with a 20 percent shareholding. The other shareholders were BHP, Amoco Minerals, and a consortium of German companies (King 1997:98). The mine began operating in 1984 and within

a decade became one of the world's largest copper producers—extracting about 30 million tons of ore. By 1996, the Papua New Guinea government owned 30 percent of shares, BHP 52 percent and Inmet, a Canadian mining company, 18 percent (King 1997:98).

Virtually all of Papua New Guinea's land is in customary ownership, with the owners grouped into small communal clans (Hancock and Omundsen 1998:1). The state, however, claims legal ownership of all mineral resources beneath customary lands. As a result, only the government and its potential corporate partners were involved in deciding whether and how to develop Mt. Fubilan's ores, assessing the Ok Tedi mine's potential environmental and social impacts, and deciding how to ameliorate those impacts (Hancock and Omundsen 1998:3).

The approximately 2,000 landowners living at the headwaters of the Ok Tedi River held customary rights to the area covered by the proposed operations (Finlayson 2002: 9). These villagers alone were included in negotiations with the mining conglomerate, agreeing to lease 7,000 hectares of land to OTML in return for a benefits and compensation package that included cash, jobs, and education and health facilities. The indigenous communities living downstream of the proposed mine were excluded from the mine consultation process. It was not until 1997, after mine waste had devastated their lives for almost a decade, that leases for these villages were finally negotiated as part of an out-of-court compensation settlement (Kirsch 2001:4).

Before the project was approved, OTML agreed to build a tailings dam to protect the Fly River as recommended in an Environmental Impact Assessment (EIA) by Australian consultants commissioned by the company. The report concluded that even with such a dam in place, copper and other heavy metals would have severe effects on fish downstream of the mine (Townsend and Townsend 1996). In January 1984, however, a landslide destroyed the dam's foundations. Under pressure from BHP not to force the expensive building of another dam, the government granted OTML temporary permission to release mine waste into the headwaters of the Ok Tedi River. In 1988, after a rebellion by indigenous landowners in Bougainville forced Papua New Guinea's other major copper mine (and revenue-earner) to close, the government renewed OTML's interim river disposal license. It is still in effect (Filer 1997:59).

Ok Tedi Mine, Fly River Basin

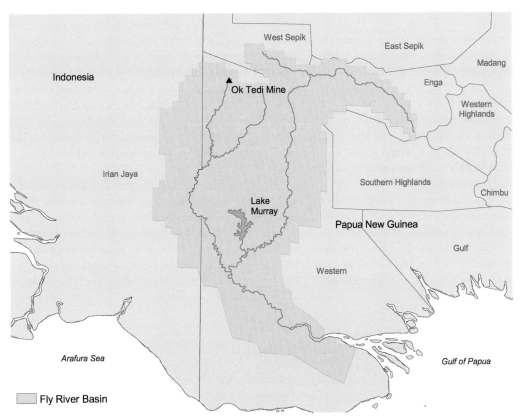

Fly River Basin

The Fallout

The well-documented environmental and social consequences of these decisions have been enormous. For almost two decades, the mine has discharged about 30 million tons of metal-tainted mine tailings and 40 million tons of waste rock a year into the Ok Tedi River, which in turn discharges its load into the Fly River. Before it reaches the Gulf of Papua in the Torres Straits, the Fly flows through dense primary tropical rain forest, wetlands, and savanna. The river system supports the greatest biological diversity in Australasia, including 128 recorded native freshwater species, with 17 unique to the Fly basin (Swales et al. 1998:100).

This chronic build-up of waste has had a devastating effect on the 50,000 people who live in the 120 villages along the two rivers and depend on them for subsistence fishing and other river-based resources. Before the mine, taro and bananas were commonly grown in village gardens and riverside sago palms often provided the mainstay of local diets. But since the early 1990s, the build-up of sediment in the rivers and subsequent flooding of forests have dramatically altered the local environment. Fish stocks have fallen by 70-90 percent, animals have migrated, and about 1,300 square kilometers of vegetation have died or become blighted, forcing villagers to hunt and fish over larger dis-

tances (BHP 1999:9; Higgins 2002:2). Copper concentrations in the water are about 30 times background levels, though the river still meets World Health Organization drinking water standards (BHP 1999:8–9).

For the Yonggom people and their neighbors living along the lower Ok Tedi and Fly rivers, the mine's ecological impact violated a centuries-old way of life. From the late 1980s, they described in interviews and anguished letters to the OTML and government officials how pollution and flooding were eroding their traditional subsistence lifestyles, forcing some villagers to relocate. "The animals living along the river banks–the pigs, cassowaries, pigeons and bandicoots–have all disappeared...now the places where turtles laid their eggs have been covered up," said one. "Before women travelled by canoe on their own, but today the river is too dangerous" (Kirsch 1997:124). An anthropologist working with the Wopkaimin people described the mine waste's impact on local wildlife and people as "ecocide" (King 1997:96).

A Voiceless People

As Ok Tedi Mining's own literature acknowledges, its arrival changed the lives of the people forever (OTDF 2001:6). The horticulturalist indigenous tribes of Papua New Guinea's Western Province had lived in small clan-based settlements

191

Chapter 8: A World of Decisions: Case Studies

for hundreds of years, cultivating small garden-farms and hunting and gathering food from the rain forest (IWT 1994:71; Kirsch 2003).

The Ok Tedi mine introduced industrial jobs, urban living, a cash economy, and supermarket food to the region, based around the company town of Tabubil. Yet, little was done to consult or prepare its indigenous residents for this upheaval (Finlayson 2002:17). Lack of communication isolated the downstream communities from their new corporate neighbor. Confusion over language, the role of customary clan leaders, and cultural and spiritual values also fed into OTML's failure to quickly recognize and deal with the environmental disaster that ensued.

When personnel in the company's environment and community affairs departments first received complaints from villagers, they found them imprecise, exaggerated, and confusing. "People are suffering from sores," stated one letter. "The rain makes us sick. The air we breathe leaves us short of breath. And the sun now burns our skin" (Kirsch 2001:5). The

often settled without formal procedures. Clan leaders who gained their legitimacy through lineage were more influential than elected local officials and members of parliament (Burton 1997:33). These clan leaders wrote letters and sent petitions to as many interested parties as they could think of, making little distinction as to who was responsible for taking action. This helped create a situation whereby even though OTML's community relations staff recorded villagers' grievances, their reports were not considered important enough for senior management to act on and instead lay "filed away in forgotten corners" until it was too late to prevent court action (Burton 1997:42,52).

When anthropologist Stuart Kirsch visited the Yonggom communities in 1992, several years after the first letters of complaint were written, little formal assessment of environmental damage had been carried out by either mining company or government. He described the villagers as "in a state of despair, feeling both frustrated and completely ignored in their efforts to obtain restitution" (Kirsch 2001:9).

villagers' letters reflected their holistic and spiritual view of nature and human society as inextricably linked. But the jumbling together of evidence of mine waste impacts with clan mythologies blunted their message and helped prevent the initiation of a political process through which the communities' grievances could be effectively heard (Burton 1997:42–44).

At the same time, local peoples had little experience with modern political environments. Traditionally, disputes were

Seeking Redress

The unresponsiveness of both OTML and the government provided a crash course in politicization for the Yonggom people and their neighbors. Through local church and environmental groups, they made contact with the Australian Conservation Foundation and the Geneva-based World Conservation Union, which funded environmental audits of the Fly River. In 1992, the Wau Ecology Institute helped a group of indigenous landowners present their grievances against OTML to the International Water Tribunal in The Hague. The tribunal's judgments lack legal force. But its finding, issued in 1992, that the Papua New Guinea government should either prevent further damage or close the mine (IWT 1994:85), brought Ok Tedi into the international spotlight. This in turn encouraged local villagers and their nongovernmental allies to seek legal remedy (Kirsch 2001:7–8).

In 1994–95, Australian law firm Slater and Gordon launched a series of lawsuits in the Victoria Supreme Court in Melbourne, where BHP was incorporated, on behalf of 30,000 villagers from 600 clans affected by the mine (Gordon 1997:143). The "David and Goliath" suit against one of Australia's biggest corporations received widespread media coverage, mostly unfavorable to BHP. Lawyers for the villagers argued that they had suffered damaging "loss of amenity" because of the waste's impact on their subsistence economy and spiritual and cultural connections to the land (Kirsch 2001:13, 17). In 1996, the two sides reached an out-of-court settlement, which included compensation and a BHP commitment to contain mine tailings. The agreed payout included 110 million kina (US$36 million) over the life of the mine for the 34,000 people living along the Ok Tedi and Fly Rivers, and 40 million kina (US$13 million) for the 15 villages most affected (Kirsch 2001:17).

In 1999, OTML began a river dredging operation 80 kilometers downstream of the mine. The same year BHP, as the major shareholder, publicly acknowledged the mine's "unexpected and significant environmental impacts" (BHP 1999:4). The timing of this announcement coincided with the publication of a risk assessment study commissioned by the company which identified the mine's closure in 2000–10 years ahead of schedule–as one of several options (BHP 1999:14). In the event, BHP chose to disinvest from the mine, arguing that the impacts of riverine disposal were not compatible with its contemporary corporate standards (BHP 1999:4).

Whatever the company's rationale for withdrawing from the Ok Tedi mine, its public admission of responsibility came 11 years after the first letters of complaint. How had such a significant failure of corporate governance and government oversight been allowed to take place, and over such a long period of time? The answer lies partly, of course, in the company's internal dynamics, but also in the political and economic climate in which it was operating.

Weak Nations, Powerful Corporations, and a Failure of Governance

Central Government: A Conflicting Role

Papua New Guinea is a country with a democratic process, freedom of information laws, and a constitution that enshrines environmental protection as a key national goal. The latter requires, for example, that "all necessary steps be taken to give adequate protection to our valued birds, animals, fish, insects, plants and trees" (Taylor 1997:15).

Yet, when it came to Ok Tedi, the government agreed first to delay and then to forego construction of a tailings dam and to permit waste dumping in the river. How did the constitution take a backseat to economic development? Why was the likelihood of ecological damage deemed acceptable? And why was there no consultation with downstream communities before permitting river dumping?

The answer lies primarily in the linkage of the mine with nation-building and economic and social development, and in the government's conflicting role as both mine shareholder and regulator.

In the 1980s, it was not unusual for developing country governments to take equity stakes in new mining ventures operated by transnational corporations. The aim was to ensure that as many benefits as possible–revenues, profits, mining taxes–remained in the host countries. Yet, by juggling the roles of mine owner and mining industry regulator, these governments opened themselves up to a major conflict of interest (Temu 1997:192–193).

Strict oversight measures are necessary to neutralize such conflicts. At Ok Tedi, however, the Papua New Guinea government's conflict of interest played itself out to damaging effect. According to critics, the state's direct financial stake undermined its role as independent arbiter of the mine's environmental and social impacts and contributed to its failure to honor the constitution. As a mine owner, the government was also seen by local communities as at least partly responsible for environmental damage caused in the pursuit of profit and as having relinquished its role as the government (Taylor 1997:24).

The government's conflicted position was most strongly demonstrated by its failure to hold its corporate partners to their agreement to contain mine waste. When the tailings dam's foundations collapsed, start-up costs were over budget and copper prices falling. The area's geological instability made another dam potentially risky, and alternative options that environmentalists favored as more ecologically sound, such as building a 100-kilometer tailings pipeline to a stable lowlands waste dump, were expensive. At the same time, the Bougainville copper mine was in the process of closing down, with a consequent reduction in national GDP of around 20 percent (Hancock 2003).

Simultaneous closure of Ok Tedi would have undermined the country's fledgling education and health systems and exacerbated rural poverty (Hancock 2003). The mining companies could afford to walk away but the government couldn't afford to let them. When BHP warned that it would close the mine if it were required to build a new dam, the government waived the requirement rather than face major revenue, tax, and job losses and a severe blow to national pride. It chose this course of action even though complaints about the environmental effects of mine waste disposal had contributed to the rebellion that brought down the Bougainville mine (Kirsch 2001:5–6).

The government's part ownership of the Ok Tedi mine also raises key governance issues in the legislative arena. From the start, the government made its deep commitment to Ok Tedi's success clear, and seemed prepared to accept some degree of environmental degradation to accomplish that goal.

Ok Tedi was exempted from later legislation, including the Environmental Planning Act of 1978, allowing the mine to escape oversight by the Department of Environment and Conservation (Burton 1997:50). Instead, OTML was made responsible for monitoring its own impacts (Kirsch 2001:8). The Department of Mining and Petroleum oversaw Ok Tedi policy in its early years, encouraging a decision-making process dominated by senior government and OTML officials (IWT 1994:66–67).

The closeness of this collaboration was brought to light at the International Water Tribunal hearings in 1991. According to its proceedings, "one former staff member at the Department of Minerals observed that OTML management personnel had easy and frequent access to the highest Papua New Guinea government levels... Frequently, important decisions by the Cabinet were made even without consulting responsible government staff, based on information provided mainly by OTML itself" (IWT 1994:66–67). In its judgment, the tribunal accused BHP of "using its foreign earning power to influence the government to make exceptions in the application of law in its favor to the detriment of the local environment and the livelihood of the local people" (IWT 1994:84).

In 1989, the government moved to address concerns about accountability for these mines, establishing a more inclusive form of decision-making for both new and existing opera-

tions. Development Forums were established, through which national and provincial governments and local landowning communities agreed to operational terms and to the benefits, rights, and obligations of each stakeholder (Hancock and Omundsen 1998:1–3). In 1991, the retrospective Development Forum for Ok Tedi resulted in an increase in royalty payments to villagers leasing land to the mine.

According to John Strongman, World Bank Mining Advisor in Washington, DC, these Development Forums "give a very good voice to landowners and provide for a very good circulation of information. Is it possible for Ok Tedi-type problems to happen again in Papua New Guinea? Absolutely not. The consultation procedures are now probably some of the best anywhere in the world" (Strongman 2003).

Many local villagers and their allies in local and international nongovernmental organizations (NGOs), however, do not share this upbeat assessment. They point to a continuing trend in decisions by the government since the 1996 settlement that favor BHP. Most contentiously, in December 2001, the Papua New Guinea government passed the Ok Tedi Mine Continuation Ninth Supplemental Act–which included a liability waiver relieving BHP of any responsibility for damage from the mine after the company sold its shareholding.

Local Government: A Lack of Capacity

Governance failures related to the Ok Tedi mine and the short-changing of local communities have not been confined to the national government.

The rule of law is tenuous in parts of Papua New Guinea, including its Western Province, and provincial agencies often lack both the capacity and expertise to deliver much-needed health, education, and transport services. Some local government administrations have also mismanaged their finances. The Fly River Provincial Government (FRPG), which governs Western Province, has been suspended three times by the national government for inadequate financial management, the third time in September 2000. It was reinstated in October 2001 (OTDF 2001:7; Finlayson 2002:10).

The FRPG has had little success in converting its substantial mining royalties into sustainable, long-term benefits for its people. Since 1990, the provincial government has received 300 million kina (US$100 million) in Ok Tedi-related payments, including royalties and taxes (Finlayson 2002:10). Yet, according to a 2002 report commissioned by the Papua New Guinea government as part of a World Bank-funded project on institutional mining reform, little of the windfall has been used to improve "unsatisfactory" health and education services or reorganize failed administrative systems. As recently as 2001, the FRPG's Building Board,

Tenders Board, Land Board, and Transport Board all failed to function, while the Department of Works had no working equipment (Finlayson 2002:11).

The province's huge size, the existence of many isolated communities to whom service delivery is costly and difficult, and the national government's failure to assist FRPG to reform have all contributed to this situation. With mine royalties and taxes due to cease in 2010, the potential consequences are dire. The national government-commissioned report concluded that "the vast majority of people outside the mine-affected areas have not benefited from the Ok Tedi mine, either financially or through improved services. In rural areas of Western Province there is little evidence of investment in agriculture or business activities that may be sustainable after mine closure" (Finlayson 2002:17).

Corporation as Government: Filling a Vacuum

Like other transnational corporations operating in developing countries where infrastructure and services are scarce, Ok Tedi Mining Limited has effectively taken on some of the functions of local government. To enable the mine to function and to attract and retain employees, it built an airstrip at Tabubil, the town nearest the mine site. It has also set up localized power and water supplies, constructed a sewage system, and built a local road network.

The company soon became the major provider of health services within 40 kilometers of the mine, running a 24-bed hospital and funding mosquito control programs (OTML 2003a). Local infant mortality subsequently fell from 27 to 2 percent. The company also paid for 133 community halls, 40 classrooms, 600 water tanks, and 15 aid posts in village communities (BHP 1999:11–12). Between 1982 and 2001, the Ok Tedi mine provided 3.39 billion kina (US$2.13 billion) in benefits to Papua New Guinea (Finlayson 2002:6).

By the early 1990s, it became clear that the Ok Tedi mine had, through its existence in a highly under-developed region, created a dependency in the Western Province on the economic activity it generated. According to David Wissink, manager of the Ok Tedi Development Foundation, "OTML provided the area around the mine site in particular with the sort of social and physical infrastructure that would ordinarily have been provided by representative government. OTML provided this to meet its own needs, but also as part of the compensation arrangements for its mining activity" (Wissink 2003).

The company's assumption of this role clearly benefited those living closest to the mine, many of whom also worked there. The bigger downstream communities suffering the brunt of ecological damage, however, received little direct benefit from the mine until after the compensation settlement. Moreover, their early efforts to win redress were hampered both by the weakness of the local government and by the absence of democratic process created by the national

government's conflicting role as a mine owner.

Acting like a surrogate government, whether intentionally or not, raises serious governance questions about the proper role of un-elected transnational corporations operating in developing countries. On one hand, local citizens often welcome the new services and infrastructure that such companies can bring. On the other, such benefits can quickly erode once the companies depart.

In Papua New Guinea, the government was warned in August 2002 by an independent expert that "unless the capacity of the provincial government is greatly enhanced in the immediate future, the [Ok Tedi] Foundation will be seen as replacing the role of government for a large proportion of Western Province's population" (Finlayson 2002:18). His report also warned that the viability of the modern infrastructure that local people had come to rely on—from water and power to roads—would be jeopardized once OTML ceased to maintain them (Finlayson 2002:15).

Ok Tedi Today: A Just Outcome?

Both the Papua New Guinea government and local communities viewed the possibility of the mine's early closure as the worst of all worlds, depriving local residents of income and the region of royalties to mitigate ecological problems and fund alternative employment programs.

A World Bank report commissioned by the national government in late 1999 concluded that closing the mine quickly would be the "best environmental option," but would create a "potentially disastrous" social situation (World Bank 2000). BHP's shareholders wanted to close the mine in 2000, but the company agreed instead to write off its investment. In February 2002, its 52 percent equity was transferred to a new trust— the Papua New Guinea Sustainable Development Program Company—whose dividend income would be spent on development programs for up to 40 years (Kirsch 2001:1; MMSD Mining et al. 2002:348). For its part, the newly-merged BHP Billiton, now one of the world's largest mining corporations, received indemnity from future pollution liability.

Legislation and agreements sealing this deal followed 2 years of consultations between OTML and Fly River communities. According to the company, each village chose two representatives to act on its behalf. By 2002, OTML had negotiated Mine Continuation Agreements with 142 of the 155 villages in the affected area (Higgins 2002:4). The agreements provide compensation for future environmental damage between 2002 and 2010. About 60,000 people—or 40 percent of Western Province's inhabitants—will benefit, with 180 million kina (US$50 million) split between cash payments (16 percent); health, education and job creation projects (58 percent); and trust funds for future generations (26 percent) (Finlayson 2002:14).

The bulk of development assistance will be managed by the new Ok Tedi Foundation, which has become a vehicle for improved company communications with the Fly River

communities. During 2002, around 150 village planning committees were set up to jointly review proposed projects with foundation staff. Agreed-upon projects are presented to one of nine community development trusts for funding approval. These trusts have an average of eight trustees, at least four of whom are local community representatives (Wissink 2003).

It is too early to judge how this new partnership approach will play out in terms of successful sustainable development and job creation before and after the mine closes. What is not in question, however, is that both the contested 1996 settlement and BHP's early exit from the mine raise crucial issues of environmental governance, accountability, and social justice that continue to reverberate throughout the region and the country.

Two issues generate most anger. First, many villagers still living with the daily outpouring of mine waste believe that BHP Billiton should not have been allowed to escape responsibility for continuing environmental damage after its exit. A pending court case in Australia alleging breach of the 1996 settlement will attempt to force both BHP Billiton—which remains bound by its terms—and OTML to implement more comprehensive tailings containment measures and pay out more compensation (Hardwick 2003). Both companies are contesting the case, expected to reach trial in early 2004.

Second, there is widespread confusion and upset among villagers over the terms of the Community Mine Continuation Agreements (CMCAs) signed on their behalf. According to local NGOs and the Australian lawyers acting for commu-

nity leaders, many villagers claim they did not understand that legal documents were being signed by two representatives on behalf of entire communities, or that they barred individuals from taking part in the second lawsuit against BHP and OTML. Fourteen hundred villagers subsequently signed affidavits disowning the agreements (Hardwick 2003).

Ongoing distrust among the mining company, provincial government, and communities is also reflected in concerns about the accountability of the Papua New Guinea Sustainable Development Program Company. Bob Danaya, governor of Western Province, has strongly objected to the lack of a provincial representative on the Board of Directors, whose membership has been appointed exclusively by BHP Billiton and the national government (Danaya 2003).

2002–2010: Crunch Time

The history of poor governance—national, local and corporate—surrounding the Ok Tedi mine and Western Province has left a legacy of distrust, disaffection, and environmental degradation. Further, Papua New Guinea remains a heavily mineral-dependent economy, despite hopes that the revenue from Ok Tedi and other mines would help the country diversify its economy.

Although Ok Tedi has generated significant income for local communities and the Fly River Provincial Government, there is little to show for it in terms of new, durable infrastructure or services (Finlayson 2002:15). Meanwhile, mine

Beyond Ok Tedi: Progress Toward Sustainable Mining?

The mining industry has rapidly consolidated in the last 20 years, creating companies that are larger than some national economies. A few giant mining transnationals based in Australia, Canada, the United States, and the UK now dominate the market. They include BHP Billiton, Rio Tinto, Placer Dome, Newmont, Freeport, and Anglo American.

These companies wield enormous power, especially in developing countries anxious to generate income. Under-resourced governments, as in Papua New Guinea, can fail to provide adequate oversight and protection for local people and resources. Some assume the potentially conflicting roles of mine regulator and shareholder. A number of questions suggest how such power imbalances among corporations, developing country governments, and local communities might be righted.

■ Would a global code of conduct agreed by governments and mining companies improve the industry's social and environmental performance?

■ How can developing country governments make informed decisions on whether to approve a mine when they are acting on information provided by the prospective mining company?

■ What better efforts can be made to ensure the full understanding and prior informed consent of communities living in or around potential mine sites?

■ Should governments be part-owners of mining projects, given the potential conflict between the roles of mine regulator and shareholder?

■ What measures can be taken to ensure that mine closures do not result in social dislocation and deprivation, especially in regions where local government is weak and companies are major service providers?

■ Should companies remain accountable for future pollution from their mining operations, even if they divest themselves of ownership?

tailings continue to pour daily into the local rivers, affecting food supplies and making it harder for people to return from a semi-cash economy to subsistence lifestyles.

Between 2001 and 2010, 40 percent of the predicted 1.5 billion kina (US$0.5 billion) total income from Ok Tedi mine will flow into Western Province (Finlayson 2002:18). Clearly, greater cooperation and better relations are urgently needed between mine, foundation, national, and provincial governments to ensure that this money is used to maximum effect.

Seven short years remain to put right the wrongs done to the people and environment of Ok Tedi. If this is not achieved, ecological disruption and cultural dislocation–not sustainable development–will be the mine's lasting legacy.

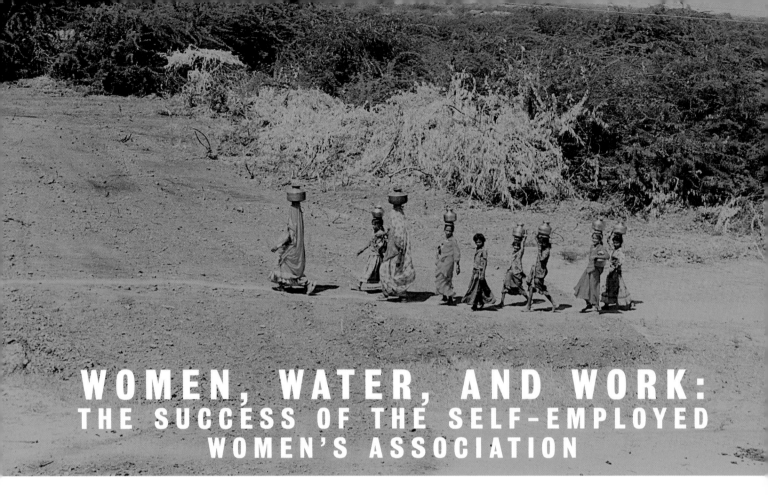

WOMEN, WATER, AND WORK:
THE SUCCESS OF THE SELF-EMPLOYED WOMEN'S ASSOCIATION

In villages of the desert district of Banaskantha in Gujarat, India, many local women have taken control of the key resource they need for their livelihoods and their families' survival: water. They have demonstrated how water resources can be governed efficiently for economic and ecological gains. In these areas, agricultural productivity has increased, outmigration in times of drought has substantially declined, and animals and birds have returned to rejuvenated habitats. In a society that is patriarchal and dominated by the state, this has not been an easy task. Yet, guided by their all-women trade union, the Self-Employed Women's Association (SEWA), they have established innovative grassroots governance structures and effectively linked them to mainstream government agencies. They have acquired new management and technical skills, and learned to influence state authorities, resulting in greater self-respect, and a more influential voice not only within the community but also inside their own homes.

The underlying strategy behind this success has been the linking of environmental protection with livelihoods. For rural women, economic benefit often depends on the health of the natural resources they use. Mainstream governance institutions, however, treat these two issues separately and, too often, as mutually exclusive. SEWA's work has shown that rural communities are motivated to rebuild their environmental bases only if they see some tangible economic benefit in doing so.

The Self-Employed Women's Association (SEWA) is a trade union of over 300,000 women in India. Of these, more than 200,000 are poor, self-employed women working in the informal sector in Gujarat. Founded by Elaben Bhatt, SEWA was registered in 1972 with the two-fold objective of providing full employment to its members and making them self-reliant. SEWA has members in 11 of the 25 districts of Gujarat. Two thirds of its members are based in rural areas.

SEWA's membership broadly comprises three types of self-employed women:

1. Hawkers, vendors, and small businesswomen who buy and sell vegetables, fruits, fish, eggs, other food items, household goods, and clothes.

2. Home-based workers like weavers, potters, *bidi* and *agarbatti* workers, *papad* rollers, ready-made garment makers, women who process agricultural products, and artisans.

3. Manual laborers and service providers like agricultural laborers, construction workers, contract laborers, handcart-pullers, hand-loaders, domestic workers, and laundry workers.

Women belonging to different occupations are organized either as unions or cooperatives. These groups are then federated at the district level into "local associations" run by district-level executive committees. At the state level, SEWA is led by a 25-member executive committee made up of representatives from various districts and occupations. The executive committee is elected every 3 years.

SEWA is both an organization and a movement to empower poor, illiterate, and vulnerable women. It organizes women to ensure that through full employment its members obtain work security, income security, food security, and social security (at least healthcare, child care, and shelter). SEWA often works like an NGO for the welfare of its members. But because it is a trade union, all its activities are mandated by the members themselves.

SEWA has offshoots in other states in India. In the northern state of Uttar Pradesh, for instance, SEWA-Lucknow works with women embroiderers who export their exquisite work. SEWA has also spawned similar organizations in other developing countries in Africa, East Asia, and South America, and has established a strong global network that has lobbied international decision-making bodies such as the International Labour Organization, for the rights of home-based workers.

Gujarat, India

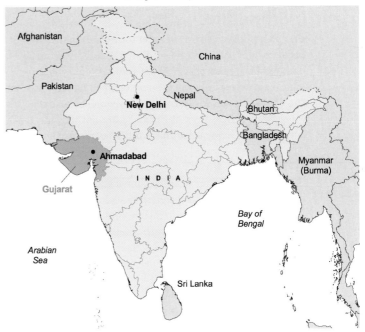

Map data courtesy of Disaster Mitigation Institute, Ahmedabad, Gujarat, India

The Harsh Environment of Banaskantha

Climatic conditions in arid Banaskantha District are hostile, with saline land and water, flash floods, sand storms, and frequent droughts. Rainfall is less than 7 inches per year. The region is also prone to cyclones and earthquakes. The Banaskantha River runs through the district but remains dry for most of the year. During the rainy season, it floods the villages bordering its banks. Droughts are common and the groundwater table has been receding by 6.5 feet a year as withdrawals exceed natural replenishment. Over 75 percent of the district's villages have been declared "no source" villages by the State Water Board, because they do not have reliable sources of fresh water. Salinity is widespread and many villages rely on mobile water tankers sent infrequently by the state's water supply agency, the Gujarat Water Supply and Sewerage Board (GWSSB).

Water, for drinking and irrigation, is a perennial problem for rural communities that subsist on rain-fed agriculture and livestock rearing. Water scarcity has led to low agricultural productivity, reduced fodder production, and low milk yields. Nearly 90 percent of the district's people live in villages, but during the long summer and the recurrent droughts water shortages force large-scale migration to towns throughout the state.

Ironically, Gujarat is home to the Sardar Sarovar dam, one of 30 major, 135 medium, and about 3,000 minor dams planned to be built on the river Narmada. Currently under construction, it will be one of the world's largest water projects with an extensive canal and irrigation system. It is expected to supply water and electricity to Gujarat and the neighboring states of Madhya Pradesh and Maharashtra. The priority intended water use is domestic consumption, but an independent review commissioned by the World Bank found that plans for the delivery of water to villagers in the drought-prone regions of Gujarat were only in the early stages of development. The review observes that a sound and reliable hydrological analysis is lacking and cites "compelling evidence that the Sardar Sarovar Projects will not operate as planned." In other words, the waters of Narmada are not likely to reach rural villagers in Banaskantha or other poor, arid districts.

Women and Water

Fetching and carrying water is women's work in rural India. Women in Banaskantha spend up to six hours a day bringing water from distant sources to their homes. They carry up to 15 liters on their heads on each trip, walking barefoot through treacherous terrain. This affects their health: women often complain of chronic backache, painful feet, general weakness, and fatigue. Ill health, in turn, lowers their productivity. In addition to domestic consumption, women need water for their enterprises and professions such as horticulture, dairy farming, food processing, handicrafts, and midwifery.

Despite the vital role of village women in the country's water supply, it was not until the eighth five-year plan (1992–1997) that the federal government formally recognized the need to involve rural communities in managing water resources, and only in 1999 did it establish guidelines for involving women. Guidelines included reserving 30 percent of places in government technical water training schemes and village-level water committees for women. However, women in Gujarat began taking their first steps toward self-governance in water issues in the mid-1980s, thanks to SEWA.

Enter SEWA

In 1986, the State Water Board of Gujarat invited SEWA to use its grassroots base to strengthen village-level water committees (called *pani panchayats*) so that rural people could take over the operation and management of failing water supply systems. After 3 consecutive years of drought, the Water Board believed that proactive local communities might succeed where more centralized management had failed. SEWA agreed to take on the task, because the organization realized that water supply was a critical issue affecting the productivity and quality of life of its membership: Two thirds of SEWA's members live in rural Gujarat.

Initial work began in two sub-districts or *talukas* of Banaskantha district, Santhalpur and Radhanpur. An existing water supply scheme funded by the Dutch government provided water to 107 villages via pipelines from 6 tube wells more than 60 miles away. These villages had formed water committees, but a preliminary survey by SEWA revealed that water committee members were far from active. Indeed, many people had not been consulted and did not even know

they were on the committees. Women tended to be members in name only, because male members excluded them from all activities. SEWA found that village-level government officials, water engineers, and water committee members themselves were generally ignorant about the powers and role of the water committees. The majority did not even know how water reached their own villages. Not surprisingly, much of the water supply system in the two sub-districts was nonfunctional. SEWA found that there was almost no easy access to safe drinking water in the whole of Santhalpur and in about half of Radhanpur.

As a first step, SEWA arranged several meetings between water engineers and villagers so that villagers could understand the water supply scheme. A group of men and women from different villages was taken to the Santhalpur headwaters to see the source of their water supply. Two of the most

Water Management in Rural India: Governance Lessons

Water resources are owned and managed by the government in India, and responsibility for day-to-day implementation of water-related policy is divided among a host of agencies ranging from different ministries in the capital, New Delhi, to administrative agencies at the state, district, and sub-district levels. In addition, recent years have seen the entry of the private sector into water delivery services. At the village level, water wells, pipes, and other infrastructure have traditionally been maintained by men. Water supply in many rural areas, however, remains inadequate and the burden of keeping fields and families supplied with daily water has fallen on women. In the state of Gujarat, in northern India, SEWA has worked for over 15 years to mobilize village women, many untrained and illiterate, to build, maintain, and manage small-scale water supply systems. While small in comparison to the vastness of the Indian subcontinent, the progress made by these women has yielded compelling lessons.

■ Decentralizing control of India's natural resources began, in principle, decades ago, but the growth of actual local control required initiative on the part of civil society.

■ Helping poor, uneducated women acquire skills needed for natural resource management takes time and represents a greater challenge than the physical construction of new water infrastructure.

■ Capacity-building efforts must be persistently applied over time if they are to take root and lead to genuine empowerment.

■ Poor women are more likely to participate in natural resource management projects if they are explicitly linked to economic development.

■ Despite official skepticism, locally driven watershed management projects in Gujarat have proven that uneducated women can navigate the complexities of government and deal effectively with mainstream institutions.

■ Successful management of a natural resource by women translates into growing respect for those women in village government, in social activities, and in the home. However, maintaining this respect against the traditions of a patriarchal society presents an ongoing challenge.

successful, and fully attended trips were to two milk cooperatives, Amul and the National Dairy Development Board. The visits were planned so that the villagers could appreciate the democratic functioning of these two thriving collective enterprises. Another visit to Indian Petro-Chemical Limited (IPCL), a government company manufacturing plastics, demonstrated how a village water supply pond could be lined with a special plastic film, to prevent the ingress of salinity. Water in an unlined pond is gradually contaminated by salts leached from the desert soils, becoming undrinkable after a few months. In later years, lining ponds with agri-film became a cornerstone of many village water maintenance projects.

SEWA's efforts to rally women and men were, however, impeded by massive seasonal distress migration due to lack of water and jobs. At times, whole villages were deserted. In others, only the elderly, the disabled, and some young children were left behind. The question that confronted SEWA was how to stop people from leaving their homes, so they could develop their village resources. The village-level water meetings thus led to the articulation of two urgent needs of the villagers: The need to find non-water based economic work, and the need to conserve water, revive traditional sources like surface wells and ponds, and create alternative water sources like roof rainwater harvesting structures.

Women and Water Governance

SEWA's leadership understood that it would be easier to recruit its members to water development activities if they were clearly linked to economic improvement. Accordingly, from 1986 on, SEWA mobilized village women into about 50 groups organized around 8 economic activities, ranging from embroidery and gum collection from the forest to rainwater harvesting for anti-desertification measures. These groups were formed under the Development of Women and Children in Rural Areas (DWCRA) Program, a joint effort of the Indian government and UNICEF. By 2000, nearly 200 such groups existed with their own district federation, helping women with economic and business development.

At first, however, women were reluctant to come forward because water infrastructure was regarded as male territory. Most men were also uncooperative. They were critical of women entering the public domain on this issue, and several went so far as to say they would not drink water from a source created by women. Many threatened not to work on water harvesting structures that would be managed by women. Some men openly said women would make financial blunders and force them to mortgage their lands (almost all land titles are in men's names) to repay their debts.

SEWA persisted, however, and facilitated the formation of women-dominated water users committees called *pani samities*. Instead of the stipulated 30 percent quota for women, these were either all-women committees or had at least an equal number of men and women members. Women slowly

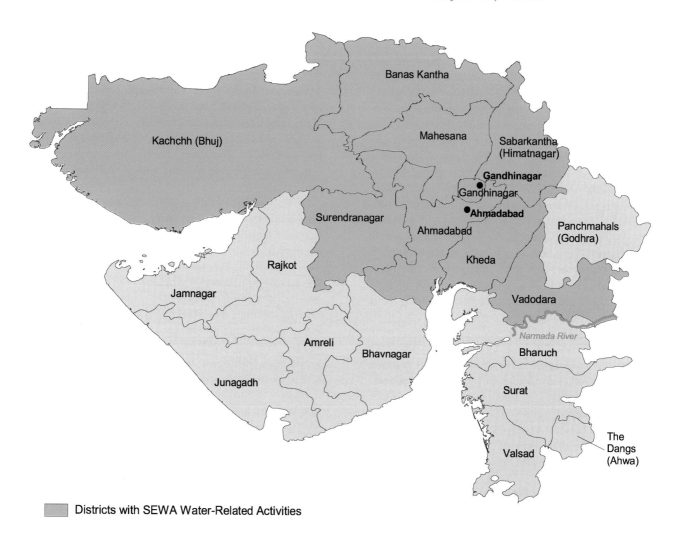

Districts with SEWA Water-Related Activities

gained confidence as they began to lead water activities, raise their productivity, and see their incomes increase. A year after the water activities were initiated, the promising results prompted more women to join in. Poonamben of Bharvad village, Radhanpur, recounts how no one wanted to join the *pani samities* initially. "Now we've learned so much about measurements, maps, and surveying methods that everyone wants to become a member and know about these things." SEWA's argument is that because women are primarily responsible for fetching and using water–for domestic purposes, cattle, and kitchen gardens–it is necessary to give them prominent roles in water governance. This fact also made it easier for SEWA to take on water-related activities because, as a trade union, it can only undertake activities that are mandated by its members.

Many different kinds of activities were undertaken in the first phase of SEWA's work. The initial 42 *pani samities* took over maintenance of the piped water system in the San-thalpur and Radhanpur sub-districts, including collecting user fees. Simultaneously, the village women applied themselves to revive and maintain their traditional community sources of water. *Pani samities* began constructing check dams, deepening existing ponds, and lining ponds with plastic film to prevent salt penetration.

The results of this early partnership between SEWA and the State Water Board were mixed, but successful enough to encourage SEWA to take up other water-related activities throughout Banaskantha and other districts of Gujarat. These first years laid the foundation for SEWA's Millennium Water Campaign, which began in 1995 (see below).

Navigating the Government Labyrinth

In Gujarat, rural drinking water supply is controlled primarily by the State Water Board. Decentralization began in 1957, when a government-instituted committee recommended devolvement of political and administrative power

Who Controls and Manages Water in Gujarat?

The state of Gujarat owns all surface water and groundwater that falls within its jurisdiction. To administer its water resources, the state has set up a maze of departments at the state, district, and village levels.

At the state level, there are three ministries and four departments in charge of water resources in different ways. The structure is complicated, the roles overlap, and there is no institutionalized manner of interdepartmental coordination. The seven bodies governing water at the state level are:

1. **Ministry of Narmada** (currently this charge is with the Chief Minister, the highest elected representative of the state).

2. **Ministry of Irrigation** (irrigation other than from Narmada waters).

3. **Ministry of Drinking Water Supply** (other than from Narmada waters).

4. **Narmada and Water Resources Department.** In this department are different secretaries for irrigation and for drinking water, but they report not to the head of the department but to the Minister of Irrigation and Minister of Drinking Water Supply respectively.

5. **Gujarat Water Supply and Sewerage Board (GWSSB)** is a separate implementing body headed by a chairman (an administrative post) and a member secretary (a technical post) and is under the charge of the Chief Secretary of the state.

6. **Sardar Sarovar Narmada Nigam** is a body responsible for the implementation of the Sardar Sarovar series of dams on the river Narmada in Gujarat. This is the only big dam in the state; all other irrigation is through smaller projects and is, therefore, known as "minor irrigation."

7. **Panchayats, Rural Housing, and Rural Development Department** has two secretaries, in charge of *panchayats* and rural development respectively. They are responsible for overseeing water resource schemes implemented directly by the *zilla panchayats* (elected self-governing bodies at the *zilla*, or district, level), the District Rural Development Agency (DRDA), and by the village-level *panchayats*.

At the **district level**:

1. "Minor" irrigation schemes are implemented by the **Minor Irrigation Department**.

2. *Zilla Panchayats* directly implement some small irrigation schemes, small drinking water supply projects delegated by the GWSSB, and small water harvesting projects.

3. Some watershed development projects are implemented directly by the **District Rural Development Agencies**, or through sub-contracting to *panchayat* institutions, private parties, NGOs, or community-based organizations like SEWA.

At the **sub-district (*taluka*) level**:
Some drinking water supply projects are delegated by the GWSSB to be implemented directly by the *taluka panchayat*.

At the **village level**:
Village *panchayats* are responsible for maintenance and distribution of village-level drinking water supply projects delegated to them by district or sub-district level *panchayats* and the DRDA.

Within village *panchayats*, *pani panchayats*, or water committees, are constituted to oversee the drinking water supply and watershed projects.

---

to the village level through the establishment of local self-governing bodies called *panchayats.* The new institutions evoked an extraordinary response from the people and the *panchayats* were given formal recognition in 1993 by means of amendments to the Indian constitution.

Panchayat representatives are members of village-level natural resource management committees and can exercise real influence over the installation, operation, and maintenance of drinking water supplies. However, *panchayats* still have limited administrative and financial control. In addition to the State Water Board and village-level *panchayats*, district committees and sub-district development offices are also responsible for overseeing some irrigation systems and watershed development projects. (See: Who Controls and Manages Water in Gujarat?)

The *pani samities* quickly learned that reviving and maintaining their traditional sources of water would not be an easy task. First, village-level water management schemes fell under the jurisdiction of *panchayats,* which often were not equipped with the required managerial and technical know-how. Second, the sheer number of government agencies dealing with different aspects of water delivery and maintenance was overwhelming. The women had to learn about the different roles of these agencies, decide what agency to approach, and when and how to approach them. Under such conditions, it was a challenge for SEWA to activate *pani samities,* keep them motivated, and sustain community participation.

Over the course of the decade 1986–1995, SEWA and the *pani samities* learned to navigate these difficult waters. Many of their experiences demonstrate the complicated alliances that had to be constructed before water projects could get off the ground.

For example, in the village of Madhutra, the *pani samiti* decided to reconstruct an old check dam that had been washed away in the floods of 1990. The *samiti,* the village *panchayat,* engineers from the Minor Irrigation Department, and SEWA employees sat together to plan, design, and construct the dam. It was agreed that the villagers would bear the cost of materials transport. The Irrigation Department would pay for the raw materials and for labor. The *panchayat* would be responsible for maintaining the dam and collecting water user charges from beneficiary farmers. This plan was carried out successfully.

Government Recognition and the Millennium Water Campaign

By 1995, SEWA had accumulated a great deal of experience in the water sector, and its projects were yielding tangible economic, social and environmental benefits throughout the state of Gujarat. In that year, the state government invited SEWA to take part in a watershed development project in the role of Principal Implementing Agency (PIA)– the body with authority to carry out the work. This was the first time that a trade union had been invited to take on such a role.

SEWA used this unprecedented opportunity to launch a watershed development program of its own, dubbed Water, Women, and Work: the Millennium Campaign. However, before SEWA decided to participate in the government program, it used its hard-won respect to bargain hard with the authorities. SEWA members discussed the government guidelines in great detail. They wanted more than the reserved 30 percent representation for women on the watershed committees because otherwise, they said, they would not be able to influence the decision-making process. The state agency in charge initially refused to entertain any modification of the guidelines. This led to protracted negotiations. State officials said that women were uneducated and unqualified, and would not be able to supervise technical works (Banaskantha has a very low literacy rate, just 11 percent). SEWA argued that it was equally difficult to find highly educated or qualified men in the villages. Finally, the state agreed to allow the formation of women-dominated village watershed committees.

Then began the second phase of negotiations. SEWA wanted the watershed development program to be integrated, linking economic development with ecological regeneration. They reached agreement that the watershed program would encompass six economic-ecological activities:

- Land development (land contouring, land leveling, plugging small furrows caused by erosion);

- Water conservation (check dams, well recharging, pond construction and repair, small lift irrigation, drip irrigation);

- Forestry (plantations on private land and on common wasteland, growing of fodder, nursery raising);

- Agriculture development (dryland horticulture, distribution of fodder kits including seeds and information capsules, improved agricultural tools, crop demonstration);

- Livestock rearing (immunization, primary health education, disease prevention interventions); and

- Capacity building (organizing the community, basic administrative skills, essential financial management).

A Successful Campaign

Between 1995 and 2001, SEWA's water campaign spread to a total of 502 villages in nine districts (see map). SEWA used funds from the national government's Integrated Desert Area Development Program to structure a watershed development program that maximized the participation of women and incorporated the lessons learned over the previous 10 years. Women comprised 80 percent or more of the membership of most of the new water users committees, and committee activities revolved around issues of particular interest to women—fodder growing, nursery plantation, improved agriculture, rainwater harvesting and capacity-building.

In Banaskantha, SEWA's program focused on 8 villages in 2 sub-districts and aimed to treat a total of 4,000 hectares. Each village was given a grant of 2.5 million rupees (Rs) (approximately US$53,000) for a four-year period. The villages were required to contribute 10 percent of this sum, in cash or as free labor. The cash was deposited in a bank as a Village Fund controlled by the water committee to be used for future repairs and maintenance. Twenty percent of the fund (Rs 0.5 million or US$10,600) was spent on technical services (for example, GIS analysis) and the salaries of SEWA employees.

Results of the water campaign in Banaskantha have been impressive. Aquifers in 18 villages have been recharged. A total of 150 wells, including surface wells, tube wells and farm wells, have been recharged in 8 villages. In Porana village alone, for instance, a total of 25 wells have been recharged. Salinity has decreased in the treated land thanks to various innovative and low-cost mechanisms for sweetening and recharging the groundwater. In Porana village, a polyvinylchloride (PVC) pipe was constructed to drain excess rainwater that collected in the corner of a sloping field. The rainwater was channeled into the ground and filtered using a traditional sand and stone layered filtration system. The pipe was plugged when not in use. This method has turned the saline groundwater sweet and it is now available in wells for drinking and irrigation. Groundwater is lifted with a water pump for irrigation and farmers are able to grow three crops annually instead of one. The investment was just Rs 5,000 (US$106) for each system.

Interestingly, some of the water harvesting structures built under the watershed development program are not recognized as technically sound by the government engineers.

SEWA's Millennium Water Campaign has brought grassroots governance to the water sector.

However, during the first torrential rains, 25 check dams built by the state irrigation department were swept away while all those constructed by SEWA survived. The state officials concede that the check dams may not adhere to stipulated norms, but that they are functional and secure.

New plantations have greened the desert around the eight villages and birds that had lost their habitat have returned. The pond in Barara village today resembles a bird colony. A rough count shows at least 28 species of birds, none of which was visible before the watershed program began. Wild animals such as deer and rabbit are now easily visible. Soil ecology has improved and the invasive growth of *prosopis* (a variety of acacia) has been contained as villagers now grow crops that they can sell in the local market.

Not least, distress out-migration has stopped completely in the eight villages. Villagers from Datrana and Gokhantar, for instance, stopped migrating once they lined the ponds in their villages with plastic film, sweetening the water. Out-migration has also declined substantially in the two sub-districts as a whole because an average of four villages around each of the eight targeted villages have benefited from the augmentation of the water supply. Migration, in other words, has been contained in at least 32 of the villages in and around the total watershed area.

SEWA's integrated watershed development program was implemented efficiently, enabling the available funds to be stretched to cover additional land. In Datrana village, for instance, the villagers, led by an 8-woman, 3-man watershed development committee, treated a total of 600 hectares from funds provided for the treatment of 500 hectares of village land. Throughout Banaskantha, an additional 30 percent over the designated area benefited from the program.

The success of the watershed program led to SEWA's nomination in 1998 to the state-level Advisory Committee for Recharging of Water Sources. SEWA immediately pushed for a novel policy change that would allow for the construction of roof rainwater harvesting systems in the arid districts of Gujarat. Government funds would be given only to women, meaning that women would benefit from drinking water storage tanks in their homes and they would own the water infrastructure. The State Water Board adopted this recommendation and, for the first time, sanctioned the construction of 1,000 such tanks by SEWA. Later, the Water Board gave permission to other agencies to build similar systems.

The guidelines for the roof rainwater harvesting systems stipulate a 30 percent contribution, in cash or as labor, by the beneficiary. For those living below the official poverty line–and many SEWA members belong to this category–the beneficiary has to contribute only one-tenth of the total cost. By mid-2001, 80 roof rainwater tanks had been built in seven villages of Banaskantha. A full tank, about 15,000 to 20,000 liters, serves a family of 5 for at least 2 months. The tanks became popular because, in times of drought, women could also store water from the mobile water tankers directly in their roof tanks. Increased water storage in the roof tanks contributed to reduced migration rates during the scorching summer months. And many villagers went back to the tradition of keeping a trough of water for the local birds. As Puriben of Vauva village explained, "If we don't get water we can always clamor for mobile water tankers. But the birds would die of thirst if they did not get water from us during the dry season."

Institution-Building for Grassroots Water Management

SEWA's watershed development program has helped to institutionalize grassroots governance in the water sector. Institution-building begins at the village level because two thirds of SEWA's members live in villages. The village-level water and watershed committees, the *pani samities*, which are at least 80 percent women, form the first building blocks of SEWA's three-tier governance system. *Pani samiti* members are identified and selected at a meeting of all village adults. This meeting is called by SEWA in collaboration with the village governing body (*panchayat*). Participants at the meeting discuss village water problems in detail and chalk out a viable plan of action. The *pani samiti* is given the responsibility of carrying out and overseeing the day-to-day tasks of water-related activities and is accountable to all village adults.

The *pani samiti* sends representatives to a district-level "water spearhead team" of 10–12 members. The spearhead teams include one or two SEWA members, one of whom is a team leader stationed at district headquarters. The team leader acts as a friend, motivator, and expert counselor while the spearhead team is still new. As *pani samiti* members gain experience and confidence, the role of the team leader diminishes.

Spearhead teams in turn report to a state-level water coordinator stationed at Ahmedabad, the former capital of Gujarat. Each team member is also a member of SEWA's district-level executive committee of the Federation of Women's Occupational Groups. This membership broadens the scope of the water campaign and enables *pani samiti* members to take advantage of other services offered by SEWA. For example, savings and credit spearhead teams are able to make "water loans" for constructing roof rainwater harvesting systems in their members' homes. In Banaskantha, for example, when the government failed to provide its grant for the systems on time, the poor women took out water loans from their savings and credit groups and repaid the loans when they received the subsidy from the government.

New Competencies, New Challenges

SEWA's water management work has yielded rich dividends and been able to face tough challenges because of two inherent strengths. First, women have been continually trained and supported to deal with the technical, social, institutional, and cultural demands of water-related activities. Second, new institutions dominated by women have been created with strong links to mainstream governing institutions. These strategies have empowered women both at the individual level and within their communities.

Women have learned to handle finances; funding is now given directly to *pani samities*. Technical training has created a cadre of "barefoot" managers, accountants, and technical experts. Women now know how to build a contour earthen dam, how much to deepen a pond, and how to line a pond with plastic film, among other things. SEWA itself has been able to develop a good database on water sources and their status in villages.

Socially, women have earned more respect within their families and their communities. Their voices are heard more and their opinions are more in demand. Handpump mechanics, for example, recount how villagers' perceptions have changed from distrust, wariness, and mockery to respect and even awe. In local politics, some women *panchayat* members have found that working with the water campaign has strengthened their own efforts to contest *panchayat* elections.

There has also been some shift in attitudes toward rural women on the part of mainstream institutions. The Gujarat Jalseva Training Institute, the technical training arm of the State Water Board, has changed its rules to accommodate illiterate women in its training program. The minimum qualification for applying to training programs was reduced, and sometimes waived for promising candidates. To accommodate women's needs, training programs are now sometimes held in villages and sub-district headquarters rather than at the Institute's campus.

SEWA's success has prompted villagers and civil society groups to question India's trend toward privatizing water distribution services. There is some sign that government agencies are beginning to trust the "people's sector" to handle water supply activities, despite their skepticism that poor, illiterate women could prove competent. The Gujarat Water Board has recently decided to abandon its private sector contract for managing piped water supply systems in Surendranagar, and handed responsibility directly to a people's organization.

Alongside the development of a promising institutional framework, expanding governance skills, and continuous capacity-building, however, there remain formidable challenges. For instance, not all women's district-level federations are registered. Even where they are registered, they are not recognized by government agencies. Thus, government departments prefer to sign agreements with SEWA, the parent body, rather than with the federations directly.

Although women's groups work with village *panchayats*, these relationships can be tenuous and dependent on individual rapport. In many villages, women's groups face resistance from elected *panchayat* representatives whose signatures are necessary for many of the projects to be implemented at the village level.

The governance capabilities of the women's groups themselves need to be strengthened. Dealing with the varied problems of the water sector and the many government water authorities is a skill that many of the water spearhead team members have yet to master. Faced with unresponsive government officials and bureaucratic delays in delivery of government services, many women lose heart and find it difficult to win the confidence of villagers. The technical cadre of women "barefoot" engineers also needs to be expanded and their skills upgraded.

There is an urgent need to sensitize government agencies to larger issues that would benefit women. For example, construction of roof rainwater harvesting systems could be included as part of the government's housing policy, especially in arid areas. Indigenous transport systems need to be developed so that women do not have to trek long distances carrying heavy loads on their heads. More institutes imparting technical training in rural water supply systems need to revisit their admission rules so as to include illiterate but competent female candidates.

As the water sector is opened to privatization by the government, pricing of water services is a critical issue that SEWA has not yet addressed. SEWA argues that women's labor should be translated into economic terms because it forms part of the total cost of collecting water. But how should this be done? And what are the other pricing issues that will come into play if water services are opened to the "people's sector"?

In spite of their many successes, the women behind SEWA's watershed campaign in Gujarat, and women elsewhere in India, face an ongoing struggle to overcome the entrenched patriarchy of their society and the proliferation of government bureaucracy that stifles innovation by local people.

Contributed by Aditi Kapoor, Independent Journalist and Fellow, Leadership for Environment and Development (LEAD), New Delhi, India.

EARTH CHARTER:
CHARTING A COURSE FOR THE FUTURE

The Earth Charter, a set of 16 overarching ethical principles and 61 supporting principles, was launched in June 2000 in The Hague. Its sponsor was an international commission led by two influential, international figures: Mikhail Gorbachev, president of Green Cross International, and Maurice Strong, Secretary-General of the 1992 UN Conference on Environment and Development.

A Manifesto for Earth

Environmental governance operates through a range of social structures, from government laws and agencies, to nongovernmental organizations (NGOs), to customary rights, responsibilities, and behaviors. But there is also a less tangible side to environmental governance. The decades since the 1972 Stockholm Conference have witnessed the emergence of global norms of good environmental governance. These norms are not formally defined, but they are characterized around the world by a decreased tolerance for corruption and increased expectations of transparency and public participation in decision-making (see also Chapter 1). Such norms are rooted in the idea that broad ethical, moral, and behavioral shifts are required by governments, corporations, and communities, if good governance is to become a universal reality.

The Earth Charter represents an attempt to codify such norms of good governance in a statement of universal applicability. It is a unique document, both in its ambitions and in its mode of development. The Earth Charter grew out of ideas and opinions expressed by thousands of individuals; it was not mandated by an intergovernmental process or body, nor does it yet have any official status. It represents something new in global governance: a genuinely public expression of the beliefs and values that should, ideally, govern decision-making for the benefit of humans and the rest of the living world. The document is characterized by strengths and weaknesses:

- The extensive participation and consultation processes undertaken around the world give the Earth Charter legitimacy.

- The genuine effort of the Earth Charter Commission to build consensus among all parties confers credibility on the final document.

- The Earth Charter's high aspirations may not be fully realizable, but their wording was not compromised by realpolitik.

- The Earth Charter has no legal status and no powers of enforcement, and will therefore be regarded by some parties as irrelevant.

- The document's lack of specificity makes it hard to translate aspirations into practical actions.

Ten years in the making, and the result of collaboration by civil society organizations across the globe, the Earth Charter builds on a succession of UN documents including the 1987 Brundtland Commission report, the 1992 Rio Declaration on Environment and Development, and the UN Millennium Declaration. In just over 2,400 carefully-crafted words, it lays out an ethical foundation for building a just and sustainable world—one based on respect for nature and people, universal human rights, social and economic justice, democratic and participatory societies, and non-violent conflict resolution.

As a set of principles to live by, rather than a prescription for action, the Earth Charter stands apart from the many other UN-driven declarations and treaties that address environment and development. And it does so in ways that have direct impact on issues of governance.

First, it presents a holistic worldview driven by such ethical concerns as respect for nature, rather than the economics-and science-driven "environment-by-numbers" approach that most businesses and governments take toward sustainable development. This holistic approach views the strengthening of democratic institutions, the transparency and accountability of governing institutions, and inclusive, participatory decision-making as inseparable from environmental protection and social and economic justice.

Second, the Earth Charter is largely a bottom-up rather than a top-down initiative, shaped and adopted primarily by civil society and local government institutions rather than central governments. Third, because it is not a policy-making document which may be ratified by some governments and flouted or rejected by others, the Earth Charter's framers hope it will reach directly to citizens the world over. The aim is to generate changes in attitude and behavior across a wide constituency including individuals, communities, local governments, schools and universities, non-governmental organizations (NGOs), and businesses.

The Earth Charter: Main Principles

I. RESPECT AND CARE FOR THE COMMUNITY OF LIFE

1 Respect Earth and life in all its diversity.

2 Care for the community of life, with understanding, compassion, and love.

3 Build democratic societies that are just, participatory, sustainable, and peaceful.

4 Secure Earth's bounty and beauty for present and future generations.

II. ECOLOGICAL INTEGRITY

5 Protect and restore the integrity of Earth's ecological systems, with special concern for biological diversity and the natural processes that sustain life.

6 Prevent harm as the best method of environmental protection and, when knowledge is limited, apply a precautionary approach.

7 Adopt patterns of production, consumption, and reproduction that safeguard Earth's regenerative capacities, human rights, and community well-being.

8 Advance the study of ecological sustainability and promote the open exchange and wide application of the knowledge acquired.

III. SOCIAL AND ECONOMIC JUSTICE

9 Eradicate poverty as an ethical, social, and environmental imperative.

10 Ensure that economic activities and institutions at all levels promote human development in an equitable and sustainable manner.

11 Affirm gender equality and equity as prerequisites to sustainable development and ensure universal access to education, healthcare, and economic opportunity.

12 Uphold the right of all, without discrimination, to a natural and social environment supportive of human dignity, bodily health, and spiritual well-being with special attention to the rights of indigenous peoples and minorities.

IV. DEMOCRACY, NON-VIOLENCE AND PEACE

13 Strengthen democratic institutions at all levels, and provide transparency and accountability in governance, inclusive participation in decision-making, and access to justice.

14 Integrate into formal education and life-long learning the knowledge, values, and skills needed for a sustainable way of life.

15 Treat all living beings with respect and consideration.

16 Promote a culture of tolerance, non-violence, and peace.

Source: Earth Charter Secretariat 2000

In an international arena crowded with environmentally driven initiatives, it is perhaps easier to define the Earth Charter by what it is not than by what it is. It is not a practical to-do list for achieving ecological protection or sustainable development on national or local levels. Nor is it (at least as yet) a formal intergovernmental agreement. On both counts, it differs from Agenda 21, the main outcome of the 1992 Earth Summit in Rio de Janeiro, which lays out a broad sustainable development plan of action for governments.

Earth Charter advocates describe inspirational documents like the French Declaration of the Rights of Man and the UN Universal Declaration of Human Rights as the closest parallels to what they hope to achieve.

These so-called "soft law" documents are not legally binding. But when adopted by state governments they become morally binding, providing standards by which nations measure their civilizations. Human rights, for example, were placed firmly on the international agenda in 1948 when the UN General Assembly declared them to be "universal" and a "common standard of achievement" (United Nations 1948). While stated in very broad terms, the declaration has successfully codified human rights standards and is used to hold nations accountable in the court of public opinion. The Earth Charter Commission hopes that it, similarly, will become a common standard for ethical, just, and environmentally sound behavior "by which the conduct of all individuals, organizations, businesses, governments and transnational institutions is to be guided and assessed" (Earth Charter Secretariat 2000).

Such sweeping goals, coupled with the charter's broad language and high-minded principles, are easy to criticize as too general to be useful and too open-ended to be monitored for effectiveness. But to do so misses the value of such behavior-changing initiatives. No one today, for example, seriously disputes the authority or effectiveness of the Universal Declaration of Human Rights, although it took many years for its principles to be translated into legally binding conventions adopted by nations.

By early 2003, the Earth Charter had been translated into 27 languages. More than 2,000 NGOs and 1,000 local governments have endorsed its principles (Rockefeller 2003), while 54 countries have formed Earth Charter national committees (Smith 2002:30). Its name recognition is limited and it remains well below the radar of most national governments. Yet among local governments and within the emerging global civil society–linked by common aims of ecological protection, social justice, and peaceful internationalism, and connected by the Internet–it is beginning to find a strong foothold.

Earth Charter Snapshots

There is no such thing as a standard Earth Charter program. Around the world, communities, individuals, businesses, educational establishments, and local governments are using different means to translate symbolic support for the charter into practical action and behavioral change.

In Parliaments and Town Halls...
Three years after its launch, actual adoption of the Earth Charter by local governments remains limited, with the most enthusiasm demonstrated in the United States, Eastern Europe, Spain, and parts of Africa, Latin America, and the Middle East. In April 2001, the parliament of Tatarstan, a semi-autonomous Russian Federation republic, became the first provincial government to embrace the Earth Charter as a guide for state policy and practice. With a mixed and potentially volatile population of Muslims and Orthodox Christians, the republic has made non-violent resolution of conflict a cornerstone of its constitution and its leaders view the Earth Charter as a means to this end. The Tatarstan government has analyzed its key laws and policies against Charter principles and is introducing the document into school curricula (Earth-Ethics 2002:36).

In April 2002, Puerto Rico's senate followed suit, voting to support the principles established in the Earth Charter, to adopt them as a guidance system in its "formulation of public laws and politics," and to exhort the territory's government,

educational system, and business, science, and media organizations to do likewise (Alvarez 2002). The document has also been endorsed by 99 cities and towns in the nation of Jordan (Earth Charter Initiative 2002:8).

In the United States, where Local Agenda 21 has generally been slow to take off, the Charter has made significant inroads into local government consciousness. It has been endorsed, among others, by the 1,000-member U.S. Conference of Mayors and the 400-member Florida League of Cities (Earth Charter Initiative 2003).

At a global level, the International Council of Local Environmental Initiatives (ICLEI) endorsed the Charter and is encouraging its 380 municipal members to apply its principles (Earth Charter Initiative 2003). Some local authorities are already doing this in practical ways. The city government of San José, Costa Rica, for example, has implemented an Earth Charter training program for over 1,800 employees, including the police, sanitation, and health departments. Workers are encouraged to incorporate its principles into their daily activities (Earth Charter Secretariat 2003).

In Classrooms...
The Earth Charter's ethical framework has struck a strong chord with educational institutions. The Charter is central to the UN Educational, Scientific and Cultural Organization's efforts to develop teacher training programs on sustainable development for schools and universities. Its principles have

Creating the Earth Charter: A Lesson in Global Democracy

In itself, the Earth Charter embodies two of the good governance themes emphasized throughout this report as prerequisites to successful sustainable development: the right of citizens to participate in decision-making and the transparency of organizations and processes. The process by which it came about could be described as textbook participatory democracy in action.

The concept of an Earth Charter, laying out "independent principles for a sustainable way of life," first surfaced in recommendations made by the 1987 Brundtland Commission. Five years later the world's heads of state gathered for the UN Conference on Environment and Development (commonly known as the Earth Summit) in Rio de Janeiro. But the charter idea failed to take root there, prompting its Secretary-General Maurice Strong and former Soviet president Mikhail Gorbachev to launch an Earth Charter Initiative in 1994, with the support of the Dutch government.

Under Maurice Strong's leadership, in his role as chairman of the Earth Council, consultations began on developing the Charter as a "people's treaty" rather than an intergovernmental document. The aim was to tap into the ideas and energies of a global civil society movement blossoming in the wake of Communist collapse in Eastern Europe and the emergence of new communications technologies (EarthEthics 2002:16–19).

At the invitation of the Earth Charter Commission, established in 1997, several thousand individuals and organizations around the world took part in a rolling process of consultation, drafting, further consultation, and re-drafting. Efforts were made to reach wide audiences via the media and Internet-based conferencing. Participants included local governments, environmental and social justice NGOs, religious, educational, and indigenous people's organizations, scientists, ethicists, and legal experts. One on-line drafting session involved representatives of 300 universities and 78 countries (Earth Charter USA 2003a).

To give the Charter a firm foundation in existing international agreements, its core team of drafters, led by Steven Rockefeller, professor of religion and ethics at Middlebury College, Vermont, drew on a wide variety of sources. These included 50 existing international law instruments, the findings of the seven UN summits held during the 1990s, and the contents of about 200 nongovernmental declarations and people's treaties on environment and development (Earth Charter USA 2003a).

The Charter's wording was shaped by contemporary science, international law, religious teachings and philosophical

also been endorsed by the International Baccalaureate Association and by dozens of university departments and hundreds of schools worldwide.

In universities, the Charter is being used both as a framework for philosophical discussion and as a starting point for developing practical policies. At Michigan State University, for example, a course entitled "Earth Charter: Pathway to a Sustainable Future" grounds environmental study in real world problems. Students are given practical projects which reflect Charter principles, including designing and building a composting system, transforming cafeteria food waste into nitrogen-rich compost, and developing a campus recycling strategy (Earth Charter USA 2003b).

In Communities...

The United States has seen some of the strongest and most spontaneous reactions to the Earth Charter's call for a new, ethical world order. A diverse group of strangers including a Philadelphia printer, a single mother in Portland, a Buddhist in San Francisco, and a former mayoral candidate in Indianapolis pooled resources over the Internet to launch community networking summits under the umbrella "The Earth Charter: A Declaration of Interdependence" (Roberts 2001). Around 700 U.S. organizations representing 40 million members have endorsed the Charter, including the Sierra Club and Humane Society of the United States.

In other nations, the Earth Charter is being used as a community development tool. Elizabeth Ramirez, an environmental educator in Costa Rica, has used its principles in working with impoverished village women in the remote, mountainous regions of Laguna Hule and Río Cuarto.

After studying individual Charter principles, villagers have planned and carried out activities that protect local landscapes, enhance women's status, and reinforce traditional cultural and social values. A children's movement, the *Defensores Verdes* or Green Defenders, has also been formed. Its members act as guardians of the natural environment within their homes, schools, and communities, creating vegetable gardens and wildlife refuges, replanting a forest area, and opposing the development of a lake, among other activities (Vilela 2003).

In the Business World...

In general, engaging with the business community has not been a priority for the Earth Charter Initiative; nor have trade associations, other than the World Federation of Engineering Organizations, flocked to endorse its prescription for change. One exception is the Australian investment banking industry, members of which met with 40 civil society groups in October 2001 to discuss using the Charter as a framework of principles for the ethical investment industry (Manning 2001). While no industry-wide agreement was reached, Earth Charter Australia is now working with individual corporations on establishing broad sustainability criteria to evaluate companies' performances. The Calvert Group, a leader in the field of socially responsible investment, has unilaterally endorsed the Earth Charter as an ethical guide.

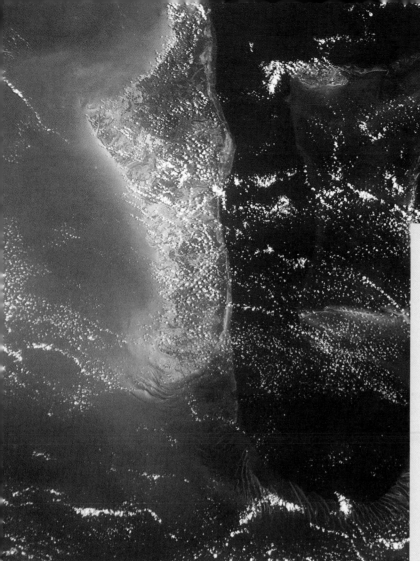

traditions, the global ethics movement, and best practices for building sustainable communities. But as it progressed, the text was continuously adapted and extended to encompass the consensus view of a broad range of organizations and individuals that commented on several globally circulated drafts.

"Whenever I got recommendations from this group, so long as they were not scientifically unsound or completely out of step with international law, we considered them in the drafting committee," says Steven Rockefeller. "Principle 10, for example, caused a lot of discussion because developing country advocates were passionate about referring to economic justice. It went through 25 or 30 drafts until we got a formula that was both consistent with international law and acceptable to all parties in the advisory group" (Rockefeller 2003).

Initially Mikhail Gorbachev and other Earth Charter commissioners wanted to develop a short statement with a few punchy principles. However, developing country activists such as Wangari Maathai, the Kenyan founder of the Green Belt Movement, argued strongly for a more detailed ethical framework that could be used to hold their governments to account for their actions.

Measuring Progress: Earth Charter Indicators

To succeed on its own terms, the Earth Charter must act as a tool to promote good environmental governance, ecological protection, social progress, and ethical business practice on a global scale. Yet many communities struggle with how to give its principles the practical application this entails. To help bridge this gap, the World Resources Institute (WRI) is developing a set of indicators that can act both as a road map to sustainability for local government and as a practical checklist for community activists to track local progress against Earth Charter principles.

Each indicator will describe a specific step, tied to an Earth Charter principle, for local governments to take along the path to sustainable living. For example, compliance with Earth Charter Principle 11(a) (to "secure the human rights of women and girls and end all violence against them") would be measured by the presence or absence of legislation granting women equal rights (WRI 2002:18).

In 2004, the Earth Charter indicators will be piloted in a few communities. WRI will help them adapt the indicators so that they will be meaningful in their particular local context. The accessibility of data at the local level will be a key to applying the indicators successfully. "The more locally you apply indicators, the more likely you are to force change as a result," argues Christian Layke, indicators project coordinator at WRI. "You are operating close enough to the decision-making level to really make a difference."

"There was a continuous tension between having a short document that would have an emotional and poetic impact and a document that would give people on the front line the concrete help they needed," recalls Rockefeller (Rockefeller 2003).

The drafting committee of international environmental law experts, scientists, ethicists, and grassroots representatives met three times in New York between 1997 and 2000 to refine a text acceptable to the Earth Charter commissioners. A final version was approved in Paris in March 2000.

Vision Versus Reality

It is hard to quarrel with the Earth Charter's sentiments, but how influential can such an aspirational document realistically hope to be? In a world riven by nationalism and religious hatred, it promotes peace, tolerance, and the interdependence of nations. In a world where natural resources are indiscriminately exploited and nonhuman species are in retreat, it urges respect for nature and ecological protection. In a world where the income gap between rich and poor nations and individuals grows ever wider, it calls for economic justice and the eradication of poverty. The task of achieving such moral and cultural shifts in the global mindset is truly Herculean.

Acting Globally

The Earth Charter's positioning outside the mainstream intergovernmental process on sustainable development is proving both a strength and a weakness. On one hand, those working to implant the document in the public consciousness can point to its grounding in civil society as a source of legitimacy arguably greater than that wielded by a small elite of international policy-makers.

They can also point to strong support for the Charter among developing countries, many of whom frequently clash with industrialized nations over the content and tone of formal international agreements on environment and development. Approximately 41 developing nations have so far begun Earth Charter-related activities, compared with about 20 developed or transition countries. Host president Thabo Mbeki of South Africa was among several developing country representatives urging support for the Earth Charter's ethical principles at the 2002 World Summit on Sustainable Development (WSSD) in Johannesburg.

At the same time, the Charter risks irrelevance, or a permanent place on the sidelines, if it becomes entrenched too far outside the formal international process. With so many environment-based treaties and statements of intent now published by the UN, by national governments, and by international and national alliances of NGOs, the Earth Charter needs to stake its claim at every level–including the intergovernmental. The Universal Declaration of Human Rights, for example, became such a powerful, behavior-changing tool precisely because it was adopted by the United Nations on behalf of all the world's countries. Pressure could then be applied by the many on the few nations who continued to defy its standards.

One of the initiative's four avowed goals was to mirror the progress of the human rights declaration by winning endorsement by the UN General Assembly at the 2002 Johannesburg summit. However, the charter's visionary worldview fell victim to business as usual. In his opening address, President Mbeki of South Africa cited the Earth Charter as part of "the solid base from which the Johannesburg World Summit must proceed," and the draft Johannesburg Declaration on Sustainable Development, to be signed by heads of state, referred to "the relevance of the challenges posed in the Earth Charter." However, the reference was later deleted, in a closed-door session, on the last day of the summit (Earth Charter Secretariat 2002:2).

This setback underlines the difficulty the Charter's exponents face in winning acceptance for an ethical framework to guide global action on environment and development. While applying a set of agreed values to policy-making might seem a logical step in our increasingly interdependent and resource-depleted world, persuading governments to limit their freedom of action by formally adopting them will not be easy. According to Earth Charter commissioners who attended the summit, there was little interest in discussing ethical principles at all, while some governments actively opposed references to the need for global ethics (Earth Charter Secretariat 2002:3).

The Earth Charter's penultimate paragraph calls for the implementation of its principles through a legally binding international instrument. Such a vehicle already exists in the form of the Draft Covenant on Environment and Development drafted by the Commission on Environmental Law of the World Conservation Union (IUCN), which synthesizes all existing international law in the field. Yet the Covenant has languished before the United Nations since 1995, with no nation so far willing to step forward and propose its adoption.

The Earth Charter commissioners believe incremental advances, rather than wholesale endorsement or recognition, may well prove the route to acceptability for both the Charter and the Covenant. One such advance was WSSD's formal acceptance of an educational partnership between the Earth Charter Initiative and the United Nations. This will involve UNESCO, the governments of Costa Rica, Honduras, Mexico, and Niger, and 13 international NGOs in using Earth Charter principles to help train community leaders to implement sustainable development (Earth Charter Secretariat 2002:4).

A second incremental step was the use of wording almost identical to that in the Charter's preamble in the Johannesburg summit's political declaration, namely: "We declare...our responsibility to one another, to the greater community of life and to our children" (United Nations 2002a). This reference to "the community of life" is the first of its kind in a UN document of law. As such, according to Steven Rockefeller, it marks "a critical moral step" by governments toward accepting environmental responsibility "not just toward human beings but to the larger living world" (Rockefeller 2003).

Acting Locally

By building strong grassroots support in many countries, the Earth Charter is creating the potential to revolutionize attitudes to local governance and stewardship of natural resources. At the 2002 World Summit on Sustainable Development, its principles were endorsed by mayors and other local government representatives from around the world. To channel this potential, however, local communities, businesses, and governing authorities need to translate their symbolic support into concrete plans and policies.

In some places, this is happening by itself. The cities of Burlington, Vermont, Toronto, Canada, San José, Costa Rica, Jundaloop, Western Australia, and Urbino, Italy are either measuring city programs against Earth Charter principles or using the principles to guide municipal practice. In Canada's biggest and most ethnically diverse city, the Toronto Regional Conservation Authority has measured its policies on minorities against the Charter's Principle 12 and taken action accordingly. In response to Principle 12(a), which calls for the elimination of "discrimination in all its forms," for example, the city has committed itself to measure and address instances of "environmental racism," such as higher pollution levels in ethnic neighborhoods. It has also pledged to provide opportunities for all minorities to have equal access to recreation, education, and green spaces in the city (King 2002:1).

Many local government organizations that have endorsed the charter, however, have done little concrete with it. "Groups such as the U.S. Conference of Mayors are coming to us and saying, 'We love the Earth Charter, how do we use it?'" says Richard Clugston, executive director of the Center for Respect of Life and Environment in Washington, DC, and a member of the Earth Charter's international steering committee (Clugston 2003). In response, the committee is now developing toolkits on using the Charter in teaching or as part of local government sustainability programs.

Such practical guidance is essential to expanding the Charter's reach, according to grassroots activists like Gwendolyn Hallsmith, a pastor who successfully led efforts to persuade more than 20 town meetings in Vermont to endorse it. "Getting a local city council to make a symbolic gesture of support for the Earth Charter is one thing, but really putting the principles to work in a municipality is another thing altogether. It requires a substantial commitment to participatory planning and action on the part of the municipality and often takes some dedicated resources to see it through" (Hallsmith 2002).

A second challenge for the Earth Charter secretariat and steering committee is delineating what role the document should play alongside other community-based sustainable development initiatives. Since the 1992 Earth Summit, for example, around 2,000 (mostly European) local governments have developed specific plans of action under the umbrella of Local Agenda 21, including recycling, water conservation, and energy efficiency programs (Hallsmith 2002).

Mirian Vilela, executive director of the Earth Charter International Secretariat, based in Costa Rica, concedes that some local authorities see no need to endorse the Charter—either because they are actively implementing Agenda 21 or

because sustainable development is not seen as a priority. She contends, however, that the Charter can legitimately complement Local Agenda 21 programs in two ways: First by providing a missing ethical framework within which decisions and policies can be made; and second by expanding sustainable development programs beyond their usual limited focus on combating environmental problems to include social and economic justice and democratic decision-making. "I describe Local Agenda 21 as providing the body of community sustainable development while the Earth Charter is the soul. You need the one to complete the other" (Vilela 2003).

This argument was endorsed somewhat less poetically by the world's governments in the 2002 Johannesburg Summit's Plan of Implementation, which emphasizes "the need to consider ethics in the implementation of Agenda 21" (United Nations 2002b). To what extent the Earth Charter will fulfil this role for local sustainability initiatives around the world, however, remains an open question.

Charting a Course for Earth's Future?

Throughout history, the power of words has shaped human actions and outlooks. By planting and spreading ideals of acceptable behavior that gradually become idée fixes in diverse cultures across the globe, inspirational texts can prove more powerful and permanent than conquering armies. Yet to achieve this, the Earth Charter needs to succeed on many levels. It must inspire with its words, acting as a driver for behavioral change and a roadmap for practical action.

How likely is this to happen? The simple answer is that it's too early to say. In a world deeply divided by geopolitics, religion, and warfare, the Earth Charter may become a guide for those who seek a partnership of nations dedicated to maintaining global peace, social and economic justice, and ecological security. Or it may simply prove too idealistic as a guide for practical behavior, and give way to a new set of values and beliefs that more accurately reflect the global zeitgeist.

"My view is that the Earth Charter provides a very useful vision of the way the world—governments, business, communities, and individuals—need to think about global issues and fold them into everyday life," reflects Daniel Esty, a governance expert at Yale University. "But it's a very big challenge to get people to re-engineer their thinking, and that process has only just begun. There is also still a good bit of work to be done to consolidate at the international level a new set of environmental norms for people to endorse and live by" (Esty 2003).

UN General Assembly endorsement would help the Earth Charter's bid to become this internationally accepted ethical framework. But the measure of real change, says Esty, will be "the extent to which the norms the Earth Charter puts forward penetrate into real life" by persuading people and governments to change their behavior (Esty 2003).

TOWARD A BETTER BALANCE

Balance means making environmental decisions that foster ecosystem health, treat people fairly, and make economic sense. Global environmental trends show that we have yet to find this balance. Environmental governance still relies on government institutions whose missions and structures are ill-matched to the task of managing ecosystems and don't always acknowledge the importance of public participation or the need for equity. Private sector performance is likewise driven by short-term economic goals that often conflict with the long-term needs of the environment. Public transparency and accountability can help resolve this conflict, but are relatively new imperatives for most companies.

How do we move toward a better balance? At least five steps must define our drive for better environmental governance.

Adopt Environmental Management Approaches that Respect Ecosystems

To match human needs with Earth's biological capacities, governance structures must adapt to the innate constraints of living systems. Ecosystems are the planet's primary biological units–the sources of all the environmental goods and services we rely on for life, and the ultimate foundations of the global economy. They must therefore become the ultimate points of reference for our environmental decisions. Such an ecosystem-level focus defines what we can call an "ecosystem approach" to environmental management (Young 2002:55).

An ecosystem approach includes explicit consideration of people's needs for food, shelter, employment, and all the varied economic and spiritual benefits we derive from nature. To accomplish this, social and economic goals must be integrated with biological information about the functions and limitations of ecosystems. Our environmental governance must provide the mechanism to negotiate this difficult integration–by giving each stakeholder a voice without losing track of what the ecosystem itself is saying about its capacity for alteration and human use. This means creating a forum where ecosystem science and monitoring can influence management goals and inform public input into environmental decisions. It demands an equal role for social science–tracking the social outcomes of decisions in order to maintain a focus on equity.

Making ecosystems the fundamental units of environmental management will require innovative approaches. One such approach is to promote decentralized management of natural resources, so that local stakeholders take a primary role in governing the ecosystems around them. Larger, regional associations–such as river basin authorities linking users across many jurisdictions–may also be useful. In practice, a variety of new institutional and economic arrangements will be needed to connect people with the ecosystems they depend on, to the benefit of both.

In Quito, Ecuador, for example, city water users pay a small fee into a special fund used to protect the watershed in the Antisana Reserve–the source of the city's water supply. This arrangement allows city residents to see themselves as stakeholders in a distant ecosystem who have decided to help manage and pay for the vital service the ecosystem renders. A similar plan, where downstream users elect to pay for upstream services, is being considered to help manage the watershed that feeds Panama City and the Panama Canal Authority (Zurita 2002).

On a much larger scale, the Mesoamerican Biological Corridor project links local community planning efforts with management of protected areas in the seven Central American countries along the corridor route. The project seeks to find economic uses of the land that will also help maintain its ecological richness–activities such as low-intensity agriculture and forestry. The plan effectively combines regional ecosystem-based goals with a decentralized, community-based approach to landscape management.

Restoration of the Chesapeake Bay on the East Coast of the United States demonstrates that managing a regional resource in a complex social setting can require a battery of governance innovations, such as new partnerships among government agencies and community organizations, new economic incentives, and a new role for science. The Chesapeake's enormous watershed spans 4 states and over 1,600 individual communities. With the help of a citizens' advisory board and a panel of science advisors, state agencies and the federal government have forged a common set of Bay restoration goals and biological benchmarks to measure their progress across all jurisdictions. Each state has pursued its own regulatory approach to this Chesapeake Bay Compact, as the regional agreement is called. These approaches include tax incentives, land use restrictions, and harvest limits on fish and shellfish. Meanwhile, a number of local nongovernmental organizations (NGOs) have played important roles in helping farmers, fishermen, and Bay communities embrace the effort and actually carry out much of the restoration work (WRI et al. 1996:74; Chesapeake Bay Program 2003).

These examples suggest the governance innovations possible with an ecosystem approach to environmental management. In some cases, adopting ecosystem-level management practices will mean reconfiguring existing agencies or creating new institutions and relationships that better reflect ecosystem realities. This need not mean wholesale abandonment of the centralized model of most state agencies, which will continue to fulfill important coordinating, monitoring, or oversight functions. But it does imply more flexibility to assign discretionary powers to other levels in order to match management structures to ecosystems.

Sound knowledge is also needed to support decision-making at the ecosystem level. In response, government agencies and other environmental management organizations could support data collection consistent with an ecosystem approach, or pool data from different organizations to get a comprehensive economic and environmental picture of the whole ecosystem.

Build the Capacity for Public Participation

Reformulating our natural resource management to respect ecosystems requires vigilant application of the principles of access and participation. In this context, public participation means not only wide access to information and direct participation in decision-making, but also effective representation, judicial redress, and other mechanisms that enable meaningful, democratic environmental governance.

Managing ecosystems inevitably involves trade-offs among different ecosystem uses. For instance, a forest can be managed to maximize timber and pulp production through intensive harvesting, but only by trading off some of its

To match human needs with Earth's biological capacities, governance structures must adapt to the innate constraints of living systems.

potential to support biodiversity, agroforestry, or nature-based tourism. Public participation–at the appropriate level–provides the best means to negotiate such trade-offs equitably and to make sure the goals that drive the day-to-day actions of natural resource agencies reflect the priorities of the community of stakeholders.

Too often, however, government agencies, private businesses, NGOs, and the media fail to play their parts in promoting transparent and inclusive decision-making. Even where the political will is present, public participation is hampered by these institutions' lack of capacity to supply relevant information, coordinate the public input process, and digest the results. At the same time, the public often doesn't know its rights to environmental access or how to use them, and doesn't understand the full context of the decisions that affect their lives. Both problems require attention.

A first step is to make sure that public institutions recognize, as part of their core missions, the need to build the capacity for public participation. That means committing staff and budget resources for training and outreach to ensure that opportunities for access are clear and straightforward. It also means committing to build basic environmental literacy among the public, as in South Africa, where the government incorporates environmental education programs into public school curricula and adult education programs (Petkova et al. 2002:107).

Decentralizing natural resource management is another way governments can empower citizens and increase public participation in the decisions that affect them most. Care must be taken however, to devolve power to local institutions in a way that actually benefits natural resources and favors democratization. That requires, first and foremost, that governments transfer authority only to those bodies that are accountable at the local level. But it also requires a commitment to strengthen local institutions by providing technical expertise, training in skills like land use planning and

resource mapping, guidance in participatory methods at town meetings, and support for the inclusion of women and other underrepresented groups. Instituting minimum environmental standards to guide local resource decisions may also be necessary to make sure these actions do not compromise larger environmental goals.

One important way governments can build public capacity for participation in environmental decision-making is to provide good foundations for the growth and maturation of NGOs and other civil society groups. This means strengthening their rights of access to information through freedom of information laws, and recognizing their right to represent their members in whatever forum decisions are being made. It also requires recognizing–and funding–the ability of NGOs to respond quickly to community needs and provide services the government can't efficiently provide. Empowering civil society groups as environmental stewards thus means more than just official tolerance–it implies active support for partnerships among these groups, government agencies, and businesses.

Nonetheless, as civil society groups gain in influence, they must practice the same good governance principles of transparency and accountability they demand of governments and businesses. These include openness about funding sources, operations, goals, and accomplishments. NGOs that purport to advocate in the public interest should take care to maintain contact with the communities they serve through public consultations, newsletters, and formal progress reports and financial statements that foster accountability. Only when NGOs are transparent and accountable to their constituencies can they effectively facilitate participation.

For the business community, facilitating public participation starts with support for and compliance with regulations governing information disclosure. Companies can go further by adopting corporate codes of conduct that recognize community interests, following clear environmental reporting processes that make data publicly available, and establishing

**The public often doesn't know its access rights
or how to use them.**

community liaisons. As guardians of transparency, media companies should adopt their own ethical codes of conduct, report all their lobbying activities, and disclose commercial ties that could influence their editorial decisions.

Building capacity for more effective public participation is a critical first step toward better environmental governance, but not one that is sufficient in and of itself.

Recognize All Affected Stakeholders in Environmental Decisions

Who should have standing to influence decisions affecting an ecosystem or negotiate for rights to ecosystem goods and services? Traditionally, the parties with influence and access have been few, creating public tension, local resistance to decisions, and a grossly unequal distribution of burdens and rewards. A commitment to building the capacity for public participation must include broadening the definition of who the "affected public" is. Public acceptance of environmental management decisions—and greater fairness in those decisions—will only emerge if a broader approach to environmental standing takes root.

One useful model might be the "rights and risks" approach recently put forward by the World Commission on Dams to guide decisions on large dams that affect a wide array of stakeholders. In this approach, anyone holding a right (such as a water right) or facing a risk from a proposed action (such as displacement by a dam) must have the opportunity to participate in the decision-making process. This includes not just those who reside in the affected ecosystem, but also those who depend on or value that ecosystem, no matter where they live. It is also important to recognize the standing of those who can speak for the ecosystem itself—whether they be scientists, natural resource managers, or members of an environmental or recreation-focused NGO.

As governments begin to broaden their conceptions of standing, civil society's role in representing the public inter-est in decision-making takes on greater significance. It is imperative to remember that civil society is not monolithic, but wildly diverse. It may be appropriate to seek the input of several different groups in a participatory process, since a single NGO, labor union, or neighborhood group rarely reflects the pluralism of public opinion. For example, the World Commission on Dams included representatives from three different categories of civil society on its Advisory Forum—indigenous groups, public interest advocacy groups, and environmental groups. This was intended to reflect the diversity of stakeholders in the dam debate (Dubash et al. 2001:7).

Integrate Environmental Sustainability in Economic Decision-Making

Many of today's environmental impacts originate in decisions about economic development, trade, and investment—decisions outside the traditional "environment" sector. To make progress in reversing environmental decline, governments and businesses—not just natural resource agencies—must accept environmental sustainability as a principal mandate. That means assessing how each policy and investment strategy will affect equity and the environment.

Examining the equity and environmental impacts of privatization, for example, could bring immediate benefits. Governments privatize responsibility to deliver water or provide electric power largely for reasons of economy and efficiency. But they must also make sure to transfer responsibility for environmental stewardship and equitable service as they cede control over these essential tasks. Contracts should be structured to require or reward saving water, generating green power, extending service to low-income areas, and other beneficial practices. This same principle must apply when governments grant forest, mining, grazing, or other resource concessions to private interests.

Some companies are already exploring ways to integrate environmental objectives into their businesses. Fully incorporating "sustainability" into business thinking will take time, but embracing standardized procedures for measuring environmental performance–and relating this to financial and social performance–is a critical first step. Only by evaluating this data against social norms and their own expectations can companies effectively guide their investments in sustainable business practices. The Global Reporting Initiative offers one well-accepted framework for this kind of performance measurement, including a combination of guiding principles and core indicators that companies can use to prepare "sustainability reports." A growing list of the world's major corporations have accepted the Initiative's voluntary guidelines, which emerged from consultations among businesses, advocacy groups, accounting bodies, trade unions, and investor groups.

Negotiating forums such as the World Trade Organization (WTO) and financial institutions such as export credit agencies must also adopt environmental sustainability as a guiding principle. This means that they must explicitly recognize environmental protection as a critical factor in trade and investment policies, making sure these policies do not undermine current international environmental agreements and national environmental laws. Greater transparency and participation in these institutions' internal decision-making practices, which are now largely hidden from public view, will also be important.

The WTO's current negotiating round, called the Doha round, may make a start at greening global trade rules. Negotiators have promised to look into reconciling trade rules with international environmental treaties, and to address environmentally harmful subsidies that also interfere with trade, such as fishery and agricultural subsidies. Global economic growth increasingly depends on trade–so the WTO has a special responsibility to ensure that the rules are crafted in a way that builds environmental responsibility and equity into the world's economic engine.

Strengthen Global Environmental Cooperation

Efforts to manage environmental impacts and develop sustainable systems for Earth's future suffer from a lack of coordination at the global level. This is evident in the nearly 200 international environmental treaties that exist independently, and in nations' uneven efforts to implement Agenda 21, the Rio Summit's plan of action for achieving sustainable development. The community of nations also lacks a strong central institution to carry the environmental agenda forward–nations have shown little interest in embracing a World Environment Organization, or similar institution with executive and enforcement powers. Nevertheless, improved integration of environmental efforts is possible even within the array of existing treaties and institutions.

Stressing the link between poverty and environment will be important in strengthening global environmental gover-

nance. Global support for environmental activities is enhanced whenever they coincide with poverty eradication goals like those established by the UN Millenium Declaration. Integration of the precautionary principle and the ecosystem approach into national development plans and environmental treaties is likewise an essential part of making global environmental governance more effective.

One first step in this process is to increase the global commitment to environmental monitoring and threat assessment. Science-based assessments by the Intergovernmental Panel on Climate Change, the Millennium Ecosystem Assessment and others have set the stage for global consensus on urgent environmental problems, and can also guide national development onto more sustainable paths. Through an integrated approach that looks across ecosystems, using predictive models and scenarios, these assessments show the effects of different land use patterns, energy strategies, and regulatory regimes on national well-being. Increased commitment must translate not only into regular funding for environmental assessments, but also into involvement by nations in their design and conduct, so that the results will be seen as valid and useful at the national level.

To make progress in reversing environmental decline, governments and businesses– not just natural resource agencies–must accept environmental sustainability as a principal mandate.

A second step in improving global environmental coordination will be a concerted effort to harmonize and strengthen international environmental treaties. These agreements represent our collective will to address environmental challenges jointly, and embody the primary legal obligations to carry out this will. Harmonizing these treaties entails exploring the complementarity between them, identifying where greater coordination of obligations, action plans, and financing could bring heightened impact and reduced administrative costs. Strengthening environmental treaties involves negotiating meaningful benchmarks for progress and firm deadlines for attaining them. These will be meaningless, however, without standard monitoring protocols to measure progress, robust enforcement mechanisms to encourage compliance, and mechanisms for settling disputes among signatories. The Montreal Protocol's success in reducing emissions of ozone-depleting gases, for example, depended strongly on careful monitoring and well-enforced national initiatives (GEF 2002:15-16). Existing regional entities such as the European Union (EU), the Organization of American States (OAS), and the Association of Southeast Asian Nations (ASEAN), or new organizations, such as river basin authorities, may be useful in helping to implement and monitor agreements.

The United Nations Environment Programme's mandate is to provide an institutional home for coordinated action on the environment. However, fulfilling this mandate requires more adequate funding and a clearer framework for its role as coordinator. Strengthening the Global Ministerial Environmental Forum, UNEP's forum for deliberation among national environment ministers–perhaps by expanding the Forum's work to include ministers from outside the environment sector (Hyvarinen and Brack 2000:56)–could be one way to accomplish this. The Commission on Sustainable Development (CSD) could also serve as an institutional focal point for global environmental action, if it were transformed from a forum for policy and political debate to a mechanism for monitoring and enforcing accountability for government commitments. Over the long term, however, other institutional options for better global environmental governance should be explored.

No matter how governments decide to strengthen global environmental institutions, greater use of multi-stakeholder processes to give voice to civil society and business and build consensus on contentious issues will be key. Institutionalizing such processes in the CSD and other environmental bodies is an important first step. But multi-stakeholder processes must also be improved to more effectively facilitate interaction between governments and other stakeholders. Useful changes might include clearer rules on selection of participants, fuller integration into official conference agendas, creative facilitation to ensure that real dialogue takes place, and,

perhaps most important, accountability mechanisms to ensure that the results are taken seriously by governments.

Civil society's role in global environmental governance is not limited to participation in multi-stakeholder processes. Indeed, such processes are just one vehicle for their involvement. NGOs can also provide objective information and new ideas, and hold governments, through media and political action, accountable for their commitments. Doing so effectively requires strong global civil society coalitions that bring together NGOs from the North and the South as well as from non-environmental interest areas, such as global justice.

Finally, global environmental governance can be strengthened by improving the financial mechanisms that underlie the present system. The Global Environment Facility has proven a useful mechanism for supporting implementation of environmental treaties and piloting innovative approaches, but its resources are dwarfed by those channeled through other public and private sources. Accordingly, mainstreaming the objectives of environmental sustainability into the decision-making of public and private development finance is important, as are new mechanisms to respond to environmental needs.

The principle of Common but Differentiated Responsibility, which enshrines the idea that nations differ in their capacity to respond to international environmental threats and to finance obligations under environmental treaties, was a key outcome of the Rio Earth Summit. It calls upon developed economies with greater means and higher consumption levels to do more, at least initially, to meet global environmental challenges. It also obligates high-income nations to help developing nations increase their capacity to comply with environmental agreements. This approach has worked well in such treaties as the Montreal Protocol to address ozone destruction, but has been one of the main stumbling blocks in negotiations on the Kyoto Protocol to control green-

There is growing dissatisfaction with environmental governance in countries around the world.

house gas emissions. At the recent World Summit on Sustainable Development in Johannesburg, many nations offered only tepid or conditional endorsement of this principle. Though contentious, this principle remains a powerful tool to address questions of equity at the global level. Reaffirming this would seem an important precursor to joint action.

Decisions for the Earth

Governance is on the global agenda today as never before. As democratic movements flourish and NGOs awaken to new activism, issues of transparency and fairness have come into sharper focus. This is true in the environmental arena as well. In fact, there is growing dissatisfaction with environmental governance in countries around the world. A 2000 Gallup International poll found that in 55 of 60 countries surveyed, the majority of people thought their governments were doing too little to address environmental issues. "Corrupt" and "bureaucratic" were the two most common descriptions people used to characterize their governments. Corporate governance has also come under greater fire as globalization gains momentum, with increasing calls for a global agreement on corporate accountability.

At the same time, global consensus has emerged on the basic principles of good environmental governance: access, participation, transparency, appropriate scale, and an ecosystem basis. These elements form the basic toolkit for environmentally empowered and educated citizens—the most potent driver for better environmental decisions.

The future lives in the decisions we make now. Moving toward greater transparency and accountability in our decision-making, toward more participation and equity in our environmental choices, is the way we make better decisions for the Earth.

Recommendations

In the following sections, we bring together recommendations and other opportunities for action drawn from this volume as a whole. These recommendations amount to an action summary that can improve environmental governance and decision-making.

Opening Up Access

How can we improve access to information, participation, and justice?

Government agencies can:

- Support independent assessment and monitoring of government performance in applying the access principles.

- Continue efforts to establish the legal framework for access, and to elaborate these laws in well-defined administrative procedures.

- Specify which classes of information are in the public domain and which are confidential, in order to reduce administrative discretion in releasing information.

- Introduce common reporting standards for industrial facilities and procedures for public access to facility-level reports.

- Establish mechanisms for public notice and comment on projects and policies beyond the narrowly defined "environmental" arena.

- Extend participation procedures into the earliest phases of the decision-making cycle, as well as into the implementation and review stages.

- Broaden the interpretation of "the public" and "legal standing" to allow legal challenges by public interest groups and citizens who may not be able to prove direct harm.

- Invest in training judges and other officials to ensure that they are familiar with rapidly changing laws related to environmental rights.

- Create favorable conditions for the formation and activities of public interest groups and media outlets.

- Implement their commitments to improved access under the Rio Declaration, Agenda 21, and the WSSD Plan of Implementation, as well as under related provisions in global environmental agreements and regional instruments such as the Aarhus Convention.

Civil society organizations can:
- Undertake independent assessments and regular monitoring using a framework of governance indicators such as The Access Initiative framework.

- Collaborate with government and other stakeholders to identify gaps in national practices of access and to set priorities for action.

- Stimulate and channel public demand for access to information, participation, and justice.

- Build their own capacity, and the capacity of the communities they live in, to access the public participation system.

Media outlets can:
- Investigate and call attention to lapses in performance by governments in providing access.

- Provide high-quality coverage of environmental issues and a forum for diverse views on environmental decisions.

Donor agencies can:
- Support continued improvement of an indicator framework for national assessments, and mechanisms for exchange of best practices.

- Provide financial, institutional, and political support for development of national public participation systems.

- Support capacity building on both the "demand" and "supply" sides.

- Model best practices of information disclosure, participation, and accountability in their own operations.

International environmental treaties and trade agreements can:
- Incorporate provisions mandating best practices of information disclosure, participation, and accountability with regard to obligations carried out under the treaty or agreement, and in on-going deliberations on the treaty.

How can we create a climate conducive to civic organizing and the inclusion of NGOs and other civil society groups in environmental decision-making?

Governments can:
- Enact or strengthen freedoms of expression and association.

- Eliminate or simplify laws governing NGOs and other civic groups, including removing barriers to registration, eliminating burdensome reporting requirements, and dropping limits on NGO longevity.

- Remove restrictions on Internet and press freedoms.

Civil society organizations can:
- Embrace the same policies of accountability and transparency that they advocate for governments and corporations, including openness about their funding, operations, purposes, goals, and accomplishments.

- Participate in NGO networks to increase communication among themselves and share successful practices.

- Join in consensus-building coalitions of NGOs that maximize their voice and increase their influence in public decision-making and multi-stakeholder processes.

- Foster greater contact with and accountability to the communities they serve through public consultations, newsletters, and formal progress reports.

- Work with the media to encourage more and higher quality environmental reporting, including the presentation of issues in greater depth, and from more perspectives.

Donors can:
- Increase NGO access to communications tools such as the Internet as a source of environmental empowerment.

- Support capacity building for NGOs, with particular attention to developing the ability of smaller groups to fundraise, build coalitions, and develop relationships at the grassroots level.

Greening Corporate Environmental Performance

How can we encourage corporations to factor the environment into their business strategies and respond to local concerns about their environmental practices?

Corporations can:
- Embrace voluntary environmental disclosure practices, including environmental auditing and sustainability

reporting. Using standardized formats such as the Global Reporting Initiative guidelines can increase the credibility of such reporting and its usefulness to shareholders, communities, and the companies themselves.

■ Work to quantify the financial benefits (as opposed to just the costs) of corporate environmental programs, thus advancing the business rationale for these programs to company managers and shareholders.

■ Establish company liaisons or ombudsmen to the communities in which they are located in order to respond to local concerns.

■ Encourage their chains of suppliers and distributors to adopt sustainable manufacturing or extraction practices, green disclosure practices, and sensitivity to community concerns.

■ Pursue corporate philanthropy that promotes employee awareness of the environment-business connection, builds employee capacity for better environmental choices, or mitigates environmental impacts caused by their business activities.

Industry trade groups can:
■ Support laws and regulations that reward companies for superior environmental performance.

■ Formulate industry guidelines and codes of conduct–including enforcement mechanisms and training programs to increase compliance–to encourage good environmental practices among their members.

■ Actively participate in and endorse environmental labeling and certification schemes that increase consumer information and choice.

■ Promote industry-wide disclosure, transparency, and community-engagement practices.

■ Participate in civil society efforts to forge consensus around new corporate performance norms.

Governments can:
■ Require companies to publicly report on emissions in key areas by establishing Pollutant Release and Transfer Registries (PRTRs), or publicly rate companies' pollution mitigation efforts in order to highlight their environmental performance.

■ Require companies to disclose environmental liabilities such as hazardous material use, toxic waste disposal, or environmental restoration costs (for extractive indus-

tries) to make it easier for investors to assess a company's potential environmental risks and thus increase incentives for improved performance.

■ Send the right economic signals to companies by removing or modifying government subsidies for water, fishing, energy exploitation, mining, pesticide use, and other environmentally harmful activities.

Consumers and shareholders can:
■ Make use of environmental labels and certifications to purchase products whose harvesting, extraction, manufacture, or disposal is environmentally sound, thus rewarding good corporate environmental performance.

■ Introduce resolutions at shareholder meetings to raise the profile of environmental concerns among top company management and encourage environment-friendly policies and investments.

NGOs can:
■ Act as industry watchdogs by compiling, analyzing, and publicizing corporate environmental performance data.

■ Initiate certification and labeling schemes to guide consumer purchase of sustainably manufactured, harvested, or extracted products.

■ In concert with industry, detail best practices necessary to achieve environmentally benign products or to receive green product certification.

■ Partner with corporations to identify targets for corporate environmental philanthropy and to design ecosystem-friendly land management practices on corporate manufacturing and office sites.

Encouraging Decentralization that Supports Sustainability
How can governments and communities develop appropriate decentralized systems for natural resource management?

National decision-makers can:
■ Create local elected bodies, and give them a mandate to define local natural resource priorities within the state's overall framework for sustainable development.

■ Strengthen the local capacity for governance and natural resource management by providing training for local government staff in key skills such as budgeting, revenue collection, conducting town meetings and other local consultations, land use planning, and mapping and cataloging the local environmental resource base.

- Reorient state extension agencies to provide services to local people in response to needs and concerns articulated directly by the people and their local representatives, or restructure them to be accountable to local elected authorities.

- Create positive incentives for good local government performance and sound resource management, such as awards for innovative programs and targeted budget allocations for demonstrated delivery of services.

- Require local elected and administrative authorities to practice transparency in their operations and budgeting procedures.

- Educate citizens on their right to be represented, the services they should expect from local authorities, their responsibility to participate in local decisions, and how they can hold local officials accountable.

- Develop and apply standardized measures of service delivery and community satisfaction to assess local governance

Box 9.1 New Collaborations: The Partnership for Principle 10

One of the themes of the World Summit on Sustainable Development was the power of collaboration across stakeholder groups, both to build consensus on the way forward, and to implement the sustainable development agenda on the ground. Multi-stakeholder processes such as the World Commission on Dams have demonstrated that representatives of constituencies with widely different perspectives can find common ground on contentious issues. Local efforts to implement Agenda 21 around the world have demonstrated the ability of businesses and civic groups to collaborate with government agencies to share responsibilities for environmental protection and stewardship of natural resources.

One initiative unveiled at the Summit—the Partnership for Principle 10 (PP10)—is specifically aimed at improving conditions for good environmental governance at the national level. Principle 10 of the Rio Declaration, adopted by 178 nations at the Earth Summit in 1992, commits national governments to an inclusive process of public participation in environmental decisions. The Partnership, formed a decade after Rio, is an effort to help nations live up to this commitment to good governance. It provides a common forum for governments, civil society organizations, donors, and other groups to design and implement practical strategies to enhance citizen access to environmental information, participation, and justice (the access principles).

The Partnership builds on the work of the Access Initiative (see Chapter 3), which has designed a framework of governance indicators to assess how well nations have translated Principle 10 into action. The first requirement of the Partnership is to support such national assessments of public access. Once NGOs have independently assessed a nation's performance using the Access Initiative framework or another acceptable method, the Partnership's work begins in earnest. Partners work together to plan, finance, and carry out projects tailored to each country's need as identified in its national assessment. That may mean financing the development of a new public information system, committing to a

program to enhance environmental literacy, or designing a training program to help public employees encourage and properly digest input from advocacy and neighborhood groups.

The Partnership for Principle 10 is targeted to the range of groups actively involved in environmental governance:

- *Civil society groups* interested in applying The Access Initiative's framework for assessing government performance on the access principles.

- *Governments* (including national and local agencies) interested in collaborating with civil society groups to improve access to information, participation, and justice.

- *Donors* interested in providing development assistance for the Partnership itself and for independent assessment and capacity building at the national level.

- *International institutions* interested in promoting the access principles in their own operations as well as through their engagements with member governments.

Commitments, Not Rhetoric

The Partnership for Principle 10 is built around a set of shared commitments. These serve as a statement of the Partnership's values and principles and set the parameters for the scope of work of the Partnership.

By joining the PP10, all partners commit to support the accelerated and enhanced implementation of Principle 10 at the national level and in their own policies and practice related to access to information, public participation, and justice by:

- Encouraging credible and independent assessments of policies and practice using a framework of indicators—such as those developed by the Access Initiative—to identify strengths and weaknesses in implementation;

statewide and help local governments identify gaps in their performance.

- Increase the voice of traditionally marginalized groups, such as women and the poor. This may include reserving seats in local decision-making bodies or creating separate opportunities to solicit their input.

- Ensure that the authority over resources exists at the appropriate ecosystem level (e.g., the watershed) so that the impacts of different land uses and development activities can be assessed and managed in an integrated manner. If this results in the formation of a new institution, such as a regional river basin authority, ensure that this institution is accountable to governments at different levels, including the local level.

- Institute minimum environmental standards to guide local resource decisions and to make sure these decisions conform to statewide environmental laws.

- Collaborating with partners and other stakeholders to improve policies and practice by prioritizing opportunities and implementing programs to strengthen capacity and enhance performance;

- Developing individual specific commitments and being accountable for them.

Specific commitments could include:

- *For governments:* developing a new Freedom of Information Law; training judges and lawyers on environmental procedural rights; developing a new public legal aid program for environmental laws and regulations; crafting procedures to introduce public participation earlier in the decision-making cycle; developing environmental education programs; developing and implementing Pollutant Release and Transfer Registers.

- *For nongovernmental organizations:* repeating a national-level assessment every two years; contributing to the Access Initiative process of refining access indicators and assessment methods.

- *For governments and NGOs together:* committing to engage in a process of consultation and dialogue to identify priorities and develop joint activities, such as training courses for government officials responsible for providing environmental information or conducting environmental impact assessments.

- *For donors:* providing a specific level of funding to support the Partnership itself or to support capacity building in specific countries.

- *For international institutions:* mainstreaming activities that support the access principles in their country offices; adopting internal policies specifying transparent and accountable practices, as well as mechanisms for public participation, in all the institution's activities.

Progress toward meeting these commitments must be measured regularly and reported to all partners and to the general public. Commitments should be achievable within a specified time period, and are expected to differ depending on the kind of organization and the income level of the country where they are located.

Joining the Partnership for Principle 10, then, is one way groups of all calibers can work locally to advance open and equitable decision-making.

Members of the Partnership include governments, international organizations, and national and international NGOs. World Resources Institute is the acting Secretariat. As of April 2003, PP10 members included:

- Governments: Chile, Hungary, the European Commission, Italy, Mexico, Sweden, Uganda, and the United Kingdom

- International Organizations: IUCN—World Conservation Union, the United Nations Development Programme, the United Nations Environment Programme, and the World Bank

- Nongovernmental Organizations: Advocates Coalition for Development and Environment (Uganda), Corporación Participa (Chile), Environmental Management and Law Association (Hungary), European Environmental Bureau (EU), Recursos e Investigación para el Desarrollo Sustentable (Chile), Thailand Environment Institute, The Access Initiative–Mexico, and World Resources Institute (USA)

PP10 also allows potential partners to obtain observer status. Observers include the Government of Thailand, the South Africa Environmental Justice Network Forum, the Swedish Society for Nature Conservation, and the International Network for Environmental Compliance and Enforcement.

New partners continue to join PP10, please visit our website at **www.pp10.org** for a complete list of current partners.

- Strengthen or accelerate the creation of a justice system that is independent and accessible to the general public.

- Make sure contracts for privatizing environmental services such as water provision also contain clauses conferring the responsibility to meet minimum environmental standards, to work within an accepted framework of sustainable development, and to deliver services equitably. Contracts awarding logging, mining, or grazing concessions should contain similar commitments to environmental stewardship and equitable service.

Local officials can:

- Commit to transparency in operations and budgeting, and make sure that opportunities for public participation are well-advertised.

- Identify which households or groups in the community find it difficult to participate in the consultative process and make special efforts to facilitate their participation.

- Collaborate with adjacent jurisdictions to manage transboundary ecosystems.

Communities can:

- Demand accountability from their local government representatives.

- Mobilize to articulate common goals for local development.

- Enlist NGOs or community groups to carry out independent monitoring of nearby forest, mining, and other concessions to discourage corruption and increase the community's voice in how these concessions are managed.

- Promote positive exchange with other communities regarding natural resource issues of common concern.

Better Global Environmental Governance

How can we build better global institutions that catalyze collective action on the environment and foster sustainable national development?

Governments can:

- *Remember the poverty-environment link.* Prioritize environmental activities that restore or mitigate the loss of resources that the poor most depend on, such as in rural areas, on marginal lands, or in informal periurban settlements. Achievement of the Millennium Development Goals will represent a key milestone in realizing sustainable and equitable development.

- *Commit to comprehensive monitoring.* Enhance the capacity for global environmental monitoring and scientific assessment of environmental trends, including their interlinkages and probable impacts on ecosystems as well as on national food supplies, economies, and settlements.

- *Implement the "Precautionary Principle."* Reaffirm the "Precautionary Principle" of applying caution to environmental decisions where environmental risks are uncertain, but carry potentially large costs. Commit to applying this approach when configuring national development plans and crafting international environmental treaties.

- *Adopt an "Ecosystem Approach."* Use ecosystems as the fundamental unit of natural resource management and governance at the local, regional, national, and international levels. Incorporate ecosystem thinking–framing threats and responses in terms of how they affect the delivery of ecosystem goods and services–into negotiations on current and future environmental treaties.

- *Strengthen and harmonize environmental agreements.* Strengthen international environmental agreements (treaties and protocols) with deadlines for significant progress, robust enforcement mechanisms to encourage compliance, competent monitoring protocols to assess progress, and binding mechanisms for dispute resolution. Harmonize and coordinate the action plans of these treaties and streamline their administration. Ensure that trade and environmental agreements are mutually supportive.

- *Enable institutional leadership.* Provide the United Nations Environment Programme with a clearer and stronger framework for its current coordinating role and adequate funding to pursue this role. Reorient the CSD to serve as a monitoring and accountability mechanism for government commitments.

- *Build and support regional mechanisms.* Support existing regional institutions or design and implement new regional mechanisms such as river basin authorities, and, where appropriate, devolve monitoring and implementation functions to such regional bodies.

- *Make decision-making inclusive.* Strengthen multi-stakeholder processes–where stakeholders of all stripes are included in decision processes–so that civil society groups can effectively participate at the international level in setting environmental priorities, specifying the terms and timelines for international action, and crafting environmental treaties.

- *Hold business and industry accountable.* Promote corporate responsibility and accountability by developing and implementing intergovernmental agreements, international initiatives, public-private partnerships, and appropriate national regulations.

■ *Pursue new partnerships.* Join in partnerships with civil society groups and businesses to achieve well-defined environmental objectives. Such partnerships should magnify the efforts of governments, rather than substitute for a lack of government commitment.

NGOs can:

■ *Provide objective information.* Advise governments on environmental issues by identifying, assessing, and disseminating scientific and other relevant information.

■ *Build coalitions.* Pursue coalitions with each other and with like-minded stakeholders to increase their leverage on governments. Priority attention should be given to expanding alliances with NGOs from developing countries and with social movements engaged in global justice work worldwide. In appropriate cases, as in the case of climate change, working with business and industry on a common objective can yield enormous political and practical benefits.

More Transparent Finance

How can multilateral development banks, export credit agencies, and private international financial institutions make their investments transparent and promote good governance practices among loan recipients?

Multilateral Development Banks can:

■ Articulate information disclosure rules for project planning documents and environmental assessment reports, permitting external parties such as NGOs and public interest groups to track project decisions.

■ Open to the public the process of developing "country assistance strategies" or other national development plans that determine how development aid is allocated, as well as institutional policies and strategies that determine how assistance is conditioned.

■ Establish mechanisms such as ombudsmen or formal dispute procedures to address and resolve complaints by civil society groups and communities that are affected by project loans and investments.

■ Relax the application of blanket confidentiality rules on loan negotiations and dispute settlements to create a more transparent decision-making process.

■ Finance structural adjustment and sectoral adjustment loans in ways that encourage a broad agenda of good governance reforms and transparency practices in client nations.

Export Credit Agencies can:

■ Adopt a set of common environmental guidelines for Export Credit Agency (ECA) investments that include robust transparency, disclosure, and public participation standards. These could include:

■ Annual disclosure of project details (including company, location, financing amount and vehicle) at the level of individual transactions;

■ Publicly disclosing environmental assessments and screening exercises;

■ Allowing periods for public comment on pending financing decisions;

■ Requiring project environmental assessments to include consultation with governments and potentially affected populations;

■ Communicating mitigation measures adopted;

■ Reporting basic environmental indicators for projects receiving ECA support.

Both Multilateral Development Banks and Export Credit Agencies can:

■ Commit not only to "do no harm" to the environment through their policies and lending, but to prioritize investments that will positively benefit the environment. For example, Export Credit Agencies can expand their support for energy efficiency and renewable energy projects rather than funding investments that put countries on paths toward fossil fuel dependency.

■ Consider the implications of financing decisions on global systems, such as biodiversity and climate, in addition to local environmental impacts at project sites. For example, international financial institutions should collaborate with other stakeholders to agree on mechanisms for assigning responsibility for the carbon emissions resulting from individual transactions.

The World Trade Organization can:

■ *Reconcile environment and trade.* Recognize environmental protection as a shaping factor in global trade policies. In the short term, this means acting with dispatch and openness on the environmental agenda set forth in the current round of WTO trade negotiations (the Doha round). Specific measures include:

■ Granting observer status at the WTO to the UN Environment Programme and to the secretariats of international environmental treaties.

- Incorporating the precautionary principle into WTO rules, allowing countries to apply national standards higher than the lowest common denominator of international standards in the health and environmental arenas.

- Granting favored trade status to environmentally beneficial technologies such as clean energy technology.

- Permitting the use of eco-labels or certifications for environmentally benign products and services, while building the capacity of developing countries to take advantage of this new market opportunity.

- Acting to reduce environmentally harmful subsidies that also interfere with trade and sustainable development, such as fishery and agricultural subsidies.

- *Adopt transparent and inclusive processes.* Commit to transparent and open processes in the manner of the multilateral development banks, including better public disclosure practices, a more transparent dispute resolution process, and consultation with civil society groups.

Private International Financial Institutions can:

- Adopt information disclosure and environmental assessment procedures consistent with international norms.

- Adopt investment policies with strong environmental criteria to ensure that their investments support sustainable development.

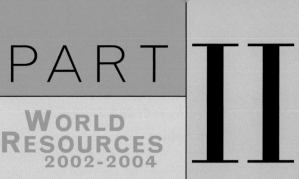

PART II

WORLD RESOURCES 2002-2004

DATA TABLES

Information about the
World Resources 2002–2004
Data Tables

Country groupings are based on lists developed by the Food and Agriculture Organization of the United Nations (FAO), (developed and developing countries), the World Bank (high-, medium-, and low-income countries), and the World Resources Institute (WRI) (regional classifications). See pages 282–283 for a full listing.

Several general notes apply to all the data tables in the report (except where noted otherwise):

- ".." in a data column signifies that data are not available or are not relevant (for example, country status has changed, as with the former Soviet republics)

- Negative values are shown in parentheses

- **0** appearing in a table indicates a value of either zero or one-half the unit of measure used in the table; **(0)** indicates a value less than zero and greater than negative one-half.

- Except where identified by a footnote, regional totals are calculated using regions designated by the World Resources Institute. Totals represent either a summation or a weighted average of available data. Weighted averages of ratios use the denominator of the ratio as the weight. Regional totals are published only if more than 85% of the relevant data are available for a particular region. Missing values are not imputed.

- The regional totals published here use data from all 222 countries and territories in the World Resources/EarthTrends database (some of these countries are omitted from the current tables). Regional summations and weighted averages calculated with only the 155 countries listed in these data tables will therefore not match the published totals.

- Except where identified with a footnote, world totals are presented as calculated by the original data source (which may include countries not listed in WRI's database); original sources are listed after each data table.

- Comprehensive technical notes are available in the pages following each data table.

World Resources Information and Statistics Available On-line and via CD-ROM

The 12 data tables published on the following pages are a subset of a larger on-line data collection, the World Resources/EarthTrends Database. This on-line data source includes more than 30 tables, along with country profiles, maps, feature stories, and a searchable database with over 600 statistical indicators spanning 30-plus years. Access this data source in one of the following ways:

EarthTrends: The Environmental Information Portal

http://earthtrends.wri.org

EarthTrends is a free on-line collection of environmental, social, and economic information. The website offers statistical, graphic, and analytical data from over 40 internationally recognized sources. Detailed metadata documents the data collection, research methodologies, and reliability of all of EarthTrends' content.

EarthTrends for Low-Bandwidth Users

http://earthtrends.wri.org/text

In an effort to broaden global access to sustainable development information, WRI has developed a low-bandwidth companion to the EarthTrends site. View the entire EarthTrends collection of information without high-resolution graphics.

EarthTrends via E-mail

EarthTrends via E-mail provides a way for users to receive environmental and sustainable development information through simple, structured e-mail requests. Send an e-mail to enviro_info@wri.org with "Instructions" in the message body, or view full instructions at http://earthtrends.wri.org/text/webinvoke.htm.

World Resources/EarthTrends Data CD-ROM

Gain instant, portable access to EarthTrends' database on global conditions and trends with the EarthTrends CD-ROM. This time-saving research and reference tool contains all of the economic, population, natural resource, and environmental statistics contained in the EarthTrends website and the print edition of *World Resources 2002–2004*.
Available by order from http://www.wristore.com

TerraViva! World Resources, 2003 Edition

The next generation in the World Resources/EarthTrends series, *TerraViva!* World Resources integrates the comprehensive World Resources/EarthTrends Database with state-of-the-art mapping and analytical tools to make world data come alive visually. Compare hundreds of environmental, social, and economic variables, generating maps, graphs, tables, or text as output.
Available by order from http://www.wristore.com

Governance and Access to Information

Sources: Freedom House, Polity IV Project, Inter-Parliamentary Union, Transparency International, Union of International Associations, Privacy International, World Bank, International Telecommunications Union

	Level of Freedom (free (F), partly free (PF), not free (NF))		Level of Civil Liberties (1=most free, 7= least free)		Polity Index of Democracy/ Autocracy (-10=fully auto-cratic, 10=fully democratic)	Percent of Parlia-mentary Seats Held by Women	Corruption Perceptions Index (10=least corrupt, 0= most corrupt)	Non-Governmental Organizations (NGOs) Per Million Population		Press Freedom (1-30=free, 31-60=partly free, 61-100= not free)	Freedom of Infor-mation Legisla-tion, Status in	Radios Per 1,000 Popu-lation	Internet Users Per 1,000 Popu-lation
	1991-1992	2001-2002	1991-1992	2001-2002	2000	2002	2001	1990	2000	2001	2002	1997	2001
WORLD	..	..	..	..	..	14	..	30	43	..	..	419	81
ASIA (EXCL. MIDDLE EAST)	..	..	..	..	..	15	..	6	9	..	..	258	42
Armenia	PF	PF	5	4	5	3	..	..	129	60	pending	225	..
Azerbaijan	PF	PF	5	5	-7	11	2.0	..	45	77		22	3
Bangladesh	F	PF	3	4	6	2	0.4	6	9	63	pending	49	1
Bhutan	PF	NF	5	6	-8	9	..	108	62	72	..	50	1
Cambodia	NF	NF	6	5	2	9	..	8	30	68		119	1
China	NF	NF	7	6	-7	22	3.5	1	2 a	80	..	339	26
Georgia	NF	NF	5	4	5	7	..	..	125	53	in effect	556	5
India	PF	F	4	3	9	9	2.7	2	3	42	pending	121	7 b
Indonesia	PF	PF	5	4	7	8	1.9	6	9 c	53	pending	157	19
Japan	F	F	2	2	10	10	7.1	19	28	17	in effect	956	455
Kazakhstan	PF	NF	4	5	-4	11	2.7	..	26	69	..	422	..
Korea, Dem People's Rep	NF	NF	7	7	-9	20	..	8	10	96	..	154	..
Korea, Rep	F	F	3	2	8	6	4.2	28	45	30	in effect	1,033	518
Kyrgyzstan	PF	NF	4	5	-3	7	..	..	48	68	..	111	..
Lao People's Dem Rep	NF	NF	7	6	-7	..	..	22	43	82	..	148	2
Malaysia	PF	PF	4	5	3	15	5.0	63	83	71	..	420	252
Mongolia	F	F	3	3	10	11	..	55	140	31	..	154	16
Myanmar	NF	NF	7	7	-7	..	..	6	9	96	..	92	0
Nepal	F	NF	3	4	6	6	..	20	33	60	pending	39	3
Pakistan	PF	NF	5	5	-6	..	2.3	9	10	57	pending	105	3
Philippines	PF	F	3	3	8	17	2.9	20	26	30	in effect	161	26
Singapore	PF	PF	4	5	-2	12	9.2	382	477	68	..	672	365
Sri Lanka	PF	PF	5	4	5	4	..	53	69	63	pending	208	8
Tajikistan	PF	NF	3	6	-1	12	..	..	28	80	..	141	1
Thailand	PF	F	4	3	9	10	3.2	20	29	30	in effect	235	56
Turkmenistan	PF	NF	5	7	-9	26	..	..	32	91	..	256	2
Uzbekistan	PF	NF	5	6	-9	7	2.7	..	14	84	in effect d	456	6
Viet Nam	NF	NF	7	6	-7	26	2.6	4	10	82	..	109	5
EUROPE	..	..	..	..	..	18	..	..	163	..	..	732	196
Albania	PF	PF	4	4	5	6	..	28	227	48	in effect	243	3
Austria	F	F	1	1	10	25	7.8	350	529	24	in effect	753	322
Belarus	PF	NF	4	6	-7	18	..	..	72	82	..	299	42
Belgium	F	F	1	2	10	25	6.6	365	541	9	in effect	793	281
Bosnia and Herzegovina	..	PF	..	4	..	5	..	..	128	53	in effect	257	11
Bulgaria	F	F	3	3	8	26	3.9	111	244	29	in effect	543	77
Croatia	PF	F	4	2	7	16	3.9	..	390	33	pending	340	..
Czech Rep	..	F	..	2	10	14	3.9	..	292	25	in effect	803	136
Denmark	F	F	1	1	10	38	9.5	654	914	9	in effect	1,139	450
Estonia	F	F	3	2	6	18	5.6	..	1,007	18	in effect	708	312
Finland	F	F	1	1	10	37	9.9	540	829	10	in effect	1,492	432 e
France	F	F	2	2	9	11	6.7	80	118	17	in effect	950	263
Germany	F	F	2	2	10	31	7.4	66	75	15	..	948	366
Greece	F	F	2	3	10	9	4.2	209	335	30	in effect	478	132
Hungary	F	F	2	2	10	8	5.3	153	329	23	in effect	690	149
Iceland	F	F	1	1	10	35	9.2	4,161	5,819	8	in effect	956	693
Ireland	F	F	1	1	10	14	7.5	596	941	16	in effect	695	233
Italy	F	F	1	2	10	9	5.5	66	98	27	in effect	878	278
Latvia	F	F	3	2	8	17	3.4	..	499	19	in effect	713	71
Lithuania	F	F	3	2	10	11	4.8	..	358	19	in effect	513	68
Macedonia, FYR	..	PF	..	4	6	7	..	..	300	46	pending	205	34
Moldova, Rep	PF	PF	4	4	7	13	3.1	..	103	59	in effect d	747	14
Netherlands	F	F	1	1	10	33	8.8	271	392	15	in effect	980	333
Norway	F	F	1	1	10	36	8.6	649	918	9	in effect	915	602
Poland	F	F	2	2	9	21	4.1	45	87	18	in effect	523	99
Portugal	F	F	1	1	10	19	6.3	234	390	15	in effect	304	359 f
Romania	PF	F	5	2	8	9	2.8	39	100	35	in effect	319	45
Russian Federation	PF	PF	3	5	7	6	2.3	..	19	60	..	418	30
Serbia and Montenegro	NF	PF	5	3	7	6	..	150	137	45	pending	297	57
Slovakia	..	F	..	2	9	14	3.7	..	359	22	in effect	966	..
Slovenia	F	F	3	2	10	12	5.2	..	904	20	pending	405	302
Spain	F	F	1	2	10	27	7.0	86	134	17	in effect	333	185
Sweden	F	F	1	1	10	43	9.0	370	559	8	in effect	932	521
Switzerland	F	F	1	1	10	22	8.4	479	673	8	pending	1,002	407
Ukraine	PF	PF	3	4	7	8	2.1	..	28	60	in effect	889	12
United Kingdom	F	F	2	2	10	17	8.3	85	128	18	in effect g	1,432	403
MIDDLE EAST & N. AFRICA	..	..	..	..	..	4	..	42	49	..	..	258	22
Afghanistan	NF	NF	7	7	-7	..	..	7	7	..	..	114	..
Algeria	PF	NF	4	5	-3	4	..	28	33	62	..	244	2
Egypt	PF	NF	5	6	-6	2	3.6	24	28	77	..	339	9
Iran, Islamic Rep	NF	NF	5	6	3	3	..	12	14	75	..	279	6
Iraq	NF	NF	7	7	-9	8	..	29	22	96	..	222	..
Israel	F	F	2	3	10	13	7.6	401	383 h	30	in effect	526	243
Jordan	PF	PF	4	5	-2	3	4.9	180	133	60	..	372	42
Kuwait	NF	PF	5	5	-7	0	..	253	369	49	..	650	101
Lebanon	PF	NF	4	5	interruption	2	..	182	291	74	..	687	..
Libyan Arab Jamahiriya	NF	NF	7	7	-7	..	..	78	78	88	..	273	4
Morocco	PF	PF	5	5	-6	1	..	37	47 i	58	..	243	13
Oman	NF	NF	6	5	-9	..	..	117	148	68	..	621	46
Saudi Arabia	NF	NF	6	7	-10	..	..	39	48	80	..	326	14
Syrian Arab Rep	NF	NF	7	7	-7	10	..	36	36	78	..	276	4
Tunisia	PF	NF	5	5	-3	12	5.3	102	125	73	..	143	42
Turkey	PF	PF	4	5	7	4	3.6	22	33	58	..	181	37
United Arab Emirates	NF	NF	5	5	-8	0	..	191	295	74	..	318	339 j
Yemen	PF	NF	5	6	-2	1	..	25	18	65	..	65	1

	Level of Freedom (free (F), partly free (PF), not free (NF))		Level of Civil Liberties (1=most free, 7= least free)		Polity Index of Democracy/ Autocracy (-10=fully auto-cratic, 10=fully democratic)	Percent of Parlia-mentary Seats Held by Women	Corruption Perceptions Index (10=least corrupt, 0= most corrupt)	Non-Governmental Organizations (NGOs) Per Million Population		Press Freedom (1-30=free, 31-60=partly free, 61-100= not free)	Freedom of Infor-mation Legisla-tion, Status in	Radios Per 1,000 Popu-lation	Internet Users Per 1,000 Popu-lation
	1991-1992	2001-2002	1991-1992	2001-2002	2000	2002	2001	1990	2000	2001	2002	1997	2001
SUB-SAHARAN AFRICA	..	..	..	..	..	12	..	40	59	..	..	198	..
Angola	PF	NF	4	6	-3	16	..	28	38	79	..	52	4
Benin	F	F	3	2	6	6	..	85	115	30	..	107	4
Botswana	F	F	2	2	9	17	6.0	283	419	30	pending	155	..
Burkina Faso	NF	PF	5	4	-3	11	..	45	58	39	..	35	2
Burundi	NF	NF	6	6	-1	20	..	52	71	77	..	69	1
Cameroon	NF	NF	6	6	-4	6	2.0	53	70	68	..	163	3
Central African Rep	PF	PF	5	5	6	7	..	90	115	69	..	80	1
Chad	NF	NF	6	5	-2	2	..	38	51	74	..	236	0
Congo	PF	PF	4	4	-6	12	..	173	198	53	..	123	..
Congo, Dem Rep	NF	NF	5	6	interregnum	..	..	17	117	86	..	386	0
Côte d'Ivoire	PF	PF	4	4	4	9	2.4	58	67	66	..	153	4
Equatorial Guinea	NF	NF	7	6	-5	5	..	270	362	80	..	427	2
Eritrea	..	NF	..	6	-6	15	..	..	40	79	..	318	3
Ethiopia	PF	PF	5	5	1	8	..	9	13	61	..	197	0
Gabon	PF	PF	3	4	-4	11	..	355	422	52	..	183	..
Gambia	F	PF	2	5	-5	..	..	359	385	65	..	165	13
Ghana	NF	F	6	3	2	9	3.4	55	60	27	pending	244	2
Guinea	NF	NF	5	5	-1	9	..	43	67	74	..	52	2
Guinea-Bissau	PF	PF	5	5	6	8	..	124	213	56	..	44	3
Kenya	NF	NF	6	5	-2	4	2.0	43	54	67	pending	109	16
Lesotho	PF	PF	4	4	in transition	11	..	187	233	46	..	53	2
Liberia	NF	NF	6	6	0	11	..	170	140	77	..	274	0
Madagascar	PF	PF	4	4	7	8	..	42	44	31	..	216	2
Malawi	NF	PF	6	3	7	9	3.2	47	59	54	pending	269	2
Mali	PF	F	4	3	6	12	..	43	55	23	..	56	3
Mauritania	NF	NF	6	5	-6	..	..	130	155	61	..	149	3
Mozambique	PF	PF	4	4	6	30	..	20	31	48	..	44	1
Namibia	F	F	3	3	6	20	5.4	108	372	34	pending	141	25
Niger	PF	PF	5	4	4	1	..	38	46	49	..	70	1
Nigeria	PF	PF	4	5	4	3	1.0	12	14	57	pending	200	..
Rwanda	NF	NF	6	6	-4	26	..	45	68	87	..	76	3
Senegal	PF	PF	3	4	8	19	2.9	103	118	39	..	141	10
Sierra Leone	PF	PF	5	5	interregnum	9	..	115	132	62	..	237	2
Somalia	NF	NF	7	7	interregnum	..	..	29	23	88	..	60	0
South Africa	PF	F	4	2	9	28	4.8	38	67	23	in effect	338	70
Sudan	NF	NF	7	7	-7	10	..	23	25	87	..	257	2
Tanzania, United Rep	NF	PF	5	4	2	22	2.2	27	32	49	pending	281	8
Togo	NF	PF	5	5	-2	5	..	124	146	68	..	227	11
Uganda	NF	PF	6	5	-4	25	1.9	33	45	42	..	127	2
Zambia	F	PF	3	4	1	12	2.6	84	105	65	pending	109	2
Zimbabwe	PF	PF	4	6	-5	10	2.9	81	114	83	in effect k	96	8
NORTH AMERICA	..	..	..	..	..	19	..	23	33	..	..	2,012	493
Canada	F	F	1	1	10	24	8.9	96	133	16	in effect	1,047	435
United States	F	F	1	1	10	14	7.6	15	22	16	in effect	2,118	500
C. AMERICA & CARIBBEAN	..	..	..	..	..	19	..	72	89	..	..	317	35
Belize	F	F	1	2	..	14	..	1,270	2,010	24	in effect	613	78
Costa Rica	F	F	1	2	10	..	4.5	300	348	17	..	274	93
Cuba	NF	NF	7	7	-7	28	..	54	89	96	..	353	11
Dominican Rep	F	F	3	2	8	15	3.1	91	106	30	..	181	22 l
El Salvador	PF	F	4	3	7	10	3.6	105	132	35	..	465	..
Guatemala	PF	PF	5	4	8	9	2.9	82	92	49	pending	79	17
Haiti	NF	NF	7	6	-2	9	..	65	74	72	..	55	4
Honduras	F	PF	3	3	7	6	2.7	108	124	43	..	412	..
Jamaica	F	F	2	3	9	16	..	287	347	17	in effect g	476	38
Mexico	PF	F	4	3	8	16	3.7	21	27	40	in effect g	330	35
Nicaragua	PF	PF	3	3	8	21	2.4	130	151	32	pending	265	..
Panama	PF	F	2	2	9	10	3.7	318	354	30	in effect d	300	..
Trinidad and Tobago	F	PF	1	3	10	17	5.3	488	625	30	in effect	532	92
SOUTH AMERICA	..	..	..	..	..	13	..	44	55	..	..	460	60
Argentina	F	PF	3	3	8	31	3.5	57	74	37	pending	681	80
Bolivia	F	F	3	3	9	10	2.0	116	141	25	pending	676	..
Brazil	F	PF	3	3	8	7	4.0	14	18	32	..	433	46
Chile	F	F	2	2	9	10	7.5	103	140	22	..	354	201
Colombia	PF	PF	4	4	7	12	3.8	36	45	60	in effect	524	27 m
Ecuador	F	PF	3	3	6	15	2.3	84	101	40	..	377	25
Guyana	PF	F	4	2	6	20	..	482	583	23	..	561	124
Paraguay	PF	PF	3	3	7	8	..	144	171	51	pending	182	11
Peru	PF	F	5	3	in transition	18	4.1	55	66	30	in effect	273	115 n
Suriname	PF	F	4	2	..	18	..	634	832	25	..	729	35
Uruguay	F	F	2	1	10	12	5.1	328	450	25	pending	603	119
Venezuela	F	F	3	5	7	10	2.8	68	76	44	..	472	53
OCEANIA	..	..	..	..	..	22	..	209	291	..	..	1,065	..
Australia	F	F	1	1	10	27	8.5	138	196	10	in effect	1,376	372 o
Fiji	PF	PF	4	3	in transition	6	..	538	797	33	pending	639	18
New Zealand	F	F	1	1	10	31	9.4	489	687	8	in effect	997	287
Papua New Guinea	F	F	3	3	10	2	..	121	149	26	pending	86	..
Solomon Islands	F	F	1	4	..	0	..	477	631	24	..	141	4
DEVELOPED	..	..	..	..	..	18	..	..	112	..	..	1,028	286
DEVELOPING	..	..	..	..	..	12	..	17	24	..	..	245	26

a. Data for China include Tibet, but not Hong Kong or Macao. **b.** Estimates are for fiscal year beginning 1 April. **c.** Data for Indonesia include East Timor. **d.** Although Freedom of Information laws exist, weaknesses in the legislation have prompted criticism. **e.** As of June, 2001. **f.** As of September, 2001. **g.** Law enacted but not yet in force. **h.** Data for Israel include the occupied territories. **i.** Data for Morocco include Western Sahara. **j.** Internet dial-up customers. **k.** The main thrust of the law passed in Zimbabwe was to give the government extensive powers to control the media by requiring the registration of journalists and prohibiting the "abuse of free expression." **l.** Data as of 30 September. **m.** Ministry of Communications' estimate. **n.** OSIPTEL estimate. **o.** Source: Australian Bureau of Statistics.

VARIABLE DEFINITIONS AND METHODOLOGY

Level of Freedom is designated by Freedom House as Free (F), Partly Free (PF), or Not Free (NF). In Free countries, a broad range of political rights and civil liberties are respected. Partly Free countries have a mixed record on political rights and civil liberties, often accompanied by corruption, weak rule of law, and the inordinate political dominance of a ruling party. In Not Free countries, basic political rights and civil liberties are denied. A country's freedom rating reflects both political rights and civil liberties, each measured on a scale of 1 to 7. If a country's combined average political rights and civil liberties ranking is between 1 and 2.5, the country is "Free." Countries with averages between 3 and 5.5 are "Partly Free"; greater than 5.5, "Not Free." For more information, please refer to the web page maintained by Freedom House: http://www.freedom house.org/research/freeworld/2001/methodology.htm.

Level of Civil Liberties is rated on a scale of 1 to 7, with 1 representing the most free and 7 representing the least free. Countries with a rating of 1 generally have an established and equitable rule of law with free economic activity. A rating of 2 indicates some deficiencies, while a rating of 3, 4, or 5 indicates varying degrees of censorship, political terror, and prevention of free association. Countries with a rating of 6 experience severely restricted freedom of expression and association coupled with political terror (e.g., political prisoners). A rating of 7 indicates virtually no freedom. Freedom House notes that a poor rating for a country "is not necessarily a comment on the intentions of the government, but may indicate real restrictions on liberty caused by non-governmental terror." To determine each rating, researchers answer a series of survey questions. The survey team may make some small adjustments for factors such as extreme violence. The 14 civil liberties questions, available on-line at http://www.freedomhouse.org/research/freeworld/2001/methodology3.htm, are classified in four categories: Freedom of Expression and Belief, Association and Organizational Rights, Rule of Law and Human Rights, and Personal Autonomy and Economic Rights.

The **Polity Index of Democracy/Autocracy** is a scale from -10 to +10 measuring the degree to which a nation is either autocratic or democratic. A score of +10 indicates a strongly democratic state; a score of -10 a strongly autocratic state. A fully democratic government has three essential elements: fully competitive political participation, institutionalized constraints on executive power, and guarantee of civil liberties to all citizens in their daily lives and in political participation. A fully autocratic system sharply restricts or suppresses competitive political participation. The chief executives are chosen by an elite group and exercise power with few institutionalized constraints. Some countries are labeled "interruption," indicating an interruption in government due to foreign occupation; "interregnum," marking an interregnum period after the complete collapse of a centralized political authority; or, "in transition," indicating a transitional or provisional government in control as new institutions are planned. The Polity index does not measure impacts unless they affect the central governing structure. A complete explanation of the index is available in the Polity IV Project Dataset User's Manual, on-line at http://www.bsos.umd.edu/cidcm/inscr/polity/polreg.htm.

Percent of Parliamentary Seats Held by Women is calculated based on the total number of seats in parliament and the number of seats occupied by women. When there is both an Upper House (Senate) and a Lower House of parliament, the total number of women in both houses is divided by the total number of seats in both houses. Data are current as of March 1, 2002. The Interparliamentary Union compiles these data based on information provided by national parliaments.

The **Corruption Perceptions Index** (CPI) measures the degree to which corruption is perceived to exist among public officials and politicians. Ratings range in value from 10 (least corrupt) to 0 (most corrupt). The survey measures public sector corruption—the abuse of public office for private gain. In the CPI, data from 14 surveys are combined to measure the perceptions of local residents, expatriates, business people, academics, and risk analysts. Assessments from the past three years (1999–2001) are combined. A country is included in the CPI only if there are data available from three or more surveys. For further information, please consult: J.G. Lambsdorff. 2001. Background Paper to the 2001 Corruption Perceptions Index. Available on-line at http://www.transparency.org/cpi/2001/dnld/methodology.pdf.

Nongovernmental Organizations (NGOs) Per Million Population is the number of NGOs with offices or members in a particular country divided by the population. NGOs are identified by the Union of International Associations based on seven organizational aspects: aims, membership, structure, officers, finance, relations with other organizations, and activities. The following types of organizations are included in this data set: federations of international organizations; universal membership organizations; intercontinental membership organizations; regionally defined membership organizations; organizations emanating from places, persons, or other bodies; and organizations having a special form, including foundations and funds.

Press Freedom is an index, defined by Freedom House as "the degree to which each country permits the free flow of information" on a scale of 1 to 100. Countries with a score between 1 and 30 are considered to have a "Free" media; 31 to 60, "Partly Free"; and 61 to 100, "Not Free." Freedom House emphasizes that this survey does not measure press responsibility; rather, it measures the degree of freedom in the flow of information. Data are collected from overseas correspondents, staff travel, international visitors, the findings of human rights organizations, specialists in geographic and geopolitical areas, the reports of governments, and a variety of domestic and international news media. The final index measures three separate categories of influence on the media: national laws and administrative decisions; censorship and intimidation; and quotas, licensing biases, or government funding.

Freedom of Information (FOI) Legislation requires disclosure of government records to the public. There are now 48 countries with comprehensive general applicability FOI laws, plus a dozen or so countries with FOI-related constitutional provisions that can be used to access information. A country's guarantee of public access to information is classified in one of three categories:

In Effect: These countries legally guarantee public access to government records through constitutional provisions or FOI legislation.

Pending: Thirty additional countries are considering adopting freedom of information acts.

No Data: Marked by "..", these are countries where no FOI legislation exists or no data are available concerning FOIA status.

Data are collected by Privacy International on a country-by-country basis and were last updated in July, 2002.

Radios Per 1,000 Population is the number of radio receivers used for broadcast to the general public, divided by a country's population in thousands. Private sets installed in public places are also included, as well as communal receivers. The World Bank obtains their data from statistical surveys conducted by the United Nations Educational, Scientific, and Cultural Organization (UNESCO).

Internet Users Per 1,000 Population measures the number of people per thousand of a country's population who have used the internet at any point in time during a specific year. Data are supplied by annual questionnaires sent to telecommunication authorities and operating companies. These results are supplemented by annual reports and statistical yearbooks of telecommunication ministries, regulators, operators, and industry associations. In some cases, estimates are derived from International Telecommunications Union background documents or other references.

FREQUENCY OF UPDATE BY DATA PROVIDERS

All data sets are updated annually, with the exception of the parliamentary and Internet data. These data sets are updated every 2–4 months. Data on radio receivers have not been collected on a global scale since 1999 (survey year 1997), when UNESCO discontinued their Statistical Yearbook.

DATA RELIABILITY AND CAUTIONARY NOTES

Many of the data in this table are index calculations and therefore contain an unavoidable amount of subjectivity. Indices can measure ideas and behaviors instead of a discrete physical quantity. While these data can illustrate rough comparisons and trends over time, rigid score comparisons and rankings are discouraged.

Polity Index of Democracy/Autocracy. The Polity IV data are subject to substantial cross-checking and inter-coder reliability checks. The least reliable calculations are typically the most recent, due to "the fluidity of real-time political dynamics and the effects this immediacy may have on the assignment of Polity codes in a semi-annual research cycle".

Percent of Parliamentary Seats Held by Women. Data change with each national election; for the most recent statistics, please consult the IPU website at http://www.ipu.org/wmn-e/classif.htm. Some governments and political parties have established formal or informal quotas for women in various legislative positions. For more information on gender quotas, please consult the International Institute for Democracy and Electoral Assistance (IDEA) on-line at http://www.idea.int/gender/quotas.htm.

Corruption Perceptions Index (CPI). CPI is based solely on perceptions instead of hard empirical data such as cross-country comparisons of prosecutions, or media coverage of corruption. Empirical data are not used because they may measure the extent of anti-corruption efforts instead of the extent of corruption. A spreadsheet with standard deviations, permutation test results, and a list of the surveys used for each country is available on-line at http://www.gwdg.de/~uwvw/2001.htm.

Nongovernmental Organizations Per Million Population. The compilation of such a massive data set inevitably leads to misreporting and underreporting of organizations. Many of the data are self-reported and not evaluated for accuracy by the Union of International Associations. Government-controlled NGOs, criticized for their ability to benefit government officials and subvert the original purpose of a non-governmental organization, may be included in some country totals. Regional totals may include double counting of NGOs present in more than one country. Comparisons between countries should be made with care, as actual estimates of the number of NGOs vary widely.

Freedom of Information Legislation. While the FOI data have been thoroughly researched, there are unavoidable difficulties in assigning each country to one of three categories. Some countries have laws guaranteeing access, but the laws are not enforced. Still others guarantee access to government documents in specific sectors, but exclude access in other sectors. For a complete description of the FOI status for each country, please refer to the Freedom of Information web site maintained by Privacy International http://www.privacy international.org/issues/foia.

Radios Per 1,000 People. In some countries, definitions, classifications, and methods of enumeration do not entirely conform to UNESCO standards. In addition, many countries impose radio license fees to help pay for public broadcasting, discouraging radio owners from declaring ownership.

SOURCES

Level of Freedom and Civil Liberties: Freedom House. 2001. Freedom in the World 2001–2002: The Democracy Gap. New York: Freedom House. Data available on-line at http://www.freedomhouse.org/research/survey2002.htm. **Polity Index:** Polity IV Project. 2002. Polity IV Project: Political Regime Characteristics and Transitions. College Park: University of Maryland. Available on-line at http://www.bsos.umd.edu/cidcm/inscr/polity/index.htm. **Parliamentary Seats Held by Women:** Inter-Parliamentary Union (IPU). 2002. Women in National Parliament. Geneva: IPU. Available on-line at http://www.ipu.org/wmn-e/classif.htm. **Corruption Perceptions Index:** Transparency International. 2001. 2001 Corruption Perceptions Index. Berlin: Transparency International. Available on-line at http://www.transparency.org/cpi/2001/cpi2001.html. **NGOs Per Million Population:** Center for the Study of Global Governance. 2001. Global Civil Society 2001. Oxford: Oxford University Press. Available on-line at http://www.lse.ac.uk/Depts/global/Yearbook/. Data were collected from the Union of International Associations' Yearbook of International Organizations by the Center for the Study of Global Governance. **Press Freedom:** Freedom House. 2002. The Annual Survey of Press Freedom 2002. New York: Freedom House. Available on-line at http://www.freedomhouse.org/pfs2002/pfs2002.pdf. **Freedom of Information Legislation:** David Banisar. 2002. Freedom of Information and Access to Government Records Around the World. Washington, D.C.: Privacy International. Available on-line at http://www.privacyinternational.org/issues/foia/foia-survey.html. **Radios Per 1,000 People:** Development Data Group, World Bank. 2002. World Development Indicators 2002 Online. Washington, D.C.: The World Bank. Available at http://www.worldbank.org/data/. **Internet Users Per 1,000 People:** International Telecommunications Union (ITU). 2002. World Telecommunications Indicators 2002. Geneva: ITU. Available on-line at http://www.itu.int/ITU-D/ict/publications/world/world.html.

Global Governance: Participation in Major Multilateral Agreements

Sources: Office of the United Nations High Commissioner for Human Rights, Convention on the International Trade in Endangered Species, United Nations Framework Convention on Climate Change, Convention on Biodiversity, United Nations Convention to Combat Desertification, Stockholm Convention on Persistent Organic Pollutants, United Nations Economic Commission for Europe, World Trade Organization, United Nations Commission on Sustainable Development, International Council for Local Environmental Initiatives.

	Covenant on Civil and Political Rights	Covenant on Economic, Social, and Cultural Rights	CITES {a} (species trade)	UNFCCC {b} (climate change)	Kyoto Protocol (CO$_2$)	CBD {c} (bio-diversity)	Bio-Safety Protocol	CCD {d} (desertification)	Stockholm Convention (POPs) {e}	Aarhus Convention	Year of WTO {f} Membership (or status of membership)	National Reporting Status in 2002 (n.r.= non-reporting)	Municipalities 1996	Municipalities 2001
WORLD													1812	6416
ASIA (EXCL. MIDDLE EAST)													87	461
Armenia	1993	1993	n.p.	1993	n.p.	1993	n.p.	1997	[2001]	2001	observer	pending	..	..
Azerbaijan	1992	1992	1998	1995	2000	2000	n.p.	1998	n.p.	2000	observer	n.r.	..	..
Bangladesh	2000	1998	1981	1994	2001	1994	[2000]	1996	[2001]	n.p.	1995	submitted	..	2
Bhutan	n.p.	n.p.	2002	1995	2002	1995	2002	n.p.	n.p.	n.p.	observer	n.r.	..	..
Cambodia	1992	1992	1997	1995	2002	1995	n.p.	1997	[2001]	n.p.	observer	n.r.	..	..
China	[1998]	2001	1981	1993	2002	1993	[2000]	1997	[2001]	n.p.	2001	pending	14	25
Georgia	1994	1994	1996	1994	1999	1994	n.p.	1999	[2001]	2000	2000	pending	..	..
India	1979	1979	1976	1993	2002	1994	[2001]	1996	[2002]	n.p.	1995	pending	20	14
Indonesia	n.p.	n.p.	1978	1994	[1998]	1994	[2000]	1998	[2001]	n.p.	1995	submitted	6	8
Japan	1979	1979	1980	1993	2002	1993	n.p.	1998	2002	n.p.	1995	submitted	26	110
Kazakhstan	n.p.	n.p.	2000	1995	[1999]	1994	n.p.	1997	[2001]	2001	observer	submitted	..	..
Korea, Dem People's Rep	1981	1981	n.p.	1994	n.p.	1994	[2001]	n.p.	2002	n.p.	n.p.	n.r.	..	..
Korea, Rep	1990	1990	1993	1993	[1998]	1994	[2000]	1999	[2001]	n.p.	1995	submitted	9	172
Kyrgyzstan	1994	1994	n.p.	2000	n.p.	1996	n.p.	1997	[2002]	2001	1998	pending	..	..
Lao People's Dem Rep	[2000]	[2000]	n.p.	1995	n.p.	1996	n.p.	1996	[2002]	n.p.	observer	n.r.	..	..
Malaysia	n.p.	n.p.	1977	1994	2002	1994	[2000]	1997	[2002]	n.p.	1995	pending	..	9
Mongolia	1974	1974	1996	1993	1999	1993	n.p.	1996	[2002]	n.p.	1997	pending	..	22
Myanmar	n.p.	n.p.	1997	1994	n.p.	1994	[2001]	1997	n.p.	n.p.	1995	submitted	..	..
Nepal	1991	1991	1975	1994	n.p.	1993	[2001]	1996	[2002]	n.p.	observer	submitted	1	4
Pakistan	n.p.	n.p.	1976	1994	n.p.	1994	[2001]	1997	[2001]	n.p.	1995	submitted	..	1
Philippines	1986	1974	1981	1994	[1998]	1993	[2000]	2000	[2001]	n.p.	1995	submitted	3	28
Singapore	n.p.	n.p.	1986	1997	n.p.	1995	n.p.	1999	[2001]	n.p.	1995	submitted	..	1
Sri Lanka	1980	1980	1979	1993	2002	1994	[2000]	1998	[2001]	n.p.	1995	submitted	..	24
Tajikistan	1999	1999	n.p.	1998	n.p.	1997	n.p.	1997	[2002]	2001	observer	submitted	..	..
Thailand	1996	1999	1983	1994	2002	[1992]	n.p.	2001	[2002]	n.p.	1995	submitted	6	21
Turkmenistan	1997	1997	n.p.	1995	1999	1996	n.p.	1996	n.p.	1999	n.p.	n.r.	..	..
Uzbekistan	1995	1995	1997	1993	1999	1995	n.p.	1995	n.p.	n.p.	observer	submitted	..	..
Viet Nam	1982	1982	1994	1994	[1998]	1994	n.p.	1998	2002	n.p.	observer	pending	2	20
EUROPE													1576	5291
Albania	1991	1991	n.p.	1994	n.p.	1994	n.p.	2000	[2001]	2001	2000	pending	1	7
Austria	1978	1978	1982	1994	2002	1994	2002	1997	2002	[1998]	1995	submitted	2	64
Belarus	1973	1973	1995	2000	n.p.	1993	2002	2001	n.p.	2000	observer	pending	..	..
Belgium	1983	1983	1983	1996	2002	1996	[2000]	1997	[2001]	[1998]	1995	submitted	5	106
Bosnia and Herzegovina	1993	1992	2002	2000	n.p.	2002	n.p.	2002	[2001]	n.p.	observer	n.r.	..	1
Bulgaria	1970	1970	1991	1995	2002	1996	2000	2001	[2001]	[1998]	1996	submitted	..	22
Croatia	1992	1991	2000	1996	[1999]	1996	2002	2000	[2001]	[1998]	2000	submitted	1	20
Czech Rep	1993	1993	1993	1993	2001	1993	2001	2000	2002	[1998]	1995	submitted	..	42
Denmark	1972	1972	1977	1993	2002	1993	2002	1995	[2001]	2000	1995	pending	147	216
Estonia	1991	1991	1992	1994	[1998]	1994	[2000]	n.p.	n.p.	2001	1999	pending	1	29
Finland	1975	1975	1976	1994	2002	1994	[2000]	1995	2002	[1998]	1995	submitted	88	303
France	1980	1980	1978	1994	2002 g	1994	[2000]	1997	[2001]	2002	1995	submitted	15	69
Germany	1973	1973	1976	1993	2002	1993	[2000]	1996	2002	[1998]	1995	pending	30	2042
Greece	1997	1985	1992	1994	2002	1994	[2000]	1997	[2001]	[1998]	1995	submitted	13	39
Hungary	1974	1974	1985	1994	2002	1994	[2000]	1999	[2001]	2001	1995	submitted	12	9
Iceland	1979	1979	2000	1993	2002	1994	[2001]	1997	2002	[1998]	1995	submitted	..	37
Ireland	1989	1989	2002	1994	2002	1996	[2000]	1997	[2001]	[1998]	1995		22	29
Italy	1978	1978	1979	1994	2002	1994	[2000]	1997	[2001]	2001	1995	submitted	22	429
Latvia	1992	1992	1997	1995	2002	1995	n.p.	n.p.	[2001]	2002	1999	pending	1	5
Lithuania	1991	1991	2001	1995	[1998]	1996	[2000]	n.p.	[2002]	2002	2001	submitted	..	14
Macedonia, FYR	1994	1994	2000	1998	n.p.	1997	[2000]	2002	[2001]	1999	observer	pending	..	..
Moldova, Rep	1993	1993	2001	1995	n.p.	1995	[2001]	1999	[2001]	1999	2001	pending	..	..
Netherlands	1978	1978	1984	1993	2002	1994	2002	1995	2002	[1998]	1995	submitted	143	100
Norway	1972	1972	1976	1993	2002	1993	2001	1996	2002	[1998]	1995	submitted	415	283
Poland	1977	1977	1989	1994	[1998]	1996	[2000]	2001	[2001]	2002	1995	submitted	3	70
Portugal	1978	1978	1980	1993	2002	1993	[2000]	1996	[2001]	[1998]	1995	submitted	10	27
Romania	1974	1974	1994	1994	2001	1994	[2000]	1998	[2001]	2000	1995	submitted	2	12
Russian Federation	1973	1973	1992	1994	[1999]	1995	n.p.	n.p.	[2002]	n.p.	observer	submitted	5	29
Serbia and Montenegro	2001	2001	2002	2001	n.p.	2002	n.p.	n.p.	[2002]	n.p.	observer	submitted	..	20
Slovakia	1993	1993	1993	1994	2002	1994	[2000]	2002	2002	n.p.	1995	submitted	3	30
Slovenia	1992	1992	2000	1995	2002	1996	[2000]	2001	[2001]	[1998]	1995	submitted	1	3
Spain	1977	1977	1986	1993	2002	1993	2002	1996	[2001]	[1998]	1995	submitted	29	359
Sweden	1971	1971	1974	1993	2002	1993	2002	1995	2002	[1998]	1995	submitted	307	289
Switzerland	1992	1992	1974	1993	[1998]	1994	2002	1996	[2001]	[1998]	1995	pending	2	83
Ukraine	1973	1973	1999	1997	[1999]	1995	n.p.	2002	[2001]	1999	observer	submitted	10	9
United Kingdom	1976	1976	1976	1993	2002	1994	[2000]	1996	[2001]	[1998]	1995	pending	285	425
MIDDLE EAST & N. AFRICA													8	98
Afghanistan	1983	1983	1985	2002	n.p.	2002	n.p.	1995	n.p.	n.p.	n.p.	n.r.	..	..
Algeria	1989	1989	1983	1993	n.p.	1995	[2000]	1996	[2001]	n.p.	observer	pending	..	3
Egypt	1982	1982	1978	1994	[1999]	1994	[2000]	1995	[2002]	n.p.	1995	submitted	1	7
Iran, Islamic Rep	1975	1975	1976	1996	n.p.	1996	[2001]	1997	[2001]	n.p.	pending	pending	..	2
Iraq	1971	1971	n.p.	n.p.	n.p.	n.p.	n.p.	n.p.	n.p.	n.p.	n.p.	pending	..	..
Israel	1991	1991	1979	1996	[1998]	1995	n.p.	1996	[2001]	n.p.	1995	submitted	..	3
Jordan	1975	1975	1978	1993	n.p.	1993	[2000]	1996	[2002]	n.p.	2000	submitted	..	4
Kuwait	1996	1996	2002	1994	n.p.	2002	n.p.	1997	[2001]	n.p.	1995	n.r.	..	1
Lebanon	1972	1972	n.p.	1994	n.p.	1994	n.p.	1996	[2001]	n.p.	observer	pending	..	6
Libyan Arab Jamahiriya	1970	1970	n.p.	1999	n.p.	2001	n.p.	1996	n.p.	n.p.	n.p.	n.r.	..	2
Morocco	1979	1979	1975	1995	2002	1995	[2000]	1996	[2001]	n.p.	1995	submitted	3	5
Oman	n.p.	n.p.	n.p.	1995	n.p.	1995	n.p.	1996	[2002]	n.p.	2000	n.r.	..	1
Saudi Arabia	n.p.	n.p.	1996	1994	n.p.	2001	n.p.	1997	[2002]	n.p.	observer	submitted	..	4
Syrian Arab Rep	1969	1969	n.p.	1996	n.p.	1996	n.p.	1997	[2002]	n.p.	n.p.	submitted	..	2
Tunisia	1969	1969	1974	1993	n.p.	1993	[2001]	1995	[2001]	n.p.	1995	submitted	1	1
Turkey	[2000]	[2000]	1996	n.p.	n.p.	1997	[2000]	1998	[2001]	n.p.	1995	submitted	3	50
United Arab Emirates	n.p.	n.p.	1990	1995	n.p.	2000	n.p.	1998	2002	n.p.	1996	n.r.	..	2
Yemen	1987	1987	1997	1996	n.p.	1996	n.p.	1997	[2001]	n.p.	observer	n.r.	..	2

	Year of Ratification of Major Multilateral Agreements (year in brackets = country is signatory to treaty; "n.p."= country is not a party to treaty)										Year of WTO {f} Member-ship (or status of mem-bership)	Agenda 21 Process		
	Covenant on Civil and Political Rights	Covenant on Economic, Social, and Cultural Rights	CITES {a} (species trade)	UNFCCC {b} (climate change)	Kyoto Proto-col (CO_2)	CBD {c} (bio-diver-sity)	Bio-Safety Proto-col	CCD {d} (desert-ification)	Stock-holm Con-vention (POPs) {e}	Aarhus Con-vention		National Reporting Status in 2002 (n.r.= non-reporting)	Number of Municipalities Involved in Local Agenda 21 — 1996	2001
SUB-SAHARAN AFRICA													**35**	**133**
Angola	1992	1992	n.p.	2000	n.p.	1998	n.p.	1997	n.p.	n.p.	1996	n.r.	..	..
Benin	1992	1992	1984	1994	2002	1994	[2000]	1996	[2001]	n.p.	1996	submitted	..	1
Botswana	2000	n.p.	1977	1994	n.p.	1995	2002	1996	[2001]	n.p.	1995	pending	..	..
Burkina Faso	1999	1999	1989	1993	n.p.	1993	[2000]	1996	[2001]	n.p.	1995	submitted	..	..
Burundi	1990	1990	1988	1997	2001	1997	n.p.	1997	[2002]	n.p.	1995	n.r.	..	2
Cameroon	1984	1984	1981	1994	2002	1994	[2001]	1997	[2001]	n.p.	1995	pending	..	1
Central African Rep	1981	1981	1980	1995	n.p.	1995	[2000]	1996	[2002]	n.p.	1995	n.r.	..	..
Chad	1995	1995	1989	1994	n.p.	1994	[2000]	1996	[2002]	n.p.	1996	n.r.	..	..
Congo	1983	1983	1983	1996	n.p.	1996	[2000]	1999	[2001]	n.p.	1997	n.r.	..	..
Congo, Dem Rep	1976	1976	1976	1995	n.p.	1994	n.p.	1997	n.p.	n.p.	1997	submitted	..	2
Côte d'Ivoire	1992	1992	1994	1994	n.p.	1994	n.p.	1997	[2001]	n.p.	1995	pending	..	..
Equatorial Guinea	1987	1987	1992	2000	2000	1994	n.p.	1997	n.p.	n.p.	n.p.	n.r.	..	..
Eritrea	2002	2001	1994	1995	n.p.	1996	n.p.	1996	n.p.	n.p.	n.p.	n.r.	..	..
Ethiopia	1993	1993	1989	1994	n.p.	1994	[2000]	1997	[2002]	n.p.	observer	n.r.	..	..
Gabon	1983	1983	1989	1998	n.p.	1997	n.p.	1996	[2002]	n.p.	1995	n.r.	..	1
Gambia	1979	1978	1977	1994	2001	1994	[2000]	1996	[2001]	n.p.	1996	submitted	..	..
Ghana	2000	2000	1975	1995	n.p.	1994	n.p.	1996	[2001]	n.p.	1995	submitted	1	3
Guinea	1978	1978	1981	1993	2000	1993	[2000]	1997	[2001]	n.p.	1995	n.r.	..	..
Guinea-Bissau	[2000]	1992	1990	1995	n.p.	1995	n.p.	1995	[2002]	n.p.	1995	pending	..	..
Kenya	1972	1972	1978	1994	n.p.	1994	2002	1997	[2001]	n.p.	1995	pending	4	11
Lesotho	1992	1992	[1974]	1995	2000	1995	2001	1995	2002	n.p.	1995	n.r.	..	..
Liberia	[1967]	[1967]	1981	[1992]	n.p.	2000	2002	1998	2002	n.p.	n.p.	n.r.	..	..
Madagascar	1971	1971	1975	1999	n.p.	1996	[2000]	1997	[2001]	n.p.	1995	submitted	..	5
Malawi	1993	1993	1982	1994	2001	1994	[2000]	1996	[2002]	n.p.	1995	submitted	6	4
Mali	1974	1974	1994	1994	2002	1995	2002	1995	[2001]	n.p.	1995	n.r.	..	2
Mauritania	n.p.	n.p.	1998	1994	n.p.	1996	n.p.	1996	[2001]	n.p.	1995	n.r.	..	1
Mozambique	1993	n.p.	1981	1995	n.p.	1995	2002	1997	[2001]	n.p.	1995	n.r.	2	2
Namibia	1994	1994	1990	1995	n.p.	1997	n.p.	1997	n.p.	n.p.	1995	submitted	..	5
Niger	1986	1986	1975	1995	[1998]	1995	[2000]	1996	[2001]	n.p.	1996	pending	..	..
Nigeria	1993	1993	1974	1994	n.p.	1994	[2000]	1997	[2001]	n.p.	1995	pending	1	5
Rwanda	1975	1975	1980	1998	n.p.	1996	[2000]	1998	2002	n.p.	1996	n.r.	..	1
Senegal	1978	1978	1977	1994	2001	1994	[2000]	1995	[2001]	n.p.	1995	submitted	1	3
Sierra Leone	1996	1996	1994	1995	n.p.	1994	n.p.	1997	n.p.	n.p.	1995	n.r.	..	..
Somalia	1990	1990	1985	n.p.	n.p.	n.p.	n.p.	2002	n.p.	n.p.	n.p.	n.r.	..	..
South Africa	1998	[1994]	1975	1997	2002	1995	n.p.	1997	2002	n.p.	1995	pending	10	20
Sudan	1976	1986	1982	1993	n.p.	1995	n.p.	1995	[2001]	n.p.	observer	n.r.	..	1
Tanzania, United Rep	1976	1976	1979	1996	2002	1996	n.p.	1997	[2001]	n.p.	1995	pending	3	13
Togo	1984	1984	1978	1995	n.p.	1995	[2000]	1995	[2001]	n.p.	1995	n.r.	..	2
Uganda	1995	1987	1991	1993	2002	1993	2001	1997	n.p.	n.p.	1995	submitted	2	5
Zambia	1984	1984	1980	1993	[1998]	1993	n.p.	1996	[2001]	n.p.	1995	n.r.	1	4
Zimbabwe	1991	1991	1981	1992	n.p.	1994	[2001]	1997	[2001]	n.p.	1995	pending	4	39
NORTH AMERICA													**26**	**101**
Canada	1976	1976	1975	1992	[1998]	1992	[2001]	1995	2001	n.p.	1995	pending	7	14
United States	1992	[1977]	1974	1992	[1998]	[1993]	n.p.	2000	[2001]	n.p.	1995	submitted	19	87
C. AMERICA & CARIBBEAN													**..**	**26**
Belize	1996	[2000]	1986	1994	n.p.	1993	n.p.	1998	[2002]	n.p.	1995	n.r.	..	..
Costa Rica	1968	1968	1975	1994	2002	1994	[2000]	1998	[2002]	n.p.	1995	pending	..	4
Cuba	n.p.	n.p.	1990	1994	2002	1994	2002	1997	[2001]	n.p.	1995	submitted	..	2
Dominican Rep	1978	1978	1986	1998	2002	1996	n.p.	1997	[2001]	n.p.	1995	pending	..	..
El Salvador	1979	1979	1987	1995	1998	1994	[2000]	1997	[2001]	n.p.	1995	submitted	..	..
Guatemala	1992	1988	1979	1995	1999	1995	n.p.	1998	[2002]	n.p.	1995	n.r.	..	..
Haiti	1991	n.p.	n.p.	1996	n.p.	1996	[2000]	1996	[2001]	n.p.	1996	submitted	..	..
Honduras	1997	1981	1985	1995	2000	1995	[2000]	1997	[2002]	n.p.	1995	submitted	..	6
Jamaica	1975	1975	1997	1995	1999	1995	[2001]	1997	[2001]	n.p.	1995	pending	..	5
Mexico	1981	1981	1991	1993	2000	1993	2002	1995	[2001]	n.p.	1995	submitted	..	2
Nicaragua	1980	1980	1977	1995	1999	1995	2002	1998	[2001]	n.p.	1995	submitted	..	5
Panama	1977	1977	1978	1995	1999	1995	2002	1996	[2001]	n.p.	1997	pending	..	..
Trinidad and Tobago	1978	1978	1984	1994	1999	1996	2000	2000	n.p.	n.p.	1995	n.r.	..	1
SOUTH AMERICA													**34**	**93**
Argentina	1986	1986	1981	1994	2001	1994	[2000]	1997	[2001]	n.p.	1995	submitted	..	1
Bolivia	1982	1982	1979	1994	1999	1994	2002	1996	[2001]	n.p.	1995	pending	13	1
Brazil	1992	1992	1975	1994	2002	1994	n.p.	1997	[2001]	n.p.	1995	submitted	8	36
Chile	1972	1972	1975	1994	2002	1994	[2000]	1997	[2001]	n.p.	1995	submitted	1	15
Colombia	1969	1969	1981	1995	2001	1994	[2000]	1999	[2001]	n.p.	1995	submitted	4	6
Ecuador	1969	1969	1975	1993	2000	1993	[2000]	1995	[2001]	n.p.	1996	submitted	3	13
Guyana	1977	1977	1977	1994	n.p.	1994	n.p.	1997	n.p.	n.p.	1995	pending	..	1
Paraguay	1992	1992	1976	1994	1999	1994	[2001]	1997	[2001]	n.p.	1995	submitted	..	..
Peru	1978	1978	1975	1993	[1998]	1993	[2000]	1995	[2001]	n.p.	1995	submitted	5	17
Suriname	1976	1976	1980	1996	n.p.	1996	n.p.	2000	[2002]	n.p.	1995	pending	..	..
Uruguay	1970	1970	1975	1994	2001	1993	[2001]	1999	[2001]	n.p.	1995	pending	..	..
Venezuela	1978	1978	1977	1994	n.p.	1994	2002	1998	[2001]	n.p.	1995	submitted	..	3
OCEANIA													**44**	**213**
Australia	1980	1975	1976	1992	[1998]	1993	n.p.	2000	[2001]	n.p.	1995	pending	40	176
Fiji	n.p.	n.p.	1997	1993	1998	1993	2001	1998	2001	n.p.	1996	submitted	..	..
New Zealand	1978	1978	1989	1993	[1998]	1993	[2000]	2000	[2001]	n.p.	1995	pending	3	37
Papua New Guinea	n.p.	n.p.	1975	1993	2002	1993	n.p.	2000	[2001]	n.p.	1996	n.r.	1	..
Solomon Islands	n.p.	1982	n.p.	1994	[1998]	1995	n.p.	1999	n.p.	n.p.	1996		..	..
DEVELOPED													**1681**	**5738**
DEVELOPING													**131**	**678**

Data in brackets indicate that a treaty is not yet ratified and show the year in which a country has signed a treaty. Years without brackets show the year of ratification of a major multilateral agreement. This table shows the status of agreements as of September 2002. **a.** Convention on International Trade in Endangered Species. **b.** The United Nations Framework Convention on Climate Change. **c.** The United Nations Convention on Biological Diversity. **d.** The United Nations Convention to Combat Desertification. **e.** Persistent Organic Pollutants. **f.** The World Trade Organization. **g.** Excludes overseas territories.

239

TECHNICAL NOTES

The ten treaties described below are a small subset of the hundreds of multilateral agreements drafted in recent decades at the global level. The table indicates the year that a country has either signed or ratified a particular agreement. By signing a treaty, a state recognizes the authentic text, intends to complete the procedures for becoming legally bound by it, and is committed not to act against the treaty's objectives before ratification. Ratification (or its equivalents of acceptance, approval, or accession) binds the state to observe the treaty. Depending on a country's system of governance, signing the treaty may be simply an executive decision while ratification requires legislative approval. Treaties vary both in international levels of participation and the extent to which they are legally binding. To a large extent, compliance lies with the individual countries and depends on informed self-interest, peer pressure from other countries, and public opinion. Effectiveness of any international convention or treaty is determined not only by the number of country ratifications, but also by the rigor of its implementation, monitoring, and enforcement.

The International Covenant on Civil and Political Rights.
This covenant details the basic civil and political rights of individuals and nations. The rights of nations include: the right to self determination, and the right to own, trade, and dispose of their property freely, and not be deprived of their means of subsistence. Among the rights of individuals are the right to life; the right to liberty and freedom of movement; the right to equality before the law; the right to presumption of innocence until proven guilty; the right to appeal a conviction; the right to privacy; freedom of thought, conscience, and religion; freedom of opinion and expression; and freedom of assembly and association. For more information, please see http://www.hrweb.org/legal/undocs.html.

The International Covenant on Economic, Social, and Cultural Rights. This covenant describes the basic economic, social, and cultural rights of individuals and nations, including the rights to self-determination; wages sufficient to support a minimum standard of living; equal pay for equal work; equal opportunity for advancement; form trade unions; strike; paid or otherwise compensated maternity leave; free primary education and accessible education at all levels; and copyright, patent, and trademark protection for intellectual property. In addition, this convention forbids exploitation of children, and requires all nations to cooperate to end world hunger. For more information, please see http://www.hrweb.org/legal/undocs.html.

CITES: The Convention on International Trade in Endangered Species of Wild Fauna and Flora, or CITES, is an international agreement between governments to ensure that the survival of wild animals and plants is not threatened by international trade. It has been in force for almost 30 years; today, it accords varying degrees of protection to more than 30,000 species of animals and plants, whether they are traded as live specimens, fur coats, or dried herbs. CITES is legally binding on countries that have joined the Convention and provides a framework to be respected by each Party, which has to adopt its own domestic legislation to make sure that CITES is implemented at the national level. More information is available at http://www.cites.org.

UNFCCC: The United Nations Framework Convention on Climate Change (UNFCCC) is the centerpiece of global efforts to combat global warming. Adopted in 1992 at the Rio Earth Summit, its ultimate objective is the "stabilization of greenhouse gas concentrations in the atmosphere at a level that would prevent dangerous anthropogenic (human-made) interference with the climate system. Such a level should be achieved within a

time-frame sufficient to allow ecosystems to adapt naturally to climate change, to ensure that food production is not threatened and to enable economic development to proceed in a sustainable manner." For more information, please consult the UNFCCC Secretariat at http://www.unfccc.int/resource/docs/convkp/conveng.pdf.

Kyoto Protocol: The Kyoto Protocol was established in 1997 by the third session of the Conference of Parties (COP-3) to the UNFCCC. With ratification, developed countries commit themselves to reducing their collective emissions of six greenhouse gases. Emissions need to be at least 5 percent lower than 1990 levels by a deadline ranging from 2008 to 2012. Compared to emissions levels that would be expected by 2010 without emissions-control measures, the Protocol target represents a 30 percent cut. Both developed and developing countries agree to take measures to limit emissions and promote adaptation to future climate change impacts; submit information on their national climate change program and inventories; promote technology transfer; cooperate on scientific and public research; and promote public awareness, education, and training. The rules for entry into force of the Kyoto Protocol require 55 Parties to the Convention to ratify the Protocol, including Annex I Parties accounting for 55 percent of that group's carbon dioxide emissions in 1990. As of September 2002, 94 countries had ratified the Protocol, but only 37 percent of Annex I (industrialized country) emissions were represented. More information is available in A Guide to the Climate Change Convention Process, on-line at http://www.unfccc.int/resource/process/guideprocess-p.pdf.

CBD: The United Nations Convention on Biological Diversity is one of the key agreements adopted at the 1992 Earth Summit in Rio de Janeiro. The Convention establishes three main goals: the conservation of biodiversity, sustainable use of the components of biodiversity, and sharing the benefits arising from the commercial and other utilization of genetic resources in a fair and equitable way. The convention is legally binding; countries that join it are obliged to implement its provisions, such as reporting on what has been done to implement the accord and the effectiveness of these activities. The national reports, particularly when seen together, are one of the key tools for tracking progress in meeting the Convention's objectives. More information is available on-line at http://www.biodiv.org/doc/publications/guide.asp.

Biosafety Protocol: Adopted in January 2000 as a subsidiary agreement to the CBD, the Cartagena Protocol on Biosafety allows governments to signal whether or not they are willing to accept imports of agricultural commodities that include Living Modified Organisms (LMOs). Living Modified Organisms— often known as genetically modified organisms (GMOs)—are becoming part of an increasing number of products, including foods and food additives, beverages, drugs, adhesives, and fuels. In addition, the treaty deals with access to and sharing of the benefits from commercial use of genetic material, such as pharmaceutical products. More information is available on-line at http://www.biodiv.org/doc/publications/guide.asp.

CCD: The United Nations Convention to Combat Desertification is an international Convention dedicated to addressing the problems of land degradation in the world's drylands, caused primarily by human activities and climatic variations. Since the Convention entered into force in 1996, countries affected by desertification are implementing the Convention by developing and carrying out national, sub-regional, and regional action programs. The Convention states that these programs must adopt a democratic, bottom-up approach designed to allow local people to help themselves reverse land degradation. More information is available at http://www.unccd.int/main.php.

Stockholm Convention: The Stockholm Convention on Persistent Organic Pollutants (POPs) is a global treaty to protect human health and the environment from POPs, which remain intact in the environment for long periods of time, become widely distributed geographically, accumulate in the fatty tissue of living organisms, and are toxic to humans and wildlife. The Convention was adopted in May 2001. Upon signature of the Convention, the first step toward implementation is the development of national action plans to eliminate or reduce the release of POPs into the environment. For more information, please consult the Stockholm Convention website at http://www.pops.int.

Year of World Trade Organization Membership indicates the year in which a country joined the World Trade Organization (WTO). The WTO began in 1995, expanding on the international trade rules set forth by its predecessor, the General Agreement on Tariffs and Trade (GATT). The WTO's purpose is to help trade flow as freely as possible without any undesirable side effects and to ensure that trade rules and tariffs are transparent and equitable among nations. It also serves as a forum for trade negotiations and dispute settlements. In theory, any state or customs territory having full autonomy in the conduct of its trade policies may join the WTO, after lengthy negotiations concerning market access, tariff rates, and other policies in goods and services. Governments marked as "observers" are expected to start accession negotiations within five years of becoming observers.

Aarhus Convention: The UN Economic Commission for Europe (UNECE) Convention on Access to Information, Public Participation in Decision-making and Access to Justice in Environmental Matters, or Aarhus Convention, was first adopted in June 1998. The Convention is open to the 55 members of the UNECE as well as to non-member states. According to UN Secretary-General Kofi Annan, "Although regional in scope...the Aarhus Convention is global. It is by far the most impressive elaboration of principle 10 of the Rio Declaration, which stresses the need for citizen's participation in environmental issues and for access to information on the environment held by public authorities..." The Convention will include regular reporting requirements and biennial meetings among member states. More information is available on-line at http://www.unece.org/env/pp.

Agenda 21, created as a result of the 1992 Earth Summit, is a comprehensive plan of action to be taken globally, nationally, and locally by organizations of the United Nations system, governments, and major groups in every area with human impacts on the environment.

National Agenda 21 Reporting Status indicates if a country has submitted a report on the status of its implementation of Agenda 21 in relation to the specific themes. Countries with reports "pending" submission are participants in the Agenda 21 process that have not yet submitted reports in 2002. "Nonreporting" countries are not participating in the Agenda 21 process. Country reports focus on social, economic, and environmental issues, including: combating poverty; energy; health; transport; agriculture; atmosphere; biodiversity; forests; freshwater; hazardous, solid, and radioactive wastes; land management; oceans; and toxic chemicals.

Local Agenda 21 Municipalities: The number of municipalities involved in the Local Agenda 21 (LA21) process denotes the number of government authorities that have made a formal commitment to LA21 or are actively undertaking the process.

As part of the Agenda 21 process, local governments are called to create their own agenda outlining local priorities. The following criteria were used to identify local authorities undertaking the LA21 process: The International Council for Local Environmental Initiatives (ICLEI) conducted two separate surveys of global LA21 participation—in 1996 and in 2001. While the data can provide a rough approximation of the number of municipalities involved in LA21s, it does not indicate either (1) the extent of a municipality's involvement or (2) the size of the municipality. Many of the local participants were "self-reported" adherents to LA21 practices, introducing some degree of reporting bias. The survey did not have a clearly defined sample size, so rigorous statistical analysis of the results is not possible.

SOURCES

Covenants for Human Rights (Civil and Political; Economic, Social and Cultural): Office of the United Nations High Commissioner for Human Rights (UNHCHR). 2002. Status of Ratifications of the Principal International Human Rights Treaties. Geneva: UNHCHR. Available on-line at http://www.unhchr.ch/pdf/report.pdf. **CITES:** Convention on International Trade in Endangered Species of Wild Fauna and Flora. 2002. List of Contracting Parties. Geneva: CITES Secretariat. Available on-line at http://www.cites.org/eng/parties/alphabet.shtml. **UNFCCC:** United Nations Framework Convention on Climate Change (UNFCCC). 2001. UNFCCC Status of Ratification. Bonn: UNFCCC. Available on-line at http://unfccc.int/resource/conv/ratlist.pdf. **Kyoto Protocol:** UNFCCC. 2002. Kyoto Protocol Status of Ratification. Bonn: UNFCCC. Available on-line at http://www.unfccc.int/resource/kpstats.pdf. **CBD and the Biosafety Protocol:** Convention on Biodiversity. 2002. Parties to the Convention on Biological Diversity/Cartagena Protocol on Biosafety. Montréal: CBD. Available on-line at http://www.biodiv.org/doc/publications/guide.asp. **CCD:** United Nations Secretariat of the Convention to Combat Desertification. 2002. Status of Ratification and Entry into Force of the UNCCD. Bonn: UNCCD Secretariat. Available on-line at http://www.unccd.int/convention/ratif/doeif.php. **Stockholm Convention:** Stockholm Convention on Persistent Organic Pollutants (POPs). 2002. List of Signatories and Parties to the Stockholm Convention. Nairobi: UNEP. Available on-line at http://www.pops.int/documents/signature/. **Aarhus Convention:** United Nations Economic Commission for Europe (UNECE). 2002. Convention on Access to Information, Public Participation in Decision-Making and Access to Justice in Environmental Matters: Participants. Geneva: UNECE. Available on-line at http://www.unece.org/env/pp/ctreaty.htm. **WTO Membership:** World Trade Organization (WTO). 2002. Organization Members and Observers. Geneva: WTO. Available on-line at http://www.wto.org/english/thewto_e/whatis_e/tif_e/org6_e.htm.

National Agenda 21 Reporting: United Nations Commission on Sustainable Development (UNCSD). 2002. National Implementation of Agenda 21: The Report. New York: UNCSD. Available on-line at http://www.un.org/esa/agenda21/natlinfo/wssd/NIA_REPORT.pdf. **Agenda 21 Municipalities:** International Council for Local Environmental Initiatives (ICLEI). 2001. Second Local Agenda 21 Survey: Background Paper Number 15. New York: United Nations Department of Economic and Social Affairs (UNDESA). International Council for Local Environmental Initiatives (ICLEI) in cooperation with the United Nations Department for Policy Coordination and Sustainable Development (UNDPCSD). 1997. A Study of Responses by Local Authorities and Their National and International Associations to Agenda 21. Toronto: ICLEI.

Financial Flows, Government Expenditures, and Corporations

Sources: The World Bank, Stockholm International Peace Research Institute, United Nations Conference on Trade and Development, International Standards Organization.

	Foreign Direct Investment, Net Inflows (million current $US) {a}		Exports as a Percent of GDP	Balance of Trade (million current $US)	External Debt as a Percent of GNI	Government Expenditure as a Percent of GDP			Off'l. Development Assistance (ODA) Receipts 1998-2000 {a}		Number of Transnational Corporations 1994-2000 {b}		Corporations With ISO 14000 Certification (number)
	1988-1990 {a}	1998-2000 {a}	1998-2000 {a}	1998-2000 {a}	1998-2000 {a}	Military 2000	Public Health 1998	Education 1998	Million Current $US	as a % of GNI	Parent Corporations	Foreign Affiliates	2000
WORLD	**180,445**	**918,158**	**23**	**..**	**..**	**5.4**	**4.5**	**59,073**	**..**	**63,312**	**821,818**	**22,897**	
ASIA (EXCL. MIDDLE EAST)	**13,703**	**76,746**	**22 c**	**184,697 c**	**..**	**1.5**	**4.6**	**3.5**	**..**	**..**	**9,434**	**452,675**	**7,723**
Armenia	..	161	21	(567)	46	4.4	3.1	2.0	189	10.0	..	1,604	..
Azerbaijan	..	554	31	(639)	22	2.7	0.9	3.4	136	3.0	..	2	..
Bangladesh	2	217	14	(2,389)	35	1.3	1.7	..	1,217	2.7	..	161	..
Bhutan	0	0	31	(101)	42	..	3.2	..	59	13.1	..	2	..
Cambodia	0	130	37	(283)	75	2.4	0.6	5.5	338	11.3	..	598	..
China	3,358	40,301	23	33,802	16	2.1	2.0	..	2,189	0.2	379	364,345	510
Georgia	..	159	28	(508)	48	0.9 d	0.9	..	195	6.2	..	190	..
India	168	2,373	12	(12,250)	23	2.4	..	..	1,529	0.4	187	1,416	257
Indonesia {e}	784	(2,550)	42	10,885	118	1.1	0.8	1.4 f	1,747	1.4	313	2,241	77
Japan	86	7,935	10 c	70,716 c	..	1.0	5.7	3.5 f	..	..	217	1,106	5,556
Kazakhstan	..	1,329	44	499	32	0.7	3.5	..	195	1.1	..	1,865	..
Korea, Dem People's Rep	..	..	..	..	..	..	..	..	128	..	..	..	26
Korea, Rep	973	8,010	46	27,751	33	2.8	2.4	4.1	(101)	(0.0)	7,460	6,486	544
Kyrgyzstan	..	50	41	(231)	110	1.9	2.9	5.4	241	18.7	..	4,004	..
Lao People's Dem Rep	4	66	36 g	(145) g	162	..	1.2	2.4 f	286	20.1	..	669	..
Malaysia	1,573	1,792	121	18,212	53	1.9	1.4	..	133	0.2	..	15,567	174
Mongolia	..	27	61	(137)	87	2.5	..	..	215	22.9	..	1,400	..
Myanmar	56	274	0 c	..	..	1.7	0.2	.. f	87	..	..	299	..
Nepal	3	7	23	(446)	54	0.9 d	1.3	2.5	383	7.3	..	224	..
Pakistan	213	449	16	(2,624)	54	4.5	1.0	.. f	830	1.4	59	644	4
Philippines	676	1,630	53	127	64	1.2	1.5	3.2 f	635	0.8	..	14,802	46
Singapore	4,039	6,634	168	16,517	..	4.8	1.2	..	1	0.0	..	24,114	100
Sri Lanka	36	181	37	(1,309)	59	4.5 d	1.4	..	349	2.2	..	305	2
Tajikistan	..	25	63	(61)	110	1.2	5.2	..	124	11.8	..	..	..
Thailand	1,775	5,631	61	14,347	76	1.6	1.9	4.7	785	0.7	..	2,721	310
Turkmenistan	..	130 g	45	(414)	..	3.8	4.1	..	26	0.8	..	..	..
Uzbekistan	..	120	37	111	41	..	3.4	..	167	1.9	..	4	..
Viet Nam	9	1,460	..	..	69	..	0.8	..	1,435	4.9	..	1,544	9
EUROPE	**80,031**	**445,655**	**34**	**121,923**	**..**	**2.0**	**6.5**	**5.2**	**..**	**..**	**38,595**	**299,691**	**10,926**
Albania	..	76	15	(782)	22	1.2	3.5	..	356	9.9	..	2,422	..
Austria	559	5,578	44 c	(1,145) c	..	0.8	5.8	6.3	..	..	896	2,464	203
Belarus	..	246	62	(788)	4	1.3	4.6	5.6	39	0.1	..	393	..
Belgium	2,804	13,188	80	9,055	..	1.4	6.1	..	..	..	..	..	130
Bosnia and Herzegovina	..	0 h	28	(1,486)	..	4.2	7.9	..	906	19.5	..	7	..
Bulgaria	1	782	50	(663)	88	3.0	3.5	3.4	274	2.3	26	918	..
Croatia	..	1,112	42	(1,600)	55	3.0	..	..	51	0.3	70	353	8
Czech Rep	155	4,865	64	(1,163)	43	2.0	6.5	4.2	404	0.8	660	71,385	116
Denmark	908	17,660	38	6,855	..	1.5	6.8	8.2	..	..	9,356	2,305	580
Estonia	..	424	80	(359)	57	1.6	..	6.8	79	1.6	..	3,066	18
Finland	611	8,601	40	11,419	..	1.3	5.3	..	..	..	1,200	2,006	508
France {i}	10,659	39,772	27	30,604	..	2.6	7.3	5.9	..	..	1,695	9,494	710
Germany	3,567	89,422	31	20,138	..	1.5	7.8	4.7	..	..	8,492	12,042	1,260
Greece	888	825 h	20 c	(10,736) c	..	4.9	4.7	..	..	..	..	798 j	42
Hungary	0	1,902	55	(1,353)	63	1.5	5.2	4.6	247	0.5	..	28,772	164
Iceland	(7)	120	35 c	(380) c	..	..	7.0	7.1	..	..	78	47	2
Ireland	268	17,476	87 c	11,328 c	..	0.7	5.2	4.5	..	..	39	1,140	163
Italy	5,126	7,584	27	25,758	..	2.1	5.5	4.7 f	..	..	806	1,769	521
Latvia	..	371	47	(706)	47	1.0 d	4.1	6.8	96	1.5	..	107	4
Lithuania	..	597	44	(1,033)	44	1.8	4.9	6.4	122	1.2	16	1,893	10
Macedonia, FYR	..	108	43	(503)	39	2.1	5.3	..	207	5.8	..	..	..
Moldova, Rep {k}	..	82	50	(317)	73	0.4	4.3	..	90	6.7	..	..	..
Netherlands	8,005	44,494	61 c	20,264 c	..	1.6	6.0	4.9	..	..	1,608	2,259 l	784
Norway	934	6,046	41	12,285	..	1.8	7.1	7.7	..	..	900	3,100	227
Poland	38	7,659	27	(9,692)	38	1.9	4.2	5.4	1,153	0.7	58	35,840	66
Portugal	1,756	3,464	31	(11,718)	..	2.1	5.1	5.7 f	..	..	1,100	3,500	47
Romania	0	1,366	29	(2,348)	28	2.1	3.1	4.4	395	1.1	20	71,318	5
Russian Federation	0	2,929	40	32,498	63 m	3.6	..	..	1,529	0.7	..	7,793	3
Serbia and Montenegro	33	0	32 n	(1,589) n	..	5.9 d	..	4.2	628	6.9	..	..	2
Slovakia	0	990	65	(1,289)	47	1.8 d	5.7	4.3	196	1.0	..	5,560	36
Slovenia	..	202	56	(610)	..	1.2	6.7	5.8	45	0.2	..	1,195	88
Spain	9,811	21,156	28	(6,819)	..	1.3 d	5.4	4.5	..	..	857	7,465	600
Sweden	1,823	33,641	45	13,779	..	2.1	6.6	8.0	..	..	5,118	4,324	1,370
Switzerland	2,804	13,188	41 c	11,833 c	..	1.1	7.6	5.5	..	..	4,506	5,774	690
Ukraine	..	611	52	726	34	3.6	3.6	4.5	525	1.6	..	7,362	..
United Kingdom	29,240	98,820	27	(21,434)	..	2.5 o	5.7	4.7	..	..	1,094	2,683	2,534
MIDDLE EAST & N. AFRICA	**..**	**..**	**31**	**(876)**	**..**	**6.0**	**..**	**..**	**5,731**	**0.7**	**4,925**	**7,898**	**340**
Afghanistan	..	..	..	..	..	..	..	..	146	..	..	3	4
Algeria	8	7	31	3,932	60	3.5 d	2.6	6.0	215	0.5	..	99	78
Egypt	1,058	1,125	16	(7,509)	36	2.3	..	..	1,622	1.8	..	16	12
Iran, Islamic Rep	(107)	33	24	5,794	10	3.8 p	1.7	4.6	152	0.1	..	16	12
Iraq	..	..	..	..	..	3.8	..	..	98	..	..	..	..
Israel	182	3,014	36	(8,649)	..	8.0	6.0	7.7	924	0.9	4,334	3,321	60
Jordan {q}	20	342	44	(1,728)	109	9.5	3.6	.. f	465	5.8	..	8	16
Kuwait	..	49	49	3,305	..	8.2	..	6.5 f	5	0.0	..	6	..
Lebanon	3	249	12	(4,524)	51	3.6	2.2	2.1	210	1.2	..	24	5
Libyan Arab Jamahiriya	..	..	..	..	..	..	..	.. f	10	..	..	..	..
Morocco	139	8	30	(1,613)	56	4.2	1.2	..	543	1.6	..	156	4
Oman	115	48	..	..	..	9.7	2.9	3.9 f	43	..	92	351	2
Saudi Arabia	..	..	42	22,224	..	11.6	..	..	28	0.0	..	1,461 r	6
Syrian Arab Rep	89	94	34	202	151	5.5	0.9	..	181	1.2	..	5	3
Tunisia	72	584	43	(607)	57	1.7	2.2	7.6	208	1.1	142	2,086	3
Turkey	567	902	24	(9,356)	54	4.9	3.5	..	118	0.1	357	136	91
United Arab Emirates	..	..	..	..	..	2.6 d	0.8	2.0	4	..	..	59	48
Yemen	(44)	(205)	38	(212)	84	5.2	2.0	6.7	345	5.3	..	4	..

	Foreign Direct Investment, Net Inflows (million current $US) {a}		Exports as a Percent of GDP	Balance of Trade (million current $US)	External Debt as a Percent of GNI	Government Expenditure as a Percent of GDP			Off'l. Development Assistance (ODA) Receipts 1998-2000 {a}		Number of Transnational Corporations 1994-2000 {b}		Corporations With ISO 14000 Certification (number)
	1988-1990 {a}	1998-2000 {a}	1998-2000 {a}	1998-2000 {a}	1998-2000 {a}	Military 2000	Public Health 1998	Education 1998	Million Current $US	as a % of GNI	Parent Corporations	Foreign Affiliates	2000
SUB-SAHARAN AFRICA	..	6,903	30	(7,167)	70	2.1	2.5	5.2	12,413	4.1	966	4,413	143
Angola	(1)	1,761	78	(90)	306	21.2 s	..	2.6	343	10.3	..	21	..
Benin	1	36	17	(280)	72	..	1.6	2.6	220	9.9	..	5	..
Botswana	59	54	31 c	(110) c	9	3.7	2.5	9.1	66	1.4	..	8	..
Burkina Faso	0	11	12	(431)	57	1.6	1.3	3.0	378	16.0	..	8	..
Burundi	1	5	9	(90)	137	5.4	0.6	3.9	81	11.0	..	3	..
Cameroon	(44)	40	27	149	109	1.3	1.1	2.6	413	4.9	..	47	..
Central African Rep	(1)	8	14	(50)	86	..	2.0	1.9	104	10.3	..	4	..
Chad	7	15	17	(225)	70	..	2.3	1.7	162	10.5	..	3	..
Congo	3	8	72	455	303	..	2.0	4.7	80	4.7	..	20	..
Congo, Dem Rep	(7)	1	..	..	..	..	..	..	147	2.5	..	4	..
Côte d'Ivoire	39	270	44	689	131	..	1.2	4.2	533	5.3	..	91	..
Equatorial Guinea	4	88	97	84	67	..	..	1.8	22	4.9	..	1	..
Eritrea	..	34	14	(483)	32	..	..	5.0	164	21.8	..	..	..
Ethiopia	5	134	15	(851)	111	..	1.7	4.3	665	10.4	..	21	..
Gabon	59	47	43	160	99	..	2.1	3.3	35	0.9	..	33	..
Gambia	5	14	48	(61)	109	1.1	1.9	4.9	40	9.7	..	5	..
Ghana	12	76	38	(1,122)	98	1.0	1.8	4.0	640	9.9	..	54	..
Guinea	15	48	23	(154)	99	1.5	2.3	1.8	250	7.6	..	..	..
Guinea-Bissau	1	1	24	(47)	475	..	..	0.0	76	38.2	..	1	..
Kenya	40	45	26	(815)	63	1.8	2.4	6.6	433	4.1	..	96	2
Lesotho	17	182	26	(634)	61	..	..	13.0	46	4.0	..	411	..
Liberia	0	13	..	..	..	..	..	..	78	..	..	..	..
Madagascar	13	53	24	(328)	122	1.2 p	1.1	1.9 f	392	10.6	..	17	..
Malawi	0	58	29	(203)	136	0.8	2.8	4.6	442	25.9	..	1	..
Mali	3	37	25	(297)	121	2.5	2.1	3.0	354	14.5	3	33	..
Mauritania	4	2	40	(128)	245	..	1.4	4.3	201	21.6	..	2	..
Mozambique	6	245	12	(847)	204	2.5	2.8	2.9	907	24.8	..	12	..
Namibia	..	..	47 c	(328) c	..	3.3	3.7	8.1	170	4.9	..	2	4
Niger	(1)	8	16	(149)	83	..	1.2	2.7 f	230	11.7	..	5	..
Nigeria	949	1,046	41	569	99	0.9	0.8	.. f	180	0.6	..	48	1
Rwanda	15	8	6	(321)	64	3.0 d	..	..	348	18.3	..	2	..
Senegal	24	112	31	(340)	78	1.4 d	2.6	3.5	487	10.8	..	27	..
Sierra Leone	10	2	15	(64)	186	1.4	0.9	1.0	121	18.9	..	1	..
Somalia	(26)	0	..	..	..	..	..	..	100	..	..	..	..
South Africa	..	1,005	27	2,951	18	1.5	3.3	6.1	514	0.4	941	2,044	126
Sudan	1	378	10	(668)	175	3.0	..	3.7	226	2.5	..	3	..
Tanzania, United Rep {t}	3	183	14	(1,001)	93	..	1.3	2.1	1,012	11.7	..	27	..
Togo	7	34	34	(184)	108	..	1.3	4.5	90	6.7	..	5	..
Uganda	1	217	11	(784)	54	1.8	1.9	1.6	686	10.7	..	22	..
Zambia	153	187	27	(477)	197	0.6 d	3.6	2.3	589	20.4	2	1,179	2
Zimbabwe	(13)	194	41	(53)	70	4.8	..	10.8	234	4.0	8	36	4
NORTH AMERICA	64,718	292,463	13 c	(189,082) c	..	3.0	5.8	5.1	..	..	5,109	23,812	1,517
Canada	6,559	36,830	43 c	13,418 c	..	1.2 o	6.5	5.6	..	..	1,722	4,562	475
United States	58,159	255,633	11 c	(202,500) c	..	3.1 o	5.8	5.0	..	..	3,387	19,103	1,042
C. AMERICA & CARIBBEAN	3,563	17,503	32	(17,414)	39	0.5	2.7	..	2,165	0.4	..	10,245	194
Belize	17	28	50	(86)	57	..	2.3	..	25	3.7	..	4	..
Costa Rica	129	564	49	294	31	..	5.2	6.1	11	0.1	..	111	20
Cuba	..	..	16	..	..	..	..	..	61	..	..	..	..
Dominican Rep	116	997	30	(1,528)	29	..	1.9	..	126	0.8	..	92	1
El Salvador	11	507	26	(1,645)	32	0.7	2.6	..	182	1.5	..	225 u	..
Guatemala	151	353	19	(1,533)	25	0.8	2.1	2.0	263	1.4	..	287 r	2
Haiti	9	18	12	(636)	30	..	1.4	..	293	7.4	..	6	..
Honduras	48	206	44	(632)	108	..	3.9	4.0	529	9.9	..	30	2
Jamaica	61	450	43	(765)	64	..	3.1	6.3	2	0.0	..	177	..
Mexico	2,755	12,171	31	(9,001)	37	0.5	2.6	..	9	0.0	..	8,420 l	159
Nicaragua	0	246	37	(1,052)	358	1.1	8.5	4.2 f	606	31.0	..	21	..
Panama	39	850	33	(736)	77	..	4.9	..	18	0.2	..	279	..
Trinidad and Tobago	107	671	55	339	39	..	2.5	..	13	0.2	..	65	1
SOUTH AMERICA	4,612	61,310	13	(14,862)	42	1.5	2.8	..	2,124	0.2	2,019	16,345	521
Argentina	1,337	14,314	10	(4,689)	51	1.3 s	2.2	..	87	0.0	..	635	114
Bolivia	(3)	902	18	(846)	70	1.5	4.1	..	558	6.9	..	257	1
Brazil	1,742	31,089	10	(11,341)	36	1.3	2.9	4.6	281	0.0	1,225	8,050	330
Chile	673	5,845	29	(349)	48	3.3	2.7	3.7	75	0.1	478	3,173	11
Colombia	426	2,224	19	(1,558)	38	2.3	5.2	..	219	0.3	302	2,220	21
Ecuador	95	738	35	798	89	..	1.7	..	158	1.0	..	121	1
Guyana	0	54	97	(82)	228	..	4.5	..	94	14.4	4	59	..
Paraguay	32	170	24	(1,218)	36	1.0	1.7	4.5	79	1.0	..	109	1
Peru	42	1,658	15	(1,749)	54	..	2.4	3.2	453	0.9	10	1,183	13
Suriname	..	..	18	8	..	..	..	..	43	4.8	..	9	..
Uruguay	16	232	19	(233)	38	1.1	1.9	2.6	22	0.1	..	123	22
Venezuela	251	4,083	24	6,398	41	1.2	2.6	..	54	0.1	..	406	7
OCEANIA	9,511	9,932	21 c	(11,000) c	..	1.6	6.0	5.1	..	..	610	3,209	1,112
Australia	7,582	7,758	19 c	(9,486) c	..	1.7	6.0	4.8	..	..	610	2,539	1,049
Fiji	44	25	68	66	10	..	2.9	..	34	2.2	..	151	..
New Zealand	1,693	1,937	31 c	(52) c	..	1.0	6.3	7.2 f	..	..	..	81	63
Papua New Guinea	171	179	48 c	143 c	69	0.8	2.5	..	284	7.9	..	345	..
Solomon Islands	8	10	..	..	50	..	..	..	50	16.5	..	56	..
DEVELOPED	154,292	762,210	21 c	2,829 c	..	2.1	6.1	4.8	..	..	49,806	340,116	19,297
DEVELOPING	25,534	154,670	34	74,191	37	2.4	2.3	..	34,450	0.6	11,852	478,172	3,179

a. Data are averaged over a range of three years. **b**. Data are from a single year within the indicated range of years. **c**. Data are from 1998 and 1999 only. **d**. Military expenditures are underreported for these countries. **e**. Economic data for Indonesia include East Timor. **f**. Partial estimate of education expenditure. **g**. Data are from 1998 only.
h. Data are from 1999 and 2000 only. **i**. National accounts data exclude overseas territories. **j**. Data are from 1991. **k**. National accounts data exclude Transnistria.
l. Data are from 1993. **m**. Debt of the former Soviet Union is included as a liabiliy of the Russian Federation. **n**. Data are from 2000 only. **o**. Figures are for the fiscal year rather than the calendar year. **p**. Military expenditures are overreported for these countries. **q**. Economic data for Jordan refer to the East Bank only. **r**. Data are from 1985.
s. Military expenditure data are highly uncertain. **t**. Economic data cover mainland Tanzania only. **u**. Data are from 1990.

VARIABLE DEFINITIONS AND METHODOLOGY

Foreign Direct Investment (FDI) is the net inflow of investment to acquire a lasting management interest (10 percent or more of voting stock) in an enterprise operating in an economy other than that of the investor. It is the sum in million current U.S. dollars of equity capital, reinvestment of earnings, other long-term capital, and short-term capital, as shown in the balance of payments. FDI can show foreign perceptions of investment opportunities in a given country. Data are based on balance of payments information reported by the International Monetary Fund (IMF), supplemented by data from the OECD and official national sources.

Exports of Goods and Services as a Percent of GDP represents the value of all goods and other market services provided to the rest of the world as a proportion of Gross Domestic Product (GDP). Exports include the value of merchandise, freight, insurance, transport, travel, royalties, license fees, and other services, such as communication, construction, financial, information, business, personal, and government services. They exclude labor and property income (formerly called factor services) as well as transfer payments. These data show, among other things, the level to which a country's economy is susceptible to world price fluctuations.

Balance of Trade is the net exports (exports minus imports) in million current U.S. dollars of goods and services for a particular country. It includes all transactions between residents of a country and the rest of the world involving a change in ownership of goods and services. If a country's exports exceed its imports, it has a trade surplus—a "positive" trade balance. If imports exceed exports, the country has a trade deficit—a "negative" trade balance. A change in the trade balance may indicate a change in a country's economic health or in the relative cost of domestic products when compared with international prices. Data are based on International Monetary Fund (IMF) databases, supplemented with estimates by World Bank staff. More information can be found in the IMF's Balance of Payments Manual 1993 (available on-line at http://www.imf.org/external/np/sta/bop/BOPman.pdf). Sources include customs data, monetary accounts of the banking system, external debt records, information provided by enterprises, surveys to estimate services transactions, and foreign exchange records.

External Debt as a Percent of GNI is the total debt owed to nonresidents repayable in foreign currency, goods, or services as a percentage of gross national income (GNI). It is the sum of public, publicly guaranteed, and private nonguaranteed long-term debt, use of International Monetary Fund (IMF) credit, and short-term debt. GNI is the sum of value added by all resident producers plus any product taxes not included in the valuation of output plus net receipts of primary income from abroad. Data are gathered by the World Bank using loan-by-loan reports on long-term public and publicly guaranteed borrowing, along with information on short-term debt collected by the countries, or from creditors through the reporting systems of the Bank for International Settlements and the OECD. These data are supplemented by information on loans and credits from major multilateral banks, loan statements from official lending agencies in major creditor countries, and estimates from World Bank and IMF staff.

Military Expenditure as a percent of GDP is defined by the Stockholm International Peace Research Institute (SIPRI) as "all current and capital expenditure on: (a) the armed forces, including peacekeeping forces; (b) defense ministries and other government agencies engaged in defense; (c) paramilitary forces associated with military operations; and (d) military space activities" as a proportion of gross domestic product. Expenditures include the cost of procurements, personnel, research & development, construction, operations, maintenance, and military aid to other countries. Civil defense, veteran's benefits, demobilization and destruction of weapons are not included as military expenditures. SIPRI obtains military expenditure data from primary sources, secondary sources quoting primary data, and other sources, including specialist journals and newspapers. When a country's definition of military expenditure differs from SIPRI's, estimates are made based on analysis of official government budget statistics.

Public Health Expenditure as a percent of GDP is the proportion of the gross domestic product (GDP) used for recurrent and capital spending from government budgets and social health insurance funds. Health expenditures include preventative and curative health services, family planning activities, nutrition activities, and emergency aid designated for health. Provision of water and sanitation are not included. Health expenditure estimates are those provided to the World Bank from the World Health Organization's World Health Report in 2000 and 2001. These data are supplemented with information from The European Observatory on Health Care Systems, OECD, and World Bank country and sector studies.

Public Education Expenditure as a percent of GDP is the proportion of gross domestic product (GDP) used for public spending on public education plus subsidies to private education at the primary, secondary, and tertiary levels. Foreign aid for education is excluded; spending for religious schools, which constitutes a sizable portion of educational spending in some developing countries, may also be excluded. According to the World Bank, education expenditure as a share of GDP reflects a country's "effort in education." Education expenditure estimates are provided to the World Bank by the United Nations Educational, Scientific and Cultural Organization (UNESCO) Institute for Statistics. UNESCO compiles their data from annual financial reports of central governments and state, provincial, or regional administrations.

Official Development Assistance (ODA) records the actual receipts of financial resources or of goods or services valued at the cost to the donor, less any repayments of loan principal during the same period. Data are reported in million current US dollars. Grants by official agencies of the members of the Development Assistance Committee (DAC) are included, as are loans with a grant element of at least 25 percent, and technical cooperation and assistance. The data on development assistance are compiled by the DAC and published in its annual statistical report, Geographical Distribution of Financial Flows to Aid Recipients, and the DAC annual Development Co-operation Report. **Official Development Assistance as a percent of GNI** is calculated as a proportion of gross national income (GNI, formerly GNP), and can be used to measure the level of importance of foreign aid to a country's economy.

A **Parent Corporation** is the portion of a transnational corporation (TNC) that controls assets of other entities outside of its home country. Typically, "control" is defined as an ownership of more than 10 percent of a corporation's equities or its equivalent for an unincorporated enterprise. A TNC is defined by the United Nations Conference on Trade and Development (UNCTAD) as an "incorporated or unincorporated enterprise composed of parent enterprises and their foreign affiliates." **Foreign Affiliates** are corporations in which an investor residing in another country has a lasting interest in the management of the enterprise, typically owning more than 10 percent of a corporation's equities or its equivalent for an unincorporated enterprise. UNCTAD requests data from national governments and publishes data precisely as reported.

Corporations with ISO 14000 Certification is defined as the number of companies in each country that have received ISO 14000 certification by December of any given year. National standards institutes from individual countries have created the ISO 14000, which provides voluntary environmental management systems standards. Companies adhering to the ISO 14000 implement environmental management systems, conduct environmental audits, and evaluate their environmental performance. Their products adhere to environmental labeling standards, and waste streams are managed through life cycle assessments. The International Organization for Standardization compiles data on all countries through an annual survey.

FREQUENCY OF UPDATE BY DATA PROVIDERS
All data sets are updated annually, with the exception of the data on transnational corporations and education expenditure. These are updated intermittently. Most data updates include revisions of past data.

DATA RELIABILITY AND CAUTIONARY NOTES
Foreign Direct Investment. Because of the multiplicity of sources, definitions, and reporting methods, data may not be comparable across countries. Data do not include capital raised locally, which has become an important source of financing in some developing countries. In addition, data only capture cross-border investment flows when equity participation is involved and thus omit nonequity cross-border transactions.
Exports as a percent of GDP. Data on exports are compiled from customs reports and balance of payments data. Although the data on exports and imports from the payments side provide reasonably reliable records of cross-border transactions, they may not adhere strictly to appropriate definitions of valuation and timing, or correspond with the change-of-ownership criterion. Neither customs nor balance of payments data usually capture the illegal transactions that occur in many countries. Goods carried by travelers across borders in legal but unreported shuttle trade may further distort trade statistics.

Balance of Trade. Because of the variety of sources, data may be inconsistent. Differences in collection methods—such as timing, definitions of residences and ownership, and exchange rate valuations—contribute to net errors and omissions. In addition, smuggling and other illegal or quasi-legal transactions may be unrecorded or misreported.

External Debt as a percent of GNI. Variations in reporting rescheduled debt affect cross-country comparability. Other areas of inconsistency include country treatment of arrears and of nonresident national deposits denominated in foreign currency. With the widening spectrum of debt instruments and investors and the expansion of private nonguaranteed borrowing, data are increasingly difficult to measure. Military debt is often underreported.

Military Expenditure as a percent of GDP. Many values are uncertain or estimated. SIPRI cautions that military expenditure does not relate directly to military capability or security.

Public Health Expenditure as a percent of GDP. Data on public spending at the sub-national level are not aggregated in all countries, making total health expenditure difficult to measure. Few developing countries have health accounts that are methodologically consistent with national accounting procedures. Health care systems are not always defined clearly.

WHO cautions that these data should only be used for an "order of magnitude" estimate; cross-country comparisons should be avoided.

Education Expenditure as a percent of GDP. In some cases, data refer only to the Ministry of Education's expenditures, excluding other authorities that spend money on educational activities. The World Bank cautions that these data do not measure effectiveness or levels of attainment in a particular educational system.

Official Development Assistance. Because data are based on donor country reports, they do not provide a complete picture of the resources received by developing and transition economies for three reasons. First, flows from DAC members are only part of the aggregate resource flows to these economies. Second, the data that record contributions to multilateral institutions measure the flow of resources made available to those institutions by DAC members, not the flow of resources from those institutions to developing and transition economies. Third, because some of the countries and territories on the DAC recipient list are normally classified as high-income, the reported flows may overstate the resources available to low- and middle-income economies.

Parent Corporations and Foreign Affiliates. Regional and global totals represent a sum of available data and may therefore be incomplete. Some countries count the number of foreign-sponsored projects instead of the number of actual companies; in this case, some double counting has occurred. Because of the range of survey years and the acceptance of survey data "as-is" from national governments, cross-country comparisons should be made with caution.

ISO 14000 Certification. A small amount of double counting occurs due to joint assessments of a single company. In addition, some underreporting may occur in all countries. No distinction is made between accredited and non-accredited institutions, and certifications may be for a single site or for multiple sites. Survey data are only as reliable as the reports of each national institute, and ISO does not ensure the accuracy of this data. The ISO 14000 standards have been criticized because they do not require companies to provide public reports on their environmental performance.

SOURCES
Foreign Direct Investment, Exports as a percent of GDP, Balance of Trade, External Debt, Public Health and Education Expenditure, and Official Development Assistance data: Development Data Group, The World Bank. 2002. World Development Indicators 2002 online. Washington, D.C.: The World Bank. Available on-line at http://www.worldbank.org/data. **Military Expenditure as a Percent of GDP:** Stockholm International Peace Research Institute (SIPRI). 2002. The SIPRI Military Expenditure Database (available on-line http://projects.sipri.se/milex/mex_database1.html). Stockholm: SIPRI. **Transnational Corporations:** United Nations Conference on Trade and Development (UNCTAD). 2001. World Investment Report 2001: Promoting Linkages, pp. 239–243. New York and Geneva: UNCTAD. Available on-line at www.unctad.org/wir/index.htm. **ISO Certification:** International Organization for Standardization (ISO). 2001. The ISO Survey of ISO 9000 and ISO 14000 Certificates. Available on-line at http://www.iso.ch/iso/en/iso9000-14000/pdf/survey10thcycle.pdf. Geneva: ISO.

Economic Indicators

Sources: World Bank, United Nations Population Division

	Gross Domestic Product (GDP)					Distribution by Sector {a} (percent)			Income Inequality				International Poverty Line			Savings Rate (percent of GNI)	
	Total GDP (1995 US$)		GDP per Capita (1995 US$)		GDP per Capita PPP					Gini Index {b}	Percent Share of Income				Percent Under		Net	Adjusted Net
	Total Value (millions) 2000	Average Annual Growth Rate (percent) 1991-2000	Total Value (dollars) 2000	Average Annual Growth Rate 1991-2000	(current int'l $) 2000	Agri-culture 2000	Ind-ustry 2000	Ser-vices 2000	Sur-vey year 2000	(0= perfect equality) 2000	Poorest 20%	Richest 20%	Sur-vey year	$1/ Day	$2/ Day	National Savings 2000	Savings 2000
WORLD	34,109,900	2.8	5,632	1.4	7,416	5	31	64 c	..	..	..	..	..	..	..	10.2	12.0
ASIA (EXCL. MIDDLE EAST)	8,913,075	2.8	2,670	1.4	4,327	6	35	59 c	..	..	..	..	..	..	34	16.9	18.9
Armenia	3,711	0.7	980	0.1	2,570	25	36	39	'96 d	44.4	5.5	50.6	'96	8	34	(5.7)	(5.0)
Azerbaijan	4,071	(4.6)	506	(5.7)	2,939	19	38	43	'95 e	36.0	6.9	43.3	'95	2	10	9.5	
Bangladesh	48,906	4.9	356	2.6	1,527	25	24	51	'96 d	33.6	8.7	42.8	'96	29	78	17.2	16.3
Bhutan	428	6.8	205	4.5	545	33	37	29								14.2	16.7
Cambodia	3,565	4.6	272	1.4	1,326 f	37	20	42	'97 d	40.4	6.9	47.6				10.0	11.3
China	1,040,312	10.1	816	9.0	3,936	16	51	33	'98 e	40.3	5.9	46.6	'99	19	53	30.6	26.8
Georgia	2,505	(9.9)	476	(9.6)	2,544	32	13	55	'96 e	37.1	6.1	43.6	'96	2	2	(7.0)	(6.1)
India	466,682	6.3	463	4.4	2,374	25	27	48	'97 d	37.8	8.1	46.1	'97	44	86	13.9	12.2
Indonesia	209,098	3.5	986	2.0	3,019	17	47	36	'99 d	31.7	9.0	41.1	'99	8	55	15.9	2.9
Japan	5,687,635	1.3	44,751	1.0	26,707	1	32	66 c	'93 e	24.9	10.6	35.7				13.5	18.0
Kazakhstan	22,487	(3.3)	1,390	(2.9)	5,398	9	43	48	'96 d	35.4	6.7	42.3	'96	2	15	11.5	(29.6)
Korea, Dem People's Rep	..	..	..	..	..												
Korea, Rep	617,513	5.5	13,212	4.6	17,579	5	43	53	'93 d	31.6	7.5	39.3	'93	2	2	19.2	21.9
Kyrgyzstan	4,350	(2.8)	884	(3.9)	2,708	39	26	34	'99 d	34.6	7.6	42.5				(3.2)	(2.9)
Lao People's Dem Rep	2,376	6.6	450	4.0	1,576 f	53	23	24	'97 d	37.0	7.6	45.0	'97	26	73	8.5	10.1
Malaysia	111,617	6.6	5,024	4.3	9,497	11	45	44	'97 e	49.2	4.4	54.3				30.4	22.5
Mongolia	1,027	2.1	405	0.9	1,688	33	19	48	'95 d	33.2	7.3	40.9	'95	14	50	11.5	
Myanmar	..	..	..	..	..	60	9	31 c									
Nepal	5,560	4.8	241	2.4	1,327	40	22	37	'96 d	36.7	7.6	44.8	'95	38	83	19.7	16.6
Pakistan	71,278	3.5	505	0.9	1,884	26	23	51	'97 d	31.2	9.5	41.1	'96	31	85	4.7	1.9
Philippines	88,232	3.6	1,166	1.4	3,967	16	31	53	'97 d	46.2	5.4	52.3				20.8	22.2
Singapore	113,426	7.7	28,229	4.5	23,356	0	34	66								38.2	39.9
Sri Lanka	16,658	5.3	880	4.2	3,611	20	27	53	'95 d	34.4	8.0	42.8	'95	7	45	16.5	18.0
Tajikistan	2,381	(9.2)	391	(10.4)	1,167	19	26	55	'98 d	34.7	8.0	40.0				7.8	5.2
Thailand	170,338	3.5	2,712	2.1	6,190	10	40	49	'98 d	41.4	6.4	48.4	'98	2	28	15.4	16.2
Turkmenistan	7,157	(4.3)	1,511	(6.7)	4,342	27	50	23	'98 d	40.8	6.1	47.5	'98	12	44	19.6	
Uzbekistan	12,007	0.1	483	(1.8)	2,429	35	23	42	'98 d	44.7	4.0	49.1	'93	3	27	5.9	
Viet Nam	27,934	7.9	357	6.1	2,006	24	37	39	'98 d	36.1	8.0	44.5				21.4	13.6
EUROPE	11,139,956	1.8	15,327	1.5	16,525	3	30	68 c	..	..	..	..	..	..		8.6	11.5
Albania	3,068	5.3	979	6.0	3,816	51	26	23								4.7	5.9
Austria	265,716	2.1	32,886	1.7	26,866	2	33	65 c	'95 e	31.0	6.9	38.0				9.8	14.5
Belarus	27,618	(0.8)	2,711	(0.7)	7,409	15	37	47	'98 d	21.7	11.4	33.3	'98	2	2	13.5	16.4
Belgium	316,070	2.2	30,838	1.9	27,185	2	27	72	'96 e	28.7	8.3	37.3				9.4	12.2
Bosnia and Herzegovina	6,068	27.3 g	1,526	24.3 g		12	26	62									
Bulgaria	12,277	(1.6)	1,544	(0.7)	5,866	15	28	58	'97 e	26.4	10.1	36.8	'97	2	22	1.1	0.5
Croatia	22,538	2.5	4,843	2.2	7,615	10	33	58	'98 e	29.0	8.8	38.0	'98	2	2	8.4	
Czech Rep	54,561	1.6	5,312	1.6	13,993	4	41	55	'96 e	25.4	10.3	35.9	'96	2	2	14.1	17.0
Denmark	205,551	2.7	38,637	2.3	27,710	3	26	71	'92 e	24.7	9.6	34.5				9.2	16.4
Estonia	6,066	1.1	4,354	2.4	9,889	6	27	67	'98 e	37.6	7.0	45.1	'98	2	5	3.1	6.2
Finland	165,787	3.6	32,056	3.3	25,021	4	34	62	'91 e	25.6	10.0	35.8				11.7	18.4
France	1,755,614 h	1.8 h	29,637 h	1.4 h	24,082	3	26	71	'95 e	32.7	7.2	40.2				9.0	14.3
Germany	2,680,002	1.5	32,676	1.2	25,144	1	31	68	'94 e	30.0	8.2	38.5				6.2	10.2
Greece	138,386	2.2	13,043	1.8	16,423	8	24	69 c	'93 e	32.7	7.5	40.3				7.8	9.4
Hungary	54,371	2.5	5,455	2.9	12,484	6	34	.. i	'98 d	24.4	10.0	34.4	'98	2	7	13.3	16.3
Iceland	8,796	3.2	31,496	2.2	29,762	..	..	..									
Ireland	105,248	8.0	27,674	7.0	29,795	4	36	60 c	'87 e	35.9	6.7	42.9				18.5	23.5
Italy	1,204,868	1.7	20,943	1.5	23,692	3	30	68	'95 e	27.3	8.7	36.3				7.0	11.2
Latvia	6,160	(1.3)	2,545	(0.2)	6,904	4	25	70	'98 e	32.4	7.6	40.3	'98	2	8	9.5	15.0
Lithuania	7,597	(1.7)	2,055	(1.5)	7,104	8	33	59	'96 d	32.4	7.8	40.3	'96	2	8	4.8	8.9
Macedonia, FYR	5,138	(0.1)	2,526	(0.7)	5,078	12	33	55								3.8	
Moldova, Rep	2,722 j	(8.3) j	634 j	(8.1) j	2,103	28	20	52	'97 e	40.6	5.6	46.8	'97	11	38	4.9	9.0
Netherlands	492,956	2.9	31,074	2.3	25,746	3	27	70 c	'94 e	32.6	7.3	40.1				14.1	18.4
Norway	170,452	3.7	38,141	3.1	30,065	2	43	55	'95 e	25.8	9.7	35.8				20.6	19.5
Poland	163,236	5.3	4,228	5.2	9,062	4	36	60	'98 d	31.6	7.8	39.7	'98	2	2	9.6	12.7
Portugal	128,039	2.8	12,784	2.7	17,277	4	31	66	'95 e	35.6	7.3	43.4	'94	2	2	2.9	8.1
Romania	32,748	0.1	1,460	0.4	6,422	13	36	51	'98 d	31.1	8.0	39.5	'94	3	28	5.3	2.8
Russian Federation	357,322	(4.1)	2,456	(3.8)	8,381	7	39	54	'98 d	48.7	4.4	53.7	'98	7	25	25.1	(13.4)
Serbia and Montenegro	13,187	0.6 k	1,250	0.6 k		..	..	..								15.9	18.8
Slovakia	22,471	3.5	4,162	3.2	11,250	4	31	65	'92 e	19.5	11.9	31.4	'92	2	2	12.6	17.2
Slovenia	23,177	3.7	11,660	3.3	17,370	3	38	58	'98 e	28.4	9.1	37.7	'98	2	2	10.1	14.4
Spain	702,395	2.7	17,599	2.6	19,255	4	31	66	'90 e	32.5	7.5	40.3				6.7	14.0
Sweden	276,768	2.3	31,301	2.0	24,351	2	29	69 i	'92 e	25.0	9.6	34.5				19.0	23.6
Switzerland	335,570	1.0	46,799	0.6	28,808	2	30	68 i	'92 e	33.1	6.9	40.3				4.7	(4.2)
Ukraine	44,352	(8.8)	895	(8.3)	3,810	14	38	48	'99 d	29.0	8.8	37.8	'99	3	31	3.6	7.0
United Kingdom	1,294,359	2.8	21,785	2.5	23,637	1	29	70	'95 e	36.8	6.1	43.2					
MIDDLE EAST & N. AFRICA	826,705	2.7	2,364	0.6	5,500	..	..	..	..	..	..	..	..	..	..	15.4	(1.7)
Afghanistan	..	..	..	..	..												
Algeria	48,819	2.2	1,612	0.2	5,326 f	9	60	31	'95 d	35.3	7.0	42.6	'95	2	15		
Egypt	78,422	4.8	1,155	2.9	3,426	17	34	49	'95 d	28.9	9.8	39.0	'95	3	53	13.2	11.3
Iran, Islamic Rep	104,986	3.2	1,493	1.4	5,326	19	22	59								24.9	(12.5)
Iraq	..	..	..	..	..												
Israel	106,383	4.8	17,612	1.9	20,773	..	..	..	'97 e	38.1	6.1	44.2				0.1	6.0
Jordan	7,899 l	4.6 l	1,608 l	0.6 l	3,945	2	25	73	'97 d	36.4	7.6	44.4	'97	2	7	11.4	15.8
Kuwait	26,880	3.2 m	14,041	3.5 m	16,377 f	..	..	..								36.1	(8.4)
Lebanon	12,511	4.5	3,578	1.9	5,333	12	22	66								(10.8)	(9.8)
Libyan Arab Jamahiriya	..	..	..	..	..												
Morocco	39,324	2.4	1,316	0.4	3,407	14	32	54	'99 d	39.5	6.5	46.6	'90-91	2	8	14.0	17.6
Oman	..	..	..	..	..												
Saudi Arabia	139,438	1.1	6,853	(1.7)	11,578	7	48	45 i								21.3	(27.3)
Syrian Arab Rep	13,578	5.4	839	2.7	3,556	24	30	46								10.3	(27.9)
Tunisia	23,623	4.7	2,497	3.2	6,433	12	29	59	'95 d	41.7	5.7	47.9	'95	2	10	14.7	15.6
Turkey	204,651	3.7	3,070	2.0	6,830	16	25	59	'94 d	41.5	5.8	47.7	'94	2	18	13.2	15.3
United Arab Emirates	..	..	..	..	..												
Yemen	5,496	6.0	300	1.3	852	15	46	38	'98 d	33.4	7.4	41.2	'98	16	45	26.7	(18.2)

	Gross Domestic Product (GDP)					Distribution by Sector {a} (percent)			Income Inequality				International Poverty Line			Savings Rate (percent of GNI)	
	Total GDP (1995 US$)		GDP per Capita (1995 US$)		GDP per Capita PPP					Gini Index {b}	Percent Share of Income						Net National	Adjusted Net
	Total Value (millions) 2000	Average Annual Growth Rate (percent) 1991-2000	Total Value (dollars) 2000	Average Annual Growth Rate 1991-2000	(current int'l $) 2000	Agriculture 2000	Industry 2000	Services 2000	Survey year	(0= perfect equality)	Poorest 20%	Richest 20%	Survey year	Percent Under $1/ Day	$2/ Day	Savings 2000	Savings 2000
SUB-SAHARAN AFRICA	362,493	2.6	617	0.4	1,797	17	31	53	..	..	..	..	..	..	..	4.6	(1.1)
Angola	6,647	2.3	506	(1.8)	2,187 f	6	76	18								(17.9)	
Benin	2,598	4.8	414	1.7	991	38	14	48								2.6	3.4
Botswana	6,330	4.7	4,107	2.4	7,467	4	44	52					'85-86	33	61	1.2	8.1
Burkina Faso	2,842	4.8	246	2.4	954 f	35	17	48	'98 d	55.1	4.6	60.4	'94	61	86	16.8	16.7
Burundi	958	(2.8)	151	(3.6)	633 f	51	18	31	'98 d	42.5	5.1	48.0				(5.5)	(5.8)
Cameroon	10,044	2.4	675	(0.8)	1,703	44	20	36	'96 d	47.7	4.6	53.1	'96	33	64	6.8	(0.5)
Central African Rep	1,258	2.5	339	(0.3)	1,172 f	55	20	26	'93 d	61.3	2.0	65.0	'93	67	84	4.5	5.9
Chad	1,676	2.1	213	(0.8)	850 f	39	14	47								(2.6)	(0.6)
Congo	2,539	(0.6)	841	(3.4)	825	5	71	24								28.5	
Congo, Dem Rep	..	..	..	..	f											(11.3)	(13.5)
Côte d'Ivoire	11,890	3.9	743	1.0	1,630	29	22	48	'95 d	36.7	7.1	44.3	'95	12	49	(1.9)	0.8
Equatorial Guinea	731	24.8	1,600	18.9	15,083	7	88	5									
Eritrea	635	3.9 m	174	1.9 m	937 f	17	29	54 c									
Ethiopia	7,451	5.4	118	1.8	683	52	11	37	'95 d	40.0	7.1	47.7	'95	31	76	2.8	(7.3)
Gabon	5,385	2.8	4,378	0.1	6,237	6	53	40								2.3	(37.6)
Gambia	483	3.2	371	(0.3)	1,649 f	38	13	49	'98 d	50.2	4.0	55.3	'98	59	83	(1.6)	1.5
Ghana	7,978	4.2	413	1.8	1,964 f	35	25	39	'99 d	40.7	5.6	46.7	'99	45	79	6.1	5.3
Guinea	4,474	4.5	549	1.3	1,802	24	37	39	'94 d	40.3	6.4	47.2				5.8	2.2
Guinea-Bissau	251	0.8	210	(1.2)	755	59	12	29	'91 d	56.2	2.1	58.9					
Kenya	9,876	2.2	322	(0.6)	1,003	20	19	61	'97 d	44.9	5.6	51.2	'94	27	62	3.4	8.1
Lesotho	1,122	4.1	552	2.1	2,031 f	17	44	39	'87 d	56.0	2.8	60.1	'93	43	66	12.1	16.9
Liberia	..	..	..	..	..												
Madagascar	3,815	2.6	239	(0.9)	817	35	13	52	'99 d	38.1	6.4	44.9	'99	49	83	(0.4)	1.2
Malawi	1,739	3.9	154	2.0	560	42	19	39								(7.6)	(8.1)
Mali	3,119	4.0	275	1.2	761	46	17	37	'94 d	50.5	4.6	56.2	'94	73	91	3.6	5.7
Mauritania	1,321	4.3	496	1.2	1,677	22	31	47	'95 d	37.3	6.4	44.1	'95	29	69	22.7	3.7
Mozambique	3,380	7.0	185	3.2	826 f	24	25	50	'97 d	39.6	6.5	46.5	'96	38	78	2.5	5.9
Namibia	4,230	3.9	2,408	1.7	6,433 f	11	28	61 c					'93	35	56	14.2	22.5
Niger	2,197	2.8	203	(1.0)	746 f	39	18	44	'95 d	50.5	2.6	53.3	'95	61	85	(5.6)	(6.3)
Nigeria	32,184	2.3	283	(0.4)	998	30	46	25	'97 d	50.6	4.4	55.7	'97	70	91	21.2	(31.8)
Rwanda	2,057	0.9	270	(1.3)	1,055	44	21	35	'85 d	28.9	9.7	39.1	'83-85	36	85	6.9	6.0
Senegal	5,806	4.1	616	1.1	1,527	18	27	55	'95 d	41.3	6.4	48.2	'95	26	68	5.3	8.1
Sierra Leone	741	(4.2)	168	(4.9)	560	47	30	23	'89 d	62.9	1.1	63.4	'89	57	75		
Somalia	..	..	..	..	..												
South Africa	170,568	2.3	3,938	0.2	9,291 f	3	31	66	'94 d	59.3	2.9	64.8	'96	12	36	1.7	4.5
Sudan	9,922	8.4	319	5.7	1,797	37	18	45								(6.7)	(6.2)
Tanzania, United Rep	6,419 n	3.2	183 n	(0.1)	501	45	16	39	'93 d	38.2	6.8	45.5	'93	20	60	6.9	10.1
Togo	1,479	2.9	327	(0.5)	1,442	38	22	40								2.6	5.2
Uganda	7,728	7.2	332	3.9	1,152 f	42	19	38	'96 d	37.4	7.1	44.9				3.9	3.7
Zambia	3,959	0.6	380	(2.1)	755	27	24	49	'98 d	52.6	3.3	56.6	'98	64	87		
Zimbabwe	7,838	2.7	621	0.4	2,635	18	25	57	'95 d	50.1	4.7	55.7	'90-91	36	64		
NORTH AMERICA	9,701,656	3.7	30,898	2.3	33,341	..	..	..	..	..	..	..	..	..	..	6.5	9.6
Canada	693,149	3.2	22,537	1.8	27,834	..	..	..	'94 e	31.5	7.5	39.3				12.3	13.7
United States	9,008,507	3.7	31,806	2.4	33,939	..	..	..	'97 e	40.8	5.2	46.4				6.1	9.3
C. AMERICA & CARIBBEAN	475,273	2.0	3,035	0.5	7,226	6	28	66	..	..	..	..	..	..	..	9.8	8.2
Belize	754	3.9	3,330	2.0	5,945	21	27	52								10.9	15.3
Costa Rica	14,908	5.3	3,705	2.4	8,193	9	31	59	'97 e	45.9	4.5	51.0	'98	13	26	7.2	11.6
Cuba	..	..	..	..	..	7	46	47									
Dominican Rep	17,264	6.4	2,062	4.2	6,033	11	34	55	'98 e	47.4	5.1	53.3	'96	3	16	14.2	14.9
El Salvador	10,995	4.6	1,751	2.6	4,496	10	30	60	'98 e	52.2	3.3	56.4	'98	21	45	3.8	5.0
Guatemala	17,742	4.1	1,558	1.4	3,821	23	20	57	'98 e	55.8	3.8	60.6	'98	10	34	2.4	1.6
Haiti	2,923	(0.2)	359	(2.2)	1,434 f	28	20	51								0.1	(1.1)
Honduras	4,563	3.0	711	0.4	2,454	18	32	51	'98 e	56.3	2.2	59.4	'98	24	45	25.8	28.6
Jamaica	4,701	0.0	1,825	(0.4)	3,720	6	31	62	'00 d	37.9	6.7	46.0	'96	3	25	11.4	15.5
Mexico	374,141	3.1	3,784	1.3	8,941	4	28	67	'98 e	53.1	3.5	57.4	'98	16	38	10.1	8.1
Nicaragua	2,361	3.9	466	0.6	2,366 f	32	23	45	'98 d	60.3	2.3	63.6				4.7	5.9
Panama	9,365	3.6	3,279	2.3	6,001	7	17	76	'97 d	48.5	3.6	52.8	'98	14	29	14.2	18.5
Trinidad and Tobago	6,665	3.3	5,149	2.4	9,010	2	43	55	'92 e	40.3	5.5	45.9	'92	12	39	6.1	(24.3)
SOUTH AMERICA	1,457,476	3.2	4,218	1.7	7,374	8	29	63	..	..	..	..	..	..	..	6.0	3.8
Argentina	293,770	3.6	7,933	3.0	12,377	5	28	68								1.1	1.7
Bolivia	7,926	4.0	952	1.6	2,424	22	15	63	'99 d	44.7	4.0	49.1	'99	14	34	3.5	2.9
Brazil	788,025	3.0	4,624	1.5	7,625	7	29	64	'98 e	60.7	2.2	64.1	'98	12	27	4.7	6.3
Chile	81,445	6.4	5,354	5.2	9,417	11	34	56	'98 e	56.7	3.3	61.0	'98	2	9	12.7	8.9
Colombia	96,864	2.8	2,301	1.1	6,276	14	31	56	'96 e	57.1	3.0	60.9	'98	20	36	2.7	(3.8)
Ecuador	18,021	1.5	1,425	(0.3)	3,203	10	40	50	'95 d	43.7	5.4	49.7	'95	20	52	22.1	(5.5)
Guyana	716	5.1	942	5.0	3,965	35	28	36	'93 d	40.2	6.3	46.9					
Paraguay	9,344	2.1	1,700	(0.4)	4,426 f	21	27	52 c	'98 e	57.7	1.9	60.7	'98	20	49	0.2	3.3
Peru	60,774	4.8	2,368	2.9	4,799	8	27	65	'96 d	46.2	4.4	51.2	'96	16	41	7.4	7.0
Suriname	414	3.5	993	2.9	3,797 f	10	20	70								(7.8)	(5.4)
Uruguay	20,405	3.2	6,115	2.6	9,035	6	27	67	'89 e	42.3	5.4	48.3	'89	2	7	(0.3)	2.3
Venezuela	79,772	1.1	3,300	(0.6)	5,794	5	36	59	'98 e	49.5	3.0	53.2	98	23	7	21.8	(0.7)
OCEANIA	540,969	4.0	17,934	2.3	20,057	4	26	70 c	..	..	..	..	..	..	..	3.3	5.2
Australia	457,255	4.3	23,893	2.8	25,753	3	26	71 c	'94 e	35.2	5.9	41.3				2.7	4.3
Fiji	1,944	1.5	2,390	0.4	4,658	18	29	53								7.4	11.7
New Zealand	67,222	3.1	17,793	1.8	20,350	..	..	..								7.5	12.2
Papua New Guinea	4,756	3.0	989	1.5	2,432 f	26	44	30	'96 d	50.9	4.5	56.5				8.6	
Solomon Islands	287	1.9	642	(1.1)	1,646 f	..	..	..									
LOW INCOME {o}	1,146,787	2.6	417	1.8	1,898	24	32	44	..	..	..	..	..	..	..	11.9	4.7
MIDDLE INCOME {o}	5,844,681	3.7	1,829	1.9	5,224	9	36	55	..	..	..	..	..	..	..	14.9	9.1
HIGH INCOME {o}	27,116,800	3.5	29,575	2.4	27,119	..	..	..	..	..	..	..	..	..	..	9.2	12.8

a. Data may not sum to 100 percent due to rounding. **b.** If every person in a country earned the same income, the Gini Index would be zero; if all income was earned by one person, the Gini Index would be 100. **c.** Distribution of GDP by sector data are from 1999. **d.** Ranked by per capita expenditure. **e.** Ranked by per capita income. **f.** Estimates are based on regression. **g.** Data refer to the growth rate from 1994-2000. **h.** National accounts data include French Guiana, Guadeloupe, Martinique, and Réunion. **i.** Data on distribution of GDP by sector are from 1998.
j. National accounts data exclude Transnistria. **k.** Data refer to the growth rate from 1995-2000. **l.** Data refer to the East Bank only. **m.** Data refer to the growth rate from 1992-2000. **n.** Economic data cover mainland Tanzania only. **o.** Data for high, middle, and low-income countries are as reported by World Bank, except for per capita and growth rate calculations which are done by WRI.

VARIABLE DEFINITIONS AND METHODOLOGY

Gross Domestic Product (GDP), Constant 1995 Dollars is the sum of gross value added by all resident and nonresident producers in the economy plus any taxes and minus any subsidies not included in the value of the products. Data are expressed in millions of U.S. dollars. The gross domestic product estimates at purchaser values (market prices) are the sum of GDP at purchaser values (value added in the agriculture, industry, and services sectors) and indirect taxes, less subsidies. It is calculated without making deductions for depreciation of fabricated assets or for depletion and degradation of natural resources. National accounts indicators for most developing countries are collected from national statistical organizations and central banks by visiting and resident World Bank missions. The data for high-income economies come from OECD data files (see the OECD's National Accounts, 1988–1999, volumes 1 and 2). The United Nations Statistics Division publishes detailed national accounts for United Nations member countries in National Accounts Statistics: Main Aggregates and Detailed Tables and updates in the Monthly Bulletin of Statistics. To obtain comparable series of constant price data, the World Bank rescales GDP and value added by industrial origin to a common reference year, currently 1995. WRI calculates **GDP per Capita by** dividing World Bank GDP figures by the population estimates of the United Nations Population Division.

Average Annual Growth Rate is a calculation of the average percent growth between (and including) 1991 and 2000, using least-squares growth rate calculation. Growth rates are calculated by WRI using a least-squares regression. The least squares growth rate is estimated by fitting a linear regression trend line to the logarithmic annual values of the variable in the relevant period. The calculated growth rate is an average rate that is representative of the available observations over the entire period. It does not necessarily match the actual growth rate between any two periods.

Purchasing Power Parity, per capita is gross domestic product, per person, converted to international dollars using Purchasing Power Parity (PPP) rates. An international dollar has the same purchasing power in a given country as a United States dollar in the United States. In other words, it buys an equivalent amount of goods or services in that country. The estimates are a blend of extrapolated and regression-based numbers, using the results of the International Comparison Programme (ICP). The ICP benchmark studies are essentially multilateral pricing exercises. For 62 countries data come from the most recent round of surveys (1996); the rest are from the 1993 round and have been extrapolated to the 1996 benchmark. Estimates from countries not included in the surveys are derived from statistical models. PPP studies recast traditional national accounts through special price collections and the disaggregation of GDP by expenditure components. National statistical offices report ICP details. The international dollar values, which are different from the U.S. dollar values of GDP, are obtained using special conversion factors designed to equalize the purchasing powers of different currencies. This conversion factor, the PPP, is defined as the number of units of a country's currency required to buy the same amounts of goods and services in the domestic market as $1 would buy in the United States. PPP estimates tend to lower per capita GDPs in industrialized countries and raise per capita GDPs in developing countries. Data are expressed in current international dollars.

Distribution by Sector is the percent of total output of goods and services which are a result of value added by a given sector. These goods and services are for final use occurring within the domestic territory of a given country, regardless of the allocation to domestic and foreign claims. Value added is the net output of a sector after adding up all outputs and subtracting intermediate inputs. It is calculated without making deductions for depreciation of fabricated assets or depletion and degradation of natural resources. The industrial origin of value added is determined by the International Standard Industrial Classification (ISIC) revision 3.

Agriculture corresponds to ISIC divisions 1–5 and includes forestry and fishing. **Industry** corresponds to ISIC divisions 10–45 and includes manufacturing (ISIC divisions 15–37). It comprises value added in mining, manufacturing, construction, electricity, water, and gas. **Services** correspond to ISIC divisions 50–99 and they include value added in wholesale and retail trade (including hotels and restaurants), transport, and government, financial, professional, and personal services such as education, health care, and real estate services. Also included are imputed bank service charges, import duties, and any statistical discrepancies noted by national compilers as well as discrepancies arising from rescaling.

Income Inequality data is taken from household surveys collected by World Bank regional offices or government agencies. It is based on either income or expenditure. Data are compiled by the World Bank's Development Research Group using primary household survey data obtained from government statistical agencies and World Bank country departments. The Gini index and income distribution for high income countries are calculated directly from the Luxemburg Income Study database, using an estimation method consistent with that applied for developing countries. Data are collected through nationally representative household surveys administered between 1985 and 2000. They are based either on expenditure or per capita income, depending on the survey. Each distribution is based on percentiles of population—rather than of households—with households ranked by income or expenditure per person. **Survey Year** is the year in which the survey that collected the data was administered.

The **Gini Index** is a measure of income inequality. A score of zero implies perfect equality while a score of 100 implies perfect inequality. If every person in a country earned the same income, the Gini Index would be zero; if all income was earned by one person, the Gini Index would be 100. The Gini index is calculated by compiling income distribution (or expenditure) data to attain a single number which indicates the extent of income inequality within a country. A Lorenz curve plots the cumulative percentages of total income received against the cumulative number of recipients, starting with the poorest individual or household. Graphically, this displays the amount of wealth that segment of the population earns. The Gini index measures the area between the Lorenz curve and a hypothetical (45-degree) line of absolute equality, expressed as a percentage of the maximum area under the line.

Percent Share of Income is equal to the percentage share of all income in a given country which is earned by a given fifth of the population. Where the original data from household surveys were available, they have been used to directly calculate the income (or consumption) share by quintile. Otherwise, shares have been estimated from the best available grouped data. The distribution indicators have been adjusted for household size, providing a more consistent measure of per capita income or consumption.

International Poverty Line data are based on nationally representative primary household surveys conducted by national statistical offices or by private agencies under the supervision of government or international agencies and obtained from government statistical offices and World Bank country departments. **Population Living Below $1/day** is the percent of the population of a country living on less than $1.08 a day at 1993 international prices, (equivalent to $1 in 1985 prices, adjusted for purchasing power parity). **Population Living Below $2/day** is the percent of the population of a country living on less than $2.15 a day at 1993 international prices, (equivalent to $2 in 1985 prices, adjusted for purchasing power parity). These poverty measures are based on surveys conducted mostly between 1994 and 1999, by the World Bank's Development Research Group. The commonly used $1 a day (or $2/day) standard, measured in 1985 international prices and adjusted to local currency using purchasing power parities (PPPs) is used because it is typical of the poverty lines in low-income countries. PPP exchange rates, such as those from the Penn World Tables or the World Bank, are used because they take into account the local prices and goods and services not traded internationally. These data are based on surveys which were administered to households in each individual country. Surveys asked households to report either their consumption or their income. Whenever possible, consumption has been used as the welfare indicator for deciding who is poor. When only household income was available, average income has been adjusted to accord with either a survey-based estimate of mean consumption (when available) or an estimate based on consumption data from national accounts.

Net National Savings as a Percent of GNI: Net national savings are equal to gross national savings (gross domestic product minus final consumption plus net income and net current transfers from abroad) minus the value of consumption of fixed capital (the replacement value of capital used up in the process of production). The United Nations system of national accounts defines gross national income as "the aggregate value of the balances of gross primary incomes for all sectors; (gross national income is identical to gross national product as hitherto understood in national accounts generally)."

Adjusted Net Savings as a Percent of GNI: Adjusted net savings (previously "genuine savings") are equal to net national savings plus education expenditure and minus energy depletion, mineral depletion, net forest depletion, and carbon dioxide damage. Adjusted Net Savings is an indicator of sustainability. Persistently negative rates of savings must lead, eventually, to declining well-being. It measures the true rate of savings in an economy after taking into account investments in human capital, depletion of natural resources, and damage caused by pollution. For a more complete description of the methodology used by the World Bank, please visit the World Bank website on Adjusted Net Savings: http://lnweb18. worldbank.org/ESSD/essdext.nsf/44ByDocName/Green Accounting AdjustedNetSavings.

FREQUENCY OF UPDATE BY DATA PROVIDERS
The World Bank publishes the World Development Indicators each year in April. The United Nations Population Division publishes the World Population Prospects every two years. Most data updates include revisions of past data. Data may therefore differ from those reported in past editions of the World Resources Report.

DATA RELIABILITY AND CAUTIONARY NOTES
Gross Domestic Product: The World Bank produces the most reliable global GDP estimates available. However, it should be noted that these data do not account for differences in purchasing power. (To see national accounts data without these differences, see PPP (purchasing power parity) estimates.) Informal economic activities sometimes pose a measurement problem, especially in developing countries, where much economic activity may go unrecorded. Obtaining a complete picture of the economy requires estimating household outputs pro-

duced for local sale and home use, barter exchanges, and illicit or deliberately unreported activity. Technical improvements and growth in services sector are both particularly difficult to measure. How consistent and complete such estimates will be depends on the skill and methods of the compiling statisticians and the resources available to them.

Income Inequality and International Poverty: Because the underlying household surveys differ in method and in the type of data collected, the distribution indicators are not strictly comparable across countries. These problems are diminishing as survey methods improve and become more standardized, but achieving strict comparability is still impossible. Two sources of noncomparability should be noted. First, surveys can differ in many respects, including whether they use income or consumption expenditure as the living standard indicator. The distribution of income is typically more unequal than the distribution of consumption. In addition, the definition of income usually differs among surveys. Consumption is usually a much better welfare indicator, particularly in developing countries. Second, households differ in size (number of members) and in the extent of income sharing among members. And individuals differ in age and consumption needs. Differences among countries in these respects may bias comparisons of distribution.

International Poverty Line: Many issues arise in measuring household living standards. The choice between income and consumption as a welfare indicator is one issue. Income is generally more difficult to measure accurately, and consumption accords better with the idea of the standard of living. But consumption data are not always available, and when they are not there is little choice but to use income. Household income can also differ widely, for example, in the number of distinct categories of consumer goods identified. Survey quality varies and even similar surveys may not be strictly comparable. Comparisons across countries at different levels of development also pose a potential problem because of differences in the relative importance of consumption of nonmarket goods. The local market value of all consumption in kind (including consumption from own production, particularly important in underdeveloped rural economies) should be included in the measure of total consumption expenditure. Similarly, the imputed profit from production of nonmarket goods should be included in income. Most survey data now include valuations for consumption or income from own production. Nonetheless, valuation methods vary. For example, some surveys use the price in the nearest market, while others use the average farm gate selling price.

Adjusted Net Savings (ANS): The data which were used to calculate ANS are mostly from official sources, and are generally considered to be reliable. Due to methodological or data limitations, the calculation omits several important resources including soils, fish, water resources, and water and air pollutants. The calculation is at best an approximation and should not be used as a stand-alone measure of the savings rate of a particular country. These data are useful as a comparison measure and to demonstrate trends over time.

SOURCES
Economic data are taken from the World Bank's World Development Indicators. World Bank. 2002. World Development Indicators. Washington: World Bank. Data are available from World Bank on CD-ROM, or on-line at http://publications.worldbank. org/ecommerce/catalog/product?item_id=631625. **Population** (used to calculate per capita values): Population Division of the Department of Economic and Social Affairs of the United Nations Secretariat, 2002. World Population Prospects: The 2000 Revision. New York: United Nations.

Agriculture and Food

Sources: Food and Agriculture Organization of the United Nations, United Nations Population Division.

	Average Production of Cereals		Average Cereal Crop Yields		Variation in Domestic Cereal Production	Net Trade of Cereals (imports - exports) as	Average Meat Production Per Capita {a}		Irrigated Land as a	Average Annual Fertilizer Use			Average Daily Per Capita Calorie Supply {a,b}	
	000 Metric Tons 1999-2001 {c}	Percent Change Since 1989-91	Kg Per Hectare 1999-2001 {c}	Percent Change Since 1989-91	(% variation from mean) 1992-2001	a Percent of Consumption 2000 {d}	Kg Per Person 1999-2001 {c}	Percent Change Since 1989-91	Percentage of Total Cropland 1999	Kg/ha of Crop-land 1997-99 {c}	Percent Change Since 1987-89		Kilocalories, 1999 Total	From Animal Products
WORLD	2,075,387	9	3,096	15	3	(1)	39	13	18	92	(3)		2,808	460
ASIA (EXCL. MIDDLE EAST)	951,041	19	3,678	13	4	4	26	55	35	144	35		2,710	367
Armenia	301	..	1,675	..	13	67	13	..	51	14	..		2,167	309
Azerbaijan	1,528	..	2,373	..	20	34	14	..	73	9	..		2,224	358
Bangladesh	39,002	39	3,322	31	13	4	3	12	47	143	69	e	2,201	67
Bhutan	159	56	1,456	34	12	13	4	(12)	25	0	(73)	e	..	..
Cambodia	4,197	62	2,050	43	18	1	15	20	7	3	2,621		2,000	148
China {f}	422,218	8	4,869	16	5	(1)	50	87	40	267	42		3,044	567
Georgia	554	..	1,576	..	22	71	21	..	44	35	..		2,347	370
India {g}	234,313	20	2,321	21	5	(1)	5	5	35	101	66	e	2,417	192
Indonesia {h}	58,954	15	3,860	1	4	10	8	(1)	16	82	8		2,931	132
Japan	12,450	(11)	6,147	9	9	67	24	(17)	55	296	(20)	e	2,782	574
Kazakhstan	14,049	..	1,162	..	33	(111)	39	..	8	1	..		2,181	587
Korea, Dem People's Rep	3,550	(51)	2,753	(39)	41	33	9	(43)	73	88	(78)		2,100	130
Korea, Rep	7,559	(10)	6,500	10	4	63	36	65	61	476	11		3,073	439
Kyrgyzstan	1,657	..	2,726	..	13	12	39	..	75	21	..		2,833	541
Lao People's Dem Rep	2,279	58	2,978	33	17	1	16	47	18	7	1,572	e	2,152	140
Malaysia	2,212	17	3,075	13	3	64	49	39	5	185	41	e	2,947	563
Mongolia	156	(78)	716	(35)	37	35	110	(5)	6	3	(78)		1,963	877
Myanmar	21,322	51	3,082	13	9	(1)	9	45	18	16	65	e	2,803	117
Nepal	6,874	21	2,089	11	8	3	10	0	38	32	25	e	2,264	160
Pakistan	28,682	36	2,305	29	8	(4)	12	3	82	122	46	e	2,462	429
Philippines	16,917	18	2,571	27	8	18	25	39	15	73	41	e	2,357	345
Singapore	..	..	..	..	..	..	30	(38)	..	..	..	e	..	..
Sri Lanka	2,901	22	3,270	12	9	30	5	56	35	123	13		2,411	150
Tajikistan	383	..	1,025	..	30	..	5	..	84	56	..		1,927	144
Thailand	29,647	25	2,659	24	7	(20)	31	21	26	90	155		2,411	286
Turkmenistan	1,358	..	1,771	..	23	..	28	..	106	63	..	i	2,746	487
Uzbekistan	3,907	..	2,603	..	19	15	21	..	88	176	..		2,871	434
Viet Nam	33,909	69	4,075	33	13	(8)	25	54	41	250	206		2,564	272
EUROPE	393,862	..	4,187	..	5	(5)	70	..	8	78	..		3,230	906
Albania	558	(30)	2,622	0	11	41	21	37	49	19	(87)		2,717	733
Austria	4,611	(10)	5,629	3	4	(14)	111	2	0	168	(17)	e	3,639	1,184
Belarus	4,261	..	1,722	..	17	20	61	..	2	139	..		3,171	884
Belgium	..	..	..	..	..	..	..	..	..	..	..	e	..	..
Bosnia and Herzegovina	1,112	..	3,034	..	17	36	7	..	0	50	..		2,960	413
Bulgaria	5,016	(43)	2,696	(35)	14	(7)	60	(29)	18	36	(82)		2,847	679
Croatia	2,889	..	4,355	..	7	(13)	28	..	0	141	..		2,617	495
Czech Rep	6,941	(43)	4,277	(14)	9	(10)	77	(49)	1	88	..	e	3,241	850
Denmark	9,187	(0)	6,032	2	8	(16)	380	25	19	176	(28)	e	3,317	1,229
Estonia	556	..	1,704	..	14	20	41	..	0	26	..		3,154	821
Finland	3,550	(8)	3,071	(9)	11	1	65	(5)	3	144	(36)	e	3,143	1,195
France	63,527	10	7,088	14	7	(90)	109	7	11	249	(20)	e	3,575	1,353
Germany	46,651	23	6,749	22	10	(32)	79	(10)	4	244	(37)	e	3,411	1,067
Greece	4,430	(19)	3,527	(5)	6	16	47	(10)	37	125	(23)		3,689	829
Hungary	12,120	(17)	4,392	(15)	12	(22)	106	(29)	4	79	(68)		3,437	1,058
Iceland	..	..	..	..	..	..	87	15	..	..	..		3,313	1,347
Ireland	2,044	5	7,241	14	8	21	273	15	..	637	(5)	e	3,649	1,195
Italy	20,584	15	4,920	23	3	23	72	5	24	161	(7)	e	3,629	937
Latvia	882	..	2,090	..	12	2	25	..	1	25	..		2,904	721
Lithuania	2,333	..	2,480	..	13	(1)	51	..	0	51	..		2,959	669
Macedonia, FYR	598	..	2,711	..	12	19	17	..	9	68	..		2,878	489
Moldova, Rep	2,082	..	2,437	..	19	(0)	21	..	14	23	..		2,728	400
Netherlands	1,611	21	7,701	11	8	68	183	2	60	517	(25)	e	3,243	1,178
Norway	1,290	(8)	3,928	(0)	6	19	58	14	14	225	(11)	e	3,425	1,132
Poland	25,107	(9)	2,861	(11)	8	8	74	(4)	1	111	(51)	e	3,368	894
Portugal	1,548	(8)	2,729	35	7	62	74	31	24	94	5	e	3,768	1,067
Romania	14,687	(20)	2,569	(17)	16	2	51	(25)	27	31	(77)		3,254	742
Russian Federation	67,270	..	1,767	..	21	5	30	..	4	11	..		2,879	654
Serbia and Montenegro	7,716	..	3,518	..	14	(11)	81	..	1	51	..		2,805	946
Slovakia	2,836	..	3,559	..	11	(18)	56	..	11	66	..	e	3,101	800
Slovenia	489	..	4,912	..	8	55	87	..	1	376	..		3,089	1,015
Spain	20,274	5	3,047	22	17	18	125	42	20	121	19	e	3,353	929
Sweden	5,417	(5)	4,557	(1)	11	(29)	63	7	4	102	(23)	e	3,141	1,030
Switzerland	1,123	(16)	6,204	(2)	5	31	59	(15)	6	273	(37)	e	3,258	1,086
Ukraine	28,856	..	2,226	..	18	(1)	33	..	7	15	..		2,809	611
United Kingdom	21,698	(4)	6,836	11	7	(11)	58	1	2	342	(5)	e	3,318	1,050
MIDDLE EAST & N. AFRICA	78,527	(1)	2,585	14	6	44	21	13	28	62	7		3,003	301
Afghanistan	3,257	18	1,285	7	10	..	15	(12)	30	1	(91)	e	1,755	373
Algeria	1,819	(27)	929	9	44	89	17	1	7	14	(35)		2,966	300
Egypt	19,657	55	7,238	30	10	33	21	53	100	347	(6)	e	3,323	241
Iran, Islamic Rep	12,990	0	1,806	32	10	44	21	24	39	58	(10)	e	2,898	269
Iraq	1,408	(45)	530	(43)	25	78	5	(59)	64	69	117		2,446	91
Israel	197	(40)	2,411	(19)	23	94	59	14	45	277	22	e	3,542	660
Jordan	50	(53)	1,949	87	31	96	27	37	19	61	9		2,834	318
Kuwait	3	114	2,260	(45)	26	100	42	111	100	..	..		3,167	737
Lebanon	95	19	2,415	24	6	89	35	10	39	198	156		3,256	460
Libyan Arab Jamahiriya	215	(24)	637	(6)	13	88	35	13	22	26	(36)		3,277	386
Morocco	3,492	(53)	670	(50)	49	72	19	7	14	33	(8)		3,010	198
Oman	5	9	2,266	7	2	98	12	(18)	81	90	20		..	..
Saudi Arabia	2,293	(46)	3,649	(13)	35	75	28	6	43	89	(39)		2,953	446
Syrian Arab Rep	3,990	54	1,304	95	16	33	22	23	22	65	42	e	3,272	407
Tunisia	1,581	(3)	1,109	(0)	36	68	26	43	7	21	(0)		3,388	322
Turkey	28,829	2	2,187	6	6	1	20	(3)	17	75	21		3,469	374
United Arab Emirates	0	(85)	598	(69)	64	100	34	25	57	262	47	e	3,182	798
Yemen	679	(2)	1,094	26	10	75	9	(16)	29	17	69		2,002	129

Data Table 5 continued

More Agriculture and Food data tables are available. Log on to http://earthtrends.wri.org/datatables/agriculture or send an e-mail to enviro_info@wri.org with "Instructions" in the message body.

| | Average Production of Cereals | | Average Cereal Crop Yields | | Variation in Domestic Cereal Production | Net Trade of Cereals (imports - exports) as | Average Meat Production Per Capita {a} | | Irrigated Land as a | Average Annual Fertilizer Use | | | Average Daily Per Capita Calorie Supply {a,b} Kilocalories, 1999 | |
	000 Metric Tons 1999-2001 {c}	Percent Change Since 1989-91	Kg Per Hectare 1999-2001 {c}	Percent Change Since 1989-91	(% variation from mean) 1992-2001	a Percent of Consumption 2000 {d}	Kg Per Person 1999-2001 {c}	Percent Change Since 1989-91	Percentage of Total Cropland 1999	Kg/ha of Cropland 1997-99 {c}	Percent Change Since 1987-89		Total	From Animal Products
SUB-SAHARAN AFRICA	**87,715**	**18**	**1,221**	**6**	**7**	**13**	**12**	**(8)**	**4**	**12**	**(5)**		**2,238**	**152**
Angola	570	91	630	86	24	42	11	2	2	1	(83)	e	1,873	146
Benin	882	56	1,047	22	14	17	10	(22)	1	24	528	e	2,489	92
Botswana	21	(64)	146	(52)	52	86	42	(11)	0	12	457	e	2,288	386
Burkina Faso	2,594	31	880	23	8	8	11	3	1	14	167	e	2,376	113
Burundi	261	(12)	1,290	(5)	7	11	4	(28)	7	3	(7)	e	1,628	41
Cameroon	1,350	52	1,842	56	12	18	14	(4)	0	6	13		2,260	127
Central African Rep	184	78	1,217	30	23	20	25	14	..	0	(30)		1,978	182
Chad	1,181	74	555	(4)	15	4	15	(13)	1	4	153	e	2,206	145
Congo	8	(32)	782	8	16	97	9	(6)	0	21	321		2,212	124
Congo, Dem Rep	1,616	10	782	(2)	3	16	5	(24)	0	0	(78)		1,637	46
Côte d'Ivoire	1,878	53	1,307	49	16	27	10	(3)	1	12	119		2,582	89
Equatorial Guinea	..	..	..	..	..	..	1	(5)	..	0	..	e	..	..
Eritrea	227	..	671	..	49	32	8	..	4	17	..		1,646	105
Ethiopia {j}	8,812	50	1,164	(6)	21	1	10	(18)	2	15	192		1,803	104
Gabon	27	16	1,638	2	5	77	26	(10)	3	0	(89)		2,487	322
Gambia	172	73	1,298	20	25	45	5	(25)	1	8	(18)		2,598	124
Ghana	1,702	47	1,305	21	6	21	8	(15)	0	3	17		2,590	97
Guinea	1,052	67	1,311	25	14	17	5	47	6	2	186	e	2,133	71
Guinea-Bissau	157	(5)	1,271	(18)	10	22	15	1	5	1	(18)	e	2,245	160
Kenya	2,869	(1)	1,477	(6)	9	21	14	(10)	1	31	25		1,886	231
Lesotho	322	90	1,337	66	38	32	12	(25)	0	17	26	e	2,300	109
Liberia	188	(2)	1,278	24	43	42	7	(19)	1	0	(100)		2,089	66
Madagascar	2,583	2	1,831	(6)	4	6	17	(17)	35	2	(3)		1,994	206
Malawi	2,650	70	1,634	48	28	4	4	(3)	1	25	(6)		2,164	52
Mali	2,690	27	1,113	23	11	5	19	0	3	8	12		2,314	208
Mauritania	177	36	718	(14)	17	..	24	(23)	10	1	(81)	e	2,703	412
Mozambique	1,656	163	929	130	33	21	5	(18)	3	2	108	e	1,939	55
Namibia	106	3	347	(28)	36	..	49	0	1	0	..	e	2,096	235
Niger	2,718	28	358	5	16	11	12	(5)	1	0	(61)	e	2,064	110
Nigeria	22,797	26	1,197	3	4	9	8	(10)	1	6	(46)		2,833	82
Rwanda	239	(17)	891	(23)	19	17	5	5	0	0	(66)	e	2,011	54
Senegal	1,061	6	854	4	11	44	18	16	3	11	42	e	2,307	206
Sierra Leone	241	(57)	1,092	(11)	25	55	5	2	5	2	27	e	2,017	71
Somalia	278	(44)	544	(24)	20	30	20	(14)	19	0	(83)		1,555	621
South Africa	11,123	(13)	2,334	14	24	6	36	(8)	9	49	(12)		2,805	351
Sudan	3,268	18	484	(3)	22	14	22	29	12	4	(11)		2,360	462
Tanzania, United Rep	3,787	(8)	1,273	(8)	11	13	9	(12)	3	7	(78)		1,940	125
Togo	745	48	1,096	36	12	29	7	(21)	0	7	32	e	2,528	105
Uganda	2,200	38	1,605	8	10	5	11	(3)	0	0	413		2,238	133
Zambia	1,055	(28)	1,437	(8)	22	7	11	(7)	1	9	(44)		1,934	90
Zimbabwe	2,175	(9)	1,221	(18)	30	1	14	4	3	53	3		2,076	105
NORTH AMERICA	**384,394**	**11**	**5,525**	**26**	**7**	**(35)**	**132**	**18**	**10**	**101**	**16**		**3,696**	**1,038**
Canada	49,839	(6)	2,772	12	5	(69)	130	29	2	58	23	e	3,161	927
United States	334,554	14	5,824	27	7	(32)	133	17	13	111	16	e	3,754	1,050
C. AMERICA & CARIBBEAN	**33,983**	**17**	**2,529**	**14**	**3**	**38**	**37**	**26**	**19**	**66**	**(13)**		**2,850**	**460**
Belize	46	67	1,912	17	18	28	43	(0)	3	58	(22)	e	2,889	618
Costa Rica	319	22	4,023	45	14	70	46	(4)	21	371	91		2,761	506
Cuba	541	(1)	2,601	11	23	..	22	(26)	19	41	(75)		2,490	348
Dominican Rep	659	24	4,105	4	11	69	39	25	17	65	25		2,334	341
El Salvador	796	1	2,098	14	9	46	36	158	5	109	(4)		2,463	310
Guatemala	1,165	(18)	1,779	(9)	10	35	20	21	7	112	67	e	2,331	197
Haiti	415	2	899	(10)	6	54	11	28	8	12	290		1,978	117
Honduras	589	(11)	1,327	(5)	10	44	22	24	4	79	298	e	2,396	384
Jamaica	2	(39)	1,183	(4)	29	100	39	28	9	85	(34)		2,708	455
Mexico	28,405	21	2,765	18	4	32	45	33	24	64	(8)		3,168	562
Nicaragua	682	50	1,706	15	10	22	21	11	3	15	(44)		2,314	166
Panama	347	3	2,732	45	7	49	50	19	5	56	(4)		2,496	549
Trinidad and Tobago	12	(28)	2,928	4	30	94	23	(2)	2	64	111		2,703	435
SOUTH AMERICA	**106,762**	**45**	**3,004**	**39**	**8**	**(4)**	**71**	**34**	**9**	**74**	**42**		**2,845**	**603**
Argentina	37,398	87	3,397	45	17	(157)	109	1	6	30	406		3,177	1,010
Bolivia	1,217	44	1,577	16	9	27	48	21	4	3	(8)	e	2,237	410
Brazil	49,886	32	2,825	51	6	19	85	60	4	90	36		3,012	642
Chile	2,624	(12)	4,453	15	9	42	59	52	78	200	119		2,858	611
Colombia	3,622	(11)	3,236	31	6	38	33	(4)	19	140	42		2,567	436
Ecuador	1,985	40	2,212	29	7	19	35	41	29	54	116		2,679	439
Guyana	564	159	3,960	24	18	(54)	20	138	30	30	2		2,569	412
Paraguay	1,153	41	2,092	14	15	(7)	79	(1)	3	29	326	e	2,588	610
Peru	3,603	82	2,977	20	22	39	35	51	28	53	(1)		2,621	344
Suriname	170	(26)	3,830	2	13	(8)	18	(52)	76	107	49		2,604	394
Uruguay	2,055	67	3,796	57	12	(67)	178	21	14	100	96		2,862	1,109
Venezuela	2,465	21	3,341	35	8	46	43	7	16	71	(54)		2,229	355
OCEANIA	**35,238**	**59**	**2,976**	**37**	**16**	**(124)**	**170**	**3**	**..**	**53**	**57**		**2,969**	**825**
Australia	34,332	61	2,058	24	16	(145)	195	9	5	44	52	e	3,150	961
Fiji	17	(43)	2,619	14	18	89	27	(1)	1	61	(42)		2,934	561
New Zealand	870	11	6,303	29	6	21	344	(4)	9	201	123	e	3,152	1,048
Papua New Guinea	11	169	4,079	75	21	97	15	9	..	15	(40)	e	2,186	234
Solomon Islands	5	..	3,999	..	123	88	6	(16)	..	0	..	e	2,222	172
DEVELOPED	**860,966**	**..**	**4,479**	**..**	**3**	**(16)**	**79**	**..**	**10**	**81**	**..**		**3,242**	**861**
DEVELOPING	**1,210,555**	**17**	**3,131**	**15**	**4**	**8**	**27**	**44**	**24**	**100**	**38**		**2,684**	**346**

a. Data are collected from Oct. 1 to Sept. 30. Data from 1999, for example, are actually from October 1998 to September 1999. **b.** 1 kilocalorie = 1 Calorie (U.S.) = 4.19 kilojoules. Figures represent the average supply available for the population as a whole and do not account for variations among individuals. **c.** Data from three years are averaged to produce the above values. **d.** Includes food aid. **e.** Data are collected from July 1 to June 30. Data from 1999, for example, are actually from July 1999 to June 2000. **f.** Data for China include Taiwan. **g.** Data relating to Kashmir-Jammu are generally included under India and excluded from figures for Pakistan. Data for Sikkim are included under India. **h.** Most data for recent years include those from East Timor. **i.** Inconsistencies with cropland or irrigated land data can cause values to erroneously be reported as greater than 100%. **j.** Data before 1993 include Eritrea.

VARIABLE DEFINITIONS AND METHODOLOGY

Data on agricultural production, yield, and trade published by the Food and Agriculture Organization of the United Nations (FAO) are generally gathered by surveys sent to, and filled out by, individual country governments or agencies. These results are compiled by FAO, who supplement missing or inaccurate data with their own estimates.

Average Production of Cereals refers to the amount of cereals produced in a given country or region each year. Data are reported in thousand metric tons. **Cereals** include wheat, barley, maize, rye, oats, millet, sorghum, rice, buckwheat, alpiste/canary seed, fonio, quinoa, triticale, wheat flour, and the cereal component of blended foods. Data relate to crops harvested for dry grain only. Harvesting losses, threshing losses, and unharvested portions of the crop are not included. Production therefore includes the quantities of the commodity sold in the market (marketed production) and the quantities consumed or used by the producers (auto-consumption). Cereal crops harvested for hay or harvested green for food, feed, or silage or used for grazing are excluded, although mixed grains and buckwheat are included. The time reference on crop production is based on the calendar year (Jan. to Dec.). That is to say, the data for any particular crop are reported under the calendar year in which the entire harvest or the bulk of it took place. In a number of cases, crops harvested during a split year (starting in November and ending in February, for example) may appear under two different calendar years.

Average Cereal Crop Yields refers to the amount of grain produced per unit of harvested area of cereals in a given country or region each year (i.e. average yield=total production/harvested area). Data are reported in kilograms per hectare of cropland. Area data relate to harvested area. Some countries report sown or cultivated area instead; however, in these countries the sown or cultivated area does not differ significantly in normal years from the area actually harvested, either because practically the whole area sown is harvested or because the area surveys are conducted around the harvest period. For most countries, FAO does not directly record yield data but instead divides production data by the area harvested for a particular country and year. In all cases, yields are computed from detailed area and production data.

Variation in Domestic Cereal Production, expressed as a percentage, is found by taking the average variation (absolute deviation from mean) of cereal production between 1992 and 2001 and dividing this by the mean production. This is an indicator of whether cereal production is stable enough to ensure a predictable food supply. Please refer to the definition of cereal production for more information.

Net Trade of Cereals as a Percent of Consumption indicates whether countries are able to produce sufficient grain for domestic consumption. It is calculated by dividing net imports (imports minus exports) by total cereal consumption (production + imports – exports). Import and export data have, for the most part, been supplied to FAO by governments through magnetic tapes, national publications and, most frequently, FAO questionnaires. Official trade data have sometimes been supplemented with data from unofficial sources, or trade information supplied by other national or international agencies or organizations. Cereal food aid shipments are included in FAO's import and export calculations. Information on food aid shipments has been provided to FAO by the World Food Program (please see http://www.wfp.org).

Average Meat Production Per Capita refers to the mass of meat in kilograms produced annually per person in a given country. Values were calculated by dividing the amount of meat

produced (in kilograms) by the population of a given country in a given year. Total meat production comprises horse meat, poultry meat and meat from all other domestic or wild animals such as camels, rabbits, reindeer, and game animals. Both commercial and farm slaughter are included. Meat production for most species is calculated by multiplying the number of animals slaughtered by the average dressed carcass weight. Dressed carcass weights exclude offal and slaughter fats. Data relate to animals slaughtered within national boundaries, irrespective of their origin. Production data were collected mostly from annual FAO surveys completed by governments. Data have been grouped in 12-month periods ending 30 September of the years stated in the tables. For example, animals enumerated in a given country at any time between 1 October and 30 September of the following year are shown under the latter year.

Irrigated Land as a Percentage of Total Cropland refers to the proportion of cropland equipped to provide water to crops. These include areas equipped for full and partial control irrigation, spate irrigation areas, and equipped wetland or inland valley bottoms.

Cropland includes arable and permanent cropland. Arable land is land under temporary crops (double-cropped areas are counted only once), temporary meadows for mowing or pasture, land under market and kitchen gardens, and land temporarily fallow (less than five years). Abandoned land resulting from shifting cultivation is not included in this category. Permanent cropland is land cultivated with crops that occupy the land for long periods and need not be replanted after each harvest, such as cocoa, coffee, and rubber; this category includes land under flowering shrubs, fruit trees, nut trees, and vines, but excludes land under trees grown for wood or timber. Data on land use are reported by country governments in questionnaires distributed by the FAO. However, for this variable, a significant percentage of data is based on FAO estimates, and some data are based on unofficial estimates.

Average Annual Fertilizer Use measures the amount of the nutrients nitrogen (N), potash (K_2O), and phosphate (P_2O_5) consumed annually per unit of cropland (see above for more information on cropland data). Data are reported in kg per hectare of cropland. Some countries report data based on the fertilizer year, from 1 July–30 June. For these countries, 1999 data were actually collected from 1 July 1999 to 30 June 2000. Data are collected through the FAO fertilizer questionnaire.

Average Daily Per Capita Calorie Supply refers to the amount of available food per person, per day, expressed in kilocalories (1 kilocalorie = 1 Calorie = 4.19 kilojoules). **Calorie Supply From Animal Products** refers to the amount of available food from animal products per person, per day. Animal products include: all types of meat and fish; animal fats and fish oils; edible offal; milk, butter, cheese, and cream; and eggs and egg products. FAO compiles statistics on apparent food consumption based on Supply/Utilization Accounts (SUAs) maintained in FAOSTAT. SUAs are time series data dealing with statistics on supply and utilization. For each product, the SUA traces supplies from production, imports, and stocks to utilization in different forms—addition to stocks, exports, animal feed, seed, processing for food and non-food purposes, waste (or losses), and lastly, as food available to the population, where appropriate. For internal consistency, total supply balances with total utilization. In many cases, commodities are not consumed in the primary form in which they are presented, e.g., cereals enter the household mainly in processed form like flour, meal, husked or milled rice. To take this fact into account, the caloric value has been derived by applying the appropriate food composition factors to the quantities of the processed commodities, not by examining primary commodities. Per capita supplies are derived from the total supplies available for human consumption by dividing the quantities of food by the total population actually partaking of the food supplies during the reference period. In almost all cases, the population figures used are the mid-year estimates published by the United Nations Population Division.

FREQUENCY OF UPDATE BY DATA PROVIDERS
Data from FAO are updated annually, with the exception of production data, which are updated three times each year, and trade data, which are updated semiannually. Population data used in per capita calculations are updated every two years by the United Nations Population Division. These updates often include revisions of past data.

DATA RELIABILITY AND CAUTIONARY NOTES
Agricultural data on production and trade reported to FAO are governed by established accounting practices and are therefore generally considered to be reliable. However, countries vary in the quality of data they have available to report. In addition, problems arise in compiling these data into internationally comparable agricultural statistics and in estimating data that are missing. Each variable in FAO's database can have as many as 30,000 data points associated with it for different countries and years. Officials need to ascertain, based on limited information, which one of various figures reported by various sources (national publications, FAO questionnaires, international publications, etc.) is the most recent or the most reliable. Variable definitions and coverage do not always conform to FAO recommendations, and therefore may not always be completely consistent across countries.

Production of subsistence crops and livestock is seldom reported in records of sales and processing, resulting in missing data points. Estimates of missing data are usually made by following the observed trend of the commodity in question in previous years, while also considering the trends in neighboring countries. When a complete time series is missing for a particular data set, FAO officials base their estimates on first-hand accounts through country visits and data from neighboring

countries. For more information, please refer to http://www.fao.org/ES/ESS/index.htm.

Cereal Production and Yields rely on accurate estimates of the sown and harvested crop area. However, in many countries, governments change the area sown each year to control prices and production through subsidies and other programs. Weather, soil quality, and seed availability often affect crop area in developing countries.

Average Meat Production estimates rely on accurate production figures from processing plants and import/export figures of live animals. Trade data are usually given by number rather than by weight, and the size of most domestic animals can vary by a factor of 10 or more depending on the age and condition of the animal. As a result, estimates of "average carcass weight" used to determine meat production vary in accuracy.

Average Annual Fertilizer Use data are excluded for some countries with a relatively small area of cropland, such as Iceland and Singapore. In these cases, the calculation of fertilizer consumed per hectare of cropland yields an unreliable number.

Per Capita Calorie Supply figures shown in the commodity balances represent only the average supply available for the population as a whole and do not necessarily indicate what is actually consumed by individuals. Even if data are used as approximations of per capita consumption, it is important to note that there could be considerable variation in consumption among individuals. Food supply data are only as accurate as the underlying production, trade, and utilization data.

SOURCES
Agricultural Variables: Food and Agriculture Organization of the United Nations (FAO). 2002. FAOSTAT On-line Statistical Service. Rome: FAO. Data available on-line at: http://apps.fao.org/. **Population** (used to calculate per capita values): Population Division of the Department of Economic and Social Affairs of the United Nations Secretariat. 2002. World Population Prospects: The 2000 Revision. New York: United Nations. Data set on CD-ROM.

Biodiversity and Protected Areas

Sources: United Nations Environment Programme-World Conservation Monitoring Centre (UNEP-WCMC), Ramsar Convention Bureau, United Nations Educational, Scientific and Cultural Organization (UNESCO), World Conservation Union (IUCN), Convention on International Trade in Endangered Species of Wild Flora and Fauna (CITES).

| | Nationally Protected Areas | | | | | Known and Threatened Species (1992-2002) | | | | | | International Legal Net Trade Reported by CITES, 2000 (imports minus exports) {b} | | |
| | Protected Areas Under IUCN Management Categories I - VI (1992-2003) {a} | | | Wetlands of Int'l Importance Area (000 ha) 2002 | Biosphere Reserves Area (000 ha) 2002 | Mammals | | Birds | | Higher Plants | | | | |
	Total Number	Percent of Land Protected	Number of Marine Areas {c}			Known Species	Number Threatened	Breeding Bird Species	Number Threatened	Known Species	Number Threatened	Live Primates	Live Parrots	Animal Skins {d}
WORLD {e}	**63,478**	**11.3**	..	**102,283**	**439,000**	..	..	..	..	..	..	**35,421**	**518,577**	**3,698,726**
ASIA (EXCL. MIDDLE EAST)	**3,655**	**7.6**	..	**5,641**	..	..	..	..	..	..	..	**(19,366)**	**(136,381)**	**(1,406,468)**
Armenia	5	7.6	..	492	..	84	11	236	4	3,553	1		(2)	
Azerbaijan	35	6.1	3	100	..	99	13	229	8	4,300	0			
Bangladesh	10	0.8	3	606	..	125	23	166	23	5,000	12		89	
Bhutan	10	25.1	..	..	..	160	22	209	12	5,468	7			
Cambodia	23	18.5	1	55	1,481	123	24	183	19		29	(200)		
China	809	7.8	30	2,548	3,316	394	79	618	74	32,200	168	(10,519)	(192,459)	67,287
Georgia	17	2.3	1	34	..	107	13	208	3	4,350	..		(1)	
India	497	5.2	60	195	1,515	390	88	458	72	18,664	244		4	0
Indonesia	1,080	20.6	95	243	2,062	515	147	929	114	29,375	384	(3,324)	25,025	(834,103)
Japan	96	6.8	19	84	116	188	37	210	34	5,565	11	4,863	27,417	427,978
Kazakhstan	73	2.7	1	..	..	178	16	379	15	6,000	1	7	3	
Korea, Dem People's Rep	31	2.6	..	..	132	..	13	150	19	2,898	3	25	4	1,828
Korea, Rep	30	6.9	7	1	39	49	13	138	25	2,898	0	51	370	57,126
Kyrgyzstan	78	3.6	..	..	4,335	83	7	168	4	4,500	1			
Lao People's Dem Rep	20	12.5	..	..	..	172	31	212	20	8,286	18			(4)
Malaysia	190	5.7	63	38	..	300	50	254	37	15,500	681	76	11,297	(772,717)
Mongolia	42	11.5	..	631	6,139	133	14	274	16	2,823	0			
Myanmar	4	0.3	1	..	..	300	39	310	35	7,000	37	(4)	67	
Nepal	15	8.9	..	18	..	181	31	274	25	6,973	6	2	135	
Pakistan	83	4.9	2	284	66	188	19	237	17	4,950	2	20	(17,274)	
Philippines	43	5.7	7	68	1,174	153	50	404	67	8,931	193	(2,085)	788	1,009
Singapore	5	4.9	..	..	..	85	3	142	7	2,282	54	83	5,484	(301,905)
Sri Lanka	110	13.5	13	8	36	88	22	126	14	3,314	280	(3)	476	
Tajikistan	19	4.2	..	95	..	84	9	210	7	5,000	2			
Thailand	158	13.9	18	132	85	265	37	285	37	11,625	78	63	2,587	(36,938)
Turkmenistan	23	4.2	1	..	35	103	13	204	6	..	0			
Uzbekistan	11	2.0	..	..	57	97	9	203	9	4,800	1	(1)	98	
Viet Nam	107	3.7	7	12	333	213	40	262	37	10,500	126	(3,149)	(2,751)	(109,458)
EUROPE	**39,432**	**8.3**	..	**19,248**	**128,034**	..	..	..	..	..	..	**13,583**	**305,812**	**1,868,230**
Albania	52	3.8	7	20	..	68	3	193	3	3,031	0			
Austria	719	33.0	..	118	47	83	7	230	3	3,100	3	4	(3)	401
Belarus	903	6.3	..	204	305	74	7	194	3	2,100	0			
Belgium	73	X	2	8	..	58	11	191	2	1,550	0	792	6,841	230
Bosnia and Herzegovina	21	0.5	..	7	..	72	10	205	3		1			
Bulgaria	127	4.5	1	3	38	81	14	248	10	3,572	0	(3)	41	(2)
Croatia	195	7.5	13	80	200	76	9	224	4	4,288	0	18	15	
Czech Rep	1,789	16.1	..	42	435	81	8	205	2	1,900	4	101	(14,058)	3
Denmark	255	34.0	52	2,283	97,200	43	5	196	1	1,450	3	(9)	(365)	1,632
Estonia	219	11.8	3	216	1,560	65	4	204	3	1,630	0	(3)	0	122
Finland	270	9.3	3	139	770	60	5	243	3	1,102	1		6	
France	1,325	13.3	70	795	900	93	18	283	5	4,630	2	3,437	12,422	310,941
Germany	7,315	31.9	..	829	1,559	76	11	247	5	2,682	12	1,129	4,927	403,919
Greece	88	3.6	10	164	9	95	13	255	7	4,992	2	58	19,717	281
Hungary	186	7.0	..	154	129	83	9	208	8	2,214	1	(33)	(275)	19,858
Iceland	79	9.8	5	59	..	11	6	93	0	377	0	(40)	197	1
Ireland	73	1.7	3	67	11	25	5	143	1	950	1	1	13	
Italy	427	7.9	28	57	204	90	14	250	5	5,599	3	270	27,557	776,148
Latvia	209	13.4	2	43	474	83	4	216	3	1,153	0	(15)	(4)	
Lithuania	79	10.3	3	50	..	68	5	201	4	1,796	0		155	
Macedonia, FYR	26	7.1	..	19	..	78	11	199	3	3,500	0			
Moldova, Rep	63	1.4	..	19	..	68	6	175	5	1,752	0			
Netherlands	86	14.2	10	327	260	55	10	192	4	1,221	0	1,364	1,094	73
Norway	178	6.8	10	70	..	54	10	241	2	1,715	2	(2)	7,386	42
Poland	579	12.4	4	90	398	84	15	233	4	2,450	4	54	683	(735)
Portugal	58	6.6	16	66	1	63	17	235	7	5,050	15	14	79,785	618
Romania	157	4.7	7	665	662	84	17	257	8	3,400	1	11	11	18
Russian Federation	10,863	7.8	14	10,324	20,532	269	45	528	38	11,400	7	2,112	3,001	(457)
Serbia and Montenegro	104	3.3	..	40	..	96	12	238	5	4,082	1	2,047	(1)	
Slovakia	1,040	22.8	..	38	241	85	9	199	4	3,124	2	1	(2,519)	4
Slovenia	32	6.0	1	1	..	75	9	201	1	3,200	0		1,187	140
Spain	328	8.5	27	158	1,181	82	24	281	7	5,050	14	452	152,460	251,411
Sweden	3,632	9.1	46	515	97	60	7	259	2	1,750	3	(10)	(6,145)	12
Switzerland	2,177	30.0	..	7	212	75	5	199	2	3,030	2	(40)	129	18,893
Ukraine	5,182	3.9	10	716	343	108	16	245	2	5,100	1	3	89	3
United Kingdom	579	20.9	95	855	30	50	12	229	2	1,623	13	1,881	7,828	84,667
MIDDLE EAST & N. AFRICA	**561**	**9.2**	..	..	..	..	..	..	..	..	..	**(296)**	**50,330**	**2,428**
Afghanistan	7	0.3	..	..	..	119	13	181	11	4,000	1			
Algeria	18	5.0	4	1,866	7,312	92	13	183	6	3,164	2		4	(3)
Egypt	35	9.7	12	106	2,456	98	13	123	7	2,076	2	(13)	(17)	(1)
Iran, Islamic Rep	78	4.8	6	1,476	2,753	140	22	293	13	8,000	1	55	2	
Iraq	8	0.0	..	..	..	81	11	140	11	..	0			
Israel	188	15.8	8	0	27	116	14	162	12	2,317	0	(273)	6,852	1
Jordan	11	3.4	..	7	31	71	10	117	8	2,100	0	(4)	373	
Kuwait	5	1.5	2	..	..	21	1	35	7	234	0		16,278	0
Lebanon	3	0.5	1	1	..	57	5	116	7	3,000	0	2	1,926	528
Libyan Arab Jamahiriya	8	0.1	3	..	..	76	8	76	1	1,825	1		0	
Morocco	12	0.7	4	14	9,754	105	16	206	9	3,675	2	(5)	48	38
Oman	6	14.0	2	..	..	56	9	109	10	1,204	6	14	22	
Saudi Arabia	78	38.3	3	..	..	77	8	125	15	2,028	3	86	9,699	438
Syrian Arab Rep	X	X	..	10	..	63	4	145	8	3,000	0		(1)	
Tunisia	7	0.3	2	13	74	78	11	165	5	2,196	0	5	432	
Turkey	78	1.6	14	159	..	116	17	278	11	8,650	3	6	2,147	1,422
United Arab Emirates	2	0.0	..	..	..	25	3	34	8	..	0	29	9,241	5
Yemen	X	X	..	..	..	66	5	93	12	1,650	52			

| | Nationally Protected Areas | | | | | Known and Threatened Species (1992-2002) | | | | | | International Legal Net Trade Reported by CITES, 2000 (imports minus exports) {b} | | |
| | Protected Areas Under IUCN Management Categories I - VI (1992-2003) {a} | | | Wetlands of Int'l Importance Area (000 ha) 2002 | Biosphere Reserves Area (000 ha) 2002 | Mammals | | Birds | | Higher Plants | | | | |
	Total Number	Percent of Land Protected	Number of Marine Areas {c}			Known Species	Number Threatened	Breeding Bird Species	Number Threatened	Known Species	Number Threatened	Live Primates	Live Parrots	Animal Skins {d}
SUB-SAHARAN AFRICA	**1,486**	**8.8**	..	..	..	..	..	..	..	..	..	**(12,677)**	**(201,235)**	**(399,556)**
Angola	14	6.6	4			276	19	265	15	5,185	19	..	(8)	..
Benin	5	11.4	..	139	623	188	8	112	2	2,500	11	1	2	..
Botswana	12	18.5	..	6,864		164	6	184	7	2,151	0	..	349	(85)
Burkina Faso	13	11.5	..	299	186	147	7	138	2	1,100	2	(1)	(3)	(1)
Burundi	13	5.7	1	1	..	107	6	145	7	2,500	2	..	..	..
Cameroon	18	4.5	2	..	876	409	40	165	15	8,260	155	(36)	(18,057)	(12)
Central African Rep	14	8.7	..	..	1,640	209	14	168	3	3,602	10	..	(19)	..
Chad	9	9.1	..	1,843	..	134	17	141	5	1,600	2	..	1	(76,139)
Congo	12	5.0	..	439	246	200	15	130	3	6,000	33	(2)	(2,102)	..
Congo, Dem Rep	43	6.5	..	866	283	450	40	345	28	11,007	55	(22)	(15,780)	..
Côte d'Ivoire	12	6	3	19	1,770	230	19	252	12	3,660	101	(5)	(2,727)	(5)
Equatorial Guinea	X	X	..	..	..	184	16	172	5	3,250	23	(1)	(5)	..
Eritrea	3	4.3	..	..	..	112	12	138	7	..	3	..	..	..
Ethiopia	39	16.9	..	..	..	277	35	262	16	6,603	22	..	..	(931)
Gabon	3	0.7	2	1,080	15	190	15	156	5	6,651	71	42	(42)	..
Gambia	6	2.3	5	20	..	117	3	154	2	974	3	1	15	..
Ghana	16	5.6	..	178	8	222	14	206	8	3,725	115	(44)	(2)	(15)
Guinea	3	0.7	..	4,779	261	190	12	109	10	3,000	21	(27)	(17,584)	(16,012)
Guinea-Bissau	X	X	..	39	110	108	3	235	0	1,000	4	..	(7)	..
Kenya	68	8.0	11	91	1,335	359	51	344	24	6,506	98	(218)	(32)	(2,465)
Lesotho	1	0.2	..	..	..	33	3	123	7	1,591	0	..	..	..
Liberia	2	1.7	1	..	..	193	17	146	11	2,200	46	..	(3,000)	(1)
Madagascar	62	4.3	2	53	293	141	50	172	27	9,505	162	0	(3,899)	(5,601)
Malawi	9	11.2	..	225	45	195	8	219	11	3,765	14	..	2	(199)
Mali	13	3.7	..	162	2,500	137	13	191	4	1,741	6	..	(6,829)	(69,323)
Mauritania	9	1.7	3	1,231	..	61	10	172	2	1,100	0	..	10	(1)
Mozambique	12	8.4	6	..	..	179	14	144	16	5,692	36	(1)	(57)	(758)
Namibia	21	13.6	4	630	..	250	15	201	11	3,174	5	2	1,007	(261)
Niger	6	7.7	..	715	25,128	131	11	125	3	1,460	2	17	2	..
Nigeria	27	3.3	..	58	131	274	27	286	9	4,715	119	..	0	(3)
Rwanda	6	6.2	..	..	13	151	9	200	9	2,288	3	..	..	..
Senegal	14	11.6	6	100	1,094	192	12	175	4	2,086	7	(154)	(30,283)	8,950
Sierra Leone	6	2.1	..	295	..	147	12	172	10	2,090	43	..	(1,108)	(75)
Somalia	10	0.8	1	..	..	171	19	179	10	3,028	17	..	..	..
South Africa	542	5.5	20	499	3,371	247	42	304	28	23,420	45	(342)	(99,390)	(26,761)
Sudan	27	5.2	1	..	1,251	267	23	280	6	3,137	17	..	51	(152,270)
Tanzania, United Rep	98	29.8	..	4,272	5,228	316	42	229	33	10,008	236	(4,424)	(82)	(1,582)
Togo	9	7.9	..	194	..	196	9	117	0	3,085	9	..	(436)	(4,079)
Uganda	54	24.6	..	15	247	345	20	243	13	4,900	33	..	..	(508)
Zambia	77	31.9	..	333	..	233	11	252	11	4,747	8	2	54	(12,428)
Zimbabwe	68	12.1	..	..	..	270	11	229	10	4,440	14	(1)	(1,226)	(53,403)
NORTH AMERICA	**7,412**	**23.4**	..	**14,241**	**35,943**	..	..	..	..	..	..	**15,476**	**26,860**	**213,733**
Canada	3,822	11.1	109	13,052	4,373	193	14	310	8	3,270	1	629	2,716	1,839
United States	3,481	25.9	229	1,190	31,570	428	37	508	55	19,473	..	14,845	24,034	211,894
C. AMERICA & CARIBBEAN	**1,476**	**15.1**	..	**3,186**	**15,729**	..	..	..	..	..	..	**(530)**	**(3,400)**	**710,492**
Belize	53	45.1	11	7	..	125	4	161	2	2,894	28	..	(68)	..
Costa Rica	130	23.0	14	313	729	205	14	279	13	12,119	109	2	118	..
Cuba	321	69.1	43	452	1,384	31	11	86	18	6,522	160	1	(15,944)	..
Dominican Rep {f}	61	51.9	12	20	..	20	5	79	15	5,657	29	6	662	..
El Salvador	3	0.4	2	2	..	135	2	141	0	2,911	23	6	0	(50)
Guatemala	42	20.0	3	503	2,350	250	6	221	6	8,681	77	(5)	3,757	..
Haiti	8	0.4	..	..	..	20	4	62	14	5,242	27	..	..	..
Honduras	72	6.4	10	172	800	173	10	232	5	5,680	108	4	1,412	..
Jamaica	143	84.6	2	6	..	24	5	75	12	3,308	206	..	..	2
Mexico	224	10.2	34	1,157	6,770	491	70	440	39	26,071	..	500	10,190	694,613
Nicaragua	73	17.8	4	406	2,182	200	6	215	5	7,590	39	(6)	(6,327)	(3,164)
Panama	33	21.7	10	111	1,515	218	20	302	16	9,915	193	38	1,084	19,090
Trinidad and Tobago	25	6.0	6	6	..	100	1	131	1	2,259	1	0	147	..
SOUTH AMERICA	**1,697**	**10.6**	..	**23,360**	**163,832**	..	..	..	..	..	..	**(1,812)**	**(50,450)**	**(1,023,927)**
Argentina	320	6.6	26	2,670	2,848	320	34	362	39	9,372	42	2	(18,474)	(326,123)
Bolivia	23	13.4	..	5,504	735	316	24	504	28	17,367	70	..	(2)	..
Brazil	802	6.7	70	6,346	125,042	394	81	686	114	56,215	..	14	31	18,460
Chile	87	18.9	26	100	2,479	91	21	157	22	5,284	40	(2)	547	..
Colombia	101	10.2	11	439	3,338	359	41	708	78	51,220	213	(4)	97	(544,565)
Ecuador {f}	27	18.3	4	83	17,375	302	33	640	62	19,362	197	(1)	(1)	(2)
Guyana	1	0.3	..	..	..	193	11	242	2	6,409	23	(1,220)	(12,562)	..
Paraguay	20	3.5	..	775	280	305	10	233	26	7,851	10	..	(1,477)	(171,373)
Peru	36	6.1	4	6,759	3,268	460	49	695	76	17,144	269	(321)	(2,171)	(3)
Suriname	18	4.9	4	12	..	180	12	235	1	5,018	27	(283)	(9,410)	..
Uruguay	13	0.3	4	407	200	81	6	115	11	2,278	1	..	(8,929)	..
Venezuela	195	63.8	16	264	8,266	323	26	547	24	21,073	67	3	1,901	(321)
OCEANIA	**7,759**	**13.2**	..	**5,944**	**5,478**	..	..	..	..	..	..	**0**	**(4,496)**	**(13,443)**
Australia {f}	4,071	13.4	285	5,310	5,478	252	63	497	37	15,638	38	102	(75)	(10,440)
Fiji	15	1.1	2	..	..	4	5	47	12	1,518	65	..	(1)	(70)
New Zealand	3,515	29.6	67	39	..	2	8	190	63	2,382	21	0	(4,004)	50
Papua New Guinea	29	2.3	9	595	..	214	58	414	32	11,544	142	..	(1)	(2,980)
Solomon Islands	1	0.3	1	..	..	53	20	111	23	3,172	16	..	(406)	..
DEVELOPED	**55,408**	**12.0**	..	**40,142**	**177,396**	..	..	..	..	..	..	**33,413**	**263,460**	**2,472,791**
DEVELOPING	**8,070**	**10.7**	..	**60,580**		..	..	..	..	..	..	**(34,641)**	**(276,420)**	**(2,521,302)**

a. Does not include data protected under international agreements. Data on Total Number and Percent of Land Protected are from a preliminary version of the World Database on Protected Areas and are incomplete for many countries. Please consult UNEP-WCMC for an updated version of this data set. **b.** CITES trade is expressed as the balance of imports minus exports. Exports are shown as negative balance (in parentheses). **c.** Includes both marine and littoral areas with substantial terrestrial components that reach the shore. **d.** Trade in animal skins includes the skins of crocodiles, wild cats, lizards, and snakes. **e.** World totals include countries that are not listed here; World values for CITES trade data represent net exports **f.** Extent of protected areas may include marine components that artificially inflate the percentage of land area protected.

255

VARIABLE DEFINITIONS AND METHODOLOGY

An **IUCN Management Protected Area** is defined by IUCN as "an area of land and/or sea especially dedicated to the protection and maintenance of biological diversity, and of natural and associated cultural resources, and managed through legal or other effective means." As of Fall 2002 a World Database on Protected Areas (WDPA) consortium has been working to produce an improved and updated database available in the public domain. Summary information presented in the WDPA, of which UNEP-WCMC is the custodian, includes the legal designation, name, IUCN Management Category, size in hectares, location (latitude and longitude), and the year of establishment for over 100,000 sites. On May 9, 2003, UNEP-WCMC provided WRI with preliminary—and incomplete—protected areas data. IUCN categorizes protected areas by management objective and has identified six distinct categories of protected areas:

Category Ia. Strict nature reserve: A protected area managed mainly for scientific research and monitoring; an area of land and/or sea possessing some outstanding or representative ecosystems, geological or physiological features and/or species.

Category Ib. Wilderness area: A protected area managed mainly for wilderness protection; a large area of unmodified or slightly modified land and/or sea retaining its natural character and influence, without permanent or significant habitation, which is protected and managed so as to preserve its natural condition.

Category II. National park: A protected area managed mainly for ecosystem protection and recreation; a natural area of land and/or sea designated to: (a) protect the ecological integrity of one or more ecosystems for present and future generations; (b) exclude exploitation or occupation inimical to the purposes of designation of the area; and (c) provide a foundation for spiritual, scientific, educational, recreational, and visitor opportunities, all of which must be environmentally and culturally compatible.

Category III. Natural monument: A protected area managed mainly for conservation of specific natural features; an area containing one or more specific natural or natural/cultural features that is of outstanding or unique value because of its inherent rarity, representative or aesthetic qualities, or cultural significance.

Category IV. Habitat/species management area: A protected area managed mainly for conservation through management intervention; an area of land and/or sea subject to active intervention for management purposes so as to ensure the maintenance of habitats and/or to meet the requirements of specific species.

Category V. Protected landscape/seascape: A protected area managed mainly for landscape/seascape conservation and recreation; an area of land, with coast and sea as appropriate, where the interaction of people and nature over time has produced an area of distinct character with significant aesthetic, ecological, and/or cultural value, and often with high biological diversity.

Category VI. Managed mainly for the sustainable use of natural ecosystems. These areas contain predominantly unmodified natural systems, managed to ensure long-term protection and maintenance of biological diversity, while also providing a sustainable flow of natural products and services to meet community needs.

IUCN defines a **Marine Protected Area** as: "any area of intertidal or subtidal terrain, together with its overlying water and associated flora and fauna, historical and cultural features, which has been reserved by law or other effective means to protect part or all of the enclosed environment."

These marine protected areas (MPAs) include areas that are fully marine and areas that have only a small percentage of intertidal land. Many MPAs have large terrestrial areas. The extent of the marine portion of most protected areas is rarely documented. The degree of protection varies from one country to another, and may bear little relationship to the legal status of any site. "Littoral" is defined as any site which is known to incorporate at least some intertidal area.

Ramsar Sites, or Wetlands of International Importance, are defined under the Wetlands Convention, signed in Ramsar, Iran, in 1971. In order to qualify as a Ramsar site, an area must have "international significance in terms of ecology, botany, zoology, limnology or hydrology." The Convention on Wetlands is an intergovernmental treaty that provides the framework for national action and international cooperation for the conservation and wise use of wetlands and their resources. There are presently 133 Contracting Parties to the Convention, with 1,179 wetland sites totaling 102.1 million hectares, designated for inclusion in the Ramsar List of Wetlands of International Importance.

Biosphere Reserves are terrestrial and coastal/marine environments recognized under UNESCO's Man and the Biosphere Programme. Selected for their value to conservation, they are intended to foster the scientific knowledge and skills necessary for improving the balance between people and nature, and for promoting sustainable development. Ideally, fully functional biosphere reserves perform three main roles: (i) conservation in situ of natural and semi-natural ecosystems and landscapes; (ii) the establishment of demonstration areas for ecologically and socio-culturally sustainable resource use; and (iii) the provision of logistic support for research, monitoring, education, training, and information exchange. Each biosphere reserve consists of three elements: a minimally disturbed core area for conservation and research; a buffer zone where traditional land uses, research, and ecosystem rehabilitation may be permitted; and a transition area. This data table lists the acreage of all three elements; however, only the core area requires legal protection. Biosphere reserves are nominated by national governments and remain under the sovereign jurisdiction of the state where they are located. As of August 2002, there are 408 biosphere reserves in 94 countries. Several countries share transboundary biosphere reserves. These sites are counted only once in regional and world totals.

The **Total Number of Known Species** refers to the total number of a particular type of species in a given country. Data on **known mammals** exclude marine mammals. Data on **known birds** include only birds that breed in that country, not those that migrate or winter there. The number of **known higher plants** includes ferns and fern allies, conifers and cycads, and flowering plants that have been classified as threatened by IUCN.

The number of known species is collected by WCMC from a variety of sources, including, but not limited to: national reports from the convention on biodiversity, other national documents, independent studies, and other texts. Data are updated on a continual basis as they become available; however, updates vary widely by country. While some countries (WCMC estimates about 12) have data that were updated in the last 6 months, other species estimates have not changed since the data were first collected in 1992.

The **Number of Threatened Species** listed for all countries includes full species that are "Critically Endangered, Endangered, or Vulnerable," but excludes introduced species, species whose status is insufficiently known (categorized by IUCN as "data deficient"), those known to be extinct, and those for which status has not been assessed (categorized by IUCN as "not evaluated").

CITES Trade Data: The international trade in wildlife and wildlife products, worth billions of dollars annually, causes serious declines in the numbers of many species of animals and plants. In response, the Convention on International Trade in Endangered Species of Wild Fauna and Flora (CITES) was drawn up in 1973 to protect wildlife against such overexploitation and to prevent international trade from threatening species with extinction. Species are listed in appendixes to CITES on the basis of their degree of rarity and the threat posed by trade. International trade in either the listed species themselves or in products derived from the species requires permits or certificates for export, import, and re-export.

Parties to the Convention are required to submit annual reports, including trade records, to the CITES Secretariat. These trade records are compiled in the CITES Trade Database and were given to WRI by UNEP-WCMC.

Net Trade in 2000 is the balance of imports minus exports. Exports are shown as a negative balance in parentheses. Figures are for trade reported in 2000. Data on net exports and net imports as reported by CITES correspond to legal international trade and are based on permits issued, not actual items traded. Figures may be overestimates if not all permits are used that year. Some permits issued in one year are used at a later date; therefore, numbers of exports and imports may not match exactly for any given year. World totals show the total number of exports, since calculating the balance of trade for the world would have canceled most figures.

Number of live primates includes all species of monkeys, apes, and prosimians listed under CITES that were traded live in 2000. **Number of live parrots** includes individuals from the Psittaciformes species listed under CITES that were traded live in 2000. **Number of animal skins** includes whole skins of all crocodile, cat, lizard, and snake species that were traded in 2000.

FREQUENCY OF UPDATE BY DATA PROVIDERS

Protected Areas Data. At the time of publication, the **WDPA** was under revision. The current version is expected to be finalized prior to the World Parks Congress in September 2003. Please contact UNEP-WCMC for more information. **Known species** of plants and mammals are updated when new information is provided to WCMC (see above); contact WCMC for the latest data. **Threatened species** data are updated by IUCN on a continual basis. **CITES trade data** refer to annual reports. Table data is for the calendar year 2000. Data are updated annually.

DATA RELIABILITY AND CAUTIONARY NOTES:

Protected areas serve a vital function in protecting the earth's resources. But they face many challenges—external threats associated with pollution and climate change, irresponsible tourism, infrastructure developments and the ever

increasing demands for land and water resources. Protected areas are also particularly susceptible to invasive species. In addition, many areas lack political support and have inadequate financial and other resources. Due to variations in consistency and methodology of collection, data on protected areas are highly variable among countries. Some countries update their information with greater regularity; others may have more accurate data on extent of coverage. Additionally, at the time of publication, the protected areas data set was under revision and incomplete. Many countries have an underreported number and/or extent of protected areas within their borders. Please contact UNEP-WCMC for a revised data set.

Data on **known species of mammals, birds and plants** are preliminary estimates based on a compilation of available data from a large variety of sources. They are not based on species checklists. Data have been collected over the last decade without a consistent approach to taxonomy. Additionally, while the number of species in each country does change, not all countries have been updated; some data may not reflect recent trends. Finally, users should be aware of greater inconsistency and less reliability with the higher plants data than with mammals and birds.

Biosphere Reserves include three zones: a core area or areas, a buffer zone or zones, and an outer transition area. According to the Statutory Framework, the transition area does not have to be clearly defined. Therefore, the area of the biosphere reserves presented in this table may not correspond exactly to the actual territory concerned.

Species traded within national borders and illegal trade in wildlife and wildlife products are not reflected in these figures. Illegal trade in wildlife products is estimated to be in the billions of dollars annually. CITES trade data also do not reflect legal trade between non-CITES members. In addition, data on mortality of individuals during capture or collection, transit, or quarantine are also not reflected in these numbers.

SOURCES

Protected Areas (IUCN management categories, marine protected areas): World Database on Protected Areas (WDPA), compiled by the World Database on Protected Areas Consortium, unpublished data (UNEP-WCMC, Cambridge, U.K., May, 2003). **Ramsar Sites (Wetlands of International Importance):** Ramsar Convention Bureau, Gland, Switzerland. Available on-line at: http://ramsar.org/sitelist.pdf. **Biosphere Reserves:** United Nations Educational, Scientific, and Cultural Organization (UNESCO) Man and the Biosphere Programme, List of Biosphere Reserves available on-line at: http://www.unesco.org/mab/wnbr.htm. **Known Species of Mammals, Plants, and Breeding Birds:** World Conservation Monitoring Centre (WCMC) Species Database, unpublished data (WCMC, Cambridge, U.K., July, 2002). **Endangered Species of Mammals, Plants and Birds:** IUCN Redlist available on-line at http://www.redlist.org. **International Legal Net Trade Reported by CITES:** Convention on International Trade in Endangered Species of Wild Flora and Fauna (CITES) annual report data, World Conservation Monitoring Centre (WCMC) CITES Trade Database (WCMC, Cambridge, U.K., July 2002).

Climate and Atmosphere

Sources: Carbon Dioxide Information Analysis Center (CDIAC), International Energy Agency (IEA), Netherlands Institute for Public Health (RIVM)

	Carbon Dioxide (CO2) Emissions Total (million metric tons) 1999	Total (percent change since 1990)	Per Capita (metric tons per person) 1999	Per Capita (percent change since 1990)	Cumulative (million metric tons) 1800-2000	Methane (million metric tons CO2 equivalent) 1995	Nitrous Oxide 1995	Industry	Residential	Road Transportation	Public Electricity and Heat	All Economic Sectors 1990	All Economic Sectors 1999	Industry Sector 1990	Industry Sector 1999
WORLD	23,172.2	8.9	3.9	(4.2)	1,017,359	6,340	3,570	4336.6	1802.1	4064.7	7424.4	689	582	..	..
ASIA (EXCL. MIDDLE EAST)	6,901.7	38.0	2.1	19.3	..	2,562	1,177	1915.4	471.0	789.0	2446.9	616	540	543	422
Armenia	3.0	..	0.8	..	290 a	2	1	1.1	0.0	0.1	1.5	..	347	..	384
Azerbaijan	33.2	..	4.2	..	2,300 a	10	3	4.1	4.9	0.9	13.9	..	1,756	..	653
Bangladesh	26.3	83.4	0.2	46.2	442 b	85	29	8.3	3.2	2.5	8.6	119	144	168	186
Bhutan	..	..	..	..	4	1	0								
Cambodia	..	..	..	..	16	13	4								
China	3,051.1 c	25.6 c	2.5 c	16.6 c	72,615 c	959	538	979.4 c	210.7 c	142.8 c	1247.1 c	1,355 c	700 c	1,249 c	442 c
Georgia	5.3	..	1.0	..	380 a	3	1	0.7	0.8	1.4	0.9	..	376	..	305
India	903.8	52.9	0.9	31.9	20,275	655	257	205.5	56.2	119.3	399.1	446	417	517	360
Indonesia	244.9	76.9	1.2	56.0	4,872	215	67	46.0	42.3	52.6	49.7	365	449	188	174
Japan	1,158.5	10.5	9.1	7.7	36,577 d	61	30	260.6	71.2	224.0	314.4	396	391	234	259
Kazakhstan	114.5	..	7.0	..	8,264 a	42	18	36.4	..	4.1	55.2	..	1,651	..	1,360
Korea, Dem People's Rep	214.3	(1.2)	9.7	(10.8)	6,114 e	10	8	158.4	0.7	9.1	32.3	..	..	..	..
Korea, Rep	410.4	75.5	8.8	62.2	7,120 e	27	12	75.7	24.8	59.3	94.3	546	578	385	247
Kyrgyzstan	4.7	..	1.0	..	440 a	4	3	1.2	..	0.7	1.7	..	405	..	391
Lao People's Dem Rep	..	..	..	..	11	7	4								
Malaysia	101.3	90.4	4.6	55.7	1,832 f	24	12	24.0	2.3	29.3	27.7	552	578	362	321
Mongolia	..	..	..	..	237	8	13								
Myanmar	9.0	122.2	0.2	90.0	257	50	16	1.3	0.8	3.2	2.7	41	54	102	90
Nepal	3.0	234.4	0.1	225.0	32	34	6	1.1	0.8	0.7	0.0	49	107	80	171
Pakistan	92.2	48.9	0.7	17.9	1,952 b	92	68	26.2	9.0	22.9	26.8	370	389	490	467
Philippines	66.3	69.0	0.9	39.1	1,555	44	20	11.2	3.5	20.6	19.1	180	239	106	122
Singapore	53.2	53.1	13.6	17.9	1,690 g	1	1	2.4	..	5.8	27.4	803	643	130	82
Sri Lanka	9.6	141.5	0.5	121.7	220	11	3	1.9	0.3	4.9	1.3	105	161	48	116
Tajikistan	5.7	..	0.9	..	270 a	4	2	0.0	..	3.1	0.7	..	568	..	..
Thailand	155.8	95.5	2.5	73.1	2,535	73	24	35.4	3.9	46.3	49.6	335	445	159	250
Turkmenistan	33.9	..	7.3	..	910 a	19	5	0.0	..	1.5	8.7	..	2,213	..	..
Uzbekistan	117.5	..	4.8	..	5,020	45	10	19.2	32.6	6.1	35.0	..	2,241	..	1,423
Viet Nam	36.6	103.7	0.5	74.1	1,061 h	59	20	9.7	2.2	12.2	7.2	248	259	427	198
EUROPE	5,892.3	..	8.1	..	411,552	1,164	607	1010.0	714.9	988.8	1816.4	..	568	..	320
Albania	1.5	(77.4)	0.5	(76.6)	198	2	2	0.4	0.2	0.6	0.1	667	146	585	138
Austria	60.5	6.1	7.5	1.5	4,099	8	7	13.9	8.2	16.6	9.3	365	319	250	214
Belarus	57.1	..	5.6	..	3,457 a	17	11	7.7	4.3	5.4	22.3	..	853	..	255
Belgium	118.7	11.8	11.6	8.9	10,569	10	12	32.0	20.3	23.3	21.2	517	487	440	466
Bosnia and Herzegovina	5.3	..	1.4	..	185 i	1	1	0.2	..	0.8	2.6	..	..	..	..
Bulgaria	43.8	(42.5)	5.4	(37.7)	3,144	7	9	9.7	1.4	5.2	22.2	1,545	1,147	501	924
Croatia	19.0	..	4.1	..	576 i	3	3	3.7	2.1	4.1	4.5	..	..	..	..
Czech Rep	110.6	(26.5)	10.8	(26.3)	10,139 j	16	8	25.0	7.1	10.6	51.8	1,122	860	857	458
Denmark	53.3 k	7.2 k	10.0 k	3.9 k	3,342	6	8	5.1 k	4.7 k	11.4 k	24.8 k	457 k	401 k	170 k	128 k
Estonia	14.7	..	10.4	..	349 a	2	1	1.0	0.5	1.2	10.7	..	1,294	..	315
Finland	57.8	8.4	11.2	4.8	2,001	7	6	14.0	3.9	11.2	18.0	536	495	437	349
France	361.4 l	(0.7) l	6.1 l	(4.5) l	30,997 l	50	90	79.4 l	58.6 l	128.1 l	25.1 l	320 l	276 l	227 l	224 l
Germany	821.7 m	(15.0) m	10.0 m	(17.7) m	75,606	93	78	128.7 m	118.9 m	173.8 m	274.4 m	599 m	444 m	282 m	218 m
Greece	81.5	18.2	7.7	13.4	2,390	6	14	9.6	7.0	15.8	41.6	565	556	297	253
Hungary	57.9	(14.4)	5.8	(11.4)	3,920	12	7	7.4	8.8	8.7	26.2	647	538	392	..
Iceland	2.1	3.0	7.4	(5.2)	88	0	0	0.6	0.3	0.6	0.0	345	294	261	..
Ireland	39.9	24.1	10.6	15.8	1,269	12	14	4.9	5.8	9.1	15.2	620	430	259	143
Italy	420.5	6.0	7.3	4.4	16,337 e	40	33	79.0	72.4	110.9	97.1	366	342	231	217
Latvia	6.8	..	2.8	..	470 a	2	1	1.2	0.3	1.7	2.7	..	481	..	291
Lithuania	13.0	..	3.5	..	889 a	4	2	1.9	0.6	3.2	4.8	..	560	..	251
Macedonia, FYR	10.0	4.7	5.0	(1.0)	300 i	1	1	0.9	0.3	1.1	6.2	..	..	..	..
Moldova, Rep	6.6	..	1.5	..	590 a	4	2	0.8	0.3	0.4	2.8	..	754	..	445
Netherlands	166.6 n	6.4 n	10.5 n	0.8 n	9,404	18	17	34.8 n	18.9 n	28.7 n	46.8 n	529 n	442 n	387 n	337 n
Norway	37.1	30.5	8.3	24.3	1,717	10	3	6.9	0.9	9.8	0.2	336	323	203	164
Poland	310.0	(11.0)	8.0	(12.3)	20,764	83	32	48.1	32.3	29.0	151.5	1,432	926	351	389
Portugal	61.1 o	53.1 o	6.1 o	51.6 o	1,509	8	7	12.4 o	2.1 o	15.8 o	21.4 o	319 o	390 o	235 o	237 o
Romania	86.6	(49.5)	3.9	(47.9)	6,440	29	17	18.9	6.1	7.4	35.7	1,059	696	734	389
Russian Federation	1,486.3	..	10.2	..	86,705 a	498	64	192.4	146.1	101.0	495.5	..	1,482	..	530
Serbia and Montenegro	41.9	(30.3)	4.0	(33.0)	2,390 j	10	7	7.4	0.1	4.2	26.1	..	..	..	..
Slovakia	39.4	(28.9)	7.3	(30.7)	3,644 i	6	3	14.4	3.6	4.1	10.2	1,096	718	844	818
Slovenia	15.0	17.0	7.5	12.9	455	2	1	2.2	1.8	3.8	5.7	..	..	..	..
Spain	272.0 p	28.6 p	6.8 p	26.6 p	9,151	31	36	47.7 p	16.2 p	77.5 p	76.9 p	379 p	395 p	236 p	223 p
Sweden	48.2	(0.6)	5.4	(3.9)	4,058	8	7	10.4	3.6	20.0	7.1	283	246	197	..
Switzerland	39.9 q	(3.1) q	5.6 q	(7.7) q	2,262	5	3	6.1 q	12.0 q	14.7 q	0.2 q	227 q	208 q	.. q	.. q
Ukraine	379.0	..	7.6	..	22,729 a	101	33	105.8	61.8	10.1	110.4	..	2,329	..	1,726
United Kingdom	535.3	(6.5)	9.0	(9.2)	68,803	52	66	74.4	81.6	114.4	143.5	567	440	226	205
MIDDLE EAST & N. AFRICA	1,339.2	45.0	3.6	19.7	..	289	186	299.5	118.5	233.7	395.5	655	721	374	..
Afghanistan	..	..	..	..	82	11	7								
Algeria	68.2	19.8	2.3	0.4	2,178	20	9	7.0	9.6	6.2	16.4	444	463	77	63
Egypt	110.3	33.7	1.7	13.0	2,682	27	19	29.4	11.3	16.6	32.9	580	529	612	448
Iran, Islamic Rep	263.2	45.6	3.8	23.0	6,664	67	53	58.4	45.5	66.4	62.1	765	783	647	762
Iraq	81.1	47.7	3.6	14.5	1,985	9	6	17.2	6.4	25.9	16.2	1,178	2,816	..	..
Israel	55.9	58.2	9.5	20.8	1,203	1	1	6.0	1.9	9.5	30.9	510	517	..	..
Jordan	13.4	43.1	2.8	(2.8)	286	1	1	2.0	1.7	3.3	4.9	824	744	409	427
Kuwait	46.5	122.0	25.2	157.4	1,268	7	0	15.1	3.0	6.0	21.2	1,174	1,960	796	..
Lebanon	15.6	143.6	4.5	92.8	326	1	1	2.9	1.9	4.2	6.7	717	875	..	729
Libyan Arab Jamahiriya	41.4	52.6	8.0	27.0	1,062	9	2	4.9	2.2	10.1	12.7	880	1,550	..	..
Morocco	28.0	49.9	1.0	26.7	703	9	14	5.4	3.3	1.3	9.0	243	298	157	177
Oman	21.1	104.3	8.6	48.3	307	2	1	5.7	0.2	2.5	6.3	376	519	156	..
Saudi Arabia	216.0	35.1	11.0	5.9	5,836	51	9	41.6	3.3	29.7	57.1	923	1,031	277	..
Syrian Arab Rep	48.1	49.8	3.0	17.4	898	6	8	9.7	2.3	3.7	11.2	1,051	938	413	626
Tunisia	16.7	31.3	1.8	14.1	416	4	5	3.8	1.7	3.8	5.1	350	303	308	245
Turkey	182.8	32.2	2.8	13.0	4,137	25	41	43.3	22.1	29.9	56.8	466	467	320	397
United Arab Emirates	67.1	59.8	26.2	25.8	2,047	26	1	30.0	0.3	5.4	28.3	1,014	1,347	837	..
Yemen	8.6	17.9	0.5	(22.6)	295 r	6	5	0.5	1.6	3.9	1.3	734	664	199	97

| | Carbon Dioxide (CO2) Emissions | | | | | Emissions of | | CO2 Emissions by Economic Sector (million metric tons), 1999 | | | | Carbon Intensity: CO2 Emissions per GDP (PPP) (tons CO2 per million $ intl) | | | |
| | Total | | Per Capita | | Cumu-lative | Methane | Nitrous Oxide | | | | | | All Economic Sectors | | Industry Sector | |
	(million metric tons) 1999	(percent change since 1990)	(metric tons per person) 1999	(percent change since 1990)	(million metric tons) 1800-2000	(million metric tons CO2 equivalent) 1995	1995	Industry	Resid-ential	Road Trans-portation	Public Electricity and Heat	1990	1999	1990	1999
SUB-SAHARAN AFRICA	..	..	..	..	17,665	488	378	..	..	..	..	..	..	..	..
Angola	4.8	11.6	0.4	(17.8)	219	14	5	1.6	0.3	1.2	0.4	410	428	401	185
Benin	1.2	391.7	0.2	280.0	19	3	2	0.2	0.3	0.8	0.0	54	216	62	193
Botswana	..	..	..	..	54	6	4	..	..	..	..	..	..	..	..
Burkina Faso	..	..	..	..	16	8	11	..	..	..	..	..	..	..	..
Burundi	..	..	..	..	6	2	1	..	..	..	..	..	..	..	..
Cameroon	2.6	(5.5)	0.2	(26.1)	143	11	9	0.2	0.6	1.6	0.0	131	115	36	44
Central African Rep	..	..	..	..	8	6	5	..	..	..	..	..	..	..	..
Chad	..	..	..	..	7	9	8	..	..	..	..	..	..	..	..
Congo	0.4	(53.2)	0.1	(65.7)	50	3	1	0.0	0.0	0.3	..	321	164	59	..
Congo, Dem Rep	2.5	(41.0)	0.0	(63.6)	178	29	20	0.7	0.3	0.5	0.0	74	78	56	..
Côte d'Ivoire	4.7	52.8	0.3	20.8	156	6	3	0.7	0.4	1.3	3.3	162	184	130	112
Equatorial Guinea	..	..	..	..	14	0	0	..	..	..	..	..	..	..	..
Eritrea	0.6	..	0.2	..	9	2	1	0.1	0.1	0.2	0.1	..	181	..	52
Ethiopia	2.9	22.1	0.0	(20.0)	81	42	53	0.8	0.5	1.6	0.0	86	76	170	186
Gabon	1.5	30.7	1.2	2.5	161	..	..	0.4	0.1	0.5	0.3	190	209	80	132
Gambia	..	..	..	..	5	1	0	..	..	..	..	..	..	..	..
Ghana	4.4	67.6	0.2	35.3	127	6	7	0.5	0.6	1.9	1.0	112	129	123	53
Guinea	..	..	..	..	40	5	2	..	..	..	..	..	..	..	..
Guinea-Bissau	..	..	..	..	6	1	1	..	..	..	..	..	..	..	..
Kenya	7.7	17.2	0.3	(7.4)	239	20	20	1.5	0.5	2.2	1.1	259	260	297	288
Lesotho	..	..	..	..	3	1	1	..	..	..	..	..	..	..	..
Liberia	..	..	..	..	42	1	1	..	..	..	..	..	..	..	..
Madagascar	..	..	..	..	45	17	10	..	..	..	..	..	..	..	..
Malawi	..	..	..	..	27 s	3	2	..	..	..	..	..	..	..	..
Mali	..	..	..	..	15	11	12	..	..	..	..	..	..	..	..
Mauritania	..	..	..	..	46	4	6	..	..	..	..	..	..	..	..
Mozambique	1.1	7.0	0.1	(28.6)	102	10	3	0.1	0.1	0.8	0.0	115	76	88	26
Namibia	2.2	..	1.3	..	16	4	4	0.2	..	1.1	0.0	..	252	..	12
Niger	..	..	..	..	25	6	4	..	..	..	..	..	..	..	..
Nigeria	38.4	0.4	0.3	(22.7)	2,276	70	33	9.3	3.0	15.7	5.9	480	387	160	265
Rwanda	..	..	..	..	14 t	2	1	..	..	..	..	..	..	..	..
Senegal	3.3	49.8	0.4	20.7	99	6	8	0.6	0.3	1.0	1.2	225	255	131	182
Sierra Leone	..	..	..	..	30	2	1	..	..	..	..	..	..	..	..
Somalia	..	..	..	..	26	17	22	..	..	..	..	..	..	..	..
South Africa	346.3	19.0	8.1	1.3	12,162	54	24	60.6	5.9	33.4	167.8	916	960	521	508
Sudan	5.4	(1.5)	0.2	(22.7)	166	42	42	0.7	0.2	3.5	0.9	589	316	..	266
Tanzania, United Rep	2.2	7.8	0.1	(14.3)	94	29	24	0.4	0.3	0.8	0.1	143	120	154	138
Togo	0.9	63.0	0.2	33.3	24	2	2	0.3	0.1	0.3	0.1	91	143	129	256
Uganda	..	..	..	..	38	10	8	..	..	..	..	..	..	..	..
Zambia	1.9	(22.9)	0.2	(40.0)	167 s	10	5	0.8	..	0.6	..	352	259	318	387
Zimbabwe	13.7	(6.0)	1.1	(22.0)	586	10	8	2.4	0.1	2.0	5.3	562	425	545	311
NORTH AMERICA	6,074.0	15.3	19.5	4.8	..	958	535	645.6	392.2	1528.2	2124.2	738	649	..	..
Canada	489.2	16.1	16.0	5.5	22,363	123	62	89.8	40.4	115.3	113.4	683	635	366	..
United States	5,584.8	15.2	19.9	4.7	301,279	835	473	555.8	351.8	1412.9	2010.9	743	650		
C. AMERICA & CARIBBEAN	464.3	22.1	2.8	4.1	13,376	149	105	90.6	26.5	122.8	127.7	497	463	404	300
Belize	..	..	..	..	9	0	0	..	..	..	..	..	..	..	..
Costa Rica	4.7	67.3	1.2	29.3	110	3	3	0.8	0.1	3.0	0.1	161	169	139	80
Cuba	28.4	(10.7)	2.5	(14.8)	1,179	9	9	11.9	0.9	2.1	11.2	834	906	..	760
Dominican Rep	17.8	91.1	2.2	64.1	284	6	4	1.4	2.5	5.6	3.5	342	396	93	94
El Salvador	5.3	126.9	0.9	91.1	107	3	2	1.1	0.4	2.6	1.0	138	208	119	150
Guatemala	8.3	126.7	0.8	82.9	173	6	5	1.4	0.5	3.7	0.8	136	212	147	171
Haiti	1.4	46.8	0.2	30.8	33	3	3	0.4	0.1	0.3	0.3	72	127	78	176
Honduras	4.3	97.7	0.7	54.5	93	5	3	1.2	0.1	1.9	0.8	194	290	258	246
Jamaica	10.1	26.6	3.9	17.3	282	1	1	0.8	0.4	1.4	2.2	890	1,112	159	275
Mexico	358.2	20.6	3.7	3.1	9,930	98	64	62.7	20.4	96.2	101.3	516	472	440	271
Nicaragua	3.4	94.8	0.7	51.1	85	5	4	0.4	0.1	1.3	1.2	186	282	144	80
Panama	4.8	77.5	1.7	51.3	179	3	3	0.9	0.2	1.9	1.2	264	311	328	357
Trinidad and Tobago	15.6	27.6	12.1	20.4	699	3	0	7.2	0.1	1.6	3.7	1,494	1,489	1,251	1,679
SOUTH AMERICA	744.9	41.3	2.2	22.5	..	588	433	183.2	52.2	235.8	86.2	310	330	195	276
Argentina	142.7	36.9	3.9	21.9	4,895	87	67	20.4	16.9	37.0	25.1	385	335	169	174
Bolivia	9.8	85.0	1.2	50.0	190	16	15	1.1	0.9	3.0	1.8	404	526	225	304
Brazil	305.6	52.0	1.8	34.1	8,140	302	244	87.2	17.0	109.9	17.5	222	271	158	267
Chile	59.0	92.4	3.9	68.2	1,457	16	9	11.4	3.4	14.6	16.4	431	465	207	242
Colombia	56.5	15.8	1.4	(2.2)	1,854	54	21	19.3	3.4	18.3	4.4	268	245	175	294
Ecuador	19.3	44.3	1.6	19.2	490	14	10	2.6	1.8	5.5	2.4	440	544	186	196
Guyana	..	..	..	..	57	1	1	..	..	..	..	..	..	..	..
Paraguay	4.0	101.5	0.7	60.9	69	12	10	0.3	0.2	3.4	..	108	179	34	48
Peru	21.2	18.4	0.8	1.2	984	19	15	6.6	2.8	8.8	2.3	229	188	162	214
Suriname	..	..	..	..	62	1	0	..	..	..	..	..	..	..	..
Uruguay	6.8	73.8	2.0	63.2	254	17	16	1.1	0.5	2.7	1.3	187	240	98	143
Venezuela	120.0	19.9	5.1	(1.4)	4,475	49	23	33.2	5.2	32.6	15.1	920	946	538	720
OCEANIA	..	..	..	..	11,839	133	139	..	..	..	..	..	..	..	..
Australia	321.6	23.8	17.0	10.4	10,524	101	95	50.5	6.7	63.9	166.3	779	687	420	352
Fiji	..	..	..	..	..	1	1	..	..	..	..	..	..	..	..
New Zealand	30.6	33.1	8.2	19.5	1,229	26	31	7.9	0.5	6.7	4.7	429	449	409	..
Papua New Guinea	..	..	..	..	68	3	2	..	..	..	..	..	..	..	..
Solomon Islands	..	..	..	..	4	0	0	..	..	..	..	..	..	..	..
DEVELOPED	14,196.7	..	10.8	..	..	2,494	1,367	2103.8	1231.6	2872.4	4742.2	..	594	..	..
DEVELOPING	8,020.2	37.2	1.8	18.2	197,323	3,836	2,192	2180.8	564.4	1167.5	2613.3	628	532	561	413

a. Emissions for the Former Soviet Union countries prior to 1992 are estimates. b. Emissions prior to 1972 are estimates. c. China includes the People's Republic of China and Hong Kong but excludes Taiwan. d. Includes the Ruyukui Islands only after 1949. e. Emissions prior to 1945 are estimates. f. Emissions from 1890-1949 and 1957-1969 are for Peninsular Malaysia. g. Estimates from 1950-1956 are derived from figures for the Federation of Malaya Singapore. h. Emissions prior to 1970 are estimates. i. Emissions for Former Yugoslav Republics before 1992 are estimates. j. Emissions for countries of the former Czechoslovakia prior to 1992 are estimates. k. Denmark excludes Greenland and the Danish Faroes. l. France includes Monaco, and excludes overseas departments (French Polynesia, Guadeloupe, Martinique, and La Réunion). m. Germany includes the new federal states of Germany from 1970 and Western Germany only from 1960 to 1969. n. The Netherlands excludes Suriname and the Netherlands Antilles. o. Portugal includes the Azores and Madeira. p. Spain includes the Canary Islands. q. Switzerland includes Liechtenstein. r. Emissions prior to 1980 are estimates. s. Emissions from 1950 to 1963 are estimates derived from figures for Rhodesia-Nyasaland. t. 1950-61 data includes Rwanda-Urundi.

VARIABLE DEFINITIONS AND METHODOLOGY

Total Carbon Dioxide (CO$_2$) Emissions and **Per Capita CO$_2$ Emissions** include the total and the average emissions of carbon dioxide per person, respectively, from combustion of all fossil fuels used by a country.

The CO$_2$ emissions presented here are based on the International Energy Agency's (IEA) energy data gathered and rectified for their Energy Balances of Organization for Economic Cooperation and Development (OECD) Countries and Energy Balances of non-OECD Countries databases (please see the notes for the Energy and Resource Use table in this book for more information on how these data are gathered and adjusted). Methods and emissions factors are spelled out in the Revised 1996 International Panel on Climate Change (IPCC) Guidelines for National Greenhouse Gas Inventories available at http://www.ipcc-nggip.iges.or.jp/public/gl/invs1.htm. The IPCC allows countries to use either the reference or the sectoral approach when reporting their emissions. The figures provided here are based on the reference approach, which calculates emissions using data on a country's energy supply, and captures refining, flaring, and other "fugitive emissions" that do not result directly from end-use fossil fuel combustion. In contrast, the sectoral approach estimates emissions based on the combustion rather than the supply of fossil fuels.

The reference approach accounts for the carbon in fuels supplied to the economy. Apparent consumption of fuels is calculated as production minus exports plus imports. Net stock changes are either added or subtracted. International marine and aviation bunkers (fuels used for international transport) are subtracted from the national total as well, as these figures are accounted for separately. The production of secondary fuels is not accounted for, because the carbon contained in those fuels is already included in the primary fuel. However, imports and exports of secondary fuels are included in the calculations. Stored carbon from fuels used for non-energy purposes is subtracted from the total carbon emissions. Emissions from biomass fuels are not included in these estimates because the IPCC assumes that such emissions are equal to sequestration during regrowth.

Cumulative CO$_2$ Contribution, 1800–2000 consists of the sum of CO$_2$ produced during consumption of solid, liquid, and gaseous fuels; gas flaring; and cement manufacture from 1800 to the year 2000. The variable does not include emissions from land use change, or from bunker fuels used in international transportation.

WRI calculates cumulative CO$_2$ emissions levels based on the Carbon Dioxide Information Analysis Center's (CDIAC) emissions data from 1800 to 1980, and on Energy Information Administration (EIA) data from 1980 to 2000. CDIAC and EIA both report CO$_2$ emissions as the weight of the elemental carbon portion of CO$_2$; WRI converted the values to the actual mass of CO$_2$ by multiplying the carbon mass by 3.664 (the ratio of the mass of CO$_2$ to that of carbon). CDIAC bases CO$_2$ emissions from before 1950 on several compilations of fossil fuel production and trade: World Energy Production 1800–1985 by Etemad et al. and four regional volumes of International Historical Statistics authored by B.R. Mitchell. Emissions and estimates from 1950 to the present are derived primarily from energy statistics published by the United Nations in their "Energy Statistics Yearbook." U.N. gas flaring estimates are supplemented with data from the U.S. Energy Information Administration, G. Marland at CDIAC, and a 1974 paper authored by R.M. Rotty entitled "First estimates of global flaring of natural gas." Emissions are calculated from data on fuel production, trade, and net apparent consumption by CDIAC. More information on the data, methodology, and sources used can be found at: http://cdiac.esd.ornl.gov/trends/emis/meth_reg.htm. A complete record of the formulas and

assumptions used to calculate CO$_2$ emissions is available online at http://cdiac. esd.ornl.gov/trends/emis/factors.htm.

Methane and Nitrous Oxide emissions include emissions, in million metric tons of CO$_2$ equivalent, from energy, agriculture, waste, and other sources. Energy emissions from energy comprise the production, handling, transmission, and combustion of fossil and biofuels (IPCC categories 1A and 1B). Agriculture comprises animals, animal wastes, rice production, agricultural waste burning not intended for energy production, and savanna burning (IPCC category 4). Waste includes emissions from landfills, wastewater treatment and disposal, and waste incineration not intended for energy production (IPCC category 6). Other sources include industrial process emissions, and tropical and temperate forest fires (IPCC categories 2 and 5).

The Emission Database for Global Atmospheric Research (EDGAR) uses activity data taken from international statistical data to estimate emissions of the individual gases reported by the database. Activity data were multiplied by emissions factors specific to that activity. The emissions factors were primarily from Olivier et al. (1999), "Sectoral emission inventories of greenhouse gases for 1990 on a per country basis as well as on 1° x 1°." Various factors were taken from other international and national-level sources. For more information, please see: http://www.rivm.nl/env/int/coredata/edgar/v2/index.html.

CO$_2$ Emissions by Economic Sector represents total CO$_2$ emissions from fossil fuel burning by individual economic sectors. It is important to note that emissions from electricity generation are not distributed to end users, but are treated in an independent sector. **Industry** represents CO$_2$ emissions from manufacturing industries and construction. Carbon dioxide emissions from **residential** sources include emissions from combustion of all fossil fuel types in households but excludes transportation. **Road transportation** refers to emissions from all road vehicles and agricultural vehicles while they are on highways. Emissions from **public electricity and heat** production include the sum of emissions from combustion of all fossil fuel types used for public electricity generation, public combined heat and power generation, and public heat plants. Emissions from electricity and heat production for use by the producer (autoproduction) are not included in this variable.

These data are produced by IEA in the same manner as described above under Total Carbon Dioxide Emissions.

Carbon Intensity: All Economic Sectors is the amount of CO$_2$ emitted per amount of Gross Domestic Product (GDP) in Purchasing Power Parity (PPP) terms generated by the country's economy. This measure provides an indicator of how efficiently a country performs, in carbon emission terms, relative to its wealth generation. Please see the notes after the Economic Indicators data table for more information on GDP PPP.

WRI calculated CO$_2$ emissions per GDP PPP using data from IEA. Total energy consumption in each country was divided by total GDP PPP in constant dollar terms.

Carbon Intensity: Industry Sector is the amount of CO$_2$ emitted by the sector per amount of income generated. The industry sector is defined as including International Standard Industrial Classification (ISIC) divisions 15–37 (please see http://unstats.un.org/unsd/cr/registry/regcst.asp?Cl=17 for more information on ISIC classifications). This measure provides an indicator of how efficiently, in greenhouse gas emissions terms, a country's industrial sector is able to generate wealth.

Industrial carbon intensity was calculated as follows: Industrial CO$_2$ emissions were divided by the amount of GDP PPP generated by the industry sector. Industrial GDP, as defined by the World Bank, includes ISIC divisions 15–37. WRI adjusted

IEA's value for industrial CO_2 emissions by subtracting emissions from mining and quarrying (ISIC Divisions 13–14) and construction (ISIC division 45) from IEA's total industrial CO_2 emissions figure. The only differences remaining after this adjustment are that the World Bank definition includes emissions from the manufacture of coke, petroleum products, and other derived fossil fuels (ISIC division 23), manufacture of coke oven products (ISIC group 231), manufacture of refined petroleum products (ISIC group 232), and processing of nuclear fuels. According to the IEA, however, the energy consumed for these activities, and therefore the CO_2 emissions, are captured in the energy contained in the original fuels used for these processes. The differences remaining between the World Bank and IEA definitions of the industry and manufacturing sector should therefore be small. After the definitions for industrial CO_2 emissions and the percentage of GDP generated by industry were brought into agreement, industrial GDP PPP was calculated by dividing total GDP PPP by the percentage generated by industry, and industrial CO_2 emissions was divided by this value.

FREQUENCY OF UPDATE BY DATA PROVIDERS
The IEA, World Bank, CDIAC, and IEA update their data annually. The National Institute for Public Health and the Environment (RIVM) calculates emissions of methane and nitrous oxide periodically. The UN Population Division updates population data every other year.

DATA RELIABILITY AND CAUTIONARY NOTES
CO_2 Emissions Data: The IEA CO_2 emissions data are based on well-established and institutionalized accounting methodologies and undergo thorough review and adjustments. The reference and sectoral approaches will, in most cases, give very similar results. However, because the reference approach is calculated using energy supply, it can lead to slight overestimates. For some countries, especially developing countries, statistical differences in basic data or unexplained differences in the two approaches can lead to significant discrepancies. Individual countries may use different energy figures than the IEA or treat bunker fuels differently. Countries may use specific calorific values, instead of the averages used by IEA. Also, military emissions may be treated differently by the IEA. As a result, the data shown here can differ from the numbers reported by a country to the IPCC.

Cumulative CO_2 contribution since 1900: The share of carbon emissions for recently formed countries such as the independent republics of the former Soviet Union is estimated based on each country's CO_2 emissions in the years immediately following its formation. For example, Kazakhstan was formed in 1992. Total 1992–1996 emissions for the former Soviet Union were 3,802,544 tons; Kazakhstan's emissions from 1992–1996 were 6.3% of this total. It is then assumed that Kazakhstan produced roughly 6.3% of the carbon emitted in the former Soviet Union each year before 1992. As a result, total contributions from the former Soviet republics, the former Yugoslav republics, and other newly formed countries should be taken only as rough approximations.

Methane and Nitrous Oxide Emissions: The methane and nitrous oxide emissions data are calculated using a standardized methodology and reviewed for accuracy by the United

Nations Framework Convention on Climate Change (UNFCCC). The data can therefore be used with considerable confidence in their accuracy.

Carbon Intensity Indicators: While CO_2 emissions per GDP PPP is a useful indicator of greenhouse gas efficiency at the scale of the entire economy, it does not necessarily indicate how efficient the individual elements that make up the economy are. For example, it does not differentiate between economies that are more focused on industry as opposed to services, which generally require less energy and generate comparatively more income than industry. Interpretation of between-country comparisons should therefore be made with care. In addition, a number of countries, particularly rapidly-developing countries, over-report their GDP and GDP growth rate, which makes them appear more efficient than they actually are. Given the close match achieved between the World Bank and IEA's definitions when calculating the **industrial sector** indicator, the results of WRI's calculation can serve as an acceptable indicator of how efficiently, in terms of greenhouse gas emissions, the industry sector is able to generate economic goods. However, this match is not perfect and could lead to slight distortions in some countries. In addition, while focusing in on the industry sector reduces the potential for mismatched comparisons as discussed above, industries in different countries can have different foci. Between-country comparisons should therefore be made with care.

SOURCES
Carbon Dioxide (CO_2) Emissions Variables: International Energy Agency (IEA), 2001. CO_2 Emissions from Fossil Fuel Combustion (2001 Edition). Paris: Organization for Economic Cooperation and Development (OECD). Electronic database available on-line at: http://data.iea.org/ieastore/default. asp. **Cumulative CO_2 Emissions Since 1900:** Carbon Dioxide Information Analysis Center (CDIAC), Environmental Sciences Division, Oak Ridge National Laboratory: 2001. Global, Regional, and National CO_2 Emission Estimates from Fossil Fuel Burning, Cement Production, and Gas Flaring: 1751–1998, NDP-030. Oak Ridge, Tennessee: CDIAC. Available on-line at http://cdiac. esd.ornl.gov/ftp/ndp030/. Energy Information Administration of the U.S. Department of Energy: 2001. Carbon Dioxide Emissions from Use of Fossil Fuels, International Energy Annual, 2000. Washington, DC: EIA. Available on-line at http://www. eia.doe.gov/iea/carbon.html. **Methane and Nitrous Oxide Emissions:** National Institute for Public Health (RIVM) and Netherlands Organisation for Applied Scientific Research (TNO). 2001. The Emission Database for Global Atmosphereic Research (EDGAR) 3.2: The Netherlands: RIVM. Database available on-line at http://www.rivm.nl/env/int/coredata/ edgar/index.html. **Carbon Intensity Indicators:** International Energy Agency (IEA), 2001. CO_2 Emissions from Fossil Fuel Combustion (2001 Edition). Paris: Organisation for Economic Co-operation and Development (OECD). Electronic database available on-line at: http://data.iea.org/ieastore/ default.asp. Development Data Group, The World Bank. 2002. World Development Indicators 2002 online. Washington, DC: The World Bank. Available on-line at http://www.worldbank.org/ data/onlinedbs/onlinedbases.htm. **Population** (used to calculate per capita values): Population Division of the Department of Economic and Social Affairs of the United Nations Secretariat, 2002. World Population Prospects: The 2000 Revision. New York: United Nations. Data set available on CD-ROM.

Energy

Source: International Energy Agency (IEA)

	Energy Consumption by Source								Energy Intensity: Energy Use per GDP PPP {a}			Energy Consumption (as a percent of total consumption), 1999		Electricity Consumption per Capita (kgoe) {e}
	Total from all sources			Total Fossil Fuels	Nuclear	Hydro-electric	Renewables		All Economic Sectors (toe per million $Intl)	Industry Sector	Residential per Capita (kgoe per person) {e}	Indus-trial	Trans-portation	
	(1000 metric toe) {d} 1999	Percent Change Since 1989	Per Capita (kgoe) {e} 1999	1999	1999	1999	Mod-ern {b} 1999	Tradi-tional {c} 1999	1999	1999	1999			1999
				(1000 metric toe) {d}										
WORLD	**9,702,786**	**12.7**	**1,623**	**7,689,047**	**661,901**	**222,223**	**62,750**	**1,035,139**	**244**	**167**	**309**	**22**	**18**	**174**
ASIA (EXCL. MIDDLE EAST)	**2,919,333**	**43.1**	**867**	**2,175,366**	**117,291**	**44,424**	**16,892**	**561,751**	**221**	**144**	**219**	**26**	**12**	**78**
Armenia	1,845	..	487	1,220	542	103	0	1	213	165	45	26	3	83
Azerbaijan	12,574	..	1,575	12,376	0	130	0	4	665	300	404	15	5	151
Bangladesh	17,935	44.4	133	10,395	0	72	0	7,469	98	84	65	21	7	7
Bhutan	..	..	..	..	..	..	..	..	..	..	..	..	..	..
Cambodia	..	..	..	..	..	..	..	..	..	..	..	..	..	..
China {f}	1,088,349	29.2	861	854,743	3,896	17,527	1,234	211,705	241	141	233	29	6	65
Georgia	2,573	..	487	1,944	0	554	0	70	183	144	114	13	21	107
India	480,418	38.1	484	271,806	3,409	7,004	89	198,018	222	172	202	20	9	33
Indonesia	136,121	57.3	650	86,325	0	806	2,346	46,748	250	77	299	14	15	29
Japan	515,447	23.6	4,064	416,131	82,512	7,432	3,993	4,332	174	137	391	26	18	639
Kazakhstan	35,439	..	2,180	34,581	0	527	0	73	511	395	29	30	7	193
Korea, Dem People's Rep	58,925	1.2	2,665	56,108	0	1,815	0	1,001	..	11	67	5	20
Korea, Rep	181,365	128.2	3,908	151,848	26,859	358	119	151	255	180	293	30	15	448
Kyrgyzstan	2,451	..	506	1,567	0	1,044	0	4	211	136	34	17	12	130
Lao People's Dem Rep	..	..	..	..	..	..	..	..	..	..	..	..	..	..
Malaysia	42,650	109.3	1,957	39,551	0	647	0	2,470	243	151	144	26	27	222
Mongolia	..	..	..	..	..	..	..	..	..	..	..	..	..	..
Myanmar	12,897	17.9	274	3,328	0	65	0	9,504	77	..	196	7	9	6
Nepal	8,051	37.1	358	1,002	0	98	0	6,937	287	72	316	5	3	4
Pakistan	59,830	43.6	435	34,363	74	1,931	0	23,462	253	236	188	22	14	27
Philippines	40,728	49.5	549	21,580	0	674	9,111	9,363	147	85	72	19	21	39
Singapore	22,693	130.5	5,791	22,629	0	0	0	0	274	139	121	18	19	576
Sri Lanka	7,728	41.7	412	3,181	0	359	0	4,189	130	104	178	22	24	22
Tajikistan	3,344	..	555	2,033	0	1,327	0	0	333	190	42	14	32	190
Thailand	70,415	85.3	1,136	56,128	0	278	0	13,844	201	132	129	26	26	113
Turkmenistan	13,644	..	2,943	13,764	0	0	0	0	891	21	19	1	4	89
Uzbekistan	49,383	..	2,017	48,613	0	489	0	0	942	704	595	19	8	141
Viet Nam	35,209	48.1	457	11,684	0	1,185	0	22,340	249	68	300	9	13	22
EUROPE	**2,559,701**	**..**	**3,516**	**2,117,484**	**303,885**	**60,847**	**8,471**	**56,374**	**243**	**176**	**653**	**22**	**18**	**400**
Albania	1,052	(63.5)	336	511	0	451	0	60	102	54	81	14	20	73
Austria	28,432	18.0	3,516	21,804	0	3,482	105	2,957	150	92	756	21	23	532
Belarus	23,895	..	2,337	22,484	0	2	0	794	357	253	593	30	10	228
Belgium	58,642	21.2	5,731	44,995	12,774	29	25	349	241	232	937	27	17	626
Bosnia and Herzegovina	2,008	..	522	1,676	0	138	0	175	..	..	45	3	21	47
Bulgaria	18,203	(41.0)	2,264	13,610	4,128	237	0	406	477	404	271	24	11	255
Croatia	8,156	..	1,753	7,053	0	567	0	278	..	..	370	23	19	216
Czech Rep	38,584	(21.8)	3,751	34,549	3,481	144	41	473	300	190	535	27	11	402
Denmark {g}	20,070	13.4	3,783	18,391	0	3	333	843	151	76	822	14	25	520
Estonia	4,557	..	3,231	4,101	0	0	3	505	401	213	713	14	11	290
Finland	33,372	13.9	6,463	19,038	5,987	1,099	22	6,124	286	301	..	35	14	1,236
France	255,043	14.8	4,321	139,942	102,742	6,227	561	9,440	194	133	674	18	20	546
Germany	337,196	(6.4)	4,111	286,465	44,304	1,671	715	1,361	182	119	774	21	20	490
Greece	26,894	23.8	2,539	25,370	0	395	141	911	183	116	406	16	28	330
Hungary	25,289	(16.5)	2,524	21,116	3,674	16	2	332	235	..	538	17	13	248
Iceland	3,173	57.2	11,452	899	0	520	1,753	0	444	..	2,114	20	11	1,991
Ireland	13,979	43.9	3,715	13,702	0	73	53	131	151	73	647	18	27	430
Italy	169,041	12.0	2,938	156,777	0	3,901	2,926	1,477	137	115	617	25	25	391
Latvia	3,822	..	1,569	2,504	0	237	0	913	270	183	444	19	19	158
Lithuania	7,909	..	2,137	4,885	2,627	36	0	591	340	163	383	16	15	152
Macedonia, FYR	3,058	..	1,512	2,736	0	119	31	180	..	..	248	16	13	218
Moldova, Rep	2,813	..	653	2,613	0	7	0	59	321	209	150	13	7	53
Netherlands {h}	74,068	13.7	4,690	70,145	999	8	189	267	196	186	654	26	19	516
Norway	26,606	22.3	5,980	14,862	0	10,398	6	1,343	232	178	854	28	19	2,090
Poland	93,382	(23.2)	2,417	89,664	0	185	26	3,541	279	159	503	21	12	206
Portugal {i}	23,627	47.2	2,364	21,761	0	626	99	1,158	151	136	208	29	26	311
Romania	36,432	(47.3)	1,621	30,734	1,362	1,573	18	2,816	280	195	389	26	9	130
Russian Federation	602,952	..	4,124	550,704	32,120	13,802	24	4,972	601	378	929	23	14	349
Serbia and Montenegro	13,375	..	1,266	11,862	0	1,150	0	210	..	..	130	20	12	242
Slovakia	17,991	(20.4)	3,335	14,095	3,418	390	0	76	328	333	434	33	8	363
Slovenia {j}	6,506	..	3,268	4,838	1,224	322	7	230	..	..	558	20	21	448
Spain	118,467	32.9	2,970	96,314	15,337	1,966	377	3,605	172	123	298	22	28	382
Sweden	51,094	8.9	5,773	17,513	19,073	6,157	67	8,084	261	..	903	25	16	1,217
Switzerland {k}	26,689	14.3	3,722	15,761	6,753	3,440	174	493	139	..	820	16	26	624
Ukraine	148,389	..	2,966	128,625	18,790	1,008	0	262	912	627	518	26	5	198
United Kingdom	230,324	8.8	3,886	201,296	25,091	460	773	944	189	117	716	18	22	465
MIDDLE EAST & N. AFRICA	**518,436**	**46.1**	**1,302**	**500,461**	**0**	**5,694**	**963**	**10,976**	**279**	**167**	**194**	**23**	**17**	**129**
Afghanistan	..	..	..	..	..	..	..	..	..	..	..	..	..	..
Algeria	28,280	27.8	950	28,147	0	60	0	76	192	36	165	13	12	50
Egypt	44,490	44.7	667	41,893	0	1,315	0	1,282	214	185	100	27	14	73
Iran, Islamic Rep	103,635	68.4	1,497	102,422	0	427	0	786	308	317	303	23	22	110
Iraq	28,802	17.9	1,290	28,726	0	50	0	26	1,000	..	103	22	32	114
Israel	18,493	56.9	3,129	18,053	0	3	538	4	171	..	355	16	21	505
Jordan	4,871	52.4	1,018	4,803	0	1	64	3	271	167	170	16	27	103
Kuwait	17,289	0.9	9,356	17,289	0	0	0	0	729	..	1,625	26	14	1,255
Lebanon	5,469	136.1	1,591	5,234	0	29	7	125	307	243	259	17	29	190
Libyan Arab Jamahiriya	12,254	13.1	2,368	12,117	0	0	0	136	459	..	184	26	31	333
Morocco	9,931	51.4	339	9,273	0	71	0	429	106	69	66	22	9	36
Oman	8,469	197.1	3,447	8,469	0	0	0	0	209	..	162	26	13	237
Saudi Arabia	84,907	33.2	4,322	84,902	0	0	0	0	404	..	282	17	15	416
Syrian Arab Rep	18,049	69.1	1,144	17,296	0	748	0	5	352	255	92	22	9	74
Tunisia	7,673	44.4	820	6,441	0	8	0	1,224	139	91	200	19	21	79
Turkey	70,326	43.8	1,071	60,040	0	2,982	319	6,792	180	161	251	24	17	118
United Arab Emirates	28,085	60.0	10,979	28,068	0	0	0	0	564	..	433	44	9	1,007
Yemen	3,139	8.0	178	3,061	0	0	0	77	242	..	34	5	46	9

	Energy Consumption by Source								Energy Intensity: Energy Use			Energy Consumption (as a percent of total consumption), 1999		Electricity Consumption per Capita (kgoe) {e}
	Total from all sources			Total Fossil Fuels	Nuclear	Hydro-electric	Renewables		per GDP PPP {a}		Residential per Capita (kgoe per person) {e}			
	(1000 metric toe) {d} 1999	Percent Change Since 1989	Per Capita (kgoe) {e} 1999	1999	1999	1999	Mod-ern {b}	Tradi-tional {c}	All Economic Sectors (toe per million $Intl)	Industry Sector		Indus-trial	Trans-portation	
						(1000 metric toe) {d}	1999	1999	1999	1999	1999			1999
SUB-SAHARAN AFRICA	..	..	..	..	..	..	..	..	425	193	..	..	..	..
Angola	7,591	28.7	595	2,032	0	77	0	5,482	678	83	323	9	9	7
Benin	1,973	19.5	323	433	0	0	0	1,511	355	69	164	3	15	5
Botswana	..	..	..	..	..	..	..	..	..	..	..	..	..	..
Burkina Faso	..	..	..	..	..	..	..	..	..	..	..	..	..	..
Burundi	..	..	..	..	..	..	..	..	..	..	..	..	..	..
Cameroon	6,103	22.5	419	939	0	287	0	4,877	270	214	280	16	10	16
Central African Rep	..	..	..	..	..	..	..	..	..	..	..	..	..	..
Chad	..	..	..	..	..	..	..	..	..	..	..	..	..	..
Congo	720	(31.3)	246	124	0	8	0	571	295	5	141	1	15	4
Congo, Dem Rep	14,525	26.0	293	888	0	489	0	13,238	454	..	204	20	2	4
Côte d'Ivoire	6,052	34.8	386	1,934	0	101	0	4,113	237	45	151	5	10	17
Equatorial Guinea	..	..	..	..	..	..	..	..	..	..	..	..	..	..
Eritrea {l}	681	..	193	214	0	0	0	467	205	20	108	3	11	4
Ethiopia {m}	18,227	24.9	297	1,052	0	138	22	17,016	477	65	6	2	3	2
Gabon	1,608	16.4	1,341	647	0	60	0	901	224	111	659	20	16	60
Gambia	..	..	..	..	..	..	..	..	..	..	..	..	..	..
Ghana	7,108	37.7	376	1,555	0	344	0	5,196	209	81	206	10	10	17
Guinea	..	..	..	..	..	..	..	..	..	..	..	..	..	..
Guinea-Bissau	..	..	..	..	..	..	..	..	..	..	..	..	..	..
Kenya	14,690	18.8	489	2,549	0	282	335	11,512	495	228	243	8	8	11
Lesotho	..	..	..	..	..	..	..	..	..	..	..	..	..	..
Liberia	..	..	..	..	..	..	..	..	..	..	..	..	..	..
Madagascar	..	..	..	..	..	..	..	..	..	..	..	..	..	..
Malawi	..	..	..	..	..	..	..	..	..	..	..	..	..	..
Mali	..	..	..	..	..	..	..	..	..	..	..	..	..	..
Mauritania	..	..	..	..	..	..	..	..	..	..	..	..	..	..
Mozambique	6,985	(5.5)	389	387	0	588	0	6,468	480	462	278	23	4	4
Namibia	1,108	..	643	748	0	101	0	169	127	1	98	5	41	101
Niger	..	..	..	..	..	..	..	..	..	..	..	..	..	..
Nigeria	87,286	25.7	787	14,410	0	486	0	72,390	881	258	585	10	7	8
Rwanda	..	..	..	..	..	..	..	..	..	..	..	..	..	..
Senegal	2,957	36.9	322	1,279	0	0	0	1,678	229	122	138	14	19	10
Sierra Leone	..	..	..	..	..	..	..	..	..	..	..	..	..	..
Somalia	..	..	..	..	..	..	..	..	..	..	..	..	..	..
South Africa	109,334	17.3	2,557	93,483	3,345	62	0	12,466	303	198	272	24	12	320
Sudan	15,372	52.4	505	1,851	0	95	0	13,426	900	174	205	3	8	4
Tanzania, United Rep	15,033	22.7	438	762	0	187	0	14,079	823	544	312	11	2	5
Togo	1,373	44.8	313	321	0	0	0	1,014	218	49	57	5	9	9
Uganda	..	..	..	..	..	..	..	..	..	..	..	..	..	..
Zambia	6,190	19.0	608	648	0	690	0	4,985	843	..	309	18	4	45
Zimbabwe	10,170	15.2	820	3,976	0	254	0	5,487	315	..	430	11	8	77
NORTH AMERICA	2,511,765	15.2	8,075	2,127,336	221,874	54,524	19,498	74,745	268	..	913	17	26	1,052
Canada	241,780	10.9	7,929	184,529	19,152	29,711	20	10,851	314	..	968	28	22	1,312
United States {n}	2,269,985	15.7	8,095	1,942,807	202722	24813	19,477	63,894	264	..	906	16	26	1,023
C. AMERICA & CARIBBEAN	205,471	22.9	1,207	169,759	2,607	4,236	6,235	22,586	205	148	178	24	23	105
Belize	..	..	..	..	..	..	..	..	..	..	..	..	..	..
Costa Rica	3,052	56.9	776	1,741	0	441	700	181	110	50	77	16	38	116
Cuba	12,464	(26.1)	1,117	9,619	0	8	51	2,786	398	..	65	51	9	84
Dominican Rep	7,451	86.4	905	5,960	0	95	0	1,396	166	63	247	13	28	56
El Salvador	4,005	61.6	651	1,848	0	152	514	1,470	157	94	214	18	23	49
Guatemala	6,074	46.5	548	2,812	0	229	0	3,053	155	90	270	12	21	29
Haiti	2,067	27.9	258	489	0	23	0	1,555	187	128	146	14	12	3
Honduras	3,267	36.2	522	1,439	0	183	0	1,633	221	126	251	18	20	39
Jamaica	4,136	68.6	1,619	3,495	0	10	0	631	456	200	121	14	22	200
Mexico	148,991	23.4	1,530	130,612	2,607	2,819	4,882	8,026	196	145	172	22	24	134
Nicaragua	2,664	28.9	539	1,176	0	34	88	1,361	221	115	233	14	18	23
Panama	2,347	67.1	835	1,648	0	242	0	462	152	144	195	16	28	113
Trinidad and Tobago	8,022	56.8	6,225	7,990	0	0	0	32	766	1,021	100	55	8	304
SOUTH AMERICA	383,514	34.4	1,126	272,172	2,888	43,346	7,432	57,856	170	174	154	30	25	137
Argentina	63,182	38.9	1,727	56,028	1,852	1,864	3	2,975	148	119	253	22	22	167
Bolivia	4,572	73.9	562	3,571	0	154	0	846	245	238	121	17	27	34
Brazil	179,701	30.8	1,068	107,150	1,036	25,188	7,415	35,645	159	201	121	36	27	156
Chile	25,348	95.6	1,688	20,079	0	1,222	7	4,040	200	139	305	25	23	199
Colombia	28,081	17.8	678	19,920	0	2,902	0	5,259	122	105	108	25	26	67
Ecuador	8,750	45.4	705	6,745	0	620	0	1,383	247	95	153	14	28	53
Guyana	..	..	..	..	..	..	..	..	..	..	..	..	..	..
Paraguay	4,140	28.9	773	1,351	0	4,465	7	2,269	185	233	240	33	28	68
Peru	13,101	15.3	519	7,442	0	1,251	0	4,409	116	101	198	24	26	56
Suriname	..	..	..	..	..	..	..	..	..	..	..	..	..	..
Uruguay	3,232	32.9	976	2,228	0	473	0	488	114	72	216	17	28	161
Venezuela	53,406	32.9	2,253	47,658	0	5,208	0	541	421	340	151	29	22	214
OCEANIA	..	..	..	..	..	..	..	..	235	172	..	..	..	..
Australia	107,930	26.6	5,701	101,140	0	1,434	234	4,943	231	172	466	22	25	765
Fiji	..	..	..	..	..	..	..	..	..	..	..	..	..	..
New Zealand	18,176	37.1	4,850	12,346	0	2,023	2,667	835	267	..	367	29	27	737
Papua New Guinea	..	..	..	..	..	..	..	..	..	..	..	..	..	..
Solomon Islands	..	..	..	..	..	..	..	..	..	..	..	..	..	..
DEVELOPED	5,962,100	..	4,550	5,002,071	612,157	130,499	35,401	153,852	248	170	651	20	21	568
DEVELOPING	3,597,314	38.5	771	2,604,225	39,733	90,276	27,349	833,261	232	149	212	25	13	63

a. GDP PPP is Gross Domestic Product in Purchasing Power Parity terms. b. Modern renewables include wind, solar, geothermal, wave/tide, liquids such as ethanol and gas derived from biomass. c. Traditional renewables include fuelwood, crop residues, and biomass left from industrial sources such as papermaking. d. Toe is tons of oil equivalent. e. Kgoe is kilograms of oil equivalent. f. Data for China do not include Taiwan. g. Denmark excludes Greenland and the Danish Faroes. h. The Netherlands excludes Suriname and the Netherlands Antilles. i. Portugal includes the Azores and Madeira. j. Spain includes the Canary Islands. k. Switzerland includes Liechtenstein. l. Data for Eritrea previous to 1992 are included under Ethiopia. m. Data for Ethiopia prior to 1992 include Eritrea. n. The United States includes Puerto Rico, Guam, and the Virgin Islands.

263

VARIABLE DEFINITIONS AND METHODOLOGY

Energy Consumption by Source is the total amount of primary energy consumed by each country in the year specified, and is reported in thousands of metric tons of oil equivalent (toe). Primary energy also includes losses from transportation, friction, heat loss, and other inefficiencies. Specifically, consumption equals indigenous production plus imports, minus exports plus stock changes, minus international marine bunkers. IEA calls this value Total Primary Energy Supply (TPES).

Total From All Sources is total consumption from all energy sources including fossil, nuclear, hydroelectric, modern renewables, and all renewable fuels and wastes.

Total Fossil Fuels includes energy consumption from oil and natural gas liquids, coal and coal products, and natural gas.

Nuclear energy consumption shows the primary heat equivalent of the electricity produced by nuclear power plants. Heat-to-electricity conversion efficiency is assumed to be 33% (its average in Europe). **Hydroelectric** includes the energy content of the electricity produced in hydro power plants. Hydro output excludes output from pumped storage.

Modern Renewables include energy from wind; tide, wave and ocean; thermal and photovoltaic solar; liquid biomass fuels such as ethanol; biogas from digesters; and geothermal systems. Wind includes electrical power generated from wind energy. Tide, wave, ocean represents the amount of energy from wave, ocean, and tide activity that is captured and transformed into electrical power. Thermal solar represents solar radiation exploited for hot water production and electricity generation by: (1) flat plate collectors, mainly of the thermosiphon type, for domestic hot water or for the seasonal heating of swimming pools and (2) solar thermal-electric plants. Passive solar energy for the direct heating, cooling, and lighting of dwellings or other buildings is not included. Solar from photovoltaics includes solar energy converted by photovoltaic cells to electricity. Energy from liquid biomass includes liquid derivatives from biomass used as a fuel. Biogases are gases derived principally from the anaerobic fermentation of biomass and solid wastes which are combusted to produce heat and electrical power. Landfill gases and gases from sewage and animal waste facilities are included in this category. Ethanol is the main form of liquid biomass produced.

Traditional Renewables include primary solid biomass, i.e., any plant matter used directly as a fuel or converted into other forms before combustion, including wood; vegetal waste including wood waste and crop waste used for energy; animal materials and wastes; sulphite lyes (also known as black liquor, this is a sludge that contains the lignin digested from wood for paper making); and other solid biomass.

All energy consumption values presented here are calculated and reported by the International Energy Agency (IEA) using an energy balance methodology that uses metric tons (tonnes) of oil equivalent (toe)—a common unit based on the calorific content of energy commodities. One toe is defined as 10 Exp.7 kilocalories, 41.868 gigajoules, or 11,628 giga watt-hours (GWh). This amount of energy is roughly equal to the amount of energy contained in a ton of crude oil. To account for the differences in quality between types of coal and other energy sources, the IEA has applied specific conversion factors supplied by national administrations for the main categories of energy sources and flows or uses (i.e., production, imports, exports, industry).

Energy statistics are expressed in terms of net calorific value and therefore may be slightly lower than statistics presented by other statistical compendia. The difference between the net and the gross calorific value for each fuel is the latent heat of vaporization of the water produced during combustion of the fuel. For oil and coal, net calorific value is 5 percent less than gross; for most forms of natural and manufactured gas the difference is 9–10 percent. Using net calorific values is consistent with the United Nations and European Community statistical offices.

The IEA has used the following conventions in accounting for primary energy such as nuclear, solar, geothermal, hydro, wind, etc.: (1) The first form of energy production with multiple practical uses is reported. This means that heat is the form reported for geothermal heat and electrical production, nuclear heat and electrical production, and solar heat production. Electricity is the form reported for hydro, wind, wave, and photovoltaic solar electricity production. (2) The physical energy content of the energy source is reported as energy production. For nuclear fuels, this is the heat energy produced in a nuclear reactor; for hydropower, it is the amount of energy in the electricity produced. Please refer to the original source for further information on the variables and collection methodologies.

Energy Intensity: All Economic Sectors is the amount of energy consumed per unit of Gross Domestic Product (GDP) in Purchase Power Parity (PPP) terms; the units are toe per million international dollars GDP PPP. This variable provides an indicator of how efficiently, in terms of energy, the economy generates wealth. Please see the notes in the Economic Indicators table for more information on GDP PPP.

WRI calculated energy consumption per GDP PPP using IEA's energy consumption data as defined above under Total From All Sources, and IEA's data on GDP in PPP terms. Total energy consumption in each country was divided by total GDP PPP for that country. IEA's GDP PPP data were used instead of the World Bank's figures (which were used for the Economic Indicators table) as they are reported in constant dollar terms, allowing WRI to calculate a meaningful time series (available in the EarthTrends searchable database). The calculation was made by dividing total energy consumption by total GDP PPP.

Energy Intensity: Industry Sector is the amount of energy consumed by the industry sector per unit of Gross Domestic Product (GDP) in Purchase Power Parity (PPP) terms generated by industry. This variable, reported in toe per million international dollars GDP PPP, indicates, in energy terms, how efficiently the industry sector generates wealth. The industry sector is defined as including International Standard Industrial Classification (ISIC) divisions 15–37 (please see http://unstats.un.org/unsd/cr/registry/regcst.asp?Cl=17 for more information on ISIC classifications).

Industrial energy intensity was calculated in a similar fashion as described above for all economic sectors: Industrial energy consumption was divided by the amount of GDP PPP generated by the industry sector. Unlike the indicator above which used data in the form provided by IEA, WRI adjusted some data elements to make this calculation. The definition of industry was determined by the percent of GDP generated by industry, provided by World Development Indicators. This variable defines industry as including International Standard Industrial Classification (ISIC) divisions 15–37. WRI adjusted IEA's value for industrial energy consumption by subtracting energy consumed by mining and quarrying (ISIC Divisions 13–14) and construction (ISIC division 45) from IEA's total industrial energy consumption. The only differences remaining after this adjustment are that the World Bank definition includes the manufacture of coke, petroleum products, and other derived fossil fuels (ISIC division 23), manufacture of coke oven products (ISIC group 231), manufacture of refined petroleum products (ISIC group 232), and processing of nuclear fuels. According to the IEA, however, the energy consumed for these activities is captured by the energy contained in the original fuels used for these processes. The differences remaining between the World Bank and IEA definitions of the industry and manufacturing sector should therefore be small. After the definitions for industrial energy consumption and the percentage of GDP generated by industry were brought into agreement, industrial GDP PPP was calculated by multiplying total GDP PPP by the percent generated by industry, and industrial energy consumption was divided by this value.

Residential Energy Use Per Capita, reported in kilograms of oil equivalent (kgoe) is the average amount of energy consumed per person by the residential sector. The residential sector includes all energy used for activities by households except for transportation. The variable provides an indicator of how much energy people in different countries require for housing.

Energy Consumption by Residences Per Capita was calculated by dividing the IEA data defined above by total population provided by the United Nations Population Division. Please see the Population, Health, and Human Well-Being table for more information on the population data.

Energy Consumption by Industry as a Percent of Total Consumption and Energy Consumption by Transportation as a Percent of Total Consumption is the percentage of the total amount of energy, from all sources, consumed by industry and transportation, respectively. Units for both variables are the percentage of the total energy consumed by that country.

The **industry sector** is defined for this variable as the combination of all industrial sub-sectors, such as mining and quarrying, iron and steel, construction, etc. Energy used for transport by industry is not included here but is reported under transportation.

Transportation represents both road and air transportation. Road transport includes all fuels used in road vehicles, including military, as well as agricultural and industrial highway use. The sector excludes motor gasoline used in stationary engines and diesel oil used in tractors. Air transportation includes both domestic and international transport. The domestic sector includes deliveries of aviation fuels to all domestic air transport: commercial, private, agricultural, military, etc. It also includes use for purposes other than flying, e.g., bench testing of engines, but not airline use of fuel for road transport. For many countries this also incorrectly includes fuel used by domestically owned carriers for outbound international traffic. The international air transportation sector includes deliveries of aviation fuels to all international civil aviation.

The amount of energy consumed by industry and transportation as a percent of total energy consumption was calculated by dividing the amount of energy consumed by these sectors by the total energy consumption in that country.

Electricity Consumption Per Capita is the amount of electricity consumed on average by each person, regardless of source, and is represented in kilograms of oil equivalent. The figure reported is final consumption, which measures only the amount of energy delivered to the end user. Losses due to transportation, friction, heat loss, and other inefficiencies are not included.

Final Electricity Consumption Per Capita was calculated by dividing total electricity consumption in each country by that country's total population.

FREQUENCY OF UPDATE BY DATA PROVIDERS

IEA updates their energy data annually. The UN Population Division updates the figures used for per capita calculations every other year. These updates also often include revisions of past data. Data may therefore differ from those reported in past editions of the World Resources report.

DATA RELIABILITY AND CAUTIONARY NOTES

Energy Data

The energy balances data are based primarily on well-established and institutionalized accounting methodologies, and are therefore considered reliable. One exception is fuelwood and other biomass fuels, which are estimated by the IEA based on small sample surveys or other incomplete information. The data give only a broad impression of trends and should not be strictly compared between countries. The IEA reports that it can be difficult to distinguish between agriculture, commercial, and public sectors, and there may be some overlap in these sectors. IEA data do not distinguish between "no data" (denoted in these tables with ..) and zero values. WRI has distinguished between the two where possible, but some values represented as zero should probably be indicated by .. and vice versa.

Please note that, in a departure from World Resources 2000–01, energy consumption by energy sector is based on primary energy supply as opposed to total final consumption. The figures should therefore not be used in conjunction with data from that edition to indicate change in any sector's relative energy use. Please see the EarthTrends searchable database at http://earthtrends.wri.org for a time series on energy data.

Energy Intensity Variables

As is the case with the energy data, economic data collection in most countries is well-established and institutionalized, resulting in accurate information. A number of countries, particularly rapidly developing countries, however, over-report GDP and the rate of GDP growth in their countries. This will make those countries appear more energy efficient than they actually are.

SOURCES

Energy Variables: International Energy Agency (IEA), 2001. Energy Balances of OECD Countries (2001 Edition) and Energy Balances of non-OECD Countries (2001 Edition). Paris: Organisation for Economic Co-operation and Development (OECD). Electronic database available on-line at: http://data.iea.org/.
Population (used to calculate per capita values): Population Division of the Department of Economic and Social Affairs of the United Nations Secretariat, 2002. World Population Prospects: The 2000 Revision. New York: United Nations. Data set available on CD-ROM.

Fisheries and Aquaculture

Sources: Food and Agriculture Organization of the United Nations, United Nations Population Division

	Marine Catch {a} (annual average)		Freshwater Catch {b} (annual average)		Total Aquaculture Production (annual average)		Trade in Fish and Fish Products {c} (annual average million US$)		Food Supply from Fish and Fish Products (kg/person/ year) {d}	Fish Protein as a Percent of All Animal Protein	Number of Fishers	Number of Decked Fishery Vessels {e}	Population within 100 km of the Coast (percent)
	Metric Tons (000) 1998-00	Percent Change Since 1988-90	Metric Tons (000) 1998-00	Percent Change Since 1988-90	Metric Tons (000) 1998-00	Percent Change Since 1988-90	Exports 1998-00	Imports 1998-00	1997-99	1997-99	2000	1995	1995
WORLD	**81,601.9**	**2**	**9,550.7**	**31**	**33,179.7**	**63**	**52,548.9**	**57,624.7**	**16.0**	**16**	**34,501,411**	**1,256,841**	**39**
ASIA (EXCL. MIDDLE EAST)	**36,527.8**	**20**	**5,751.2**	**61**	**26,625.3**	**62**	**15,235.0**	**20,418.1**	**18.0**	**28**	**28,890,352**	**1,057,966**	**38**
Armenia	..	..	1.0	(63)	0.7	..	0.3	1.0	0.5	1	244 f	6	0
Azerbaijan	0.0	(67)	14.8	(70)	0.2	..	1.7	1.3	0.9	1	1,500 f	..	56
Bangladesh	179.6	27	754.6	47	597.4	69	313.6	2.5	10.2	47	1,320,480	61	55
Bhutan	..	..	0.3	-	0.0	67	..	..	..	..	450 f	..	0
Cambodia	36.4	25	184.1	212	14.5	62	35.3	3.1	12.0	35	73,425 g	..	24
China	14,395.9	170	2,367.1	188	22,722.0	73	3,081.3	1,315.0	24.5	21	12,233,128 h	432,674	24
Georgia	2.2	(99)	0.2	(60)	0.1	..	0.3	1.6	1.3	2	1,900 f	82	39
India	2,726.5	33	753.5	48	2,039.2	52	1,221.4	24.0	4.7	14	5,958,744 f	56,600	26
Indonesia	3,624.7	69	375.3	18	722.5	37	1,582.2	69.7	19.0	56	5,118,571	67,325	96
Japan	4,836.3	(52)	285.1	(3)	763.0	(5)	756.2	14,406.3	65.4	45	260,200	360,747	96
Kazakhstan	0.0	(83)	23.3	(70)	1.2	..	13.2	13.3	1.9	2	16,000 f	1,970	4
Korea, Dem People's Rep	190.2	(87)	20.0	(66)	67.9	23	69.6	5.6	9.4	36	129,000 f	2,900	93
Korea, Rep	1,968.3	(16)	16.4	(59)	317.9	(30)	1,346.6	1,037.6	47.3	39	176,928 j	76,801	100
Kyrgyzstan	..	..	0.1	(79)	0.1	..	..	2.0	0.7	1	154 f	..	0
Lao People's Dem Rep	..	..	26.3	34	31.2	73	0.0	1.4	10.0	31	15,000 f	..	6
Malaysia	1,201.8	42	20.4	74	146.8	65	189.6	262.6	57.0	35	100,666 f	17,965	98
Mongolia	..	..	0.4	91	..	..	0.2	0.0	0.1	0	0	..	0
Myanmar	772.7	33	166.2	21	90.7	93	162.0	1.0	16.0	45	610,000 f	140	49
Nepal	..	..	13.8	131	13.6	48	0.2	0.3	1.1	3	50,000 f	..	0
Pakistan	448.3	28	173.9	78	17.6	50	141.9	0.4	2.5	3	272,273	5,064	9
Philippines	1,719.0	14	146.4	(37)	342.7	(5)	408.7	109.2	29.6	42	990,872 f	3,220	100
Singapore	6.5	(44)	0.04	(68)	4.3	55	413.6	483.9	..	..	364	110	100
Sri Lanka	255.3	67	32.7	4	10.2	45	103.5	66.5	21.2	54	146,188	2,990	100
Tajikistan	..	..	0.1	(81)	0.1	..	..	0.2	0.1	0	200 f	..	0
Thailand	2,654.6	14	206.5	77	664.5	61	4,180.5	841.3	28.2	37	354,495	17,600	39
Turkmenistan	0.0	(93)	9.4	(79)	0.6	(338)	0.4	0.1	1.7	2	611 i	45	8
Uzbekistan	..	..	3.0	(40)	5.9	(257)	0.0	2.0	0.5	1	4,800	..	3
Viet Nam	1,217.6	92	156.3	19	463.6	66	1,080.4	12.1	18.1	37	1,000,000	140	83
EUROPE	**15,710.1**	**(24)**	**674.7**	**(18)**	**1,726.0**	**13**	**19,063.8**	**22,875.8**	**20.6**	**10**	**855,333**	**105,324**	**40**
Albania	2.1	(73)	0.8	(64)	0.2	..	6.5	4.5	2.4	1	1,590 j	2	97
Austria	..	..	0.6	4	2.9	(37)	9.0	189.7	14.3	4	2,300	..	2
Belarus	..	..	0.5	(84)	5.6	(203)	16.4	72.8	8.5	4	5,000 f	..	0
Belgium	29.7	(27)	0.5	4	1.4	49	471.9	1,059.0	..	..	544 j	156	83
Bosnia and Herzegovina	0.0	..	2.5	..	..	..	..	8.3	1.9	2	3,500 f	..	47
Bulgaria	10.2	(87)	1.9	37	5.2	(102)	7.2	15.5	4.2	3	1,483 f	30	29
Croatia	20.6	..	0.4	..	6.3	..	40.9	38.1	5.2	5	65,151 l	305	38
Czech Rep	..	..	4.3	..	18.5	..	27	79.4	12.7	5	2,243	..	0
Denmark	1,497.3	(15)	1.5	(71)	42.9	19	2,856.3	1,804.9	26.0	10	6,711 j	4,285	100
Estonia	110.2	(72)	4.4	(36)	0.2	(286)	86.6	37.6	19.7	12	13,346	186	86
Finland	108.7	28	56.4	(16)	15.6	(14)	19.1	127.5	33.6	14	5,879	3,838	73
France	573.2	(10)	3.3	(40)	266.8	11	1,104.7	3,275.8	31.3	9	26,113 g	6,586	40
Germany	212.6	(33)	24.5	96	66.8	(1)	1,044.5	2,403.1	14.9	7	4,358	2,406	15
Greece	104.4	(16)	4.4	15	73.1	92	248.5	301.0	26.0	11	19,847	18,375	99
Hungary	..	..	7.3	(58)	11.7	(60)	8.1	45.7	4.3	2	4,900	..	0
Iceland	1,799.9	13	0.3	(57)	3.8	50	1,352.0	80.3	93.1 n	30	6,100	826	100
Ireland	290.2	38	2.6	(52)	45.8	52	356.4	113.5	16.0	6	8,478 i	1,353	100
Italy	298.7	(24)	5.2	(61)	208.8	34	370.5	2,705.7	24.2	11	48,770	16,000	79
Latvia	120.2	(77)	1.2	(43)	0.4	(853)	54.4	35.9	15.4	11	6,571	351	75
Lithuania	57.8	(85)	1.9	(63)	1.7	(152)	40.0	56.1	22.0	15	4,700 f	131	23
Macedonia, FYR	..	..	0.2	..	1.5	..	0.6	8.8	5.1	5	8,472	..	14
Moldova, Rep	..	..	0.3	(86)	1.1	(537)	2.0	4.6	3.3	4	40 f	..	9
Netherlands	513.6	27	2.1	(47)	101.4	5	1,490.2	1,237.0	19.7	9	3,743	1,008	93
Norway	2,726.8	59	1.4	(56)	458.2	74	3,668.3	635.4	52.2	26	23,552	8,664	95
Poland	211.1	(60)	19.5	23	33.1	21	266.8	293.7	12.8	11	8,640 i	445	14
Portugal	206.6	(37)	0.04	(23)	7.1	(12)	276.6	936.1	65.7	23	25,021	9,265	93
Romania	3.0	(98)	5.1	(75)	9.4	(369)	5.4	38.8	2.5	2	8,519	33	6
Russian Federation	3,700.0	(50)	488.3	(10)	68.6	(179)	1,269.1	230.6	21.7	15	316,300	3,584	15
Serbia and Montenegro	0.4	..	1.2	..	4.3	..	0.8	44.0	2.9	1	1,429 f	5	8
Slovakia	..	..	1.7	..	0.8	..	2.2	36.3	8.3	5	215	..	0
Slovenia	..	..	0.2	..	1.1	..	6.4	28.5	6.9	3	231	11	61
Spain	1,133.8	(8)	8.9	(6)	316.3	26	1,582.1	3,399.6	44.4	18	75,434 f	15,243	68
Sweden	363.2	51	3.6	(46)	5.5	(55)	472.0	688.9	30.4	14	2,783	1,240	88
Switzerland	..	..	1.8	(49)	1.1	26	3.1	374.1	18.3	7	522	..	0
Ukraine	409.3	(57)	11.6	(81)	31.0	(193)	56.4	109.6	11.4	10	120,000 f	444	21
United Kingdom	830.6	(1)	4.2	81	148.2	69	1,421.8	2,294.9	21.8	10	17,847 i	9,562	99
MIDDLE EAST & N. AFRICA	**2,348.0**	**24**	**411.0**	**74**	**355.9**	**62**	**..**	**756.3**	**7.2**	**9**	**746,955**	**21,990**	**47**
Afghanistan	..	..	1.1	10	..	..	..	..	..	..	1,500 f	..	0
Algeria	98.2	(1)	0.0	..	0.3	(35)	2.7	11.2	3.5	6	26,151 i	2,184	69
Egypt	156.0	81	219.8	44	235.3	75	1.6	157.3	11.2	19	250,000	..	53
Iran, Islamic Rep	248.3	23	140.3	424	35.2	25	48.2	56.1	4.4	7	138,965	900	24
Iraq	12.5	204	10.1	(43)	3.8	16	..	0.6	1.5	8	12,000 f	8	6
Israel	4.2	(57)	1.8	8	19.1	23	8.2	133.2	23.4	9	1,535 f	384	97
Jordan	0.1	..	0.4	10	0.5	87	..	23.4	5.1	5	721	..	29
Kuwait	5.8	(19)	1.0	127	0.3	..	5.3	16.4	12.1	5	670 j	917	100
Lebanon	3.6	122	0.0	..	0.4	75	..	24.2	8.0	7	9,825	5	100
Libyan Arab Jamahiriya	33.0	45	0.0	-	0.1	50	35.0	11.3	6.1	7	9,500 f	93	79
Morocco	782.3	43	1.8	16	2.2	89	815.3	11.3	8.4	17	106,096	3,052	65
Oman	110.1	(18)	0.0	-	5.1	22	46.6	5.3	..	..	28,003 j	390	88
Saudi Arabia	49.1	10	0.1	..	5.4	78	8.6	108.5	7.6	6	25,360	23	30
Syrian Arab Rep	2.6	81	4.6	282	6.7	58	..	48.9	1.8	2	11,292	5	34
Tunisia	90.9	(4)	1.0	291	1.5	37	94.7	13.1	9.4	12	50,815	17	84
Turkey	491.3	5	28.9	(12)	66.2	93	96.4	62.7	8.0	10	33,614 f	9,710	58
United Arab Emirates	112.5	22	0.1	82	0.0	..	36.8	27.5	25.9	12	15,543	4,050	85
Yemen	122.3	64	0.0	..	..	..	26.1	4.8	6.8	22	12,200 j	71	63

	Marine Catch {a} (annual average)		Freshwater Catch {b} (annual average)		Total Aquaculture Production (annual average)		Trade in Fish and Fish Products {c} (annual average million US$)		Food Supply from Fish and Fish Products (kg/person/year) {d}	Fish Protein as a Percent of All Animal Protein	Number of Fishers	Number of Decked Fishery Vessels {e}	Population within 100 km of the Coast (percent)
	Metric Tons (000) 1998-00	Percent Change Since 1988-90	Metric Tons (000) 1998-00	Percent Change Since 1988-90	Metric Tons (000) 1998-00	Percent Change Since 1988-90	Exports 1998-00	Imports 1998-00	1997-99	1997-99	2000	1995	1995
SUB-SAHARAN AFRICA	2806.5	15	1808.0	13	37.2	25	1,691.4	845.5	7.6	25	1,995,694 j	71	21
Angola	186.4	50	6.0	(25)			10.8	14.3	10.4	28	30,364 f	580	29
Benin	13.8	6	24.5	(6)	0.0	..	2.2	4.7	8.7	26	61,793	5	62
Botswana	..	..	0.2	(89)			0.1	5.3	6.1	5	2,620 f	..	0
Burkina Faso	..	..	8.1	7	0.0	..	0.0	1.4	1.9	6	8,300	..	0
Burundi	..	..	10.9	(18)	0.1	60	0.2	0.1	2.3	23	7,030 j	..	0
Cameroon	59.6	21	50.0	138	0.1	(117)	2.7	30.2	12.3	31	24,500	25	22
Central African Rep	..	..	14.8	14	0.1	20	..	0.4	4.2	9	5,410	..	0
Chad	..	..	84.0	31			..	..	6.9	14	300,000 g	..	0
Congo	20.6	(6)	25.5	10	0.2	(29)	2.4	19.7	21.4	46	10,500	26	25
Congo, Dem Rep	3.9	97	194.4	21	0.4	(66)	0.5	42.5	6.7	34	108,400	23	3
Côte d'Ivoire	65.5	(2)	11.5	(59)	1.0	86	171.0	171.7	14.2	42	19,707 f	63	40
Equatorial Guinea	4.5	34	1.0	162			2.8	2.1	..	..	9,218	5	72
Eritrea	7.0	..	0.0	..			1.0	0.1	0.9	3	14,500 f	..	73
Ethiopia {k}	..	..	15.2	365	0.0	..	..	..	0.2	1	6,272	..	1
Gabon	40.4	114	10.1	421	0.4	..	14.0	7.1	49.6	37	8,258	39	63
Gambia	26.5	69	2.5	(7)	0.0	..	4.9	1.3	24.1	64	2,000 f	..	91
Ghana	384.6	24	77.9	24	0.5	18	81.1	97.3	28.1	66	230,000 f	500	42
Guinea	78.9	108	4.0	33	0.0	..	23.1	14.3	11.2	51	10,707 f	15	41
Guinea-Bissau	5.1	3	..	..	..	..	3.1	0.4	4.4	14	2,500 f	8	95
Kenya	6.0	(29)	191.7	25	0.3	(188)	36.8	6.3	5.4	10	59,565	32	8
Lesotho	..	..	0.0	494	0.00	..	..	..	0.0	0	60 f	..	0
Liberia	8.5	3	4.1	(1)	0.0	..	0.0	1.9	5.9	26	5,143	14	58
Madagascar	98.9	47	30.0	(10)	5.9	96	77.0	6.4	7.5	16	83,310 j	65	55
Malawi	..	..	43.8	(41)	0.4	55	0.2	0.3	4.5	34	42,922 j	57	0
Mali	..	..	102.1	55	0.1	80	0.4	2.2	8.8	15	70,000 i	..	0
Mauritania	32.9	(51)	5.0	(17)			70.1	0.5	10.6	11	7,944 g	126	40
Mozambique	25.8	(16)	10.8	215	0.0	..	84.0	8.8	2.7	21	20,000 f	291	59
Namibia	305.0	191	1.5	49	0.0	50	266.1	..	11.6	20	2,700 f	218	5
Niger	..	..	11.4	226	0.0	(100)	0.7	0.9	0.9	3	7,983 f	..	0
Nigeria	316.4	66	136.9	46	22.6	35	4.8	231.6	8.8	32	481,264 g	318	26
Rwanda	..	..	6.6	287	0.2	65	..	0.1	1.0	7	5,690	..	0
Senegal	378.8	42	27.3	47	0.1	82	287.6	7.0	32.1	45	55,547 j	180	83
Sierra Leone	49.5	32	16.3	(0)	0.03	33	14.6	3.3	13.6	61	17,990 f	27	55
Somalia	20.7	(2)	0.2	(50)	..	..	3.7	..	2.9	2	18,900 f	12	55
South Africa	596.4	(34)	0.9	10	4.4	47	259.0	64.1	6.9	8	10,500 f	600	39
Sudan	5.7	336	44.0	52	1.0	88	0.4	0.4	1.7	2	27,700 j	..	3
Tanzania, United Rep	49.6	(4)	280.0	(18)	0.2	(30)	66.8	0.4	8.9	32	92,529	30	21
Togo	15.4	34	5.2	20	0.1	89	1.8	14.2	13.4	51	14,120	3	45
Uganda	..	..	267.5	19	0.2	80	33.8	0.1	8.9	28	57,862 j	..	0
Zambia	..	..	68.0	6	4.2	70	0.4	0.9	7.4	25	23,833 f	235	0
Zimbabwe	..	..	14.0	(41)	0.2	11	2.2	9.3	2.7	10	1,804 i	..	0
NORTH AMERICA	5457.1	(19)	419.4	(19)	559.8	32	5,682.6	10,840.9	21.5	12	303,784	45,480	41
Canada	933.5	(37)	68.9	(56)	109.1	70	2,575.9	1,318.9	23.8	10	8,696	18,280	24
United States	4365.8	(15)	350.5	(3)	450.7	23	2,847.5	9,511.3	21.3	7	290,000 f	27,200	43
C. AMERICA & CARIBBEAN	1582.5	(7)	117.0	(25)	132.8	(697)	1,529.2	423.0	8.8	14	446,390	7,161	55
Belize	37.8	..	0.0	(50)	2.5	92	27.7	2.4	13.0	13	1,872	12	100
Costa Rica	23.2	40	1.0	233	9.0	95	177.4	27.4	5.9	5	6,510 j	1,003	100
Cuba	58.4	(68)	5.0	(61)	51.5	86	90.1	26.9	13.1	16	11,865 f	1,250	100
Dominican Rep	9.2	(44)	0.6	(57)	1.2	80	0.9	52.4	12.6	10	9,286	..	100
El Salvador	7.5	2	2.6	(5)	0.3	(119)	31.9	6.9	2.9	4	24,534	80	99
Guatemala	13.7	324	6.9	477	4.0	79	29.9	7.6	1.6	3	17,275	85	61
Haiti	4.6	(9)	0.5	58	..	..	3.4	7.4	3.1	11	4,700 f	1	100
Honduras	10.8	(25)	0.1	115	8.3	62	40.2	14.8	2.9	3	21,000 i	280	65
Jamaica	6.5	(18)	0.5	1	4.0	23	13.0	56.0	25.5	20	23,465	5	100
Mexico	1130.8	(9)	98.5	(27)	47.7	60	694.0	125.2	9.6	8	262,401	3,100	29
Nicaragua	21.7	444	1.2	813	4.8	99	87.1	6.5	3.3	7	14,502	280	72
Panama	182.2	27	0.0	21	5.3	28	232.8	15.4	11.0	8	13,062	695	100
Trinidad and Tobago	9.1	12	0.0	-	0.02	..	11.8	7.7	14.2	14	7,297	19	100
SOUTH AMERICA	14649.6	1	345.7	6	318.2	61	4,980.1	687.7	8.9	12	784,051	13,106	49
Argentina	1006.7	101	24.7	133	1.3	77	824.7	86.5	8.5	4	12,320	800	45
Bolivia	0.9	(64)	5.2	59	0.4	21	0.1	5.6	1.7	2	7,754 f	..	0
Brazil	520.5	(16)	180.9	(6)	132.7	86	168.7	357.0	6.5	4	290,000 f	1,450	49
Chile	4150.8	(26)	0.0	(97)	319.6	94	1,694.4	54.1	17.6	10	50,873	563	82
Colombia	101.7	71	25.1	(37)	53.6	88	195.1	86.5	4.5	5	129,410 i	167	30
Ecuador	466.4	(18)	0.4	(32)	112.0	33	915.7	16.1	7.0	9	162,870 g	515	61
Guyana	51.2	44	0.7	(16)	0.5	92	38.6	0.7	59.9	47	6,571	55	77
Paraguay	..	..	25.0	124	0.1	44	0.1	2.3	5.5	4	4,469 g	..	0
Peru	7773.0	15	34.6	2	7.6	34	852.2	15.4	20.3	21	66,361	7,710	57
Suriname	16.0	209	0.2	(27)	0.2	..	6.9	4.1	24.6	24	3,628 f	22	87
Uruguay	117.9	11	2.2	878	0.0	..	115.0	13.4	8.6	4	4,023	958	78
Venezuela	389.9	37	46.7	41	11.1	94	126.9	45.5	18.3	19	44,302 i	866	73
OCEANIA	1110.1	75	23.0	(1)	127.6	62	1,681.7	629.9	22.7	25	85,324	1,917	87
Australia	214.6	13	4.1	9	33.9	62	885.7	518.8	21.3	7	13,800 i	246	90
Fiji	27.9	17	5.5	18	1.3	99	28.5	16.8	32.1	21	8,985 j	..	100
New Zealand	594.9	97	1.6	(20)	90.4	69	682.2	55.9	30.3	13	1,928	1,375	100
Papua New Guinea	47.1	271	11.7	(7)	0.0	..	31.7	11.5	15.1	31	16,000 f	35	61
Solomon Islands	46.8	46	0.0	-	0.0	..	0.2	0.2	52.5	52	11,000 m	130	100
DEVELOPED	27258.0	(30)	1439.3	(21)	3180.4	12	27,094.4	48,905.7	23.7	10	1,467,401	516,259	45
DEVELOPING	53010.2	32	8110.6	49	26702.3	60	24,010.7	8,571.6	13.8	20	32,640,482	740,322	

Negative values are shown in parentheses. **a.** Includes marine fish and diadromous fish caught in marine areas, as well as molluscs and crustaceans. **b.** Includes freshwater fish and diadromous fish caught in inland waters or low-salinity marine areas, as well as molluscs and crustaceans. **c.** Includes trade of all marine and freshwater catch, and total aquaculture production, excluding aquatic plants. **d.** Per capita values are expressed on a live-weight equivalent basis, which means that all parts of the fish, including bones, are taken into account when estimating consumption of fish and fishery products. **e.** Includes fishing vessels such as trawlers, long liners, etc., and non-fishing vessels such as motherships, fish carriers, etc. **f.** Data were collected between 1991 and 1996. **g.** Data are for 1997. **h.** Does not include Taiwan or Hong Kong. **i.** Data are for 1998. **j.** Data are for 1999. **k.** Data for Ethiopia before 1993 include Eritrea **l.** Since independence, data include a substantial but unquantifiable number of sport fishers. **m.** Data are for 1980. **n.** Per capita fish consumption in Iceland includes quantities of fish and fish products destined for the export market.

VARIABLE DEFINITIONS AND METHODOLOGY

Marine and Freshwater Catch data refer to marine and freshwater fish caught or trapped for commercial, industrial, and subsistence use (catches from recreational activities are included where available); data refer to fish caught by a country's fleet anywhere in the world. Statistics for mariculture, aquaculture, and other kinds of fish or shellfish farming are not included in the country totals. Marine fish includes demersal fish (flounders, halibuts, soles, etc.; cods, hakes, haddocks, etc.; redfishes, basses, congers, etc.; and sharks, rays, chimeras, etc.), pelagic fish (jacks, mullets, sauries, etc.; herrings, sardines, anchovies, etc.; tunas, bonitos, billfishes, etc.; and mackerels, snooks, cutlassfishes, etc.), and diadromous fish in marine areas (i.e., sturgeons, paddlefishes, river eels, salmons, trouts, smelt, shads, and miscellaneous diadromous fishes), marine molluscs (squids, cuttlefishes, octopuses, etc.; abalones, winkles, conchs, etc.; oysters; mussels; scallops, pectens, etc.; clams, cockles, arkshells, etc.; and miscellaneous marine molluscs) and marine crustaceans (sea-spiders, crabs, etc.; lobsters, spiny-rock lobsters, etc.; squat lobsters; shrimps, prawns, etc.; krill, planktonic crustaceans, etc.; and miscellaneous marine crustaceans).

Freshwater fish includes fish caught in inland waters (i.e., carps, barbels, and other cyprinids; tilapias and other cichlids; and miscellaneous and freshwater fishes), and diadromous fish caught in inland waters, as well as freshwater molluscs and crustaceans. Catch figures are the national totals averaged over a 3-year period.

Data are represented as nominal catches, which are the landings converted to a live-weight basis, that is, the weight when caught. Fish catch does not include discards. Landings for some countries are identical to catches. Catch data are provided annually to the Food and Agriculture Organization of the United Nations (FAO) Fisheries Department by national fishery offices and regional fishery commissions. Some recent data are provisional. If no data are submitted, FAO uses the previous year's figures or makes estimates based on other information.

Aquaculture is defined by FAO as "the farming of aquatic organisms, including fish, molluscs, and crustaceans. Farming implies some form of intervention in the rearing process to enhance production, such as regular stocking, feeding, and protection from predators, etc. [It] also implies ownership of the stock being cultivated...." Aquatic organisms that are exploitable by the public as a common property resource are included in the harvest of fisheries.

FAO's global collection of aquaculture statistics from questionnaires to national fishery offices was begun in 1984. FAO's aquaculture database has 337 "species items" that are grouped into six categories. **Total Aquaculture Production** includes marine, freshwater, and diadromous fishes, molluscs and crustaceans cultivated in marine, inland, or brackish environments. For a detailed listing of species, please refer to the original source. Aquaculture production is expressed as an annual average over a 3-year period.

Trade in Fish and Fish Products expresses the value associated with imports and exports of fish that are live, fresh, chilled, frozen, dried, salted, smoked, or canned, and other derived products and preparations. Trade includes freshwater and marine fish, aquaculture, molluscs and crustaceans, meals, and solubles. Aquatic plants are not included. Figures are the national totals averaged over a 3-year period in millions of U.S. dollars. Exports are generally on a free-on-board basis (i.e., not including insurance or freight costs). Imports are usually on a cost, insurance, and freight basis (i.e., insurance and freight costs added in).

Regional totals are calculated by adding up imports or exports of each country included in that region. Therefore, the regional totals should not be taken as a net trade for that region, since there may also be trade occurring within a region. To collate national data, FAO uses its International Standard Statistical Classification of Fishery Commodities. Commodities produced by aquaculture and other kinds of fish farming are also included.

Food Supply from Fish and Fish Products is defined as the quantity of both freshwater and marine fish, seafood and derived products available for human consumption. Data were calculated by taking a country's fish production plus imports of fish and fishery products, minus exports, minus the amount of fishery production destined to non-food uses (i.e., reduction to meal, etc.), and plus or minus variations in stocks. The quantity of fish and fish products consumed include the bones and all parts of the fish.

Fish Protein as a Percent of Animal Protein Supply is defined as the quantity of protein from both freshwater and marine fish, seafood, and derived products available for human consumption as a percentage of all available animal protein. FAO calculates food supply for all products, including fish, in its food balance sheets. FAOSTAT maintains statistics on apparent consumption of fish and fishery products, in live weight, for 220 countries in a collection of Supply/Utilization Accounts (SUAs). For each product, the SUA traces supplies from production, imports, and stocks to its utilization in different forms—addition to stocks; exports; animal feed; seed; processing for food and non-food purposes; waste (or losses); and lastly; as food available for human consumption, where appropriate. For more detailed information, please refer to the following article: "Supply Utilization Accounts and Food Balance Sheets in the Context of a National Statistical System," maintained on-line by FAO at **http://www.fao.org/es/ESS/Suafbs.htm**.

Number of Fishers includes the number of people employed in commercial and subsistence fishing (both personnel on fishing vessels and on shore), operating in freshwater, brackish and marine areas, and in aquaculture production activities. Data on people employed in fishing and aquaculture are collected by the FAO through annual questionnaires submitted to the national reporting offices of the member countries. When possible, other national and/or regional published sources are also used to estimate figures. Please refer to the original source for further information on collection methodologies (available on-line at **http://www.fao.org/fi/statist/fisoft/fishers.asp**) or to the following publication: Numbers of Fishers 1970–1997, FAO Fisheries Circular N. 929 Revision 2, Fishery Information, Data and Statistics Unit (FAO, Rome, 1999).

Decked Fishery Vessels include trawlers, purse seiners, gill netters, long liners, trap setters, other seiners and liners, multi-purpose vessels, dredgers, and other fishing vessels. Data on undecked vessels are being collected by FAO, but are not yet available. Fleet data are collected by the FAO through questionnaires submitted to the national reporting offices of the member countries. Other national or regional published sources, such as the registry of fishing vessels, are also used to estimate fleet size. The flag of the vessel is used to assign its nationality. However, in many cases vessels are flagged in one country, while the ownership, landings, and trade resides with another nation. This approach is referred to as a "flag of convenience," and fishers or corporations use this method to facilitate registration of a vessel (i.e., some countries have fewer registration restrictions), to gain access to fish in different Exclusive Economic Zones, or to avoid having to follow set fishing quotas in their own nation.

Population within 100 km of the Coast refers to estimates of the percentage of the population living within the coastal area based on 1995 population figures. These estimates were calculated using a data set that provides information on the spatial distribution of the world's human population on a 2.5-minute grid. Populations are distributed according to administrative districts, which vary in scale, level, and size from country to country. A 100-km coastal buffer was used to calculate the number of people in the coastal zone for each country. The percentage of the population in the coastal zone was calculated from 1995 United Nations Population Division totals for each country.

FREQUENCY OF UPDATE BY DATA PROVIDERS

FAO updates the FishStat database annually. Updates can be found on the FishStat website at http://www.fao.org/fi/statist/FISOFT/FISHPLUS.asp. The FAO updates the data on Food Supply variables annually; the most recent updates incorporated in these tables are from July 2002. Data on the number of fishers and decked fishery vessels are updated by the Fishery Information, Data and Statistics Unit (FIDI) of FAO.

DATA RELIABILITY AND CAUTIONARY NOTES

Marine Catch, Freshwater Catch, Total Aquaculture Production, and Trade in Fish and Fishery Products. While the FAO data set provides the most extensive, global time series of fishery statistics since 1970, there are some problems associated with the data. Funding for the development and maintenance of fisheries statistics at the national level has been decreasing in real terms since 1992, while the demand is growing for a variety of global statistics on discards, fish inventories, aquaculture, and illegal activities. Country-level data are often submitted with a 1–2 year delay, and countries are declaring an increasing percentage of their catch as "unidentified fish." Stock assessment working groups can more accurately estimate the composition of a catch; however, due to financial constraints, these groups are rare, especially in developing countries. Statistics from smaller artisanal and subsistence fisheries are particularly sparse. In addition, fishers sometimes underreport their catches because they have not kept within harvest limits established to manage the fishery. In some cases, catch statistics are inflated to increase the importance of the fishing industry to the national economy. FAO states that "general trends are probably reliably reflected by the available statistics...but the annual figures and the assessments involve a certain degree of uncertainty and small changes from year to year are probably not statistically significant." The quality of the aquaculture production estimates varies because many countries lack the resources to adequately monitor landings within their borders.

These statistics provide a good overview of regional fisheries trends. However, when reviewing the state of fisheries stocks, evaluating food security, etc., these data should be used with caution and supplemented with estimates from regional organizations, academic literature, expert consultations, and trade data. For more information, please consult Fishery Statistics: Reliability and Policy Implications, published by the FAO Fisheries Department and available on-line at http://www.fao.org/fi/statist/nature_china/30jan02.asp.

Food Supply from Fish and Fishery Products and Fish Protein as a Percent of Total Protein: Food supply as represented here is different from actual consumption. Figures do not account for discards (including bones) and losses during storage and preparation. Supply data should only be used to assess food security if it is combined with an analysis of food availability and accessibility. Per capita supply averages can also mask disparate food availability within a particular country. Nonetheless, the data are subject to "vigorous consistency checks." According to FAO, the food supply statistics, "while often far from satisfactory in the proper statistical sense, do provide an approximate picture of the overall food situation in a country and can be useful for economic and nutritional studies, for preparing development plans and for formulating related projects." For more information see Food Balance Sheets: A Handbook, maintained on-line by FAO at http://www.fao.org/DOCREP/003/X9892E/X9892E00.htm.

Number of Fishers: Numbers presented in this table are gross estimates. Many countries do not submit data on fishers, or submit incomplete information; therefore the quality of these data is poor. Apart from the gaps and the heavy presence of estimates due to non-reporting, the information provided by national statistical offices may not be strictly comparable since different definitions and methods are used in assessing the number of people engaged in fishing and aquaculture.

FAO recognizes that these statistics are incomplete and may not accurately reflect the current level of employment in the fishing sector. Specifically, it is aware that some countries failed to report for several years. Those which report regularly have occasionally omitted fish farmers from the total or included subsistence and sport fishers as well as family members living on fishing.

Decked Fishery Vessels: As with the number of fishers, FAO recognizes that these fleet statistics are incomplete and may not accurately reflect current world fishing capacity. These data may include vessels that are no longer in operation. The quality of the estimates varies because many countries lack the resources to adequately monitor and report on fleet size. For further information, please refer to the original source or to Fishery Fleet Statistics, 1970, 1975, 1980, 1985, 1989–95, Bulletin of Fishery Statistics No. 35 (FAO, Rome, 1998).

SOURCES

Catch, Aquaculture Production, and Trade in Fish and Fishery Products: Fishery Information, Data and Statistics Unit, Food and Agriculture Organization of the United Nations (FAO). 2002. FISHSTAT Plus: Universal software for fishery statistical time series, Version 2.3 Rome: FAO. Available on-line at: http://www.fao.org/fi/statist/FISOFT/FISHPLUS.asp. **Food Supply Variables:** Food and Agriculture Organization of the United Nations (FAO), FAOSTAT on-line statistical service. 2002. Rome: FAO. Available on-line at: http://apps.fao.org. **Data on the Number of Fishers:** Food and Agriculture Organization of the United Nations (FAO), Fishery Information, Data and Statistics Unit (FIDI) December, 1999. **Number of People within 100 km of the Coast:** Center for International Earth Science Information Network (CIESIN), World Resources Institute, and International Food Policy Research Institute. 2000. Gridded Population of the World, Version 2 alpha Columbia University, Palisades, NY. Available on-line at: http://sedac.ciesin.org/plue/gwp. **Population** (used to calculate per capita values): Population Division of the Department of Economic and Social Affairs of the United Nations Secretariat. 2002. World Population Prospects: The 2000 Revision. Data set on CD-ROM. New York: United Nations.

Forests, Grasslands, and Drylands

Sources: Food and Agriculture Organization of the United Nations (FAO), Forest Stewardship Council (FSC), United Nations Environment Program—Global Resource Information Database, Global Land Cover Characteristics Database (GLCCD).

	Total Forest		Natural Forest		Plantations		FSC {b} Certified		All Certification Schemes	Drylands {a}		Grassland Area		
	Area (1000 ha) 2000	Annual % Change 1990-2000	Area (1000 ha) 2000	Annual % Change 1990-2000	Area (1000 ha) 2000	Annual % Change 1990-2000	Area (1000 ha) 2002	Annual % Change 1998-2002	(1000 ha) 2000	Average Area (1000 ha) 1950-1981	Percent of Total Land Area	Shrublands (1000 km²) 1992-93	Savannas 1992-93	Herbaceous Grasslands 1992-93
WORLD	**3,869,455**	**(0.2)**	**3,682,722**	**..**	**186,733**	**..**	**27,227**	**30.9**	**80,717**	**5,060**	**..**	**23,343**	**16,013**	**10,542**
ASIA (EXCL. MIDDLE EAST)	**504,180**	**(0.1)**	**375,824**	**(0.1)**	**110,953**	**5.3**	**245**	**29.9**	**..**	**1,078**	**..**	**4,003**	**1,061**	**4,054**
Armenia	351	1.3	338	..	13	..	0		0	3	98	1	4	2
Azerbaijan	1,094	1.3	1,074	..	20	..	0		0	7	84	9	2	4
Bangladesh	1,334	1.3	709	(0.8)	625	4.4	0		0	0	0	3	0	1
Bhutan	3,016	..	2,995	(0.0)	21	4.7	0	..	0	0	0	3	0	4
Cambodia	9,335	(0.6)	9,245	(0.6)	90	3.3	0	..	0	0	0	4	3	0
China	163,480	1.2	118,397	0.6	45,083	3.0	0		0	318	34	1,829	415	1,815
Georgia	2,988	..	2,788	..	200	..	0		0	2	34	5	2	1
India	64,113	0.1	31,535	(3.8)	32,578	6.2	0		0	185	60	285	246	26
Indonesia	104,986	(1.2)	95,116	(1.5)	9,871	3.2	152	..	72	5	3	1	111	48
Japan	24,081	..	13,399	..	10,682	..	6	..	3	0	0	18	43	2
Kazakhstan	12,148	2.2	12,143	..	5	..	0		0	269	99	479	8	1,180
Korea, Dem People's Rep	8,210	..	..	..	..	..	0		0	0	0	0	45	1
Korea, Rep	6,248	(0.1)	..	..	..	..	0		0	0	0	1	37	0
Kyrgyzstan	1,003	2.6	946	..	57	..	0		0	11	55	53	4	53
Lao People's Dem Rep	12,561	(0.4)	12,507	(0.5)	54	..	0	..	0	0	0	2	6	0
Malaysia	19,292	(1.2)	17,543	(1.4)	1,750	2.2	68	4.1	55	0	0	3	0	1
Mongolia	10,645	(0.5)	..	..	..	..	0	..	0	101	65	450	45	806
Myanmar	34,419	(1.4)	33,598	(1.5)	821	5.9	0	..	0	8	43	2		
Nepal	3,900	(1.8)	3,767	(2.0)	133	5.1	0	..	0	1	9	25	4	11
Pakistan	2,361	(1.5)	1,381	(4.1)	980	3.7	0	..	0	73	83	300	1	19
Philippines	5,789	(1.4)	5,036	(2.1)	753	5.1	15	..	15	0	0	0	0	0
Singapore	2	..	..	..	..	..	0		0	0	0	0	0	0
Sri Lanka	1,940	(1.6)	1,625	(2.2)	316	1.5	5	..	13	2	24	1	0	0
Tajikistan	400	0.5	390	..	10	..	0		0	6	40	50	1	18
Thailand	14,762	(0.7)	9,842	(2.9)	4,920	6.1	0	..	0	3	7	12	33	0
Turkmenistan	3,755	..	3,743	..	12	..	0	..	0	47	100	259	0	35
Uzbekistan	1,969	0.2	1,669	..	300	..	0		0	44	99	187	0	22
Viet Nam	9,819	0.5	8,108	(0.3)	1,711	6.3	0		0	0	0	15	7	2
EUROPE {c}	**1,035,344**	**0.0**	**1,007,236**	**0.1**	**32,015**	**0.0**	**16,255**	**31.6**	**46,703**	**488**	**..**	**3,650**	**686**	**715**
Albania	991	(0.8)	889	..	102	..	0	..	0	0	0	0	1	0
Austria	3,886	0.2	..	..	..	..	0	..	550	0	0	3	0	1
Belarus	9,402	3.2	9,207	..	195	..	0		0	0	0	0	0	0
Belgium {d}	728	(0.2)	..	..	..	..	4		..	0	0	0	0	0
Bosnia and Herzegovina	2,273	..	2,216	..	57	..	0		0	0	0	0	0	0
Bulgaria	3,690	0.6	2,722	..	969	..	0	..	0	6	53	0	0	0
Croatia	1,783	0.1	1,736	..	47	..	373	..	167	0	0	0	1	0
Czech Rep	2,632	..	..	..	..	..	10	..	10	1	13	0	0	0
Denmark	455	0.2	114	..	341	..	0		0	0	0	0	0	0
Estonia	2,060	0.6	1,755	..	305	..	0		0	0	0	0	0	0
Finland	21,935	..	..	..	..	..	0	..	21,900	0	0	15	0	3
France	15,341	0.4	14,380	..	961	..	15	..	1	0	0	6	5	2
Germany	10,740	..	..	..	..	..	418	55.2	3,242	2	5	0	0	1
Greece	3,599	0.9	3,479	..	120	..	0	..	0	6	45	15	8	1
Hungary	1,840	0.4	1,704	..	136	..	0	..	0	4	46	0	0	0
Iceland	31	2.2	19	..	12	..	0	..	0	..	..	23	0	2
Ireland	659	3.0	69	..	590	..	0	..	0	0	0	0	0	0
Italy	10,003	0.3	9,870	..	133	..	11	0.0	11	6	21	47	2	3
Latvia	2,923	0.4	2,780	..	143	..	0		0	0	0	0	0	0
Lithuania	1,994	0.2	1,710	..	284	..	0		0	0	0	0	0	0
Macedonia, FYR	906	..	876	..	30	..	0		0	1	37	0	0	0
Moldova, Rep	325	0.2	324	..	1	..	0		0	3	100	0	0	0
Netherlands	375	0.3	275	..	100	..	103	..	69	0	0	0	0	0
Norway	8,868	0.4	8,568	..	300	..	0	..	5,600	0	0	76	1	17
Poland	9,047	0.2	9,008	..	39	..	3,592	16.1	2,743	6	19	0	0	0
Portugal	3,666	1.7	2,832	..	834	..	0	..	0	3	29	18	5	0
Romania	6,448	0.2	6,357	..	91	..	0	..	0	9	38	0	0	2
Russian Federation	851,392	..	834,052	..	17,340	..	216	..	33	367	22	3,323	638	667
Serbia and Montenegro	2,887	(0.1)	2,848	..	39	..	0		0	..	..	0	0	0
Slovakia	2,177	0.9	2,162	..	15	..	0		0	0	0	0	0	0
Slovenia	1,107	0.2	1,106	..	1	..	0		0	0	0	0	0	0
Spain	14,370	0.6	12,466	..	1,904	..	0	..	0	35	69	85	23	2
Sweden	27,134	..	26,565	..	569	..	10,130	35.8	11,167	0	0	34	0	4
Switzerland	1,199	0.4	1,195	..	4	..	84	73.6	49	0	0	5	0	2
Ukraine	9,584	0.3	5,159	..	4,425	..	238	..	203	39	65	0	0	6
United Kingdom	2,794	0.6	866	1.5	1,928	0.3	1,061	93.4	958	0	0	0	0	0
MIDDLE EAST & N. AFRICA	**29,104**	**0.2**	**20,448**	**..**	**6,533**	**..**	**0**	**..**	**..**	**553**	**..**	**2,476**	**76**	**596**
Afghanistan	1,351	..	..	..	..	..	0		0	60	94	310	0	161
Algeria	2,145	1.3	1,427	(0.2)	718	5.3	0		0	49	21	192	2	10
Egypt	72	3.3	0	0.0	72	3.3	0		0	8	8	6	3	4
Iran, Islamic Rep	7,299	..	5,015	(1.2)	2,284	3.2	0		0	147	90	567	10	225
Iraq	799	..	789	(0.0)	10	2.7	0		0	44	100	166	4	4
Israel	132	4.9	41	..	91	..	0		0	1	69	7	0	0
Jordan	86	..	41	(1.5)	45	1.6	0		0	6	72	46	0	0
Kuwait	5	3.5	0	..	5	3.4	0		0	2	92	4	0	0
Lebanon	36	(0.4)	34	..	2	..	0		0	1	59	2	0	2
Libyan Arab Jamahiriya	358	1.4	190	0.0	168	3.3	0		0	37	23	34	0	2
Morocco	3,025	..	2,491	(0.4)	534	2.0	0		0	37	92	155	1	15
Oman	1	5.3	0	(17.3)	1	5.1	0		0	4	14	43	0	0
Saudi Arabia	1,504	..	1,500	0.0	4	4.8	0		0	46	24	532	0	0
Syrian Arab Rep	461	..	232	(6.9)	229	..	0		0	18	98	99	0	1
Tunisia	510	0.2	308	(3.5)	202	11.7	0		0	15	94	38	1	9
Turkey	10,225	0.2	8,371	..	1,854	..	0		0	60	77	46	55	160
United Arab Emirates	321	2.8	7	..	314	0.0	0		0	6	6	0	0	0
Yemen	449	(1.9)	..	..	..	..	0		0	13	30	216	0	2

	Forest Area						Certified Forest Area			Drylands {a}		Grassland Area		
	Total Forest		Natural Forest		Plantations		FSC {b} Certified		All Certification Schemes	Drylands				
	Area (1000 ha) 2000	Annual % Change 1990-2000	Area (1000 ha) 2000	Annual % Change 1990-2000	Area (1000 ha) 2000	Annual % Change 1998-2002	Area (1000 ha) 2002	Annual % Change 1990-2000	(1000 ha) 2000	Average Area (1000 ha) 1950-1981	Percent of Total Land Area	Shrub-lands	Savan-nas (1000 km²)	Herbaceous Grasslands
												1992-93	1992-93	1992-93
SUB-SAHARAN AFRICA	486,571	(0.9)	478,576	..	6,210	..	1,070	30.5	974	1,121	..	2,513	7,749	1,830
Angola	69,756	(0.2)	69,615	(0.2)	141	0.1	0	..	0	24	19	43	537	35
Benin	2,650	(2.3)	2,538	(2.5)	112	1.0	0	..	0	10	88	0	109	0
Botswana	12,427	(0.9)	12,426	(0.9)	1	4.1	0	..	0	58	100	127	97	226
Burkina Faso	7,089	(0.2)	7,023	(0.3)	67	11.3	0	..	0	27	100	2	199	31
Burundi	94	(9.0)	21	(21.9)	73	3.4	0	..	0	0	0	1	4	0
Cameroon	23,858	(0.9)	23,778	(0.9)	80	0.3	0	..	0	6	13	0	202	2
Central African Rep	22,907	(0.1)	22,903	..	4	..	0	..	0	12	20	0	473	0
Chad	12,692	(0.6)	12,678	(0.6)	14	2.5	0	..	0	87	68	68	445	120
Congo	22,060	(0.1)	21,977	(0.1)	83	11.5	0	..	0	0	0	0	91	2
Congo, Dem Rep	135,207	(0.4)	135,110	(0.4)	97	0.1	0	..	0	1	0	7	493	4
Côte d'Ivoire	7,117	(3.1)	6,933	(3.3)	184	2.9	0	..	0	..	..	0	201	0
Equatorial Guinea	1,752	(0.6)	..	..	..	..	0	..	0	0	0	0	3	0
Eritrea	1,585	(0.3)	1,563	(0.5)	22	..	0	..	0	10	83	25	29	15
Ethiopia	4,593	(0.8)	4,377	(0.9)	216	1.0	0	..	0	65	58	410	347	57
Gabon	21,826	..	21,790	..	36	..	0	..	..	0	0	1	48	2
Gambia	481	1.0	479	..	2	..	0	..	0	1	97	0	5	0
Ghana	6,335	(1.7)	6,259	(1.8)	76	2.5	0	..	0	16	66	0	154	0
Guinea	6,929	(0.5)	6,904	(0.5)	25	7.4	0	..	0	3	14	0	205	0
Guinea-Bissau	2,187	(0.9)	2,186	..	2	..	0	..	0	0	6	1	24	0
Kenya	17,096	(0.5)	16,865	(0.5)	232	0.9	0	..	0	40	68	221	152	19
Lesotho	14	..	0	..	14	..	0	..	0	0	0	0	13	9
Liberia	3,481	(2.0)	3,363	(2.0)	119	0.1	0	..	0	0	0	0	24	1
Madagascar	11,727	(0.9)	11,378	(1.0)	350	1.7	0	..	0	14	23	1	333	43
Malawi	2,562	(2.4)	2,450	(2.6)	112	1.5	0	..	0	0	0	1	43	0
Mali	13,186	(0.7)	13,172	(0.7)	15	6.6	0	..	0	101	80	138	304	126
Mauritania	317	(2.7)	293	(3.5)	25	..	0	..	0	47	46	56	10	71
Mozambique	30,601	(0.2)	30,551	(0.2)	50	1.5	0	..	0	30	38	4	283	3
Namibia	8,040	(0.9)	8,040	..	0	..	61	..	54	75	91	356	86	168
Niger	1,328	(3.7)	1,256	(4.1)	73	4.2	0	..	0	74	62	149	42	253
Nigeria	13,517	(2.6)	12,824	(2.8)	693	4.0	0	..	0	53	58	1	662	17
Rwanda	307	(3.9)	46	(15.2)	261	0.6	0	..	0	0	0	4	4	0
Senegal	6,205	(0.7)	5,942	(0.9)	263	5.3	0	..	0	19	94	17	97	31
Sierra Leone	1,055	(2.9)	1,049	..	6	..	0	..	0	0	0	0	27	0
Somalia	7,515	(1.0)	7,512	..	3	..	0	..	0	51	80	504	50	5
South Africa	8,917	(0.1)	7,363	(0.3)	1,554	0.8	898	29.2	828	81	66	240	138	290
Sudan	61,627	(1.4)	60,986	(1.5)	641	6.3	0	..	0	168	67	84	1,029	178
Tanzania, United Rep	38,811	(0.2)	38,676	..	135	..	0	..	0	..	..	26	168	65
Togo	510	(3.4)	472	(3.8)	38	1.7	0	..	0	2	34	0	50	0
Uganda	4,190	(2.0)	4,147	(2.0)	43	3.6	0	..	0	4	16	11	92	3
Zambia	31,246	(2.4)	31,171	(2.4)	75	2.9	0	..	0	12	16	3	355	9
Zimbabwe	19,040	(1.5)	18,899	(1.6)	141	1.7	111	29.9	92	26	67	3	122	41
NORTH AMERICA	470,564	0.1	209,755	0.1	16,238	0.8	5,860	27.4	30,489	547	..	4,531	415	1,334
Canada	244,571	..	..	..	..	..	1,972	76.1	4,360	157	16	2,385	8	55
United States	225,993	0.2	209,755	0.1	16,238	0.8	3,888	19.8	26,129	390	41	2,132	407	1,279
C. AMERICA & CARIBBEAN	78,737	(1.1)	76,556	(1.2)	1,295	(0.5)	1,033	31.7	427	138	..	437	348	333
Belize	1,348	(2.3)	1,345	(2.4)	3	3.6	96	0.0	96	0	0	0	0	1
Costa Rica	1,968	(0.8)	1,790	(1.4)	178	9.6	86	38.8	41	0	0	0	3	0
Cuba	2,348	1.3	1,867	0.1	482	7.6	0	..	0	1	11	0	19	8
Dominican Rep	1,376	..	1,346	(0.3)	30	..	0	..	0	0	5	0	6	6
El Salvador	121	(4.6)	107	(6.1)	14	..	0	..	0	0	0	0	0	0
Guatemala	2,850	(1.7)	2,717	(2.2)	133	..	312	64.8	100	0	0	0	3	6
Haiti	88	(5.7)	68	(7.6)	20	5.1	0	..	0	0	3	0	3	5
Honduras	5,383	(1.0)	5,335	(1.1)	48	..	14	11.1	20	0	0	0	5	2
Jamaica	325	(1.5)	317	..	9	..	0	..	0	0	31	0	1	1
Mexico	55,205	(1.1)	54,938	(1.1)	267	..	516	36.6	169	136	69	436	293	301
Nicaragua	3,278	(3.0)	3,232	(3.2)	46	14.3	0	..	0	0	0	0	4	0
Panama	2,876	(1.6)	2,836	(1.8)	40	17.3	8	87.2	1	0	0	0	6	1
Trinidad and Tobago	259	(0.8)	244	..	15	..	0	..	0	0	4	0	0	0
SOUTH AMERICA {c}	885,618	(0.4)	875,163	(0.5)	10,455	6.7	2,110	30.3	1,551	444	..	1,674	3,168	1,101
Argentina	34,648	(0.8)	33,722	(1.1)	926	..	0	..	0	147	53	746	324	541
Bolivia	53,068	(0.3)	53,022	(0.3)	46	3.7	927	35.7	885	..	..	219	279	66
Brazil	543,905	(0.4)	538,924	(0.4)	4,982	3.2	1,183	26.9	666	131	15	251	1,751	116
Chile	15,536	(0.1)	13,519	(0.8)	2,017	5.5	0	..	0	16	21	105	23	87
Colombia	49,601	(0.4)	49,460	(0.4)	141	6.2	0	..	0	20	17	47	182	45
Ecuador	10,557	(1.2)	10,390	(1.3)	167	2.4	0	..	0	16	63	43	29	17
Guyana	16,879	(0.3)	16,867	..	12	..	0	..	0	0	0	2	13	2
Paraguay	23,372	(0.5)	23,345	(0.5)	27	11.3	0	..	0	22	55	0	247	11
Peru	65,215	(0.4)	64,575	(0.5)	640	15.2	0	..	0	48	37	240	44	134
Suriname	14,113	..	14,100	0.0	13	0.8	0	..	0	0	0	0	2	0
Uruguay	1,292	5.0	670	0.0	622	16.3	0	..	0	0	0	0	4	66
Venezuela	49,506	(0.4)	48,643	(0.5)	863	8.7	0	..	0	45	49	21	267	18
OCEANIA	201,271	(0.2)	194,718	(0.2)	2,848	0.6	654	91.9	410	661	..	4,023	2,505	567
Australia	154,539	(0.2)	153,496	(0.2)	1,043	..	0	..	0	661	86	4,007	2,397	411
Fiji	815	(0.2)	718	(1.4)	97	29.3	0	..	0	0	0	0	0	0
New Zealand	7,946	0.5	6,404	..	1,542	..	610	111.6	363	0	0	0	44	122
Papua New Guinea	30,601	(0.4)	30,511	(0.4)	90	5.9	4	0.0	4	0	1	13	56	32
Solomon Islands	2,536	(0.2)	2,486	(0.2)	50	2.2	39	..	43	0	0	2	5	0
DEVELOPED	1,725,231	0.1	1,377,765	..	63,695	..	23,630	30.9	78,386	2,168	..	13,483	3,745	4,190
DEVELOPING	1,962,481	(0.5)	1,817,491	(0.2)	122,764	4.4	3,597	31.1	2,326	2,862	..	9,825	12,263	6,341

a. Drylands area is determined using aridity zones; arid, semi-arid and dry sub-humid zones are included. Hyper-arid (bare sand deserts) are excluded. b. Forest Stewardship Council.
c. Regional totals are from the original source and are not calculated by WRI. d. Belgium includes Luxembourg.

VARIABLE DEFINITIONS AND METHODOLOGY

FAO Total Forest Area includes both natural forests and plantations, which are determined by the presence of trees and the absence of other predominant land uses, such as agroforestry. Data are presented in thousands of hectares. **Total Forests** are areas where tree crowns cover over 10 percent of the ground, and cover areas greater than 0.5 hectares. Tree height at maturity should exceed 5 meters. **Natural Forests** are forests composed primarily of indigenous (native) tree species. **Plantations** are forest stands established artificially by afforestation and reforestation, and can include either non native or indigenous (native) trees. Reforestation does not include regeneration of old tree crops.

The Food and Agriculture Organization (FAO) published the Global Forest Resources Assessment 2000 (FRA 2000) in response to international interest in a global forest assessment with a single definition of forest cover. FAO compiles country information to create one internationally comparable database, and national data gathering methodologies can be found at http://www.fao.org/forestry/fo/fra/index.jsp.

Forest statistics are based primarily on forest inventory information provided by national governments. FAO harmonized these national assessments with the 10-percent forest definition mentioned above. In tropical regions, national inventories are supplemented by a remote sensing survey. FAO analyzed high resolution Landsat satellite data from a number of sample sites covering a total of 10 percent of the tropical forest zone. Where only limited or outdated inventory data were available, FAO used linear projections and expert opinion to fill in data gaps. If no forest statistics existed for 1990 and 2000, FAO projected forward or backward in time to estimate forest area in the two reference years.

World Resources Institute (WRI) staff used data from the FRA 2000 to estimate natural forest and plantation area for 1990 and to calculate the rate of change from 1990 to 2000. FAO, assuming a fixed rate of tree planting for each country, compiled country data from various years and extrapolated forward to the year 2000. WRI reversed this approach and extrapolated backward from 2000 to 1990 by subtracting tree planting rates. Plantations area was then subtracted from total forest area to calculate natural forest area. Countries where this methodology resulted in a negative plantations area in 1990 were assigned a value of ".." (no data available). Rates of change for the decade were calculated using an exponential growth rate equation.

Certified Forest Area, expressed in thousands of hectares, includes forests certified by major forest certification schemes. **Forest Stewardship Council (FSC) Certified Forests** include all natural forests, plantations, and mixed and semi-natural forests certified as managed in accordance with the ten FSC principles and criteria. The FSC certifies forests as natural forests when most of the principal characteristics and key elements of the native ecosystems, such as complexity, structure, and diversity are still present. Forests are certified as plantations when they are the result of human activities and lack most of the principal characteristics and key elements of native ecosystems. According to FSC, certified plantations should decrease the pressures on natural forests; represent diverse species and age classes; preferentially choose native over exotic species; improve soil function, fertility and structure; and have a portion of their area managed for the restoration of natural forest cover. Semi-natural and mixed forest area includes mixed areas of natural forest and plantations. Full FSC certification involves two steps. First, the site is assessed for sustainability. Second, a chain of custody is traced from forest, to processor, to distributors, to the final consumer to ensure that only wood from the certified forests are being sold and delivered as FSC-certified.

For a complete list of the Principles and Criteria, please refer to Document 1.2 at http://www.fscoax.org/principal.htm.

Forest Area Certified by All Certification Schemes aggregates the total area of forests certified by international, regional, and national forest certification schemes, and is reported in thousands of hectares. Certifications by ISO 14000 are not included. The only, or primary, certifier in most countries with active certification programs is the Forest Stewardship Council (FSC). Other certification bodies include the American Tree Farm Program (ATFP), Canadian Standards Association (CSA), Green Tag (GT), Pan-European Forest Certification (PEFC), and the Sustainable Forestry Initiative (SFI) of the American Forest and Paper Association (AFPA). Data are compiled by FAO.

Drylands Area is the terrestrial area, in thousands of hectares, that falls within three of the world's six aridity zones—the arid, semi-arid, and dry sub-humid zones—as a percent of Earth's total terrestrial area. This definition of drylands has been adopted by the United Nations Convention to Combat Desertification (UNCCD) to identify areas where efforts combating land degradation should be focused and where methods for attaining sustainable development should be promoted.

The world is divided into six aridity zones based on the aridity index—the ratio of mean annual precipitation (PPT) to mean annual potential evapotranspiration (PET). Drylands of concern to the CCD include those lands with an aridity index between .05 and .65 (excluding polar and sub-polar regions). Ratios of less than .05 indicate hyperarid zones, or true deserts. Ratios of 0.65 or greater identify humid zones. The areas with an aridity index between .05 and .65 encompasses the arid, semi-arid, and dry sub-humid areas. See the UNCCD's website at http://www.unccd.int/main.php for more information.

Climatic data from 1950 to 1981 were used to define aridity zone boundaries for the globe with a resolution of about 50 km. The amount of land within each aridity zone for individual countries was calculated by WRI.

Grasslands Area includes five categories under the International Geosphere- Biosphere Programme (IGBP) as classified by the Global Land Cover Classification Database (GLCCD). Data are reported in thousands of square kilometers. **Shrublands** is the combination of IGBP's closed and open shrublands categories; **Savannas** is IGBP's savannas and woody savannas; **Herbaceous Grasslands** is the IGBP grassland classification.

The Global Land Cover Classification team describes the method used to classify vegetation types as a "multitemporal unsupervised classification of NDVI data with post-classification refinement using multi-source earth science data." NDVI data are a measure of "greenness" derived from satellite data. The satellite data in this study were from the Advanced Very High Resolution Radiometer (AVHRR), and have a resolution of 1 X 1 km. Other data sets used were a digital elevation model to help define ecological factors that govern natural vegetation distribution, ecoregions data, and maps of soils, vegetation, and land cover. For a description of the five-step classification process, please see technical notes available at http://earthtrends.wri.org/searchable_db/variablenotes_static.cfm?varid=750&themeid=9.

FREQUENCY OF UPDATE BY DATA PROVIDERS

FAO forestry data is compiled each decade; data in this table are from the 2000 assessment. FRA 2000 uses different definitions for total forest area than FRA 1990; the data from these two volumes cannot be directly compared. **Certified Forest Area** data are updated periodically. WRI has compiled data from these periodic updates to cover a five-year time span. The most recent data are up-to-date as of June 30, 2002. Data from 1998 were captured on December 31 of that year. **Drylands** data were prepared in 1991. Raw data for **Grassland area** estimates were recorded from April 1992 to March 1993. Data were classified, refined, and released in a database version 2.0 in 2001.

DATA RELIABILITY AND CAUTIONARY NOTES

FAO's FRA 2000 Forest Extent and Change Data: FAO acknowledges that the quality of primary data available on tropical forest resources remains very poor. The accuracy of national estimates provided to FAO is affected by two major sources of error. First, in most tropical countries, forests are not monitored comprehensively or frequently enough to map their extent accurately or to track their rate of change. In the absence of inventory data for specific dates (1990 and 2000), FAO's latest estimates of forest area and change over time are often based on projections and expert opinion and thus remain educated guesses. Just one or two satellite scenes appear to have been the prime source of new information for some countries with very poor inventory data. Second, estimates of open woodland areas are far less accurate than those of closed forest because it is difficult to monitor woodlands by remote sensing techniques, and government forestry agencies tend not to survey them as part of normal forest inventories. Differences in definitions used among countries further complicate this issue. The quality of data from developed countries is generally better than from developing countries, but problems still arise with estimates because of differences in national forestry definitions and systems of measurement, and the use of different reference periods. In Northern countries, the boundary between forest and tundra is vague, and the additional forest that should be counted under the new (globally harmonized) 10-percent crown cover threshold proved difficult to quantify. Non-production forests are classified as "other wooded land" in FRA 2000, even though many of them appear to meet the FAO definition of forests. This results in significant underreporting in some countries. For a more complete discussion of some data reliability issues associated with the FRA 2000, please see: http://www.wri.org/wri/forests/fra2000.html.

WRI-calculated natural and plantation forest area: These data are based on the FRA 2000 and are subject to all the concerns those data raise. Moreover, the calculations are based on assumptions of linear change that are not supported by field research. WRI chose to make this calculation and present the data despite FAO's decision not to include them in the FRA 2000. These data represent the only available indicators of forest change based on consistent definitions. However, the data should be used as very rough approximations.

Certified Forest Area: The certification schemes are either performance-based or systems-based. Performance-based certification requires that landowners meet performance criteria set by the certification body. Systems-based schemes require that landowners manage the forest within broad system components. While there is some disagreement about which scheme best guarantees sustainable forestry, many groups feel that those using performance-based criteria carry the most weight.

More information on certification is available at: http://eesc. orst.edu/agcomwebfile/edmat/EC1518.pdf. While the numbers reported are reliable, it is worth noting that certified forests do not represent the total area of well-managed forests. Many uncertified forests are under sound management. Increasing trends in forest certification indicate the importance that consumers attach to forest management issues rather than the total area of well-managed forests.

Drylands: The accuracy of land area totals is limited by the 50 kilometer resolution of the data set. The climate data set was derived from a limited number of field observations. Actual boundaries between aridity zones are neither abrupt nor static, making delineated borders somewhat artificial. The data should therefore be considered useful as a general indicator of the extent of drylands within each country, rather than as an exact depiction of the climatic situation on the ground.

Alternative methods for measuring extent of drylands area include use of soil moisture and agricultural production systems, although these methods may also be subject to similar problems such as low resolution data, limited field observations, and subjectivity when delineating exact boundaries on the ground.

Grasslands area: Following publication of the GLCC database version 1, a number of scientific teams assessed its accuracy by comparing the results with higher-resolution satellite imagery. These teams found that the accuracy of the GLCC's approach was in a range from 60 to nearly 80 percent—meaning that the assessment teams' classification of a given area agreed with the GLCC's classification between 60 and 80 percent of the time. Given the relatively high level of potential for misclassification, the area of land in each classification should be treated as estimated rather than an exact interpretation of the earth's surface.

SOURCES

FAO Forest Area Variables and **All Certification Schemes**: Food and Agriculture Organization of the United Nations (FAO). 2001. Global Forest Resources Assessment 2000—Main Report. FAO Forestry Paper No. 140. Rome: FAO. Data can also be obtained electronically at: http://www.fao.org/forestry/fo/fra/index.jsp. **FSC-certified Forests:** Forest Stewardship Council (FSC). 1998, 2002. Forests Certified by FSC-Accredited Certification Bodies. Document 5.3.3. Oaxaca, Mexico, FSC. Available on-line at: http://www.fscoax.org/principal.htm. **Drylands:** U. Deichmann and L. Eklundh. 1991. Global digital data sets for land degradation studies: a GIS approach. United Nations Environment Program/Global Resource Information Database (UNEP/GRID) GRID Case Study Series No. 4., Nairobi, Kenya. **Grasslands area:** T.R. Loveland, B.C. Reed, J.F. Brown, D.O. Ohlen, Z. Zhu, L. Yang, J. Merchant. 2000. Global Land Cover Characteristics Database (GLCCD) Version 2.0. Available on-line at: http://edcdaac.usgs.gov/glcc/globdoc2_0.html. Loveland, T.R., B.C. Reed, J.F. Brown, D.O. Ohlen, Z. Zhu, L. Yang, and J.W. Merchant. 2000. "Development of a global land cover characteristics database and IGBP DISCover from 1-km AVHRR data." International Journal of Remote Sensing 21: 1303–1330.

Freshwater Resources

Sources: AQUASTAT Information System on Water and Agriculture, The Blue Plan: Environment and Development in Mediterranean Countries

	Renewable Water Resources (annual) {a}						Year	Water Withdrawals (annual)						Desalinated Water Production (million m³) {g}
	Internal Renewable Water Resources (IRWR)				Natural Renewable Water Resources {b}					as a % of Renewable Water Resources	Sectoral Share (percent) {c}			
	Groundwater Recharge (km³) {e}	Surface Water (km³) {e}	Overlap (km³)	Total {d} (km³)	Total (km³)	Per Capita (m³ per person) {f}		Total (million m³)	Per Capita (m³ per person)		Agriculture	Domestic	Industry	
WORLD	11,358	40,594	10,067	43,219	..	..	1990	3,414,000	650	..	71	9	20	..
ASIA (EXCL. MIDDLE EAST)	2,472	10,985	2,136	11,321	..	..	..	..	..	..	..	..	..	..
Armenia	4.2	6.3	1.4	9.1	11	2,778	1994	2,925	784	28	66	30	4	0
Azerbaijan	6.5	6.0	4.4	8.1	30	3,716	1995	16,533	2,151	58	70	5	25	0
Bangladesh	21	84	0	105	1,211	8,444	1990	14,636	133	2	86	12	2	0
Bhutan	..	95	..	95	95	43,214	1987	20	13	0	54	36	10	0
Cambodia	18	116	13	121	476	34,561	1987	520	60	0	94	5	1	0
China	829	2,712	728	2,812	2,830	2,186	1993	525,489	439	20	78	5	18	0
Georgia	17	57	16	58	63	12,149	1990	3,468	635	5	59	21	20	0
India	419	1,222	380	1,261	1,897 h	1,822 h	1990	500,000	592	32	92	5	3	0
Indonesia	455	2,793	410	2,838	2,838	13,046	1990	74,346	407	3	93	6	1	0
Japan	27	420	17	430	430	3,372	1992	91,400	735	22	64	19	17	0
Kazakhstan	6.1	69	0	75	110	6,839	1993	33,674	2,010	29	81	2	17	1,328
Korea, Dem People's Rep	13	66	12	67	77	3,415	1987	14,160	742	22	73	11	16	0
Korea, Rep	13	62	11	65	70	1,471	1994	23,668	531	36	63	26	11	0
Kyrgyzstan	14	44	11	46	21 h	4,078 h	1994	10,086	2,231	55	94	3	3	0
Lao People's Dem Rep	38	190	38	190	334	60,318	1987	990	259	0	82	8	10	0
Malaysia	64	566	50	580	580	25,178	1995	12,733	636	3	77	11	13	0
Mongolia	6.1	33	4.0	35	35	13,451	1993	428	182	1	53	20	27	0
Myanmar	156	875	150	881	1,046	21,358	1987	3,960	103	0	90	7	3	0
Nepal	20	198	20	198	210	8,703	1994	28,953	1,451	17	99	1	0	0
Pakistan	55	47	50	52	223 h	2,812 h	1991	155,600	1,382	100	97	2	2	0
Philippines	180	444	145	479	479	6,093	1995	55,422	811	13	88	8	4	0
Singapore	..	..	..	..	..	..	1975	..	..	..	4	45	51	..
Sri Lanka	7.8	49	7.0	50	50	2,592	1990	9,770	574	22	96	2	2	0
Tajikistan	6.0	63	3.0	66	16 h	2,587 h	1994	11,874	2,096	81	92	3	4	0
Thailand	42	199	31	210	410	6,371	1990	33,132	605	10	91	5	4	0
Turkmenistan	0.4	1.0	0	1.4	25 h	5,015 h	1994	23,779	5,801	116	98	1	1	0
Uzbekistan	8.8	9.5	2	16	50 h	1,968 h	1994	58,051	2,598	132	94	4	2	0
Viet Nam	48	354	35	367	891	11,109	1990	54,330	822	7	87	4	10	0
EUROPE	1,318	6,223	986	6,590	..	..	..	..	..	..	..	..	..	..
Albania	6.2	23	2.4	27	42	13,178	1995	1,400	440	3	71	29	0	..
Austria	6.0	55	6.0	55	78	9,629	1991	2,360	303	3	9	33	58	..
Belarus	18	37	18	37	58	5,739	1990	2,734	266	5	35	22	43	0
Belgium	0.9	12	0.9	12	18	1,781	..	..	..	..	..	..	..	..
Bosnia and Herzegovina	..	..	..	36	38	9,088	1995	1,000	292	3	60	30	10	..
Bulgaria	6.4	20	5.5	21	21	2,734	1988	13,900	1,573	58	22	3	75	..
Croatia	11	27	0.5	38	106	22,654	1996	764	164	1	0	50	50	..
Czech Rep	1.4	13	1.4	13	13	1,283	1991	2,740	266	21	2	41	57	..
Denmark	4.3	3.7	2.0	6.0	6	1,123.0	1990	1,200	233	21	43	30	27	..
Estonia	4.0	12	3.0	13	13	9,413	1995	158	106	1	5	56	39	0
Finland	2.2	107	2.0	107	110	21,223	1991	2,200	439	2	3	12	85	..
France	100	177	98	179	204	3,414	1999	32,300	547	16	10	18	72	..
Germany	46	106	45	107	154	1,878	1991	46,270	579	31	20	11	69	..
Greece	10	56	7.8	58	74	6,984	1997	8,700	826	12	87	10	3	..
Hungary	6.0	6.0	6.0	6.0	104	10,541	1991	6,810	659	6	36	9	55	..
Iceland	24	166	20	170	170	599,944	1991	160	622	0	6	31	63	..
Ireland	11	48	10	49	52	13,408	1980	790	232	2	10	16	74	..
Italy	43	171	31	183	191	3,330	1998	42,000	730	22	48	19	34	..
Latvia	2.2	17	2.0	17	35	14,820	1994	285	112	1	13	55	32	0
Lithuania	1.2	15	1.0	16	25	6,763	1995	254	68	1	3	81	16	0
Macedonia, FYR	..	5.4	..	5.4	6	3,120.6	1996	1,850	936	30	74	12	15	..
Moldova, Rep	0.4	1.0	0.4	1.0	12	2,726	1992	2,963	678	25	26	9	65	0
Netherlands	4.5	11	4.5	11	91	5,691	1991	7,810	519	9	34	5	61	..
Norway	96	376	90	382	382	84,787	1985	2,030	489	1	8	20	72	..
Poland	13	53	12	54	62	1,598	1991	12,280	321	20	11	13	76	..
Portugal	4.0	38	4.0	38	69 h	6,837 h	1990	7,290	736	11	48	15	37	..
Romania	8.3	42	8.0	42	212	9,486	1994	26,000	1,141	12	59	8	33	..
Russian Federation	788	4,037 i	512	4,313 i	4,507 i	31,354 i	1994	77,100	519	2	20	19	62	0
Serbia and Montenegro	3.0	42	1.4	44	209	19,815	1995	13,000	1,233	6	8	6	86	..
Slovakia	1.7	13	1.7	13	50	9,265	1991	1,780	337	4	..	..	..	..
Slovenia	14	19	13	19	32	16,070	1996	1,280	642	4	1	20	80	..
Spain	30	110	28	111	112	2,793	1997	35,210	884	32	68	13	19	..
Sweden	20	170	19	171	174	19,721	1991	2,930	340	2	9	36	55	..
Switzerland	2.5	40	2.5	40	54	7,464	1991	1,190	172	2	4	23	73	..
Ukraine	20	50	17	53	140	2,868	1992	25,991	500	17	30	18	52	0
United Kingdom	9.8	144	9.0	145	147	2,464	1991	11,790	204	8	3	20	77	..
MIDDLE EAST & N. AFRICA	149	374	60	518	..	..	..	..	..	..	..	..	..	..
Afghanistan	..	..	..	55	65	2,790	1987	26,110	2,007	72	99	1	0	0
Algeria	1.7	13	1.0	14	14	460	1995	5,000	181	39	52	34	14	64
Egypt	1.3	0.5	0	1.8	58 h	830 h	1996	66,000	1,055	127	82	7	11	25
Iran, Islamic Rep	49	97	18	129	138	1,900	1993	70,034	1,122	59	92	6	2	2.9
Iraq	1.2	34	0	35	75 h	3,111 h	1990	42,800	2,478	80	92	3	5	0
Israel	0.5	0.3	0	0.8	2	265.0	1997	1,620	287	108	54	39	7	..
Jordan	0.5	0.4	0.2	0.7	1	169.4	1993	984	255	151	75	22	3	2.0
Kuwait	0	0	0	0	0.02	9.9	1994	538	306	3,097	60	37	2	231
Lebanon	3.2	4.1	2.5	4.8	4 h	1,219.5 h	1996	1,300	400	33	68	27	6	0
Libyan Arab Jamahiriya	0.5	0.2	0.1	0.6	1	108.5	1999	4,500	870	801	84	13	3	70
Morocco	10	22	3.0	29	29	936	1998	11,480	399	43	89	10	2	3.4
Oman	1.0	0.9	0.9	1.0	1	363.6	1991	1,223	658	181	94	5	2	34
Saudi Arabia	2.2	2.2	2.0	2.4	2	110.6	1992	17,018	1,056	955	90	9	1	714
Syrian Arab Rep	4.2	4.8	2.0	7.0	26 h	1,541 h	1995	12,000	844	55	90	8	2	0
Tunisia	1.5	3.1	0.4	4.2	5	576.5	1996	2,830	312	54	86	13	1	8.3
Turkey	69	186	28	227	229 h	3,344 h	1997	35,500	558	17	73	16	12	0.5
United Arab Emirates	0.1	0.2	0.1	0.2	0	55.5	1995	2,108	896	1,614	67	24	9	385
Yemen	1.5	4.0	1.4	4.1	4	205.9	1990	2,932	253	123	92	7	1	10

| | Renewable Water Resources (annual) {a} | | | | | | Water Withdrawals (annual) | | | | | | | Desalinated Water Production (million m³) {g} |
| | Internal Renewable Water Resources (IRWR) | | | | Natural Renewable Water Resources {b} | | | | | as a % of Renewable Water Resources | Sectoral Share (percent) {c} | | | |
	Ground-water Recharge (km³) {e}	Sur-face Water (km³) {e}	Over-lap (km³)	Total {d} (km³)	Total (km³)	Per Capita (m³ per person) {f}	Year	Total (million m³)	Per Capita (m³ per person)		Agri-culture	Dom-estic	Indus-try	
SUB-SAHARAN AFRICA	**1,549**	**3,812**	**1,468**	**3,901**	..	..	..	..	..	..	..	..	..	..
Angola	72	182	70	184	184	13,203	1987	480	54	0	76	14	10	0
Benin	1.8	10	1.5	10	25	3,741	1994	145	27	1	67	23	10	0
Botswana	1.7	1.7	0.5	2.9	14	9,209	1992	113	86	1	48	32	20	0
Burkina Faso	9.5	8.0	5.0	13	13	1,024	1992	376	40	4	81	19	0	0
Burundi	2.1	3.5	2.0	3.6	4	538.3	1987	100	19	4	64	36	0	0
Cameroon	100	268	95	273	286	18,378	1987	400	38	0	35	46	19	0
Central African Rep	56	141	56	141	144	37,565	1987	70	25	0	74	21	5	0
Chad	12	14	10	15	43	5,125	1987	180	34	1	82	16	2	0
Congo	198	222	198	222	832	259,547	1987	40	20	0	11	62	27	0
Congo, Dem Rep	421	899	420	900	1,283	23,639	1990	357	10	0	23	61	16	0
Côte d'Ivoire	38	74	35	77	81	4,853	1987	709	62	1	67	22	11	0
Equatorial Guinea	10	25	9.0	26	26	53,841	1987	10	30	0	6	81	13	0
Eritrea	..	..	..	2.8	6	1,577.7	..	..	..	..	..	..	..	0
Ethiopia	40	110	40	110	110	1,666	1987	2,200	51	3	86	11	3	0
Gabon	62	162	60	164	164	126,789	1987	60	70	0	6	72	22	0
Gambia	0.5	3.0	0.5	3.0	8	5,836.0	1982	20	29	1	91	7	2	0
Ghana	26	29	25	30	53	2,637	1970	300	35	1	52	35	13	0
Guinea	38	226	38	226	226	26,964	1987	740	132	0	87	10	3	0
Guinea-Bissau	14	12	10	16	31	24,670	1991	17	17	0	36	60	4	0
Kenya	3.0	17	0	20	30	947	1990	2,050	87	9	76	20	4	0
Lesotho	0.5	5.2	0.5	5.2	3 h	1,455.6 h	1987	50	32	2	56	22	22	0
Liberia	60	200	60	200	232	70,348	1987	130	59	0	60	27	13	0
Madagascar	55	332	50	337	337	19,925	1984	16,300	1,611	8	99	1		0
Malawi	1.4	16	1.4	16	17	1,461	1994	936	95	6	86	10	3	0
Mali	20	50	10	60	100	8,320	1987	1,360	167	2	97	2	1	0
Mauritania	0.3	0.1	0	0.4	11	4,029	1985	1,630	923	23	92	6	2	1.7
Mozambique	17	97	15	99	216	11,382	1992	605	42	0	89	9	2	0
Namibia	2.1	4.1	0.04	6.2	18 h	9,865 h	1991	249	175	2	68	29	3	0
Niger	2.5	1.0	0	3.5	34	2,891	1988	500	69	2	82	16	2	0
Nigeria	87	214	80	221	286	2,384	1987	3,630	46	2	54	31	15	0
Rwanda	3.6	5.2	3.6	5.2	5	638.2	1993	768	141	22	94	5	2	0
Senegal	7.6	24	5.0	26	39	3,977	1987	1,360	202	5	92	5	3	0
Sierra Leone	50	150	40	160	160	33,237	1987	370	98	4	89	7	4	0
Somalia	3.3	5.7	3.0	6.0	14	1,413	1987	810	119	8	97	3	0	0.1
South Africa	4.8	43	3.0	45	50	1,131	1990	13,309	366	32	72	17	11	0
Sudan	7.0	28	5.0	30	65 h	1,981 h	1995	17,800	637	32	94	4	1	0.4
Tanzania, United Rep	30	80	28	82	91	2,472	1994	1,165	39	2	89	9	2	0
Togo	5.7	11	5.0	12	15	3,076	1987	91	29	1	25	62	13	0
Uganda	29	39	29	39	66	2,663	1970	200	21	1	60	32	8	0
Zambia	47	80	47	80	105	9,676	1994	1,706	190	2	77	16	7	0
Zimbabwe	5.0	13	4.0	14	20	1,530	1987	1,220	131	9	79	14	7	0
NORTH AMERICA	**1,670**	**4,702**	**1,522**	**4,850**	..	..	..	..	..	..	..	..	..	..
Canada	370	2,840	360	2,850	2,902	92,810	1991	45,100	1,607	2	12	18	70	..
United States	1,300 j	1,862 j	1,162 j	2,800	3,051	10,574	1990	467,340	1,834	26	42	13	45	..
C. AMERICA & CARIBBEAN	**359**	**1,050**	**231**	**1,186**	..	..	..	..	..	..	..	..	..	..
Belize	..	..	..	16	19	78,763	1993	95	485	1	0	12	88	0
Costa Rica	37	75	0	112	112	26,764	1997	5,772	1,540	6	80	13	7	0
Cuba	6.5	32	0	38	38	3,382	1995	5,211	475	14	51	49	0	0
Dominican Rep	12	21	12	21	21	2,430	1994	8,339	1,102	45	89	11	0	0
El Salvador	6.2	18	6	18	25	3,872	1992	729	137	4	46	34	20	0
Guatemala	34	101	25	109	111	9,277	1992	1,158	126	1	74	9	17	0
Haiti	2.2	11	..	13	14	1,670	1991	980	139	8	94	5	1	0
Honduras	39	87	30	96	96	14,250	1992	1,520	294	2	91	4	5	0
Jamaica	3.9	5.5	0	9.4	9	3,587.5	1993	900	371	10	77	15	7	0
Mexico	139	361	91	409	457	4,490	1998	77,812	812	18	78	17	5	0
Nicaragua	59	186	55	190	197	36,784	1998	1,285	267	1	84	14	2	0
Panama	21	144	18	147	148	50,299	1990	1,643	685	1	70	28	2	0
Trinidad and Tobago	..	..	..	3.8	4	2,940.4	1997	297	233	8	6	68	26	0
SOUTH AMERICA	**3,693**	**12,198**	**3,645**	**12,246**	..	..	..	..	..	..	..	..	..	..
Argentina	128	276	128	276	814	21,453	1995	28,583	822	4	75	16	9	0
Bolivia	130	277	104	304	623	71,511	1987	1,210	197	0	87	10	3	0
Brazil	1,874	5,418	1,874	5,418	8,233	47,125	1992	54,870	359	1	61	21	18	0
Chile	140	884	140	884	922	59,143	1987	20,289	1,629	3	84	5	11	0
Colombia	510	2,112	510	2,112	2,132	49,017	1996	8,938	228	0	37	59	4	0
Ecuador	134	432	134	432	432	32,948	1997	16,985	1,423	4	82	12	6	0
Guyana	103	241	103	241	241	314,963	1992	1,460	1,993	1	99	1	1	0
Paraguay	41	94	41	94	336	58,148	1987	430	112	0	78	15	7	0
Peru	303	1,616	303	1,616	1,913	72,127	1992	18,973	849	1	86	7	7	0
Suriname	80	88	80	88	122	289,848	1987	460	1,171	0	89	6	5	0
Uruguay	23	59	23	59	139	41,065	1965	650	..		91	6	3	0
Venezuela	227	700	205	722	1,233	49,144	1970	4,100	382	0	46	44	10	0
OCEANIA	..	**1,241**	**20**	**1,693**	..	..	..	..	..	..	..	..	..	..
Australia	72	440	20	492	492	25,185	1985	14,600	933	4	33	65	2	..
Fiji	..	..	..	29	29	34,330	1987	30	42	0	60	20	20	..
New Zealand	..	..	..	327	327	85,221	1991	2,000	588	1	44	46	10	..
Papua New Guinea	..	801	..	801	801	159,171	1987	100	29	0	49	29	22	0
Solomon Islands	..	..	..	45	45	93,405	1987	..	..	..	40	40	20	..
DEVELOPED	**3,153**	**12,084**	**2,584**	**13,016**	..	..	..	..	..	..	..	..	..	..
DEVELOPING	**8,128**	**28,500**	**7,483**	**29,289**	..	..	..	..	..	..	..	..	..	..

a. Although data were obtained from FAO in 2002, they are long-term averages originating from multiple sources and years. For more information, please consult the original source at http://www.fao.org/waicent/faoinfo/agricult/agl/aglw/aquastat/water_res/index.stm. b. Natural Renewable Water Resources include Internal Renewable Water Resources plus or minus the flows of surface and groundwater entering or leaving the country. c. Sectoral withdrawal data may not add up to 100 because of rounding. d. At the country level, Total Internal Renewable Water Resources = Surface water + Groundwater - Overlap. Regional and global totals represent a sum of available country-level data. e. Groundwater and surface water cannot be added together to calculate total available water resources because of overlap--water that is counted in both the groundwater and surface water totals. f. Calculation is based on withdrawals from various years, and population data from 2002. g. Data on desalinated water originate from FAO country surveys conducted in various regions between 1992 and 2000. h. Data account for the portion of flow secured through treaties or agreements to other countries. i. River discharges in Siberia are not well documented and highly uncertain. j. Data are for the continental United States.

VARIABLE DEFINITIONS AND METHODOLOGY

Internal Renewable Water Resources (IRWR) include the average annual flow of rivers and the recharge of groundwater (aquifers) generated from endogenous precipitation—precipitation occurring within a country's borders. IRWR are measured in cubic kilometers per year (km³/year).

Groundwater Recharge is the total volume of water entering aquifers within a country's borders from endogenous precipitation and surface water flow. Groundwater resources are estimated by measuring rainfall in arid areas where rainfall is assumed to infiltrate into aquifers. Where data are available, groundwater resources in humid areas have been considered as equivalent to the base flow of rivers.

Surface Water produced internally includes the average annual flow of rivers generated from endogenous precipitation and base flow generated by aquifers. Surface water resources are usually computed by measuring or assessing total river flow occurring in a country on a yearly basis.

Overlap is the volume of water resources common to both surface and groundwater. It is subtracted when calculating IRWR to avoid double counting. Two types of exchanges create overlap: contribution of aquifers to surface flow, and recharge of aquifers by surface run-off. In humid temperate or tropical regions, the entire volume of groundwater recharge typically contributes to surface water flow. In karstic domains (regions with porous limestone rock formations), a portion of groundwater resources are assumed to contribute to surface water flow. In arid and semi-arid countries, surface water flows recharge groundwater by infiltrating through the soil during floods. This recharge is either directly measured or inferred by characteristics of the aquifers and piezometric levels.

Total Internal Renewable Water Resources is the sum of surface and groundwater resources minus overlap; in other words, IRWR = Surface Water Resources + Groundwater Recharge – Overlap.

Natural Renewable Water Resources, measured in cubic kilometers per year (km³/year), is the sum of internal renewable water resources and natural flow originating outside of the country. Natural Renewable Water Resources are computed by adding together both internal renewable water resources (IRWR—see above) and natural flows (flow to and from other countries). Natural incoming flow is the average amount of water which would flow into the country without human influence. In some arid and semi-arid countries, actual water resources are presented instead of natural renewable water resources. These actual totals, labeled with a footnote in the freshwater data table, include the quantity of flows reserved to upstream and downstream countries through formal and informal agreements or treaties. The actual flows are often much lower than natural flow due to water scarcity in arid and semi-arid regions.

Per Capita Natural Renewable Water Resources are measured in cubic meters per person per year (m³/person/year). Per capita values were calculated by using national population data for 2002. For more information about the collection methodology and reliability of the UN data, please refer to the technical notes in the population data table.

Water Withdrawals (annual), measured in million cubic meters, refers to total water removed for human uses in a single year, not counting evaporative losses from storage basins. Water withdrawals also include water from nonrenewable groundwater sources, river flows from other countries, and desalination plants.

Per Capita Annual Withdrawals were calculated using national population data for the year the withdrawal data were collected.

Water Withdrawals as a Percent of Renewable Water Resources is the proportion of renewable water resources withdrawn on a per capita basis, expressed in cubic meters per person per year (m³/person/year). The value is calculated by dividing water withdrawals per capita by actual renewable water resources per capita.

Sectoral Share of water withdrawals, expressed as a percentage, refers to the proportion of water used for one of three purposes: agriculture, industry, and domestic uses. All water withdrawals are allocated to one of these three categories.

Agricultural uses of water primarily include irrigation and, to a lesser extent, livestock maintenance.

Domestic uses include drinking water plus water withdrawn for homes, municipalities, commercial establishments, and public services (e.g. hospitals).

Industrial uses include cooling machinery and equipment, producing energy, cleaning and washing goods produced as ingredients in manufactured items, and as a solvent.

Desalinated Water Production, expressed in million cubic meters, refers to the amount of water produced by the removal of salt from saline waters—usually seawater—using a variety of techniques including reverse osmosis. Most desalinated water is used for domestic purposes.

Most Freshwater resources data were provided by AQUA-STAT, a global database of water statistics maintained by the Food and Agriculture Organization of the United Nations (FAO). AQUASTAT collects its information from a number of sources—national water resources and irrigation master plans; national yearbooks, statistics and reports; FAO reports and project documents; international surveys; and, results from surveys done by national or international research centers. In most cases, a critical analysis of the information was necessary to ensure consistency among the different data collected for a given country.

When possible, cross-checking of information among countries was used to improve assessment in countries where information was limited. When several sources gave different or contradictory figures, preference was always given to information collected at the national or sub-national level. This preference is based on the assumption by FAO that no regional information can be more accurate than studies carried out at the country level. Unless proven to be wrong, official rather than unofficial sources were used. In the case of shared water resources, a comparison among countries was made to ensure consistency at river-basin level.

For more information on the methodology used to collect these data, please refer to the original source or: Food and Agriculture Organization of the United Nations (FAO): Water Resources, Development and Management Service. October, 2001. Statistics on Water Resources by Country in FAO's AQUA-STAT Programme (available on-line at http://www.fao.org/ag/agl/aglw/aquastat/water_res/index.stm). Rome: FAO.

FREQUENCY OF UPDATE BY DATA PROVIDERS

AQUASTAT was developed by the Food and Agriculture Organization of the United Nations in 1993; data have been available on-line since 2001. Most freshwater data are not available in a time series, and the global data set contains data collected over a time span of up to 30 years. AQUASTAT updates their website as new data become available, or when FAO conducts special regional studies. Studies were conducted in Africa in 1994, the Near East in 1995–96, the former Soviet republics in 1997, selected Asian countries in 1998–99, and Latin America & the Caribbean in 2000. Data from the Blue Plan on Mediterranean water withdrawals were last updated in 2002. Most data updates include revisions of past data.

DATA RELIABILITY AND CAUTIONARY NOTES

While AQUASTAT represents the most complete and careful compilation of country-level water resources statistics to date, freshwater data are generally of poor quality. Information sources are various but rarely complete. Some governments will keep internal water resources information confidential because they are competing for water resources with bordering countries. Many instances of water scarcity are highly localized and are not reflected in national statistics. In addition, the accuracy and reliability of information vary greatly among regions, countries, and categories of information, as does the year in which the information was gathered. As a result, no consistency can be ensured among countries on the duration and dates of the period of reference. All data should be considered order-of-magnitude estimates.

Groundwater Recharge tends to be overestimated in arid areas and underestimated in humid areas.

Natural Renewable Water Resources vary with time. Exchanges between countries are complicated when a river crosses the same border several times. Part of the incoming water flow may thus originate from the same country in which it enters, making it necessary to calculate a "net" inflow to avoid double counting of resources. In addition, the water that is actually accessible to humans for consumption is often much smaller than the total renewable water resources indicated in the data table.

Renewable Water Resources Per Capita contains water resources data from a different set of years than the population data used in the calculation. While the water resources data are usually long-term averages, inconsistencies may arise when combining it with 2002 population data.

Water Withdrawals as a Percentage of Actual Water Resources are also calculated using per capita data from two different years. While this ratio can indicate that some countries are depleting their water resources, it does not accurately reflect localized over-extraction from aquifers and streams. In addition, the calculation does not distinguish between ground and surface water.

Sectoral Withdrawal Data may not add to 100 because of rounding. Evaporative losses from storage basins are not considered; users should keep in mind, however, that in some parts of the world up to 25 percent of water that is withdrawn and placed in reservoirs evaporates before it is used by any sector.

Desalinated Water Production may exist in some countries where the volume of production is indicated to be zero, since AQUASTAT assumes that production is zero if no value has been given for those countries where information on water use is available.

SOURCES

Renewable Water Resources: Food and Agriculture Organization of the United Nations (FAO): Water Resources, Development and Management Service. 2002. AQUASTAT Information System on Water in Agriculture: Review of Water Resource Statistics by Country. Rome: FAO. Available on-line at http://www.fao.org/waicent/faoinfo/agricult/agl/aglw/aquastat/water_res/index.htm.

Water Withdrawals: Food and Agriculture Organization of the United Nations (FAO): Water Resources, Development and Management Service. 2002. AQUASTAT Information System on Water in Agriculture. Rome: FAO. Available on-line at http://www.fao.org/waicent/faoinfo/agricult/agl/aglw/aquastat/dbase/index.htm. Data for Mediterranean countries were provided directly to WRI from: J. Margat, 2002. Present Water Withdrawals in Mediterranean Countries. Paris: Blue Plan.

Population Data (for per capita calculations): Population Division of the Department of Economic and Social Affairs of the United Nations Secretariat. 2002. World Population Prospects: The 2000 Revision. New York: United Nations. Data set on CD-ROM.

Population, Health, and Human Well-Being

Sources: United Nations Population Division, United Nations Children's Fund, World Health Organization, Joint United Nations Program on HIV/AIDS, United Nations Educational, Scientific, and Cultural Organization.

	Total Population (thousands) {a}		Percent of Population in Specific Age Groups 2002		Total Fertility Rate {a} (children per woman)	Mortality Under Age 5 (per 1000 live births)	Life Expectancy at Birth (years)	Health-Adjusted Life Expectancy {b} (years)	Adults Ages 15-49 Living HIV or AIDS (percent)	Access to Improved Sanitation (percent of population) 2000		Net School Enrollment Ratio 1998-1999		Adult Literacy Rate (percent) {c} 2002	
	2002	2025	Under 15	65 & Over	2000-2005	2000	2000-2005	2000	2001	Urban	Rural	Primary	Secondary	Women	Men
WORLD	6,211,082	7,936,741	29	7	2.7	83	66.0	57.0	1.2	85	40	..	..	75	86 d
ASIA (EXCL. MIDDLE EAST)	3,493,424	4,345,549	29	6	2.5	..	67.9	57.4	0.4	70	31	..	..	68	83
Armenia	3,790	3,736	21	9	1.1	30	73.4	59.0	0.2	..	..	..	..	98	99
Azerbaijan	8,147	9,076	27	7	1.5	105	72.2	55.4	<0.1	90	70	96	82	..	..
Bangladesh	143,364	210,823	38	3	3.6	82	60.7	49.3	<0.1	71	41	104 e	..	31	50
Bhutan	2,198	3,843	42	4	5.1	100	63.2	49.2	<0.1	65	70	16	5	..	..
Cambodia	13,776	22,310	43	3	4.8	135	56.2	47.1	2.7	56	10	103 e	20	59	81
China	1,294,377	1,470,787	24	7	1.8 f	40	71.2 f	62.1	0.1	69	27	91	50	80	93
Georgia	5,213	4,377	19	14	1.4	29	73.6	58.2	<0.1	100	99	..	78	..	..
India	1,041,144	1,351,801	33	5	3.0	96	64.2	52.0	0.8	61	15	..	39	47	70
Indonesia	217,534	272,911	30	5	2.3	48	67.3	57.4	0.1	69	46	..	..	83	93
Japan	127,538	123,798	14	18	1.3	4	81.5	73.8	<0.1	..	..	102 e	..	..	..
Kazakhstan	16,027	16,090	26	7	2.0	75	65.0	54.3	0.1	100	98	..	74	99	100
Korea, Dem People's Rep	22,586	25,872	26	6	2.1	30	65.1	55.4	..	99	100	..	..	..	..
Korea, Rep	47,389	52,065	20	8	1.5	5	75.5	66.0	<0.1	76	4	97	..	97	99
Kyrgyzstan	5,047	6,460	32	6	2.3	63	68.6	52.6	<0.1	100	100	85	..	..	..
Lao People's Dem Rep	5,530	8,721	42	4	4.8	105	54.5	44.7	<0.1	67	19	76	27	56	77
Malaysia	23,036	31,326	34	4	2.9	9	73.0	61.6	0.4	..	98	98	93	85	92
Mongolia	2,587	3,478	33	4	2.3	78	63.9	52.4	<0.1	46	2	85	53	98	99
Myanmar	48,956	60,243	32	5	2.8	110	56.2	49.1	..	84	57	..	..	81	89
Nepal	24,153	38,706	41	4	4.5	100	59.8	45.8	0.5	73	22	..	..	26	62
Pakistan	148,721	250,981	41	4	5.1	110	61.0	48.1 g	0.1	95	43	..	..	30	59
Philippines	78,611	107,073	37	4	3.2	40	70.0	59.0	<0.1	93	69	..	..	95	96
Singapore	4,188	4,998	21	8	1.5	4	78.1	67.8	0.2	100	..	..	..	89	97
Sri Lanka	19,287	22,529	25	6	2.1	19	72.6	61.1	<0.1	97	93	102 e	..	90	95
Tajikistan	6,177	8,066	37	5	2.9	73	68.0	50.8	<0.1	97	88	..	..	99	100
Thailand	64,344	77,480	26	6	2.0	29	70.8	59.7	1.8	96	96	77	55	94	97
Turkmenistan	4,930	6,844	36	4	3.2	70	67.1	52.1	<0.1	..	..	..	..	..	..
Uzbekistan	25,618	34,203	34	5	2.3	67	69.7	54.3	<0.1	97	85	..	..	99	100
Viet Nam	80,226	105,488	32	5	2.3	39	69.2	58.9	0.3	82	38	97	49	91	95
EUROPE	725,124	683,532	17	15	1.3	..	74.1	64.7	0.4	..	..	..	..	99	99 d
Albania	3,164	3,676	29	6	2.3	31	73.7	59.4	..	99	85	..	..	79	93
Austria	8,069	7,605	16	16	1.2	5	78.5	70.3	0.2	100	100	88	..	..	..
Belarus	10,106	9,335	17	14	1.2	20	68.5	60.1	0.3	..	..	..	..	100	100
Belgium	10,276	10,205	17	17	1.5	6	78.8	69.4	0.2	..	..	..	..	..	..
Bosnia and Herzegovina	4,126	4,165	18	11	1.3	18	74.0	63.7	<0.1	h	..	..	..	..	..
Bulgaria	7,790	6,125	15	16	1.1	16	70.9	63.4	<0.1	h	100	100	93	81	98	99
Croatia	4,657	4,519	18	15	1.7	9	74.2	64.0	<0.1	..	..	..	..	98	99
Czech Rep	10,250	9,727	16	14	1.2	5	75.4	65.6	<0.1	..	..	90	79	..	..
Denmark	5,343	5,359	18	15	1.7	5	76.6	69.5	0.2	..	..	101 e	89	..	..
Estonia	1,361	1,062	16	15	1.2	21	71.2	60.8	1.0	93	..	96	77	100	100
Finland	5,183	5,138	18	16	1.6	5	78.0	68.8	<0.1	100	100	99	95	..	..
France	59,670	62,753	18	16	1.8	5	79.0	70.7	0.3	..	..	100	94	..	..
Germany	81,990	78,897	15	17	1.3	5	78.2	69.4	0.1	..	..	87	88	..	..
Greece	10,631	10,149	15	18	1.2	6	78.5	71.0	0.2	..	..	95	86	96	99
Hungary	9,867	8,783	16	15	1.2	9	72.0	59.9	0.1	100	98	82	85	99	100
Iceland	283	319	23	12	1.9	4	79.4	71.2	0.2	..	..	99	85	..	..
Ireland	3,878	4,745	21	11	2.0	6	77.0	69.3	0.1	..	..	104 e	77	..	..
Italy	57,449	52,364	14	19	1.2	6	78.7	71.2	0.4	..	..	101 e	88	98	99
Latvia	2,392	2,090	16	15	1.1	21	71.2	57.7	0.4	..	..	94	83	100	100
Lithuania	3,682	3,418	18	14	1.2	21	72.7	58.4	0.1	..	..	94	85	100	100
Macedonia, FYR	2,051	2,067	22	10	1.5	26	73.6	64.9	<0.1	..	..	96	79	..	..
Moldova, Rep	4,273	4,052	21	10	1.4	33	66.6	58.4	0.2	100	98	..	..	99	100
Netherlands	15,990	16,571	18	14	1.5	5	78.3	69.7 g	0.2	100	100	100	93	..	..
Norway	4,505	4,800	20	15	1.7	4	78.9	70.5	0.1	..	..	102 e	96	..	..
Poland	38,542	37,254	18	13	1.3	10	73.9	61.8	0.1	h	..	..	..	..	100	100
Portugal	10,049	9,831	17	16	1.5	6	76.2	66.3	0.5	..	..	108 e	88	91	95
Romania	22,332	20,585	17	14	1.3	22	69.8	61.7	<0.1	86	10	94	76	98	99
Russian Federation	143,752	125,682	16	13	1.1	22	66.0	55.5	0.9	..	..	..	..	100	100
Serbia and Montenegro	10,522	10,044	19	14	1.6	20	73.2	64.3	0.2	100	99	..	..	100	..
Slovakia	5,408	5,317	18	12	1.3	9	73.7	62.4	<0.1	100	100	..	..	..	..
Slovenia	1,983	1,847	15	15	1.1	5	76.1	66.9	<0.1	..	..	94	89	100	100
Spain	39,924	37,395	14	17	1.1	5	78.8	70.6	0.5	..	..	105 e	92	97	99
Sweden	8,823	8,518	17	18	1.3	4	80.1	71.4	0.1	100	100	103 e	100	..	..
Switzerland	7,167	6,729	16	16	1.4	4	79.1	72.1	0.5	100	100	94	83	..	..
Ukraine	48,652	39,569	17	15	1.1	21	68.1	56.8	1.0	100	98	..	..	100	100
United Kingdom	59,657	61,243	19	16	1.6	6	78.2	69.9	0.1	100	100	102 e	94	..	..
MIDDLE EAST & N. AFRICA	423,296	631,320	35	4	3.5	64 i	68.0	56.4	..	91	70	..	..	62	81
Afghanistan	23,294	45,193	43	3	6.8	257	43.2	33.8	..	25	8	..	..	..	..
Algeria	31,403	42,738	34	4	2.8	65	70.3	58.4	0.1 h	99	81	94	58	60	78
Egypt	70,278	94,777	34	4	2.9	43	68.3	57.1	<0.1	100	96	92	..	46	68
Iran, Islamic Rep	72,376	99,343	35	3	2.8	44	69.7	58.8	<0.1	86	79	..	..	71	85
Iraq	24,246	40,298	41	3	4.8	130	64.9	52.6	<0.1	93	31	80	31	..	..
Israel	6,303	8,486	28	10	2.7	6	79.2	69.9	0.1	..	..	95	85	93	97
Jordan	5,196	8,666	40	3	4.3	34	71.0	58.5	<0.1	100	98	64	60	86	96
Kuwait	2,023	3,219	28	3	2.7	10	76.5	64.7	..	..	..	67	57	81	85
Lebanon	3,614	4,581	30	6	2.2	32	73.5	60.7	..	100	87	78	76	82	93
Libyan Arab Jamahiriya	5,529	7,972	33	4	3.3	20	70.9	58.5	0.2	97	96	..	71	71	92
Morocco	30,988	42,002	34	4	3.0	46	68.7	54.9	0.1	86	44	79	..	38	63
Oman	2,709	5,411	43	3	5.5	14	71.5	59.7	0.1	98	61	66	58	65	82
Saudi Arabia	21,701	40,473	42	3	5.5	29	72.2	59.5	..	100	100	59	..	70	84
Syrian Arab Rep	17,040	27,410	39	3	3.7	29	71.8	59.6	..	98	81	93	38	63	89
Tunisia	9,670	12,343	28	6	2.1	28	70.9	61.4	..	96	62	98	55	63	83
Turkey	68,569	86,611	30	6	2.3	45	70.5	58.7	<0.1 h	97	70	100	..	78	94
United Arab Emirates	2,701	3,468	25	3	2.9	9	75.4	63.1	..	..	..	83	70	81	76
Yemen	19,912	48,206	51	2	7.6	117	61.9	49.1	0.1	89	21	61	35	29	70

	Total Population (thousands) {a}		Percent of Population in Specific Age Groups 2002		Total Fertility Rate {a} (children per woman) 2000-2005	Mortality Under Age 5 (per 1000 live births) 2000	Life Expectancy at Birth (years) 2000-2005	Health-Adjusted Life Expectancy {b} (years) 2000	Adults Ages 15-49 Living HIV or AIDS (percent) 2001	Access to Improved Sanitation (percent of population) 2000		Net School Enrollment Ratio 1998-1999		Adult Literacy Rate (percent) {c} 2002	
	2002	2025	Under 15	65 & Over						Urban	Rural	Primary	Secondary	Women	Men
SUB-SAHARAN AFRICA	**683,782**	**1,157,847**	**44**	**3**	**5.6**	**175 i**	**49.1**	**38.8**	**9.0 j**	**72**	**44**	**..**	**..**	**56**	**71**
Angola	13,936	28,213	48	3	7.2	295	45.8	36.9	5.5	70	30	57	..	..	..
Benin	6,629	11,992	46	3	5.7	154	54.0	42.5	3.6	46	6	..	16	26	55
Botswana	1,564	1,826	42	3	3.9	101	36.1	37.3	38.8	88	43	81	57	82	76
Burkina Faso	12,207	25,227	49	3	6.8	198	48.1	34.8	6.5	39	27	34	9	16	36
Burundi	6,688	12,390	47	3	6.8	190	40.6	33.4	8.3	68	90	38	..	44	58
Cameroon	15,535	23,986	43	4	4.7	154	50.0	40.4	11.8	92	66	..	..	67	81
Central African Rep	3,844	5,886	43	4	4.9	180	44.3	34.1	12.9	38	16	53	..	38	62
Chad	8,390	16,383	47	3	6.7	198	46.3	39.3	3.6	81	13	55	7	38	55
Congo	3,206	6,284	47	3	6.3	108	51.6	42.6	7.2	14	..	..	..	77	89
Congo, Dem Rep	54,275	114,876	49	3	6.7	207	52.1	34.4	4.9	54	6	32	12	54	75
Côte d'Ivoire	16,691	25,024	41	3	4.6	173	47.9	39.0	9.7	71	35	59	..	40	61
Equatorial Guinea	483	889	44	4	5.9	156	52.0	44.8	3.4	60	46	83	26	77	93
Eritrea	3,993	7,063	44	3	5.3	114	52.4	41.0	2.8	66	1	34	19	47	69
Ethiopia	66,040	113,418	45	3	6.8	174	43.3	35.4	6.4	33	7	35	16	34	49
Gabon	1,293	2,178	41	6	5.4	90	52.9	46.6	..	55	43	..	..	..	..
Gambia	1,371	2,077	40	3	4.8	128	47.1	46.9	1.6	41	35	61	23	32	46
Ghana	20,176	30,936	40	3	4.2	102	57.2	46.7	3.0	74	70	..	..	66	82
Guinea	8,381	14,120	44	3	5.8	175	48.5	40.3	..	94	41	46	13	..	..
Guinea-Bissau	1,257	2,170	44	4	6.0	215	45.4	36.6	2.8	95	44	..	..	26	57
Kenya	31,904	44,897	42	3	4.2	120	49.3	40.7	15.0	96	82	..	..	79	90
Lesotho	2,076	2,225	39	4	4.5	133	40.2	35.3	31.0	72	40	60	14	94	74
Liberia	3,298	7,638	43	3	6.8	235	55.6	37.8	..	..	..	41	..	39	72
Madagascar	16,913	30,759	45	3	5.7	139	53.6	42.9	0.3	70	30	63	13	62	75
Malawi	11,828	19,544	46	3	6.3	188	39.3	30.9	15.0	96	70	..	7	49	76
Mali	12,019	23,461	46	3	7.0	233	52.1	34.5	1.7	93	58	42	..	17	38
Mauritania	2,830	5,351	44	3	6.0	183	52.5	41.5	..	44	19	60	..	31	52
Mozambique	18,986	28,012	44	3	5.9	200	38.0	31.3	13.0	68	26	41	7	31	62
Namibia	1,819	2,776	43	4	4.9	69	44.3	35.6	22.5	96	17	86	31	83	84
Niger	11,641	25,725	50	2	8.0	270	46.2	33.1	..	79	5	26	6	9	25
Nigeria	120,047	202,957	45	3	5.4	184	52.1	41.6	5.8	66	45	..	..	59	74
Rwanda	8,148	12,883	44	3	5.8	187	40.9	31.9	8.9	12	8	91	..	63	75
Senegal	9,908	16,511	44	3	5.1	139	54.3	44.9	0.5	94	48	59	..	30	49
Sierra Leone	4,814	9,052	45	3	6.5	316	40.5	29.5	7.0	88	53	..	..	..	..
Somalia	9,557	21,192	48	2	7.3	225	48.9	35.1	1.0	..	..	..	..	..	..
South Africa	44,203	43,772	33	4	2.9	70	47.4	43.2	20.1	93	80	..	..	85	87
Sudan	32,559	49,556	40	4	4.5	108	57.0	45.1	2.6	87	48	46	..	49	71
Tanzania, United Rep	36,820	60,395	44	3	5.0	165	51.1	38.1	7.8	99	86	48	4	69	85
Togo	4,779	8,219	44	3	5.4	142	52.2	42.7	6.0	69	17	88	23	45	74
Uganda	24,780	53,765	49	2	7.1	127	46.0	35.7	5.0	93	77	..	9	59	79
Zambia	10,872	19,026	47	3	5.7	202	42.2	33.0	21.5	99	64	73	22	74	86
Zimbabwe	13,076	18,672	45	3	4.5	117	42.9	38.8	33.7	71	57	..	..	86	94
NORTH AMERICA	**319,925**	**383,678**	**21**	**12**	**1.9**	**8**	**77.7**	**67.5**	**0.6**	**100**	**100**	**..**	**..**	**..**	**..**
Canada	31,268	36,717	19	13	1.6	6	79.0	70.0	0.3	100	99	96	94	..	..
United States	288,530	346,822	21	12	1.9	8	77.5	67.2	0.6	100	100	95	90	..	..
C. AMERICA & CARIBBEAN	**178,512**	**233,965**	**33**	**5**	**2.7**	**37 k**	**71.2**	**61.4**	**0.8**	**86**	**49**	**..**	**..**	**86**	**89**
Belize	236	324	37	4	2.9	41	74.4	59.2	2.0	71	25	99	39	94	94
Costa Rica	4,200	5,929	31	5	2.7	12	76.7	65.3	0.6	89	97	..	..	96	96
Cuba	11,273	11,733	20	10	1.6	9	76.4	65.9	<0.1	99	95	97	75	97	97
Dominican Rep	8,639	10,924	32	4	2.7	48	66.9	56.2	2.5	70	60	87	53	84	84
El Salvador	6,520	8,975	35	5	2.9	40	70.3	57.3	0.6	89	76	81	37	77	82
Guatemala	11,995	19,624	43	4	4.4	59	65.6	54.7	1.0	83	79	83	..	63	77
Haiti	8,400	11,549	39	4	4.0	125	53.3	43.1	6.1	50	16	80	..	50	54
Honduras	6,732	10,106	41	3	3.7	40	65.8	56.8	1.6	93	55	..	..	76	76
Jamaica	2,621	3,264	31	7	2.4	20	75.7	64.0	1.2	99	99	92	79	91	84
Mexico	101,842	130,194	32	5	2.5	30	73.0	64.2	0.3	88	34	102 e	56	90	94
Nicaragua	5,347	8,606	42	3	3.8	45	69.1	56.9	0.2	96	72	..	..	67	67
Panama	2,942	3,779	30	6	2.4	26	74.5	63.9	1.5	99	83	..	..	92	93
Trinidad and Tobago	1,306	1,437	23	7	1.5	20	74.8	61.7	2.5	..	..	93	72	98	99
SOUTH AMERICA	**355,695**	**460,770**	**30**	**6**	**2.4**	**37 k**	**70.2**	**59.2**	**0.6**	**86**	**51**	**..**	**..**	**90**	**91**
Argentina	37,944	47,160	27	10	2.4	21	73.8	63.9	0.7	..	..	107 e	74	97	97
Bolivia	8,705	13,131	39	4	3.9	80	63.5	51.4	0.1	86	42	97	..	81	93
Brazil	174,706	218,980	28	5	2.2	38	68.3	57.1 g	0.7	84	43	98	..	88	88
Chile	15,589	19,548	28	7	2.4	12	75.6	65.5	0.3	96	97	88	70	96	96
Colombia	43,495	59,161	32	5	2.6	30	71.9	60.9	0.4	96	56	87	..	92	92
Ecuador	13,112	17,796	33	5	2.8	32	70.5	60.3	0.3	92	74	97	46	91	94
Guyana	765	703	30	5	2.3	74	62.4	52.1	2.7	97	81	85	..	98	99
Paraguay	5,778	9,355	39	4	3.8	31	70.7	60.9	..	94	93	92	42	93	95
Peru	26,523	35,518	32	5	2.6	50	69.5	58.8	0.4	79	49	103 e	61	86	95
Suriname	421	442	29	6	2.1	33	71.1	60.6	1.2	99	75	..	..	..	..
Uruguay	3,385	3,871	25	13	2.3	17	75.0	64.1	0.3	95	85	92	66	98	97
Venezuela	25,093	34,775	33	5	2.7	23	73.3	62.3	0.5 h	71	48	..	..	93	94
OCEANIA	**31,281**	**40,020**	**24**	**10**	**2.3**	**25**	**74.8**	**66.3**	**0.2**	**97**	**92**	**..**	**..**	**98**	**99 d**
Australia	19,536	23,523	20	12	1.8 l	6	79.2 l	71.5	0.1	100	100	..	..	..	..
Fiji	832	954	33	4	3.0	22	69.8	59.6	0.1	75	12	101 e	76	92	95
New Zealand	3,837	4,302	23	12	2.0	6	78.0	70.8	0.1	..	..	..	..	..	..
Papua New Guinea	5,032	8,023	40	2	4.3	112	57.7	46.8	0.7	92	80	85	22	59	72
Solomon Islands	479	943	45	3	5.3	25	69.2	59.0	..	98	18	..	..	..	..
DEVELOPED	**1,321,286**	**1,359,805**	**19**	**14**	**1.6**	**..**	**74.6**	**65.1**	**1.1**	**..**	**..**	**..**	**..**	**99**	**99 d**
DEVELOPING	**4,889,753**	**6,576,876**	**32**	**5**	**3.0**	**91**	**65.3**	**54.8**	**1.2**	**73**	**37**	**..**	**..**	**68**	**82**

a. Medium variant population projections. **b.** Health-Adjusted Life Expectancy (HALE) is number of years that a newborn can expect to live in full health based on current rates of ill-health and mortality. **c.** Includes all adults aged 15 years and over. **d.** Regional values were interpolated by WRI from UNESCO's literacy data for 2000 and 2005. **e.** Inconsistencies with enrollment or population numbers can skew enrollment ratios, erroneously reporting them to be greater than 100% (see the technical notes for more information). **f.** Data for China do not include Hong Kong and Macao. **g.** Figure not yet endorsed by Member States as official statistics. **h.** Data are from 1999. **i.** Regional totals were calculated by UNICEF; the countries included may be slightly different from those in WRI's regional definitions. **j.** Regional estimate calculated by UNAIDS. **k.** Regional totals were calculated by UNICEF and combine South America, Central America, and the Caribbean. **l.** Including Christmas Island, Cocos (Keeling) Islands, and Norfolk Island.

VARIABLE DEFINITIONS AND METHODOLOGY

Total Population is the mid-year population projected for a specific country, area or region, measured in thousands of people. The values are estimated using models based on various demographic parameters: a country's population size, age and sex distribution, fertility and mortality rates by age and sex groups, growth rates of urban and rural populations, and levels of internal and international migration.

Percent of Population Under Age 15 is the proportion of the total population younger than 15 years of age.

Percent of Population Age 65 and Over is the proportion of the total population 65 years of age and older.

Total Fertility Rate is an estimate of the average number of children a woman would have over the course of her entire life if current age-specific fertility rates remained constant during her reproductive years.

Life Expectancy at Birth is the average number of years that a newborn baby is expected to live if the age-specific mortality rates effective at the year of birth apply throughout his or her lifetime.

For the variables defined above, the U.N. Population Division evaluates census and survey results from all countries. These data are adjusted for over-enumeration and under-enumeration of certain age and sex groups (e.g., infants, female children, and young males), misreporting of age and sex distributions, and changes in definitions, when necessary. These adjustments incorporate data from civil registrations; population surveys; earlier censuses; and, when necessary, population models based on information from economically similar countries. After the figures for population size and age/sex composition have been adjusted, these data are scaled to 1990. Historical data are used when deemed accurate, also with adjustments and scaling. However, accurate historical data do not exist for many developing countries. In such cases, the U.N. Population Division uses available information and demographic models to estimate the main demographic parameters. Projections are based on estimates of the 1990 base-year population. Age- and sex-specific mortality rates are applied to the base-year population to determine the number of survivors at the end of each 5-year period. Births are projected by applying age-specific fertility rates to the projected female population. Births are distributed by an assumed sex ratio, and the appropriate age- and sex-specific survival rates are applied. Future migration rates are also estimated on an age- and sex-specific basis. Combining future fertility, mortality, and migration rates yields the projected population size. Assumptions about future mortality, fertility, and migration rates are made on a country-by-country basis and, when possible, are based on historical trends. The U.N. Population Division publishes projections for high-, medium- and low-fertility scenarios; all projections in this table are for the medium-case fertility scenario.

Mortality Under Age 5 is the probability of a child dying between birth and age five expressed per 1,000 live births. The data on mortality of children after infancy is typically obtained from population census information, civil registration records on deaths of young children, United Nations Childrens' Fund (UNICEF) Multiple Indicator Cluster Surveys (MICS) and Demographic and Health Surveys (DHS). For each country, UNICEF and its partners plotted all data from 1960 to the present on a graph; a curve was fitted through this data using a weighted least-squares regression model. The basic model assumes that the rate of change of mortality is linear with respect to time.

Health-Adjusted Life Expectancy (HALE) is defined as the number of years that a newborn can expect to live in full health

based on current rates of ill health and mortality. Healthy life expectancy combines information on mortality and disability, making it a valuable policy tool for assessing health burdens internationally. These data are the product of more than 15 years of work by WHO to measure severity-weighted incidences of ill health. To determine healthy life expectancies, regular life expectancy is first calculated for each age group in a population according to standard methodologies. Next, the frequency of different states of health is measured along with the severity of these disabilities. Finally, the length of time that a population is affected by disabilities compared to full health is valued and reported in years.

Adults Ages 15–49 Living With HIV or AIDS is the estimated percentage of people aged 15–49 living with HIV/AIDS. These estimates include all people with HIV infection—whether or not they have developed symptoms of AIDS—who are alive at the end of the year specified. Data for adults ages 15 to 49 captures those in their most sexually active years. While the risk of HIV infection continues beyond the age of 50, the vast majority of people with substantial risk behavior are likely to have become infected by this age. Measuring infection within this age range also makes populations with different age structures more comparable. In order to estimate prevalence rates of HIV, prevalence estimates for a single point in time and the starting date of the epidemic were used to plot an epidemic curve charting the spread of HIV in a particular country. Prevalence data were collected in developing countries with generalized epidemics using surveillance data from antenatal clinics; in other cases, epidemiologists examined high risk populations (sex workers, intravenous drug users, homosexual males).

Access to Improved Sanitation measures the percentage of the population with access to any of the following excreta disposal facilities: connection to a public sewer, connection to a septic tank, pour-flush latrine, simple pit latrine, and ventilated improved pit latrine. A poor water supply and sanitation system can lead to a number of diseases, including diarrhoea, intestinal worms, and cholera. Examples of an unimproved sanitation system include: open pit latrines, public or shared latrines, and service or bucket latrines (where excreta are manually removed). WHO emphasizes that these data measure access to an improved excreta disposal system—access to a sanitary system cannot be adequately measured on a global scale. Data were collected from assessment questionnaires and household surveys and plotted on a graph for each country to show coverage in available years (not necessarily 1990 and 2000). A trend line was drawn and reviewed by a panel of experts to determine the level of sanitation available in 1990 and 2000. Particular care was taken with the 40 most populous developing countries.

Net School Enrollment Ratio (NER) is defined as the enrollment of the official age group for a given level of education expressed as a percentage of the population from the same age group. The theoretical maximum value is 100%. A high NER denotes a high degree of participation of the official school-age population. If the NER is below 100%, users should not assume that the remaining school-aged population is not enrolled in any school; they could be enrolled in school at other grade levels. Primary Education is defined by the International Standard Classification of Education (ISCED) as the "beginning of systematic apprenticeship of reading, writing and mathematics." Programs are typically six years long and represent the beginning of compulsory education in many countries. Secondary education follows primary education, and is characterized as being subject-oriented with specialized fields of learning. Programs may be vocational or technical in nature, and students achieve a full implementation of basic skills. Net enrollment ratio is calculated by dividing the number of pupils enrolled who are of the official age group for a given level of education by the total population of the same age group. National governments provide the United Nations Educational, Scientific, and Cultural Organization (UNESCO) with enrollment data based on a series of electronic questionnaires. When data from national governments are not available or are of inferior quality, UNESCO will estimate enrollment ratios from background data, if available.

Adult Literacy Rate is the proportion of adults aged 15 years and over who can both read and write with understanding a short, simple statement on their everyday life. Most literacy data are collected during national population censuses and supplemented by household surveys, labor force surveys, employment surveys, industry surveys, and agricultural surveys when they are available. UNESCO uses this data to graph a logistic regression model. Male and female literacy rates are modeled separately. When census and survey data are not available, literacy rates for a specific country are estimated based on neighboring countries with similar characteristics.

FREQUENCY OF UPDATE BY DATA PROVIDERS
Both the UN Population Division and the Joint United Nations Program on HIV/AIDS (UNAIDS) publish country-level statistics every two years with annual revisions of key estimates. UNICEF publishes the most recent available data each year. Other data sets in this table are updated irregularly—educational statistics are updated as new country-level data are sent to UNESCO, and healthy life expectancy was calculated for the first time in 2001. Most updates include revisions of past data.

DATA RELIABILITY AND CAUTIONARY NOTES
Total Population, Fertility, and Life Expectancy: Although projections cannot factor in unforeseen events (e.g. famine), U.N. demographic models are based on surveys and censuses with well-understood qualities, which make these data fairly reliable.

Mortality Under Age 5: Estimates were calculated based on a wide variety of sources of disparate quality. For information on the underlying data for each country's regressions, refer to the country estimates and new country data available from UNICEF on-line at http://www.childinfo.org/cmr/kh98meth.html.

Health-Adjusted Life Expectancy: Some estimates have not yet been endorsed by Member States as official statistics. The data will improve as national governments become involved in providing data and survey results. WHO has estimated the uncertainty in HALE for each country; these results are published in the World Health Report 2001 (available on-line at http://www.who.int/whr2001/2001/).

Adults Ages 15–49 Living with HIV or AIDS: While the HIV surveillance systems are generally more extensive than those for other diseases, problems do remain with the data. Data are often very weak for marginalized risk groups such as intravenous drug users or homosexual males. Infection rates in the general population are calculated based on infection rates in childbearing women; other women and men are then assumed to have the same rate of infection. Prevalence of HIV is assumed to be uniform in periurban and urban areas. The original source material captures some of these uncertainties with estimates of low and high values for the total number of HIV/AIDS infections. For a detailed description of the collection methodology and limitations of this data, please see: B. Schwartlander et al. 1999. "Country-specific estimates and models of HIV and AIDS: methods and limitations." AIDS, 13: 2445–2458.

Access to Improved Sanitation: These data have become more reliable as WHO and UNICEF shift from provider-based information (national census estimates) to consumer-based information (survey data). Nonetheless, estimates were calculated based on a wide variety of sources of disparate quality. Definitions of urban and rural are not consistent across countries. In addition, regions with higher overall levels of service tend to implement a stricter definition of "adequate" sanitation.

Net School Enrollment: Even though UNESCO has applied the same methodology to analyze all of the country data, definitions of "schooling" and "enrollment" are not strictly comparable among countries. As net enrollment ratios approach 100%, inconsistencies with enrollment and/or population data are more likely to skew the resulting ratios. As a result, some net enrollment ratios are greater than 100%. Difficulties also arise when a substantial proportion of students begin school earlier than the prescribed age, or when the reference date for entry into primary education does not coincide with the birthdays of all eligible students.

Adult Literacy Rate: The availability and quality of national statistics on literacy vary widely, particularly for developing countries. National census and survey data are typically collected only once every decade. In addition, many industrialized countries have stopped collecting literacy data in recent years, based on the sometimes incorrect assumption that universal primary education means universal literacy. When census and survey data are not available for a particular country, estimates are sometimes made based on neighboring countries. Actual definitions of adult literacy are not strictly comparable among countries. Some countries equate persons with no schooling with illiterates, or change definitions between censuses. In addition, UNESCO's definition of literacy does not include people who, though familiar with the basics of reading and writing, do not have the skills to function at a reasonable level in their own society. Practices for identifying literates and illiterates during actual census enumeration may also vary, and errors in literacy self-declaration can affect data reliability.

SOURCES
Population, Total Fertility and Life Expectancy: Population Division of the Department of Economic and Social Affairs of the United Nations Secretariat. 2002. World Population Prospects: The 2000 Revision. New York: United Nations. Data set on CD-ROM. **Mortality under Age 5 and Access to Improved Sanitation:** United Nation's Children's Fund (UNICEF). 2001. State of the World's Children 2002. New York: UNICEF. Data available on-line at http://www.unicef.org/sowc02/. Improved Sanitation data were collected under the UNICEF-World Health Organization (WHO) Joint Monitoring Programme. **Health-Adjusted Life Expectancy:** World Health Organization (WHO). 2001. World Health Report 2001: Annex Table 4. Geneva: WHO. Data available on-line at http://www.who.int/whr/2001/main/en/annex/annex4.htm. **Adults Living with HIV or AIDS:** Joint United Nations Programme on HIV/AIDS. July 2002. UNAIDS Barcelona Report on the Global HIV/AIDS Epidemic. Geneva: UNAIDS. Data available on-line at http://www.unaids.org/barcelona/presskit/barcelona%20report/contents.html. **Net School Enrollment:** United Nations Educational, Scientific, and Cultural Organization (UNESCO) Institute for Statistics. 2002. Unpublished data. UNESCO: Montreal. **Adult Literacy Rate:** United Nations Educational, Scientific, and Cultural Organization (UNESCO) Institute for Statistics, Literacy and Non Formal Education Sector. 2002. Adult illiteracy for population aged 15 years and above, by country and by gender 1970–2015. Paris: UNESCO. Data available on-line at http://www.uis.unesco.org/en/stats/stats0.htm.

Regional Groupings of Countries

Countries are listed according to their primary regional classification, assigned by the World Resources Institute.

World Bank income designations follow the country names: "H" represents high-income countries, "M" middle-income countries, and "L" low-income countries.

Developed countries are labeled with a "D"; developing countries are not labeled. WRI uses the Food and Agriculture Organization of the United Nations' definitions of developed and developing countries.

ASIA (EXCLUDING THE MIDDLE EAST)
Armenia L D
Azerbaijan L D
Bangladesh L
Bhutan L
Brunei Darussalam H
Cambodia L
China M
East Timor L
Georgia M D
Hong Kong H
India L
Indonesia M
Japan H D
Kazakhstan M D
Korea, Dem People's Rep M
Korea, Rep H
Kyrgyzstan L D
Lao People's Dem Rep L
Macau H
Malaysia M
Maldives M
Mongolia L
Myanmar L
Nepal L
Pakistan L
Philippines M
Singapore H
Sri Lanka M
Taiwan, Province of China
Tajikistan L D
Thailand M
Turkmenistan L D
Uzbekistan M D
Viet Nam L

EUROPE
Albania L D
Andorra H D
Austria H D
Belarus M D
Belgium H D
Bosnia and Herzegovina L D
Bulgaria M D

Channel Islands H D
Croatia M D
Czech Rep M D
Denmark H D
Estonia M D
Faeroe Islands H D
Finland H D
France H D
Germany H D
Gibraltar D
Greece H D
Hungary M D
Iceland H D
Ireland H D
Isle of Man M D
Italy H D
Latvia M D
Liechtenstein H D
Lithuania M D
Luxembourg H D
Macedonia, FYR M D
Malta M D
Moldova, Rep L D
Monaco H D
Netherlands H D
Norway H D
Poland M D
Portugal H D
Romania M D
Russian Federation M D
San Marino H D
Serbia and Montenegro M D
Slovakia M D
Slovenia H D
Spain H D
Sweden H D
Switzerland H D
Ukraine M D
United Kingdom H D

MIDDLE EAST AND NORTH AFRICA
Afghanistan L
Algeria M
Bahrain M
Cyprus H
Egypt M
Iran, Islamic Rep M
Iraq M
Israel H D
Jordan M
Kuwait H
Lebanon M
Libyan Arab Jamahiriya M
Morocco M
Oman M
Qatar H
Saudi Arabia M
Syrian Arab Rep M
Tunisia M
Turkey M
United Arab Emirates H
West Bank M
Western Sahara M
Yemen L

SUB-SAHARAN AFRICA
Angola L
Benin L
Botswana M
Burkina Faso L
Burundi L
Cameroon L
Cape Verde M
Central African Rep L
Chad L
Comoros L
Congo L
Congo, Dem Rep L
Côte d'Ivoire L
Djibouti M
Equatorial Guinea M
Eritrea L
Ethiopia L
Gabon M

Gambia L
Ghana L
Guinea L
Guinea-Bissau L
Kenya L
Lesotho L
Liberia L
Madagascar L
Malawi L
Mali L
Mauritania L
Mauritius M
Mozambique L
Namibia M
Niger L
Nigeria L
Réunion H
Rwanda L
Saint Helena
Sao Tome & Principe L
Senegal L
Seychelles M
Sierra Leone L
Somalia L
South Africa M D
Sudan L
Swaziland M
Tanzania L
Togo L
Uganda L
Zambia L
Zimbabwe L

NORTH AMERICA
Bermuda H
Canada H D
Greenland H
Saint Pierre and Miquelon
United States H D

CENTRAL AMERICA AND THE CARIBBEAN
Antigua and Barbuda M
Aruba H
Bahamas H
Barbados M
Belize M
British Virgin Islands
Cayman Islands H
Costa Rica M
Cuba M
Dominica M
Dominican Rep M
El Salvador M
Grenada M
Guadeloupe M
Guatemala M
Haiti L
Honduras L
Jamaica M
Martinique H
Mexico M
Netherlands Antilles H
Nicaragua L
Panama M
Puerto Rico M
Saint Kitts and Nevis M
St. Lucia M
St. Vincent & Grenadines M
Trinidad and Tobago M
Turks and Caicos Islands
Virgin Islands H

SOUTH AMERICA
Argentina M
Bolivia M
Brazil M
Chile M
Colombia M
Ecuador M
Falkland Islands
French Guiana H
Guyana M
Paraguay M
Peru M
Suriname M
Uruguay M
Venezuela M
American Samoa M

OCEANIA
Australia H D
Cook Islands
Fiji M
French Polynesia H
Guam H
Kiribati M
Marshall Islands M
Micronesia, Fed States M
Nauru
New Caledonia H
New Zealand H D
Niue
Northern Mariana Islands H
Palau M
Papua New Guinea M
Samoa M
Solomon Islands M
Tonga M
Vanuatu M

Acknowledgments

World Resources 2002–2004 is the result of a unique partnership between the United Nations Environment Programme (UNEP), the United Nations Development Programme (UNDP), The World Bank, and the World Resources Institute (WRI). It is the only instance where UN agencies, a multilateral financial institution, and an NGO work together to determine the content, conclusions, and recommendations of a major environmental report.

INSTITUTIONS

For our tenth edition in the *World Resources* series, the *World Resources* staff gives special thanks to the Metanoia Fund, the Netherlands Ministry of Foreign Affairs, the Swedish International Development Cooperation Agency (SIDA), and the Earth Charter Initiative for their generous support. The Ford Motor Company, The David and Lucile Packard Foundation, SIDA, UNDP, UNEP, the V. Kann Rasmussen Foundation, The World Bank, and WRI also provided additional support for EarthTrends, the companion website to the *World Resources* series, which offers environmental data, indicators, and information on-line.

We are particularly grateful to the Access Initiative, a global coalition of civil society groups. In 2000, the Access Initiative partners set out to measure the public's ability to participate in decisions about the environment. Their findings became a key part of this report.

THE ACCESS INITIATIVE PARTNERS

Advocates Coalition for Development and Environment (ACODE), Uganda
Agricultural Cooperative Development International (ACDI), Uganda
Austral Center for Environmental Law, Chile
Centro de Investigación y Planificación del Medio Ambiente (CIPMA), Chile
Centro Mexicano de Derechos Ambientales (CEMDA), Mexico
Comunicación y Educación Ambiental, Mexico
Corporación PARTICIPA, Chile
Cultural Ecológica, Mexico
Ecological Institute for Sustainable Development (Miskolc), Hungary
Environmental Justice Networking Forum (EJNF), South Africa
Environmental Law and Management Clinic of Technikon Pretoria, South Africa
Environmental Law Institute (ELI), USA
Environmental Management and Law Association (EMLA), Hungary
Environmental Partnership for Central Europe (ÖKOTÁRS), Hungary

Fundación RIDES, Chile
Fundación Terram, Chile
Indonesian Center for Environmental Law (ICEL)
King Prajadhipok's Institute (KPI), Thailand
NGO-Coordinating Committee on Development (NGO-COD), Thailand
Ohio Citizen Action, USA
Presencia Ciudadana, Mexico
Silicon Valley Toxics Coalition (SVTC), USA
Society for Participatory Research in Asia (PRIA), India
Sustainable Development Institute, Hungary
Thailand Environment Institute
Uganda Wildlife Society
World Resources Institute, USA

INDIVIDUALS

Many individuals contributed to the development of this report by providing expert advice, data, or careful review of manuscripts. While final responsibility for the contents rests with the *World Resources* staff, the report reflects valuable contributions from all of the following individuals and organizations. In particular, special thanks go to Mirjam Schomaker (consultant) of UNEP, Kirk Hamilton of the World Bank, and Jake Werksman of UNDP, who coordinated the input of many experts throughout their organizations including:

UNEP

Adnan Amin, Meryem Amar-Samnotra, Charles Arden-Clarke, Marion Cheatle, Munyaradzi Chenje, Dan Claasen, Gerry Cunningham, Arthur Dahl, Volodymyr Demkine, Halifa Drammeh, Eric Falt, Hiremagalur Gopalan, Tessa Goverse, Michael Graber, Sherry Heileman, John Hilborn, Anja Jaenz, Cornis Lugt, Timo Maukonen, Elizabeth Migongo-Bake, Patrick M'mayi, Masa Nagai, Werner Obermeyer, Neil Pratt, Naomi Poulton, Daniel Puig, Anisur Rahman, Denis Ruysschaert, Nelson Sabogal, Vijay Samnotra, Megumi Seki, Rajendra Shende, David Smith, Eric Usher, Isabelle Vanderbeck, Marceil Yeater

UNDP

Ali Farzin, Sergio Feld, Linda Ghanime, Pascal Girot, Hossein Jafari Giv, Peter Hazlewood, John Hough, Selim Jahan, Mehdi Kamyab, Arun Kashyap, Charles McNeill, Joseph Opio Odongo, Usha Rao, Nadine Smith

THE WORLD BANK

Kristalina Georgieva, Magda Lovei, Saeed Ordoubadi, Stefano Pagiola, Gunars Platais

Special thanks go to Allen Hammond who graciously stepped in as acting Editor-in-Chief to guide the Report to final publication.

World Resources staff also gratefully acknowledges the guidance of Anthony Janetos (WRI) in project planning and Dan Tunstall (WRI) in overseeing the review process.

PART I

CHAPTER 1 ENVIRONMENTAL GOVERNANCE: WHOSE VOICE? WHOSE CHOICE?

Contributors and reviewers: Nikolai Denisov (UNEP/GRID-Arendal), Sofie Flensborg (UN Economic Commission for Europe), Allen Hammond (WRI), Norbert Henninger (WRI), Somrudee Nicro (Thailand Environment Institute), Gustavo Alanis Ortega (Centro Mexicano de Derecho Ambiental), Elena Petkova (WRI), Jesse Ribot (WRI), Alejandra Serrano P. (Centro Mexicano de Derecho Ambiental), Frances Seymour (WRI), Peter Veit (WRI), Jeremy Wates (UN Economic Commission for Europe)

CHAPTER 2 ENVIRONMENTAL GOVERNANCE TODAY

Contributors and reviewers: Frank Ahern (Terrevista Earth Imaging), Linda Shaffer Bollert (WRI), Carl Bruch (Environmental Law Institute), Dirk Bryant (WRI), Andrew Buchman (WRI), Jean-Gael Collomb (WRI), Gayle Coolidge (WRI), Hamid R. Davoodi (IMF), Linda Delgado (WRI), Katie Frohardt (African Wildlife Foundation), Allen Hammond (WRI), Massimo Mastruzzi (World Bank Institute), Emily Matthews (WRI), Crescie Maurer (WRI), Erin McAlister (WRI), Becky Milton (WRI), Susan Minnemeyer (WRI), Judy Oglethorpe (WWF-US), Elena Petkova (WRI), Jesse Ribot (WRI), James Shambaugh, Frances Seymour (WRI), Peter Veit (WRI)

CHAPTER 3 PUBLIC PARTICIPATION AND ACCESS

Contributors and reviewers: The Access Initiative, Tom Beierle (Resources for the Future), John Coyle (WRI), Gretchen Hoff (WRI), Bill LaRocque (WRI), Elena Petkova (WRI), Lina Maria Ibarra Ruiz (WRI)

CHAPTER 4 AWAKENING CIVIL SOCIETY

Contributors and reviewers: Richard Andrews (University of North Carolina), L. David Brown (Harvard University), Grant Curtis (ADB), Robert Dobias (ADB), Alan Fowler (INTRAC), Marlies Glasius (Global Civil Society 2001), William Moody (Rockefeller Brothers Foundation), Tomas Růžička (EPCE), Tamás Scsaurszki (C.S. Mott Foundation), Robert Sinclair (consultant)

CHAPTER 5 DECENTRALIZATION: A LOCAL VOICE

Contributors and reviewers: Jon Anderson (USAID), Krister Par Andersson (Indiana University), Richard Andrews (University of North Carolina), Nate Badenoch (WRI), Navroz Dubash (WRI), Mairi Dupar Gore (WRI), Fredrich Kahrl (WRI), Anne M. Larson (CIFOR), Jamie Pittock (WWF International), Jesse Ribot (WRI), Frances Seymour (WRI), Barbara Wyckoff-Baird (Aspen Institute)

CHAPTER 6 DRIVING BUSINESS ACCOUNTABILITY

Contributors and reviewers: Shakeb Afsah (International Resources Group), Rick Bunch (WRI), Cary Coglianese (Harvard University), Julie Gorte (Calvert Group), Chris Herlugson (BP-Amoco), Jacky Higgins (HSBC), David Hillyard (Earthwatch), Fran Irwin (WRI), William Kramer (WRI), Steve Lippman (Trillium Asset Management), Nick Maybury (HSBC), Elena Petkova (WRI), Janet Ranganathan (WRI), Don Reed (Ecos Corporation), David Wheeler (World Bank)

CHAPTER 7 INTERNATIONAL ENVIRONMENTAL GOVERNANCE

Contributors and reviewers: Linda Shaffer Bollert (WRI), Duncan Brack (RIIA), Anne Marie DeRose (WRI), Charles Di Leva (World Bank), Navroz Dubash (WRI), Lindsey Fransen (WRI), Mairi Dupar Gore (WRI), Allen Hammond (WRI), Fredrich Karhl (WRI), Tony La Viña (WRI), Crescie Maurer (WRI), Frances Seymour (WRI)

CHAPTER 8 A WORLD OF DECISIONS: CASE STUDIES

Contributors and reviewers: Bharti Bhavsar (SEWA), Melissa Boness (WRI), George Branch (University of Cape Town), Mauricio Castro (Secretaría General del Sistema de la Integracíon Centroamericana), Angela Cassar (Environmental Law Institute), Elsa Chang (Advocacy Institute), Rick Clugston (Center for Respect of Life and Environment, and Earth Charter), Malcolm Douglas, Geoff Evans (Mineral Policy Institute), Ali Farzin (UNDP), Polly Ghazi, Gwendolyn Hallsmith, Graeme Hancock (Department of Mining, PNG), Ben Hardwick (Slater & Gordon Lawyers), Jean Harris (Ezemvelo KwaZulu-Natal Wildlife), Maria Hauck (University of Cape Town), Aditi Kapoor (Alternative Futures), Stuart Kirsch (University of Michigan), Harvey Locke, Emily Matthews (WRI), Kenton Miller (WRI), Marta Miranda (WRI), Mohit Mukherjee (Earth Charter International Secretariat), Reema Nanavaty (SEWA), Steven C. Rockefeller (Middlebury College), Phil Shearman, John E. Strongman (The World Bank), Asghar Tahmasebi, Anil Prabhakar Tambay (BAIF Development Research Foundation), Patricia Townsend, Peter Veit (WRI), Mirian Vilela (Earth Charter Secretariat), Peter Wilshusen (Bucknell University of Pennslyvania), David Wissink (OK Tedi Mining Limited)

CHAPTER 9 TOWARD A BETTER BALANCE

Contributors and reviewers: Navroz Dubash (WRI), Mairi Dupar Gore (WRI), Gretchen Hoff (WRI), Tony La Viña (WRI), Allen Hammond (WRI), Elena Petkova (WRI), Jesse Ribot (WRI), Frances Seymour (WRI)

PART II

DATA TABLES

Institutions and Governance
Reviewers and contributors: David Banisar (Privacy International), Maryam Niamir-Fuller (UNDP), Norbert Henninger (WRI), Frances Irwin (WRI), Tundu Lissu (WRI), Crescencia Maurer (WRI), Elena Petkova (WRI), Frances Seymour (WRI), Peter Veit (WRI)

Economic Indicators
Reviewers and contributors: Duncan Austin (WRI), Christian Averous (OECD), Katherine Bolt (World Bank), Alan Brewster (Yale), Rashid M. Hassan (CEEPA), Dan Tunstall (WRI), Monika Zurek (FAO)

Agriculture and Food
Reviewers and contributors: Suzie Greenhalgh (WRI), Marta Iglesias (FAO), Allan Lines (USDA), Emily Matthews (WRI)

Biodiversity and Protected Areas
Reviewers and contributors: Phillip Fox (WCMC), Dwight Peck (Ramsar), Carmen Revenga (WRI), Katarina Vestin (UNESCO), Robin White (WRI)

Climate and Atmosphere
Reviewers and contributors: Kevin Baumert (WRI), Tom Boden (CDIAC), Emily Matthews (WRI), Karen Treanton (IEA)

Fisheries and Aquaculture
Reviewers and contributors: Adele Crispoldi (FAO), Luca Garibaldi (FAO), Yumiko Kura (WRI), Carmen Revenga (WRI), Mirjam Schomaker (UNEP)

Energy
Reviewers and contributors: Kevin Baumert (WRI), Tom Boden (CDIAC), Emily Matthews (WRI), Karen Treanton (IEA)

Forests, Grasslands, and Drylands
Reviewers and contributors: Nigel Dudley (Equilibrium), Peter Gilruth (Raytheon), Suzie Greenhalgh (WRI), Peter Holmgren (FAO), Alexander Korotkov (UNECE), Emily Matthews (WRI)

Freshwater Resources
Reviewers and contributors: Lauretta Burke (WRI), Åse Eliasson (FAO), Jean-Marc Faurès (FAO), Yumiko Kura (WRI), Jean Margat (Plan Bleu), Sandra Postel (Global Water Policy Project), Carmen Revenga (WRI)

Population, Health, and Human Well-Being
Reviewers and contributors: Nada Chaya (PAI), Don Doering (WRI), Robert Johnston (UNDP), Craig Hanson (WRI), Olivier Labe (UNESCO), Douglas Lynd (UNESCO), Amanda Sauer (WRI), Dan Tunstall (WRI), Tessa Wardlaw (UNICEF)

The *World Resources* staff also wishes to extend thanks to the following individuals for their contributions: Andy Brown (Appalachian Trail Conference), Strachan Donnelley (The Hastings Center), Charles H.W. Foster (Harvard University), Lawrence Harrison (Tufts Fletcher School of Diplomacy), Jack Hogan (Johns Hopkins SAIS), Denis Hynes (Johns Hopkins SAIS), Bob Sacha (Bob Sacha Photography), Nigel Sizer (TNC), Robb Turner (SAMAB)

PUBLISHING SUPPORT AND ASSISTANCE

We are grateful to The Magazine Group and to Jarboe Printing Company in Washington, DC for publishing support and assistance. Our special thanks to Richard Creighton, Glenn Pierce, Judy Gibson, Brenda Waugh, and the proofreading team at The Magazine Group. At Jarboe Printing we are especially grateful to Stephen Jarboe, Robert Gray, Jane Fierstein, and Timothy O'Connor. Thanks also go to our indexer Leonard Rosenbaum. Finally, we say thank you to our colleague Bill LaRocque for creating the access icons used in Chapter 3.

References

Chapter 1 Text

Andersen, S., and K.M. Sarma. 2002. *Protecting the Ozone Layer: The United Nations History*. London: Earthscan.

Bailey, E. 2002. "Administration May Cut Klamath's Flow Again." *Los Angeles Times* (11 October):10.

Bowles, I., and C. Kormos. 1995. "Environmental Reform at the World Bank: The Role of the U.S. Congress." *Virginia Journal of International Law* 35:777–839.

Bruch, C. 2001. "Charting New Waters: Public Involvement in the Management of International Watercourses." *Environmental Law Reporter* 31:11389–11416.

Centre for Science and the Environment (CSE). 2002. "Centre for Science and Environment Welcomes Recent Supreme Court Ruling." Press Release. 6 April. Cited 16 May 2003. On-line at: http://www.cseindia.org/html/cmp/air/press_20020406.htm.

Dupar, M., and N. Badenoch. 2002. *Environment, Livelihoods, and Local Institutions: Decentralization in Mainland Southeast Asia*. Washington, DC: World Resources Institute.

Forest Watch Indonesia (FWI) and Global Forest Watch (GFW). 2002. *The State of the Forest: Indonesia*. Bogor, Indonesia: FWI and Washington, DC: GFW.

Friends of the Earth UK (FOE-UK). 2002. "Big Cuts in Cancer Gases Achieved." Press Release. 6 March. Cited 15 May 2003. On-line at: http://www.foe.co.uk/pubsinfo/infoteam/pressrel/2002/20020306000113.html.

Hofer, J. 1997. "Up in Arms in Bukidnon." Pp: 236–238 in *Saving the Earth: The Philippine Experience*. C. Balgos, ed. Manila, Philippines: Philippine Center for Investigative Journalism.

Kaufmann, D., A. Kray, and P. Zoido-Lobatón. 2002. "Governance Matters II: Updated Indicators for 2000/01." Policy Research Working Paper Series, No. 2772. Washington, DC: The World Bank. Cited 18 June 2003. On-line at: http://econ.worldbank.org/files/11783_wps2772.pdf.

Keohane, R. 2003. "The Concept of Accountability in World Politics and the Use of Force." *Michigan Journal of International Law* (Forthcoming).

Schoch, D. 2001. "Klamath Farmers Thwarted in Plea for Irrigation Water." *Los Angeles Times* (14 July):9.

World Conservation Monitoring Centre (WCMC), and United Nations Environment Programme (UNEP). 2003. "World Database on Protected Areas, Sustainable Parks Map." Unpublished data. Cambridge, UK: UNEP-WCMC.

World Resources Institute. 2002. "WRI, Cameroon Ink Pact to Monitor Forests, Curb Illegal Logging." Press Release. 6 June. Cited 19 March 2003. On-line at: http://newsroom.wri.org/newsreleases.cfm.

World Resources Institute (WRI) in collaboration with United Nations Environment Programme (UNEP), United Nations Development Programme (UNDP), and World Bank. 2000. *World Resources 2000–2001: People and Ecosystems: The Fraying Web of Life*. Washington, DC: WRI.

Box 1.1 Who Governs Nature?

Evans, J. 2002. "The Role of Community Initiative and Traditional Leadership in the Establishment of Marine Protected Areas (Ra'ui) on Rarotonga, Cook Islands." World Resources Institute Lecture, 19 June. Washington, DC: World Resources Institute.

Farah, D. 2002. "Liberian Leader Again Finds Means to Hang On." *Washington Post* (4 June):A1.

Global Witness. 2001a. "Liberia Breaches UN Sanctions–Whilst Its Logging Industry Funds Arms Imports and RUF Rebels." Press Release. 6 September. Cited 19 March 2003. On-line at: http://www.globalwitness.org/campaigns/forests/display2.php?id=114.

Global Witness. 2001b. *Taylor-made: The Pivotal Role of Liberia's Forests and Flag of Convenience in Regional Conflict*. London: Global Witness.

Global Witness. 2001c. "UN Expert Recommendation on Liberia's Timber Industry Leaves a Platform for Continued Arms Trade." Press Release. 30 October. Cited 19 March 2003. On-line at: http://www.globalwitness.org/campaigns/forests/liberia/display2.php?id=116.

Global Witness. 2002. "Liberia's Logs of War: Underpinning Conflict." Briefing Document. London: Global Witness. 13 December. Cited 20 March 2003. On-line at: http://www.globalwitness.org/campaigns/forests/liberia/pressreleases.php.

Rumansara, A. 2000. "Indonesia: The Struggle of the People of Kedung Ombo." Pp: 123–149 in *The Struggle for Accountability: The World Bank, NGOs, and Grassroots Movements*. J. Fox and L.D. Brown, eds. Cambridge, MA: MIT Press.

Box 1.2 Governance and Ecosystems

Bryant, D., D. Nielsen, and L. Tangley. 1997. *The Last Frontier Forests: Ecosystems and Economies on the Edge*. Washington, DC: World Resources Institute.

Food and Agriculture Organization of the United Nations (FAO). 2000. *The State of World Fisheries and Aquaculture, 2000*. Rome: FAO.

Revenga, C., J. Brunner, N. Henninger, K. Kassem, and R. Payne. 2000. *Pilot Analysis of Global Ecosystems: Freshwater Systems*. Washington, DC: World Resources Institute.

Williams, M. 1996. *The Transition in the Contribution of Living Aquatic Resources to Food Security*. Food, Agriculture, and the Environment Discussion Paper 13. Washington, DC: International Food Policy Research Institute (IFPRI).

Wood, S., K. Sebastian, and S. Scherr. 2000. *Pilot Analysis of Global Ecosystems: Agroecosystems*. Washington, DC: World Resources Institute.

World Commission on Forests and Sustainable Development (WCFSD). 1999. *Our Forests, Our Future*. Cambridge, UK: Cambridge University Press.

World Resources Institute (WRI) in collaboration with United Nations Environment Programme (UNEP), United Nations Development Programme (UNDP), and World Bank. 2000. *World Resources 2000–2001: People and Ecosystems: The Fraying Web of Life*. Washington, DC: WRI.

Box 1.4 What About Ownership?
Property Rights and Governance

Agbosu, L.K. 2000. "Land Law in Ghana: Contradiction between Anglo-American and Customary Conceptions of Tenure and Practices." Working Paper No. 33. Madison, WI: Land Tenure Center, University of Wisconsin–Madison.

Bruce, J. 1998a. "Country Profiles of Land Tenure: Africa, 1996." Research Paper No. 130. Madison, WI: Land Tenure Center, University of Wisconsin–Madison.

Bruce, J. 1998b. "Review of Tenure Terminology." Tenure Brief No. 1. Madison, WI: Land Tenure Center, University of Wisconsin–Madison.

Burger, J., E. Ostrom, R. Norgaard, D. Policansky, and B. Goldstein, eds. 2001. *Protecting the Commons: A Framework for Resource Management in the Americas*. Washington, DC: Island Press.

Feeny, D., F. Berkes, B. McCay, and J. Acheson. 1990. "The Tragedy of the Commons: Twenty-Two Years Later." *Human Ecology* 18(1):1–19.

Hardin, G. 1968. "The Tragedy of the Commons." *Science* 162(3859):1243–1248.

Jensen, M. 2000. "Common Sense and Common-Pool Resources." *BioScience* 50(8):638–644.

Land Trust Alliance (LTA). 2003. *About Land Trusts*. Website. Cited 18 September 2002. On-line at http://www.lta.org/aboutlt/index.html.

McCay, B. 2000. "Property Rights, The Commons, and Natural Resource Management." Pp: 67–82 in *Property Rights, Economics, and the Environment*. M. Kaplowitz, ed. Stamford, CT: Jai Press.

Ostrom, E. 1990. *Governing the Commons: The Evolution of Institutions for Collective Action*. Cambridge, UK: Cambridge University Press.

Ostrom, E., J. Berger, C. Field, R. Norgaard, and D. Polcansky. 1999. "Revisiting the Commons: Local Lessons, Global Challenges." *Science* 284:278–282.

Rukuni, M. 1999. "Land Tenure, Governance and Prospects for Sustainable Development in Africa." Policy Brief No. 6. Washington, DC: Natural Resources Policy Consultative Group for Africa.

Seno, S., and W. Shaw. 2002. "Land Tenure Policies, Maasai Traditions, and Wildlife Conservation in Kenya." *Society and Natural Resources* 15:79–88.

Suyanto, S., T. Tomich, and K. Otsuka. 2001. "Land Tenure and Farm Management Efficiency: The Case of Smallholder Rubber Production in Customary Land Areas of Sumatra." Policy Brief, Gender and Forest Resource Management: A Comparative Study in Selected Areas of Asia and Africa. Washington, DC: International Food Policy Research Institute (IFPRI).

Toulmin, C., and J. Quan, eds. 2000. *Evolving Land Rights, Policy and Tenure in Africa*. London: Department for International Development–UK (DFID), International Institute for Environment and Development (IIED), National Resources Institute (NRI).

Trust for Public Land (TPL). 2003. Website. Cited 15 May 2003. On-line at http://www.tpl.org.

World Resources Institute (WRI) in collaboration with United Nations Environment Programme (UNEP), United Nations Development Programme (UNDP), and World Bank. 2000. *World Resources 2000–2001: People and Ecosystems: The Fraying Web of Life*. Washington, DC: WRI.

Box 1.5 Poverty and Environmental Governance

Cavendish, W. 1999. "Empirical Regularities in the Poverty-Environment Relationship of African Rural Households." Working Paper Series 99-21. Oxford, UK: Center for the Study of African Economies (CSAE).

Department for International Development–United Kingdom (DFID), Directorate General for Development–European Commission (EC), United Nations Development Programme (UNDP), and World Bank. 2002. *Linking Poverty Reduction and Environmental Management: Policy Challenges and Opportunities*. Washington, DC: World Bank.

Friends of the Earth UK (FOE-UK). 1999. *In-Depth Information About Pollution and Poverty*. Website. Cited 16 May 2003. On-line at http://www.foe.co.uk/campaigns/industry_and_pollution/factorywatch/pollution_and_poverty/indepth.html.

International Fund for Agricultural Development (IFAD). 2001. *Rural Poverty Report 2001: The Challenge of Ending Rural Poverty*. New York: Oxford University Press.

Jodha, N.S. 1995. "Common Property Resources and Dynamics of Rural Poverty in India's Dry Regions." *Unasylva* 46(180). Cited 15 May 2003. On-line at: http://www.fao.org/docrep/v3960e/v3960e00.htm#Contents.

Wheeler, D. 2000. *Greening Industry: New Roles for Communities, Markets and Governments*. New York: Oxford University Press.

World Bank. 2001. *World Development Report 2000/2001: Attacking Poverty*. New York: Oxford University Press.

World Bank. 2003. *World Development Report 2003: Sustainable Development in a Dynamic World: Transforming Institutions, Growth, and Quality of Life*. New York: World Bank.

Box 1.6 Avenues for Public Participation

Beierle, T.C., and J. Cayford. 2002. *Democracy in Practice: Public Participation in Environmental Decisions*. Washington, DC: Resources for the Future.

Environmental Law Institute (ELI). 1997. *Transparency and Responsiveness: Building a Participatory Process for Activities Implemented Jointly Under the Climate Change Convention*. Washington, DC: ELI.

Chapter 2 Text

Bacon, R. 1999. "A Scorecard for Energy Reform in Developing Countries." *Public Policy for the Private Sector* 175.

Bhatnagar, S. 2000. "Land/Property Registration in Andhra Pradesh." E*Government Case Study. Washington, DC: World Bank. Cited 8 May 2003. On-line at: http://www1.worldbank.org/publicsector/egov/cardcs.htm.

Brubaker, E. 2001. "The Promise of Privatization." Toronto, Canada: Energy Probe Research Foundation. Cited 8 May 2003. On-line at: http://www.environmentprobe.org/enviroprobe/pubs/walkerton.pdf.

Bruch, C. 2001. "Charting New Waters: Public Involvement in the Management of International Watercourses." *Environmental Law Reporter* 31:11389–11416.

Commission on Sustainable Development (CSD). 2002. "Second Local Agenda 21 Survey." Background Paper No. 15 for the Second Preparatory Committee for the World Summit on Sustainable Development, New York, 28 January–8 February.

Convention on Biological Diversity (CBD). 2002. "The Hague Ministerial Declaration of the Conference of Parties to the Convention on Biological Diversity." Cited 6 June 2003. On-line at: http://www.biodiv.org/doc/meetings/cop/cop-06/other/cop-06-min-decl-en.pdf.

Davis, D., and P. Saldiva. 1999. "Urban Air Pollution Risks to Children: A Global Environmental Health Indicator." Environmental Health Notes. Washington, DC: World Resources Institute.

Denisov, N., and L. Christoffersen. 2001. "Impact of Environmental Information on Decision-Making Processes and the Environment." Occasional Paper 01-2001. Arendal, Norway: UNEP and GRID-Arendal.

Dodds, S., W.B. Chambers, and N. Kanie. 2002. "International Environmental Governance: The Question of Reform: Key Issues and Proposals, Preliminary Findings." Tokyo, Japan: United Nations University Institute of Advanced Studies. Cited 12 May 2003. On-line at: http://www.ias.unu.edu/binaries/NYPrepComReport3.pdf.

Dubash, N., ed. 2002. *Power Politics: Equity and Environment in Electricity Reform*. Washington, DC: World Resources Institute.

Dupar, M., and N. Badenoch. 2002. *Environment, Livelihoods, and Local Institutions: Decentralization in Mainland Southeast Asia*. Washington, DC: World Resources Institute.

Forest Watch Indonesia (FWI) and Global Forest Watch (GFW). 2002. *The State of the Forest: Indonesia*. Bogor, Indonesia: FWI and Washington, DC: GFW.

Frankel, J. 2000. "Globalization of the Economy." Pp. 45–71 in *Governance in a Globalizing World*. J. Nye and J. Donahue, eds. Washington, DC: Brookings Institution Press.

Freedom House. 2003. "Liberty's Expansion in a Turbulent World: Thirty Years of the Survey of Freedom." *Freedom in the World 2003: The Annual Survey of Political Rights and Civil Liberties*. Cited 12 May 2003. On-line at: http://www.freedomhouse.org/research/freeworld/2002/webessay2003.pdf.

Gleick, P., G. Wolff, E. Chalecki, and R. Reyes. 2002. *The New Economy of Water: The Risks and Benefits of Globalization and Privatization of Fresh Water*. Oakland, CA: Pacific Institute.

Global Environment Facility (GEF). 2002. "Focusing on the Global Environment: The First Decade of the GEF: Second Overall Performance Study (OPS2)." Washington, DC: GEF. Cited 24 June 2003. On-line at: http://www.gefweb.org/1Full_Report-FINAL-2-26-02.pdf.

Global Reporting Initiative (GRI). 2003. *Global Reporting Initiative: Organisations Using the Guidelines*. Website. Cited 12 May 2003. On-line at http://www.globalreporting.org/guidelines/reporters_all.asp.

International Institute for Sustainable Development (IISD) and World Wildlife Fund (WWF). 2001. *Private Rights, Public Problems: A Guide to NAFTA's Controversial Chapter on Investor Rights*. Winnipeg, Manitoba, Canada: IISD.

Klopp, J. 2000. "Pilfering the Public: the Problem of Land Grabbing in Contemporary Kenya." *Africa Today* 47(1). Cited 20 May 2003. On-line at: http://iupjournals.org/africatoday/aft47-1.html.

La Viña, A., G. Hoff, and A. DeRose. 2003. "The Outcomes of Johannesburg: Assessing the World Summit on Sustainable Development." *SAIS Review* 23(1):53–70.

Lieberthal, K. 1997. "China's Governing System and its Impact on Environmental Policy Implementation." *China Environment Series* 1:3–8.

Maurer, C., and R. Bhandari. 2000. *The Climate of Export Credit Agencies*. Climate Notes. Washington, DC: World Resources Institute.

Owen, D. 2001. "Second Chance for Private Water?" *Privatisation International* 149:14–17.

Ribot, J. 2002. *Democratic Decentralization of Natural Resources: Institutionalizing Popular Participation*. Washington, DC: World Resources Institute.

Rose, A. 2000. "Does a Currency Union Boost International Trade?" *California Management Review* 42(2):52–62.

Scorecard. 2003. Website. Cited 8 May 2003. On-line at http://www.scorecard.org.

Streck, C. 2001. "The Global Environment Facility—A Role Model for International Governance?" *Global Environmental Politics* 1(2):71–94.

Transparency International. 2003. Website. Cited 15 May 2003. On-line at http://www.transparency.org/.

Union of International Associations (UIA). 2000. "International Organizations by Year and Type 1909–1999." *Yearbook of International Organizations*. Cited 28 January 2003. On-line at: http://www.uia.org/statistics/organizations/ytb299.php.

Union of International Associations (UIA). 2001. *Yearbook of International Organizations 2001–2002*. New York: Saur.

United Nations Department of Economic and Social Affairs (DESA). 2003. *Economic and Social Council: Non-Governmental Organizations Section*. Website. Cited 8 May 2003. On-line at http://www.un.org/esa/coordination/ngo/ngosection.htm.

Upton, S. 2002. "The International Framework for Action—Is the CSD the Best We Can Do?" Pp. 20–29 in *Words Into Action*. L. Chatterjee, ed. Washington, DC: International Institute for Environment and Development (IIED).

Walsh, D. 2002. "Kenyans Fear Harvest of Tree-cutting." *Boston Globe* (10 February):A4.

Willetts, P., ed. 1996. *The Conscience of the World: The Influence of Non-Governmental Organisations in the UN System*. London: Hurst and Washington.

Willetts, P. 2002. "The Growth in the Number of NGOs in Consultative Status with the Economic and Social Council of the United Nations." Cited 8 May 2003. On-line at: http://www.staff.city.ac.uk/p.willetts/NGOS/NGO-GRPH.HTM#data.

Wolfensohn, J. 1996. "People and Development." Annual Meeting Address. Washington, DC: World Bank. 1 October. Cited 15 May 2003. On-line at: http://www.worldbank.org/html/extdr/extme/jdwams96.htm.

World Bank. 1997. *Clear Water, Blue Skies: China's Environment in the New Century*. Washington, DC: World Bank.

World Bank. 2002a. *Global Development Finance 2002: Financing the Poorest Countries*. Washington, DC: World Bank.

World Bank. 2002b. *Globalization, Growth, and Poverty: Building an Inclusive World Economy*. A World Bank Policy Research Report. New York: Oxford University Press.

World Bank. 2003. *World Development Indicators*. Database. Cited 12 February 2003. On-line at http://www.worldbank.org/data/onlinedbs/onlinedbases.htm.

Box 2.1 Armed Conflict: Killing Governance

Blom, A., and J. Yamindou. 2001. *A Brief History of Armed Conflict and its Impact on Biodiversity in the Central African Republic (CAR)*. Washington, DC: Biodiversity Support Program.

Creative Associates International Inc. (CAII), and the Greater Horn of Africa Initiative. 1997. *Preventing and Mitigating Violent Conflicts: A Revised Guide for Practitioners*. Website. Cited 4 February 2003. On-line at http://www.caii-dc.com/ghai.

Global Witness. 2003. Website. Cited 4 February 2003. On-line at http://www.globalwitness.org.

Hatton, J., M. Couto, and J. Oglethorpe. 2001. *Biodiversity and War: A Case Study from Mozambique*. Washington, DC: Biodiversity Support Program.

Interdisciplinary Research Programme on Root Causes of Human Rights Violations (PIOOM). 2002. "World Conflict & Human Rights Map 2000–2001." Databank. Leiden, The Netherlands: PIOOM. Cited 19 June 2003. On-line at: http://www.iimcr.org/imgs/conflictmap%202001-g.pdf.

Jacobs, M., and C. Schloeder. 2001. *Impacts of Conflict on Biodiversity and Protected Areas in Ethiopia*. Washington, DC: Biodiversity Support Program.

Kalpers, J. 2001. *Overview of Armed Conflict and Biodiversity in Sub-Saharan Africa: Impacts, Mechanisms and Responses*. Washington, DC: Biodiversity Support Program.

Matthew, R., M. Halle, and J. Switzer, eds. 2002. *Conserving the Peace: Resources, Livelihoods and Security*. Winnipeg, Manitoba, Canada: International Institute for Sustainable Development.

McNeely, J. 2000. "War and Biodiversity: An Assessment of Impacts." Pp. 353–369 in *The Environmental Consequences of War: Legal, Economic, and Scientific Perspectives*. J. Austin and C. Bruch, eds. Cambridge: Cambridge University Press.

Messer, E., M. Cohen, and J. D'Costa. 2000. "Armed Conflict and Hunger." *Hunger Notes Online* Fall 2000. Cited 19 March 2003. On-line at: http://www.worldhunger.org/articles/fall2000/messer1.htm.

Oglethorpe, J. 2002. Director, Conservation Strategies Unit, World Wildlife Fund. Personal Communication. E-mail. 30 December.

Omar, S., E. Briskey, R. Misak, and A. Asem. 2000. "The Gulf War Impact on the Terrestrial Environment of Kuwait: An Overview." Pp. 316–337 in *The Environmental Consequences of War: Legal, Economic, and Scientific Perspectives*. J. Austin and C. Bruch, eds. Cambridge: Cambridge University Press.

Orr, R. 2002. "Governing When Chaos Rules: Enhancing Governance and Participation." *The Washington Quarterly* 25(4): 139–152.

Paul Richards Technology and Agricultural Development Group (PRTADG). 1999. "The Silent Casualties of War." *The UNESCO Courier* July/August:12–14.

Plumptre, A., M. Masozera, and A. Vedder. 2001. *The Impact of Civil War on the Conservation of Protected Areas in Rwanda*. Washington, DC: Biodiversity Support Program.

Regional Environmental Center (REC). 1997. *Problems, Progress and Possibilities: A Needs Assessment of Environmental NGOs in Central and Eastern Europe*. Szentendre, Hungary: REC.

Renner, M. 2002. *The Anatomy of Resource Wars*. Worldwatch Paper 162. Washington, DC: Worldwatch.

Shambaugh, J., J. Oglethorpe, and R. Ham with contributions from S. Tognetti. 2001. *The Trampled Grass: Mitigating the Impacts of Armed Conflict on the Environment*. Washington, DC: Biodiversity Support Program.

Smith, D. 2001. "Trends and Causes of Armed Conflicts." *Berghof Handbook for Conflict Transformation*. Berlin: Berghof Research Center for Constructive Conflict Management. Cited 20 March 2003. On-line at: http://www.berghof-handbook.net/smith/final.pdf.

Squire, C. 2001. *Sierra Leone's Biodiversity and the Civil War.* Washington, DC: Biodiversity Support Program.

Stockholm International Peace Research Institute (SIPRI). 2002. "SIPRI Yearbook 2002." Chapter Summaries. Cited 4 February 2003. On-line at: http://editors.sipri.se/pubs/yb02/pr02.html.

United Nations Environment Programme (UNEP). 2002. *Global Environment Outlook 3.* London: Earthscan.

United Nations Environment Programme (UNEP). 2003. *Afghanistan: Post-Conflict Environmental Assessment.* Geneva, Switzerland: UNEP.

United Nations Environment Programme (UNEP), and United Nations Centre for Human Settlements (UNCHS). 1999. *The Kosovo Conflict: Consequences for the Environment and Human Settlements.* Geneva, Switzerland: UNEP and UNCHS.

United Nations High Commission on Refugees (UNHCR). 2002. *Statistical Yearbook 2001.* Geneva, Switzerland: UNHCR.

United Nations Population Division. 2003. "International Migration 2002." Wallchart. New York: United Nations. On-line at: http://www.un.org/esa/population/publications/ittmig2002/Migration2002.pdf.

Box 2.2 Open Accounts? The Transparency of Multilateral Development Banks

Fox, J., and L.D. Brown, eds. 1998. *The Struggle for Accountability: The World Bank, NGOs, and Grassroots Movements.* Cambridge, MA and London: MIT Press.

Gwin, C. 2001. "Development Assistance." Pp: 151–195 in *Managing Global Issues: Lessons Learned.* P.J. Simmons and C. Oudraat, eds. Washington, DC: Carnegie Endowment for International Peace.

Maurer, C., S. Ehlers, and A. Buchman. 2003. *Aligning Commitments: Public Participation, International Decision-Making, and the Environment.* WRI Issue Brief. Washington, DC: World Resources Institute.

Organisation for Economic Co-operation and Development (OECD). 2002. "Development Cooperation Report 2002, Statistical Annex, Table 1." Paris: OECD. Cited 20 March 2003. On-line at: http://www.oecd.org/EN/document/0,,EN-document-59-2-no-1-2674-0,00.html.

Tussie, D., and M.F. Tuozzo. 2001. "Opportunities and Constraints for Civil Society Participation in Multilateral Lending Operations: Lessons from Latin America." Pp: 105–117 in *Global Citizen Action.* M. Edwards and J. Gaventa, eds. London: Earthscan.

World Bank. 2002a. *Global Development Finance 2002: Financing the Poorest Countries.* Washington, DC: World Bank.

World Bank. 2002b. *World Bank Annual Report 2002. Vol. 1, Year in Review.* Washington, DC: World Bank.

Box 2.3 More Democracy, Better Environment?

Barrett, S., and K. Graddy. 2000. "Freedom, Growth, and the Environment." *Environment and Development Economics* 3:433–456.

Esty, D., J. Goldstone, T. Gurr, B. Harff, M. Levy, G. Dabelko, P. Surko, and A. Unger. 1998. "State Failure Task Force Report: Phase II Findings." McLean, VA: Science Applications International Corporation.

Forest Watch Indonesia (FWI) and Global Forest Watch (GFW). 2002. *The State of the Forest: Indonesia.* Bogor, Indonesia: FWI and Washington, DC: GFW.

Freedom House. 1999. "Democracy's Century: A Survey of Global Political Change in the 20th Century." Press Release. Cited 15 May 2003. On-line at: http://www.freedomhouse.org/reports/century.html.

Freedom House. 2003. "Liberty's Expansion in a Turbulent World: Thirty Years of the Survey of Freedom." *Freedom in the World 2003: The Annual Survey of Political Rights and Civil Liberties.* Cited 12 May 2003. On-line at: http://www.freedomhouse.org/research/freeworld/2002/webessay.pdf.

Gore, A. 1992. *Earth in the Balance: Ecology and the Human Spirit.* New York: Houghton Mifflin.

Grossman, G., and A. Kreuger. 1995. "Economic Growth and the Environment." *Quarterly Journal of Economics* 110:353–377.

Max-Neef, M. 1995. "Economic Growth and Quality of Life: A Threshold Hypothesis." *Ecological Economics* 15:115–118.

Petkova, E., and P. Veit. 2000. *Environmental Accountability Beyond the Nation-State: The Implications of the Aarhus Convention.* Environmental Governance Note. Washington, DC: World Resources Institute.

Torras, M., and J. Boyce. 1998. "Income, Inequality, and Pollution: A Reassessment of the Environmental Kuznets Curve." *Ecological Economics* 25:147–160.

Box 2.4 Undue Influence: Corruption and Natural Resources

Andvig, J., O. Fjeldstad, I. Amudsen, T. Sissener, and T. Søreide. 2000. "Research on Corruption: A Policy Oriented Survey." Bergen, Norway: Chr. Michelsen Institute (CMI) and Norwegian Institute of International Affairs (NUPI).

Ascher, W. 2000. "Understanding Why Governments in Developing Countries Waste Natural Resources." *Environment* 42(2):8–18.

Bryant, D., D. Nielsen, and L. Tangley. 1997. *The Last Frontier Forests: Ecosystems and Economies on the Edge.* Washington, DC: World Resources Institute.

Callister, D. 1999. "Corrupt and Illegal Activities in the Forestry Sector: Current Understandings, and Implications for World Bank Forest Policy: Draft for Discussion." Washington, DC: World Bank. Cited 19 May 2003. On-line at: http://lnweb18.worldbank.org/eap/eap.nsf/Attachments/FLEG_OB6/$File/OB+6+FPR+Paper+-+Illegal+Actions+-+Debra+Callister.pdf.

Contreras-Hermosilla, A. 2001. "Illegal Forest Activities in the Asia Pacific Rim." Markets for Forest Conservation Brief. Washington, DC: Forest Trends. Cited 19 May 2003. On-line at: http://www.forest-trends.org/resources/pdf/pri_illegallogging2.pdf.

Contreras-Hermosilla, A., and M. Rios. 2002. "Social, Environmental and Economic Dimensions of Forest Policy Reforms in Bolivia." Washington, DC: Forest Trends and Bogor, Indonesia: Center for International Forestry Research. Cited 19 May 2003. On-line at: http://www.forest-trends.org/whoweare/pdf/Bolivia English.pdf.

Eigen, P. 2002. "Multinationals' Bribery Goes Unpunished." *International Herald Tribune* (12 November):6.

Food and Agriculture Organization of the United Nations (FAO). 2001. *State of the World's Forests 2001.* Rome: FAO.

Forest Watch Indonesia (FWI) and Global Forest Watch (GFW). 2002. *The State of the Forest: Indonesia.* Bogor, Indonesia: FWI and Washington, DC: GFW.

Global Witness. 2002. *All the Presidents' Men: The Devastating Story of Oil and Banking in Angola's Privatised War.* London: Global Witness.

Gray, C., and D. Kaufman. 1998. "Corruption and Development." Pp: 21–31 in *New Perspectives on Combating Corruption.* Transparency International and World Bank, eds. Washington, DC: Transparency International and World Bank.

Hawley, S. 2000. "Exporting Corruption: Privatisation, Multinationals and Bribery." Briefing Paper 19. Dorset, UK: The Corner House.

Kaufmann, D. 1997. "Corruption: The Facts." *Foreign Policy* 107: 114–131.

Mbaku, J. 1996. "Bureaucratic Corruption in Africa: The Futility of Cleanups." *Cato Journal* 16(1):99–118.

Organisation for Economic Co-operation and Development (OECD). 1998. "Convention on Combating Bribery of Foreign Public Officials in International Business Transactions." Cited 16 June 2003. On-line at: http://www.imf.org/external/np/gov/2001/eng/091801.pdf.

Organisation for Economic Co-operation and Development (OECD). 2003. "Steps Taken and Planned Future Actions by Participating Countries to Ratify and Implement the Convention on Combating

Bribery of Foreign Public Officials in International Business Transactions." Paris: OECD. Cited 19 May 2003. On-line at: http://www.oecd.org/pdf/M00025000/M00025443.pdf.

Pearce, J. 2002. "IMF: Angola's 'Missing Millions'." *BBC News Online*. 18 October. Cited 19 May 2003. On-line at: http://news.bbc.co.uk/2/hi/world/africa/2338669.stm.

Schloss, M. 1998. "Combating Corruption for Development: The Role of Government, Business, and Civil Society." Pp: 1–20 in *New Perspectives on Combating Corruption*. Transparency International and World Bank, eds. Washington, DC: Transparency International and World Bank.

Smith, W. 2003. "Combating Illegal Logging: A Review of Initiatives and Monitoring Tools." Internal working draft. Washington, DC: World Resources Institute.

Tanzi, V. 1995. "Corruption: Arm's-length Relationships and Markets." Pp: 161–180 in *The Economics of Organised Crime*. G. Fiorentini and S. Pelzman, eds. Cambridge, UK: Cambridge University Press.

Tanzi, V., and H. Davoodi. 1998. "Roads to Nowhere: How Corruption in Public Investment Hurts Growth." Pp: 33–42 in *New Perspectives on Combating Corruption*. Transparency International and World Bank, eds. Washington, DC: Transparency International and World Bank.

Transparency International. 2001. *Global Corruption Report 2001*. Berlin: Transparency International.

Transparency International. 2002. "Corrupt Political Elites and Unscrupulous Investors Kill Sustainable Growth in Its Tracks, Highlights New Index." Press Release. Berlin: Transparency International. 28 August. Cited 19 May 2003. On-line at: http://www.transparency.org/pressreleases_archive/2002/2002.08.28.cpi.en.html.

Vogl, F. 1998. "The Supply Side of Global Bribery." Pp: 55–64 in *New Perspectives on Combating Corruption*. Transparency International and World Bank, eds. Washington, DC: Transparency International and World Bank.

Walsh, D. 2002. "Kenyans Fear Harvest of Tree-cutting." *Boston Globe* (10 February):A4.

World Bank. 2003. *World Bank Listing of Ineligible Firms: Fraud and Corruption*. Website. Cited 19 May 2003. On-line at http://www.worldbank.org/html/opr/procure/debarr.html.

Box 2.5 Information Technology: A Map to Accountability

Bryant, D. Director, Global Forest Watch, World Resources Institute. 2001. Personal Communication. 18 December.

Global Forest Watch. 2000. *An Overview of Logging in Cameroon*. Washington, DC: World Resources Institute.

Vasset, P. 2000. "Les Déboiseurs." *La Lettre Du Continent* 356.

Vasset, P. 2001. "Les Barons du Bois." *La Lettre Du Continent* 374.

World Resources Institute. 2002. "WRI, Cameroon Ink Pact to Monitor Forests, Curb Illegal Logging." Press Release. 6 June. Cited 19 March 2003. On-line at: http://newsroom.wri.org/newsreleases.cfm.

Chapter 3 Text

African Centre for Technology Studies (ACTS), Environmental Law Institute (ELI), Lawyers' Environmental Action Team (LEAT), and World Resources Institute (WRI). 2000. "Environmental Procedural Rights in Africa: An Agenda for Reform." An Information Document Prepared for Africa's Ministers of the Environment at the Fifth Conference of the Parties to the Convention on Biological Diversity, Nairobi, Kenya, 15–26 May.

Banisar, D. 2002. *Freedom of Information and Access to Government Records Around the World*. Washington, DC: Privacy International.

National Security Archive. 2001. "The U.S. Freedom of Information Act at 35: Nearly 2 Million Requests Last Year at a Cost of One Dollar per Citizen." *National Security Archive Electronic Briefing Book 51*. Cited 19 March 2003. On-line at: http://www.gwu.edu/~nsarchiv/NSAEBB/NSAEBB51.

Box 3.1 Measuring Access

Kaufmann, D., A. Kray, and P. Zoido-Lobatón. 2002. "Governance Matters II: Updated Indicators for 2000/01." Policy Research Working Paper Series, No. 2772. Washington, DC: The World Bank. Cited 18 June 2003. On-line at: http://econ.worldbank.org/files/11783_wps2772.pdf.

Prescott-Allen, R. 2001. *The Wellbeing of Nations: A Country-by-Country Index of Quality of Life and the Environment*. Washington, DC: Island Press.

Russian Journalists' Union. 2001. *General Expertise: Freedom of Speech in Russia Project*. Website. Cited 20 March 2003. On-line at http://www.freepress.ru/win.

United Nations Commission on Sustainable Development (UNCSD). 2002. *Indicators of Sustainable Development: Guidelines and Methodologies – 2001*. New York: United Nations.

United Nations Development Programme (UNDP). 2002. *Human Development Report 2002: Deepening Democracy in a Fragmented World*. New York: Oxford University Press.

World Economic Forum in collaboration with the Yale Center for Environmental Law and Policy, Yale University and the Center for International Earth Science Information Network, Columbia University. 2002. "2002 Environmental Sustainability Index." New York: Yale Center for Environmental Law and Policy. Cited 18 June 2003. On-line at: http://www.ciesin.columbia.edu/indicators/ ESI.

Box 3.2 The Merits of Meaningful Participation

Beierle, T.C., and J. Cayford. 2002. *Democracy in Practice: Public Participation in Environmental Decisions*. Washington, DC: Resources for the Future.

Fülöp, S. Executive Director and Managing Attorney, Environmental Management and Law Association. 2002. Personal Communication. E-mail. November 5.

Box 3.3 Comparing Environmental Impact Assessment Laws in Latin America and the Caribbean

Ibarra, L. 2002. "Public Participation Provisions in Environmental Impact Assessment Law and Policies of Latin American and the Caribbean Countries." Mimeo. Prepared for the World Resources Institute.

Box 3.4 Access and the Internet

Environmental Law Alliance Worldwide (E-LAW). 2002. " 'Right to Know' Takes Hold in Mexico." *E-Law Impact* 22 August. Cited 19 March 2003. On-line at: http://www.elaw.org/custom/custompages/viewpage.asp?webpage_id=19&profile_id=1191.

International Telecommunications Union (ITU). 2002. *World Telecommunications Indicators Database*. Geneva: ITU.

Population Division of the Department of Economic and Social Affairs of the United Nations Secretariat. 2002. *World Population Prospects: The 2000 Revision. Dataset on CD-ROM*. New York: United Nations.

United Nations Economic and Social Council. 2000. "Furthering the Implementation of the Aarhus Convention through the Use of Electronic Tools and Media." CEP/WG.5/2000/11. Economic Commission for Europe, Committee on Environmental Policy. May 2.

World Bank. 2002. *World Development Indicators 2002*. Washington, DC: World Bank.

Box 3.5 Public Interest Groups in Africa: Supported or Thwarted?

Viet, P. 1999. "Protecting Environmental Advocacy NGOs in Africa." *Innovation* 6(2).

Chapter 4 Text

Anand, P. 2000. "Co-operation and the Urban Environment: An Exploration." *Journal of Development Studies* 36(5):30–58.

Anheier, H., M. Galsius, and M. Kaldor, eds. 2001. *Global Civil Society 2001*. Oxford: Oxford University Press.

Atkinson, R., and J. Messing. 2002. *Planning for Sustainability: Supporting NGO Self-financing Ventures*. Szentendre, Hungary: Regional Environmental Center for Central and Eastern Europe (REC).

Baron, B. 2002. "Opening Remarks for the Workshop on the Legal Framework for Civil Society in East and Southeast Asia." Washington, DC: Catholic University of America. 12 April. Cited 20 March 2003. On-line at: http://www.asiafoundation.org/pdf/bbaron_41202.pdf.

Belize Audubon Society (BAS). 2003. *National Parks Managed by the Belize Audubon Society*. Website. Cited 18 March 2003. On-line at http://www.belizeaudubon.org/html/parks.html.

Boli, J., and G. Thomas, eds. 1999. *Constructing World Culture: International Nongovernmental Organizations since 1875*. Stanford, CA: Stanford University Press.

Boyle, A., and M. Anderson, eds. 1996. *Human Rights Approaches to Environmental Protection*. New York: Oxford University Press.

Brown, L.D. Lecturer in Public Policy and Associate Director for International Programs, John F. Kennedy School of Government, Harvard University. 2002. Personal Communication. E-mail. 17 November.

Brown, L.D., and A. Kalegaonkar. 2002. "Support Organizations and the Evolution of the NGO Sector." *Nonprofit and Voluntary Sector Quarterly* 31(2):231–258.

Brown, L.D., S. Khagram, M. Moore, and P. Frumkin. 2000. "Globalization, NGOs and Multi-Sectoral Relations." The Hauser Center for Nonprofit Organizations, Harvard University, Working Paper No. 1. Cited 18 June 2003. On-line at: http://papers.ssrn.com/sol3/papers.cfm?abstract_id=253110.

Carothers, T. 1999. *Aiding Democracy Abroad: the Learning Curve*. Washington, DC: Carnegie Endowment for International Peace.

Christensen, J. 2002. "Fiscal Accountability Concerns Come to Conservation." *New York Times* (5 November):D2.

Diamond, L. 1994. "Rethinking Civil Society: Toward Democratic Consolidation." *Journal of Democracy* 5(3):4–17.

Edwards, M., and J. Gaventa, eds. 2001. *Global Citizen Action*. London: Earthscan.

Florini, A., ed. 2000. *The Third Force: The Rise of Transnational Civil Society*. Washington, DC: Japan Center for International Exchange and the Carnegie Endowment for International Peace.

Fowler, A. 1997. *Striking a Balance: A Guide to Enhancing the Effectiveness of Nongovernmental Organizations in International Development*. London: Earthscan.

Gan, L. 2000. "Energy Development and Environmental NGOs: The Asian Perspective." Pp: 109–129 in *The Global Environment in the Twenty-First Century: Prospects for International Cooperation*. P. Chasek, ed. New York: United Nations University.

Gemmill, B., and A. Bamidele-Izu. 2002. "The Role of NGOs and Civil Society in Global Environmental Governance." Pp: 77–99 in *Global Environmental Governance: Options & Opportunities*. D. Esty and M. Ivanova, eds. New Haven, CT: Yale School of Forestry and Environmental Studies.

Global Witness. 2002. *All the Presidents' Men: The Devastating Story of Oil and Banking in Angola's Privatised War*. London: Global Witness.

Hanson, C. Senior Associate, World Resources Institute. 2003. Personal Communication. E-mail. 19 May.

Ho, P. 2001. "Greening Without Conflict? Environmentalism, NGOs and Civil Society in China." *Development and Change* 32:893–921.

Independent Sector. 2001. *The New Nonprofit Almanac in Brief: Facts and Figures on the Independent Sector in 2001*. Washington, DC: Independent Sector.

InterAction. 2003. Website. Cited 20 March 2003. On-line at http://www.interaction.org/.

Jiang, J. 2002. "Nature Conservancy, Paper Mill Reach Deal." *Boston Globe* (2 September):B2.

Jordan, L., and P. van Tuijl. 2000. "Political Responsibility in Transnational NGO Advocacy." *World Development* 28(12): 2051–2065.

Jubilee 2000. 2003. *About Jubilee 2000*. Website. Cited 29 January 2003. On-line at http://www.jubilee2000uk.org/about/about.htm.

Keohane, R., and J. Nye. 2001. *Power and Interdependence*. Glenview, IL: Scott Foresman.

Khagram, S. 2000. "Toward Democratic Governance for Sustainable Development: Transnational Civil Society Organizing Around Big Dams." Pp: 83–114 in *The Third Force: The Rise of Transnational Civil Society*. A. Florini, ed. Washington, DC: Japan Center for International Exchange and the Carnegie Endowment for International Peace.

Kothari, A. 2000. "Conserving Nature with Communities: Lessons from Real Life Experiences in South Asia." A paper presented at the 2nd World Conservation Congress of IUCN, Amman, Jordan, 3–11 October.

Kovach, H., C. Neligan, and S. Burall. 2003. *The Global Accountability Report 2003: Power Without Accountability?* London: One World Trust.

Kunguru, J., D. Kokonya, and C. Otiato. 2002. "Evaluation of the Development Cooperation Activities of Finnish NGOs in Kenya: Final Report." Helsinki: Ministry for Foreign Affairs of Finland. Cited 14 February 2003. On-line at: http://global.finland.fi/julkaisut/hae_evaluointi.php?id=37&kieli=1.

Kuroda, K. 1998. "The Current Status of Civil Society in Japan." Pp: 7–9 in *A Changing Asia: Women in Emerging Civil Societies*. San Francisco, CA: The Asia Foundation.

Lissu, T. 2002. "Interrogating Tanzania's Gold Boom: A 3-Year Inquiry into the Economics, Politics, Environment and Governance in Tanzania's Goldfields." A WRI Lecture. Washington, DC: World Resources Institute. 20 September.

Mathews, J. 1997. "Power Shift: The Rise of Global Civil Society." *Foreign Affairs* 76(1):50–67.

Mekata, M. 2000. "Building Partnerships Toward a Common Goal: Experiences of the International Campaign to Ban Landmines." Pp: 143–176 in *The Third Force: The Rise of Transnational Civil Society*. A. Florini, ed. Washington, DC: Japan Center for International Exchange and the Carnegie Endowment for International Peace.

Norwegian Forum for Environment and Development (FwF). 2002. "Forum's Position Paper on Freshwater." Oslo, Norway: FwF. Cited 7 February 2003. On-line at: http://www.verdenstoppmotet2002.no/Posisjonspapier/Freshwater.pdf.

Organisation for Economic Co-operation and Development (OECD). 1999. *Environment in the Transition to a Market Economy: Progress in the Central and Eastern Europe and the New Independent States*. Paris: OECD.

Paxton, P. 2002. "Social Capital and Democracy: An Interdependent Relationship." *American Sociological Review* 76:254–277.

Pesticide Action Network North America (PANNA). 2001. "Farmers and NGOs Monitoring the World Bank in Indonesia Get Results." *Pesticide Action Network Updates Service (PANUPS)*. Cited 19 March 2003. On-line at: http://panna.igc.org/resources/panups/panup_20010511.dv.html.

Petkova, E., C. Maurer, N. Henninger, and F. Irwin. 2002. *Closing the Gap: Information, Participation, and Justice in Decision-making for the Environment*. Washington, DC: World Resources Institute.

Pinter, F. 2001. "Funding Global Civil Society Organizations." Pp: 195–217 in *Global Civil Society 2001*. H. Anheier, M. Galsius and M. Kaldor, eds. Oxford: Oxford University Press.

Putnam, R. 1993. *Making Democracy Work: Civic Traditions in Modern Italy*. Princeton, NJ: Princeton University Press.

Regional Environmental Center (REC). 1997. *Problems, Progress and Possibilities: A Needs Assessment of Environmental NGOs in Central and Eastern Europe*. Szentendre, Hungary: REC.

Risse, T. 2000. "The Power of Norms Versus the Norms of Power: Transnational Civil Society and Human Rights." Pp: 177–209 in

The Third Force: The Rise of Transnational Civil Society. A. Florini, ed. Washington, DC: Japan Center for International Exchange and the Carnegie Endowment for International Peace.

Robinson, D. 1997. "New Zealand." Pp. 100–103 in *The New Civic Atlas: Profiles of Civil Society in 60 Countries.* L. Poinier, ed. Washington, DC: Civicus.

Runyon, C. 1999. "Action on the Front Lines." *World Watch* November/December:12–21.

Salamon, L. 1994. "The Rise of the Nonprofit Sector: A Global 'Associational Revolution'." *Foreign Affairs* 73(4):109–123.

Salamon, L., and H. Anheier. 1996. "The Nonprofit Sector: A New Global Force." Working Paper of the Johns Hopkins Comparative Nonprofit Sector Project, 21. Baltimore, MD: The Johns Hopkins Institute for Policy Studies. Cited 18 June 2003. On-line at: http://www.jhu.edu/~ccss/pubs/pdf/globalfo.pdf.

Salamon, L., H. Anheier, R. List, S. Toepler, and S. Sokolowski, eds. 1999. *Global Civil Society: Dimensions of the Nonprofit Sector.* Baltimore, MD: Johns Hopkins Center for Civil Society Studies.

Secretariat of the United Nations Convention to Combat Desertification (UNCCD). 2003. *Conference Sessions Official Documents.* Cited 3 February 2003. On-line at http://www.unccd.int/cop/officialdocs/menu.php.

Silk, T., ed. 1999. *Philanthropy and Law in Asia: A Comparative Study of the Nonprofit Legal Systems in Ten Asia Pacific Societies.* San Francisco: Jossey-Bass Publishers.

Sinclair, R. Capacity Development Consultant, Nairobi, Kenya. 2002. Personal Communication. E-mail. 12 November.

Swilling, M., and B. Russell. 2002. *The Size and Scope of the Nonprofit Sector in South Africa.* Durban, South Africa: Centre for Civil Society, University of Natal.

Union of International Associations (UIA). 2000. "International Organizations by Year and Type 1909–1999." *Yearbook of International Organizations.* Cited 28 January 2003. On-line at: http://www.uia.org/statistics/organizations/ytb299.php.

Union of International Associations (UIA). 2001. *Yearbook of International Organizations 2001–2002.* New York: Saur.

United Nations Development Programme (UNDP). 2002. *Human Development Report 2002: Deepening Democracy in a Fragmented World.* New York: Oxford University Press.

Valderrama, M. 1999. "Latin American NGOs in an Age of Scarcity When Quality Matters." A paper presented at the Third International NGO Conference, Birmingham, UK, 10–13 January.

Vanasselt, W. 2002. "Promoting North-South NGO Collaboration in Environmental Negotiations." Pp. 154–171 in *Transboundary Environmental Negotiation: New Approaches to Global Cooperation.* L. Susskind, W. Moomaw and K. Gallagher, eds. San Francisco: Jossey-Bass.

Wapner, P. 1997. "Governance in Global Civil Society." Pp. 65–84 in *Global Governance: Drawing Insights from the Environmental Experience.* O. Young, ed. Cambridge, MA: MIT Press.

Weiss, T., and L. Gordenker, eds. 1996. *NGOs, the UN, and Global Governance.* Boulder: Lynne Rienner.

Willetts, P. 2002. "The Growth in the Number of NGOs in Consultative Status with the Economic and Social Council of the United Nations." Cited 8 May 2003. On-line at: http://www.staff.city.ac.uk/p.willetts/NGOS/NGO-GRPH.HTM#data.

Wixley, S. 2002. "Campaign Celebrates Progress on Mine Ban Treaty Fifth Anniversary." *ICBL News* 3 December. Cited 20 March 2003. On-line at: http://www.icbl.org/news/2002/263.php.

World Bank. 1996. *Investing in People: The World Bank in Action.* Cited 29 January 2003. On-line at http://www.worldbank.org/html/extdr/hnp/health/inv_ppl/contents.htm.

World Bank. 1997. *Cooperation between the World Bank and NGOs: FY96 Progress Report.* Washington, DC: World Bank.

World Bank. 2001. *The World Bank Annual Report 2001: Volume 1, Year in Review.* Washington, DC: World Bank.

World Bank and The International Center for Nonprofit Law (ICNL). 1997. *Handbook on Good Practices for Laws Relating to Non-Governmental Organizations.* Environment Department Work in Progress.

World Watch. 1999. "NGO–Friend or Foe." *World Watch* March/April:2.

World Wide Fund for Nature (WWF). 2003. Website. Cited 28 January 2003. On-line at http://www.worldwildlife.org.

Zarsky, L., ed. 2002. *Human Rights and the Environment: Conflicts and Norms in a Globalizing World.* London: Earthscan.

Box 4.1 Democracy and Civic Renaissance in Central and Eastern Europe

Atkinson, R., and J. Messing. 2002. *Planning for Sustainability: Supporting NGO Self-financing Ventures.* Szentendre, Hungary: Regional Environmental Center for Central and Eastern Europe (REC).

Organisation for Economic Co-operation and Development (OECD). 1999. *Environment in the Transition to a Market Economy: Progress in the Central and Eastern Europe and the New Independent States.* Paris: Organisation for Economic Co-operation and Development (OECD).

Regional Environmental Center (REC). 1997. *Problems, Progress and Possibilities: A Needs Assessment of Environmental NGOs in Central and Eastern Europe.* Szentendre, Hungary: REC.

Salamon, L., H. Anheier, R. List, S. Toepler, and S. Sokolowski, eds. 1999. *Global Civil Society: Dimensions of the Nonprofit Sector.* Baltimore, MD: Johns Hopkins Center for Civil Society Studies.

Tolles, R., and A. Beckmann. 2000. *A Decade of Nurturing the Grassroots: The Environmental Partnership for Central Europe, 1991–2000.* Staré Mesto, Czech Republic: Environmental Partnership for Central Europe.

Box 4.2 Partnering for the Environment in Central Europe

Beckmann, A. 2000. *Caring for the Land: A Decade of Promoting Landscape Stewardship in Central Europe.* Staré Mesto, Czech Republic: Environmental Partnership for Central European Consortium and QLF/Atlantic Center for the Environment.

Růžička, T. Project Manager, Nadace Partnerstvi / Environmental Partnership for Central Europe, Czech Republic. 2002. Personal Communication. 19 November.

Scsaurszki, T. Associate Program Officer, Czech Republic, Hungary, Poland, and Slovakia, C.S. Mott Foundation. 2002. Personal Communication. 10 December.

Tolles, R., and A. Beckmann. 2000. *A Decade of Nurturing the Grassroots: The Environmental Partnership for Central Europe, 1991–2000.* Staré Mesto, Czech Republic: Environmental Partnership for Central Europe.

Box 4.3 New Communication Tools for Environmental Empowerment

Bray, J. 1998. "Web Wars: NGOs, Companies and Governments in an Internet-Connected World." *Greener Management International* 24:115–129.

Freedom House. 2001. *How Free? The Web and the Press: The Annual Survey of Press Freedoms.* New York: Freedom House.

International Telecommunications Union (ITU). 2002. *World Telecommunications Indicators Database.* Geneva, Switzerland: ITU.

Keohane, R., and J. Nye. 2001. *Power and Interdependence.* Glenview, IL: Scott Foresman.

Naughton, J. 2001. "Contested Space: The Internet and Global Civil Society." Pp. 147–168 in *Global Civil Society 2001.* J. Anheier, M. Glasius and M. Kaldor, eds. Oxford: Oxford University Press.

Norris, P. 2001. *Digital Divide: Civic Engagement, Information Poverty, and the Internet Worldwide.* Cambridge: Cambridge University Press.

Pigato, M. 2001. "Information and Communication Technology, Poverty and Development in Sub-Saharan Africa and South Asia." Africa Region Working Paper Series 20. Washington, DC: World

Bank. Cited 18 June 2003. On-line at: http://www.worldbank.org/afr/wps/wp20.pdf.

Sinclair, R. Capacity Development Consultant, Nairobi, Kenya. 2002. Personal Communication. E-mail. 12 November.

Smith, P., and E. Smythe. 2000. "Globalization, Citizenship, and Technology: The MAI Meets the Internet." A paper presented at the 2000 International Studies Association Annual Meeting, Los Angeles, CA, 14–18 March. International Studies Association. Cited 16 January 2003. On-line at: http://www.ciaonet.org/isa/smp01.

United Nations Development Programme (UNDP). 2001. *Human Development Report 2001: Making New Technologies Work for Human Development*. New York: Oxford University Press.

Box 4.4 In a Clear Voice: Press and Internet Freedoms

Asian Development Bank (ADB). 2001. *Asian Environment Outlook 2001*. Manila: ADB.

Freedom House. 2001. *How Free? The Web and the Press: The Annual Survey of Press Freedoms*. New York: Freedom House.

Regional Environmental Center (REC). 2001. "International Law and the Baia Mare Cyanide Spill." Szentendre, Hungary: REC. Cited 16 January 2003. On-line at: http://www.rec.org/REC/Programs/EnvironmentalLaw/BaiaMareReport.PDF.

Sussman, L., and K. Karlekar. 2002. *The Annual Survey of Press Freedom 2002*. New York: Freedom House.

SustainAbility, United Nations Environment Programme (UNEP), and Ketchum. 2002. *Good News and Bad: The Media, Corporate Responsibility and Sustainable Development*. London: SustainAbility.

Box 4.5 African NGOs: A Kaleidoscope of Efforts

Government of Kenya Ministry of Health. 2001. *Health Management Information Systems: Report for the 1996–1999 Period*. Nairobi, Kenya: Ministry of Health, Health Management Information Systems.

Hakkarainen, O., H. Katsui, C. Kessey, T. Kontinen, T. Kyllonen, S. Rovaniemi, and R. Wamai. 2002. "Voices From the Southern Civil Societies: Interplay of National and Global Contexts in the Performance of Civil Society Organisations in the South: A Report Prepared for the Department for International Development Cooperation, the Ministry for Foreign Affairs of Finland." Helsinki, Finland: NGO Research Group, University of Finland. Cited 24 February 2003. On-line at: http://www.valt.helsinki.fi/kmi/Tutkimus/Projektit/voices/index.htm.

Sinclair, R. Capacity Development Consultant, Nairobi, Kenya. 2003. Personal Communication. E-Mail. 20 March.

Box 4.6 Russia's NGOs: Learning to Engage

Wernstedt, K. 2002a. "Environmental Management in the Russian Federation: A Next Generation Enigma." Discussion Paper 02-04. Washington, DC: Resources for the Future. Cited 17 June 2003. On-line at: http://www.rff.org/disc_papers/PDF_files/0204.pdf.

Wernstedt, K. 2002b. "Who is Protecting Russia's Natural Resources? Why Should We Care?" *Resources* 148:22–27.

Chapter 5 Text

Agrawal, A. 2001. "The Regulatory Community: Decentralization and the Environment in the Van Panchayats (Forest Councils) of Kumaon." *Mountain Research and Development* 21(3):208–211.

Agrawal, A., and J. Ribot. 1999. "Accountability in Decentralization: A Framework with South Asian and West African Cases." *Journal of Developing Areas* 33:473–502.

Brinkerhoff, D., and G. Honadle. 1996. "Co-Managing Natural Resources in Africa: Implementing Policy and Institutional Changes in Five Countries." Implementing Policy Change (IPC) Monograph No.4. Washington, DC: United States Agency for International Development (USAID).

Brunner, J., F. Seymour, N. Badenoch, and B. Ratner. 1999. "Forest Problems and Law Enforcement in Southeast Asia: The Role of Local Communities." Resources Policy Brief. Washington, DC: World Resources Institute.

Caldecott, J., and E. Lutz. 1998. "Decentralization and Biodiversity Conservation." Pp: 175–185 in *Agriculture and the Environment: Perspectives on Sustainable Rural Development*. E. Lutz, ed. Washington, DC: World Bank.

CAMPFIRE. 2003. *What is CAMPFIRE?* Website. Cited 13 June 2003. On-line at http://www.campfire-zimbabwe.org/more_01.html.

Contreras-Hermosilla, A., and M. Rios. 2002. "Social, Environmental and Economic Dimensions of Forest Policy Reforms in Bolivia." Washington, DC: Forest Trends and Bogor, Indonesia: Center for International Forestry Research. Cited 19 May 2003. On-line at: http://www.forest-trends.org/whoweare/pdf/Bolivia English.pdf.

Conyers, D. 2002. "Decentralization in Zimbabwe: A Local Perspective." *Public Administration and Development* 23(1):115-124.

Crook, R., and A. Sverrisson. 2001. "Decentralisation and Poverty-Alleviation in Developing Countries: A Comparative Analysis *or* is West Bengal Unique?" IDS Working Paper 130. Brighton, UK: Institute of Development Studies.

Department for International Development–United Kingdom (DFID), Directorate General for Development–European Commission (EC), United Nations Development Programme (UNDP), and World Bank. 2002. *Linking Poverty Reduction and Environmental Management: Policy Challenges and Opportunities*. Washington, DC: World Bank.

Dupar, M., and N. Badenoch. 2002. *Environment, Livelihoods, and Local Institutions: Decentralization in Mainland Southeast Asia*. Washington, DC: World Resources Institute.

Enters, T., and J. Anderson. 1999. "Rethinking the Decentralization and Devolution of Biodiversity Conservation." *Unasylva* 50(4). Cited 29 May 2003. On-line at: http://www.fao.org/docrep/x3030e/x3030e00.htm.

Goldsmith, W. 1999. "Participatory Budgeting in Brazil." Paper from the International Meeting on Democracy, Equality and Quality of Life, Puerto Alegre, Brazil, 5–8 December. Cited 28 May 2003. On-line at: http://www.plannersnetwork.org/htm/pub/working-papers/brazil/brazil_goldsmith.pdf.

International Council on Human Rights Policy (ICHRP). 2002. *Local Rule: Decentralisation and Human Rights*. Versoix, Switzerland: ICHRP.

Kaimowitz, D., and J. Ribot. 2002. "Services and Infrastructure Versus Natural Resource Management: Building a Discretionary Base for Democratic Decentralization." Paper prepared for the Conference on Decentralization and the Environment, Bellagio, Italy, 18–22 February.

Larson, A. 2002. "Decentralization and Natural Resource Management: A Nicaraguan Case Study." Paper prepared for the Conference on Decentralization and the Environment, Bellagio, Italy, 18–22 February.

Larson, A. 2003a. "Decentralization and Forest Management in Latin America: Toward a Working Model." Forthcoming. *Public Administration and Development*.

Larson, A. 2003b. Research Associate, Center for International Forestry Research, Indonesia and Nitlapan Research Institute, Universidad Centroamericana, Nicaragua. Personal Communication. E-mail. 5 May.

Manor, J. 2002. "Democratic Decentralization and the Issue of Equity." Paper prepared for the Conference on Decentralization and the Environment, Bellagio, Italy, 18–22 February.

Pacheco, P. 2002. "The Implications of Decentralization in Forest Management: Municipalities and Local Forest Users in Lowland Bolivia." Paper prepared for the Conference on Decentralization and the Environment, Bellagio, Italy, 18–22 February.

Resosudarmo, I. 2002. "Closer to People and Trees: Will Decentralization Work for the People and the Forests of Indonesia?" Paper prepared for the Conference on Decentralization and the Environment, Bellagio, Italy, 18–22 February.

Ribot, J. 1995. "Local Forest Control in Mali: An Institutional Analysis of Participatory Policies." Review of Policies in the Traditional Energy Sector (RPTES): A Forestry Sector Policy Report. Washington, DC: World Bank.

Ribot, J. 1999. "Framework for Environmental Governance." A paper presented at the Workshop on Environmental Governance in Central Africa, World Resources Institute, Washington, DC, 26–27 April.

Ribot, J. 2000. "Representation and Accountability in Decentralized Sahelian Forestry: Legal Instruments of Political-Administrative Control." *Georgetown International Environmental Law Review* 12(2):447–491.

Ribot, J. 2002a. "African Decentralization: Local Actors, Powers and Accountability." Democracy, Governance and Human Rights Paper No. 8. Geneva, Switzerland: United Nations Research Institute for Social Development (UNRISD) and International Development Research Centre (IDRC).

Ribot, J. 2002b. "Decentralization and the Environment: Power Transfer and Institutional Choice: Some Observations from Bellagio." Mimeo. Washington, DC: World Resources Institute.

Ribot, J. 2002c. *Democratic Decentralization of Natural Resources: Institutionalizing Popular Participation*. Washington, DC: World Resources Institute.

Ribot, J. 2003. "Democratic Decentralisation of Natural Resources: Institutional Choice and Discretionary Power Transfers in Sub-Saharan Africa." *Public Administration and Development* 23(1):55–65.

Smoke, P. 2000. "Beyond Normative Models and Development Trends: Strategic Design and Implementation of Decentralization in Developing Countries." Prepared for the Management Development and Governance Division, United Nations Development Programme (UNDP).

Souza, C. 2002. "Participatory Budgeting in Brazil: Decentralization and Policy Innovation." Washington, DC: World Movement for Democracy. Cited 28 May 2003. On-line at: http://www.wmd.org/action/oct-nov02/souza.html.

United Nations Environment Programme (UNEP). 2002. *Global Environment Outlook 3*. London: Earthscan.

United States Agency for International Development (USAID), with the Center for International Forestry Research (CIFOR), Winrock, World Resources Institute (WRI), and International Resources Group (IRG). 2002. *Nature, Wealth, and Power: Emerging Best Practice for Revitalizing Rural Africa*. Washington, DC: USAID.

Watt, D., R. Flanary, and R. Theobald. 2000. "Democratisation or the Democratisation of Corruption? The Case of Uganda." Pp. 37–64 in *Corruption and Democratisation*. A. Doig and R. Theobald, eds. Portland, OR: Frank Cass.

World Bank. 1999. *World Development Report 1999/2000: Entering the 21st Century*. New York: World Bank.

World Bank. 2001. "Decentralization and Governance: Does Decentralization Improve Public Service Delivery?" PREMnote No. 55. Washington, DC: World Bank. On-line at: http://www1.worldbank.org/prem/PREMNotes/premnote55.pdf.

World Bank. 2002. *World Development Report 2002: Building Institutions for Markets*. New York: Oxford University Press.

World Bank. 2003. *World Development Report 2003: Sustainable Development in a Dynamic World: Transforming Institutions, Growth, and Quality of Life*. New York: World Bank.

Box 5.1 Tracing Decentralization in Developing Countries

Agrawal, A. 2001. "The Regulatory Community: Decentralization and the Environment in the Van Panchayats (Forest Councils) of Kumaon." *Mountain Research and Development* 21(3):208–211.

Contreras-Hermosilla, A., and M. Rios. 2002. "Social, Environmental and Economic Dimensions of Forest Policy Reforms in Bolivia." Washington, DC: Forest Trends and Bogor, Indonesia: Center for International Forestry Research. Cited 19 May 2003. On-line at: http://www.forest-trends.org/whoweare/pdf/Bolivia English.pdf.

Dillinger, W. 1994. "Decentralization and its Implications for Service Delivery." Urban Management and Municipal Finance Working Paper No. 16. Washington, DC: World Bank Urban Management Programme.

Dupar, M., and N. Badenoch. 2002. *Environment, Livelihoods, and Local Institutions: Decentralization in Mainland Southeast Asia*. Washington, DC: World Resources Institute.

Manor, J. 2002. "Civil Society and Democratic Decentralization: The Increasing Importance of 'User Committees'." Civil Society and Governance Programme Policy Brief. Brighton, UK: Institute of Development Studies. Cited 29 May 2003. On-line at: http://www.ids.ac.uk/ids/civsoc/PolicyBriefs/policy.html.

Namara, A., and X. Nsabagasani. 2003. "Decentralization and Wildlife Management: Devolving Rights or Shedding Responsibility? Bwindi Impenetrable National Park, Uganda." Environmental Governance in Africa Working Paper No. 9. Washington, DC: World Resources Institute.

Pantana, P., M. Real, and B. Resurreccion. 2001. "Officializing Strategies: Participatory Processes and Gender in ADB's Capacity-Building in Thailand's Water Resources Sector." Pp. 34–51 in *Mekong Regional Environmental Governance: Perspectives on Opportunities and Challenges: Papers from the Mekong Regional Environmental Governance Research and Dialogue Group*. Resources Policy Support Initiative (REPSI), ed. Washington, DC: REPSI.

Resosudarmo, I. 2002. "Closer to People and Trees: Will Decentralization Work for the People and the Forests of Indonesia?" Paper prepared for the Conference on Decentralization and the Environment, Bellagio, Italy, 18–22 February.

Smoke, P. 2000. "Beyond Normative Models and Development Trends: Strategic Design and Implementation of Decentralization in Developing Countries." Prepared for the Management Development and Governance Division, United Nations Development Programme (UNDP).

World Bank. 1999. *World Development Report 1999/2000: Entering the 21st Century*. New York: World Bank.

Box 5.2 Defining Decentralization

United States Agency for International Development (USAID). 2003. *Building Democracy in El Salvador*. Website. Cited 23 May 2003. On-line at http://www.usaid.gov/democracy/lac/elsalvador.html.

Box 5.3 Privatization: Can the Private Sector Deliver Public Goods?

Birdsall, N., and J. Nellis. 2002. "Winners and Losers: Assessing the Distributional Impact of Privatization." Working Paper No. 6. Washington, DC: Center for Global Development. Cited 29 May 2003. On-line at: http://www.cgdev.org/wp/cgd_wp006.pdf.

Doukov, D., N. Dubash, and E. Petkova. 2002. "Bulgaria: Supply-Led Versus Efficiency-Led Electricity Reform." Pp. 97–115 in *Power Politics: Equity and Environment in Electricity Reform*. N. Dubash, ed. Washington, DC: World Resources Institute.

Dubash, N., ed. 2002. *Power Politics: Equity and Environment in Electricity Reform*. Washington, DC: World Resources Institute.

Dubash, N., and S. Rajan. 2002. "Electricity Reform Under Political Restraints." Pp. 51–71 in *Power Politics: Equity and Environment in Electricity Reform*. N. Dubash, ed. Washington, DC: World Resources Institute.

Finnegan, W. 2002. "Leasing the Rain." *The New Yorker*:43–53.

Gleick, P., G. Wolff, E. Chalecki, and R. Reyes. 2002. *The New Economy of Water: The Risks and Benefits of Globalization and Privatization of Fresh Water*. Oakland, CA: Pacific Institute.

Hall, D. 2001. "Water in Public Hands: Public Sector Water Management–A Necessary Option." London, UK: Public Services International. Cited 29 May 2003. On-line at: http://www.psiru.org/reportsindex.asp.

Kessler, T. 2002. "Tools for Advocacy: Putting the Private Sector in its Place–Part II: Assessing the Feasibility of Private Sector Participation in Basic Services." Takoma Park, MD: Citizen's Network on Essential Services (CNES). Cited 29 May 2003. On-line at: http://www.challengeglobalization.org/html/tools/Policy_Analysis_Series_2.shtml.

Lovei, M., and B. Gentry. 2002. "The Environmental Implications of Privatization." World Bank Discussion Paper No. 426. Washington, DC: World Bank.

Megginson, W., and J. Netter. 2001. "From State to Market: A Survey of Empirical Studies on Privatization." *Journal of Economic Literature* 39(2):321–390.

Newbery, D., and M. Pollitt. 1997. "The Restructuring and Privatisation of Britain's CEGB–Was It Worth It?" *Journal of Industrial Economics* 65(3):269–303.

Ram Mohan, T. 2001. "Privatisation: Theory and Evidence." *Economic and Political Weekly* 36(52):4865–4871.

Ribot, J. 1995. "Mali." Review of Policies in the Traditional Energy Sector (RPTES): A Forestry Sector Policy Report. Washington, DC: World Bank.

World Bank. 2001. *Global Development Finance 2001: Building Coalitions for Effective Development Finance*. Washington, DC: World Bank.

Box 5.4 Why Does a Local Voice Matter?

Agrawal, A. 2000. "Small is Beautiful, but Is Larger Better? Forest-Management Institutions in the Kumaon Himalaya, India." Pp: 57–85 in *People and Forests: Communities, Institutions, and Governance*. C. Gibson, M. McKean and E. Ostrom, eds. Cambridge, MA: MIT Press.

Kothari, A. 2000. "Conserving Nature with Communities: Lessons from Real Life Experiences in South Asia." A paper presented at the 2nd World Conservation Congress of IUCN, Amman, Jordan, 3–11 October.

Larson, A. 2002. "Decentralization and Natural Resource Management: A Nicaraguan Case Study." Paper prepared for the Conference on Decentralization and the Environment, Bellagio, Italy, 18–22 February.

McKean, M. 2000. "Common Property: What Is It, What Is It Good For, and What Makes It Work?" Pp: 27–55 in *People and Forests: Communities, Institutions, and Governance*. C. Gibson, M. McKean and E. Ostrom, eds. Cambridge, MA: MIT Press.

Ribot, J. 2001. *Democratic Decentralization of Natural Resources: Institutionalizing Popular Participation*. Washington, DC: World Resources Institute.

Rohter, L. 2000. "Where Darwin Mused, Strife Over Ecosystem." *New York Times* (27 December):A1.

Box 5.5 Namibia's Conservancies: Nature in the Hands of the People

Anderson, J. 2003. Natural Resource Policy Advisor, United States Agency for International Development (USAID). Personal Communication. E-mail. 23 May.

United States Agency for International Development (USAID) with the Center for International Forestry Research (CIFOR), Winrock, World Resources Institute (WRI), and International Resources Group (IRG). 2002. *Nature, Wealth, and Power: Emerging Best Practice for Revitalizing Rural Africa*. Washington, DC: USAID.

Chapter 6 Text

Aaronson, S. 2001. "Oh Behave! Voluntary Codes Can Make Corporations Model Citizens." Washington, DC: National Policy Association. Cited 17 April 2003. On-line at: http://www.multinationalguidelines.org/csr/oh_behave!.htm.

Adams, R., M. Houldin, and S. Slomp. 1999. "Towards a Generally Accepted Framework for Environmental Reporting." Pp: 314–329 in *Sustainable Measures: Evaluation and Reporting of Environmental and Social Performance*. M. Bennett and P. James, eds. Sheffield, UK: Greenleaf.

American Chemistry Council (ACC). 2001. *Guide to Community Advisory Panels*. Arlington, VA: ACC.

American Chemistry Council (ACC). 2002. "A History of Accomplishment, A Future of Promise: Responsible Care–Good Chemistry At Work." Brochure. Arlington, VA: ACC.

American Chemistry Council (ACC). 2003. *Responsible Care Practitioners Site*. Website. Cited 18 April 2003. On-line at http://www.americanchemistry.com/rc.nsf/open?OpenForm.

Amnesty International. 1998. "Human Rights Principles for Companies." London: Amnesty International. Cited 17 April 2003. On-line at: http://web.amnesty.org/aidoc/aidoc_pdf.nsf/Index/ACT700011998ENGLISH/$File/ACT700198.pdf.

Andrews, R., N. Darnall, D. Gallagher, S. Keiner, E. Feldman, M. Mitchell, D. Amaral, and J. Jacoby. 2001. "Environmental Management Systems: History, Theory, and Implementation Research." Pp: 31–60 in *Regulating From the Inside: Can Environmental Management Systems Achieve Policy Goals*. C. Coglianese and J. Nash, eds. Washington, DC: Resources for the Future.

Antweiler, W., and K. Harrison. 2003. "Toxic Release Inventories and Green Consumerism: Empirical Evidence from Canada." *Canadian Journal of Economics* 36(2):495–520.

Association of British Insurers (ABI). 2001. *Investing in Social Responsibility: Risks and Opportunities*. London: ABI.

Austin, D., and A. Sauer. 2002. *Changing Oil: Emerging Environmental Risks and Shareholder Value in the Oil and Gas Industry*. Washington, DC: World Resources Institute.

Baue, W. 2003. "Australia to Require Investment Firms to Disclose How They Take SRI into Account." *Social Investment News (SocialFunds.com)* 3 January. Cited 20 March 2003. On-line at: http://socialfunds.com/news/article.cgi/article998.html.

Baxter International Inc. 2001. *Balance: Baxter International Inc. Sustainability Report 2000*. Deerfield, IL: Baxter International Inc.

Bennett, M., and P. James, eds. 1999. *Sustainable Measures: Evaluation and Reporting of Environmental and Social Performance*. Sheffield, UK: Greenleaf.

Bouvret, F. 2003. Help-desk Coordinator, European Union Eco-labelling Board (EUEB). Personal Communication. E-mail. 15 April.

Broad, R., and J. Cavanagh. 1998. "The Corporate Accountability Movement: Lessons and Opportunities." A Study for the World Wildlife Fund's Project on International Financial Flows and the Environment. Cited 2 April 2003. On-line at: http://www.umass.edu/peri/pdfs/broad.pdf.

Burson-Marsteller. 2000. "The Responsible Century: Summary of the International Opinion Leader Survey on Corporate Social Responsibility." London: The Prince of Wales Business Leaders Forum.

Butler, L. 2003. Senior Manager, Worldwide Communications, Levi Strauss & Co. Personal Communication. E-mail. 13 March.

Chiquita Brands International Inc. 2000. *2000 Corporate Responsibility Report*. Cincinnati, OH: Chiquita Brands International, Inc.

Coglianese, C., and J. Nash, eds. 2001. *Regulating From the Inside: Can Environmental Management Systems Achieve Policy Goals*. Washington, DC: Resources for the Future.

Commission for Environmental Cooperation of North America (CEC). 2002. *Taking Stock 1999: North American Pollutant Releases and Transfers: Summary*. Montréal, Canada: CEC.

Commission on Sustainable Development (CSD). 2000. "Changing Consumption and Production Patterns: Organic Agriculture." Background Paper No. 4. Commission on Sustainable Development, Eighth Session, 24 April–5 May 2000. New York: United Nations Department of Economic and Social Affairs.

Cortese, A. 2002. "As the Earth Warms, Will Companies Pay?" *New York Times* (18 August):C6.

Danish Environmental Protection Agency. 2003. "The Danish Green Accounts: Experiences and Internal Effects." Copenhagen, Denmark: Danish Ministry of the Environment. Cited 18 April 2003. On-line at: http://www.mst.dk/indu/05050000.htm.

Dasgupta, S., B. Laplante, and N. Mamingi. 1998. "Capital Market Responses to Environmental Performance in Developing Countries." Development Research Group Working Paper 1909. Washington, DC: The World Bank.

Ditz, D., and J. Ranganathan. 1997. *Measuring Up: Toward a Common Framework for Tracking Corporate Environmental Performance*. Washington, DC: World Resources Institute.

Domini, A. 2001. *Socially Responsible Investing: Making a Difference and Making Money*. Chicago, IL: Dearborn Trade.

Elkington, J., N. Kreander, and H. Stibbard. 1999. "A Survey of Company Environmental Reporting: The 1997 Third International Benchmark Survey." Pp: 330–343 in *Sustainable Measures: Evaluation and Reporting of Environmental and Social Performance*. M. Bennett and P. James, eds. Sheffield, UK: Greenleaf.

Environics International Ltd. in cooperation with The Prince of Wales Business Leaders Forum and The Conference Board. 1999. "The Millennium Poll on Corporate Social Responsibility: Executive Briefing." Toronto, Canada: Environics International Ltd. Cited 20 March 2003. On-line at: http://www.environics international.com/news_archives/MPExecBrief.pdf.

Environmental Defense Fund. 1999. "McDonald's & Environmental Defense Fund Mark 10th Anniversary of Landmark Alliance." Press Release. New York: Environmental Defense Fund. 21 December. Cited 20 March 2003. On-line at: http://www.environmental defense.org/pressrelease.cfm?ContentID=1299.

Environmental News Service (ENS). 2002. "Against SEC Rules, Firms Hide Environmental Risks." *ENS* 30 September. Cited 18 April 2003. On-line at: http://ens-news.com/ens/sep2002/2002-09-30-09.asp.

European ECO-Forum. 2003. "The UNECE Pollutant Release and Transfer Register Protocol Report from the 8th and Final Working Group Meeting (January 2003)." Geneva, Switzerland: European ECO-Forum.

European Union Eco-labelling Board (EUEB). 2003. *The EU Eco-label*. Website. Cited 18 April 2003. On-line at http://www.eco-label.com/.

Florida, R., and D. Davison. 2001. "Why Do Firms Adopt Advanced Environmental Practices (And Do They Make a Difference)?" Pp: 82–104 in *Regulating from the Inside: Can Environmental Management Systems Achieve Policy Goals*. C. Coglianese and J. Nash, eds. Washington, DC: Resources for the Future.

Forest Stewardship Council (FSC). 2003. *Certification*. Website. Cited 17 April 2003. On-line at http://www.fscoax.org/principal.htm.

Frankel, C. 1998. *In Earth's Company: Business, Environment and the Challenge of Sustainability*. Gabriola Island, Canada: New Society Publishers.

Grote, U. 2002. "Environmental Standards in Developing Countries." Pp: 285–306 in *Public Concerns, Environmental Standards and Agricultural Trade*. F. Brouwer and D. Ervin, eds. Oxon, UK: CABI Publishing.

Hamilton, J. 1995. "Pollution as News: Media and Stock Market Reactions to the Toxics Release Inventory Data." *Journal of Environmental Economics and Management* 28:98–113.

Hamilton, J. 1999. "Exercising Property Rights to Pollute: Do Cancer Risks and Politics Affect Plant Emission Reductions?" *Journal of Risk and Uncertainty* 18(2):105–124.

Harrison, K. 1999. "Voluntarism and Environmental Governance." Vancouver, British Columbia, Canada: University of British Columbia, Centre for Research on Economic and Social Policy. Cited 20 March 2003. On-line at: http://www.arts.ubc.ca/cresp/khvolun.pdf.

Hill and Knowlton. 2001. *2001 Hill & Knowlton Corporate Citizen Watch Survey*. Chicago: Hill & Knowlton.

Innovest Strategic Value Advisors (Innovest). 2002. *Value at Risk: Climate Change and the Future of Governance*. CERES Sustainable Governance Project Report. Boston, MA: Coalition for Environmentally Responsible Economies (CERES).

International Council of Chemical Associations (ICCA). 1999. "Responsible Care Implementation Guide For Associations." Brussels: ICCA.

Irwin, F. 2003. Fellow, World Resources Institute. Personal Communication. E-mail. 4 April.

Irwin, F., T. Natan, W. Muir, E. Howard, L. Lobo, and S. Martin. 1995. *A Benchmark for Reporting on Chemicals at Industrial Facilities*. Washington, DC: World Wildlife Fund (WWF).

Jenkins, R. 2002. "Corporate Codes of Conduct: Self-Regulation in a Global Economy." Pp: 1–59 in *Voluntary Approaches to Corporate Responsibility: Readings and a Resource Guide*. New York, NY: United Nations Non-Governmental Liaison Service (NGLS).

Kenya Flower Council. 2003. Website. Cited 19 March 2003. On-line at http://www.kenyaflowers.co.ke/.

Konar, S., and M. Cohen. 1997. "Information As Regulation: The Effect of Community Right to Know Laws on Toxic Emissions." *Journal of Environmental Economics and Management* 32(1): 109–124.

KPMG. 2002. *KPMG International Survey of Corporate Sustainability Reporting 2002*. De Meern, The Netherlands: KPMG.

Levi Strauss & Co. 2003. *Social Responsibility / Sourcing Guidelines*. Website. Cited 12 March 2003. On-line at http://www.levi strauss.com/responsibility/conduct.

Metzenbaum, S. 2001. "Information, Environmental Performance, and Environmental Management Systems." Pp: 146–180 in *Regulating from the Inside: Can Environmental Management Systems Achieve Policy Goals?* C. Coglianese and J. Nash, eds. Washington, DC: Resources for the Future.

Nash, J., and J. Ehrenfeld. 2001. "Factors That Shape EMS Outcomes in Firms." Pp: 61–81 in *Regulating from the Inside: Can Environmental Management Systems Achieve Policy Goals?* C. Coglianese and J. Nash, eds. Washington, DC: Resources for the Future.

Organisation for Economic Co-operation and Development (OECD). 2000. *The OECD Guidelines for Multinational Enterprises*. Paris: OECD.

Organisation for Economic Co-operation and Development (OECD). 2001. *OECD Environmental Outlook*. Paris: OECD.

Organisation for Economic Co-operation and Development (OECD). 2002. "PRTR Implementation: Member Country Progress." ENV/EPOC(2000)8/FINAL. Paris: OECD. Cited 21 April 2003. On-line at: http://www.olis.oecd.org/olis/2000doc.nsf/LinkTo/env-epoc(2000)8-final.

Organisation for Economic Co-operation and Development (OECD). 2003. *About: Guidelines for Multinational Enterprises*. Website. Cited 18 April 2003. On-line at http://www.oecd.org/EN/about/0,,EN-about-93-3-no-no-no-0,00.html.

Ortega, D. 1995. "Broken Rules: Conduct Codes Garner Goodwill for Retailers, But Violations Go On." *The Wall Street Journal* (3 July):A1.

Orum, P. 1994. "Reports Using Toxics Release Inventory (TRI) Data." *Working Notes on Community Right-To-Know* July/August:1–11.

Outen, R. 1999. "Designing Information Rules to Encourage Better Environmental Performance." A paper presented at the conference on Environmental Policies in the New Millennium: Incentive-Based Approaches, 2–3 November. Washington, DC: World Resources Institute.

Petkova, E., C. Maurer, N. Henninger, and F. Irwin. 2002. *Closing the Gap: Information, Participation, and Justice in Decision-making for the Environment*. Washington, DC: World Resources Institute.

Ranganathan, J. 1998. *Sustainability Rulers: Measuring Corporate Environmental & Social Performance*. Sustainable Enterprise Perspectives. Washington, DC: World Resources Institute.

Ranganathan, J. 1999. "Signs of Sustainability: Measuring Corporate Environmental and Social Performance." Pp: 475–495 in *Sustainable Measures: Evaluation and Reporting of Environmental and Social Performance.* M. Bennett and P. James, eds. Sheffield, UK: Greenleaf.

Reed, D. 2001. *Stalking the Elusive Business Case for Corporate Sustainability.* Sustainable Enterprise Perspectives. Washington, DC: World Resources Institute.

Repetto, R., and D. Austin. 2000. *Coming Clean: Corporate Disclosure of Financially Significant Risks.* Washington, DC: World Resources Institute.

Rikhardsson, P. 1998. "Corporate Environmental Performance Measurement: Systems and Strategies." PhD Thesis Series. Aarhus, Denmark: Aarhus School of Business. Cited in M. Bennett and P. James, eds. 1999. *Sustainable Measures: Evaluation and Reporting of Environmental and Social Performance.* Sheffield, UK: Greenleaf, p.53.

Salzhauer, A. 1991. "Obstacles and Opportunities for a Consumer Ecolabel." *Environment* 33(9):10–15, 33–37.

Schmidneiny, S., R. Chase, and L. De Simone. 1997. "Business Progress Toward Sustainable Development." Pp: 143–156 in *Bridges to Sustainability: Business and Government Working Together for a Better Environment.* L. Gomez-Echeverri, ed. Yale School of Forestry and Environmental Studies Bulletin Series 101. New Haven, CT: Yale School of Forestry and Environmental Studies.

Skillius, Å., and U. Wennberg. 1998. *Continuity, Credibility and Comparability: Key Challenges for Corporate Environmental Performance Measurement and Communication.* European Environment Agency (EEA).

SmartWood. 2003. Website. Cited 7 March 2003. On-line at http://www.smartwood.org.

Social Investment Forum (SIF). 2001. *2001 Report on Socially Responsible Investing Trends in the United States.* Washington, DC: SIF.

SRI World Group Inc. 2001a. "Americans Increasingly Interested in Corporate Citizenship." *SRI-adviser.com.* Cited 17 April 2003.

SRI World Group Inc. 2001b. *Leading Social Investment Indicators Report 2001.* Brattleboro, VT: SRI World Group, Inc.

SRI World Group Inc. 2003. "News Briefs." *Social Investment News (SocialFunds.com)* 8 April. Cited 8 April 2003. On-line at: http://www.socialfunds.com/news.

SustainAbility and United Nations Environment Programme (UNEP). 2002. *Trust Us: The Global Reporters 2002 Survey of Corporate Sustainability Reporting.* London: SustainAbility.

The Blue Angel. 2003. Website. Cited 18 April 2003. On-line at http://www.blauer-engel.de.

Tietenberg, T., and D. Wheeler. 1998. "Empowering the Community: Information Strategies for Pollution Control." A paper presented at the Frontiers of Environmental Economics Conference, Airlie House, VA, 23–25 October.

United Nations. 2003. *The Global Compact.* Website. Cited 17 April 2003. On-line at http://www.unglobalcompact.org/.

United Nations Conference on Trade and Development (UNCTAD). 2001. "Ways to Enhance the Production and Export Capacities of Developing Countries of Agriculture and Food Products, Including Niche Products, Such as Environmentally Preferable Products." TD/B/COM.1/EM.15/2. Background note for the Expert Meeting with the same name, Geneva, Switzerland, 16–18 July. Cited 20 March 2003. On-line at: http://www.unctad.org/en/docs/c1em15d2.en.pdf.

United Nations Economic and Social Council (ECOSOC). 2000. "Furthering the Implementation of the Aarhus Convention through the Use of Electronic Tools and Media." CEP/WG.5/2000/11. Geneva, Switzerland: Economic Commission for Europe (ECE), Committee on Environmental Policy.

United Nations Economic Commission for Europe (UNECE). 2003. "34 Countries Sign New Protocol on Pollutant Release and Transfer Registers." Press Release. Geneva, Switzerland: UNECE. 21 May. Cited 18 June 2003. On-line at: http://www.unece.org/press/pr2003/03env_p16e.htm.

United Nations Economic Commission for Europe (UNECE). 2003b. "Governments Reach Agreement on New United Nations Treaty on Pollution Information Disclosure." Press release. Geneva, Switzerland: UNECE. 31 January. Cited 16 April 2003. On-line at: http://www.unece.org/env/pp/press.releases/prtr.31.01.03.pdf.

United Nations Economic Commission for Europe (UNECE). 2003. "More Signatories to the New UNECE Protocols as Fifth Ministerial Conference "Environment for Europe" Wraps up in Kiev." Press Release. Geneva, Switzerland: UNECE. 23 May. Cited 18 June 2003. On-line at: http://www.unece.org/press/pr2003/03env_p17e.htm.

United Nations Environment Programme (UNEP). 2002. *Industry as a Partner for Sustainable Development: 10 Years after Rio: the UNEP Assessment.* Paris: UNEP.

United Nations Institute for Training and Research (UNITAR). 2003. *Design and Implementation of National Pollutant Release and Transfer Registers (PRTRs).* Website. Cited 18 April 2003. On-line at http://www.unitar.org/cwm/homepage/b/prtr/index.htm.

United States Environmental Protection Agency (USEPA). 2002. "2000 Toxics Release Inventory (TRI) Public Data Release Report: Executive Summary." Washington, DC: USEPA. Cited 20 March 2003. On-line at: http://www.epa.gov/tri/tridata/tri00/press/execsummary_final.pdf.

Utting, P. 2002. "Regulating Business via Multistakeholder Initiatives: A Preliminary Assessment." Pp: 61–130 in *Voluntary Approaches to Corporate Responsibility: Readings and a Resource Guide.* New York, NY: UN Non-Governmental Liaison Service (NGLS).

White, A., and D. Zinkl. 1999. "Standardisation: The Next Chapter in Corporate Environmental Performance Evaluation and Reporting." Pp: 117–131 in *Sustainable Measures: Evaluation and Reporting of Environmental and Social Performance.* M. Bennett and P. James, eds. Sheffield, UK: Greenleaf.

World Business Council for Sustainable Development (WBCSD). 2002. *Sustainable Development Reporting: Striking the Balance.* Geneva, Switzerland: WBCSD.

World Resources Institute (WRI) in cooperation with the United States Environmental Protection Agency (USEPA). 2000. "Environmental Policies in the New Millennium: Incentive-Based Approaches to Environmental Management and Ecosystem Stewardship: A Conference Summary." Washington, DC: WRI.

Box 6.1 Growing Corporate Influence

Center for Responsive Politics. 2003. *Soft Money for Energy & Natural Resources in 2002.* Website. Cited 2 April 2003. On-line at http://www.opensecrets.org/softmoney/softindus.asp?ind=E.

Panayotou, T. 1997. "The Role of the Private Sector in Sustainable Infrastructure Development." Pp: 46–69 in *Bridges to Sustainability: Business and Government Working Together for a Better Environment.* L. Gomez-Echeverri, ed. Yale School of Forestry and Environmental Studies Bulletin Series 101. New Haven, CT: Yale School of Forestry and Environmental Studies.

United Nations Conference on Trade and Development (UNCTAD). 2002. *World Investment Report 2002: Transnational Corporations and Export Competitiveness.* New York: United Nations.

World Bank. 2001. *Global Development Finance 2001: Building Coalitions for Effective Development Finance.* Washington, DC: World Bank.

World Bank. 2002. "Private Infrastructure: A Review of Projects with Private Participation, 1990–2001." *Public Policy for the Private Sector* 250.

World Bank. 2003. *World Development Indicators.* Database. Cited 12 February 2003. On-line at http://www.worldbank.org/data/onlinedbs/onlinedbases.htm.

Box 6.2 A Community's Right to Know: The U.S. Toxics Release Inventory

Doa, M. 2003. "How Are the Toxics Release Inventory Data Used?" Pp: 93–117 in *How PRTRs Affect Environmental Policy: Past and Future: Abstracts.* Tokyo, Japan: Ministry of the Environment of Japan.

Hamilton, J. 1995. "Pollution as News: Media and Stock Market Reactions to the Toxics Release Inventory Data." *Journal of Environmental Economics and Management* 28:98–113.

Harrison, K., and W. Antweiler. 2001. "Environmental Regulation vs. Environmental Information: A View From Canada's National Pollutant Release Inventory." Vancouver, British Columbia, Canada: University of British Columbia, Centre for Research on Economic & Social Policy. Cited 20 March 2003. On-line at: http://www.arts.ubc.ca/cresp/environ.pdf.

Konar, S., and M. Cohen. 1997. "Information As Regulation: The Effect of Community Right to Know Laws on Toxic Emissions." *Journal of Environmental Economics and Management* 32(1):109–124.

Robins, J. 1990. *The World's Greatest Disasters*. London: Hamlyn.

Scorecard. 2003. *Pollution Locator: Which Pollution Sources Are Covered by TRI?* Website. Cited 18 March 2003. On-line at http://www.scorecard.org/general/tri/tri_source.html.

Shrivastava, P. 1996. "Long-term Recovery From the Bhopal Crisis." Pp: 121–147 in *The Long Road to Recovery: Community Responses to Industrial Disaster*. J. Mitchell, ed. Tokyo; New York: United Nations University Press.

United States Environmental Protection Agency (USEPA). 2002. "2000 Toxics Release Inventory (TRI) Public Data Release Report: Executive Summary." Washington, DC: USEPA. Cited 20 March 2003. On-line at: http://www.epa.gov/tri/tridata/tri00/press/execsummary_final.pdf.

United States Environmental Protection Agency (USEPA). 2002b. *Toxics Release Inventory (TRI): 2000 TRI Data Release*. Website. Cited 3 March 2003. On-line at http://www.epa.gov/tri/tridata/tri00/index.htm.

United States Environmental Protection Agency (USEPA). 2003. *Toxics Release Inventory (TRI) Explorer*. Database. Cited 18 March 2003. On-line at http://www.epa.gov/triexplorer/.

Box 6.3 The Polluters Exposed: The Power of Indonesia's Public Ratings Program

Afsah, S. 1998. "PROPER: Program for Pollution Control Evaluation and Rating: A Model for Promoting Environmental Compliance and Strengthening Transparency and Community Participation in Developing Countries." Washington, DC: International Resources Group Ltd. Cited 20 March 2003. On-line at: http://www.worldbank.org/nipr/work_paper/PROPER2.pdf.

Afsah, S. 2003. Consultant, International Resources Group. Personal Communication. Telephone interview. 4 April.

Afsah, S., A. Blackman, and D. Ratunanda. 2000. "How Do Public Disclosure Pollution Control Programs Work? Evidence from Indonesia." Discussion Paper 00-44. Washington, DC: Resources for the Future.

Wheeler, D. 2000. *Greening Industry: New Roles for Communities, Markets and Governments*. New York: Oxford University Press.

Wheeler, D. 2003. Development Research Group, World Bank. Personal Communication. E-mail. 3 April.

Box 6.4 The Global Reporting Initiative

Global Reporting Initiative (GRI). 2002. *Sustainability Reporting Guidelines*. Boston, MA: GRI.

Global Reporting Initiative (GRI). 2003. *Global Reporting Initiative: Organisations Using the Guidelines*. Website. Cited 12 May 2003. On-line at http://www.globalreporting.org/guidelines/reporters_all.asp.

SustainAbility and United Nations Environment Programme (UNEP). 2002. *Trust Us: The Global Reporters 2002 Survey of Corporate Sustainability Reporting*. London: SustainAbility.

Box 6.5 ISO 14001: A Standard for Environmental Management Systems

Andrews, R., N. Darnall, D. Gallagher, S. Keiner, E. Feldman, M. Mitchell, D. Amaral, and J. Jacoby. 2001. "Environmental Management Systems: History, Theory, and Implementation Research." Pp. 31–60 in *Regulating From the Inside: Can Environmental Management Systems Achieve Policy Goals*. C. Coglianese and J. Nash, eds. Washington, DC: Resources for the Future.

International Organization for Standards (ISO). 2002. *The ISO Survey of ISO 9000 and ISO 14000 certificates, Eleventh cycle, 2001*. Geneva, Switzerland: ISO.

Panayotou, T. 2001. "Environmental Management Systems and the Global Economy." Pp. 105–122 in *Regulating from the Inside: Can Environmental Management Systems Achieve Policy Goals?* C. Coglianese and J. Nash, eds. Washington, DC: Resources for the Future.

Box 6.6 Covenants: Voluntary Industry— Government Agreements in Europe

Business and the Environment (BAE). 2003. "EU Opens Probe of the Dutch Packing Agreement; Product Stewardship and Takeback." *Business and the Environment* 14(1):11.

European Partnership for the Environment (EPE). 1996. *EPE Sourcebook*. Website. Cited 5 March 2003. On-line at http://epe.be/workbooks/sourcebook/index.html.

EUROPEN. 2002. "Regulatory News: Dutch Industry Meets Packaging Targets." *EUROPEN Bulletin* 18:3–4.

Harrison, K. 1999. "Voluntarism and Environmental Governance." Vancouver, British Columbia, Canada: University of British Columbia, Centre for Research on Economic and Social Policy. Cited 20 March 2003. On-line at: http://www.arts.ubc.ca/cresp/khvolun.pdf.

Box 6.7 The Growth of Socially Responsible Investing

Association for Sustainable & Responsible Investment in Asia (ASrIA). 2003. Website. Cited 5 March 2003. On-line at http://www.asria.org.

Association of British Insurers (ABI). 2001. *Investing in Social Responsibility: Risks and Opportunities*. London: ABI.

Domini, A. 2001. *Socially Responsible Investing: Making a Difference and Making Money*. Chicago, IL: Dearborn Trade.

Kendall, R. 2001. "World SRI Estimated at $US 1.42 Trillion." *Ethical Investor* 14 September. On-line at: http://www.ethicalinvestor.com.au/news/story.asp?Story_ID=236.

Social Investment Forum (SIF). 2001. *2001 Report on Socially Responsible Investing Trends in the United States*. Washington, DC: SIF.

Social Investment Organization (SIO). 2003. *About Socially Responsible Investing*. Website. Cited 24 April 2003. On-line at http://www.socialinvestment.ca/.

Box 6.8 A Binding Convention on Corporate Accountability

Broad, R., and J. Cavanagh. 1998. "The Corporate Accountability Movement: Lessons and Opportunities." A Study for the World Wildlife Fund's Project on International Financial Flows and the Environment. Cited 2 April 2003. On-line at: http://www.umass.edu/peri/pdfs/broad.pdf.

Bruno, K., and J. Karliner. 2002. "Marching to Johannesburg." San Francisco, CA: CorpWatch. 21 August. Cited 2 April 2003. On-line at: http://www.corpwatch.org/campaigns/PCD.jsp?articleid= 3588.

Friends of the Earth International (FOEI). 2002. "Towards Binding Corporate Accountability." Briefing. Amsterdam, The Netherlands: FOEI. Cited 2 April 2003. On-line at: http://www.foei.org/publications/corporates/accountability.html.

Gardiner, R. 2002. "Governance for Sustainable Development: Outcomes from Johannesburg." WHAT Governance Program, Paper 8. Paper prepared for Global Governance 2002: Redefining Global Democracy, Montreal, Canada, 13–16 October. Cited 2 April 2003. On-line at: http://www.earthsummit2002.org/es/issues/Governance/wssdgovernanceoutcomes.pdf.

Journal of Corporate Citizenship. 2002. "World Review: Convention-al Warfare?" *Journal of Corporate Citizenship* 8:4.

La Viña, A., G. Hoff, and A. DeRose. 2002. *The Success and Failure of Johannesburg: A Story of Many Summits.* WRI Working Paper. Washington, DC: World Resources Institute.

Phillips, M. 2002. "Global Rules for Corporate Accountability: The Proposal to Establish a Corporate Accountability Convention." *Multinational Monitor* 23(10/11). Cited 2 April 2003. On-line at: http://multinationalmonitor.org/mm2002/02oct-nov/oct-nov02corp2.html.

United Nations. 2002. "Report of the World Summit on Sustainable Development: Johannesburg, South Africa, 26 August-4 September 2002." New York: United Nations. Cited 6 June 2003. On-line at: http://ods-dds-ny.un.org/doc/UNDOC/GEN/N02/636/93/PDF/N0263693.pdf.

Box 6.9 Banking on Ecosystems: HSBC's Corporate Gamble

Beck, R. 2002. Head of Group External Relations, HSBC. Personal Communication. Telephone interview. 21 February.

Bond, J., Chairman HSBC. 2002. "Investing in Nature News Conference." London: HSBC. 21 February. Cited 7 March 2002. On-line at: http://media.corporate-ir.net/media_files/lse/hsba.uk/nature.html.

Carrell, S. 2002. "Bank's Pounds 35M Gift for WWF Angers Greens." *The Independent* (London) (7 April):6.

Combes, A. 2002. Manager, HSBC in the Community, HSBC. Personal Communication. Telephone interview. 31 May.

Higgins, J. 2002. HSBC Publications Manager, Hong Kong. Personal Communication. Telephone interview. 31 May.

Hillyard, D. 2002. Head of Corporate Programmes, EarthWatch. Personal Communication. Telephone interview. 29 May.

HSBC Group (HSBC). 2001. *HSBC in the Community: Sharing our Success 2000.* London, UK: HSBC.

HSBC Group (HSBC). 2002. *HSBC Holdings plc Annual Report and Accounts 2002.* London, UK: HSBC.

HSBC Group (HSBC). 2003. *HSBC in the Community: Sharing our Success 2002.* London, UK: HSBC.

HSBC Group (HSBC), Botanic Gardens Conservation International (BGCI), EarthWatch, and World Wide Fund for Nature (WWF). 2003. *Investing in Nature.* Website. Cited 7 April 2003. On-line at http://www.investinginnature.org.

Neville, A. 2002. WWF-UK Head of Press and Campaigns. Personal Communication. Telephone interview. 29 May.

O'Brien, T. 2002. Manager, Inserting Services, HSBC. Personal Communication. Telephone interview. 6 May.

Box 6.10 Encouraging Green Power

Fischlowitz-Roberts, B. 2002. "Green Power Purchases Growing by Leaps and Bounds." *Eco-Economy Update* 2002-5. Cited 20 March 2003. On-line at: http://www.earth-policy.org/Updates/Update9.htm.

Chapter 7 Text

Agarwal, A., S. Narain, A. Sharma, and A. Imchen. 2001. *Poles Apart: Global Environmental Negotiations 2.* New Delhi: Centre for Science and Environment.

Andonova, L., and M. Levy. 2003. "Franchising Global Governance: Making Sense of the Johannesburg Type Two Partnerships." In *Yearbook of International Co-operation on Environment and Development 2003/2004* (Forthcoming). O. Stokke and Ø. Thommessen, eds. London: Earthscan.

Barrett, S. 2002. *Environment and Statecraft: The Strategy of Environmental Treaty-Making.* New York: Oxford University Press.

Baumert, K., and N. Kete. 2001. *The U.S., Developing Countries, and Climate Protection: Leadership or Stalemate?* Issue Brief. Washington, DC: World Resources Institute.

Benedick, R. 1991. *Ozone Diplomacy: New Directions in Safeguarding the Planet.* Cambridge, MA: Harvard University Press.

Bernstein, J. 2001. "Analysis of UNEP Executive Director's Report on International Environmental Governance (UNEP/IGM/1/2)." WHAT Governance Program, Paper 2. Paper prepared for the UNEP Civil Society Consultations on International Environmental Governance, Nairobi, Kenya, 22–25 May. Cited 24 June 2003. On-line at: http://www.earthsummit2002.org/es/issues/Governance/UNEPCritique.PDF.

Brack, D. 2000. "Global Regimes in Conflict? Environmental Treaties and the WTO." Paper presented at the International Trade and Environment Seminar, University of Calgary, Calgary, Canada, October.

Brack, D. 2001. "International Environmental Disputes: International Forums for Non-Compliance and Dispute Settlement in Environment-Related Cases." London: Royal Institute of International Affairs. Cited 6 June 2003. On-line at: http://www.riia.org/pdf/research/sdp/envdisputes.pdf.

Brack, D. 2004. "Trade and the Environment." In *Trade Politics.* B. Hocking and S. McGuire, eds. In Press. London: Routledge.

Bush, G. 2002. "President Outlines U.S. Plan to Help World's Poor: Remarks by the President at United Nations, Financing for Development Conference, Cintermex Convention Center, Monterrey, Mexico." Press Release. Washington, DC: The White House. Cited 11 June 2003. On-line at: http://www.whitehouse.gov/news/releases/2002/03/20020322-1.html.

Cheatle, M. 2003. Head, Global Environment Outlook Section, Division of Early Warning and Assessment (DEWA), United Nations Environment Programme. Personal Communication. Interview. 28 May.

Commission on Sustainable Development (CSD). 2002. "Vice-Chairs' Summary of the Informal Meeting on Partnerships." Summary prepared following the Third Preparatory Committee Meeting of the World Summit on Sustainable Development, New York, 25 March–5 April. Cited 19 June 2003. On-line at: http://www.un.org/esa/sustdev/partnerships/vice_chairman_summary.htm.

Commission on Sustainable Development (CSD). 2003a. *Commission on Sustainable Development, 11th Session New York, 28 April–9 May 2003.* Website. Cited 11 June 2003. On-line at http://www.un.org/esa/sustdev/csd/csd11/CSD11.htm.

Commission on Sustainable Development (CSD). 2003b. *Partnerships for Sustainable Development.* Website. Cited 7 June 2003. On-line at http://www.un.org/esa/sustdev/partnerships/partnerships.htm.

Convention on Biological Diversity (CBD). 2002. "The Hague Ministerial Declaration of the Conference of Parties to the Convention on Biological Diversity." Cited 6 June 2003. On-line at: http://www.biodiv.org/doc/meetings/cop/cop-06/other/cop-06-min-decl-en.pdf.

Dodds, F. 2001a. "The Context: Multi-Stakeholder Processes and Global Governance." Pp. 26–38 in *Multi-Stakeholder Processes for Governance and Sustainability—Beyond Deadlock and Conflict.* M. Hemmati, ed. London: Earthscan.

Dodds, F. 2001b. "Inter-Linkages Among Multilateral Environmental Agreements." WHAT Governance Program, Paper 3. Paper prepared for the World Summit on Sustainable Development (WSSD) International Eminent Persons Meeting on Interlinkages, Tokyo, Japan, 3–4 September. Cited 6 June 2003. On-line at: http://www.earthsummit2002.org/es/issues/Governance/interlinkages.PDF.

Dodds, S., W.B. Chambers, and N. Kanie. 2002. "International Environmental Governance: The Question of Reform: Key Issues and Proposals Preliminary Findings." Tokyo, Japan: United Nations University Institute of Advanced Studies. Cited 12 May 2003. On-line at: http://www.ias.unu.edu/binaries/NYPrepComReport3.pdf.

Drammeh, H. 2003. Deputy Director, Division of Policy Development and Law, United Nations Environment Programme (UNEP). Personal Communication. Interview. 29 May.

Dubash, N., M. Dupar, S. Kothari, and T. Lissu. 2001. *A Watershed in Global Governance? An Independent Assessment of the World Com-*

mission on Dams. Washington, DC: World Resources Institute.

Focus on the Global South. 2003. "NGOs Call on Trade Ministers to Reject Exclusive Mini Ministerials and Green Room Meetings in the Run Up to and at the 5th WTO Ministerial." Petition. Cited 17 June 2003. On-line at: http://www.focusweb.org/gb/guestbook.html.

Food and Agriculture Organization of the United Nations (FAO). 2003. "Aquaculture Rapidly Growing." Press Release. Rome: FAO. 20 February. Cited 6 June 2003. On-line at: http://www.fao.org/english/newsroom/news/2003/14203-en.html.

Gale, L. 2002. "Greenpeace International." Pp: 251–262 in *The Cartagena Protocol on Biosafety: Reconciling Trade in Biotechnology with Environment and Development?* C. Bail, R. Falkner and H. Marquard, eds. London: The Royal Institute of International Affairs.

Global Environment Facility (GEF). 2002. "Focusing on the Global Environment: The First Decade of the GEF: Second Overall Performance Study (OPS2)." Washington, DC: GEF. On-line at: http://www.gefweb.org/1Full_Report-FINAL-2-26-02.pdf.

Grubb, M., C. Vrolijk, and D. Brack. 1999. *The Kyoto Protocol: A Guide and Assessment*. London: The Royal Institute of International Affairs.

Gupta, J. 1997. *The Climate Change Convention and Developing Countries: From Conflict to Consensus*. Dordrecht, Netherlands: Kluwer Academic Publishers.

Haas, P., M. Levy, and E. Parson. 1992. "Appraising the Earth Summit: How Should We Judge UNCED's Success?" *Environment* 34(8):6–11, 26–33.

Haas, P., and J. Sundgren. 1993. "Evolving International Environmental Law: Changing Practices of National Sovereignty." Pp: 401–429 in *Global Accord: Environmental Challenges and International Responses*. N. Choucri, ed. Cambridge, MA: MIT Press.

Henderson, D. 1999. "The MAI Affair: A Story and its Lessons." London: Royal Institute for International Affairs.

Holdgate, M. 1999. *The Green Web: A Union for World Conservation*. London: Earthscan.

Hyvarinen, J., and D. Brack. 2000. *Global Environmental Institutions: Analysis and Options for Change*. RIIA Briefing Paper. London, UK: Royal Institute of International Affairs (RIIA), Energy and Environmental Programme.

Intergovernmental Panel on Climate Change (IPCC). 1995. *IPCC Second Assessment: Climate Change 1995*. Geneva, Switzerland: IPCC.

Intergovernmental Panel on Climate Change (IPCC). 2001. *Climate Change 2001: Synthesis Report: Summary for Policymakers*. Geneva, Switzerland: IPCC.

International Centre for Trade and Sustainable Development (ICTSD). 2002. "NAFTA Tribunal Fines Canada 6 Million Over Law Banning Toxic Waste Exports." *Bridges* 6(36). Cited 6 June 2003. On-line at: http://www.ictsd.org/weekly/02-10-24/inbrief.htm.

International Commission for the Protection of the Danube River (ICPDR). 2003. *GEF Strategic Partnership on the Black Sea/Danube Basin*. Website. Cited 11 June 2003. On-line at http://www.icpdr.org/undp-drp/.

International Institute for Sustainable Development (IISD) and World Wildlife Fund (WWF). 2001. *Private Rights, Public Problems: A Guide to NAFTA's Controversial Chapter on Investor Rights*. Winnipeg, Manitoba, Canada: IISD.

Khor, M. 2002. "WSSD Survives WTO Takeover." Penang, Malaysia: Third World Network. Cited 24 June 2003. On-line at: http://www.twnside.org.sg/title/twr145b.htm.

La Viña, A. 2003. Senior Fellow, Institutions and Governance Program, World Resources Institute. Personal Communication. Interview. 6 June.

La Viña, A., G. Hoff, and A. DeRose. 2003. "The Outcomes of Johannesburg: Assessing the World Summit on Sustainable Development." *SAIS Review* 23(1):53–70.

La Viña, A., and V. Yu. 2002. "From Doha to Cancun: The WTO Trade Negotiations and its Implications to Communities." Washington, DC: World Resources Institute. Cited 13 June 2003. On-line at: http://pdf.wri.org/lavina_doha_trade_workingpaper.pdf.

Liebenthal, A. 2002. *Promoting Environmental Sustainability in Development: An Evaluation of the World Bank's Performance*. Washington, DC: World Bank.

Malhotra, K. 2002. "Doha: Is it Really a Development Round?" Trade, Environment, and Democracy, Issue 1. Washington, DC: Carnegie Endowment for International Peace. Cited 24 June 2003. On-line at: http://www.ceip.org/files/pdf/TED_1.pdf.

Maurer, C. 2002. "The Transition from Fossil to Renewable Energy Systems: What Role for Export Credit Agencies?" Paper prepared for the German Advisory Council on Global Change, Berlin, Germany.

Maurer, C., S. Ehlers, and A. Buchman. 2003. *Aligning Commitments: Public Participation, International Decision-Making, and the Environment*. WRI Issue Brief. Washington, DC: World Resources Institute.

Nagai, M. 2003. Head, International Legal and Other Instruments Unit, Environmental Law Branch, Division of Policy Development and Law, United Nations Environment Programme (UNEP). Personal Communication. E-mail.

Nile Basin Initiative (NBI). 2001. "Development on the Nile Goes the Next Step–Details Worked out on a $122m Package." Press Release. Entebbe, Uganda: NBI. 17 October. Cited 10 June 2003. On-line at: http://www.nilebasin.org/pressreleases.htm.

North American Free Trade Agreement Secretariat (NAFTA Secretariat). 1992. "North American Free Trade Agreement: Preamble." Cited 7 June 2003. On-line at: http://www.nafta-sec-alena.org/english/nafta/preamble.htm.

Organisation for Economic Co-operation and Development (OECD). 2002. *The DAC Guidelines: Integrating the Rio Conventions into Development Co-operation*. Paris: OECD.

Paoletto, G. 1999. "Capacity Building Systems for Inter-Linkages." Paper prepared for Inter-Linkages: International Conference on Synergies and Coordination Between Multilateral Environmental Agreements, Tokyo, Japan, 14–16 July. Cited 9 June 2003. On-line at: http://www.geic.or.jp/interlinkages/docs/Paoletto.pdf.

Petkova, E., and P. Veit. 2000. *Environmental Accountability Beyond the Nation-State: The Implications of the Aarhus Convention*. Environmental Governance Note. Washington, DC: World Resources Institute.

Phillips, M., and M. Pacelle. 2003. "Banks Accept 'Equator Principles'." *Wall Street Journal* (3 June):A1.

Porter, G., and J. Brown. 1996. *Global Environmental Politics*. Boulder, CO: Westview.

Public Citizen and Friends of the Earth (FOE). 2001. *NAFTA Chapter 11 Investor-to-State Cases: Bankrupting Democracy: Lessons for Fast Track and the Free Trade Area of the Americas*. Washington, DC: Public Citizen.

Régnier, M. 2001. "Trade and Sustainable Development at Doha: Meeting Report." London: The Royal Institute of International Affairs. Cited 6 June 2003. On-line at: http://oikosinternational.org/centers_of_excellence/itas/Lidija.pdf.

Sampson, G. 2002. "The World Trade Organization and Global Environmental Governance." International Environmental Governance (Gaps and Weaknesses/Proposals for Reform) Working Paper. Tokyo: United Nations University Institute of Advanced Studies. Cited 7 June 2003. On-line at: http://www.ias.unu.edu/binaries/IEG_Sampson.pdf.

Sand, P. 2001. "Environment: Nature Conservation." Pp: 281–309 in *Managing Global Issues: Lessons Learned*. P. Simmons and C. Oudraat, eds. Washington, DC: Carnegie Endowment for International Peace.

Secretariat of the Convention on Biological Diversity (CBD Secretariat). 2000. "Cartagena Protocol on Biosafety." Cited 9 June 2003. On-line at: http://www.biodiv.org/biosafety/protocol.asp.

Secretariat of the Multilateral Fund for the Implementation of the Montreal Protocol (UNMFS). 2003. *General Information.* Website. Cited 6 June 2003. On-line at http://www.unmfs.org/general.htm.

Seymour, F., L. Dreier, and L. Donge. 2002. "Private Finance." Pp: 173–195 in *Stumbling Towards Sustainability.* J. Dernbach, ed. Washington, DC: Environmental Law Institute.

Seymour, F., and N. Dubash. 2000. *The Right Conditions: The World Bank, Structural Adjustment, and Forest Policy Reform.* Washington, DC: World Resources Institute.

Sokona, Y., A. Najam, and S. Huq. 2002. "Climate Change and Sustainable Development: Views from the South." World Summit on Sustainable Development Briefing Paper. London: International Institute for Environment and Development (IIED). Cited 16 June 2003. On-line at: http://www.iied.org/pdf/wssd_07_climate-change_long.pdf.

Speth, J. 2002. "A New Green Regime: Attacking the Root Causes of Global Environmental Deterioration." *Environment* 44(7):16–25.

Stokke, O., and Ø. Thommessen, eds. 2002. *Yearbook of International Co-operation on Environment and Development 2002/2003.* London: Earthscan.

Streck, C. 2001. "The Global Environment Facility–A Role Model for International Governance?" *Global Environmental Politics* 1(2):71–94.

The Equator Principles. 2003. *World Bank and IFC Specific Guidelines (Exhibit III of The Equator Principles).* Website. Cited 16 June 2003. On-line at http://www.equator-principles.com/exhibit3.shtml.

Thrupp, L., G. Bergeron, and W. Waters. 1995. *Bittersweet Harvests For Global Supermarkets: Challenges in Latin America's Agricultural Export Boom.* Washington, DC: World Resources Institute.

Tolba, M., and I. Rummel-Bulska. 1998. *Global Environmental Diplomacy: Negotiating Environmental Agreements for the World, 1973–1992.* Cambridge, MA: MIT Press.

United Nations. 1992. "List of Non-Governmental Organizations Recommended for Accreditation by the Secretary General of the Conference." A/CONF.151/PC/L.28 (Add. 1–14). Preparatory Committee for the United Nations Conference on Environment and Development, Second Session, Geneva, Switzerland, 18 March–5 April.

United Nations. 1994. "The United Nations Convention to Combat Desertification." Cited 9 June 2003. On-line at: http://www.unccd.int/convention/text/convention.php.

United Nations. 2000. "United Nations Millennium Declaration." A/RES/55/2. Cited 9 June 2003. On-line at: http://www.un.org/millennium/declaration/ares552e.pdf.

United Nations. 2002a. "Accreditation of Non-Governmental Organizations and Other Major Groups to the World Summit on Sustainable Development." A/CONF.199/PC/6. Preparatory Committee for the World Summit on Sustainable Development, Third Session, New York, 25 March–5 April. Cited 19 June 2003. On-line at: http://ods-dds-ny.un.org/doc/UNDOC/GEN/N02/293/33/IMG/N0229333.pdf.

United Nations. 2002b. "Accreditation of Non-Governmental Organizations and other Major Groups to the World Summit on Sustainable Development." A/CONF.199/PC/20. Preparatory Committee for the World Summit on Sustainable Development, Fourth Session, Bali, Indonesia, 27 May–7 June. Cited 19 June 2003. On-line at: http://ods-dds-ny.un.org/doc/UNDOC/GEN/N02/392/45/PDF/N0239245.pdf.

United Nations. 2002c. "Note by the Secretary-General on International Environmental Governance." A/CONF.199/PC/3 22 March. Paper prepared for the Third Summit Preparatory Committee (PREPCOM 3) for the World Summit on Sustainable Development, New York, 25 March–5 April 2002. Cited 7 June 2003. On-line at: http://ods-dds-ny.un.org/doc/UNDOC/GEN/N02/300/57/ IMG/N0230057.pdf.

United Nations. 2003. *The United Nations Convention on the Law of the Sea: A Historical Perspective.* Website. Cited 9 June 2003. On-line at http://www.un.org/Depts/los/convention_agreements/convention_historical_perspective.htm.

United Nations Department of Economic and Social Affairs (DESA). 2002. "Johannesburg Summit 2002: Key Outcomes of the Summit." New York: DESA. Cited 11 June 2003. On-line at: http://www.johannesburgsummit.org/html/documents/summit_docs/2009_keyoutcomes_commitments.pdf.

United Nations Development Programme (UNDP). 2001. "UNDP Thematic Trust Fund: Environment." New York: UNDP. Cited 9 June 2003. On-line at: http://www.undp.org/trustfunds/Environment-English-Final.pdf.

United Nations Development Programme (UNDP). 2003a. *Cambodia: Natural Resource Management: Promoting National Policy, Legal and Regulatory Frameworks for Environmentally Sustainable Development.* Website. Cited 10 June 2003. On-line at http://www.un.org.kh/undp/index.asp?page=environment/frameworks.asp.

United Nations Development Programme (UNDP). 2003b. *The Role of the MPU.* Website. Cited 10 June 2003. On-line at http://www.undp.org/seed/eap/montreal/role.htm.

United Nations Economic and Social Council (ECOSOC). 2002. "Accreditation of Non-Governmental Organizations and Other Major Groups to the World Summit on Sustainable Development." E/CN.17/2002/PC.2/16. Preparatory Committee for the World Summit on Sustainable Development, Second Session, New York, 28 January–8 February. Cited 19 June 2003. On-line at: http://ods-dds-ny.un.org/doc/UNDOC/GEN/N02/225/30/IMG/N0222530.pdf.

United Nations Environment Programme (UNEP). 1992. "Rio Declaration on Environment and Development." Cited 9 June 2003. On-line at: http://www.unep.org/Documents/Default.asp?DocumentID=78&ArticleID=1163.

United Nations Environment Programme (UNEP). 1999. *Global Environment Outlook 2.* London: Earthscan.

United Nations Environment Programme (UNEP). 2000. "Malmö Ministerial Declaration." Cited 7 June 2003. On-line at: http://www.unep.org/malmo/malmo_ministerial.htm.

United Nations Environment Programme (UNEP). 2001a. "Global Ministerial Environment Forum: International Environmental Governance." UNEP/GCSS.VII/2 27 December. Paper prepared for the Governing Council of the United Nations Environment Program/Global Ministerial Environmental Forum, Seventh Special Session, Cartagena, Colombia, 13–15 February 2002. Cited 6 June 2003. On-line at: http://www.unep.org/governingbodies/gc/specialsessions/gcss_vii/Documents/k0200009.pdf.

United Nations Environment Programme (UNEP). 2001b. "International Environmental Governance: Multilateral Environmental Agreements (MEAs)." UNEP/IGM/2/INF/3 10 July. Paper prepared for the Open-Ended Intergovernmental Group of Ministers or Their Representatives on International Environmental Governance, Second Meeting, Bonn, Germany, 17 July 2001. Cited 7 June 2003. On-line at: http://www.unep.org/IEG/Working Documents. asp.

United Nations Environment Programme (UNEP). 2001c. "Multilateral Environmental Agreements: A Summary." UNEP/IGM/1/INF/1 30 March. Paper prepared for the Open-Ended Intergovernmental Group of Ministers or Their Representatives on International Environmental Governance, First Meeting, New York, 18 April 2001. Cited 7 June 2003. On-line at: http://www.unep.org/IEG/WorkingDocuments.asp.

United Nations Environment Programme (UNEP). 2002a. *Global Environment Outlook 3.* London: Earthscan.

United Nations Environment Programme (UNEP). 2002b. *UNEP in 2002: Environment for Development.* Nairobi, Kenya: UNEP.

United Nations Environment Programme (UNEP). 2003. *Resource Mobilization: Trust Funds.* Website. Cited 10 June 2003. On-line at http://www.unep.org/rmu/html/fund_trustfund.htm.

United Nations Environment Programme (UNEP), and International Institute for Sustainable Development (IISD). 2000. *Environment and Trade: A Handbook.* Winnipeg, Canada: IISD.

United Nations University (UNU). 1999. "Inter-Linkages: Synergies and Coordination Between Multilateral Environmental Agreements." Tokyo: UNU. Cited 6 June 2003. On-line at: http://www.geic.or.jp/interlinkages/docs/UNUReport.PDF.

United States Department of Commerce. 2003. "International Data, Table G.1, International Investment Position of the United States at Yearend, 2000 and 2001." *Survey of Current Business* 83(6):D-58. On-line at: http://www.bea.doc.gov/bea/ARTICLES/2003/06June/D-Pages/0603DpgG.pdf.

Upton, S. 2002. "The International Framework for Action—Is the CSD the Best We Can Do?" Pp: 20–29 in *Words Into Action*. L. Chatterjee, ed. Washington, DC: International Institute for Environment and Development (IIED).

Utting, P. 2001. "UN—Business Partnerships: Whose Agenda Counts?" New York: Global Policy Forum. Cited 5 June 2003. On-line at: http://www.globalpolicy.org/socecon/tncs/2001/0727twn.htm.

Victor, D. 2001. *The Collapse of the Kyoto Protocol and the Struggle to Slow Global Warming*. Princeton, NJ: Princeton University Press.

Werksman, J., K. Baumert, and N. Dubash. 2001. *Will International Investment Rules Obstruct Climate Protection Policies?* Climate Notes. Washington, DC: World Resources Institute.

Willetts, P. 2002. "The Growth in the Number of NGOs in Consultative Status with the Economic and Social Council of the United Nations." Cited 8 May 2003. On-line at: http://www.staff.city.ac.uk/p.willetts/NGOS/NGO-GRPH.HTM#data.

World Bank. 2002a. "Environment Strategy Implementation: End-Year Progress Report for FY '02." Washington, DC: World Bank. Cited 6 June 2003.

World Bank. 2002b. *Global Development Finance 2002: Financing the Poorest Countries*. Washington, DC: World Bank.

World Meteorological Organization (WMO). 2003. *Scientific Assessment of Ozone Depletion 2002: Executive Summary*. Geneva, Switzerland: WMO.

World Trade Organization (WTO). 2001a. "Doha WTO Ministerial 2001: Ministerial Declaration." WT/MIN(01)/DEC/1 20 November. Ministerial Conference Fourth Session, Doha, Qatar, 9–14 November 2001. Cited 7 June 2003. On-line at: http://www.wto.org/english/thewto_e/minist_e/min01_e/mindecl_e.pdf.

World Trade Organization (WTO). 2001b. "NGOs attending the Fourth WTO Ministerial Conference, Doha, Qatar 9–13 November 2001." Cited 7 June 2003. On-line at: http://www.wto.org/english/thewto_e/minist_e/min01_e/doha_attend_e.doc.

World Wide Fund for Nature (WWF). 2002. *Turning the Tide on Fishing Subsidies: Can the World Trade Organization Play a Positive Role?* Washington, DC: WWF.

Zarsky, L. 1997. "Stuck in the Mud? Nation-states, Globalization and the Environment." Globalisation and Environment Study, OECD Economics Division. Berkeley, CA: Nautilus Institute for Security and Sustainable Development. Cited 16 June 2003. On-line at: http://www.nautilus.org/papers/enviro/zarsky_mud.html.

Box 7.1 The World Summit on Sustainable Development: Pursuing a Global Agenda

Global People's Forum (GPF). 2002a. "Civil Society Declaration: A Sustainable World is Possible." Final declaration of the Global People's Forum, Johannesburg, South Africa, 24 August–3 September. Cited 11 June 2003. On-line at: http://www.worldsummit.org.za/policies/cs_decl.html.

Global People's Forum (GPF). 2002b. "Programme of Action: A Sustainable World is Possible!" Final report of the Global People's Forum, Johannesburg, South Africa, 24 August–3 September. Cited 11 June 2003. On-line at: http://www.worldsummit.org.za/policies/program_action.html.

International Indigenous Peoples Summit on Sustainable Development (IIPSSD). 2002. "The Kimberley Declaration." Final declaration of the Indigenous Peoples International Summit on Sustainable Development, Kimberley, South Africa, 20–24 August.

Cited 11 June 2003. On-line at: http://www.tebtebba.org/tebtebba_files/wssd/ipsummitdec.html.

International Institute for Sustainable Development (IISD). 2002. "Summary of the World Summit on Sustainable Development: 26 August–4 September 2002." *Earth Negotiations Bulletin* 22(51):1–18. Cited 11 June 2003. On-line at: http://www.iisd.ca/linkages/download/pdf/enb2251e.pdf.

La Viña, A., G. Hoff, and A. DeRose. 2003. "The Outcomes of Johannesburg: Assessing the World Summit on Sustainable Development." *SAIS Review* 23(1):53–70.

Speth, J. 2003. "Perspectives on the Johannesburg Summit." *Environment* 45(1):24–29.

United Nations Department of Economic and Social Affairs (DESA). 2002. "Johannesburg Summit 2002: Key Outcomes of the Summit." New York: DESA. Cited 11 June 2003. On-line at: http://www.johannesburgsummit.org/html/documents/summit_docs/2009_keyoutcomes_commitments.pdf.

Box 7.2 Transboundary Environmental Governance: The Ebb and Flow of River Basin Organizations

Bruch, C. 2001. "Charting New Waters: Public Involvement in the Management of International Watercourses." *Environmental Law Reporter* 31:11389–11416.

International Commission for the Protection of the Rhine (ICPR). 2003. Website. Cited 11 June 2003. On-line at http://www.iksr.org/icpr/.

International Network of Basin Organizations (INBO). 2003. *Organismes Membres et Observateurs*. Website. Cited 11 June 2003. On-line at http://www.inbo-news.org/anglais/list_org.htm.

McNally, R., and S. Tognetti. 2002. "Tackling Poverty and Promoting Sustainable Development: Key Lessons for Integrated River Basin Management." A World Wide Fund for Nature Discussion Paper. London, UK: WWF-UK. Cited 11 June 2003. On-line at: http://www.wwf.org.uk/filelibrary/pdf/irbm_report.pdf.

Milich, L., and R. Varady. 1998. "Managing Transboundary Resources: Lessons From River-Basin Accords." *Environment* 40(8):10–15, 37–41.

Pittock, J. 2003. "Establishing River Basin Organizations for Conservation and Sustainable Development of Rivers." Mimeo. Washington, DC: World Wide Fund for Nature (WWF).

Scanlon, J. 2002. "From Taking, to Capping to Returning: The Story of Restoring Environment Flows in the Murray Darling Basin in Australia." Paper prepared for the Stockholm International Water Institute Seminar 2002: Towards Upstream/Downstream Hydrosolidarity, Stockholm, Sweden, 16 August.

Turton, A., F. Curtin, R. Iyer, E. Mostert, and A. Wolf. 2000. "Transboundary River Basins: Proposed Principles and Discussion Papers." WCD Thematic Review: Institutional Processes, Volume 3. Cape Town, South Africa: Secretariat of the World Commission on Dams. Cited 11 June 2003. On-line at: http://www.damsreport.org/docs/kbase/contrib/ins224.pdf.

World Resources Institute (WRI) in collaboration with United Nations Environment Programme (UNEP), United Nations Development Programme (UNDP), and World Bank. 2000. *World Resources 2000–2001: People and Ecosystems: The Fraying Web of Life*. Washington, DC: WRI.

Box 7.3 Trading Away Public Participation?

Maurer, C., S. Ehlers, and A. Buchman. 2003. *Aligning Commitments: Public Participation, International Decision-Making, and the Environment*. WRI Issue Brief. Washington, DC: World Resources Institute.

Box 7.4 A Watershed in Global Governance?

Asmal, K. 1999. "Message from the Chair." *World Commission on Dams Newsletter* March. Cited 10 June 2003. On-line at: http://www.dams.org/news_events/newsletter2.htm.

303

Development Today. 2001. "Sida Puts up SEK 5.5m to Handle Negative Impacts of Song Hinh Dam." *Development Today* 12 February. Cited 10 June 2003. On-line at: www.damsreport.org/new_events/media273.htm.

Dubash, N., M. Dupar, S. Kothari, and T. Lissu. 2001. *A Watershed in Global Governance? An Independent Assessment of the World Commission on Dams.* Washington, DC: World Resources Institute.

Friends of the Earth (FOE). 2002. *How the World Bank is Undermining the Extractive Industries Review.* Website. Cited 10 June 2003. On-line at http://www.foe.org/camps/intl/worldbank/902undermine.html.

Hemmati, M. 2001. *Multi-Stakeholder Processes for Governance and Sustainability–Beyond Deadlock and Conflict.* London: Earthscan.

South African Steering Committee. 2002. *World Commission on Dams Report: Fourth Draft Framework Recommendation.* Website. Cited 10 June 2003. On-line at http://www.unep-dams.org/document.php?doc_id=190.

World Bank. 2001. "The World Bank Position on the Report of the World Commission on Dams." Washington, DC: World Bank. Cited 10 June 2003. On-line at: http://www.dams.org/report/reaction/reaction_wb2.htm.

World Commission on Dams (WCD). 2000. *Dams and Development: A New Framework for Decision Making: A Report of the World Commission on Dams.* London: Earthscan.

World Conservation Union (IUCN). 2003. *About IUCN.* Website. Cited 10 June 2003. On-line at http://www.iucn.org/about/.

Chapter 8

Mind Over Mussels: Rethinking Mapelane Reserve

Bailey, C., and S. Jentoft. 1990. "Hard Choices in Fisheries Development." *Marine Policy* 14:333–344.

Bennett, M., and P. James, eds. 1999. *Sustainable Measures: Evaluation and Reporting of Environmental and Social Performance.* Sheffield, UK: Greenleaf.

Davis, A., and S. Jentoft. 2001. "The Challenge and the Promise of Indigenous Peoples' Fishing Rights–From Dependency to Agency." *Marine Policy* 25.

Harris, J. 2003. Ecological Advice Coordinator, Coast Region, Ezemvelo KwaZulu-Natal Wildlife. Personal Communication. E-mail. 21 February.

Harris, J., G. Branch, C. Sibiya, and C. Bill. 2003. "The Sokhulu Subsistence Mussel-Harvesting Project: Co-Management in Action." Pp: 61–98 in *Waves of Change: Coastal and Fisheries Co-Management in South Africa.* M. Hauck and M. Sowman, eds. Lansdowne, South Africa: University of Cape Town Press.

Harris, J., and P. Radebe-Mkhize. 2003. "Intertidal GIS system for the Management of Marine Resources in KwaZulu-Natal, South Africa." Unpublished data.

Horwitz, L., T. Maggs, and V. Ward. 1991. "Two Shell Middens as Indicators of Shellfish Exploitation Pattern During the First Millennium AD on the Natal North Coast." *Natal Museum Journal of Humanities* 3:1–28.

Kamuaro, O. 1998. "State and Community Conflict in Natural Resource Management in Kenya." Pp: 301–321 in *Africa's Valuable Assets: A Reader in Natural Resource Management.* P. Veit, ed. Washington, DC: World Resources Institute.

South African National Parks (SANParks). 2002. "Greater St. Lucia Wetland Park Authority." Press Release. Pretoria, South Africa: SANParks. Cited 25 May 2003. On-line at: http://www.parks-sa.co.za/news/media_releases/2002/stluciaauthority.htm.

Sowman, M., M. Hauck, and G. Branch. 2003. "Lessons Learned From Nine Coastal and Fisheries Co-Management Case Studies." Pp: 299–340 in *Waves of Change: Coastal and Fisheries Co-Management in South Africa.* M. Hauck and M. Sowman, eds. Lansdowne, South Africa: University of Cape Town Press.

World Conservation Monitoring Centre (WCMC). 1999. *World Heritage Sites Protected Areas Programme: The Greater St. Lucia Wetland Park.* Website. Cited 25 May 2003. On-line at www.unep-wcmc.org/sites/wh/st_lucia.html.

The New Iran: Toward Environmental Democracy

Anderson, J. 2001. "Iranian Village Shapes a Model of Democracy." *The Washington Post* (2 September):A1, A24.

Djazi, H. 2002. Facilitator, Sustainable Management of Land and Water Resources Programme, Lazoor, Iran. Personal Communication. Interview. December.

Douglas, M. 2002. UNDP Consultant, Panel of Experts, Sustainable Management of Land and Water Resources Programme. Personal Communication. Interview. December.

Douglas, M., B. Paterson, N. Yazdani, and E. Kodzi. 2001. "Report of the Second Panel of Experts Mission for the National Action Programme for Sustainable Management of Land and Water Resources." United Nations Development Programme (UNDP), Food and Agricultural Organization of the United Nations (FAO).

Esfandiar, S. 2003. Development Animator, Sustainable Management of Land and Water Resources Programme, Lazoor, Iran. Personal Communication. E-mail. February.

Farzin, A. 1998. "Iran's Agriculture Sector Performance: A General Analytical Note on Performance." Prepared for the Food and Agriculture Organization of the United Nations (FAO).

Farzin, A. 2002. "The Hable Rud 'Sustainable Management of Land and Water Resources' Program In Iran." Washington, DC: World Resources Institute.

Farzin, M. 1999. "First Report–Conceptual Issues on Programming and Monitoring." Panel of Experts, First Mission, Reviewing Programme Document and Conceptual Issues. United Nations Development Programme (UNDP), Food and Agricultural Organization of the United Nations (FAO).

Jafari, H. 2003. UNDP Programme Officer for Natural Resources Management and Vulnerability Reduction in Tehran. Personal Communication. Interview. December.

Kamyab, M. 2003. Former UNDP Manager for the Sustainable Management of Land and Water Resources Programme. Personal Communication. E-mail. April.

Koohafkan, P., A. Fitzherbert, and M. Farzin. 1999. "Report of the First Panel of Experts Mission for the National Action Programme for Sustainable Management of Land and Water Resources." United Nations Development Programme (UNDP), Food and Agricultural Organization of the United Nations (FAO).

Maafi, F. 2003. Facilitator, Sustainable Management of Land and Water Resources Programme, Lazoor, Iran. Personal Communication. E-mail. February.

Roudi-Fahimi, F. 2002. "Iran's Family Planning Program: Responding to a Nation's Needs." Washington, DC: Population Reference Bureau (PRB). Cited 13 June 2003. On-line at: http://www.prb.org/pdf/IransFamPlanProg_Eng.pdf.

United Nations Office for the Coordination of Humanitarian Affairs (OCHA). 2001. "Iran: Focus on Community Empowerment." *Integrated Regional Information Networks (IRIN)*. Cited 23 May 2003. On-line at: http://www.irinnews.org/report.asp?ReportID=12958.

World Bank. 2003. *GenderStats Database.* Cited 11 June 2003. On-line at http://genderstats.worldbank.org/.

Ok Tedi Mine: Unearthing Controversy

Broken Hill Proprietary (BHP). 1999. "BHP and Ok Tedi." Discussion Paper. Melbourne, Australia: BHP. On-line at: http://basemetals.bhpbilliton.com/okTedi/docs/Colour%20Ok%20Tedi.pdf.

Burton, J. 1997. "*Terra Nugax* and the Discovery Paradigm: How Ok Tedi Was Shaped by the Way it Was Found and How the Rise of Political Process in the North Fly Took the Company by Surprise." Pp: 27–55 in *The Ok Tedi Settlement: Issues, Outcomes and Impli-*

cations. G. Banks and C. Ballard, eds. Canberra, Australia: National Center for Development Studies and Resource Management in Asia-Pacific Project–Australian National University.

Danaya, B. 2003. Governor of Western Province, Papua New Guinea. Press Statement. 31 January.

Filer, C. 1997. "West Side Story: The State's and Other Stakes in the Ok Tedi Mine." Pp: 56-93 in *The Ok Tedi Settlement: Issues, Outcomes and Implications*. G. Banks and C. Ballard, eds. Canberra, Australia: National Center for Development Studies and Resource Management in Asia-Pacific Project–Australian National University.

Finlayson, M. 2002. "Planning for Sustainable Development in the Mining Industry of Papua New Guinea: Benefit Stream Analysis." Working Paper. Submitted to the Government of Papua New Guinea under the PNG Mining Sector Institutional Strengthening Project. Canberra, Australia.

Gordon, J. 1997. "The Ok Tedi Lawsuit in Retrospect." Pp: 141–166 in *The Ok Tedi Settlement: Issues, Outcomes and Implications*. G. Banks and C. Ballard, eds. Canberra, Australia: National Center for Development Studies and Resource Management in Asia-Pacific Project–Australian National University.

Hancock, G. 2003. Project Director, World Bank Technical Assistance Project in the Mining Sector. Personal Communication. E-mail. 7 April.

Hancock, G., and T. Omundsen. 1998. "The Development Forum Process and Approval of Large Mining Projects in Papua New Guinea." Paper prepared for Mining and the Community Conference, Madang, Papua New Guinea, 27–29 July.

Hardwick, B. 2003. Solicitor, Slater and Gordon, Australia. Personal Communication. Interview. 27 February.

Higgins, R. 2002. "Ok Tedi: Creating Community Partnerships for Sustainable Development." Conference paper delivered at the Canadian Institute of Mining, Minerals and Petroleum's AGM, Vancouver, Canada, May. Cited 22 May 2003. On-line at: http://www.oktedi.com/reports/news/26/CIM_paper_Higgins.pdf.

International Water Tribunal. 1994. *Second International Water Tribunal: Mining*. Utrecht, Netherlands: International Books.

King, D. 1997. "The Big Polluter and the Constructing of Ok Tedi: Eco-Imperialism and Underdevelopment Along the Ok Tedi and Fly Rivers of Papua New Guinea." Pp: 94–112 in *The Ok Tedi Settlement: Issues, Outcomes and Implications*. G. Banks and C. Ballard, eds. Canberra, Australia: National Center for Development Studies and Resource Management in Asia-Pacific Project–Australian National University.

Kirsch, S. 1997. "Is Ok Tedi a Precedent? Implications of the Lawsuit." Pp: 118–140 in *The Ok Tedi Settlement: Issues, Outcomes and Implications*. G. Banks and C. Ballard, eds. Canberra, Australia: National Center for Development Studies and Resource Management in Asia-Pacific Project–Australian National University.

Kirsch, S. 2001. "Mining, Indigenous Peoples and Human Rights: A Case Study of the Ok Tedi Mine, Papua New Guinea (Draft)." Case study prepared for Indigenous Peoples, Private Sector Natural Resources, Energy and Mining Companies and Human Rights Workshop, Geneva, Switzerland, December.

Kirsch, S. 2002. "Litigating Ok Tedi (Again)." *Cultural Survival Quarterly* 26(3):15-19.

Kirsch, S. 2003. Assistant Professor, Department of Anthropology, University of Michigan. Personal Communication. E-mail. 4 April.

Mineral Policy Institute (MPI) and AID/WATCH. 1999. *Putting the Ethic into E.F.I.C.: A Discussion Paper on Accountability and Social and Environmental Standards Within the Export Finance and Insurance Corporation of Australia*. Sydney, Australia: MPI and AID/WATCH.

Mining, Minerals, and Sustainable Development Project. 2002. *Breaking New Ground: Mining, Minerals, and Sustainable Development: The Report of the MMSD Project*. London: Earthscan.

National Research Institute (NRI), and World Bank. 2002. "Papua New Guinea Environment Monitor." Washington, DC: World Bank. Cited 22 May 2003. On-line at: http://lnweb18.worldbank.org/eap/eap.nsf/Attachments/PNG+Enviornment+Monitor/$File/PNG+Environment+Monitor+2002.pdf.

Ok Tedi Development Foundation (OTDF). 2001. "Investing in the Future of Western Province." Tabubil, Papua New Guinea: OTDF. Cited 22 May 2003. On-line at: http://www.oktedi.com/odf/links/reports/10/SOCIAL_OTDF_Report11_01.pdf.

Ok Tedi Mining Limited (OTML). 2003a. *Community and Environment*. Website. Cited 22 May 2003. On-line at http://www.oktedi.com/community/healthServices.php.

Ok Tedi Mining Limited (OTML). 2003b. *Impacts of Mining*. Website. Cited 27 May 2003. On-line at http://www.oktedi.com/community/impactOfMining.php.

Ok Tedi Mining Limited (OTML). 2003c. "Ok Tedi Mining Limited Historical Statistics at Year Ending December 2001." Tabubil, Papua New Guinea: OTML.

Ok Tedi Mining Limited (OTML). 2003d. *OTML at a Glance*. Website. Cited 22 May 2003. On-line at http://www.oktedi.com/aboutus.

Strongman, J. 2003. World Bank Mining Advisor, Papua New Guinea. Personal Communication. E-mail. 2 April.

Swales, S., A. Storey, I. Roderick, B. Figa, K. Bakowa, and C. Tenakanai. 1998. "Biological Monitoring of the Impacts of the Ok Tedi Copper Mine on Fish Populations in the Fly River System, Papua New Guinea." *The Science of the Total Environment* 214:99-111.

Taylor, M. 1997. "Putting Ok Tedi in Perspective." Pp: 12–26 in *The Ok Tedi Settlement: Issues, Outcomes and Implications*. G. Banks and C. Ballard, eds. Canberra, Australia: National Center for Development Studies and Resource Management in Asia-Pacific Project–Australian National University.

Temu, I. 1997. "Government and Landowner Equity: Contexts for the Ok Tedi Case." Pp: 183–188 in *The Ok Tedi Settlement: Issues, Outcomes and Implications*. G. Banks and C. Ballard, eds. Canberra, Australia: National Center for Development Studies and Resource Management in Asia-Pacific Project–Australian National University.

Townsend, P., and W. Townsend. 1996. "Giving Away the River Cont.: The Environmental Impact of The Ok Tedi Mine, Papua New Guinea." Paper presented at the European Society of Oceanists Annual Conference, Copenhagen, 13–15 December.

Wissink, D. Manager, Ok Tedi Development Foundation. 2003. Personal Communication. E-mail. 4 April.

World Bank. 2000. "Technical Note on 'Mine Waste Management Project–Risk Assessment'." Washington, DC: World Bank. Cited 28 May 2003. On-line at: http://www.mpi.org.au/oktedi/world_bank_summary.html.

Earth Charter: Charting a Course for the Future

Alvarez, J. 2002. "Certification of Approval of Resolution of the Senate Number 1582 by the Senate of Puerto Rico." Cited 29 May 2003. On-line at: http://www.earthcharter.org/communities/puerto_rico.htm.

Clugston, R. Executive Director, Centre for Respect of Life and Environment, Washington, DC. 2003. Personal Communication. Interview. March.

Earth Charter Secretariat. 2000. "The Earth Charter." San José, Costa Rica: Earth Charter Secretariat. Cited 28 May 2003. On-line at: http://www.earthcharter.org/earthcharter/charter.htm.

Earth Charter Secretariat. 2002. "The Earth Charter at the Johannesburg Summit: A Report Prepared by the Earth Charter Steering Committee and International Secretariat." San José, Costa Rica: Earth Charter Secretariat. Cited 27 May 2003. On-line at: http://www.earthcharter.org/wssd/summit_report.doc.

Earth Charter Secretariat. 2003. *Local Communities: A Growing and Vibrant Network*. Cited 29 May 2003. On-line at http://www.earthcharter.org/communities/.

Earth Charter USA. 2003a. *The Earth Charter–A Brief History*. Website. Cited 28 May 2003. On-line at http://www.earthcharterusa.org/ec_history.htm.

Earth Charter USA. 2003b. *Earth Charter in Action*. Website. Cited 29 May 2003. On-line at http://www.earthcharterusa.org/ecin action.html.

EarthEthics. 2002. "History of the Earth Charter." *EarthEthics* Winter:16–20.

Esty, D. 2003. Director, Yale Center for Environmental Law and Policy. Personal Communication. Interview. April.

Hallsmith, G. 2002. "Earth Charter: Local Government Strategy." San José, Costa Rica: Earth Charter Secretariat.

King, L. 2002. "Earth Charter for the Living City." Prepared for the Toronto and Region Conservation Authority (TRCA). Toronto, Canada: TRCA.

Layke, C. 2003. Senior Associate, Information Program, World Resources Institute. Personal Communication. Interview. March.

Manning, P. 2001. "Earth Charter Push Underway." *Ethical Investor News* 22 October. On-line at: http://www.ethicalinvestor.com/au/news/story.asp?Story_ID=254.

Roberts, J. 2001. "Local Communities: Overview of the Community Summits." Institute for Ethics and Meaning: Earth Charter Community Summits. Cited 29 May 2003. On-line at: http://www.earthchartersummits.org/2001summits.htm.

Rockefeller, S. 2003. Professor Emeritus of Religion, Middlebury College. Personal Communication. Interview. March.

Smith, S. 2002. "Earth Charter in Action." *EarthEthics* Winter: 30–39.

United Nations. 1948. "Universal Declaration of Human Rights." Cited 28 May 2003. On-line at: http://www.un.org/Overview/rights.html.

United Nations. 2002a. "Johannesburg Declaration on Sustainable Development." Cited 27 May 2003. On-line at: http://www.un.org/esa/sustdev/documents/WSSD_POI_PD/English/POI_PD.htm.

United Nations. 2002b. "WSSD Plan of Implementation." Cited 29 May 2003. On-line at: http://www.un.org/esa/sustdev/documents/WSSD_POI_PD/English/POIChapter1.htm.

Vilela, M. 2003. Executive Director, Earth Charter Secretariat, San José, Costa Rica. Personal Communication. Interview. March.

World Resources Institute (WRI). 2002. "The Earth Charter Indicators: Helping Communities Move Toward Sustainability." Mimeo. Washington, DC: WRI.

Chapter 9 Text

Chesapeake Bay Program. 2003. *Chesapeake 2000 Agreement*. Website. Cited 12 May 2003. On-line at http://www.chesapeakebay.net/c2k.htm.

Dubash, N., M. Dupar, S. Kothari, and T. Lissu. 2001. *A Watershed in Global Governance? An Independent Assessment of the World Commission on Dams: Executive Summary*. Washington, DC: World Resources Institute.

Global Environment Facility (GEF). 2002. "Focusing on the Global Environment: The First Decade of the GEF: Second Overall Performance Study (OPS2)." Washington, DC: GEF. On-line at: http://www.gefweb.org/1Full_Report-FINAL-2-26-02.pdf.

Hyvarinen, J., and D. Brack. 2000. *Global Environmental Institutions: Analysis and Options for Change*. RIIA Briefing Paper. London, UK: Royal Institute of International Affairs (RIIA), Energy and Environmental Programme.

Petkova, E., C. Maurer, N. Henninger, and F. Irwin. 2002. *Closing the Gap: Information, Participation, and Justice in Decision-making for the Environment*. Washington, DC: World Resources Institute.

World Resources Institute (WRI), United Nations Environment Programme (UNEP), United Nations Development Programme (UNDP), and World Bank. 1996. *World Resources 1996–1997: A Guide to the Global Environment: The Urban Environment*. New York: Oxford University Press.

Young, O. 2002. *The Institutional Dimensions of Environmental Change: Fit, Interplay, and Scale*. Cambridge, MA: MIT.

Zurita, P. 2002. Associate, World Resources Institute. Personal Communication. Interview. 14 July.

Index

L

Labeling programs, ecological. *See* Eco-labeling

Latin America, Environmental Impact Assessment laws in, 60

Latin American nongovernmental organizations (NGOs), 83

Laws, 7

    and plans, national environmental, 53

Lazoor, 183–84

    participatory planning in action, 183

Legal standing, 49

Liberalization, 24

Liberia, 3

Local management capacity, building, 108

Logging. *See also* Forestry laws and practices

    illegal, 37

Logging rights, 3

M

Maafi, Fatemeh, 184–85

Mapelane Nature Reserve, 177. *See also* Sokhulu

    governance lessons from, 175

    invisible users, 176

    rethinking, 174–76

Marine resource management, 3

Markets, 7

Media. *See also* Press freedom

    access and the, 63

Media outlets, 222

Mekong River Commission (MRC), 159

Mining. *See also* Ok Tedi

    progress toward sustainable, 197

Mobile phone use, 77

Montreal Protocol on Substances that Deplete the Ozone Layer, 12, 14, 149, 160

Multilateral Agreement on Investment (MAI), 76–77, 164

Multilateral agreements, participation in major, 238–39

Multilateral development banks (MDBs), 30–31, 165, 227

    transparency in regional and, 30

Multilateral Environmental Agreements (MEAs), 145–49

    changing face of, 148–49

    growth in numbers of parties to, 148

    harmonizing and strengthening, 155–56

    limitations, 150–51

    problems of scale and unequal influence, 151–52

    strengths, 149–50

Multi-stakeholder processes (MSPs), 167–68

Municipalities, 102, 103

Murray-Darling Basin Commission (MDBC), 158

Mussels. *See* Mapelane Nature Reserve

N

Namibia's conservancies, 106

National Pollutant Release Inventory (NPRI), 113

National sectoral policies, 53

Natural resource management, 186. *See also* Environmental governance

    poor, 3, 5

Natural resources, corruption and, 36–38

Nature, who governs, 3

Nepal

    access to information by the poor in, 76

    who is empowered to manage Terai, 104

Netherlands, 124

Nghe An, 100

Nicaragua, decentralization in, 102

Nongovernmental organizations (NGOs), 8, 27, 31, 63, 66, 117. *See also* Civil society

    African, 84

    are not perfect, 75, 78

        contention and discord, 78–79

    beyond, 70–71

    in Central and Eastern European region, 67

    and citizen action, 69–70

    coalitions, 75

        and alliances, 87–88

    decentralization and, 94, 107

    developing local support, 82–83

    empowered *vs.* marginalized, 79–81

    government action, 82

    growth of, 24, 35–36, 71, 72

        NGO sector growth, 71

    lend fresh perspectives, 58

    multitude of roles, 71, 73–75

        educating and informing, 71, 73

        implementing programs and providing services, 71

        joining in global environmental governance, 74–75

        promoting participation and increasing equity, 73, 74

        watchdogs for accountability, 73

        working with private sector, 73–74

    nurturing new, 81–82

    power in numbers, 66, 68–71

    specialized support organizations, 86–87